AND SUDDENLY EVERYTHING STARTED CHANGING

Liquor was outlawed and organized crime got the go-ahead. Women had the vote, short hair, short skirts, and their first heady taste of liberation. Writers widened the boundaries of expression and artistry. Athletes became idols. Booming business became the national religion and buying on credit the universal pastime. Song lyrics inescapably lodged themselves in the American mind, and the movies, radio, and tabloids became the muscle of the new mass media.

This is just part of what will pass before your eyes in marvelous essays, stories, and lyrics that vividly record and recall all that happened in the decisive decade of the 1920s, from the wild, wacky and wonderful fads to the profound and far-reaching changes that continue to affect us all.

AIN'T WE GOT FUN?

BARBARA H. SOLOMON teaches English at Iona College. Her other notable anthologies include *The Awakening and Selected Stories of Kate Chopin, Short Fiction of Sarah Orne Jewett and Mary Wilkins Freeman,* and *The Experience of the American Woman,* all available in Signet Classic and Mentor editions.

MENTOR and SIGNET CLASSIC Books of Special Interest

☐ **THE EXPERIENCE OF THE AMERICAN WOMAN: 30 Stories** edited and with an Introduction by Barbara H. Solomon. A century of great fiction about the place and the role of women in America. Works by Kate Chopin, William Faulkner, Toni Cade Bamabra, Katherine Anne Porter, and many other fine writers are included. (#ME1808—$2.95)

☐ **SHORT FICTION OF SARAH ORNE JEWETT AND MARY WILKINS FREEMAN** edited and with an Introduction by Barbara H. Solomon. Includes the novel and four stories about the fictional town of Dunnet Landing that make up Jewett's classic, *The Country of the Pointed Firs;* plus five other dramatic tales about outwardly placid lives; and fourteen stories by Freeman that take us into the world of women fighting for dignity and independence. (#CE1192—$2.95)

☐ **THE AWAKENING AND SELECTED STORIES OF KATE CHOPIN** edited and with an Introduction by Barbara H. Solomon. Chopin's female characters are unconventional women who refuse to play the standard role of the passive sexual partner. *The Awakening* and the seventeen short stories included here vividly depict the problems of a woman's place in marriage and society. (#CJ1234—$1.95)

☐ **THE SECRET SHARER AND OTHER GREAT STORIES** edited by Abraham H. Lass and Norma L. Tasman. Brilliant examples of some of the finest writers such as Prosper Merimee, Bernard Malamud, Dorothy Parker, Willa Cather, and Stephen Vincent Benet. (#MJ1801—$1.95)

Buy them at your local bookstore or use this convenient coupon for ordering.

THE NEW AMERICAN LIBRARY, INC.,
P.O. Box 999, Bergenfield, New Jersey 07621

Please send me the SIGNET CLASSIC and MENTOR BOOKS I have checked above. I am enclosing $_____ (please add 50¢ to this order to cover postage and handling). Send check or money order—no cash or C.O.D.'s. Prices and numbers are subject to change without notice.

Name _____

Address _____

City_____ State_____ Zip Code_____

Allow 4-6 weeks for delivery.
This offer is subject to withdrawal without notice.

AIN'T WE GOT FUN?

Essays, Lyrics, and Stories of the Twenties

EDITED AND WITH AN
INTRODUCTION BY
Barbara H. Solomon

A MENTOR BOOK
NEW AMERICAN LIBRARY
TIMES MIRROR
New York and Scarborough, Ontario

NAL BOOKS ARE AVAILABLE AT QUANTITY DISCOUNTS
WHEN USED TO PROMOTE PRODUCTS OR SERVICES. FOR
INFORMATION PLEASE WRITE TO PREMIUM MARKETING DIVISION,
THE NEW AMERICAN LIBRARY, INC., 1633 BROADWAY,
NEW YORK, NEW YORK 10019.

Copyright © 1980 by Barbara H. Solomon

All rights reserved

Library of Congress Catalog Card Number: 80-81025

PERMISSIONS ACKNOWLEDGMENTS

Essays

"Personality Craze" by Jules Abels from *In the Time of Silent Cal.* Copyright © 1969 by Jules Abels. Reprinted by permission of G. P. Putnam's Sons.

"Coolidge Prosperity" by Frederick Lewis Allen from *Only Yesterday.* Copyright 1931 by Frederick Lewis Allen, renewed 1959 by Agnes Rogers Allen. Reprinted by permission of Harper & Row, Publishers, Inc.

"Where the Booze Came From" by Herbert Asbury from *The Great Illusion: An Informal History of Prohibition.* Copyright 1950 by Herbert Asbury. Reprinted by permission of Doubleday & Co., Inc.

"Early Radio Successes" by Erik Barnouw from *A Tower in Babel: A History of Broadcasting in the United States,* Vol. 1. Copyright © 1966 by Erik Barnouw. Reprinted by permission of Oxford University Press, Inc.

"The Popularity of the Tabloid: *The Daily News* of 1926" by Simon Michael Bessie from *Jazz Journalism: The Story of the Tabloid Newspapers.* Copyright 1938, 1966 by Simon Michael Bessie. Reprinted by permission of Russell & Russell.

"Era of Wonderful Nonsense" from *Remember When* by Allen Churchill. Copyright © 1967 by Western Publishing Company, Inc., and the Ridge Press. Reprinted by permission.

"Revolution in Baseball: Ruth Reaches New York" by Robert W. Creamer from *Babe: The Legend Comes to Life.* Copyright © 1974 by Robert W. Creamer. Reprinted by permission of Simon & Schuster, Inc.

"Popular Music of the Decade" by David Ewen from *The Life and Death of Tin Pan Alley.* Copyright © 1974 by David Ewen. Reprinted by permission of Harper & Row, Publishers, Inc.

(The following pages constitute an extension of this copyright page.)

"Woman as Consumer: Advertising in the 1920s" by Stuart Ewen from *Captains of Consciousness*. Copyright © 1976 by Stuart Ewen. Reprinted by permission of McGraw Hill Co., Inc.

"Smoking and Dancing as Symbols of Liberation" by Paula S. Fass from *The Damned and the Beautiful*. Copyright © 1977 by Oxford University Press. Reprinted by permission.

"Film as Big Business" by Lewis Jacobs from *The Rise of the American Film: A Critical History*. Copyright © 1939, 1948, and 1967 by Lewis Jacobs. Reprinted by permission of author and Teachers College Press.

"Trials of the Twenties" by Paul Sann from *The Lawless Decade*. Copyright © 1957 by Crown Publishers, Inc. Reprinted by permission of Bonanza Books.

"New Social Types" by Elizabeth Stevenson from *Babbitts and Bohemians*. Copyright © 1967 by Elizabeth Stevenson. Reprinted by permission of Macmillan Publishing Co., Inc.

Lyrics

"The Varsity Drag" and "The Best Things in Life are Free" copyright © 1927, "Button Up Your Overcoat" copyright © 1928, all by Buddy DeSylva, Lew Brown, and Ray Henderson. Copyright renewed, assigned to Chappell & Co., Inc. International copyright secured, all rights reserved. Reprinted by permission.

"Can't Help Lovin' Dat Man" by Jerome Kern and Oscar Hammerstein II copyright © 1927 by T. B. Harms Company. Copyright renewed c/o The Welk Music Group, Santa Monica, California. International copyright secured, all rights reserved. Reprinted by permission.

"Look for the Silver Lining" by Jerome Kern and Buddy DeSylva copyright © 1920 by T. B. Harms Company. Copyright renewed c/o The Welk Music Group, Santa Monica, California. International copyright secured, all rights reserved. Reprinted by permission.

"Ain't We Got Fun?" by Richard Whiting, Gus Kahn and Raymond B. Egan copyright © 1921 by Warner Bros., Inc. Copyright renewed. All rights reserved. Reprinted by permission.

"Let's Do It (Let's Fall in Love)" by Cole Porter © 1928 by Warner Bros. Inc. Copyright renewed. All rights reserved. Reprinted by permission.

"I Guess I'll Have To Change My Plan" by Arthur Schwartz and Howard Dietz copyright © 1929 by Warner Bros., Inc. Copyright renewed. All rights reserved. Reprinted by permission.

"That New-Fangled Mother of Mine" by George Gershwin and Desmond Carter copyright © 1924 by New World Music Corporation. Copyright renewed. All rights reserved. Reprinted by permission of Warner Bros. Music.

"Tea for Two" by Vincent Youmans and Irving Caesar copyright © 1924 by Warner Bros., Inc. Copyright renewed. All rights reserved. Reprinted by permission.

"The Man I Love" by George and Ira Gershwin copyright © 1924 by New World Music Corporation. Copyright renewed. All rights reserved. Reprinted by permission of Warner Bros. Music.

"Mountain Greenery" by Richard Rodgers and Lorenz Hart copyright © 1926 by Warner Bros., Inc. Copyright renewed. All rights reserved. Reprinted by permission.

"Star Dust" by Hoagy Carmichael and Mitchell Parish copyright © 1929 by Mills Music, Inc. Copyright renewed. All rights reserved. Reprinted by permission.

"I Can't Give You Anything But Love" by Dorothy Fields and Jimmy McHugh copyright © 1928 by Mills Music, Inc. Copyright renewed. All rights reserved. Reprinted by permission.

"Second Hand Rose" by James F. Hanley and Grant Clarke copyright © 1921 by Shapiro Bernstein and Co., Inc. and Fisher Music Corporation. Copyright renewed. All rights reserved. Reprinted by permission.

"Makin' Whoopee" by Gus Kahn and Walter Donaldson copyright © 1928. Copyright renewed. All rights reserved. Reprinted by permission of Gus Kahn Music Co., Inc. and Donaldson Publishing Co. in U.S.; in Canada by permission of Bregman, Vocco and Conn. Inc.

Stories

"The Egg" by Sherwood Anderson copyright 1926 by B. W. Huebsch, Inc., renewed 1948 by Eleanor Anderson. Reprinted by permission of Harold Ober Associates Inc.

"There's Money in Poetry" by Konard Bercovici copyright © 1928 by *Harper's Magazine,* copyright renewed. Reprinted from October 1928 issue by permission.

"Night Club" by Katharine Brush copyright 1928 by *Harper's Magazine,* copyright renewed 1956 by Thomas S. Brush. Reprinted by permission of Thomas S. Brush.

"Each in His Generation" by Maxwell Struthers Burt copyright 1920 by Charles Scribner's Sons. Reprinted by permission of Mrs. Julia Burt Atteberry.

"The Cracked Teapot" by Charles Caldwell Dobie copyright © 1923 by *Harper's Magazine,* copyright renewed. Reprinted from January 1924 issue by permission.

"A Jazz-Age-Clerk" by James T. Farrell copyright © 1956 by James T. Farrell. Reprinted from *An Omnibus of Short Stories* by author with permission of publisher, Vanguard Press, Inc.

"Hey! Taxi!" by Edna Ferber copyright © 1947 by Edna Ferber, renewed 1975 by Harriet F. Pilpel, Executrix. All rights reserved. Reprinted by permission of Harriet F. Pilpel.

"Bernice Bobs Her Hair" by F. Scott Fitzgerald copyright 1920 by Charles Scribner's Sons, renewed 1948 by Zelda Fitzgerald. Reprinted from *Flappers and Philosophers* by permission of Charles Scribner's Sons.

"Fame for Mr. Beatty" by James Norman Hall copyright 1929 by James Norman Hall, renewed 1957 by Mrs. James N. Hall. Reprinted by permission.

"The Golden Honeymoon" by Ring Lardner copyright 1922, 1950 by Ellis A. Lardner. Reprinted by permission of Charles Scribner's Sons.

"Manicure" by Margaret Leech copyright © 1928 by *Harper's Magazine*. Copyright renewed. Reprinted from October 1928 issue by permission.

"A Matter of Business" by Sinclair Lewis copyright 1921 by Harper & Bros., renewed 1948 by Sinclair Lewis. Reprinted by permission of the Estate of Sinclair Lewis.

"The Dummy-Chucker" by Arthur Somers Roche copyright 1921 by Arthur Somers Roche, renewed 1949 by Clyde Roche. Reprinted by permission.

"Romance in the Roaring Forties" copyright 1929 by Damon Runyon. Reprinted by permission of American Play Company.

"Midwestern Primitive" by Ruth Suckow copyright 1928 by *Harper's Magazine*. Reprinted by permission of the Estate of Ruth Suckow.

MENTOR TRADEMARK REG. U.S. PAT. OFF. AND FOREIGN COUNTRIES
REGISTERED TRADEMARK—MARCA REGISTRADA
HECHO EN CHICAGO, U.S.A.

SIGNET, SIGNET CLASSICS, MENTOR, PLUME, MERIDIAN
AND NAL BOOKS are published *in the United States* by
The New American Library, Inc.,
1633 Broadway, New York, New York 10019,
in Canada by
The New American Library of Canada Limited,
81 Mack Avenue, Scarborough, Ontario M1L 1M8.

First Printing, June, 1980

1 2 3 4 5 6 7 8 9

PRINTED IN THE UNITED STATES OF AMERICA

For Anita, Mel, and Michael Hochster

Acknowledgments

I wish to express my gratitude for the information about the songs of the Twenties supplied by my husband, Stanley, as well as for his very helpful reading of the manuscript.

Professors Gary F. Kriss and Thomas Pendleton of Iona College suggested useful sources and Eileen Liebeskind of Ryan Library secured copies of materials. I also wish to thank Mary A. Bruno and the following members of the staff of the college's secretarial center: Marian Casali, Barbara Ferry, Hyacinth Fyffe, Patti Heiles, and Teresa Martin, as well as Guylaine Rocourt, an English Department student secretary; and Janet B. Thaden of New Rochelle.

Contents

Introduction ... 1

Essays

Personality Craze ... 39
Jules Abels

Coolidge Prosperity ... 65
Frederick Lewis Allen

Where the Booze Came From ... 83
Herbert Asbury

Early Radio Successes ... 106
Erik Barnouw

The Popularity of the Tabloid: The *Daily News* of 1926 ... 124
Simon Michael Bessie

Era of Wonderful Nonsense ... 129
Allen Churchill

Revolution In Baseball: Ruth Reaches New York ... 133
Robert W. Creamer

Popular Music of the Decade ... 142
David Ewen

Woman As Consumer: Advertising in the 1920s ... 164
Stuart Ewen

Smoking and Dancing as Symbols of Liberation ... 172
Paula S. Fass

Film as Big Business ... 189
Lewis Jacobs

Trials of the Twenties ... 203
Paul Sann

New Social Types ... 234
Elizabeth Stevenson

Lyrics

Ain't We Got Fun? *Gus Kahn and Raymond B. Egan;* *Richard A. Whiting*	252
Second Hand Rose *Grant Clarke; James F. Hanley*	255
The Best Things in Life Are Free *Buddy DeSylva, Lew Brown, and* *Ray Henderson*	257
Can't Help Lovin' Dat Man *Oscar Hammerstein II; Jerome Kern*	258
Let's Do It (Let's Fall in Love) *Cole Porter*	260
Look for the Silver Lining *Buddy DeSylva; Jerome Kern*	264
Makin' Whoopee *Gus Kahn; Walter Donaldson*	265
The Man I Love *Ira Gershwin; George Gershwin*	267
Mountain Greenery *Lorenz Hart; Richard Rodgers*	269
Star Dust *Mitchell Parish; Hoagy Carmichael*	272
Tea for Two *Irving Caesar; Vincent Youmans*	273
That New-Fangled Mother of Mine *Desmond Carter; George Gershwin*	275
The Varsity Drag *Buddy DeSylva, Lew Brown, and* *Ray Henderson*	277
I Can't Give You Anything But Love *Dorothy Fields; Jimmy McHugh*	279
I Guess I'll Have To Change My Plan *Howard Dietz; Arthur Schwartz*	281
Button Up Your Overcoat *Buddy DeSylva, Lew Brown, and* *Ray Henderson*	283

Stories

The Egg *Sherwood Anderson*	287
"There's Money in Poetry" *Konrad Bercovici*	297
Night Club *Katharine Brush*	306
Each in His Generation *Maxwell Struthers Burt*	319
The Cracked Teapot *Charles Caldwell Dobie*	337
A Jazz-Age Clerk *James T. Farrell*	352
Hey! Taxi! *Edna Ferber*	360
Bernice Bobs Her Hair *F. Scott Fitzgerald*	379
Mendel Marantz—Housewife *David Freedman*	403
Fame for Mr. Beatty *James Norman Hall*	421
The Golden Honeymoon *Ring W. Lardner*	431
Manicure *Margaret Kernochan Leech*	447
A Matter of Business *Sinclair Lewis*	459
The Dummy-Chucker *Arthur Somers Roche*	477
Romance in the Roaring Forties *Damon Runyon*	491
Midwestern Primitive *Ruth Suckow*	503
SELECTED BIBLIOGRAPHY	520

AIN'T WE GOT FUN?

Introduction

The decade of the 1920s has become virtually a mythic era of American life. It was a period of enormous social and cultural change, as well as one of extraordinary economic growth, national expansiveness, and unlimited confidence in American potential.

For a year or two after the Armistice (1918), the country had been plagued by problems of unemployment and inflation. But as factories switched from wartime production to peacetime manufacturing conditions, large numbers of Americans found satisfactory jobs and began to participate in the era's economic resurgence.

By 1923 factory workers were averaging twice the cash incomes they had earned in 1914. A sense of well-being was also promoted among workers by management's growing practice of making company stocks more available to them. More than $100,000,000 in United States Steel stock was owned by company employees in 1925, and many of the 300,000 shareholders of Standard Oil and its subsidiaries were its own employees, who had been encouraged to buy company stock.

Industrial expansion was accompanied by booms in both the stock market and in the real-estate market. The growth in paper value of the New York Stock Exchange's companies during the Twenties is now legend. At the peak of the market in September 1929, a single share of United States Steel was selling at 261¾, almost twice the price of a year before; Westinghouse E&M was 289⅞, or triple the price of a year earlier. In 1919 a new record of two million shares had been traded in a single day on the Exchange. By 1928 that number had more than tripled as hordes of Americans, convinced that the market's climb would never end, rushed to invest their savings and even their as-yet-unearned wages as they bought stock on margin. The fever of speculation had become a national epidemic.

A somewhat shorter boom in Florida real estate had already run its course, making some fabulously wealthy and leaving others penniless. At its peak, in 1925, the population of Miami was double what it had been in 1920. Binders, agreements to purchase property that cost a fraction of the actual price of the property, were sold and resold, each time at a higher price. Land speculators sold their visions of populous new towns and luxurious vacation resorts rising from Florida's swamps and marshes, and optimistic Americans bought them. The inevitable collapse of the boom was accelerated by a hurricane in 1926 that destroyed the railroad to Key West and damaged developments around Miami. Speculators were not completely discouraged; they simply looked elsewhere for new dreams to sell.

An ever-increasing proportion of the population became urban dwellers, leaving behind the isolation and grueling routines of farm life. Spread out before these workers in the city was a dazzling array of goods, housing, comfortable restaurants, luxurious movie houses, and shiny new cars. An era of national advertising and installment buying gave desirable objects an even greater appeal.

Whereas at the turn of the century there were a very limited number of products that were nationally known or that could be purchased anywhere in the country, the Twenties witnessed the unprecedented triumph of advertising campaigns for nationally available products. A look at the fortunes of the Lambert Pharmaceutical Company, makers of Listerine, readily demonstrates the effectiveness of one advertising strategy. In 1922 the son of the owner of the company, Gerald B. Lambert, was $700,000 in debt. Determined to improve the sales of Listerine, a mild antiseptic developed in 1879, he and two employees of the firm's advertising agency launched a campaign designed around a word they had come across in the British medical journal *Lancet*: "halitosis." The resulting advertisements proclaimed "Even Your Best Friend Won't Tell You," and the profits poured in. By 1928 Lambert's debt had been paid off and his company's advertising budget was five million dollars a year.[*]

Closely linked to aggressive advertising campaigns was the use of installment-plan buying. After the consumer had been convinced of the desirability of that new refrigerator, radio,

---

[*]James Playsted Wood, *The Story of Advertising* (New York: The Ronald Press Co.), 1958, pp. 384–85.

washing machine, or vacuum cleaner, the next important step in the sales process was to persuade him to make his purchase as soon as possible. Prior to the 1920s the public had held generally negative attitudes toward credit purchasing. Young people were warned against burdening themselves with a lifetime of debt and were made fearful of losing their possessions should they fail to make payments on time. In the Twenties all that was turned around. Advertisers promised an acquisitive public that it needed no money down and could get liberal terms. Millions of ready buyers were convinced that there was no need to deprive themselves of the magnificent new appliances and machines of this age of progress. In 1927 six billion dollars' worth of goods (about 15 percent of all sales) were bought on installment plans. And the factories kept on producing more merchandise.

The general sense of prosperity, coupled with the disillusionment with wartime idealism, became the basis of a new theme that dominated the age. The mass of Americans believed that they had an inalienable right to the good life and particularly to "a good time." And a good time they determined to have. Never before had a generation set out to be so self-consciously different from their forebears.

Young people rejected many of the values and ideals, and all of the fashions, of the preceding generation, much to the dismay of bewildered parents. Within a few years after the war, women had radically altered their appearance, adopting short skirts, flesh-colored stockings, makeup, and bobbed hair. They began to smoke in public. Together men and women sought out the ubiquitous speakeasy, whereas only a few years before, the saloon had been a masculine preserve with only an occasional small corner set aside for female intruders (who usually had to enter through a separate side door).

This generation danced its new dances to a new music called jazz. The older generation might reminisce about the days of the dignified waltz and innocent polka; the younger generation wanted to excel at the shimmy and the Charleston and took dance lessons from a talented New York instructor, Arthur Murray.

Soon a new source of excitement about dancing appeared. In March of 1923 the first marathon dance was held, during which a world record was set by Alma Cummings, who danced a total of twenty-seven hours. In the same year the first fatality attributed to a marathon dance occurred when a young man, Homer Morehouse, collapsed and died after eighty-seven hours on the dance floor.

Americans, discovering they had a penchant for contests and record-breaking activities of all kinds, designed contests to test the endurance not merely of dancers, swimmers, and runners but of pie eaters, coffee drinkers, piano players, flagpole sitters and even of long-distance expectorators.

Each succeeding year of the Twenties brought new attendance records at sporting events, as pleasure-loving Americans flocked to well-publicized matches. When in 1923 heavyweight champion Jack Dempsey fought Argentina's Luis Firpo at the Polo Grounds in New York, the gate receipts were an incredible $1,082,600. But only four years later the Dempsey-Tunney fight in Chicago drew a crowd of 145,000 spectators and gate receipts of $2,600,000. Americans would keep on making and breaking records throughout the decade as they pursued their "good time" with a vengeance. Football was a favorite crowd-pleaser, and both golf and tennis could boast of such popular champions as Bobby Jones and William T. Tilden. But baseball was the sport that came to dominate the era, and its hero, unquestionably, was Babe Ruth. He virtually revitalized the game, which had suffered from public suspicion after the "Black Sox Scandal" of 1919. Once a pitcher-dominated, low-scoring sport, baseball changed radically in the Ruth era and became an exciting, hitter-dominated spectacle, a change aided by such developments as the use of a livelier ball and the banning of the spitball. In 1915 a total of 384 home runs were hit in major-league games; ten years later the number was 1167. It was a decade of home-run fever.

Ruth's role in the growth of the sport cannot be overstated. In 1920, his first year with the New York Yankees, Ruth hit 54 home runs, easily breaking his own record of 29, set the year before, when he was playing for the Boston Red Sox. The effect on his new ball club was magical: attendance at Yankee games doubled that of the preceding year, with a record breaking 1,289,422 paid admissions. Ruth became the sports idol of the age as fans swarmed to the parks to see "the Sultan of Swat," "the Bambino," "the Babe."

A more readily available and cheaper source of entertainment than baseball drew even larger numbers of Americans away from home in the 1920s: the movies. The Kinetoscope had begun as an oddity in 1889—a black, hand-cranked box with a lens through which a viewer could watch thirty seconds of moving film. But by 1920 motion pictures had grown into the fifth-largest industry in the country. Fascinated audiences across the nation delighted in the performances of such stars as Harold Lloyd, Charlie Chaplin, Buster Keaton, Laurel and Hardy, Mary Pickford, Douglas Fairbanks, Greta Garbo, Norma Talmadge, Tom Mix, Rudolph Valentino, and Gloria Swanson. Classic films of the era included D. W. Griffith's *Way Down East* (1920) and *Orphans of the Storm* (1922); Charles Chaplin's *The Kid* (1921) and *The Gold Rush* (1925); King Vidor's *The Big Parade* (1925); Erich von Stroheim's *Greed* (1925); Buster Keaton's *The General* (1926); and Cecil B. De Mille's *The King of Kings* (1927).

From a cultural (though not aesthetic) point of view, the most important film of the decade was a Warner Brothers experiment in sound-synchronized motion pictures, *The Jazz Singer* (1927). Starring Al Jolson, probably the most dynamic performer of the Twenties, this only partially synchronized "talkie" almost overnight created an enormous demand for the sound film. Within a few months a mammoth industry at the height of its commercial and artistic success redesigned its product, reevaluated (usually downward) all its proven formulas and its box-office stars, and embarked in new directions that permanently altered the nature of the motion-picture medium.

By 1927 there were more than 20,000 theaters in the country, and most of them changed their programs on a daily basis. About 800 commercial feature films were produced that year (as opposed to the 100 or so currently produced), and there were more than 50,000,000 paid admissions to the movies per week, at a time when the nation's population totaled 117,000,000. The movie houses themselves were often not merely comfortable theaters but places of extravagant showiness.

The Roxy, for example, built in New York City in 1927, had 6000 seats, 125 well-drilled ushers, a ballet troupe, and a 110-piece orchestra. Over the decade, it is estimated that more than 500 of the movie theaters built cost at least $1,-000,000. When the moviegoer bought his ticket, he often bought as well a luxurious experience of crystal chandeliers, thick carpets, and a profusion of mirrors, pictures, and plush furniture in an enormous lobby. The dreams that were manufactured in Hollywood were projected on the walls of dream palaces throughout the country.

The public, however, did not always head anyplace special

when they left home in the Twenties, for automobiling had become a national pastime in its own right. By 1929 more than 26,000,000 automobiles were on the road; one of every five Americans had a car. Never before had people so obsessively and fully identified with a single possession. In his novel *Babbitt* (1922) Sinclair Lewis described the American preoccupation with the auto:

> A family's motor indicated its social rank as precisely as the grades of the peerage determined the rank of an English family. . . . The details of precedence were never officially determined. There was no court to decide whether the second son of a Pierce Arrow limousine should go into dinner before the first son of a Buick roadster, but of their respective social importance there was no doubt.

The Twenties brought improvements in the appearance and performance of the automobile. At the opening of the decade cars were painted dark colors, required laborious crank-starting, had complicated controls such as low-speed and reverse pedals, and were for the most part open models. But by the middle of the decade closed cars with a newly invented pyroxylin finish could be purchased in light blue, cream, and violet shades, with automatic starters, simplified controls, lower, cleaner lines, and balloon tires. When Henry Ford unveiled his Model A in December of 1927, almost a million New Yorkers jammed the area around the Ford premises hoping for a glimpse of the car that was to succeed the old Model T in the hearts of faithful drivers.

Even when Americans chose to remain at home, they were certain of a considerable assortment of new pleasures to select from. Radio broadcasting had made an undramatic debut around 1920 in the remodeled barn of Dr. Frank Conrad, a Westinghouse engineer. From his early programs of baseball scores and phonograph music, heard on crystal sets that cost about a dollar, a multimillion-dollar industry burgeoned with astounding speed.

This new medium, which had 30,000,000 regular listeners by 1927, transformed sports and cultural and political activities into national events. Among the major broadcasts of that year was a coast-to-coast program featuring Secretary of Commerce Herbert Hoover, who discussed relief efforts to help the 700,000 victims of the catastrophic floods that had occurred in the Mississippi Valley and in Vermont. In the same year, Charles Lindbergh went on the air soon after his solo transatlantic flight, the Rose Bowl was heard coast to coast for the first time, and the second Tunney-Dempsey fight was broadcast from Chicago. An estimated 40,000,000 Americans tuned in to the fight, and it was reported that five listeners died of heart attacks brought on by the excitement of the bout. The Federal Radio Commission was created by Congress in 1927 for the purpose of settling disputes concerning the wavelengths and airspace of competing stations. By the end of the decade, among the popular voices that had been heard over the radio were those of Will Rogers, Lowell Thomas, Eddie Cantor, Rudy Vallee, and Al Jolson.

Another lively source of home entertainment, the daily newspaper, took on added dimensions in the Twenties. It now regularly provided comic strips, health- and household-advice columns, sports features, Hollywood gossip, advice to the lovelorn, dramatic photographs, cartoons, and editorials. The country's first tabloid, the *Daily News*, was founded in 1919, and it was followed by others such as the *Mirror* and the *Daily Graphic*. The newspapers of the decade discovered that the public had an insatiable appetite for ballyhoo—for human-interest stories rife with every element of sensationalism. Among the first of these stories was the ordeal of Floyd Collins, who in 1925 became trapped by a cave-in near Cave City, Kentucky. His predicament became a national preoccupation after W. B. Miller, of the Louisville *Courier-Journal*, published an interview with Collins, which he had secured by descending into the cave. Unfortunately, the extraordinary interest generated in Collins through daily vivid newspaper accounts of the rescue operation could not save the explorer's life; searchers reached Collins on the eighteenth day, one day too late. Other national frenzies were created through newspaper publicity about the journey of Balto, an Alaskan dog that led a team of sled dogs carrying diphtheria antitoxin to a victim of the disease in icebound Nome and, in 1926, about the death of the Hollywood movie idol Rudolph Valentino. Even the process of bringing criminals to justice or of testing the nation's laws became a favorite source of newspaper sensationalism. Detailed reports were published of the proceedings at the Scopes "monkey trial" in Dayton, Tennessee; the annulment suit of multimillionaire Kip Rhinelander; the separation case of Peaches and Daddy Browning; the Hall-Mills murder trial; and the Snyder-Gray murder trial. Personal scandals and brutal crimes became juicy American spectacles.

Contributing to the sense of excitement and progress of the decade were the considerable alterations within the American home itself. As with the look of the automobile, the appearance of apartments and houses changed radically in the decade. Architects, influenced by technology and the need for fewer servants, produced smaller houses. Many changes resulted from the growing number of such electrical appliances as toasters, fans, irons, and vacuum cleaners. Between 1913 and 1927 the number of customers for electricity increased by 465 percent. Kerosene lamps that required filling and trimming were replaced by bright electric lights; the cool cellar that served as a storage area for food was replaced first by the icebox and shortly afterward by the electric refrigerator; cumbersome iron cookware was replaced by polished aluminum pots; and goods and services that hitherto could be obtained only through back-breaking drudgery in the home were now provided by the local delicatessen, bakery, and steam laundry.

Liberation from time-consuming traditional labor in the home was frequently matched by similar liberation in the world of work. In 1923, for example, the head of United States Steel, bowing to pressure from President Harding, reduced the twelve-hour workday to eight hours, and the rest of the steel industry quickly adopted this new policy.

No wonder, then, that the public had an overwhelming sense of American progress and superiority, of material well-being, and unprecedented reverence for business. Men and women, busy pursuing individual success and acquiring possessions, turned away from political and social concerns and developed a distrust of all but the blandest cultural achievements. The nation complacently witnessed the sometimes brutal treatment of striking workers and the oppression and prejudice that victimized minorities and the foreign-born.

Interestingly, at a time when a Babbitt-dominated America seemed to be one of the most uncongenial places for the arts to flourish, a great creative surge gathered momentum throughout the decade as American artists came of age spectacularly. Two of the forms in which they excelled are represented in this volume: popular music and the short story.

INTRODUCTION

In a most profound way, songwriters of the 1920s occupied a central place in the popular culture that has no equivalent even today, when music seems all-pervasive. True, in the 1920s people did not carry their music with them through the streets nor work to the accompaniment of an insistent rhythmic background. But though music then was not a continuous subconscious life-support system, it nevertheless functioned as a powerful force for shaping perceptions of contemporary reality and social relationships.

More than just capturing the spirit of the age, popular music helped direct the developing values of the Twenties—a tribute both to the diversity of its subject matter and to the enormous flourishing of creative genius in composition and lyric writing. In the 1920s eight of the greatest masters of American popular music were actively writing songs: Irving Berlin, Jerome Kern, George Gershwin, Ira Gershwin, Richard Rodgers, Lorenz Hart, Oscar Hammerstein, and Cole Porter. And there were at least two dozen other superb lyricists and composers (among them, Vincent Youmans, Gus Kahn, Walter Donaldson, Arthur Schwartz, Howard Dietz, Buddy DeSylva, Lew Brown, Ray Henderson, Dorothy Fields, Jimmie McHugh, Otto Harbach, Bert Kalmar, Harry Ruby, Irving Caesar, Sigmund Romberg, Rudolf Friml, Richard Whiting, Arthur Freed, Nacio Herb Brown, Harry Warren, and Fats Waller) who produced songs that are still constantly recorded and performed today. (This list excludes some truly major songwriters, such as Harold Arlen and Yip Harburg, who, though they wrote in the Twenties, did not begin to produce their famous work until the Thirties.) A list of the classic songwriters who published only after 1929 (from Johnny Mercer to Stephen Sondheim) would be much shorter than the one above. Despite all the radical changes in musical style over the past sixty years, the attitudes of innumerable songs of the 1920s seem to have become so thoroughly absorbed into our immediate musical heritage that we think in terms of 1920s' values when we think about popular music at all.

In our popular music our recollections are nostalgic:

> I dream of her and Avalon
> From dusk till dawn.

> I wonder what's become of Sally, that old gal of mine.

Sometimes I wonder why I spend the lonely night
Dreaming of a song . . .
And I am once again with you

Our need for love can reduce to total insignificance our need for money:

>   Who cares what banks fail in Yonkers
>   As long as you've got the kiss that conquers?

>   Poverty may come to me, that's true,
>   But what care I as long as I have you?

>   The things I long for are simple and few,
>   A cup of coffee, a sandwich, and you.

The weather mirrors our emotional state:

>   Liza, Liza, skies are gray.
>   If you return to me
>   All the clouds will roll away.

>   Whenever skies are gray,
>   Don't worry or fret,
>   A smile will bring the sunshine
>   And you'll never get wet.

>   When you're laughing, when you're laughing,
>   The sun comes shining through,
>   But when you're crying, you bring on the rain . . .

>   Knee deep in flowers we'll stay.
>   We'll keep the showers away . . .
>   Come tip-toe through the tulips with me.

Our loneliness, resulting from a lack of love, is devastating:

>   And while I'm waiting here
>   This heart of mine is singing,
>   "Lover come back to me!"

>   True love, true love, what have I done
>   That you should treat me so? . . .

Weary totin' such a load,
Trudging down that lonesome road.

All by myself in the night.
I sit alone with a table and a chair,
So unhappy there,
Playing solitaire.

When day is done and grass is wet with twilight's dew,
My lonely heart is sinking with the sun.

As recordings and radio broadcasting and, eventually, movies in the Twenties greatly expanded the availability of new popular music—which in an earlier decade had relied mainly on sheet music and theatrical performance for dissemination—the public perception of music changed in both obvious and subtle ways. A successful song had at one time been associated primarily or exclusively with the one performer who popularized it in a Broadway play or a vaudeville routine. But by the late Twenties, songs were performed on the radio or distributed on records, and many people had access to them within a short period of time. Therefore, the road companies of musical plays or the touring vaudeville acts were featuring familiar, rather than new, material as they traveled to diverse parts of the country. Vaudeville singers now had to change their repertory more often than they did in the past. With more singers using more songs, not even the singer whose hit version may have sold a million recordings could be exclusively associated with that song. There were, of course, 1920s performers who sang the definitive versions of songs for the era—Al Jolson with "My Mammy," Eddie Cantor with "If You Knew Susie Like I Know Susie," Fanny Brice with "My Man," Helen Morgan with "Bill," and several others—but it was no longer an era in which individuals owned songs exclusively. The media had democratized the industry. (As all new fashions finally give way to the old, it is notable that in the 1970s popular music frequently reverted to a turn-of-the-century association of song and performer.)

A more significant change in public perception resulted from a change in the idiom of song lyrics, from a manner before the Twenties expressive of general or objective notions to one reflecting a passionate sensibility or at least a singular viewpoint. In other words, songs now projected a singer's private feelings, not necessarily generalized public attitudes. Even subjects overtly impersonal were transformed into personal statements. For example, consider the treatment of popular music in an earlier song, Irving Berlin's famous "Alexander's Ragtime Band" (1911). The point of this song, simply enough, is to take someone "up to the man who's the leader of the band"—to share an appreciation for a fine musical experience. Similarly, in Shelton Brooks's "The Darktown Strutters' Ball" (1917), the singer instructs his date to be ready on time because "I want to be there when the band starts playin'." Such attitudes of appreciation are generalized responses that anyone might have. But the response to music in songs of the Twenties often became an obsessive internal preoccupation—the expression of an intense drive that comes to define the singer—particularly in the jazz music of George and Ira Gershwin:

> Fascinating rhythm . . .
> What a mess you're making!
> The neighbors want to know
> Why I'm always shaking
> Just like a flivver.
>
> I've got fidgety feet, fidgety feet . . .
>
> You'll dance until you totter;
> You're sure to get the fever,
> For nothing could be hotter—
> Oh, that Sweet and Low-down!

The development of an increasingly personal idiom in song lyrics reflected an interest in certain themes that are especially characteristic of the Twenties. One of the most meaningful of these themes, as embodied in a musical legacy that continued to be relevant to the musical fashions of the succeeding six decades, was developed primarily by Irving Berlin around the subject of the forsaken lover. His lyrics describing a wistful longing after the unattainable often contained a phrase or image or analogy that was exactly right for the age's view of a forlorn and impassioned lover:

> What'll I do, with just a photograph
> To tell my troubles to?

> You and the song are gone,
> But the melody lingers on.
>
> And maybe
> A baby
> Will climb upon your knee
> And put its arms about you,
> But how about me?
>
> And just when I learned to care a lot,
> You promised that you'd forget me not,
> But you forgot to remember.

Although Berlin contributed most to the shaping of this theme (of the type, his "What'll I Do?" and "Remember" are probably the most frequently performed today), other lyricists and composers also handled the concept of the singer's revelation of his deeply felt sense of loss, as in "Moanin' Low" (Ralph Rainger, music; Howard Dietz, lyrics), "Am I Blue?" (Harry Akst, music; Grant Clarke, lyrics), "Lover, Come Back to Me" (Sigmund Romberg, music; Oscar Hammerstein, lyrics), and "I Guess I'll Have to Change My Plan" (Arthur Schwartz, music; Howard Dietz, lyrics).

One significant variation on the unrequited-love theme appears most prominently in the works of George and Ira Gershwin, in which people—usually women—elaborate on their anticipation or hope of finding love.

> Someday he'll come along,
> The man I love ...
> And when he comes my way,
> I'll do my best to make him stay.
>
> There's a somebody I'm longing to see:
> I hope that he
> Turns out to be
> Someone to watch over me.

Even when women were not searching for a new love or suffering from the loss of an old one, they still did not fare too happily in many of the distinguished songs of the era. Women were desperately in love, poorly treated, or undervalued in most of those songs written to be sung by women. This reflects a prevailing assumption of the age: that women committed themselves more intensely to love relationships than did men and so were vulnerable to all kinds of suffering—for no tangible reward but to be around their beloved, as in "My Man":

Oh my man, I love him so—he'll never know . . .

Some of the titles communicate the theme most directly: "What Wouldn't I Do for That Man," "I Must Have That Man," and "Can't Help Lovin' Dat Man." The last song, of course, endures as one of the most poignant romantic statements in our language (though "that" is now invariably substituted for "dat"). Oscar Hammerstein's lyric creates a simple and yet profound analogy for a woman's commitment to a man who may not be worthy of it:

> Fish got to swim and
> Birds got to fly,
> I got to love one
> Man till I die,
> Can't help lovin' dat man of mine.

The bulk of songs of the 1920s, however, were neither sorrowful nor complaining; rather, they mirrored, and perhaps even created, the exuberant attitude of the period. It was the era of joyful expectations, a striving after "fun":

> Good news,
> You're what I waited for,
> I wasn't slated for blues.
>
> Happy days are here again . . .
>
> I'm sitting on top of the world,
> Just rolling along, just rolling along.
>
> I'm singin' in the rain,
> Just singin' in the rain,
> What a glorious feeling,
> I'm happy again.

It was a time to dispel gloom by dispersing clouds, to look for and find what is really there waiting to be discovered—a dark cloud's silver lining—because "A heart full of joy and gladness will always banish sadness and strife." By 1927 even

Irving Berlin was finally able to participate in the revival of good weather:

> Blue days, all of them gone;
> Nothing but blue skies from now on.

The good feelings embodied in popular songs were expressive not only of the prosperity of the period. A surprising number of famous songs (including "Who Cares?" "I Can't Give You Anything But Love," and "Sunday") dealt with the nonmaterialistic aspect of love, as in the seemingly compelling logic of a DeSylva-Brown-Henderson song: "love can come to ev'ryone/The best things in life are free." It was as if the spirit of the time required people to sing about their defiance of the materialism they accepted in fact.

> Not much money,
> Oh, but honey,
> Ain't we got fun?

In *The Great Gatsby*, "Ain't We Got Fun" is used by Fitzgerald to supply an ironic commentary when it is played for Gatsby and Daisy on the day they are reunited, after five years of separate and empty existences. Similarly, in her famous story "Big Blonde," Dorothy Parker refers to the main character Hazel Morse's dislike of this song, which her neighbor plays incessantly on the phonograph. Since Hazel struggles dutifully to have fun, to be a good sport and desirable companion in order to attract and please men, "Ain't We Got Fun?" understandably repels her.

To have fun, to be highly susceptible to the lure of parties, amusements, entertainments, was a proof of having the kind of sensibility overtly valued in the Twenties. It was more than acceptable to sing of one's self-indulgence in the frenetic pursuit of pleasure ("Runnin' wild—lost control"). Usually the self-indulgence expressed in song was innocuous enough, but occasionally it challenged the prevailing mores of the older generation implicitly—or directly, as in the now-classic remarks on marriage in Walt Donaldson and Gus Kahn's "Makin' Whoopee":

> Ev'ry time I hear that march from Lohengrin
> I am always on the outside lookin' in. . . .

Weddings make a lot of people sad,
But if you're not the groom they're not so bad.

Although always developed within a humorous context, the new morality could be daringly expressed, as in Cole Porter's "Let's Do It," which brilliantly manipulates the *double entendre* of the pronoun "it," and the grammatical necessity of relating the word to an impeccable moral modifier:

> ... birds do it, bees do it,
> Even educated fleas do it,
> Let's do it,
> Let's fall in love.

More commonly, the creed of the new morality appears in less suggestive contexts, as in Carter and Gershwin's "That New-Fangled Mother of Mine":

> And thanks to that mother of mine,
> The nightclubs I have to resign
> 'Cause I hate to have to answer
> That the exhibition dancer
> Is that new-fangled mother of mine.

The theme of "letting go" in the Twenties was quite often presented in terms of one's exaggerated response to music. Music, indeed, became the all-purpose excuse for one's behavior, whether it was eccentric (in which case you could allude to your body's possession by "Crazy Rhythm") or just slightly grandiose ("With a song in my heart, I behold your adorable face;/Just a song at the start, but it soon is a hymn to your grace"—an unusual excess by Rodgers and Hart). One way people responded to music in the Twenties was to sing about dancing: "Black Bottom," "Charleston," "I'd Rather Charleston," "Charleston Is the Best Dance After All," "I'm Gonna Charleston Back to Charleston," "Doin' the New Low-Down," and "When Francis Dances with Me." The dancing-song fashion was a carry-over from the previous decade, but in the Twenties it took a position of prominence. It even became, in a satirical sense, a standard for behavior in college:

> Stay after school,
> Learn how it goes;

INTRODUCTION

Everybody do the Varsity Drag.

Another aspect of the "search for fun" theme can be seen in a rather large number of songs that contain elements of the absurd or the nonsensical. The titles alone say it all:

1920 "So Long! oo-Long" ("How long while you're away?")
"All She'd Say Was 'Umh Hum'"
"Where Do They Go When They Row, Row, Row?"
"Who Ate Napoleons with Josephine When Bonaparte Was Away?"

1921 "Ma—He's Making Eyes at Me"

1922 "Ooo Ernest—Are You Earnest with Me?"
"You Tell Her, I S-t-u-t-t-e-r"

1923 "Barney Google" (With his goo-goo-googly eyes")
"Yes! We Have No Bananas"

1924 "Does the Spearmint Lose Its Flavor on the Bedpost Over Night?"

1925 "Keep Your Skirts Down, Mary Ann"
"Down by the Winegar Woiks"
"Who Takes Care of the Caretaker's Daughter While the Caretaker's Busy Taking Care?"

1926 "Where Do You Work-a, John?"

1927 "Mississippi Mud" ("It's a treat to beat your feet on the Mississippi mud")

1928 "I Faw Down an' Go Boom"
"I Love to Dunk a Hunk of Sponge Cake"

1929 "I Got a 'Code' in My 'Dose'"

But beyond this level of the farcical and the ludicrous, the 1920s certainly was a thriving time for witty lyricists. It was a decade in which Ira Gershwin, Lorenz Hart, and Cole Porter created on Broadway a still-unsurpassed standard for clever, allusive, literate—and even slangy—lyrics that fully retain their humor today. However, their songs were not necessarily comic. The wit of the songwriters was often used for the purposes of sentiment or even sorrow. This may be seen from the handling of the theme of the love nest, an innocuous enough variation on the classic literary theme of retirement that evolved from the Latin poet Horace. A popular theme in the Twenties, perhaps as an unconscious protest over increasing urbanization, the idea of two lovers escaping from the rest of the world, as in "My Blue Heaven" ("Just Molly and me, and baby makes three"), was an innocent fantasy. But the theme could also be handled in more self-consciously ironic terms, as when Irving Caesar begins the verse of "Tea for Two" with

> I'm discontented
> With homes that are rented,
> So I have invented
> My own.

He projects his song's love nest in terms not of specified locations but of pleasurable conditions without "friends or relations on weekend vacations." Similarly, Lorenz Hart's lovers' paradise is no make-believe castle; it is a plausibly tempting invitation to create a private place in the landscape of the mind:

> How we love sequestering
> Where no pests are pestering,
> No dear mama holds us in tether!
>
> Mosquitos here
> Won't bite you, dear;
> I'll let them sting
> Me on the fing-er
>
> We could find no cleaner re-
> Treat from life's machinery,
> Than our mountain greenery home!

The achievement of popular American music in the 1920s defies adequate summation. Much of the music remains with us, perennially relevant to our own emotional life; some of it has been permanently engraved in our memory of what songs are supposed to sound like. In any case, even aside from their very high musical quality and their ability to produce pleasure, the songs of the Twenties are certain to remain as an invaluable source, providing historical and sociological clues to the life-styles of that era.

The literary achievements of the decade are equally impressive. Among the American writers who had already begun to publish before America entered World War I (and who continued to produce important literature throughout most of the decade) were Theodore Dreiser, Edith Wharton, Upton Sinclair, Willa Cather, Dorothy Canfield Fisher, Ellen Glasgow, James Branch Cabell, Ring Lardner, Sinclair Lewis, Gertrude Stein, Sherwood Anderson, Edna Ferber, William Carlos Williams, Vachel Lindsay, Amy Lowell, H. D. (Hilda Doolittle), E. A. Robinson, Robert Frost, Carl Sandburg, Edna St. Vincent Millay, Edgar Lee Masters, Robinson Jeffers, Conrad Aiken, Wallace Stevens, Elmer Rice, and Eugene O'Neill. And an astonishing number of major young writers emerged at the end of the war. Many, such as Ernest Hemingway, F. Scott Fitzgerald, John Dos Passos, E. E. Cummings, William Faulkner, T. S. Eliot, Archibald MacLeish, Maxwell Anderson, and Laurence Stallings, depicted either their experiences during the fighting or the resulting battle scars and disillusionments of their generation. Later in the decade they were joined by, among others, Thornton Wilder, Dorothy Parker, Damon Runyon, Katherine Anne Porter, and Thomas Wolfe.

As a result of the contributions of a number of these writers, of their experiments with both style and theme, American literature displayed an originality and vitality that influenced authors around the world. American writers were greatly responsible for the shaping of concepts of what modern writing was all about. Of course, the themes and attitudes of these writers were myriad, but they also reflected the cultural, economic, and social conditions of the nation. The stories that appear in this collection are examples of some of the typical preoccupations of American writers of fiction. For purposes of discussion I have, perhaps arbitrarily, grouped the stories into seven categories: "A New Generation," "The Roles of Women," "American Voices," "A Couple of Con Men," "The Business World," "The Pulse of the City," and "The American Dream." Although there may be some overlapping of themes—for example, Lewis's "A Matter of Business" concerns the urban experience of an American as well as the matter of his business ethics—the categories are useful for identifying and emphasizing some of the patterns of the literature of the decade.

A New Generation

Maxwell Struthers Burt's story "Each in His Generation" (1920) dramatizes a young man's awareness that he exists in a world much different from that of the previous generation. It portrays the passing of that generation through a detailed comparison of the behavior and ideals of two conspicuously different sets of characters. Adrian and Cecil McCain, the younger set, ridicule and scorn the values of Adrian's uncle and guardian, Henry McCain, and Mrs. Denby, the married woman Henry has loved over a period of twenty years. Adrian believes that his uncle epitomizes

> the main and minor vices of a generation for which Adrian found little pity in his heart; a generation brittle as ice; a generation of secret diplomacy; a generation that in its youth had covered a lack of bathing by a vast amount of perfume. That was it—! That expressed it perfectly! The just summation! Camellias, and double intentions in speech, and unnecessary reticences, and refusals to meet the truth, and a deliberate hiding of uglinesses!

The actions of his uncle that Adrian finds most offensive stem from the relationship of Henry McCain and Mrs. Denby. She has continued to live with her husband in her fashionable house in New York City, where Henry presents himself each afternoon to take her riding, to pay her extravagant compliments, to fulfill his role as her faithful but discreet lover. Having avoided even a hint of a scandal, they remained socially acceptable.

Henry McCain and Mrs. Denby personify the well-bred, wealthy American social class that came of age long before World War I. Significantly, Henry and Adrian can never agree about the experience of that war. Adrian had lost some of his illusions: "there had been too much sweat, too much crowding, too much invasion of dignity. . . ." Henry regrets the loss of the professional armies of history. His analysis of the changes that have taken place indicates that he is quite perceptive about the qualities of modernity he has rejected. He explains:

> But this modern war, and this modern craze for self-revelation! Naked! Why, these books—the young men kept their fingers on the pulses of their reactions. It isn't clean; it makes the individual cheap. War is a dreadful thing; it should be as hidden as murder.

The author provides numerous details that support Adrian's accusations of the emptiness and hypocrisy of Henry McCain's world, but the story is not one-sided. The author is not convinced that the younger generation has the claim of right and progress entirely on its side. Although a radical change has taken place, the values that are being discarded are not to be glibly dismissed.

The Roles of Women

Outwardly, the Twenties wrought revolutionary changes in the lives of women, especially those who were just coming of age at the end of the war. The new feminine ideal was to be a bold and provocative woman who could wear her skirts above the knee, freely apply rouge, and take a swig now and then from her date's hip flask. This new woman often had a position in an office or department store—jobs that had not been open to women a few decades earlier.

But although the new role of the flapper offered a great deal of real freedom, it also held out the seductive promise of a new kind of existence, a false promise that could rarely be fulfilled. Even the most carefree debutante knew that after a few seasons of dating and dancing, of weekends at Harvard and Yale, her ultimate goal was a serious matter of business: securing a proposal from an eligible bachelor. Her future would be shaped, by and large, by the status of the man who had chosen her. F. Scott Fitzgerald's "Bernice Bobs Her Hair" (1920) is virtually a handbook of advice on how to become a successful flapper. In "Manicure" (1929) Margaret Kernochan Leech dramatizes the experience of another unmarried woman, a manicurist who is determined to have a good time and to get the most out of life.

In both the Fizgerald and Leech stories, the all-consuming topic that draws women together is the problem of attracting and holding the attention of a desirable man. The image of the successful flapper that Fitzgerald more than anyone else created early in the Twenties became a model that women imitated for more than four decades. The women he extolled, like Marjorie Harvey in "Bernice Bobs Her Hair," were self-confident, strong-willed, adventurous, witty, and fun-loving. Still, the extent of his heroines' success is measured by how attractive they can be to men. Using her beauty as a kind of capital she can draw upon, Marjorie has consciously molded herself into an exciting, challenging companion for men, and she works hard to maintain her popularity. As a flapper, she cares little about the trait of sincerity, and values much more highly the skillful manipulation of males.

One of Fitzgerald's notions about the new woman appears early in the story when we are told that Marjorie has "no female intimates" and that "she considered girls stupid." When this accomplished flapper takes on the task of teaching her cousin Bernice how to become popular, she seems motivated more by the pleasure of the challenge than by any feeling of pity for her unhappy cousin. Marjorie criticizes Bernice's old-fashioned definition of femininity as she asserts:

> "Girls like you are responsible for all the tiresome colorless marriages; all those ghostly inefficiencies that pass as feminine qualities. What a blow it must be when a man with imagination marries the beautiful bundle of clothes that he's been building ideals round, and finds that she's just a weak, whining, cowardly mass of affectations!"

Bernice becomes a popular flapper after Marjorie provides her with a series of shocking remarks to use as her "line." Unfortunately, Bernice makes the mistake of using her newly acquired techniques on Warren McIntyre, a longtime beau of Marjorie's. Since there is really little goodwill between the two girls, Marjorie has no qualms about reasserting her supremacy in a way that humiliates her cousin. Though temporarily defeated, Bernice through her subsequent revenge indicates that she now possesses the kind of courage and self-image that will make her a formidable flapper. "Bernice Bobs Her Hair" celebrates the transformation of an undistin-

INTRODUCTION

guished girl into the type of lively and daring heroine so highly prized by the author himself.

Leech's "Manicure" opens with a detailed description of the women who have appointments at Leon and Jules, a luxurious beauty salon located in an expensive New York hotel. Two types of women frequent the salon—working women and those supported by wealthy men:

> The Saturday afternoon patrons were persons well up in the world. Here were buyers, smartly dressed and deftly rouged. Here were well-informed private secretaries, in dark woolen dresses. Here were women executives with lines of worry between their brows. They looked prosperous, even affluent. But some grace was lacking—some glaze of exquisiteness which leisure and years of infinite luxury impart. On Saturday afternoons there was none of the casual elegance of an enameled cigarette case, of a glimpse of *binche* at the bosom, of a square emerald sliding negligently around a thin finger. And it might have been observed that on Saturday afternoons the deference of the girls at Leon and Jules fell a shade short. For these women were not silken creatures from some incredible Aladdin's palace. After all, they worked for a living. They might be wise and friendly, but they were not opening doors of vivid life, and they were not clear windows through which to peep into a fairyland of riches.

The manicurist Nina, like the other girls who worked in the salon, is stirred only by imagining the luxury and leisure of the weekday patrons and is a little bored with the working women on Saturday afternoons. Only the women who are supported by wealthy men are envied.

As she manicures the nails of a new blond customer one Saturday, she discovers that this stranger knows a great deal about her and her current lover, Peter Koch, the attractive assistant manager of the hotel. First the blond discusses a woman named Adele who was forced to give up her job at Leon and Jules because of her passion for Koch. Nina criticizes the foolish Adele, who was incautious enough to visit Koch's room in the hotel. Obviously, Nina's affair with him is proceeding in much less public places. The patron then reveals that she too has been betrayed by Koch. Perhaps she hopes that Nina will be sufficiently disillusioned to give Koch up when she learns the truth. She seems really to want to save Nina from the same suffering she experienced during the six years of her relationship with the womanizing manager.

The author portrays Nina as a new kind of woman, one who plans to use men and who will not be victimized by them. In this story the pleasure-seeking flapper has hardened into a ruthless and cold social climber. When the blonde advises Nina to return to her boy friend and get married, the manicurist scorns the suggestion:

"Married? Say, what's getting married? Kids. No clothes. No fun. Washing and ironing and mending his clothes, instead of just your own. Cooking and cleaning and losing your looks. And him not as nice to you as before you were married." She thrust her face close to the blonde woman's. "I'm going to have things," she said. Her little voice was shrill and vibrant. "No thirty-dollar clerk for me when I marry. I've been studying, educating myself to speak nice, and everything. I gave the boy friend the air six months ago. Do you think I'm going to throw myself away?"

Nina—who has changed her name from Nellie in addition to changing the way she speaks—is more than a match for Koch. In a way Leech's story seems to be a fantasy of feminine invulnerability. The old-fashioned girl who wanted to marry a man like Koch could be deceived or destroyed by him. But now he has become the vulnerable one who will have to deal with a cold, calculating woman.

American Voices

Although "The Golden Honeymoon" (1924), by Ring Lardner, and "Romance in the Roaring Forties" (1929), by Damon Runyon, are celebrations of very different kinds of experiences, they are remarkable examples of the same literary technique: the first-person narrative in which the speaker is vividly characterized by the way he describes his perceptions. The narrator in each story has an unmistakably American voice—a pattern of phrasing, a choice of wording, a way of thinking, that makes him an American original.

INTRODUCTION

In "The Golden Honeymoon," the narrator, Charley, a middle-class married man of seventy-two, takes his wife, Lucy, to St. Petersburg, Florida, to celebrate their fiftieth anniversary. He is an unreliable narrator in that his descriptions of his own character and the actions of others are distorted by his own egotism and prejudices. The core of Lardner's story reveals itself in the way the reader comes to an understanding of Charley, which is far superior to Charley's own analysis of his behavior.

For example, in St. Petersburg Charley and Lucy meet the Hartsells, who are from Michigan. Frank Hartsell had been Lucy's fiancé more than fifty years before and had been displaced by Charley. Although both men are over seventy, Charley is still competitive and vain as he describes the man who was once his rival:

> Him and I is the same age to the month, but he seems to show it more, some way. He is balder for one thing. And his beard is all white, where mine has still got a streak of brown in it.

Charley can't resist criticizing Frank's appearance as he tells him that his beard "looks like a regular blizzard." Frank retorts that Charley's beard would be as white as his if it were dry-cleaned, suggesting that Charley's dark streak is merely a tobacco stain.

While the couples spend a great deal of time together, Charley perpetually compares the Hartsells to him and Lucy, noting their inferiority in every respect. When the four of them attend a church social sponsored by the Michigan Society, Charley finds the entertainment—music, and bird imitations—to be quite dull. But when his own New York-New Jersey Society provides an evening of similar entertainment, Charley enthusiastically describes the performance of Mrs. Newell, a bird imitator, saying " 'You could really tell what they was the way she done it.' " Charley has the dubious ability of going blissfully through life unaware that he is continually irritating others or that they are putting him down. He is a marvelous caricature, exemplifying the narrow one-sidedness everyone occasionally displays.

In "Romance in the Roaring Forties" the distinctive world of the unnamed narrator is communicated by the story's opening lines:

> Only a rank sucker will think of taking two peeks at Dave the Dude's doll, because while Dave may stand for the first peek, figuring it is a mistake, it is a sure thing he will get sored up at the second peek, and Dave the Dude is certainly not a man to have sored up at you.

This narrator's domain is the area of Manhattan around Broadway from Forty-second to Forty-ninth Streets. The location of nightclubs, restaurants, and theaters, it is inhabited by characters with names such as Waldo Winchester, One-eyed Solly, Slugsy Sachs, Missouri Martin, and Lola Spaola. This story is the first of Runyon's very popular tales of gangsters, gamblers, bootleggers, and showgirls who speak their own dialect and live by their own special code. The narrator is a good-natured observer of the relationships among Dave the Dude, who is a bootlegger; Waldo Winchester, a reporter; and Miss Billy Perry, a nightclub tap dancer. He makes extensive use of the local dialect in which "the old equalizer" is a gun, giving someone the "leather" is kicking him when he's down, and a fake message is "nothing but the phonus bolonus." Learning that after being rejected by Billy Perry, Dave has taken to drinking at the Chicken Club, the narrator discusses Dave's behavior and makes us feel that we are among the insiders who make up the Broadway crowd:

> This is regarded as a very bad sign indeed, because while everybody goes to the Chicken Club now and then to give Tony Bertazolla, the owner, a friendly play, very few people care to do any drinking there, because Tony's liquor is not meant for anybody to drink except the customers.

In this gangster fantasy land of Runyon's, a criminal like Dave the Dude can be so deeply in love that he reveals his heart of gold. Desiring Billy's happiness above all else, he wants to make it possible for her to marry Waldo by buying the engagement ring, paying for the wedding, and staking the couple to a good start with a few thousand dollars. At the scene of the wedding he displays another gentlemanly trait—he won't shoot a lady, not even one who has socked him a few times. Dave the Dude is appropriately rewarded as true love triumphs at Big Nig Skolsky's roadhouse.

A Couple of Con Men

Two stories in this collection depict dishonest characters: "The Dummy-Chucker" (1920), by Arthur Somers Roche, and "The Cracked Teapot" (1924), by Charles Caldwell Dobie. There is a significant degree of humanity and responsiveness about each of these con artists. Both men turn out to have a highly moral point of view and make important value judgments by the conclusion of their adventures.

Roche's "dummy-chucker" (a person who chucks a dummy is one who puts something over on a naïve victim) is distinctly a character of Manhattan. He carefully chooses an appropriate spot outside a theater where he will have a good chance of arousing pity with his phony epileptic fit:

> If he tried to do business with a flock of people that had just seen Charlie Chaplin, he'd fail. He knew. Fat women who'd left the twins at home with the neighbor's cook in order that they might have a good cry at the Concorde—these were his mutton-heads.

The unnamed "dummy-chucker" is a close observer of human nature. Thus, when he is hired to trick a young woman by pretending to be drunk, he judges the ruthlessness of his employer's character and acts on his conviction that the wealthy young suitor is unfit to become the girl's husband.

The transformation of the con artist into a gentleman of high standards and compassion is accomplished when he is supplied with expensive clothes and other appurtenances of luxury. The story conveys a particularly American theme, because it suggests the possibility of extraordinary social mobility and the potential of any individual to create a new and better self when he has sufficient material wealth to satisfy his imagination.

In "The Cracked Teapot" Dobie depicts a tense encounter between an itinerant con man, Finderson, and his intended victim, a pregnant farm wife. The woman arouses Finderson's admiration by her unexpected strength of character. The one weakness that makes her vulnerable is that the stranger, who has eaten a meal in her kitchen, has discovered her secret hoard of money, collected over the years through the occasional sale of a few eggs or a chicken. Finderson is gleeful when he discovers the money in the teapot, since he plans to blackmail the woman and bilk the couple, as he has done with other farm couples in the past. The con man is an experienced strategist who relishes the cat-and-mouse game he plays with the woman, exploiting her overwhelming fear that her husband will learn of her "dishonesty." Finderson's chief weapon is his knowledge of the underlying power struggle between husbands and wives. In justifying her accumulation of the secret money, the wife asks whether it is right that a woman has to "*ask* for every nickel" and asserts, " 'If men make thieves of women, why that's their lookout.' " And when she threatens to tell her husband that Finderson had insulted her, in order to get him thrown out of the house, he predicts that her life will be miserable as a result, since her husband will forever berate her for not obeying his rules about feeding vagabonds.

She acknowledges that this outsider is right about the price she would be forced to pay. Clearly, her husband is difficult to live with. Finderson appears to reflect the author's view that the wife's attempt to achieve a small degree of financial independence will inevitably lead to far-reaching corruption of family life. This is a somewhat unusual theme; in many nineteenth-century stories farm wives often use "egg money" as their special income, and husbands generally understand the rightness of this personal resource. Yet in this twentieth-century story a more restrictive role for a wife is advocated. The con man becomes a moral agent who demonstrates to the pregnant woman how any of her actions that do not have her husband's approval will lead to serious failures on her part as a mother and as a wife.

The Business World

The problems associated with standardized production of cheap goods as well as questions of business ethics were significant themes of the Twenties, reflecting the burgeoning of American industrial forces. In a decade of enormous acquisition of material goods, many authors made inevitable comparisons between the quickly manufactured, mass-produced clothing and furniture that flooded the stores and the homemade and sometimes artistically impressive articles that many Americans had known as children. Two stories, Sinclair Lewis's "A Matter of Business" (1920) and Ruth Suckow's "Midwestern Primitive" (1929), offer serious criticisms of mass-produced goods and of a new standardized national culture of bland mediocrity. A third story, " 'There's Money in Poetry' " (1929), by Konrad Bercovici, ridicules the values of an immigrant father stunned by the prospect that one of his sons may become a poet instead of a businessman. For him there could be no greater tragedy.

Readers familiar with Lewis's *Babbitt* will recognize the similarities between James T. Candee, of Vernon, and George F. Babbitt, of Zenith. For example, Candee makes all sorts of plans to improve himself and his surroundings, but these plans, like those of George Babbitt to stop smoking, are never carried out.

Candee is inexplicably attracted to the group of carved wooden dolls he glimpses at a roadside stand. Haunted by a dreamlike quality in the dolls, he returns to the stand and arranges with Emile Jumas, a frustrated sculptor, to buy the entire collection to retail in Candee's Novelty Stationery Shop in the city. Although Papa Jumas's dolls sell well enough, Candee finds himself faced with a dilemma when a salesman suggests that the shop ought to become an exclusive outlet for a new doll, the Skillyoolly—"a simpering, star-eyed, fluffy, chiffon-clothed lady doll." Although this doll is cheaply made, it is not cheaply priced. Candee realizes he must choose between selling what he considers rubbish at a considerable profit or remaining true to his own affection for the Papa Jumas dolls, which have not been very profitable. Clearly the Jumas dolls appeal to people of superior taste, but most of the characters in the story, including Mrs. Candee, prefer the Skillyoolly dolls. During lunch at the Boosters Club, Jimmy consults his friend Frank Darbin about his difficulty in deciding between the two varieties of dolls. Frank's response is that Candee should of course "pick the kind that brings in the most money."

Candee, in contrast, believes he has a moral responsibility to sell items that are well made, imaginative, and solid. Yet like Babbitt, the character for whom he was a prototype, he is insecure, vacillating, and fearful. Within a year or so a more disillusioned Lewis would depict the American businessman as having no moral qualms as he joyfully profits from corrupt land purchases. Babbitt will live in a house that epitomizes the indifference of the American middle class toward individuality and toward any attempt at a meaningful cultural existence. Candee, with the two dolls set before him, is a transitional figure of the period.

In Ruth Suckow's "Midwestern Primitive" a woman, Bert Statzer, opens a country tea room called the Hillside Inn in the small town of Shell Spring. She copies many of her ideas about serving guests from a magazine photograph and has prepared a special meal for some new patrons, an author and four of his companions. Bert's ambition centers around doing things correctly, as they are done in the Eastern cities:

> The shining glasses twinkled up at her, the sweet peas were rosy and stiff, the dishes looked so nice, the little napkins were so pretty . . . was everything right? She had got ideas wherever she could, but was she sure? She wanted to show these people that even if she did live out here in Shell Spring, she knew how things ought to be. She was going to have a *real* tea room some day. . . . If she could only have the kind of things that other people had, do things the way that other people did them! She was going to do it even if she was stuck here. It had to be right.

Ashamed of her old-fashioned immigrant mother, Bert supplies the same undistinguished fare her guests have traveled so far to escape. The contrast between daughter and mother is that of a younger woman attempting to piece together a new identity and life-style based on glimpses of a sophisticated world she does not know first-hand, and a casual older woman, secure in her lifelong interests and pleasures and expecting the world to appreciate the possessions and scenes she has always considered beautiful. For her, time cannot alter their value.

In the portrait of Bert, Suckow captures the intense desire of rural Americans to have exactly the same possessions and eat the same food as their urban counterparts. Bert's pretensions and ideals are obviously empty and destructive. The guests are not at all impressed by her; instead they are charmed by her unpretentious mother. They admire the mother's garden and are interested in all the reminders of the past. If Bert has her way, however, all the individual touches of her home will soon disappear and the standards of the magazine editors will prevail. Her future guests will never be able to tell the difference between her tea room and thousands of others just like it across the country.

In " 'There's Money in Poetry,' " Bercovici satirizes America's infatuation with business in the Twenties, as well as its anti-intellectual climate. The story is framed by two narrators. A successful businessman named Levine corners a fellow passenger on a steamship, a writer, and insists on telling him about his friend Kantrowitz's ordeal. Kantrowitz and Levine, both immigrants, had become successful silk wholesalers in America. Kantrowitz's ordeal starts when he discovers that his younger son, Izzy, has no interest in the family business but instead writes and occasionally publishes his poems. Levine shares Kantrowitz's horror at this aberration. When Levine questions his friend as to whether there has ever been a poet in his family before, Kantrowitz replies, " 'No bankrupts and no poets.' " This genuine contempt for the arts is echoed by Levine, who several times reassures the narrator to whom he has been describing this near-tragedy that the latter's profession—that of writer—is nothing to be ashamed of.

Bercovici's satire is rather mild as he dramatizes the way in which Izzy finally wins family approval while putting his poetic talents to work. The way that Izzy finds to make poetry pay is not merely entertaining; it provides a kind of archetypal model of the way in which an ever larger number of people would put their creative talents to work in the business world.

The Pulse of the City

A significant number of stories in the Twenties explored life in the large cities. By the middle of the decade more than 57 percent of the populace had become city dwellers, some dazzled by the bustling stores, glamorous night spots, and exotic restaurants, but others made desperate by airless tenements, littered alleys, and impersonal crowds.

Two of the stories in this collection that depict urban adventures are structured quite similarly: "Night Club" (1927), by Katharine Brush, and "Hey! Taxi!" (1928), by Edna Ferber. In each story the author records a character's Saturday work shift in New York City. In the first, Mrs. Brady arrives at the Club Français, where she is the attendant in the women's lounge; in the second, Ernest Stewig goes to work, driving his own cab. In "Night Club" Brush sketches the emotional crises of six women who enter the lounge during the course of the evening, suggesting that many of the other women who stand before the mirrors there have equally dramatic stories of their own. Among the actions we, along with Mrs. Brady, witness are a married woman's preparations to embark on an affair, the arrangements made by a girl who has just decided to elope with a man she has known for less than a week, and the quick recovery of a girl who is on drugs and has got her "fix" in the lounge. Mrs. Brady, however, has little interest in her patrons—in the misery experienced by a wife who has just discovered that her husband is unfaithful or in the terror felt by another woman who needs to arm herself with a pair of scissors before rejoining the male who waits outside for her. Insensitive to the real-life problems around her, Mrs. Brady waits for her opportunity to experience her own sort of drama: that of the stories in the magazine she has brought to work with her.

In "Hey! Taxi!" we follow Ernest Stewig as he begins work on a typical Saturday in November with a routine fare, driving two older women to a movie theater and collecting a nickel tip. As the day wears on, Ernie has a series of adventures that include transporting bootleg liquor, reluctantly driving a notorious underworld figure to Brooklyn, and heroically getting an injured milk-wagon driver to the hospital. Ernie's quick thinking results in the apprehension of the automobile driver who caused the accident. But, like Mrs. Brady, Ernie is oblivious of the significance of the miniature dramas that have occurred in and around his cab.

An isolated moment of excitement occurs in the life of Herbert Beatty in "Fame for Mr. Beatty" (1929), by James Norman Hall. Beatty, who has cheerfully performed his work as a bookkeeper for more than twenty years, leads a lonely life of dull routines. He might be described as a "mass-produced man," one of three thousand consumers served daily between twelve and two o'clock in the same restaurant by waitresses who never recognize him. One of the great pleasures of his day is reading the *Morning Post*:

> Mr. Beatty was one of the numberless army of men and women who have made possible the success of the mod-

ern American newspaper, whose reading is confined almost entirely to its columns. It amused him, instructed him, thought for him. He found there satisfaction for all his modest needs, spiritual and cultural.

In this tale of Beatty's brief moment of glory, Hall touches upon two concerns that troubled thoughtful Americans of the Twenties. First, they were made uncomfortable by the extraordinary hold that newspapers had established over the public by the middle of the decade. Americans could now get all their opinions ready made from the newspapers as quickly as they could purchase their standardized lunches in colorless fast-food establishments. The second vital issue is reflected in the question the *Morning Post*'s inquiring reporter asks of Mr. Beatty: "Do you favor restricted immigration?" The answers supplied by the four men queried on this issue are an excellent index of the range of the opinions of the age and the contradictions of the American way of life.

The American Dream

It is no wonder that a considerable number of stories of the Twenties deal with the dream, and sometimes the attainment, of extraordinary success. For most of the decade Americans were busy acquiring new possessions, among them some objects that had not even existed a few years earlier. As radios, automobiles, phonographs, vacuum cleaners, and sparkling new kitchens and bathrooms glittered seductively in the pages of popular magazines, buying on credit was fast becoming a national pastime. Virtually every American was aware of the incredible fortune being amassed by Henry Ford, and no doubt each could reel off the names of a dozen others who had risen from a working-class existence to become extremely wealthy or perhaps merely enviably comfortable. F. Scott Fitzgerald captured the American dreamer's preoccupation with creating a successful self-image in the character of Jay Gatsby. In *The Great Gatsby* (1925) we have a list of resolutions drawn up by young James Gatz as he dreams of entering a new world of beautiful people. By such methods as studying electricity and "needed inventions," practicing elocution and poise, reading "one improving book or magazine per week," would he not be guaranteed a place in the elusive world of his dreams? The dreamers in some of the stories in this volume might well have made up similar lists for themselves if they had thought such resolutions would help in their quests.

Two of the stories in this collection, Sherwood Anderson's "The Egg" (1920) and James T. Farrell's "A Jazz-Age Clerk" (1932), portray the failures, the disappointed seekers after glamour and success, who are all the more pathetic because they believe that most others are living the pleasurable and exciting lives that have eluded them. In a third story, "Mendel Marantz—Housewife" (1922), by David Freedman, the dreamer is rewarded with the success he craves, and the reader is reassured that nothing is impossible in America.

The narrator of "The Egg" summarizes his family's history of failures, but the central event of the tale is the dramatic failure of his father that occurs one evening. This event is so crucial that the narrator believes it has shaped his own character and outlook. His father, who had once been a contented farmhand, had experienced numerous disappointments as a chicken farmer. The forces of the universe seem diabolically to conspire to prevent the farmer from bringing his chickens to a profit-producing maturity. Leaving the farm, he acquires a small restaurant near the railroad station. He becomes obsessed with the idea of turning his isolated and unsuccessful restaurant into a mecca of gaiety for the young people of the nearby town.

> It was father's notion that a passion for the company of himself and mother would spring up in the breasts of the younger people of the town of Bidwell. In the evening bright happy groups would come singing down Turner's Pike. They would troop shouting with joy and laughter into our place. There would be song and festivity.

Since the narrator's father is a rather cheerless, uncommunicative man who has decorated his restaurant with jars of deformed chicks floating in alcohol, this dream of success involves a great deal more than the profitable selling of food. It is a fantasy of the rebirth of the hardworking, pessimistic chicken farmer as the joyful, popular center of social activities. He dreams of changing the gloomy pattern of his life through an act of will.

An even greater dreamer is the central character of James

INTRODUCTION

T. Farrell's "A Jazz-Age Clerk." Jack Stratton, a Chicago clerk, habitually fills his vacant moments with dreams of being loved by beautiful women and of possessing great wealth. Occasionally, Jack admits to himself that beneath his jaunty air, his snatches of the latest hit songs, his fashionable dance steps, the image he has is badly in need of bolstering. He sits in the lobby of the luxurious Potter Hotel daydreaming that one day a bellboy will call him to the phone, where he will make a profitable deal with a millionaire. Afterward,

> he would be waiting for this movie actress more beautiful than even Gloria Swanson, thinking how when he had been nothing but a punk clerk at the express company he'd come to sit in the same lobby, wearing shabby clothes, dreaming of the day when things would happen to him.

Jack's vocabulary is a compendium of the slang of the Twenties. He thinks of pretty women as "shebas," "mamas," "queens," or "broads" and is incapable of imagining himself in a realistic relationship with one of them. In his dreams he wins the love of one of these sex objects by supplying her with expensive gifts. He resents his co-workers, who don't even try to be "cake-eaters" and who have nicknamed him "Jenny." Discontented with his prospects and ashamed of his shabby appearance, Jack feeds his spirit on nebulous dreams of future success.

Among the plethora of Twenties stories celebrating the varieties of American success is Freedman's "Mendel Marantz—Housewife," the story of an immigrant Jewish couple, Mendel and Zelde, who with their six children are struggling to survive in desperate straits because Mendel has never been able to hold on to a job for long. Although he has worked as an insurance agent, a night watchman, and a candy-stand owner, he is an incurable dreamer who can never repeat any manual labor without trying to invent a device that will perform the same work for him. Freedman's story is punctuated by Mendel's running commentary on the world. He asks himself a series of philosophical questions about life and answers them in his own antithetical way:

> " 'What is love? A conquest. What is marriage? An inquest.' "

" 'What is success? Fifth Avenue. What is failure? Fifth floor.' "

" 'What is a woman? A lot of thunder, but a little rain.' "

In an unusual reversal of roles, Zelde goes out into the world to earn a living for her family while the imaginative Mendel is forced to care for the house and his three younger children. His remarkable invention to handle the repetitious and backbreaking chores of keeping a household in order must have been pleasing to readers for two reasons: first, a struggling immigrant demonstrates that by being true to his dreams, he can succeed; second, his invention reflects the promise of material progress that pervaded the nation during the decade, as new roads were built, new movie theaters opened, and new technologies such as the radio and vacuum cleaner became available. What if Mendel's marvelous machine was today only a figment of the author's imagination? Tomorrow it would surely be on sale for a few dollars down and a few easy payments. Weren't luxury and ease the birthright of every American who was willing to work for them?

BARBARA H. SOLOMON
Iona College
New Rochelle, New York

Essays

Personality Craze

by Jules Abels

Absorption with personality was so much a hallmark of the age that even Calvin Coolidge became a personality that fascinated the public. Walter Lippmann, in an article he wrote in 1926, conjectured that in Coolidge the public was rediscovering rugged virtues of our past that it feared we had lost. Americans now craved luxury and were buying it furiously, largely on the installment plan, but they liked the idea of having a simple, frugal man as their symbol in the White House.

> They are delighted with the oil lamps in the farmhouse at Plymouth, and with fine, old Colonel Coolidge and his chores and his antique grandeur . . . they are delighted that the President comes of such stock, and they even feel, I think, that they are stern, ascetic and devoted to plain living because they vote for a man who is. . . . Thus we have attained a Puritanism de luxe in which it is possible to praise the classic virtues, while continuing to enjoy all the modern conveniences.

Certainly, if the American press and public could find glamor in a drab personality like that of Coolidge, it could become ecstatic about personalities with some flair. It would be futile to explore the rationality of it all. There was an exuberance in the air, a *joie de vivre* that found expression in identification with other human beings. Most ambrosial was the delight of sharing vicariously in the experience of superior human beings, those who stood above the mass.

After the dramatic solo flight of Charles A. Lindbergh across the Atlantic Ocean in May, 1927, the mail that poured in to President Coolidge reflected the thrill America felt at the feat. Among the requests made to the President were the following:

1. That he forbid Lindbergh to fly back home across the Atlantic (a project that had undoubtedly never occurred to Lindbergh).
2. That the day of the flight, May 21, be a legal holiday, Lindbergh Day.
3. That Lindberg be declared exempt from federal income taxes.
4. That he be appointed Secretary of Aviation in the Cabinet (a post that did not exist).
5. That he be appointed an ambassador-at-large, with the portfolio of ambassador of goodwill.
6. That his portrait be put beside that of George Washington on the three-cent stamp.
7. That the name of a bright star in the heavens be renamed Lindbergh.

As always, Coolidge was matter of fact and coldly logical. He addressed an inquiry to the Department of Commerce. Should not a medal be given to the designer of Lindbergh's plane, the *Spirit of St. Louis*? A letter to him from William P. MacCracken, Assistant Secretary of Commerce, replied that this did not seem practical. If the designer of the plane were thus honored, then the inventor of the earth inductor compass that Lindbergh used should also be honored, and if that were done, the inventors of other gadgets would have to be recognized. (The earth inductor compass, a new device, enabled Lindbergh to steer a straight line through fog or dark since its coil, rotating on a vertical axis, showed any deviation in relation to the lines of force around the globe.)

Coolidge arranged Lindbergh's return to Washington. He was to arrive immediately after noon on a Saturday when government offices let out, thus making it unnecessary to declare a holiday. The President had sent the cruiser *Memphis* to carry him and his plane home from Europe. The ship was met 100 miles at sea by four destroyers and was escorted up Chesapeake Bay by two Army blimps and forty airplanes. At the Navy Yard pier he was greeted by three members of the Cabinet and former Secretary of State Charles Evans Hughes, top Army and Navy brass, including the Chiefs of the Army and Navy Air Forces, his mother, and Commander Richard E. Byrd. There was a parade to the Washington Monument, and Coolidge in a long speech hailed our "ambassador without portfolio," voiced "the gratitude of the Republic," awarded him the Distinguished Flying Cross, and made him a

Personality Craze

colonel in the Army Reserve Corps. In a press conference in Washington's largest auditorium, he was presented by Postmaster General New with the Lindbergh airmail stamp, the first living man so honored.

He was a weekend guest at the temporary White House on Dupont Circle. (The White House was undergoing repairs, and the Coolidges were occupying "Cissy" Patterson's mansion.) At the dinner there on Saturday night, one of the guests, Coolidge's friend Dwight Morrow, father of Anne Morrow, met Lindbergh, thereby enabling Coolidge unwittingly to play cupid to one of the most famous love matches of the era. The next morning Lindbergh went to church with the Coolidges. When he appeared in a light suit, the President discreetly hinted that darker clothes might be more appropriate, and Lindbergh reluctantly changed. He invariably accepted suggestions with the word "check."

The next morning he flew an Army pursuit plane to Mitchell Field in New York. (The *Spirit of St. Louis* had been damaged by salt air on the ocean trip.) The trip to New York took two hours and four minutes; this conveys an idea of the primitiveness of the planes of that day. From there he went by amphibious plane to the Narrows, where he transferred to the municipal welcoming boat, the *Macom*, and with Grover Whalen, the city's official greeter, he proceeded up the harbor with an escort of 400 ships, with every whistle screeching. "My mind is ablaze with noise, terrible noise," wrote Lindbergh of the welcome. Then up to Broadway he rode, showered with ticker tape and confetti, to City Hall, where he received the State Medal of Valor from Mayor Jimmy Walker.

The outpouring of praise from the press could hardly be surpassed. The Baltimore *Sun* said, "He has exulted the race of men." The Minneapolis *Star* said, "This was heroism worthy of the greatest that has ever entered Valhalla." The New York *Post* said, "He has flown like a poem into the heart of America. Romance lived again in him." At a dinner in New York for him, former Secretary of State Hughes said, "He has lifted us into the freer and upper air that is his home. He has displaced everything that is petty, that is sordid, that is vulgar. What is money in the presence of Charles A. Lindbergh, what is . . . etc.?" Even a worldly cynic like Heywood Broun wrote, "We came up out of slumps and slouches. There was more brotherhood in being than I have ever seen here since the Armistice."

Of the wild adulation, Lindbergh said over and over again, "Do I deserve all this?" As summarized in *The Great American Bandwagon*, by Charles Merz, in six days Lindbergh had received fifteen medals; a song, "When Lindbergh Came Home," had been written by George M. Cohan; a new dance, the Lindbergh Hop, had been invented; the Pennsylvania Railroad had named a Pullman car for him; eleven laundries in New York had sought to incorporate with his name; he had been tendered the largest dinner ever given an individual in New York at the Hotel Commodore, where 36,000 cups and plates had been used, 12,000 pieces of cake eaten, and 300 pounds of butter consumed.

In his book about Lindbergh, Kenneth Davis quotes Joseph Campbell's *The Hero with a Thousand Faces* concerning the constant factors that go into the making of a hero, "a magnification in the formula represented in the rites of passage: separation, initiation, return." In the "monomyth," a "hero ventures forth from the world of common day into a region of supernatural wonder; fabulous forces are there encountered and a decisive victory is won; the hero comes back from this mysterious venture with the power to bestow boons on his fellow men." Certainly the Lindbergh feat embodied all those elements.

Immediately after the war, a Frenchman, Raymond Orteig, had offered $25,000 for the first nonstop flight between New York and Paris in the next five years, and when there were no attempts during that time, he renewed his offer. The first efforts failed. In 1926 René Fonck's plane crashed and exploded into flames when he took off from Roosevelt Field in New York. Two of the crew perished, making a spectacular newsreel. In the spring of 1927 two French airmen, Charles Nungesser and François Coli, disappeared and presumably died after taking off from Paris. There were two pilots now waiting on Roosevelt Field for good weather: Commander Richard E. Byrd, in a plane with the most modern equipment and with a crew of three other specialists; and a longtime air barnstormer, Clarence Chamberlin, who would take along as a passenger Charles Levine, president of Columbia Aircraft Corporation.

Before they decided to leave, the lone twenty-five-year-old former Army mail pilot, after a record transcontinental flight of twenty-one hours and twenty minutes in his *Spirit of St. Louis*, beat them to it. On a murky morning, taking a risk on the weather, he flew off from a rain-soaked field, saying, "So long," as casually as if he were setting off on an automobile trip. It was problematical whether the plane, heavily loaded as it was with fuel, would get off the ground or become a fiery wreck like Fonck's aircraft. Steadily the plane ascended, and the New York *Times* report said, "The wheels of the plane cleared by a bare ten feet a tractor which lay directly in its path. A gully was ahead into which he might have plunged but which he safely left below. Over the telephone lines he passed with a scant twenty feet to spare."

The "separation" phase was over, and the "initiation" phase began when the plane headed east into the Atlantic Ocean from Newfoundland. That night during the broadcast of the Jack Sharkey–Jim Maloney fight from Yankee Stadium the voice of the announcer Joe Humphries asked the crowd to stand for a minute of silent prayer. There were songs of prayer sung on the radio that night. Will Rogers' column read, "No attempt at jokes today. A slim, tall, bashful, smiling American boy is somewhere over the middle of the Atlantic Ocean, where no lone human being has ever ventured before."

Then the news came of the landing at Le Bourget airfield! He had flown the 3,610 miles to Paris in thirty-three hours and twenty-nine minutes, a record for distance in nonstop flight. It was a triumph of personal courage and a triumph, too, of unpremeditated art in the display of personal modesty. His personal belongings on the flight were only a razor, passport, and six letters of introduction, apparently in the belief that after tidying up, he would have to make acquaintances. Then there were his frequent references, before and after the flight to himself and the plane as "We."

What "boons to his fellow men" did this hero confer on his "return" from the mysterious venture? John W. Ward, writing in 1958 of "The Meaning of Lindbergh's Flight," said, "From the moment of success there were two Lindberghs, the private Lindbergh and the public Lindbergh. The latter was the construction of the imagination of Lindbergh's time fastened to an unwilling object." A nation which had cherished moral absolutes was uneasy in an age of relativism. Lindbergh "gave the American people a glimpse of what they liked to think themselves to be at a time when they feared they had deserted their own vision of themselves . . . the response to Lindbergh involved a mass ritual in which America celebrated itself more than it celebrated Lindbergh." (This is similar to Lippmann's explanation of the Coolidge worship.)

He was the lone pioneer figure who had moved the American frontier ever westward. His feat, said Dean Howard Chandler of the Cathedral of St. John the Divine, required the "self-discipline of years," which stands out in the present age of "revolt against discipline" and the tendency to "uninhibited self-expression." He has revealed the true American, misrepresented in the newspapers, said former Secretary Hughes. "He has driven the sensation-mongerers out of the temples of our thought. He has kindled anew the fires on the eight ancient altars of that temple. Where are the stories of crime, of divorce, of the triangles that are never equilateral?"

The flight was symbolic in another sense. It was a victory for the modern machine, to be worshiped as an instrument to lead us all to a new paradise, instead of a devilish device which would enthrall mankind. There can be no doubt that the flight was the catalyst responsible for the great leap forward that aviation took in the next five years. Interest in planes had lagged. The government inaugurated airmail flight in 1918, a bomber carrying a bag of mail once a day between New York and Washington. Not until 1924 was the first airmail flight inaugurated across the continent; it took thirty-two hours and the airmail stamp cost twenty-four cents. There were many who believed that the greatest potential for the nation's defense lay in dirigibles, which could be the mother ship for planes, rather than in long-distance aircraft. After the Lindbergh flight, everybody was talking about the feasibility of networks for carrying passengers commercially. In the succeeding year and a half after the flight, the price of Wright Aeronautical Company stock soared from $25 to $245. There was even discussion about the possibility of transoceanic service, although it was the prevailing opinion that this would not be possible until there were floating airports stationed in the Atlantic Ocean.

It was natural that royalty should be the object of special attention. In 1924 the nation was agog about the prospective visit of Edward Albert Christian George Andrew Patrick David Windsor, who would be traveling incognito as Lord Renfrew, but who, everybody knew, was the Prince of Wales. Because his worldwide travels helped promote British goods, he had been dubbed the Prince of Sales. This was a Prince Charming out of *Grimm's Fairy Tales*, thirty years old, unmarried, under middle height but handsome, with the round face of a Kewpie doll.

Preceded by the shipment of eight of his polo ponies he arrived on the *Berengaria* at the end of August and managed to elude any official welcome. Then he went to pay a visit on President Coolidge, stopping off at Baltimore to visit a crippled child, while attended by the press. After alighting at Union Station in Washington, he was driven to the White House.

The prince was quite nervous. He fidgeted, standing first on one foot and then the other, his hands continually darting in and out of his pockets, smoking cigarettes one after another. He had lunch with the President, his wife and son John. Coolidge saw the nervousness of his guest and tried to make him comfortable, working to make conversation as the White House staff had never seen him work before. While the President dug deeper and deeper into his store of recollections of history, the prince merely smiled. No doubt Coolidge was relieved when the meal was finished, and he could turn the prince over to the wives of Washington officialdom who were eager to curtsy before him.

Going from Washington to Long Island, the prince embarked on a mad social whirl on the estates of the Morgans, the Vanderbilts, and the Phippses. He was a marathon dancer, driving from one party to another as the women lined up for his attentions. Once he took the place of a drummer in the band. He played polo with a patch on one eye because a pony had hoofed a clod of earth into it, went on a fox hunt, rode the steeplechase, and raced in a speedboat. All this the press reported avidly. Will Rogers accompanied him and told America, "All kidding aside, the Kid is there. He is a Regular Guy."

Was the prince fittingly called the Playboy of the Western World? The kind of publicity he was receiving so disturbed his entourage that his aide, Captain Lascelles, confided to the press that the prince was an avid reader, who was now making his way through *The Life and Letters of Walter H. Page*. Many wondered when the prince had any time for reading. One afternoon he drove in from Long Island and visited Julia Richman High School, the Museum of Natural History, and two printing plants of newspapers, again attended by the press. So much for culture!

The Reverend Thomas Kirkwood of Syracuse assailed the voguish aping of the prince: "It is a sad commentary on our democracy to see the way so many of our youths are spoiling their good hats by turning down the brim in front because the Prince does so." When he visited the International Polo Cup matches at Meadow Brook, according to the New York *Times*, "The whole stand was a fogbank from thousands and thousands of hats worn in the Prince's style. Gray hats were so numerous that even the special police could not identify him."

The prince was highly sensitive on one subject. He had fallen off his horse on at least fourteen occasions in the last two years while hunting or steeplechasing. As the great British sportsman John Jorrocks, MFH, had said, "There is no young man wot will not rather 'ave a himputation on his morality than 'is 'ossmanship." The prince explained to the press that he had never fallen "off" a horse but rather "with" his horse. If the horse falls, how could he be expected to stay upright?

In late September he departed for his ranch in Alberta, Canada, and returned briefly on his way home a month later. He visited the Ford plant in Detroit to see autos assembled, and Ford showed the prince a new electric motor which would be capable of drawing 150 coal cars at forty miles an hour. "Well, sir, it wasn't two seconds before he was asking me questions about it I couldn't answer." When Ford expressed his surprise at his technical knowledge, he said that the prince replied, "You may not know that I took four years of electrical engineering."

The greatest concern of the Empire about the prince was: When would he marry? His American trip had resulted in no progress in that direction. Cosmo Hamilton, the British playwright, in a speech to the English-Speaking Union in Philadelphia, explained that the trouble was Socialism, which had infected his companions in the gay clubs of London. "One can't be smart unless one is a Socialist. It is like the cross-word puzzle here. The Prince is up against it. He doesn't marry because there has been injected into him from all sides the virus of Socialism." The connection was not clear, since Socialists do marry.

For the remainder of the decade the prince was featured in our papers, though he never returned here. His tours over the world, to South Africa, South America, to Canada, were fully reported; so, too, were his falls from horses. Regularly photos appeared in the papers of a cut and bruised young man walking forlornly from a horse. In November, 1925, he fell twice in one week. In 1928 he hit a new record, six tumbles in five days, and a week later he fell off a horse twice in the same race. It was now abundantly clear that he was the worst horseman in the British royal line. The Empire was filled with dread when it was announced in 1929 that he had learned to fly, but was reassured when the prince promised that he would not be at the controls unless he had an experienced pilot by his side.

The years went on, and despair grew as the prince remained single. There were bubbles about Princess Astrid of Sweden, then Princess Ingrid of Sweden, Lady Curzon, Princess Beatrice of Spain. By the end of the decade he was thirty-six years old and without a permanent love interest. Mrs. Simpson was yet to appear on the scene.

A royal visitor of 1926 made a good deal more of a stir. This was Queen Marie of Rumania. At the time she was over fifty and had lost her beauty, but bejeweled photographs of her at an earlier age filled the newspapers, dazzling the viewer. Actually little of her could be seen since her neck was enclosed in strings of pearls and she wore a jeweled headdress that resembled a football helmet.

She was a granddaughter of Queen Victoria, her father having been Victoria's second son, the Duke of Edinburgh, and she was also descended from Czar Alexander II of Russia. Her husband, King Ferdinand, had equally little Rumanian blood. He was a German Hohenzollern prince, having been nominated for the job of heir apparent of Rumania because his predecessor, King Carol, had no heir. The queen had early shown her affinity for the press. When she arrived for the Versailles Peace Conference, her first words were: "Where is the press?" The Versailles Treaty almost doubled the territory of Rumania, giving it control of Bessarabia and shoving into its borders many minority groups. It was a backward country of 18,000,000 people, and the regime survived by brute force. Peasants were shot down in Bessarabia by the hundreds, freedom of speech was gone, the jails were packed with political prisoners, and the government was openly anti-Semitic.

All this was forgotten by the American public, if it had ever been known, in the ocean of publicity for the queen who for years had waged an unflagging campaign for the limelight. Her picture had long been in the newspapers, and she had written articles for the Hearst press on subjects such as "My Experience with Men," "Clothes and the Woman," "Dreams Do Come True" and "Making Marriage Durable."

And now in the fall of 1926 she would be here in the flesh with an entourage of twenty—a genuine live queen! All America was excited. The New York *World* said that this was an extraordinary event "because it brings together the world's first ultra-modern publicity engine and the world's first ultra-modern Queen. When the modern publicity engine which dotes on motion-picture Queens is actually confronted by a Queen who of her own accord has become a motion-picture version Queen because she dotes on publicity, the lid is off and almost anything can happen. Applesauce flows fast and loose."

Her reception in England was disappointing, but then the English have a queen of their own. On the ocean liner *Leviathan* she announced that she was getting ready for America. She would not touch liquor; she refused to have French soup; she insisted on eating American apple pie and American oysters. She issued statements that America was "marvellously efficient," "terribly sincere," "gloriously generous" (it was rumored that the real purpose of her visit was to get a loan of $100,000,000). In New York she received the deluxe treatment from Grover Whalen and Mayor Walker, though heavy rains held down the size of the crowds. Her stay in Manhattan was a round of receptions, dinners, and press conferences, at each of which she made profound statements such as, "Women have done so much for peace. Some day women will end war—that is if they don't start fighting among themselves." When she visited the jeweler Cartier, a plaque was set up commemorating her visit.

The queen arrived in Washington on October 18 and was driven immediately to the Rumanian Legation. Mrs. Coolidge sent flowers with her card. The next day a car drew up to the White House with an acknowledgment written by a lady-in-waiting and not by the queen, a breach of etiquette. On the twentieth the queen and her party visited the White House.

She was the first queen to visit a President, and there had been some speculation on how the Vermont farmboy would greet her. Would he bow low and kiss her hand? What happened was that she said, "I am pleased to meet you, Mr. President," and he replied, "I am pleased to meet you." (Contrary to report, he did not say "Howdy, Queen.") It had been planned that she and the President would sit on one sofa and Secretary of State Kellogg would sit on another facing them, but Marie upset plans by choosing to sit on an overstuffed chair facing the fireplace. The President had no choice but to take a small cane-seat affair next to her on which he had to sit sideways.

The President, having been coached, asked if he could see her children, Prince Nicholas and Princess Ileana, and they were produced. The queen, so the schedule read, would then take her departure, but to the surprise of all she sat down again as if prepared for a long stay. After an interval, Coolidge rose and walked off with his wife.

Following Marie's return to her legation, the Coolidges reciprocated her call. Only one photograph had been allowed in the White House, but when the Presidential party was seated in the legation, a horde of photographers emerged from behind a curtain, forcing the Coolidges to submit to endless photos. The next night there was a state dinner at the White House for forty guests. The queen, more bejeweled and beplumed than ever, sat next to Coolidge and tried to draw him out in conversation, with the usual result.

There is a story that after she left, Mrs. Coolidge saw the President staring out the window. She asked what he was looking at, and he replied, "I just wanted to be sure that she's gone." Fictional or not as this may be, he had undoubtedly found the whole thing a crashing bore. He had to put up with protocol since he had no choice. White House chief usher Ike Hoover, listing the attitude toward protocol of the various Presidents he had known, said that Coolidge regarded it all as "comedy."

As for the queen, she made a transcontinental tour in which she received an ecstatic welcome everywhere. In Kansas City, Mayor Beach said, "This is the greatest day in the history of Kansas City." When she arrived at Denver the Denver *Post* had the greeting AS ONE QUEEN TO ANOTHER across its front page. The main streets were hung with bunting of red, blue, and yellow, the Rumanian national colors. Everywhere, Marie spouted talk, despite the pleas of the syndicate which sold her column that she reserve her thoughts for her readers.

It all became very tiresome. F.P.A. (Franklin P. Adams) wrote in his diary (a column of his thoughts in the New York *World*, outwardly modeled on Pepys):

> Queen Marie is travelling about in great luxury and a vast amount of money is being expended by somebody and there are tayles of the Queen's great candor and frankness, and I think it would be a good idea to say to

her "All right. How much does your country want?" and say either Yes or No. For it seems to me that the money spent on silk hats by members of the reception committees here and there would keep Rumania in funds for years.

Soon afterward Coolidge entertained another celebrity at a White House meal, the new American operatic sensation Marion N. (for Nevada) Talley, who was in Washington to give a concert. Miss Talley, only nineteen, was seated at the right of Coolidge, who characteristically attacked his food without a word and without any sign that he was conscious of her presence. His guest of honor was frozen in shyness. William Allen White was at the luncheon, and Mrs. Coolidge whispered to him, "For heaven's sake, stir up those two at the head of the table." And so White told Coolidge that Miss Talley was going to purchase a farm in western Kansas. Mrs. Talley, Marion's mother, joined in. The silence was at last broken, and Coolidge made a quip or two.

As an operatic star, Marion Talley was synthetic, as genuine as a cultured pearl is to a real one. She was created by ballyhoo and sold as many another product was sold in that age. During the twenties, amid growing chauvinism, resentment was often expressed that in the field of music, particularly opera, America was dependent on foreigners. It was therefore satisfying to native pride when Lawrence Tibbett, a Californian who had never studied abroad, made a sensationally successful debut as Ford in *Falstaff* in 1925. In 1927 an American opera, *The King's Henchman*, music by Deems Taylor and book by Edna St. Vincent Millay, was hailed as the precursor of a new national art.

During 1925 word spread of a great new operatic soprano who had been discovered in Kansas City, Missouri, the daughter of a railroad telegrapher. Her talent had been brought to light when she was fifteen, at which time Kansas City had taken her under its wing; thus, she became a community project who might have been named the Spirit of Kansas City. A benefit concert was held to raise money to give her the best training and wealthy patrons made contributions. She had an audition at the Metropolitan in New York at seventeen and then was sent abroad to study.

She made her debut at the Metropolitan in February, 1926, after tons of publicity. She had never sung in opera before except for two small roles in a civic opera company in Kansas

City. However the house was sold out well in advance, and there were offers of $100 to $150 for a seat. Five thousand were turned away. Taxiloads of flowers were already at the door. She appeared as Gilda in *Rigoletto*, a large, unpretty girl who scampered on stage in the second act with a nervous, awkward run to thunderous applause. After "Caro Nome," she received a deafening ovation, plus twelve curtain calls after the act and twenty after the final curtain. Asked if he was pleased, manager Giulio Gatti-Casazza said over and over again, "*Sì, sì magnifico.*"

The critics however were not enthusiastic. Olin Downes of the New York *Times* said, "Miss Talley, precipitated at the age of 19 and with virtually no experience upon one of the most famous operatic stages in the world, has not at present the artistic knowledge to make the most of her gifts. The wisdom of the aforesaid precipitation may be better discussed on another occasion, and after Miss Talley has appeared a second time in a second role." Olga Samaroff of the New York *Post* said, "Miss Talley's voice with all its natural beauty, sweetness and extended range is not powerful . . . the long melodic lines last night were tremulous and lacking in the sustained power which in early youth can be achieved through real mastery."

While the critics emphasized her tender years, the fact remained that operatic stars had made successful debuts at younger ages than nineteen. Adelina Patti sang Lucia at the Brooklyn Academy of Music when she was sixteen, and Schumann-Heink and Lilli Lehmann made their debuts at seventeen.

Miss Talley appeared in other roles, and the audiences were less enthusiastic. Kansas City could not be there in force as it had been on the first night. As Eastern critics became more critical, the Midwest became more critical of the Eastern critics. The Kansas City (Missouri) *Star* said editorially, "This city is blamed for the unprecedented publicity preceding the debate. There is no reason for this. Kansas City has been altogether rational about its discovery. It has found her most interesting and promising and has done what was needed to supplement her efforts to get proper training and finally an advantageous appearance. It is quite within reason to believe that Miss Talley would have fared even better at the hands of the critics in one of the greater European capitals. New York critics evinced a timidity, due perhaps to their inexperience in judging voices which are wholly natural." The

Witchita *Beacon* said, "We have been told very often that the prairie country is hopeless from the standpoint of beauty. How can anything good come out of Nazareth?" The Jefferson City *Capital News* said, "Kansas City has faith and believes that Marion will easily become one of the famous singers of the generation. Therefore Kansas City boosts and even the people of New York respond to the spirit while Marion delivers the goods. So to hell with the critics!"

In 1928 she broke with her manager, who revealed that in two years, entirely apart from her earnings at the Metropolitan Opera, she had taken in $334,894 from concerts. In 1929 Marion Talley retired at the age of twenty-two. She became a farmer and was photographed on her tractor wearing a sombrero. She admitted frankly that she was glad to be away from singing, which she found drudgery. There was a general concession, even in Kansas City, that her voice, while sweet and lovely, was no better than that of hundreds of female church choir singers throughout the country.

Marion Talley is now over sixty. *Eheu, fugaces . . . anni. . . .*

When celebrities arrived at New York, they were given a lavish welcome. Even Charles Levine who was merely a passenger on Clarence Chamberlin's transatlantic flight received a ticker-tape welcome. The city's official greeter, Grover A. (for Aloysius) Whalen, was actually the general manager of Wanamaker's Department Store who took time off for this duty. He regarded the job seriously. When Queen Marie arrived, he issued a bulletin for the official party on proper costume: "Frock coats, striped trousers, gray cravats, black shoes, silk hats and lacquer canes."

In "Grover the Magnificent," Henry F. Pringle wrote, "Some men achieve greatness by cunning or industry of by engaging press agents. Grover Whalen rode to fame on a winning smile, irreproachable manners and a meticulous attention to his wardrobe. A lesser man would have failed. He would have been called a dude, an inconsequential clotheshorse." He was a remnant of the dear, dear days beyond recall when "the dull, plumaged male bird of today wore bright feathers, when the burgomaster sported elaborate stocks, frilled shirts, brocaded waistcoats, silken pantaloons and stockings."

After being doused by ticker tape and confetti of shredded paper from office wastebaskets before the gaze of the lunch-

Personality Craze

hour crowds lined along Broadway, the celebrity of the day was lauded in front of City Hall by the mayor, James J. "Jimmy" Walker, slim, dapper and verbally facile, who had just risen from bed for the occasion.

Walker was himself a political phenomenon of the times. This scintillating figure of lighthearted charm belonged on the stage, rather than in one of the most important jobs in the nation. The *Outlook* once said, "Jimmy translated the problems of municipal government, a series of headaches to the average citizen, into simple musical comedy terms that the average person understands. In his hands they became problems that can be solved with a jig and a jest."

When he ran for reelection in 1929 against Fiorello H. LaGuardia and won by a record majority, the *New Yorker* magazine said that while Walker himself did nothing, others, his civil service engineers, for example, accomplished such duties as paving the streets and building tunnels:

> The city struggles on. Meanwhile Walker does things of infinitely greater importance. He lives. He is carefree, obviously happy. He makes whoopee, stays up late, rises late. He dresses snappy and talks snappy. He dines with the Biddles and is photographed with Coleen Moore. Thus he becomes a symbol for some odd-million starved souls numbly seeking escape from reality. In importance he ranks ahead of Roxy's, Babe Ruth's home run score, Ziegfeld's chorus, the tabloids, the Snooks case or Lindbergh's private life. He is five hundred years ahead of his time, or maybe only one hundred at the rate we're going.

Meanwhile, New York City was being wretchedly and corruptly misgoverned. But in the halcyon years of the twenties, Walker lived a charmed life. Gene Fowler wrote, "When Walker had become the John Barrymore of the political stage, most people looked with lenient eyes upon the foibles of the city's darling, for Jim was created in New York's own image."

He was born in Greenwich Village in 1881, the son of a carpenter who went into Tammany politics. Under his father's pressure he attended New York Law School, and after interrupting his studies to play semiprofessional baseball, he managed to graduate. Having no interest in the law but great ambitions as a songwriter, he did not take the bar examinations, preferring to hang out his shingle in Tin Pan Alley. He wrote lyrics for songs such as "Goodbye Eyes of Blue," "After They Gather the Hay," and "There's Music in the Rustle of a Skirt." Then in 1908 came his smash hit, "Will You Love Me in December as You Do in May?"

His subsequent songs were flops, and to please his father, now a big wheel in Tammany circles, he entered politics. In the State Assembly he finally, at the age of thirty-one, took the bar examination and married a former actress he had known for several years. His debonair charm and wit endeared him to Charles F. Murphy, leader of Tammany Hall. He entered the State Senate and became Democratic floor leader where his best-known accomplishment was his sponsorship of the bill to legalize boxing in New York, the Walker Law.

In 1925 he ran in the Democratic primary against the incumbent mayor, John F. Hylan, who was too stuffy for New York's taste. Walker was the Broadway show business candidate. The first nominating speech for him was made by Georgie Jessel, and the demonstration that followed was led by George M. Cohan. Irving Berlin wrote a song, "We'll Walk In with Walker." To get the support of Governor Alfred E. Smith, who was a good family man, the candidate exiled his current sweetheart, actress Vonnie Shelton. He won easily.

During his first two years as mayor, Walker took seven vacations for a total of 150 days, visiting London, Paris, Berlin, Rome, Houston, Hollywood, San Francisco, Atlanta, Bermuda, Canada, Havana, and Florida. His working day did not start until noon, and he was notoriously late for appointments, once keeping President Coolidge waiting for forty minutes. Governor "Al" Smith paid a visit to City Hall in vain and said wryly, "If you make a date with Jimmy in December, he'll keep it in May." He conducted meetings of the Board of Estimate, which were public, like a stage performance. Once a heckler shouted at him "Liar," and Walker replied, "Now that you have identified yourself, we shall proceed."

He popped up at all kinds of gatherings and was always ready with a speech, often a marvel of impromptu oratory. After his Presidency, Coolidge told an associate, "Walker has the Celtic ability to put all his goods in the front window and leave none in reserve—the kind of man who, if you wake him from a sound sleep to make a speech, is able to start right in speaking. But if you examine the speech later, you will find he has said nothing worth while."

The popinjay mayor was the life of the party wherever he appeared. He took as his new sweetheart actress Betty Compton, whom he eventually married after getting a divorce. He changed clothes at least three times a day and had wardrobes in several places around town for his convenience. He pranced as thousands cheered. A New York journalist wrote, "New York wore James J. Walker in its lapel and he returned the compliment."

In the Depression, New York taxpayers took a less indulgent attitude toward the song and dance man who played mayor. Hearings before the Hofstadter committee of the state legislature revealed that he had received gifts of hundreds of thousands of dollars, and he resigned in 1932 to escape removal from office by Governor Franklin D. Roosevelt.

On August 15, 1926, Rudolph Valentino, Hollywood's greatest screen lover, was in his suite at the Ambassador Hotel in New York with his valet. Suddenly he gasped, put his hand to his body, and fainted. He was rushed to the Polyclinic Hospital, where he was operated on for a gastric ulcer and appendicitis. When he woke from the anesthetic, he asked the doctor, "Am I a pink puff?" to which the reply was, "No, indeed, you have been very brave."

His condition was serious. The hospital was inundated with telephone calls from women, and a special information booth was established on the ground floor. A bulletin was issued that he had passed the crisis, that his temperature was normal, and that he felt so strong that he was eager to leave. Then pleurisy developed, and on August 23 he was dead. He was thirty-one years of age.

Rodolpho Alfonzo Raffaelo Pierre Filibert Guglielmi di Valentina d'Antonguolla was born in 1895 in the small Italian town of Castellaneta, the son of a veterinarian. Presumably he had attended the Royal School of Agriculture in Genoa. He arrived in this country in 1913 intending to become a gardener. He worked for a while on the Long Island estate of Cornelius Bliss, Jr. Then there followed a period of penury, in which he was reduced to odd jobs in order to eat, shining the brass of autos and sweeping floors of office buildings. The headwaiter of Maxim's restaurant hired him as a dancer, part of whose job was to dance with lonely women diners. He joined a musical comedy troupe and was left stranded in San Francisco. A chance friend who was then a leading movie actor, Norman Kerry, got him a small film part playing a tough guy, and this led to minor roles on the New York stage. There he caught the eye of a woman writer who had just adapted Vicente Blasco-Ibáñez's *The Four Horsemen of the Apocalypse* for the screen, and he was given the role of Julio Desmoyers in which he scored a great success, a highlight of the film being his dancing of the tango.

He was given larger roles and scored in *Blood and Sand*, about the life and death of a toreador, and in *The Sheik*, which made "sheik" the male counterpart to "flapper" in the everyday vocabulary. There was a popular song "The Sheik of Araby." The new film idol far outsoared the late Wallace Reid, who had died suddenly in 1923. When *Son of the Sheik* opened on Broadway, a month before Valentino's death, he was mobbed by screeching females, one of whom tackled him at the ankles and tried to unlace his shoelaces for a souvenir.

Valentino was an excited, as well as an exciting, lover, as I discovered when I re-viewed *The Sheik* in my adult life.

> AGNES AYRES: Why have you abducted me?
> VALENTINO (chest madly heaving and nostrils dilating): Can't you guess?

His film producer, Adolph Zukor, wrote in a later year that his acting "was largely confined to protruding his large, almost occult eyes, until the vast areas of white were visible, drawing back the lips of his wide, sensuous mouth to bare his gleaming teeth and flaring his nostrils."

H. L. Mencken, "by one of the chances that relieve the dullness of life and make it instructive," had had a private dinner with Valentino only a week before his fatal illness. Valentino had asked for the meeting through an actress who acted as intermediary since he wanted the famous man's advice. An editorial writer for the Chicago *Tribune* had found in the men's room of a hotel a talcum powder which was colored pink, and he had written an editorial entitled "Pink Powder Puff," in which he suggested getting rid of Rudy "before the younger generation of American males replaces razors with depilatories and the ancient caveman virtues of their forefathers are replaced by cosmetics, flopping pants and slave bracelets."

Valentino arrived in Chicago at the time of publication,

Personality Craze

and, enraged about the aspersion on his manhood, challenged the writer to a duel and then to a fistfight, but in vain.

At first, Mencken advised him to forget the whole thing. Then Mencken, who had regarded the dinner as the lightest of capers, looked more closely at Valentino and discovered "what is commonly called for want of a better name, a gentleman. In brief, Valentino's agony was the agony of a man of relatively civilized feelings thrown into a situation of intolerable vulgarity." With some touch of fineness in him, "Valentino was only the hero of the rabble. Imbeciles surrounded him in a dense herd. He was pursued by women—but what women! . . . in those last days, unless I am a worse psychologist than even the professors of psychology, it was revolting him. Worse, it was making him afraid." The inscrutable gods were kind in bringing his life to a swift close. If he had lived, he would have enclosed himself in a web of deception, "of increasing pretension, of solemn artiness, of hollow hocus-pocus, deceptive only to himself."

His funeral was given over to the *vulgus ignobile*. His body was taken to Campbell's Funeral Parlor at 66th Street and Broadway, and he lay in state on a draped catafalque, surrounded by candles. When the home opened the next morning, the queue stretched eight blocks north to 74th Street, made up mostly of weeping women and girls. Forty patrolmen and six mounted police had to control the crowds. The plate-glass windows of the parlor were broken, and three persons fell through them. The casualty toll of the day was 100. At 11:40 P.M. the police cut off the line, preventing thousands from going in. That night ten black-shirted men came to the funeral home and said that as members of the Fascist League of America they would guard the body through the night. A wreath was laid by them upon instructions from Premier Benito Mussolini. The next morning the mounted police again had to hold back the mob. Finally, when a fracas between Fascists and anti-Fascists seemed inevitable, the doors were closed to the public.

A New York mother found the grief too great to bear and shot herself, a sheaf of Valentino photographs in her hand. In London a dancer did away with herself and left a note, "It is heartbreaking to live in the past when the future is hopeless. Please look after Rudolph's pictures."

The Polish actress Pola Negri announced that she had been his fiancée; this was a surprise to Valentino's closest associates since he had had such a host of marital troubles with two wives that it seemed unlikely that he would let himself in for more agony with the tempestuous Miss Negri. She arrived from Hollywood on August 29. At the coffin she conveniently swooned for the photographers. The next day a cortege of twelve cars carried the corpse to St. Malachy's Church on West 49th Street. Sobbing and wailing, Miss Negri had to be supported going into and leaving the church. During the service her baying rose higher than the notes of the pipe organ and ceased only when the reporters and photographers were requested to leave. Not until three days later was the body, accompanied by the inconsolable Miss Negri, transported to a train for the trip across the continent to Hollywood for burial.

M. M. Marberry in his article "The Overloved One," in *American Heritage*, August, 1965, described how later research found that genuine shock over the death had been artificially magnified. Much of the ballyhoo was staged by a movie studio press agent, named Oscar Dobb, since the studio wanted the interment to be made memorable in order to protect its investment in *Son of the Sheik*. Dobb revealed to the press that Rudy's last words had been, "Let the tent be struck," which had a fine, classic ring and the additional merit of linking it with the lovemaking sequences of the film. When it was discovered that they had also been the last words of General Robert E. Lee, they were amended to, "I want the sunlight to greet me." The second publicity source was the press agent for Campbell's, who initially hired thirty persons at a dollar a head to stand outside the funeral home. The third source was Valentino's own publicity manager who was involved in several books, one by himself, *As I Knew Him*; another by the film star, *How to Keep Fit*; and a third of poetry, in which Valentino, thanks to his ghostwriter, showed signs of budding into a second Shelley. Miss Negri's agent did his part, claiming that Valentino's last words were in fact, "Pola, I love you and will love you in eternity." Miss Negri announced she would enter a convent but not, of course, until after she had fulfilled her movie contract commitments.

Press agentry brought results. Valentino was in debt at the time of his death, but his heirs got $600,000 from *Son of the Sheik*. Campbell's had been a struggling funeral parlor, but now it climbed to the top. Miss Negri had a splurge in popularity until the talkies plunged her into obscurity. She married Prince Serge Mdivani a few months later and wound up suing the Valentino estate for $15,000 she alleged that she had lent her fiancé. As for Valentino himself, his second wife, Natacha Rambova, said she had a message from him in the spirit world. "I have many valuable friends up here and am happy. Caruso likes me. So does Wally Reid and Sarah Bernhardt. These spirits do the same thing as they did on earth, but of course in a different way. They act with more soul now."

Leisure time grew, and sports came into their own. A marked difference in the newspaper of the beginning of the twenties and the end is in the development of the sports section. One figure dominated each sport, Red Grange in football, Babe Ruth in baseball, Bobby Jones in golf, Bill Tilden in tennis. Huge crowds gaped at these heroes with what former sports reporter Ring Lardner called "an excess of anile idolatry."

Some were personalities who would have enriched any age, such as Tilden, who was the monarch of the courts. He had been stagestruck as a child, and his interest in the theater continued as an adult, when he invested a good deal of money in stage ventures. Once he walked up and down the aisle of a theater holding aloft a finger which he had injured in a tournament. The tennis court was his personal stage. To win support from the gallery, he would go to absurd lengths. His opponent was always the underdog, but Tilden would let him get so far ahead that defeat seemed inevitable. Seemingly he was a man crushed by despair. Then with full histrionics he would rise, straighten his sagging shoulders, slowly strip off his sweater, douse his head in ice water, and stage a spectacular come-from-behind drive that would blast his opponent off the court.

On September 22, 1927, an event occurred that wiped out of national consciousness all other issues or problems—the so-called Battle of the Century, between Gene Tunney and Jack Dempsey, for the world's heavyweight boxing championship.

In September, 1923, Dempsey had knocked out Luis Angel Firpo of Argentina in two rounds of what is regarded as the most exciting bout in boxing history. After that Dempsey had been inactive, dodging a fight against the man considered the leading contender, Harry Wills. Dempsey had the support of most of the public since Wills was a Negro and the public did not relish the possibility of another Jack Johnson as champion. Finally a fight was arranged for September 23, 1926, between Dempsey and former Marine James "Gene" Tunney in the Sesqui-Centennial Stadium in Philadelphia.

Dempsey was the 3 to 1 favorite, even though at thirty-one he was three years older than Tunney and had not been in the ring for three long years. Tunney, a good puncher and fast on his feet, had a fetish about keeping fit while Dempsey had whiled away many evenings in nightclub life with his new movie-actress wife, Estelle Taylor. The overestimation of Dempsey at this time is curious. It was probably a reflection of the period's exaltation of public personalities, which in the case of athletes gave rise to such titles as the King of Swat, the Four Horsemen, the Flying Finn. Sportswriter Grantland Rice once wrote a story commencing, "Once or twice within the course of a century a prodigy comes along to ride the crest of the world. He may be a Rembrandt or a Galileo or a Shakespeare. He may be a Da Vinci or a Milton. But there is about him an indefinable mastery that lifts him far above the puny achievements of the near great." Of what gift from heaven was he writing? "Golf has contributed this to the galaxy of masters in the person of Robert Tyre Jones who today won his third amateur championship."

Because of this superman worship and the recollection of the Firpo fight, Dempsey was regarded as the "untamed savage," the brute latent in civilized man who was sure to massacre an ordinary human in fistic combat. In training for the fight, Dempsey looked far from impressive, and it was evident to boxing writers that age and activity had taken their toll—he was woefully slow afoot, and his formerly sharp reflexes were dulled. Yet in spite of the testimony of their eyes, the odds were not affected, and an overwhelming majority of the boxing writers predicted a victory for him.

The fight was held before a mammoth crowd of 121,000, who paid a record gate of $1,895,000. Dempsey proved to be a shell of his old self and was almost helpless in facing the ring craft of Tunney. In a driving rain he was battered into helplessness. The judges gave only a decision, but he probably lost every round.

The public, refusing to be disillusioned, retained its fixation about Dempsey. Promoter Tex Rickard set up an elimination tournament and Jack Sharkey emerged as the leading contender to fight it out with Dempsey for the right to face Tunney. The fight took place before 80,000 in Yankee Stadium on July 22, 1927. By the seventh round, Dempsey was groggy from the rain of blows from the faster Sharkey; he swung wildly and hit Sharkey four times below the belt. If Sharkey had sunk to the floor, he would probably have been declared the winner on a foul. Instead, he clutched his midsection and turned complainingly to the referee, whereupon Dempsey, having a clear field, leaned back, clouted Sharkey on the jaw, and floored him. The referee, showing some doubt, counted Sharkey out, thus saving the big fight for Rickard. (Since that time, referees in New York give the familiar injunction to fighters before hostilities begin, "Protect yourself at all times.")

So the buildup was ready for the Battle of the Century to be fought on September 22 at Soldier Field, Chicago. By clear logic there should have been no doubt of the outcome. Tunney had given Dempsey a bad beating, and a year would have passed. Tunney would be a year older, too, but it was Dempsey who was obviously sliding downhill. Nonetheless, there was a surge of sentiment toward Dempsey, and enough people believed that he could win so that he entered the ring only a 7 to 5 underdog. On paper it should have been 5 to 1.

The nation was agog. The fight was the coast-to-coast topic of conversation to an extent that is impossible to convey to a later generation.

The VIP list to attend included ten governors, several United States Senators, and mayors without number. This was a far cry from the time not too far in the past when John L. Sullivan fought James J. Corbett for the championship before a few thousand in New Orleans for a side bet of $10,000; when Corbett fought Joe Choynski on a barge off San Francisco, and they cut each other to pieces for fifty rounds for a few hundred dollars; when Tex Rickard had to move the Jeffries-Johnson fight from place to place before finding a haven in Reno, Nevada. A minister brought a suit in federal court to bar the Dempsey-Tunney fight on the ground that it was "degraded and brutal." The Albany *Knickerbocker News* denounced it as a "public debauch, a Neronic monstrosity." The St. Louis *Globe-Democrat* commented:

> It is one of the amazing social phenomena of modern times that this form of combat which has become the accepted form of fighting supremacy has risen from the lowest dregs of society to a position where it is recognized, approved and supported by the great majority of all classes of society. Once, not so long ago, utterly con-

demned by the law, it is now not only sanctioned by the law but even gladly attended by the highest officers of the law.

The fight was covered by 1,200 reporters. The AP and UP leased 245,000 miles of wire. The result was reported the next day by the New York *Times* in three-line banner headlines and four columns on the right-hand side of the front page. There were twenty-four special trains run to Chicago; the Twentieth Century Limited, the day before, was run in seven sections with seventy-seven Pullman cars. Two airplanes carried passengers from New York to Chicago, making the trip in twelve hours, which was eight hours faster than the train. In a record-breaking radio hookup eighty stations broadcast the fight to an audience estimated as the greatest in history, 60,000,000. Warden Lewis Lawes of Sing Sing gave special permission to the inmates to stay up to hear the fight.

Seats cost $5 to $40, and even the $40 seats were forty rows away, back of the reporters and the VIP's. The cheaper seats were two blocks away. Most seats were sold without a seat plan on a take-it-or-leave-it basis. To those in the faraway hills of the stadium, the ring looked like a distant spot in which marionettes danced around. The crowd did not measure up to Rickard's hopes. The paid attendance was 104,000, but at the higher prices the gate was $2,658,000, a record which still stands. Tunney received (aside from radio and movie revenues) about $900,000 and Dempsey half as much.

Millions gathered around the radios. The *Life* magazine of that time ran a satiric cartoon captioned "Battle of the Century," depicting crippled war veterans listening to the fight. The result should have been cut-and-dried, and it appeared that it would go that way as Tunney pummeled Dempsey about the ring. Then came the unexpected, which H. L. Mencken once wrote was the only thing that makes life worth living. In the seventh round Graham McNamee, the announcer, was saying, "Tunney shot a hard left to Dempsey's face which he follows up with two mean lefts and as the left is in Dempsey's face, he lands a right."

There was a huge roar through which McNamee's voice could hardly be heard, "And then Dempsey comes back. Tunney is down from a barrage of lefts and rights to the face." No more could be heard for many seconds—and then

Personality Craze

McNamee's voice faintly, "The fight is going on." Ten listeners, according to the AP, died of heart failure during the fight, and seven succumbed in that round. Tunney weathered the storm and backpedaled while Dempsey motioned to him to come in and fight. In the eighth round Tunney did wade in and knocked Dempsey to the floor for a count of one. At the end of the fight McNamee said that Dempsey was out on his feet. Tunney was without doubt the winner, and he was so declared. On the radio Tunney greeted "my friends in Connecticut," by which he meant "Polly" Lauder, a wealthy young lady whom he thereafter married.

And so the Battle of the Century was over, but the rhubarb lingered on. Dempsey officially protested the fight on the ground that Tunney was on the canvas for at least fifteen seconds since the referee, Dave Barry, did not begin the count of nine until he had returned from escorting Dempsey to a neutral corner. The Illinois Boxing Commission overruled the "long count" protest. It stated that to prevent a repetition of what had happened in the Firpo fight, when Dempsey stood over Firpo and clubbed him down every time he got up, the fighters had been told before the bout that the count would not start until whoever scored a knockdown went to the farthest neutral corner.

Tunney was an unpopular champion with the public, an antihero. In the public mind of the twenties a sports hero must regard his sport as a religion; he must be proud of the role he plays. Tunney had only scorn for the base degrees by which he climbed. As described by the New York *Times* on the eve of the big fight, "Tunney thoroughly dislikes the ring but, being in it, he is imbued with the idea that he can elevate it." To the public, which saw no need of elevation, this was heresy. Then, too, the sports king must be completely democratic. Babe Ruth played sandlot ball with the boys, and Bobby Jones was buddy-buddy with his caddie. Tunney scorned contact with the ring *hoi polloi* in favor of social climbing. He was a cynic who refused to join in the acclaim for Lindbergh, saying, "He had a wonderful motor."

And then the unforgivable! On April 23, 1928, Tunney appeared before the literature class of his fishing companion, Professor William Lyon Phelps of Yale, to lecture on Shakespeare. The young man who had started out as a teamster in Greenwich Village opened his lecture by quoting Carlyle and paraphrasing Spencer. He disclosed that his acquaintance with Shakespeare began when, as a Marine, he had run across *A Winter's Tale*, which he had read ten times before he got the hang of it.

"Shakespeare was a sport," he said. He discussed *Troilus and Cressida* and combat in the Trojan War. Ajax, he said, was "a great, big, ambitious fellow like Jack Sharkey who didn't have the stuff." Of a speech by Achilles to Ulysses he said that it meant "cash in when you can," because the public memory of heroes is short.

When asked by a reporter afterward how it went, Tunney replied, "I felt a little nervous. You see it is not my métier." Those who knew Tunney well said that while he was a nice fellow, he was singularly devoid of a sense of humor.

Heywood Broun wrote sourly:

> Tunney did better against Shakespeare than anyone had a right to expect. My own student days came before the Jazz Age, and I have a residue of resentment against prize-fighters, trained seals and motion-picture stars in the classroom. The world has gone beyond the notions of us veteran classical scholars. Go-getters sit in the seats of the mighty. Harvard, I trust, will counter by asking Babe Ruth to tell the boys at Cambridge just what Milton has meant to him.

Dempsey, who was appearing in court in one of his perennial legal battles with his former manager, Jack Kearns, was asked by a reporter what he thought of Tunney's appearance at Yale.

"I got a big kick out of it," he replied.

"What do you think of Gene as a lecturer?"

"Oh, if it helps his racket, I guess it's O.K."

"How are you getting on with Shakespeare, Jack?"

"Sorry, never had the pleasure."

The Dempsey versus Tunney argument raged on in the press. John Kieran, erudite sports columnist for the New York *Times*, wrote, "As soon as it is apparent that the letter concerns the merits or demerits of either Dempsey or Tunney, the missive should be immersed in a bucket of water, dissected at least six inches below the surface and only the lightest part allowed to float to the top." He quoted from the placid letter of one old lady who refused to haul up the white flag of surrender: "Permit me to say that Jack Dempsey's knowledge of literature, music and the arts is quite as extensive as Mr. Tunney's although not so persistently advertised."

Coolidge Prosperity

by Frederick Lewis Allen

Business was booming when Warren Harding died, and in a primitive Vermont farmhouse, by the light of an old-fashioned kerosene lamp, Colonel John Coolidge administered to his son Calvin the oath of office as President of the United States. The hopeless depression of 1921 had given way to the hopeful improvement of 1922 and the rushing revival of 1923.

The prices of common stocks, to be sure, suggested no unreasonable optimism. On August 2, 1923, the day of Harding's death, United States Steel (paying a five-dollar dividend) stood at 87, Atchison (paying six dollars) at 95, New York Central (paying seven) at 97, and American Telephone and Telegraph (paying nine) at 122; and the total turnover for the day on the New York Stock Exchange amounted to only a little over 600,000 shares. The Big Bull Market was still far in the future. Nevertheless the tide of prosperity was in full flood.

Pick up one of those graphs with which statisticians measure the economic ups and downs of the Post-war Decade. You will find that the line of business activity rises to a jagged peak in 1920, drops precipitously into a deep valley in late 1920 and 1921, climbs uncertainly upward through 1922 to another peak at the middle of 1923, dips somewhat in 1924 (but not nearly so far as in 1921), rises again in 1925 and 1926, dips momentarily but slightly toward the end of 1927, and then zigzags up to a perfect Everest of prosperity in 1929—only to plunge down at last into the bottomless abyss of 1930 and 1931.

Hold the graph at arm's-length and glance at it again, and you will see that the clefts of 1924 and 1927 are mere indentations in a lofty and irregular plateau which reaches from early 1923 to late 1929. That plateau represents nearly seven years of unparalleled plenty; nearly seven years during which men and women might be disillusioned about politics and religion and love, but believed that at the end of the rainbow there was at least a pot of negotiable legal tender consisting of the profits of American industry and American salesmanship; nearly seven years during which the business man was, as Stuart Chase put it, "the dictator of our destinies," ousting "the statesman, the priest, the philosopher, as the creator of standards of ethics and behavior" and becoming "the final authority on the conduct of American society." For nearly seven years the prosperity band-wagon rolled down Main Street.

Not everyone could manage to climb aboard this wagon. Mighty few farmers could get so much as a fingerhold upon it. Some dairymen clung there, to be sure, and fruit-growers and truck-gardeners. For prodigious changes were taking place in the national diet as the result of the public's discovery of the useful vitamin, the propaganda for a more varied menu, and the invention of better methods of shipping perishable foods. Between 1919 and 1926 the national production of milk and milk products increased by one-third and that of ice-cream alone took a 45-per-cent jump. Between 1919 and 1928, as families learned that there were vitamins in celery, spinach, and carrots, and became accustomed to serving fresh vegetables the year round (along with fresh fruits), the acreage of nineteen commercial truck vegetable crops nearly doubled. But the growers of staple crops such as wheat and corn and cotton were in a bad way. Their foreign markets had dwindled under competition from other countries. Women were wearing less and less cotton. Few agricultural raw materials were used in the new economy of automobiles and radios and electricity. And the more efficient the poor farmer became, the more machines he bought to increase his output and thus keep the wolf from the door, the more surely he and his fellows were faced by the specter of overproduction. The index number of all farm prices, which had coasted from 205 in 1920 to 116 in 1921—"perhaps the most terrible toboggan slide in all American agricultural history," to quote Stuart Chase again—regained only a fraction of the ground it had lost: in 1927 it stood at 131. Loudly the poor farmers complained, desperately they and their Norrises and Brookharts and Shipsteads and La Follettes campaigned for federal aid, and by the hundreds of thousands they left the farm for the cities.

There were other industries unrepresented in the triumphal march of progress. Coal-mining suffered, and textile-manufacturing, and shipbuilding, and shoe and leather manufacturing. Whole regions of the country felt the effects of depression in one or more of these industries. The South was held back by cotton, the agricultural Northwest by the dismal condition of the wheat growers, New England by the paralysis of the textile and shoe industries. Nevertheless, the prosperity bandwagon did not lack for occupants, and their good fortune outweighed and outshouted the ill fortune of those who lamented by the roadside.

In a position of honor rode the automobile manufacturer. His hour of destiny had struck. By this time paved roads and repair shops and filling stations had become so plentiful that the motorist might sally forth for the day without fear of being stuck in a mudhole or stranded without benefit of gasoline or crippled by a dead spark plug. Automobiles were now made with such precision, for that matter, that the motorist need hardly know a spark plug by sight; thousands of automobile owners had never even lifted the hood to see what the engine looked like. Now that closed cars were in quantity production, furthermore, the motorist had no need of Spartan blood, even in January. And the stylish new models were a delight to the eye. At the beginning of the decade most cars had been somber in color, but with the invention of pyroxylin finishes they broke out (in 1925 and 1926) into a whole rainbow of colors, from Florentine cream to Versailles violet. Bodies were swung lower, expert designers sought new harmonies of line, balloon tires came in, and at last even Henry Ford capitulated to style and beauty.

If any sign had been needed of the central place which the automobile had come to occupy in the mind and heart of the average American, it was furnished when the Model A Ford was brought out in December, 1927. Since the previous spring, when Henry Ford had shut down his gigantic plant, scrapped his Model T and the thousands of machines which brought it into being, and announced that he was going to put a new car on the market, the country had been in a state of suspense. Obviously he would have to make drastic changes. Model T had been losing to Chevrolet its leadership in the enormous low-priced-car market, for the time had come when people were no longer content with ugliness and a maximum speed of forty or forty-five miles an hour; no longer content, either, to roar slowly uphill with a weary left foot jammed against the low-speed pedal while robin's-egg blue Chevrolets swept past in second. Yet equally obviously Henry Ford was the mechanical genius of the age. What miracle would he accomplish?

Rumor after rumor broke into the front pages of the newspapers. So intense was the interest that even the fact that an automobile dealer in Brooklyn had "learned something of the new car through a telegram from his brother Henry" was headline stuff. When the editor of the Brighton, Michigan, *Weekly Argus* actually snapped a photograph of a new Ford out for a trial spin, newspaper-readers pounced on the picture and avidly discussed its every line. The great day arrived when this newest product of the inventive genius of the age was to be shown to the public. The Ford Motor Company was running in 2,000 daily newspapers a five-day series of full-page advertisements at a total cost of $1,300,000; and everyone who could read was reading them. On December 2, 1927, when Model A was unveiled, one million people—so the *Herald-Tribune* figured—tried to get into the Ford headquarters in New York to catch a glimpse of it; as Charles Merz later reported in his life of Ford, "one hundred thousand people flocked into the showrooms of the Ford Company in Detroit; mounted police were called out to patrol the crowds in Cleveland; in Kansas City so great a mob stormed Convention Hall that platforms had to be built to lift the new car high enough for everyone to see it." So it went from one end of the United States to the other. Thousands of orders piled up on the Ford books for Niagara Blue roadsters and Arabian Sand phaetons. For weeks and months, every new Ford that appeared on the streets drew a crowd. To the motor-minded American people the first showing of a new kind of automobile was no matter of merely casual or commercial interest. It was one of the great events of the year 1927; not so thrilling as Lindbergh's flight, but rivaling the execution of Sacco and Vanzetti, the Hall-Mills murder trial, the Mississippi flood, and the Dempsey-Tunney fight at Chicago in its capacity to arouse public excitement.

In 1919 there had been 6,771,000 passenger cars in service in the United States; by 1929 there were no less than 23,121,000. There you have possibly the most potent statistic of Coolidge Prosperity. As a footnote to it I suggest the following. Even as early as the end of 1923 there were two cars for every three families in "Middletown," a typical American city. The Lynds and their investigators interviewed 123 working-class families of "Middletown" and found that 60 of them had cars. Of these 60, 26 lived in such shabby-looking houses that the investigators thought to ask whether they had bathtubs, and discovered that as many as 21 of the 26 had none. The automobile came even before the tub!

And as it came, it changed the face of America. Villages which had once prospered because they were "on the railroad" languished with economic anaemia; villages on Route 61 bloomed with garages, filling stations, hot-dog stands, chicken-dinner restaurants, tearooms, tourists' rests, camping sites, and affluence. The interurban trolley perished, or survived only as a pathetic anachronism. Railroad after railroad gave up its branch lines, or saw its revenues slowly dwindling under the competition of mammoth interurban busses and trucks snorting along six-lane concrete highways. The whole country was covered with a network of passenger bus-lines. In thousands of towns, at the beginning of the decade a single traffic officer at the junction of Main Street and Central Street had been sufficient for the control of traffic. By the end of the decade, what a difference!—red and green lights, blinkers, one-way streets, boulevard stops, stringent and yet more stringent parking ordinances—and still a shining flow of traffic that backed up for blocks along Main Street every Saturday and Sunday afternoon. Slowly but surely the age of steam was yielding to the gasoline age.

The radio manufacturer occupied a less important seat than the automobile manufacturer on the prosperity bandwagon, but he had the distinction of being the youngest rider. You will remember that there was no such thing as radio broadcasting to the public until the autumn of 1920, but that by the spring of 1922 radio had become a craze—as much talked about as Mah Jong was to be the following year or cross-word puzzles the year after. In 1922 the sales of radio sets, parts, and accessories amounted to $60,000,000. People wondered what would happen when the edge wore off the novelty of hearing a jazz orchestra in Schenectady or in Davenport, Iowa, play "Mr. Gallagher and Mr. Shean." What actually did happen is suggested by the cold figures of total annual radio sales for the next few years:

1922—$ 60,000,000   (as we have just seen)
1923—$136,000,000
1924—$358,000,000
1925—$430,000,000

1926—$506,000,000
1927—$425,600,000
1928—$650,550,000
1929—$842,548,000   (an increase over the 1922 figures of 1,400 per cent!)

Don't hurry past those figures. Study them a moment, remembering that whenever there is a dip in the curve of national prosperity there is likely to be a dip in the sales of almost every popular commodity. There was a dip in national prosperity in 1927, for instance; do you see what it did to radio sales? But there was also a dip in 1924, a worse one in fact. Yet radio sales made in that year the largest proportional increase in the whole period. Why? Well, for one thing, that was the year in which the embattled Democrats met at Madison Square Garden in New York to pick a standard-bearer, and the deadlock between the hosts of McAdoo and the hosts of Al Smith lasted day after day after day, and millions of Americans heard through loud-speakers the lusty cry of, "Alabama, twenty-four votes for Underwoo-ood!" and discovered that a political convention could be a grand show to listen to and that a seat by the radio was as good as a ticket to the Garden. Better, in fact; for at any moment you could turn a knob and get "Barney Google" or "It Ain't Gonna Rain No More" by way of respite. At the age of three and a half years, radio broadcasting had attained its majority.

Behind those figures of radio sales lies a whole chapter of the life of the Post-war Decade: radio penetrating every third home in the country; giant broadcasting stations with nation-wide hook-ups; tenement-house roofs covered with forests of antennaes, Roxy and his Gang, the Happiness Boys, the A & P Gypsies, and Rudy Vallee crooning from antique Florentine cabinet sets; Graham McNamee's voice, which had become more familiar to the American public than that of any other citizen of the land, shouting across your living-room and mine: "*And* he did it! Yes, sir, he did it! It's a touch-down! Boy, I want to tell you this is one of the finest games . . ."; the Government belatedly asserting itself in 1927 to allocate wave-lengths among competing radio stations; advertisers paying huge sums for the privilege of introducing Beethoven and a few well-chosen words about yeast or toothpaste; and Michael Meehan personally conducting the common stock of the Radio Corporation of America from a 1928 low of 85¼ to a 1929 high of 549.

There were other riders on the prosperity band-wagon. Rayon, cigarettes, refrigerators, telephones, chemical preparations (especially cosmetics), and electrical devices of various sorts all were in growing demand. While the independent storekeeper struggled to hold his own, the amount of retail business done in chain stores and department stores jumped by leaps and bounds. For every $100 worth of business done in 1919, by 1927 the five-and-ten-cent chains were doing $260 worth, the cigar chains $153 worth, the drug chains $224 worth, and the grocery chains $387 worth. Mrs. Smith no longer patronized her "naborhood" store; she climbed into her two-thousand-dollar car to drive to the red-fronted chain grocery and save twenty-seven cents on her daily purchases. The movies prospered, sending their celluloid reels all over the world and making Charlie Chaplin, Douglas Fairbanks, Gloria Swanson, Rudolph Valentino, and Clara Bow familiar figures to the Eskimo, the Malay, and the heathen Chinee; while at home the attendance at the motion-picture houses of "Middletown" during a single month (December, 1923) amounted to four and a half times the entire population of the city. Men, women, and children, rich and poor, the Middletowners went to the movies at an average rate of better than once a week!

Was this Coolidge Prosperity real? The farmers did not think so. Perhaps the textile manufacturers did not think so. But the figures of corporation profits and wages and incomes left little room for doubt. Consider, for example, two significant facts at opposite ends of the scale of wealth. Between 1922 and 1927, the purchasing power of American wages increased at the rate of more than two per cent annually. And during the three years between 1924 and 1927 alone there was a leap from 75 to 283 in the number of Americans who paid taxes on incomes of more than a million dollars a year.

Why did it happen? What made the United States so prosperous?

Some of the reasons were obvious enough. The war had impoverished Europe and hardly damaged the United States at all; when peace came the Americans found themselves the economic masters of the world. Their young country, with enormous resources in materials and in human energy and with a wide domestic market, was ready to take advantage of this situation. It had developed mass production to a new point of mechanical and managerial efficiency. The Ford gospel of high wages, low prices, and standardized manufacture on a basis of the most minute division of machine-tending labor was working smoothly not only at Highland Park, but in thousands of other factories. Executives, remembering with a shudder the piled-up inventories of 1921, had learned the lesson of cautious hand-to-mouth buying; and they were surrounded with more expert technical consultants, research men, personnel managers, statisticians, and business forecasters than had ever before invaded that cave of the winds, the conference room. Their confidence was strengthened by their almost superstitious belief that the Republican Administration was their invincible ally. And they were all of them aided by the boom in the automobile industry. The phenomenal activity of this one part of the body economic—which was responsible, directly or indirectly, for the employment of nearly four million men—pumped new life into all the rest.

Prosperity was assisted, too, by two new stimulants to purchasing, each of which mortgaged the future but kept the factories roaring while it was being injected. The first was the increase in installment buying. People were getting to consider it old-fashioned to limit their purchases to the amount of their cash balance; the thing to do was to "exercise their credit." By the latter part of the decade, economists figured that 15 per cent of all retail sales were on an installment basis, and that there were some six billions of "easy payment" paper outstanding. The other stimulant was stock-market speculation. When stocks were skyrocketing in 1928 and 1929 it is probable that hundreds of thousands of people were buying goods with money which represented, essentially, a gamble on the business profits of the nineteen-thirties. It was fun while it lasted.

If these were the principal causes of Coolidge Prosperity, the salesman and the advertising man were at least its agents and evangels. Business had learned as never before the immense importance to it of the ultimate consumer. Unless he could be persuaded to buy and buy lavishly, the whole stream of six-cylinder cars, super-heterodynes, cigarettes, rouge compacts, and electric ice-boxes would be dammed at its outlet. The salesman and the advertising man held the key to this outlet. As competition increased their methods became more strenuous. No longer was it considered enough to recommend one's goods in modest and explicit terms and to place them on the counter in the hope that the ultimate consumer would make up his mind to purchase. The advertiser must plan

Coolidge Prosperity

elaborate national campaigns, consult with psychologists, and employ all the eloquence of poets to cajole, exhort, or intimidate the consumer into buying—to "break down consumer resistance." Not only was each individual concern struggling to get a larger share of the business in its own field, but whole industries shouted against one another in the public's ear. The embattled candy manufacturers took full-page space in the newspapers to reply to the American Tobacco Company's slogan of "Reach for a Lucky instead of a sweet." Trade journals were quoted by the *Reader's Digest* as reporting the efforts of the furniture manufacturers to make the people "furniture conscious" and of the clothing manufacturers to make them "tuxedo conscious." The salesman must have the ardor of a zealot, must force his way into people's houses by hook or by crook, must let nothing stand between him and the consummation of his sale. As executives put it, "You can't be an order-taker any longer—you've got to be a *salesman*." The public, generally speaking, could be relied upon to regard with complacence the most flagrant assaults upon its credulity by the advertiser and the most outrageous invasions of its privacy by the salesman; for the public was in a mood to forgive every sin committed in the holy name of business.

Never before had such pressure been exerted upon salesmen to get results. Many concerns took up the quota system, setting as the objective for each sales representative a figure 20 or 25 per cent beyond that of the previous year, and putting it up to him to reach this figure or lose his employer's favor and perhaps his job. All sorts of sales contests and other ingenious devices were used to stimulate the force. Among the schemes suggested by the Dartnell Company of Chicago, which had more than ten thousand American business organizations subscribing to its service, was that of buying various novelties and sending them to the salesman at weekly intervals: one week a miniature feather duster with a tag urging him to "dust his territory," another week an imitation cannon cracker with the injunction to "make a big noise," and so on. The American Slicing Machine Company offered a turkey at Christmas to every one of its salesmen who beat his quota for the year. "We asked each man," explained the sales manager afterward, "to appoint a child in his family as a mascot, realizing that every one of them would work his head off to make some youngster happy at Christmas. The way these youngsters took hold of the plan was amusing, and at times the intensity of their interest was almost pathetic." The sales manager of another concern reported cheerfully that "one of his stunts" was "to twit one man at the good work of another until he is almost sore enough to be ready to fight." And according to Jesse Rainsford Sprague, still another company invented—and boasted of—a method of goading its salesmen which for sheer inhumanity probably set a record for the whole era of Coolidge Prosperity. It gave a banquet at which the man with the best score was served with oysters, roast turkey, and a most elaborate ice; the man with the second best score had the same dinner but without the oysters; and so on down to the man with the worst score, before whom was laid a small plate of boiled beans and a couple of crackers.

If the salesman was sometimes under pressure such as this, it is not surprising that the consumer felt the pressure, too. Let two extreme instances (both cited by Jesse Rainsford Sprague) suffice to suggest the trend in business methods. A wholesale drug concern offered to the trade a small table with a railing round its top for the display of "specials"; it was to be set up directly in the path of customers, "whose attention," according to *Printer's Ink*, "will be attracted to the articles when they fall over it, bump into it, kick their shins upon it, or otherwise come in contact with it." And *Selling News* awarded one of its cash prizes for "sales ideas" to a vender of electric cleaners who told the following story of commercial prowess. One day he looked up from the street and saw a lady shaking a rug out of a second-story window. "The door leading to her upstairs rooms was open. I went right in and up those stairs without knocking, greeting the lady with the remark: 'Well, I am here right on time. What room do you wish me to start in?' She was very much surprised, assuring me that I had the wrong number. But during my very courteous apologies I had managed to get my cleaner connected and in action. The result was that I walked out minus the cleaner, plus her contract and check for a substantial down payment." The readers of *Selling News* were apparently not expected to be less than enthusiastic at the prospect of a man invading a woman's apartment and setting up a cleaner in it without permission and under false pretenses. For if you could get away with such exploits, it helped business, and good business helped prosperity, and prosperity was good for the country.

Coolidge Prosperity

The advertisers met the competition of the new era with better design, persuasively realistic photographs, and sheer volume: the amount of advertising done in 1927, according to Francis H. Sisson, came to over a billion and a half dollars. They met it with a new frankness, introducing to staid magazine readers the advantages of Odo-ro-no and Kotex. And they met it, furthermore, with a subtle change in technic. The copy-writer was learning to pay less attention to the special qualities and advantages of his product, and more to the study of what the mass of unregenerate mankind wanted—to be young and desirable, to be rich, to keep up with the Joneses, to be envied. The winning method was to associate his product with one or more of these ends, logically or illogically, truthfully or cynically; to draw a lesson from the dramatic case of some imaginary man or woman whose fate was altered by the use of X's soap, to show that in the most fashionable circles people were choosing the right cigarette in blindfold tests, or to suggest by means of glowing testimonials—often bought and paid for—that the advertised product was used by women of fashion, movie stars, and non-stop flyers. One queen of the films was said to have journeyed from California all the way to New York to spend a single exhausting day being photographed for testimonial purposes in dozens of costumes and using dozens of commercial articles, many of which she had presumably never laid eyes on before—and all because the appearance of these testimonials would help advertise her newest picture. Of what value were sober facts from the laboratory: did not a tooth-powder manufacturer try to meet the hokum of emotional toothpaste advertising by citing medical authorities, and was not his counter-campaign as a breath in a gale? At the beginning of the decade advertising had been considered a business; in the early days of Coolidge Prosperity its fulsome prophets were calling it a profession; but by the end of the decade many of its practitioners, observing the overwhelming victory of methods taken over from tabloid journalism, were beginning to refer to it—among themselves—as a racket.

A wise man of the nineteen-twenties might have said that he cared not who made the laws of the country if he only might write its national advertising. For here were the sagas of the age, romances and tragedies depicting characters who became more familiar to the populace than those in any novel. The man who distinctly remembered Mr. Addison Sims of Seattle. . . . The four out of five who, failing to use

Forhan's, succumbed to pyorrhea, each of them with a white mask mercifully concealing his unhappy mouth. . . . The pathetic figure of the man, once a golf champion, "now only a wistful onlooker" creeping about after the star players, his shattered health due to tooth neglect. . . . The poor fellow sunk in the corner of a taxicab, whose wife upbraided him with not having said a word all evening (when he might so easily have shone with the aid of the *Elbert Hubbard Scrap Book*). . . . The man whose conversation so dazzled the company that the envious dinner-coated bystanders could only breathe in amazement, "I think he's quoting from Shelley." . . . The woman who would undoubtedly do something about B.O. if people only said to her what they really thought. . . . The man whose friends laughed when the waiter spoke to him in French. . . . The girl who thought filet mignon was a kind of fish. . . . The poor couple who faced one another in humiliation after their guests were gone, the wife still holding the door knob and struggling against her tears, the husband biting his nails with shame (When Your Guests Are Gone—Are You Sorry You Ever Invited Them? . . . Be Free From All Embarrassment! Let the Famous *Book of Etiquette* Tell You Exactly What to Do, Say, Write, or Wear on Every Occasion). . . . The girl who merely carried the daisy chain, yet she had athlete's foot. . . . These men and women of the advertising pages, suffering or triumphant, became a part of the folklore of the day.

Sometimes their feats were astonishing. Consider, for example, the man who had purchased Nelson Doubleday's *Pocket University*, and found himself, one evening, in a group in which someone mentioned Ali Baba:

"Ali Baba? I sat forward in my chair. I could tell them all about this romantic, picturesque figure of fiction.

"I don't know how it happened, but they gathered all around me. And I told them of golden ships that sailed the seven seas, of a famous man and his donkey who wandered unknown ways, of the brute-man from whom we are all descended. I told them things they never knew of Cleopatra, of the eccentric Diogenes, of Romulus and the founding of Rome. I told them of the unfortunate death of Sir Raleigh (*sic*), of the tragic end of poor Anne Boleyn. . . .

" 'You must have traveled all over the world to know so many marvelous things.' "

Skeptics might smile, thanking themselves that they were not of the company on that interminable evening; but the advertisement stuck in their minds. And to others, less sophisticated, it doubtless opened shining vistas of delight. They, too, could hold the dinner party spellbound if only they filled out the coupon. . . .

By far the most famous of these dramatic advertisements of the Post-war Decade was the long series in which the awful results of halitosis were set forth through the depiction of a gallery of unfortunates whose closest friends would not tell them. "Often a bridesmaid but never a bride. . . . Edna's case was really a pathetic one." . . . "Why did she leave him that way?" . . . "*That's* why you're a failure," . . . and then that devilishly ingenious display which capitalized the fears aroused by earlier tragedies in the series: the picture of a girl looking at a Listerine advertisement and saying to herself, "This *can't* apply to me!" Useless for the American Medical Association to insist that Listerine was "not a true deodorant," that is simply covered one smell with another. Just as useless for the Life Extension Institute to find "one out of twenty with pyorrhea, rather than Mr. Forhan's famous four-out-of-five" (to quote Stuart Chase once more). Halitosis had the power of dramatic advertising behind it, and Listerine swept to greater and greater profits on a tide of public trepidation.

As year followed year of prosperity, the new diffusion of wealth brought marked results. There had been a great boom in higher education immediately after the war, and the boom continued, although at a somewhat slackened pace, until college trustees were beside themselves wondering how to find room for the swarming applicants. There was an epidemic of outlines of knowledge and books of etiquette for those who had got rich quick and wanted to get cultured quick and become socially at ease. Wells's *Outline of History*, the best-selling non-fiction book of 1921 and 1922, was followed by Van Loon's *Story of Mankind*, J. Arthur Thomson's *Outline of Science* (both of them best sellers in 1922), the Doubleday mail-order *Book of Etiquette* and Emily Post's *Book of Etiquette* (which led the non-fiction list in 1923), *Why We Behave Like Human Beings* (a big success of 1926), and *The*

Story of Philosophy, which ran away from all other books in the non-fiction list of 1927.

There was a rush of innocents abroad. According to the figures of the Department of Commerce, over 437,000 people left the United States by ship for foreign parts in the year 1928 alone, to say nothing of 14,000 odd who entered Canada and Mexico by rail, and over three million cars which crossed into Canada for a day or more. The innocents spent freely: the money that they left abroad, in fact (amounting in 1928 to some $650,000,000), solved for a time a difficult problem in international finance: how the United States could continue to receive interest on her foreign debts and foreign investments without permitting foreign goods to pass the high tariff barrier in large quantities.

The United States became the banker and financial arbitrator for the world. When the financial relations between Germany and the Allies needed to be straightened out, it was General Charles G. Dawes and Owen D. Young who headed the necessary international commissions—not only because their judgment was considered wise, and impartial as between the countries of Europe, but because the United States was in a position to call the tune. Americans were called in to reorganize the finances of one country after another. American investments abroad increased by leaps and bounds. The squat limestone building at the corner of Broad and Wall Streets, still wearing the scars of the shrapnel which had struck it during the 1920 explosion, had become the undisputed financial center of the world. Only occasionally did the United States have to intervene by force of arms in other countries. The Marines ruled Haiti and restored order in Nicaragua; but in general the country extended its empire not by military conquest or political dictation, but by financial penetration.

At home, one of the most conspicuous results of prosperity was the conquest of the whole country by urban tastes and urban dress and the urban way of living. The rube disappeared. Girls in the villages of New Hampshire and Wyoming wore the same brief skirts and used the same lip-sticks as their sisters in New York. The proletariat—or what the radicals of the Big Red Scare days had called the proletariat—gradually lost its class consciousness; the American Federation of Labor dwindled in membership and influence; the time had come when workingmen owned second-hand Buicks and applauded Jimmy Walker, not objecting in the least, it seemed, to his exquisite clothes, his valet, and his frequent visits to the millionaire-haunted sands of Palm Beach. It was no accident that men like Mellon and Hoover and Morrow found their wealth an asset rather than a liability in public office, or that there was a widespread popular movement to make Henry Ford President in 1924. The possession of millions was a sign of success, and success was worshiped the country over.

Business itself was regarded with a new veneration. Once it had been considered less dignified and distinguished than the learned professions, but now people thought they praised a clergyman highly when they called him a good business man. College alumni, gathered at their annual banquets, fervently applauded banker trustees who spoke of education as one of the greatest American industries and compared the president and the dean to business executives. The colleges themselves organized business courses and cheerfully granted credit to candidates for degrees in the arts and sciences for their work in advertising copy-writing, marketing methods, elementary stenography, and drug-store practice. Even Columbia University drew men and women into its home-study courses by a system of follow-up letters worthy of a manufacturer of refrigerators, and sent out salesmen to ring the door bells of those who expressed a flicker of interest; even the great University of Chicago made use of what André Siegfried has called "the mysticism of success" by heading an advertisement of its correspondence courses with the admonition to "DEVELOP POWER AT HOME, to investigate, persevere, achieve." . . . The Harvard Business School established annual advertising awards, conferring academic *éclat* upon well-phrased sales arguments for commercial products. It was not easy for the churches to resist the tide of business enthusiasm. The Swedish Immanuel Congregational Church in New York, according to an item in the *American Mercury*, recognized the superiority of the business to the spiritual appeal by offering to all who contributed one hundred dollars to its building fund "an engraved certificate of investment in preferred capital stock in the Kingdom of God." And a church billboard in uptown New York struck the same persuasive note: "Come to Church. Christian Worship Increases Your Efficiency. Christian F. Reisner, Pastor."

In every American city and town, service clubs gathered the flower of the middle-class citizenry together for weekly luncheons noisy with good fellowship. They were growing fast, these service clubs. Rotary, the most famous of them, had been founded in 1905; by 1930 it had 150,000 members and boasted—as a sign of its international influence—as many as 3,000 clubs in 44 countries. The number of Kiwanis Clubs rose from 205 in 1920 to 1,800 in 1929; the Lions Clubs, of which the first was not formed until 1917, multiplied until at the end of the decade there were 1,200 of them. Nor did these clubs content themselves with singing songs and conducting social-service campaigns; they expressed the national faith in what one of their founders called "the redemptive and regenerative influence of business." The speakers before them pictured the business man as a builder, a doer of great things, yes, and a dreamer whose imagination was ever seeking out new ways of serving humanity. It was a popular note, for in hundreds of directors' rooms, around hundreds of conference tables, the American business men of the era of Coolidge Prosperity were seeing themselves as men of vision with eyes steadfastly fixed on the long future. At the end of the decade, a cartoon in the *New Yorker* represented an executive as saying to his heavy-jowled colleagues at one of these meetings: "We have ideas. Possibly we tilt at windmills—just seven Don Juans tilting at windmills." It was a perfect bit of satire on business sentimentality. The service clubs specialized in this sort of mysticism: was not a speaker before the Rotarians of Waterloo, Iowa, quoted by the *American Mercury* as declaring that "Rotary is a manifestation of the divine?"

Indeed, the association of business with religion was one of the most significant phenomena of the day. When the National Association of Credit Men held their annual convention at New York, there were provided for the three thousand delegates a special devotional service at the Cathedral of St. John the Divine and five sessions of prayer conducted by Protestant clergymen, a Roman Catholic priest, and a Jewish rabbi; and the credit men were uplifted by a sermon by Dr. S. Parkes Cadman on "Religion in Business." Likewise the Associated Advertising Clubs, meeting in Philadelphia, listened to a keynote address by Doctor Cadman on "Imagination and Advertising," and at the meeting of the Church Advertising Department the subjects discussed included "Spiritual Principles in Advertising" and "Advertising the Kingdom through Press-Radio Service." The fact that each night of the session a cabaret entertainment was furnished to the earnest delegates from 11.30 to 2 and that part of the Atlantic City

Beauty Pageant was presented was merely a sign that even men of high faith must have their fun.

So frequent was the use of the Bible to point the lessons of business and of business to point the lessons of the Bible that it was sometimes difficult to determine which was supposed to gain the most from the association. Fred F. French, a New York builder and real-estate man, told his salesmen, "There is no such thing as a reason why not," and continued: "One evidence of the soundness of this theory may be found in the command laid down in Matthew vii:7 by the Greatest Human-nature Expert that ever lived, 'Knock and it shall be opened unto you.'" He continued by quoting "the greatest command of them all—'Love Thy Neighbor as Thyself'"—and then stated that by following such high principles the Fred F. French salesmen had "immeasurably strengthened their own characters and power, so that during this year they will serve our stockholders at a lower commission rate, and yet each one earn more money for himself than in nineteen hundred twenty-five." In this case Scripture was apparently taken as setting a standard for business to meet—to its own pecuniary profit. Yet in other cases it was not so certain that business was not the standard, and Scripture complimented by being lifted to the business level.

Witness, for example, the pamphlet on *Moses, Persuader of Men* issued by the Metropolitan Casualty Insurance Company (with an introduction by the indefatigable Doctor Cadman), which declared that "Moses was one of the greatest salesmen and real-estate promoters that ever lived," that he was a "Dominant, Fearless, and Successful Personality in one of the most magnificent selling campaigns that history ever placed upon its pages." And witness, finally, the extraordinary message preached by Bruce Barton in *The Man Nobody Knows*, which so touched the American heart that for two successive years—1925 and 1926—it was the best-selling non-fiction book in the United States. Barton sold Christianity to the public by showing its resemblance to business. Jesus, this book taught, was not only "the most popular dinner guest in Jerusalem" and "an outdoor man," but a great executive. "He picked up twelve men from the bottom ranks of business and forged them into an organization that conquered the world. . . . Nowhere is there such a startling example of executive success as the way in which that organization was brought together." His parables were "the most powerful advertisements of all time. . . . He would be a national advertiser today." In fact, Jesus was "the founder of modern business." Why, you ask? Because he was the author of the ideal of service.

The Gospel According to Bruce Barton met a popular demand. Under the beneficent influence of Coolidge Prosperity, business had become almost the national religion of America. Millions of people wanted to be reassured that this religion was altogether right and proper, and that in the rules for making big money lay all the law and the prophets.

Was it strange that during the very years when the Barton Gospel was circulating most vigorously, selling and advertising campaigns were becoming more cynical and the American business world was refusing to exercise itself over the Teapot Dome disclosures and the sordid history of the Continental Trading Company? Perhaps; but it must be remembered that in all religions there is likely to be a gap between faith and works. The business man's halo did not always fit, but he wore it proudly.

Where the Booze Came From

by Herbert Asbury

No one ever knew how much good liquor was in the United States when the country went constitutionally dry on the early morning of January 17, 1920. An unknown quantity was in the hands of private citizens and farsighted bootleggers who had bought it before the prohibition era began and stored it away for future use or sale, and the saloonkeepers and wholesale dealers had some. The largest supplies were in some eight hundred warehouses, both free and bonded, many of which were attached to distilleries. Information given out by the government about this liquor was always vague and contradictory. On January 30, 1920, the New York *Times* said that it amounted to sixty-nine million gallons, figures obviously obtained from federal sources. William G. Shepherd, a well-known journalist of the period, said in *Collier's Weekly* for March 21, 1925, that liquor stocks at the beginning of prohibition included fifty million gallons of rye and bourbon whiskey alone. Other guesses ranged from forty millions to seventy millions. Early in 1923 Roy A. Haynes, Prohibition Commissioner, made the most positive statement that any federal official had ever issued on the subject. He said that on July 1, 1922, the government held thirty-eight million gallons of pre-prohibition liquors.

This liquor was taken over by the government, but it wasn't exactly confiscated. The distillers who had put it in the warehouses still owned it, and under the law were responsible for it, but they couldn't touch it or dispose of it. As Representative James R. Mann said in a speech in Congress on January 30, 1920, "The man who owns liquor in a bonded warehouse is between the devil and deep sea. He cannot sell it for beverage purposes. He cannot withdraw it for beverage purposes. He cannot destroy it without paying the government tax upon it. If somebody steals it from him, he is required to pay the beverage tax upon it. He cannot make use of it in any way except to let it remain in the warehouse at his own risk, not the risk of the government. . . . Eventually there must be some disposition by Congress of this liquor." Congress appropriated one million dollars in 1921, and other large sums in later years, to pay for guarding the booze, but the ultimate disposition of most of it was determined by the bootleggers.

These stocks were augmented, from time to time, by confiscated liquor, and by legally manufactured whiskey, brandy, and rum. It was not true, as Wayne B. Wheeler of the Anti-Saloon League wrote in the New York *Times* of March 30, 1926, that when the liquor provisions of the Food Control Bill became effective on September 8, 1917, "the distilling of beverage liquor in the United States was ended and was never legally resumed." The production of distilled liquors continued throughout 1918; whiskey, according to government records, to the extent of 17,383,511.3 gallons. No gin was manufactured after 1918, and in 1919 no legal whiskey was distilled. In the fiscal years 1920, 1921, and 1922, however, selected distilleries—it was never explained how or why these selections were made—were permitted to operate. They produced in those years 1,303,879.49 gallons of whiskey.

The distillation of rum and brandy was never stopped, although the manufacture of both liquors was considerably curtailed after 1918. The production of rum ranged from 534,507.5 gallons in 1921 to 953,350.8 in 1928; of brandy, from 1,802,422.3 gallons in 1919 to 338,430.7 in 1927. A considerable number of wineries maintained full production throughout the dry era, and as late as 1926 four breweries were being legally operated. The excuse given by the government for permitting the distillation of whiskey was that it was needed to replenish existing supplies, which dwindled rapidly after the Eighteenth Amendment went into effect. Rum was required, principally, in the manufacture of tobacco products, and brandy was needed to fortify sacramental wines. It was solemnly explained that although millions of gallons of wine were on hand, a great deal more was needed for religious purposes and for the manufacture of vinegar. Inquisitive journalists who tried to find out why the breweries were running were ignored or brushed off, for not even a federal official with all his double talk could get around the fact that there were no legal uses for beer.

A small quantity of the liquor impounded by the government was used by industry, mostly in the manufacture of a few food products, but the great bulk of it was held for medicinal purposes and was released to wholesalers who in turn sold it to the drugstores. Both required permits, but none was issued to retailers in nineteen states because of local laws. Under the regulations as first promulgated by the Prohibition Bureau, a physician, who also had to obtain a permit, could prescribe one quart of whiskey per patient per month, on numbered blanks furnished by the government. This seemed to be a simple enough procedure, but it was so entangled in what the New York *Times* called "onerous and burdensome red tape" that many druggists and doctors announced that they would not sell or prescribe liquor because the law made it too easy for an innocent man to get into trouble. Nevertheless, by June 1920, less than five months after the Eighteenth Amendment went into effect, some fifteen thousand physicians and fifty-seven thousand druggists had applied for permits. Most of the latter were retailers.

The Prohibition Bureau announced after a few months that the new system was working perfectly; it ignored the fact, as shown by its own records, that medicinal liquor was moving out of the warehouses in enormous quantities. In 1921 well over eight million gallons of whiskey were withdrawn, probably twenty times as much as was used in any pre-prohibition year. In March 1921 the bureaucratic machinery was suddenly jammed by a ruling of the Attorney General, A. Mitchell Palmer, who said that the Volstead Act placed no restrictions upon the prescribing of beer and wine. Immediately thousands of Americans complained of ailments which could be relieved only by copious draughts of these beverages. There was a tremendous uproar from the drys, and meetings of protest were held throughout the country. The Anti-Saloon League rushed into action, and in November 1921 Congress passed the Willis-Campbell Law, which forbade a physician to prescribe beer for any purpose, or wine containing more than 24 per cent of alcohol by volume. The wine provision was a phony, as very few wines contained that much alcohol. The new law also limited a physician to a hundred prescriptions in ninety days, and no more than one half pint could be prescribed for any one person within ten days. This made legal whiskey very expensive; the doctor usually received two dollars for the prescription, and the druggist charged from three to six dollars for the half pint. And it was apt to be adulterated.

Before prohibition medicinal liquors were handled by approximately four hundred wholesale drug houses. It was a profitable business, for most doctors who prescribed booze specified drugstore whiskey, which, in those days, was almost certain to be of good quality. By the latter part of 1920 some thirty-three hundred such firms, supposedly carrying ten thousand dollars' worth of drugs each, were withdrawing medicinal liquor on permit. Most were fronts for bootleg gangs. So were many retail druggists; they cut their stocks and diverted half to the illicit liquor trade. Federal inspectors, on the rare occasions when they appeared, were concerned only with the quantity of whiskey on hand and not its strength. Much of the drugstore liquor was 25 per cent whiskey and 75 per cent water. In addition to the wholesale druggists there were a great many dealers who didn't pretend to be anything but liquor sellers; they were likewise granted permits. Mannie Kessler, who became one of the country's biggest bootleggers, was in the liquor business for fifteen years before the United States went dry, and late in 1919 he bought a thousand cases of whiskey and stored it in one of his private warehouses. The Prohibition Bureau gave him permission to sell it to drugstores, and issued another permit which enabled him to withdraw as much more as he wanted. It is very doubtful if he ever sold an ounce legitimately.

During the first six years of prohibition the Prohibition Bureau gave permits to an average of 63,891 doctors annually, and revoked 169. By 1929 the number of permits in force had risen to more than a hundred thousand. These physicians were writing about eleven million prescriptions for whiskey every year. Theoretically, all were carefully checked by agents of the bureau after they had been filled by druggists, who were also subject to rigid controls. Actually, the Prohibition Bureau never had enough agents to make even token inspections. In New York, for example, the bureau in 1925 assigned seventeen agents to watch the city's twelve hundred drugstores and check the one million prescriptions issued every year by fifty-one hundred doctors. These figures did not include the forged and counterfeit prescriptions which were circulated all over the country; on June 2, 1920, the prohibition administrator for Illinois said that three hundred thousand had been issued in Chicago alone. In 1922 federal agents in New York uncovered a counterfeiting ring which was selling prescription blanks at from twenty-five to fifty dollars a hundred to bootleggers who in turn sold them to consumers for two dollars each. All the buyers had to do was take them to drugstores; they were properly filled out and signed, supposedly by reputable doctors. Prohibition officials said the bootleggers had forged the name of almost every physician listed in the New York telephone directory.

Some of the big bootleg syndicates used more direct methods to get the liquor out of the warehouses. The largest operator in this field was George Remus, a Chicago lawyer who abandoned a lucrative practice in the latter part of 1919 to become one of the most successful illicit liquor dealers in the country. Handling nothing but medicinal whiskey, Remus made more than five million dollars in less than five years; in one period of eleven months he deposited $2,800,000 in a single Cincinnati bank. Remus's system was simple but effective—he bought distilleries; eventually he owned at least a dozen in Kentucky, Ohio, and Missouri. He thus became the legal owner of whatever whiskey was stored in the distillery warehouses. These transactions were legitimate, and Remus and his associates would have made a reasonable profit if they had continued to sell the liquor on permit under government control. But no bootlegger was ever satisfied with less than 100 per cent return on his investment, and the big syndicates made far more. For example, Remus paid $125,000 for 891 barrels of whiskey in the Jack Daniel distillery in St. Louis, or approximately fifteen dollars a barrel. He removed 890 barrels, and sold the liquor at from twenty-five to thirty dollars a gallon. The total was well over a million dollars.

Once he had obtained title to a distillery, Remus bribed everybody who might conceivably interfere with his schemes. In October 1920, when he was planning to remove liquor from a Cincinnati distillery, federal agents planted a microphone in his hotel room. In one day they heard him paying off forty-four persons, including policemen, prohibition agents, warehouse guards, politicians, officers of the Internal Revenue Bureau, and other government officials. When these matters had been arranged, Remus moved into the distillery at night with his trucks and other equipment. Occasionally the barrels of liquor were boldly loaded into the trucks and then shipped by railroad. On one occasion a single train pulled into Cincinnati with eighteen freight cars carrying Remus booze.

Usually, however, Remus was more careful. Inside the distillery he built a large wooden trough, from which a rubber hose led through a window into a shed or other outbuilding. There an electric pump was installed. The liquor was poured into the trough and then pumped through the hose into barrels waiting on Remus's trucks, which sped away to hiding places in Ohio, Kentucky, Missouri, Indiana, and Illinois. It was in these states that Remus and his associates sold most of their stolen whiskey; a great deal wound up in Chicago cutting plants, and some was sent to New York and Philadelphia. To cover up the withdrawals, Remus sometimes refilled the empty whiskey barrels with water, and enough alcohol to bring up the proof. At other times all the barrels were emptied of liquor except one, which was left near the warehouse door for the convenience of any honest government gauger—there were such—who might visit the distillery on an inspection tour. It was usually from two to four months before the theft was discovered.

The government obtained twenty-six indictments after an investigation of the Jack Daniel conspiracy, which was probably Remus's best-known adventure, and twenty-three of the defendants were convicted, including a Missouri state senator, a former Internal Revenue collector, a former circuit-court judge, and one member each of the St. Louis Democratic and Republican city committees. Remus himself turned state's evidence and was not prosecuted. However, he served five short jail sentences during his career as a rum king, and paid fines totaling eleven thousand dollars. He was released from the county jail at Portsmouth, Ohio, on April 26, 1927, and after spending a few days in New York went to his home in Cincinnati. He immediately accused his wife of having been unfaithful while he was in prison, and on October 6, 1927, shot her to death in a Cincinnati park. He conducted his own defense, and although the verdict was guilty, the jury found him insane, and the court committed him to an asylum. A few months later he convinced the Ohio Court of Appeals that he was sane, and was released. He was never resentenced or tried again.

Early in 1925 the Prohibition Bureau began to gain at least a measure of control over the medicinal liquor situation. The number of permits to wholesalers was reduced to 446, and the privilege of selling the liquor was restricted to drug houses, which were required to carry at least twenty-five thousand dollars' worth of drugs in stock and to prove that the liquor business was not more than 10 per cent of their total volume. The regulations dealing with retail drugstores were also tightened, but were never strictly enforced. By 1930 legal withdrawals from the warehouses had been reduced to about 1,500,000 gallons a year, which was still considerably more than was actually needed but was only a small fraction of the total consumption. Armed robbery of warehouses declined when the bureau, acting under laws passed by Congress in 1923, began to concentrate the booze in a smaller number of storage places. This was a slow process, but in 1928 all the legal whiskey in the country was stored in thirty-seven warehouses. By that time, however, probably two thirds of the original supply was gone; it was officially admitted in Washington that one half had been withdrawn, in one way or another, by 1926.

Approximately a hundred million gallons of alcohol a year were manufactured during the prohibition era by licensed distilleries in nineteen states, Hawaii, and the District of Columbia. Most of it was made from cane- and beet-sugar molasses, although in the Middle West corn and other grains were used. All of this alcohol, except a small proportion kept for use in its pure state, passed through denaturing plants, where it was made unfit to drink by the addition of various substances, many of them poisonous. It was then concentrated in bonded warehouses, and released for sale by the government under three main classifications—pure, specially denatured, and completely denatured. The pure variety could be withdrawn only on permits issued by the Prohibition Bureau, and upon payment of a tax of about six dollars a gallon. It was used for medicinal and scientific purposes, and in the production of pharmaceuticals, candy, spices, extracts, and other preparations intended for human consumption. Permits were also required for specially denatured alcohol, but it was tax-free. It was necessary in the manufacture of cosmetics, insecticides, soap, photographic supplies, remedies for external use, and many other products. Completely denatured alcohol was also tax-free, but there were no restrictions upon its sale, purchase, or use. Anybody could buy it, and the government had no interest in what the purchaser did with it, although of course as a good American he was supposed to obey the law and not try to drink it. The principal use for this alcohol was in the manufacture of anti-freeze solutions for automobile radiators, but it was also needed in making paints and varnishes.

Several factors combined to make the problem of controlling the flow of industrial alcohol very difficult of solution, and for a good many years almost impossible. The attempt to enforce the Volstead Act and the Eighteenth Amendment paralleled an enormous expansion of the American chemical industry, and it was the established policy of the United States Government to foster and encourage this growth. In 1906, when the laws making denatured alcohol tax-free were passed by Congress, the legitimate demand was satisfied by a production of one million gallons. By 1910 this had increased to a little less than seven million gallons, and in 1920 it jumped to almost thirty million. The increase was even greater every year thereafter. At the beginning of prohibition, because of the large and uncertain demand, no restrictions were placed upon the quantity of alcohol a manufacturer might produce. The result, of course, was a tremendous overproduction of which the government knew little or nothing, and for which there was no outlet except the illicit liquor business.

For the usual reasons of incompetence, corruption, shortage of personnel, and, particularly, political meddling, the administration of the permit system was lax and slipshod. Mrs. Mabel Walker Willebrandt, Assistant Attorney General, wrote in *The Inside of Prohibition* in 1929 that "the policy of granting permit privileges has always been subject to so much political pressure that it has been marked by vacillation and puerility." She might also have said pusillanimity and plain crookedness. In general an applicant had only to say that he was engaged, or about to engage, in the manufacture of products requiring the use of alcohol; keep silent about his criminal record, if any, and present the endorsement of a powerful politician. After 1921 it was helpful to be an enrolled Republican. If the application was refused, pressure could be brought to bear or recourse to the courts could be had; but as Mrs. Willebrandt pointed out, the Prohibition Bureau said no so seldom that few such suits were filed. In ten years only one reached the Supreme Court, where the government was upheld. In addition to the vast number of permits officially issued by the bureau, which Mrs. Willebrandt said "reached into higher mathematics" during the regime of General Lincoln C. Andrews, there was always a brisk business in forged and stolen permits, all of which were usually honored without investigation. Occasionally a permit was revoked, and the holder had to pay the politicians as high as twenty thousand dollars to get it restored.

Thousands of new companies appeared in the chemical industry; they far outnumbered the "wholesale" drug houses which were making such heavy inroads in the stocks of medicinal liquor. They were prepared and eager, they said, to manufacture anything in the chemical line, provided they were given enough alcohol. The financial backing of these concerns was usually provided by big bootleggers or gang chieftains, but as front men they frequently used politicians and federal and state officials; often they were granted permits when their political big shots solemnly asserted that they intended to manufacture something but wished to have supplies of alcohol on hand before they equipped their factories and sought customers. The vast majority of these companies never manufactured anything. They simply withdrew alcohol up to the limit of their permits, stored it awhile in warehouses, and then sent it along to the bootleggers, protecting themselves by means of fake corporations and partnerships known as "cover houses." These houses, supposedly wholesalers and jobbers, seldom possessed any more facilities for doing business than a desk, a fountain pen, and a supply of receipts.

The cover house was one of the safest and easiest methods of beating the prohibition laws ever devised, because the power of the Prohibition Bureau to investigate didn't extend beyond the original purchase of the alcohol. The holder of a permit would withdraw a certain quantity of denatured alcohol and turn it over to his bootleg principals, but his records would show that it had been used to manufacture, say, toilet water, which had been shipped to a cover house. A prohibition agent could make inquiries about the transaction between the permittee and the manufacturer of the alcohol, but the former could stop the investigation by simply producing a receipt from the cover house. If the agent called upon the cover house and asked what had become of the toilet water, he was told that it was none of his business. And under the law it wasn't. The only chance the authorities had of exposing a cover house was to intercept a shipment and find that it was alcohol and not the preparation it was supposed to be, or trace it and prove that the cover house never received it. Similar methods were used to get alcohol out of denaturing plants, which could always produce receipts for shipments of alcohol to manufacturers of cosmetics and other products. Sometimes they offered forged receipts from legitimate houses.

Diversion of industrial alcohol to the bootleggers was considerably reduced in the late 1920s by a determined attack upon the source, although it was never entirely stopped. For almost ten years no attempt was made to ascertain the actual alcohol requirements of the legitimate chemical industry, although such a survey was frequently urged by officials of the Department of Commerce. It was finally done, however, and regulations imposing production quotas were put into effect on January 1, 1928. As a further precaution against surpluses, no distillery was permitted to produce more than 40 per cent of its quota during the first six months of any year. Changes were also made in the system of handling permits; thereafter they were issued by state administrators instead of in Washington, which somewhat reduced, or at least distributed, the political pressure.

How much alcohol was diverted into the illicit liquor trade was anybody's guess, and estimates varied widely. Chester P. Mills, prohibition administrator for the New York City area, said that in 1926 sixteen denaturing plants in the metropolis turned out eleven million gallons, of which about ten million went into the manufacture of bootleg hooch. Emory R. Buckner, United States Attorney for the southern district of New York, declared that the total diversion in 1926 was sixty million gallons. He estimated the value of the booze made from industrial alcohol, in New York and Pennsylvania alone, at $3,600,000,000 a year. General Lincoln C. Andrews told a congressional committee that one million gallons a month was being diverted in Philadelphia in 1926, and that the country-wide total was enough to make 150,000,000 quarts of booze annually.

Dr. James M. Doran, then chief chemist of the Prohibition Bureau, disputed General Andrews's statement: he estimated that in 1926 the bootleggers' share of a total production of 105,000,000 gallons of alcohol was only thirteen million gallons. Dr. Doran was Prohibition Commissioner in 1928, when the quota system was established; he testified later in the year that industrial alcohol presented "only a minor enforcement problem. It has to be watched all the time," he said, "but the leakages are comparatively small." Late in 1930 the bureau estimated that in that year the booze boys managed to get hold of five million gallons, a little more than 4 per cent of the total production. During the remaining years of the dry era, according to government records, the diversion was even less.

The government eventually managed to reduce the diversion of medicinal liquor and industrial alcohol, and to make life fairly miserable for the smugglers, but it was never able to do much about the moonshiners. During the first few years of prohibition the illicit distillers made whiskey, or at least they called it whiskey, and some continued to do so, especially in isolated areas. After about 1925, however, the great majority concentrated on alcohol, which was easier to make, required no storage, and netted a larger profit. In time they became more important than all other sources combined. As General Lincoln C. Andrews gloomily put it in 1926, "When we cut off one source of supply, moonshine wells up to fill the gap." Two years later the Prohibition Commissioner said that the moonshiners were producing eight times as much alcohol as was being diverted to bootleggers from government warehouses. Many observers thought this estimate was too low.

Stills were everywhere—in the mountains, on the farms, in the small towns and villages, and in the cities. In New York, Chicago, Detroit, Pittsburgh, and other cities with large foreign populations, the pungent odor of fermenting mash and alcoholic distillate hung over whole sections twenty-four hours a day. West Madison Street in Chicago, from the edge of the Loop to Halsted Street and beyond, smelled like a distillery throughout the dry era; in 1928 the Chicago police estimated that at least a hundred stills were running full blast in every block. In many places the operations of the moonshiners created problems of waste disposal, as in North Tarrytown, New York, where the sewer inspector officially asked them not to flush the refuse from their stills down the drains. Prune pits, potato peelings, grain, and other discards were clogging the sewers.

The Rev. Francis Kasackszul, a Catholic priest of Sugar Notch, a coal-mining town in Luzerne County, Pennsylvania, told a congressional committee in 1926 that since prohibition began liquor had been manufactured in "practically every other home" in his community. "They make it, they drink it, they sell it," he said. A survey published in 1925 by the Federal Council of Churches of Christ in America said, "The illicit liquor traffic has become a means of comparative opulence to many families that formerly were on the records of relief agencies. In one New England industrial town a row of somber tenements has been adorned with Stutz and Packard cars purchased with the profits of a new-found illicit livelihood." In many foreign families the children were taught to mind the still, while Mama bought the ingredients and prepared the mash, and Papa sold the product, after liberal samplings by all members of the family.

An enormous mass of similar testimony was accumulated by congressional committees, the Wickersham Commission, and other investigating agencies. Mrs. Viola M. Anglin, deputy chief probation officer for New York City, assigned to the family court in Manhattan, quoted the sixteen deputies under her supervision. "They tell me," she said, "that in each one of their districts you can find from one hundred to one hundred and fifty, and in some of them two hundred, stills. And these stills are not operated alone in cigar stores, delicatessen stores, and all sorts of places, but they are operated also in the homes of the people who live in the tenements. You open the door of a tenement and walk in and the first thing you get is a whiff of liquor, or some kind of alcohol. . . ." Mrs. Anglin told of a case of nonsupport in which the father of a family had been sent to jail. A week or so later a probation officer called at the family's tenement home, intending to refer the mother and her three children to a relief agency. She found that they had moved into a larger apartment and were doing splendidly. The mother was operating a still in her living room, and the liquor she made was sold by her brother and brother-in-law. The children were happy, well-dressed, and much interested in the new business.

Moonshining or alky cooking in the big cities was a highly organized racket controlled by the gang leaders in association with their political henchmen, although of course there were many little independents whose operations were too small to interest the big shots. As a rule the gangsters provided the stills and the raw materials, and employed the tenement dwellers to handle the details of manufacturing, to barrel or bottle the alcohol, and to have it ready for shipment when the collecting trucks made their periodic calls. Sometimes the men who actually made the moonshine were given a small percentage of the profits, sometimes they worked on a straight wage basis, and sometimes they were simply told that they and their families would be murdered unless they ran the stills, obeyed orders, and kept their mouths shut. The gang captains sold the alcohol to wholesale bootleggers or ran it through their own cutting plants and themselves supplied the speakeasies and the retail dealers. A great deal was sold to consumers without further treatment—raw, fiery stuff that could scarcely be drunk without the addition of ginger ale or orange juice. Most people turned it into the beverage known in prohibition times as gin.

Virtually all the Italian moonshiners, who formed the largest racial group engaged in the business, worked for the Unione Siciliana, or for the gang leaders who controlled the Unione's loosely connected branches. This organization, which was more or less an offshoot of the Mafia, was founded in the early 1900s by Ignazio Saietta, a Sicilian counterfeiter and professional murderer who was also known as Ignazio Lupo and Lupo the Wolf. Under Lupo's leadership the Unione engaged in a criminal business in women, narcotics, extortion, kidnaping, burglary, bank robbery, counterfeiting, and murder. In less than half a dozen years Unione gunmen committed sixty homicides, the details of which were known to the United States Secret Service, which investigated Lupo and his followers because of their counterfeiting operations. About half of these killings occurred in the Little Italy section of New York, in the vicinity of East 125th Street. In 1920 the current leader, Joe (The Boss) Masseria, reorganized the Unione for bootlegging and moonshining, although other activities were continued and the gang also worked in the field of industrial and labor-union racketeering. The branches that Lupo the Wolf had formed in Chicago, Detroit, and other cities with large Italian districts were strengthened, but not until several bloody gang wars had been fought for control. Largely because of the protection afforded by Frankie Yale of Brooklyn and Al Capone and the murderous Genna brothers of Chicago, Joe the Boss managed to retain his national leadership until 1931, when he was shot down. Lucky Luciano, the notorious pander who was later convicted and deported, was with Masseria at the time, and succeeded Joe the Boss as the big shot of the Unione.

Criminal gangs, generally with big-city connections, also controlled moonshining in many country areas, especially in the Middle West and the South; they induced farmers, by money payments or threats, to run their stills. Typical of these outfits were the Traum gang of St. Louis and Terre Haute, Indiana, and the Stephens gang of San Antonio, Texas. The latter, protected by state and county officials and political leaders, handled the production of twenty-three large stills which had been set up on farms in the vicinity of San Antonio. Extensive aging and cutting plants were maintained, and the gang supplied most of that part of Texas with liquor. When the gang was exposed, following a pistol battle in which a prohibition agent was killed, indictments were obtained against seventy-six persons, including the assistant district attorney of Bexar County and the chief investigator for the state of Texas.

The Traum gang was a group of about a dozen St. Louis hoodlums, most of whom had served prison sentences for bank robbery in Illinois and Missouri. In 1928 these ruffians invaded Terre Haute, Indiana, where they opened offices and made the usual arrangements with state and county officials and prohibition agents. The gang handled the output of thirty-seven big stills, some of which could produce a thousand gallons of alcohol a day. All the liquor-making plants were on farms in two adjacent Indiana counties, and with their combined production the Traums supplied that part of the state and ran convoys of alcohol-laden trucks to St. Louis, East St. Louis, and Louisville. The gang owned only a few of the stills; the operators of the others, in addition to turning over their entire output, were compelled to pay a tribute of $1.50 on every barrel of mash and fifty cents on each one-hundred-pound sack of sugar. From these sources the gang collected about thirteen thousand dollars a week.

A government report on the operations of the Traums, prepared by the Department of Justice for the Wickersham Commission, said that two murders were committed by the gang. "This combine," the report continued, "owned a number of Thompson machine guns and terrorized the community, in some instances, by going to the homes of farmers, placing guns in their backs, and forcing them to put stills on their farms. . . . The deputy administrator at Indianapolis raided one of these stills, and secured a confession from the farmer on whose property the still in question was located. On the following day the farmer was killed by machine-gun fire as he drove through one of the main streets of Terre Haute." The government investigated the Traum gang early in 1930, and thirty-five members of the outfit were indicted. Of these, twenty-nine were convicted, and sentenced to serve a total of thirty-six years in prison and to pay fines aggregating twenty-five thousand dollars. This seems to be a long time and a lot of money; actually, it averaged considerably less than a year in jail and a fine of one thousand dollars for each defendant.

The hundreds of thousands of moonshine stills which operated day and night from the Atlantic to the Pacific and from the Gulf of Mexico to the Canadian border were of all sizes and types. They ranged from crude homemade contraptions with a capacity of five gallons or less to huge, well-equipped distilleries capable of producing two thousand gallons of high-proof alcohol a day. Many of the big plants were in Chicago, where the political protection was unexcelled, and some were in New York, Detroit, and other cities where politicians and gangsters were playfellows. In 1927 federal agents captured a moonshine plant in Detroit which occupied an acre of space in a Twelfth Street warehouse and had cost at least $250,000 to equip. It contained, among other things, thirty-four vats, each holding two thousand gallons of mash, and a still which could turn out fifteen hundred gallons of alcohol in twenty-four hours. This plant was discovered because, despite their huge investment and the obvious necessity for undercover operation, the moonshiners stole electric current from other tenants of the warehouse, thus saving at the most a few hundred dollars a year.

Prohibition agents seized an enormous number of stills in the course of the noble experiment; according to the records of the bureau, a total of 696,933 were captured in the five years from 1921 to 1925. Of these, 172,537 were found in 1925. General Lincoln C. Andrews presented these figures to a congressional committee in 1926 and remarked, "This means that a great many people are distilling." He estimated that five hundred thousand persons were engaged in the moonshine business, and expressed the opinion that for every still seized nine remained undiscovered. This would seem to be a very poor record, but when everything is considered, it is much better than it sounds. The Prohibition Bureau never had more than twenty-three hundred field agents, and if the entire force had done nothing but search for moonshine stills, which were widely scattered all over the United States, each man would have had to patrol 1,316 square miles of territory. State, county, and city authorities were never of much help in the never-ending quest for illicit liquor-makers; by and large, the moonshiners and the gangsters were their pals.

The Volstead Act outlawed beer, which had long been the favorite tipple of the American people, but permitted the manufacture of "cereal beverage" with an alcoholic content of not more than one half of 1 per cent, a concoction which became widely, but not favorably, known as near beer. All breweries were supposed to close when the Eighteenth Amendment went into effect, and to reopen only if granted permits to operate as cereal-beverage plants. The system under which these permits were issued was similar to that used for the withdrawal of alcohol and medicinal liquor, and was administered in the same irresponsible manner and subject to the same corruption and political pressure. When the regulations dealing with beer were being prepared by the experts of the Treasury Department, several forward-looking federal officials suggested that permits be restricted to large, long-established breweries, which had millions of dollars invested in plant and equipment, and would be more apt to obey the law than smaller concerns with little or nothing to lose. It was also proposed that permits be issued slowly until it had been determined how much near beer the country would consume. Such a policy would have greatly simplified the problem of policing the beer industry. But the politicians opposed it with great vehemence; they screamed indignantly that this was a free country and that every man should have a chance to get into the near-beer racket if he so desired. Consequently, permits were granted, as Mrs. Mabel Walker Willebrandt put it, to "any person with a nice clean face and no guns sticking out of his pockets"; he merely had to fill out an application form and present it with the endorsement of a congressman or other politician. On the rare occasions when an investigation was made, it was confined to inquiries addressed to the persons whom the applicant had named as references. Government records show that a minimum of five hundred plants made near beer throughout the dry era, forty in New York City alone. And there were many special and temporary permits which were not listed. Ten or a dozen big breweries, such as Anheuser-Busch in St. Louis, Pabst in Milwaukee, and Ruppert in New York, could have supplied all the cereal beverages needed; except in one year, 1921, the production never exceeded two hundred million gallons. This was a very small percentage of the consumption of real beer before prohibition; and, for that matter, a not much larger percentage of the consumption of real beer *during* prohibition.

The control of beer production was hopeless from the beginning, partly because of the chronic shortage of prohibition agents and partly because of a simple fact of manufacturing which nullified any serious attempt to enforce the law. In order to make near beer it was necessary first to manufacture real beer containing from 3 to 8 per cent alcohol. The excess alcohol was then drawn off until it had been reduced to the legal limit of one half of 1 per cent. The alcohol thus removed was supposed to be shipped to government warehouses for denaturing, but a great deal was diverted to bootleggers and cutting plants. There was nothing to compel the brewer to lower the alcoholic content of his beer except his conscience—and almost everybody's conscience seems to have been on vacation during the fourteen years of the Eighteenth Amendment. "If a brewer is disposed to violate the law," said the Prohibition Commissioner in 1930, "it is just a question of putting a hose in a high-powered beer tank and filling near-beer kegs with the high-powered beer and running it out as near beer. So it is a rather difficult thing to get at."

Prohibition agents were seldom able to make a case against a brewery suspected of sending out real beer unless they captured a shipment in transit; beer away from the brewery was evidence. It was comparatively easy to escape the few men assigned to watch the breweries, and enormous quantities of real beer were shipped as cereal beverage. Some of the breweries, when caught, were found to have no sales departments to handle near beer, and no customers. Many brewers honestly tried to obey the law and to build up a legitimate business in near beer, but they couldn't control all of their employees; there were always some who would accept bribes from the bootleggers and run real beer out at night. The big beer rings employed expert "beer shooters" to handle such operations. Scores of brewers sent near beer openly to the speakeasies, but followed it with secret shipments of alcohol to bring the stuff up to full strength. Sometimes this was done in speakeasy cellars by forcing the alcohol into a barrel of beer with a compression pump. In many places, however, the bartender squirted a little alcohol into each glass as it was served. This was the famous needled beer which caused so many stomach-aches and so much unpleasant drunkenness; it contained anywhere from 3 to 20 per cent alcohol, depending upon the generosity of the bartender or the speakeasy proprietor. There was a big profit in beer; a half keg cost about one dollar to make, and the brewer sold it for twenty-five to thirty dollars. At twenty-five to fifty cents a glass, over the bar, it brought from seventy-five to one hundred and twenty-five dollars.

The beer situation was further complicated by the introduction of "wort," which was first manufactured in Chicago, spread quickly to Wisconsin and thence throughout the country. Wort was simply beer in which the manufacturing processes had been halted before the addition of yeast. To make beer, the purchaser simply dropped a cake of yeast into the wort, let the mixture ferment, and then filtered it. Since wort contained no alcohol, it was a perfectly legal commodity, and was sold openly everywhere. Many breweries abandoned the production of near beer and concentrated on wort. It gave a tremendous impetus to home-brewing, and was a great help to the wildcat, or moonshine, breweries. Many of these were "alley breweries," which were really large home-brew units. They were operated by the thousands in tenement cellars, abandoned buildings, caves, and wherever else they could find concealment. In the aggregate they manufactured a great deal of bad beer, which was always sold green. The usual reaction to a few glasses of alley beer was described by a Detroit businessman to a Detroit *News* reporter in 1928: "The beer tastes wonderful, but after I've had a couple of glasses I'm terribly sleepy. Sometimes my eyes don't seem to focus and my head aches. I'm not intoxicated, understand, merely feel as if I've been drawn through a knothole."

In theory, all breweries to which near-beer permits had been refused were immediately dismantled, in such a manner as to make the manufacture of beer impossible. In practice, the dismantling usually consisted of the formal removal, by a prohibition agent, of a section of pipe. Since the government men seldom inspected a "dismantled" brewery, hundreds of brewers immediately replaced the pipe, or substituted a piece of rubber hose, and resumed the production of beer. When General Smedley D. Butler, of the Marine Corps, was assigned to clean up Philadelphia, he was told before he left Washington that he must confine his activities to alcohol and whiskey, as the federal authorities were taking care of the breweries. They were indeed. General Butler found thirteen, all supposedly dismantled, running full blast. He immediately wrote to the prohibition administrator for the Philadelphia district, describing the situation and asking what action the administraor's office intended to take. Several months later he received a letter from the assistant administrator, who wrote that little could be done because "suspicion is attached to a majority of the employees on whom we have to depend for results." General Butler then publicly threatened to raid the breweries, and was promptly notified by the United States Marshal's office that any policeman who entered a Philadelphia brewery would be shot. That angered the old war horse, and he sent cops into the breweries. They performed the operation without casualties, and brought the operators of the plants into the city courts. The cases against twelve were immediately dismissed, and a small fine was imposed upon the thirteenth.

Roy A. Haynes, Prohibition Administrator, said in 1923 that the great beer centers of the country were Chicago, New York, Detroit, Atlantic City, Philadelphia, St. Louis, Baltimore, New Orleans, and Buffalo. There were many others, however, just as important; breweries operated, either as wildcats or in the guise of near-beer manufacturers, in every state and in almost every city. One of the largest producing areas was northern Illinois; it "teemed with breweries" which made huge quantities of beer for Chicago, Detroit, and other midwestern cities. It also produced Lawrence Crowley of Joliet, Illinois, better known as Butch, who called himself King of the Beer Runners and who was one of the fantastic characters of the early years of the dry era. Crowley was the son of a Joliet dogcatcher, and when prohibition began he was working in a garage as a mechanic's helper and occasionally driving a taxicab. He started bootlegging in a small way, and as business increased spent a large part of his profits making political connections.

About the middle of 1921 Crowley suddenly bloomed as the big shot of a beer ring which controlled more than twenty breweries, scattered from Joliet to the Wisconsin line. He made an enormous lot of money—and loved to spend it. He was married early in 1922, and gave the priest one thousand dollars. He wore a four-carat diamond ring, and two platinum wrist watches, one set with diamonds. He carried a roll of fifty thousand dollars in a pants pocket, and displayed it at every opportunity. He drove a different car every day in the week; he owned eight, one a spare. He bought a fourteen-room house in an exclusive residential section of Joliet and equipped it from cellar to attic with gold doorknobs. He bought the garage where he had worked. When the Commercial Club blackballed him, he bought the business block in which the club was located and ordered it to move. He bought the Joliet *Times* and assigned the paper's best writer to turn out editorials signed "Lawrence Crowley." He buried his mother in a fifteen-hundred-dollar casket and erected a twenty-five-thousand-dollar monument over her grave.

He was a notable spender and put a great deal of money into circulation, but he made one big mistake—he did all of his splurging in his home town. Everybody talked about Butch, and eventually the gossip reached the ears of Mrs.

Mabel Reineke, a go-getting young woman who was serving her first term as Collector of Internal Revenue for the Chicago district, of which Joliet was a part. She ordered an investigation, and it was found that Crowley had never even heard of the income tax. The government thereupon unlimbered its arsenal of liens, writs, and other lethal weapons, and demanded back income taxes amounting to several hundred thousand dollars, with penalties. Within a year the federal tax hounds had stripped Crowley of his wealth, and he started all over again in the bootleg business. But he was never able to regain his former eminence.

Although wine was somewhat harder to come by than in pre-prohibition times, those who liked to tarry at the wine cup never lacked supplies for their bibbing. The framers of the Volstead Act gave them a head start in the race for booze by including a provision permitting a householder to possess two hundred gallons of grape juice or cider a year, strictly for the use of himself and his family. It was assumed that of course nature would co-operate and not let the grape juice ferment or the cider get hard. This was intended to placate the farmers, but everybody took advantage of it. The winegrowers, much gratified and anticipating a further demand, greatly increased their production of grapes; in California alone the acreage devoted to viniculture jumped from ninety-seven thousand acres in 1919 to 680,796 in 1926. Grape juice was sold in stores which specialized in materials and equipment for home liquor-making, and in grocery stores and other establishments, and by door-to-door salesmen in five- to twenty-gallon kegs. Each keg was accompanied by a printed notice warning the purchaser not to do so-and-so. "If you do," the notice said, "this grape juice will ferment and turn into wine. That would be illegal." In every home where wine was liked, the cellar, garage, or a closet usually held a keg of grape juice quietly obeying the call of nature and violating the Volstead Act. However, there was a dearth of really good wine, even though almost any bootlegger would gladly supply the finest French champagnes and still wines; that is, the bottles looked authentic and bore the labels of famous foreign producers. Actually, 99 per cent of the still wines came from tenement cellars, and almost all of the champagne was cider pumped full of air and needled with a little alcohol. Prohibition agents in New York raided forty night clubs in

1926 and seized some eight thousand cases of champagne, all of which was analyzed. Not one drop was genuine.

The most important source of professionally made wines was the large stocks stored in government warehouses and intended for the manufacture of vinegar and for religious purposes. As soon as prohibition began, new vinegar-manufacturing plants appeared all over the country, and of course had no trouble getting permits to withdraw wine. Before the dry era twenty vinegar factories supplied the needs of New York and Connecticut; by the middle of 1922 more than a hundred had received permits in these states, and were withdrawing nine hundred thousand gallons of wine a year. The government finally solved this problem by loading the wine with acetic acid before it was shipped to the plants, so that it was vinegar when the vinegar men got it. This didn't hamper the operations of those who were really making vinegar, but it was a serious blow to the fakes. They tried various reagents, but found none that was effective for more than ten days or two weeks, after which the wine became vinegar again. They lost their customers, and after struggling for a year most of them quit in disgust.

Far more serious was the leakage of sacramental wines, of which the Jews were the largest legitimate consumers. The Protestants and the Catholics caused very little trouble; they use no sacramental wines in their homes, and not very much in their church services. Most of the Protestant denominations, in fact, use unfermented grape juice. Moreover, the Protestant ministers and the Catholic priests are under the control of their bishops and can be disciplined. The Jews, on the other hand, use a great deal of sacramental wine in both their homes and synagogues. And since the Jewish faith is not organized, in the sense that the hierarchal churches are, the rabbi is under no control. Under the regulations of the Prohibition Bureau a Jewish family was permitted one gallon of wine a year for each adult member, up to a total of five gallons. They purchased the wine from the rabbi, who received a withdrawal permit upon presentation of a list of the members of his congregation and an approximate estimate of their needs.

A few real rabbis went crooked, withdrew more wine than was required, and trafficked with bootleggers, but the proportion was small. The trouble was that anyone could become a rabbi upon being certified as such by a senior rabbi, and the senior rabbis were gentle, unsuspicious old men with an abiding faith in the goodness of humanity, and easily imposed upon. Even a proper certification was not always necessary; to the Prohibition Bureau any man who dressed in solemn black, possessed a Jewish cast of countenance, and wore a beard was automatically a rabbi. Many of the membership lists were later found to have been copied from telephone directories, and contained names of Christian ministers, Irishmen, business houses, and factories. Some applicants didn't even bother to prepare lists, but bought them from the clerks in the various prohibition offices, paying ten to twenty-five cents a name. One young woman in New York did a prosperous business in lists for more than two years; she came to work in a two-thousand-dollar automobile, wore diamonds and fur coats, and lived in a big apartment. Her salary was forty dollars a week.

The result of these goings on was that the big cities swarmed with fake rabbis busily diverting wine to bootleggers. Many opened wine stores; they were supposed to sell only to members of their own congregations and to Jews certified by other rabbis. Actually, they sold to everyone. In some the stocks included such unusual sacramental items as champagne, vermouth, cordials, and even gin. Izzy Einstein, the celebrated dry sleuth, investigated almost two hundred rabbis during his five years as a prohibition agent, and found some curious things. One rabbi's synagogue consisted of a tiny hall bedroom in a tenement flat; his congregation was a mailing list for which he had paid ten dollars. Another rabbi ran a butcher shop, a second a pork store, and a third a pool parlor with dice games in the back room. Izzy bought wine from a score of stores, and was asked for no identification. Only one refused to sell, on the ground that Izzy didn't look Jewish enough. So Izzy sent another agent around to make the purchase, which he did. His name was Dennis J. Donovan.

After a series of conferences with prominent rabbis, General Lincoln C. Andrews in 1926 put in effect a new set of rules for the issuance and renewal of permits. All lists were carefully checked, and all applicants were required to submit letters from their bishops, or, in the case of Jews, from leading laymen of their congregations. Within one year withdrawals of sacramental wine had been reduced from well over two million gallons to a little more than six hundred thousand. In 1928 the Prohibition Commissioner said, "There is no troublesome situation in sacramental wine as it affects law enforcement."

Early Radio Successes

by Erik Barnouw

Dear, Dear Friends

Christmas in 1924 was widely advertised as a "radio Christmas." In the December issue of *Radio Broadcast* more than two hundred companies advertised their equipment. They vied for attention with scores of brand names, a number of which would not face another Christmas. Among pages of slogans and promises the reader could learn about RCA's Radiola radios and Radiotron tubes and also about the De Forest Radiophone ("how many radio miles did you go last night?"), the Golden-Leutz Pliodyne-6 ("the 'perfect' receiver"), the Newport radio ("makes every day a Christmas"), the Dynergy ("authorities agree on the Dynergy"), the Splitdorf 5-tube radio ("coast-to-coast with Splitdorf"), the Crosley ("of course it's a Crosley"), the Freed-Eisemann ("The difference is—finesse"), the Timmons ("housed in cabinets of rare beauty"), the Brandola ("one dial"), the Mercury ("the Stradivarius of radio"), the Sherma-Flex ("shipped on approval—send no money"), the Melco Supreme ("Aladdin had his lamp, you have the Melco Supreme"), the Marshall ("embodying a marvelous new, non-oscillating principle"), Magnavox ("the utmost in quality and value"), the Kennedy ("ask Santa to bring you a Kennedy"), not to mention such items as Na-Ald sockets and dials, the Bel-Canto loudspeaker, and the Danziger-Jones Kit of a Thousand Possibilities.[1]

What was America hearing, as 1925 began, on this profusion of equipment? Much was as it had been a year or two earlier, but there was a crucial new factor.

In its first years broadcasting had been dominated by anonymous personalities. The only people on the air regularly, the announcers, were largely nameless. In this respect

[1] *Radio Broadcast*, December 1924.

as in others, early radio resembled early film, with its "Biograph girl" and other stirring mysteries. Aside from the announcers, most performers made such fleeting appearances that few became fixed in public consciousness. The announcers, anonymous or not, became recognizable.

In the first months at WJZ, Tommy Cowan adopted the practice of identifying himself with a set of intials—ACN. *A* stood for announcer, *C* for Cowan, *N* for Newark (later New York). The practice was considered an echo of wireless, and continued at WJZ until 1925. Each new announcer and each "operator"—another wireless echo—received a set of initials, starting either with *A* for announcer or *O* for operator. Because Cowan had preempted *C*, Milton J. Cross became AJN.[2] Because Bertha Brainard was ABN, Norman Brokenshire became AON. The policy apparently appealed to management for a reason that had also operated in the early film field: the fear that performers, if identified, might become unmanageable celebrities. There was basis for the fear. As voices became familiar, listeners developd a compulsive curiosity about the people behind them. Everywhere stations received innumerable queries about them. At WHAS, Louisville, these were answered with a form letter:

> Dear Madam:
> It is against the rules of this radio station to divulge the name of our announcer.
> With deep regret, I am—[3]

This executive resistance was futile. Whether known by initials or merely by a voice, the elusive personality aroused ungovernable interest, admiration, affection, and passion.

As program patterns changed and the parade of momentary appearances gave way to weekly features, similar feelings were lavished on singers, poetry readers, and actors. As the anonymity policy broke down, unabashed idolatry followed.

The idolatry must have been furthered by changing styles of performance. In 1922 performers still imagined themselves in a vast auditorium "where rear seats are hundreds of miles from the stage," but by 1925 a cozier image was established. Many artists liked to imagine the audience as "a single per-

---

[2] Popenoe, *WJZ*, p. 16.
[3] Harris, *Microphone Memoirs*, p. 86.

son." Letters encouraged this; no other medium had ever afforded an audience this illusion of intimacy shielded by privacy.

Many a performer began getting letters by hundreds and thousands. Listeners often wrote as though he had spoken directly to them. Accepted without question was the premise that they were friends and that it was possible to speak frankly of one's problems. Many poured out their hearts. A few wrote love letters. This could be disconcerting to a beginning announcer. "The first such epistle," wrote Credo Harris of WHAS, Louisville, "nearly jumped me out of my skin. In all my young and sheltered life no woman had ever come at me like that! Its fire and fervor were terrifying."[4] Some writers, with few preliminaries, made proposals or other suggestions. To Ted Husing, who joined WJZ in 1925, a woman wrote: "Would you like to thrill a lady in person?" She explained that her husband teased her about her complete infatuation for Husing, but nothing could be done about it. Now she was to go on a trip and could arrange her itinerary to include a rendezvous.[5]

During 1924 and 1925 the spotlight of broadcasting began to center itself on idols and the business of developing them. Candidates for idolatry were numerous and flocked to the microphone. "Each announcer knew in his heart," wrote Norman Brokenshire, "that he was God's gift to radio." Brokenshire described the apparent camaraderie among WJZ announcers as pretense. "Actually each man was strictly out for himself."[6] Brokenshire exuded charm at all times and seemed to have no doubts about his destiny. His elaborate jauntiness may have masked severe doubts; between periods of success he struggled with alcoholism.

Like many a radio personality, Brokenshire was the child of a minister and was raised for religious service. Both his father and mother—daughter of a missionary—played the cornet, which almost inevitably led them to the Salvation Army and endless mission journeys. Eventually the father became a preacher in remote sections of Canada, where young Brokenshire was born near Hudson's Bay with the aid of an Indian midwife. During his childhood the family was constantly pulling up stakes. The father was strict and the boy feared him. "He was a restless, I now think unhappy, soul, irritably com-

---

[4] *Ibid.* p. 115.
[5] Husing, *Ten Years Before the Mike*, p. 196.
[6] Brokenshire, *This Is Norman Brokenshire*, p. 55.

municating to his children reflections of an inner turmoil."[7] When the boy eventually sought Broadway and then the microphone, he may have felt he was repudiating his father, while even then following in his footsteps.

As AON, making his appearance in 1924 over WJZ, Norman Brokenshire at once attracted attention. He quotes Stuart Hawkins, radio editor of the New York *Herald Tribune*, as asking, "Who is this new AON? He speaks with perfect enunciation and exceptional modulation."[8] The following year WJZ, pressed by competition, abandoned the cryptic initials. At WEAF Graham McNamee, announcing under his own name, was becoming a legendary figure. During the 1925 World Series he received 50,000 letters.[9] The WJZ staff fretted under anonymity. The RCA management relented, and AON became Norman Brokenshire. For a day or two he felt exposed and vulnerable, then he began to relish the role.

Assigned to introduce a Mrs. Heath, who was conducting one of the first series of homemaking advice, Brokenshire devised introductions that, in one way or another, injected himself into the spotlight. He might begin: "You know, Mrs. Heath, I have a confession to make; this morning I wiped my razor on one of my landlady's best towels." Mrs. Heath, playing along with this, was shocked. "But you must never, never do that. You, ladies, do remind your husbands to use a bit of tissue paper; otherwise they'll cut the fibers in your cloth towels . . ." According to Brokenshire, more and more of the mail began to be addressed to him instead of to Mrs. Heath. Through this and other assignments he was getting at least a hundred letters per day. "I would cram my pockets with them and read them between announcements and on the outside jobs."[10]

In March 1925 Brokenshire was sent to WJZ to Washington to cover the inauguration of President Coolidge. Except for the engineers, he was alone on the assignment. Without precedents, he was given no instructions except to "do the job." For WEAF, Graham McNamee went with leg men, researchers, and publicity representatives. Early on inauguration day, as Brokenshire surveyed the podium, he was asked by a press photographer: "Are you going to be the an-

---

[7] *Ibid.* p. 4.
[8] *Ibid.* p. 43.
[9] Banning, *Commercial Broadcasting Pioneer*, p. 144.
[10] Brokenshire, *This Is Norman Brokenshire*, pp. 46–56.

nouncer?" Yes indeed, Norman Brokenshire told him, and he had his picture taken standing by the podium microphones, wearing his new hat. Next day this United Press photo was in countless newspapers. Meanwhile Brokenshire had ad libbed for over two hours for the WJZ-WRC audience and displayed an inexhaustible gift for banter and bonhomie. "I used my name at every decent opportunity. For the nice listeners I think I even spelled it several times."[11]

As his mail snowballed, station manager Charles Popenoe felt it might go to Brokenshire's head. He also considered the mail to be station property, and so ordered the mail department to withhold it. Brokenshire countered this with a visit to the main New York City post office, where he rented a large mail box and filled out a change-of-address card. At WJZ Popenoe was puzzled at the sudden drop in Brokenshire mail, especially when he saw the young man walking about with huge bundles of letters.[12]

Idols and management struggled not only over mail and the use of names, but over personal appearances as well. The rising stars were deluged with invitations. Some stations permitted them to appear as station representatives but not to accept remuneration. Instead they were plied with gifts. To Brokenshire came monogrammed cigarette cases, belt buckles, pigskin wallets with gold corners. He received a plaque that held a twenty-dollar gold piece—removable. Everywhere radio personalities were treated like war heroes. Said Phillips Carlin of WEAF: "We received keys to the cities on many occasions and were met with bands and driven through the streets in automobiles . . . We were quite something."[13]

The no-fee policy could not survive. Announcing salaries were still modest. Husing began at $45 per week. Brokenshire, announcing the presidential inauguration, was getting $65 a week. The effort to keep salaries at such levels made the outside fees a bargaining point. On many stations artists worked regularly for minimal fees—and even without fees— for the sake of money earned outside via a radio buildup. In Detroit, Elton Plant of the Detroit *News* station WWJ began to appear in theaters as the Boy Baritone of the Air, dressed in patched knickers with a bundle of papers under his arm.[14]

[11] *Ibid.* pp. 60–1.
[12] *Ibid.* p. 93.
[13] Carlin, *Reminiscences*, pp. 17–18.
[14] Plant, *Reminiscences*, p. 18.

In Chicago, Patrick Barnes joined WHT in 1925 as chief announcer and was soon earning huge sums through appearances. "Very often we would get a thousand dollars in a night. Oh, it was very profitable."[15]

Among the most widely celebrated of the new idols were those featured on late-night programs, when stations were heard over great distances and Silent Night helped them win vast audiences. Many a station became known by its late-night personality. Much of the nation knew Lambdin Kay, the Little Colonel of WSB, Atlanta; George Hay, the Solemn Old Judge of WLS, Chicago; Harold Hough, the Hired Hand of WBAP, Fort Worth; and Leo Fitzpatrick, the Merry Old Chief of the Kansas City Nighthawks of WDAF. Fitzpatrick went on a personal-appearance tour that covered 101 towns in 100 days. He was famed for his sign-off, borrowing from Longfellow: "And the night shall be filled with music, and the cares that infest the day shall fold their tents like the Arabs and as silently steal away . . . Goodnight to all on the Atlantic Coast, goodnight to those on the Pacific Coast, and goodnight to everyone until tomorrow night." Fitzpatrick offered listeners membership cards in a mythical society of "Nighthawks." Two million people are said to have enrolled.[16]

That this door to greatness should have attracted to radio some strange characters is not surprising. To some extent the rise of the personality coincided with the rise of commercialism. The influx of 1924–25 included many men with something to sell.

The first program for which time was sold over WOR, Newark, brought to the air the colorful Bernarr Macfadden. Short of stature, he had become obsessed with physical culture and, through the magazine *Physical Culture,* parlayed his obsession into a magazine empire. In 1919 he had launched its fitting companion piece, *True Story*, which specialized in confessions of sex and repentance; by 1925 it had a circulation of over a million and a half copies and a year later was close to two million. Meanwhile he was adding other magazines and challenging the New York tabloid field with his daily *Graphic* and its bizarre "composographs," in which bedroom scandals of the day were restaged for the camera by models—with the proper celebrity faces inserted. These new interests had by no means reduced his concern for physical

---

[15] Barnes, *Reminiscences*, p. 10.
[16] Patt, *Reminiscences*, pp. 21–2.

culture, for in 1925 Bernarr Macfadden took over the newly launched morning calisthenics broadcasts over WOR. Started as an experiment, this series had soon won the largest following among all WOR programs.[17] During the Bernarr Macfadden regime it began at 6:45 each morning and lasted for an hour and a quarter, with alternating segments of music and exercise. Music was provided by piano, saxophone, and violin. Listeners could send for charts showing the movements; exercises were identified by number. Letters indicated that many listeners exercised with earphones on. The studio engineer, a former ship wireless operator in the British merchant marine, was John Gambling.[18] He eventually took over the program when Macfadden, with ever-larger involvements and thoughts of the Presidency, withdrew.

Macfadden paid WOR for the privilege of conducting the exercises and in return was allowed to promote the *Graphic* as well as *Physical Culture*. Sometimes he brought a chorus girl to exercise with him; she would get her picture in the *Graphic*. Sometimes the chorus girl spoke a testimonial for physical fitness. One such visitor, in refined tones, read a statement penciled for her by Gambling.

> I am so happy to be here with Mr. Macfadden. I do these exercises *every* morning, and I am sure I keep my figure and keep in condition just through these exercises. Thank you. (GASP OF RELIEF) My gawd, I'm glad that's over.[19]

There were other faddists, medicine men and messiahs who attracted audiences in the mid-1920's and played their part in the changing atmosphere of broadcasting. By far the most remarkable, and a pivotal figure in the story of radio, was John Romulus Brinkley—Dr. Brinkley.

His beginnings are lost in mist; Brinkley himself told various versions of his life. Most began in a log cabin in the Smoky Mountains with hollyhocks at the door, and a spinning wheel inside. Brinkley had a feeling for symbols of America's rural past. His mother died early, and he spent part of his childhood with an uncle, a general practitioner, picking up a smattering of medical lore. Like many later broadcasters, the boy took his first step toward radio in a

17 Barnett, *Reminiscences*, pp. 18–19.
18 Gambling, *Reminiscences*, pp. 1–7.
19 *Ibid.* pp. 21–6.

Early Radio Successes

telegraph office. Without pay he assisted the railroad agent at Sylva, N.C., and was taught telegraphy. "I was first attracted to him by his curiosity," the agent later recounted. "He just wanted to tear my instruments off the table, he was so interested in them." Brinkley subsequently worked for Western Union in Chicago, studied medicine, quit his studies, and instead bought medical diplomas from diploma mills in Kansas City and St. Louis. The Kansas City $100 parchment won him a license to practice in Kansas. Thanks to reciprocal courtesies between states, other licenses followed. He and a partner opened a medical office in Greenville, N.C., with the sign "Greenville Electro Medic Doctors." Their advertisements in the Greenville *Daily News* asked, "Are you a manly man full of vigor?"—a question Brinkley was to ask most of his life, and before long, on the air. The Greenville partners gave $25 injections of distilled colored water and after two months left town. At a later time Brinkley worked for less than a month in the medical office at Swift & Company in Kansas City, which he later said gave him an unparalleled opportunity to study animal glands.[20]

Further wandering—and brushes with the law—brought Brinkley and his wife in 1917 to Milford, Kansas, population 200. The village drugstore was empty, and Brinkley took it over for $8 a month. In back were two rooms, one of which became the Brinkley home, the other his consultation room, while Mrs. Brinkley sold patent medicines in the store. One day an elder citizen of Milford insisted that the doctor do something about his problem of failing manhood. The conversation turned to the goats Brinkley had seen at Swift & Company. "You wouldn't have any trouble if you had a pair of those buck glands in you," Brinkley said. The man asked, "Well, will you put 'em in?" Eventually it was done in the back room, and a career was launched. Other men came to say they had the same trouble as Jake had had. The Brinkley operation fee went up to $750, $1000, $1500. When Mrs. Brinkley received a legacy, they used it to build, in 1918, a small Brinkley Hospital. It was expanded rapidly.[21]

About 1922 the Brinkley legend reached the ears of Harry Chandler, who owned the Los Angeles *Times* and was also starting KHJ, Los Angeles. He persuaded Brinkley to come to California and vowed to make him famous if his treatment was good. We are told that "several staff members" of the

[20] Carson, *The Roguish World of Dr. Brinkley*, pp. 12–26.
[21] *Ibid.* pp. 30–40.

Times had the treatment and that several screen stars also became "Brinkley alumni." Besides spreading the word, the trip brought a new element into Brinkley's life. Impressed by KHJ and $40,000 richer from the California trip, Brinkley applied for a broadcasting license from the Department of Commerce and in 1923 founded KFKB, Milford. Starting with a 1000-watt transmitter, it was immediately one of the most powerful stations and its power was subsequently increased several times. Under Department of Commerce rules this entitled the station to a preferred dial position: KFKB was soon heard far and wide. On every night except Sunday a Brinkley lecture was heard; the rest of the schedule presented fundamentalist religion, guitar and banjo ensembles, accordionists, cowboy singers, yodelers, crooners, hymn-singers, story-tellers. The doctor's lectures held a vast audience spellbound. "Don't let your doctor two-dollar you to death . . . come to Dr. Brinkley." He delighted in images of rural life.

> Note the difference between the stallion and the gelding. The stallion stands erect, neck arched, mane flowing, champing the bit, stamping the ground, seeking the female, while the gelding stands around half asleep, going into action only when goaded, cowardly, listless, with no interest in anything.

Was the listener listless? The doctor recommended his "compound operation." In response to inquiries a steady stream of literature backed up the radio message. "Are you a man of your own mind? Men like Edison, Marconi, Burbank, and Brinkley have always *thought for themselves*." A daily KFKB feature, *Medical Question Box*, quoted letters from listeners describing their symptoms. If they were not candidates for the compound operation, Dr. Brinkley would tell them on the air what medicines to use. A huge mail-order drug business was developed, which was to continue for thirteen years and probably exceed the hospital business in income and profit. Shipments of goats came in from Arkansas. Shipments of drugs went out to all points of the compass. Whereas the operations catered to men, 95 per cent of the mail-order business involved women. "Now here is a letter," said the doctor on KFKB, "from a dear mother—a dear little mother who holds to her breast a babe of nine months. She should take Number 2 and Number 16 and—yes—Number 17 and she will be helped. Brinkley's, 2, 16, and 17. If her druggist hasn't got them, she should write and order them from the Milford Drug Company, Milford, Kansas, and they will be sent to you, Mother, collect. May the Lord guard and protect you, Mother. The postage will be prepaid."[22]

Dr. Brinkley was a genius in what came to be known as public service. Through his bequests a local Sunday school became the Brinkley Methodist Sunday School. Similarly a local baseball team became the Brinkley Goats. He served the children of America with a "Tell Me a Story Lady" over KFKB; she also happened to be the wife of the local banker. But his most impressive achievement was a relationship established with Kansas State College of Manhattan. A student, a go-getter named Sam Pickard, is said to have been the intermediary in making arrangements. Over KFKB the college launched a College of the Air which by 1924 had for credit enrollments from 39 states and from Canada, thanks to the vast range of the Brinkley station. Among the radio students, 311 that year received certificates from Kansas State.[23] In dealings with government agencies Dr. Brinkley could always cite beneficences such as these and present letters of praise and gratitude and plaques in his honor. "We are prospering," said Brinkley, "because our keynote is service."[24] Sam Pickard became radio director for the Department of Agriculture and then a member of the Federal Radio Commission, which may have proved helpful to Brinkley.

Meanwhile the American Medical Association was stirring itself. The diploma mills from which Brinkley had purchased his degrees were being exposed. Brinkley himself, in his applications for state licenses, was found to have made numerous false claims. The American Medical Association declared his operation a fraud. By 1925 several states took steps to revoke his licenses. Over KFKB Brinkley counterattacked; he referred to the American Medical Association as a "meat cutters' union." He also began to give his "dear, dear friends" of the radio audience a continuing autobiography, constantly elaborating the Brinkley legend and heaping scorn on his enemies—who were at the same time piecing together the details of the Brinkley career. Meanwhile he prospered, drove a 16-cylinder Cadillac, wore large diamonds, built a mansion, bought airplanes, and spent $65,000 on new and more power-

---

[22] *Ibid*. pp. 89–103. Chase, *Sound and Fury*, 61–5.
[23] Frost, *Education's Own Stations*, p. 144.
[24] Carson, *The Roguish World of Dr. Brinkley*, p. 82.

ful station equipment.[25] The famous goat-gland doctor—goateed himself—became a folk hero.

Milford became Brinkley and Brinkley Milford. He was its patron saint, and the town's life was inextricably meshed with his. The daughter of the county sheriff was his secretary. The local banker was a stockholder in the radio station. The local newspaper editor did the Brinkley printing. When exposures began to be printed in newspapers like the Kansas City *Journal-Post*, they were simply not distributed around Milford.[26]

By 1925 strong forces were arrayed against him, but Brinkley rode high and had years of success ahead of him. In a few years a station popularity contest run by *Radio Digest* of Chicago would give first place—among all the stations of the nation—to KFKB, Milford.[27] By then he would even loom as a political power.

Brinkley had already made an indelible mark on radio. He had swept aside the potted palms and spoken to a rural audience in its idiom. The radio careers of many a later figure, including that of Huey Long, were to follow a trail blazed by Dr. Brinkley.

He had done more. With his drug business—built entirely by radio—he had made clear there was gold in the kilocycles. Many had caught the message and were descending on radio. They knew what was needed—a wave length and personality.

They made their contribution to a period of crisis.

* * * *

Ain't Dat Sumpin'?

The programs NBC and CBS sent throughout the United States in 1928 and 1929 were still largely musical. Many were "concerts," although dance music—it was all called "jazz" now—was on the increase. Along with these another element was seizing attention—drama.

The dramatic series pushed in various directions. Some mined traditional "period" material: *Great Moments in History*, *Biblical Dramas*, and the continuing *Eveready Hour*, all on NBC. These had an aura of respectability paralleling that of concert music. Other dramatic series exploited a native—and equally traditional—hayseed vein: *Real Folks* on NBC, *Main Street* sketches on CBS. More contemporary was

[25] Chase, *Sound and Fury*, pp. 66–70.
[26] Carson, *The Roguish World of Dr. Brinkley*, pp. 122–3.
[27] *Ibid.* p. 143.

Early Radio Successes

True Story on CBS, sponsored by Macfadden Publications. Based on the magazine stories, neatly bowdlerized and dressed with strangely literate dialogue and philosophizing, the series was both lurid and respectable enough to be a smashing 1928–29 success. It exemplified the dictum of Peter Finley Dunne's Mr. Dooley: "The city of New York, Hennessy, sets the fashion of vice and starts the crusade against it."[1]

But all these were overshadowed by another series, in many respects a pioneering work, and considered by many the first classic of broadcasting. It became, according to some estimates,,[2] the consuming delight of forty million people. It would influence dinner hours across the nation. It would involve the attention of Presidents. And it would pose a racial issue.

Robert J. Landry in *This Fascinating Radio Business* noted resemblances between the history of broadcasting and that of film. In each of these a crude toy became an industry; fierce patent struggles erupted; public acceptance skyrocketed; business combinations won domination; anonymous idols exploded into fame.[3] A further resemblance can be added. In each the first work that explored, with startling virtuosity, the possibilities of a new medium, and won unheard-of success financially and statistically, also raised tensions on the frontier of Negro-white relations.

There was little surface resemblance between D. W. Griffith's *Birth of a Nation* and Correll and Gosden's *Amos 'n' Andy*—their moods were different—but kinship is nevertheless clear.

Freeman Fisher Gosden (Amos) was, like D.W. Griffith, a product of southern heritage. His father had belonged to a group of Confederate raiders who fought on after Appomattox. The boy Freeman was born in Richmond, Va., in 1899. He was cared for by a Negro mammy in a household that also sheltered a Negro boy called Snowball. Freeman was close to Snowball, and later said many facets of *Amos 'n' Andy* were derived from Snowball. Freeman spent his youth in Richmond, except for a year in an Atlanta military school. Then he became the first Gosden in three generations to leave the South.[4] Regarded as a virtuoso in Negro dialect stories

---

[1] Dunne, *Mr. Dooley Remembers*, p. 288.
[2] Wylie, "Amos 'n' Andy—Loving Remembrance," *Television Quarterly*, Summer 1963.
[3] Landry, *This Fascinating Radio Business*, pp. 217–18.
[4] Correll and Gosden, *All About Amos 'n' Andy*, pp. 21–2.

and banjo-playing, Gosden—after a stint on the road as tobacco salesman—landed with the Joe Bren Company, which made a business of staging local shows throughout the United States for lodges, churches, and clubs. Local talent was used; the Joe Bren Company supplied sketches, jokes, songs, costumes, and supervision. Freeman Gosden started traveling for Joe Bren, organizing reviews, minstrel shows, carnivals.

Charles J. Correll (Andy) was born in 1890 in Peoria, Illinois. He first joined his father in construction work but at night played the piano in a movie house, banging out "Hearts and Flowers" for Pearl White close-ups and a ragtime "Everybody's Doing It" for John Bunny comedies. Soft-shoe dancing was another of his talents. As a result of these abilities, he too was recruited by the Joe Bren Company. Gosden and Correll first traveled separate routes but eventually worked and roomed together, and began to work up a blackface act. When they were promoted to the Chicago headquarters, it gave them a chance to try out for WEBH in the Edgewater Beach Hotel. Still working for the Joe Bren Company, they began to broadcast weekly blackface routines, receiving free dinners.

Someone at the Chicago *Tribune* suggested they work up something like *Andy Gump*, transferring the comic strip form to radio. This led them first to the creation of *Sam 'n' Henry*, which landed them a paid spot on WGN and enabled them to leave Joe Bren. The series ran two years—586 five-a-week episodes. They expected renewal but, according to one account, could find no one at the *Tribune* who could deal with them.[5] This allowed WMAQ at the Chicago *Daily News* to sign them, at $150 per week for each.[6] Because the title *Sam 'n' Henry* was owned by WGN the team became *Amos 'n' Andy*. Besides a raise, they won from WMAQ a concession of importance in the development of broadcasting economics. Correll and Gosden had the notion they would like to make recordings of their programs and sell them to other stations; this had been prevented by the WGN arrangement. WMAQ approved, provided the Chicago broadcasts were live. Each program was recorded in two five-minute parts at the Marsh studios in Chicago. The pioneering syndication—Correll and Gosden called it a "chainless chain"—was handled by the

[5] Hedges, *Reminiscences*, p. 25.
[6] Wylie, "Amos 'n' Andy—Loving Remembrance," *Television Quarterly*, Summer 1963.

Chicago *Daily News*. Starting early in 1928, it soon involved some thirty stations.[7] By 1929 Amos 'n' Andy were already widely celebrated. According to one account, Coolidge did not like to be disturbed at the White House while they were on the air.[8] Rand McNally decided to publish an *Amos 'n' Andy* autobiography, in which Correll and Gosden told about themselves and their characters. It was here that Gosden discussed Snowball, calling him the inspiration for Amos and to some extent other characters. The book included script excerpts illustrated with photographs in which Correll and Gosden, in burnt-cork make-up, gave an idea of how they visualized their creations. The book began:

> QUESTION: Who are Amos 'n' Andy?
> ANSWER: Freeman F. Gosden and Charles J. Correll.
> QUESTION: Are they white or colored?
> ANSWER: White.[9]

The radio characters were described as follows:

> AMOS: Trusting, simple, unsophisticated. High and hesitating in voice. It's "Ain't dat sumpin'?" when he's happy or surprised, and "Awa, awa, awa," in the frequent moments when he's frightened or embarrassed. . . . Andy gives him credit for no brains but he's a hard, earnest worker and has a way of coming across with a real idea when ideas are most needed. He looks up to and depends on
> ANDY: Domineering, a bit lazy, inclined to take credit for all of Amos' ideas and efforts. He's always "workin' on the books" or "restin' his brain," upon which (according to Andy) depends the success or failure of all the boys' joint enterprises. He'll browbeat Amos, belittle him, order him around, but let anyone else pick on the little one—then look out!

The boys hail from Atlanta and have come to the big city to make fame and fortune. After a year in Chicago they have to their credit one broken-down topless automobile, one business enterprise—the Fresh-Air Taxicab Company of America, Incorpulated—one desk (not paid

[7] Hedges, *Reminiscences*, p. 25.
[8] Slate and Cook, *It Sounds Impossible*, p. 76.
[9] Correll and Gosden, *All About Amos 'n' Andy*, p. 13.

for), one swivel chair for the president to rest in and think...[10]

In addition to the Fresh-Air Taxicab Company, the action revolved around a South Side rooming house and a brotherhood called the Mystic Knights of the Sea, presided over by a character called the Kingfish. An important early sequence involved the widow Parker, alias Snookems, and her breach-of-promise suit against Andy.

Correll and Gosden wrote every word. One typed while the other, often pacing, tried out dialogue, always in dialect. All speeches were put down as pronounced. "I'se regusted." "Recordin' to my figgers in de book . . ." "Splain dat to me." A script averaged 1500–2000 words and took ten minutes. There was no rehearsal before broadcast. Having thought the story through jointly, they felt rehearsal would reduce spontaneity. Under their method of working, neither could completely anticipate how the other would play a scene, and actual interaction resulted. Each occasionally ended a broadcast in tears. Gosden would say concerning Amos: "I feel so sorry for that poor ignorant fellow."[11]

They sat while broadcasting. Correll as Andy performed with furrowed brow and protruding lip. Gosden as Amos wore a vacant, naïve look. For several years no other actors took part. In the widow Parker breach-of-promise episodes—in later years there was another breach-of-promise sequence—Correll played Andy, Attorney for the Defense, Judge, Policeman, Court Clerk; Gosden played Amos, Prosecuting Attorney, Bailiff, Kingfish, Consulting Attorney. Each actor changed his position, pitch, and volume for each character. Each could on occasion produce animal sounds. Women characters, though vividly real to the audience, appeared for some time only by reference; they were also illuminated by long phone conversations in which the women were not heard.

Correll and Gosden claimed not to depend on jokes, but repetitive gag lines were frequent. In a court sequence Andy was advised by his lawyer: "Now Brown, you can occasionally use the expression, 'I don't remember.' Don't make it noticeable, but occasionally say, 'I don't remember.' " The result was:

---

[10] *Ibid.* pp. 43–4.
[11] *Ibid.* pp. 53–4, 86, 114.

Early Radio Successes

BAILIFF: Raise your right hand.
ANDY: I don't remembeh.
BAILIFF: Raise your right hand.
ANDY: Yessah, yessah.
BAILIFF: Do you solemnly swear that the evidence you are about to give in this case is the truth, the whole truth, and nothing but the truth, so help you God?
ANDY: I don't remembeh.
BAILIFF: Say "I do."
ANDY: I do.
BAILIFF: Sit down!
JUDGE (*in distance*): Attorney for the plaintiff will proceed with the cross examination.
ATTORNEY: Your name is Andrew Brown?
ANDY: I don't remembeh.

Word-distortion humor was often used. As Amos added up the day's receipts, Andy asked: "Wait a minute heah! Whut is you doin'? Is you mulsiflyin' or revidin'?"[12]

Correll and Gosden wrote that they made frequent contact with "colored folk" to keep the characters "true to life." They posed for publicity pictures making such contact. They felt their most important equipment for the series was "a thorough understanding of the colored race."[13]

The *Amos 'n' Andy* series broke new ground in several ways. It established syndication as a mechanism, even though recordings were still of doubtful quality and limited to five-minute lengths. The feasibility of the continued story was also overwhelmingly shown. A basic dilemma continuing for weeks, far from alienating listeners, enmeshed ever-widening rings of addicts. Throughout the breach-of-promise crises *Amos 'n' Andy*—echoing Dickens's success with this theme in the serialized *Pickwick Papers*—built audience frenzy and became mealtime and commuting train talk across the continent. All this would bring a flood of radio serials in succeeding years.

Two broadcasting triumphs, said John S. Cohen of the Atlanta *Journal* and its station WSB, did most to make radio a national medium: the 1924 Democratic convention and *Amos 'n' Andy*.[14]

By 1929 their fame had given birth to a daily *Amos 'n'*

[13] *Ibid.* pp. 51–2.
[12] *Ibid.* pp. 67–8, 118.
[14] Arnold, *Broadcast Advertising*, p. 226.

Andy comic strip syndicated by the Chicago *Daily News* and to *Amos 'n' Andy* phonograph records marketed by Victor, and NBC was ready to pay $100,000 a year for their services. They went on the network that summer, sponsored by Pepsodent. That fall *Amos 'n' Andy* sent hordes to radio shops; sales of radio sets and parts went from $650,550,000 in 1928 to $842,548,000 in 1929.[15] The program began on the network at a late hour but was soon shifted to 7:00 to 7:15 Eastern time, where it dominated all radio listening. In the spring, when daylight saving time began, some communities found themselves getting *Amos 'n' Andy* at 6 P.M. Crisis resulted. Forty factories in Charlotte, N.C., agreed to shift their closing time from 6:00 to 5:45 P.M.[16] When national telephone surveys began soon afterward, more than half of all those phoned were found listening to *Amos 'n' Andy*.[17]

During this staggering rise to fame, what had happened to Snowball? Repeated mention of Snowball in the 1929 autobiography suggests that he was on Gosden's mind. But the problem was not only Gosden's but the nation's.

In the 1920's the ghetto was well established and fortified. The Negro lived in his, the white man in his. Reasons and conditions differed, but the result was insulation. Except for Negro domestics, few crossed over. In New York white intellectuals taxied to Harlem to see Negro stars in nightclubs owned by white gangsters. Occasional Negro performers—musicians, dancers, actors—played "the white time." But when in that period Ethel Waters and other Negro girls went on tour in a musical—in "burnt-cork" make-up—they had to be lodged at each stop in a brothel; no other place would take them.[18]

In the South the boy growing up with a Snowball was called on in puberty for that total repudiation—Faulkner wrote of this—seldom required of shielded northerners. It involved a deep sense of guilt that had to be combated and overlaid with endless fantasy: stories, jokes, burnt-cork comedy. In retrospect it is easy—at the time it was less easy—to see the stories and *Amos 'n' Andy* as part of the ghetto system. All of it was more readily accepted and maintained if one could hold on to this: "they" were lovely people, essentially happy people, ignorant and somewhat

---

15 *Broadcasting*, 1939 Yearbook, p. 11.
16 Wallace, *The Development of Broadcasting in North Carolina*, p. 237.
17 Summers (ed.), *A Thirty-Year History of Programs*, p. 21.
18 Waters, *His Eye Is on the Sparrow*, p. 139.

shiftless and lazy in a lovable, quaint way, not fitting in with higher levels of enterprise, better off where they were (the Fresh-Air Taxicab Company, Incorpulated), essentially happy, happy. The more one remembered Snowball, the more the fantasy was needed. It could make South Side poverty somehow charming and fitting. The nation needed the fantasy. It was a wall buttressed by decades of jokes, vaudeville sketches, cartoons, and joke books sold by millions of copies in 5&10¢ stores with titles like *Minstrel Jokes, Coon Jokes, Darky Jokes,* how-to-do books like *The Amateur Minstrel* and *Burnt Cork*.[19] So ingrained was all this that the idea of Negro objections to *Amos 'n' Andy* was at first received with disbelief. Was it not known that Negroes loved *Amos 'n' Andy*?

There was some truth in this, although statistics are scarce. The Negro writer William Branch remembered sitting in a family group roaring with laughter over *Amos 'n' Andy*. Those seemed very funny people. There was another memory: the father did not laugh. Only gradually the boy learned why. Those people were supposed to be "us."[20]

James Baldwin put this Negro experience vividly. At movies he always cheered wildly with others as heroes pursued and slaughtered Indians. Then he learned he was the Indian.

During the fantastic rise of *Amos 'n' Andy*, Secretary of Commerce Herbert Hoover was elected President of the United States. As he settled into the White House, *Amos 'n' Andy* led in program popularity. Presidential recognition followed in due course. At Hoover's invitation, Merlin Aylesworth brought the two men to the White House. Correll and Gosden told some of their best jokes. Hoover, in upright collar, warmed to the occasion and caused surprise by telling some himself—for more than an hour.[21]

It was not an accident that *Amos 'n' Andy* was a national triumph. It was virtually a national self-expression, a vivid amusement-park image of its time.

---

[19] Wehman Bros. publications sold throughout the 1910's and 1920's.
[20] Interview, William Branch.
[21] Gross, *I Looked and Listened,* p. 155.

The Popularity of the Tabloid: The *Daily News* of 1926

by Simon Michael Bessie

In March of 1926 the six-year-old *Daily News* entered journalism's promised land with the attainment of a circulation of 1,000,000 and there it has remained ever since. For this, and for other reasons, the year 1926 makes a good period for insight into the character and ways of the *News*. In many ways, the tabloid is an expression of America's post-war moods and no year of the decade was more emphatically "post-war" than 1926. Almost everything that characterized the period between the War and the depression can be found symbolized in the events of 1926 many of which were so peculiarly products of the epoch that it is doubtful whether they would have achieved front page notice at any other time. A résumé of the stories featured by the *News* in 1926 affords adequate materials for the dissection of the era, and, what is more important for our purposes, gives a picture of tabloid in action under ideal circumstances. As an overture, the orchestra plays the current song hits "Dinah", "Brown Eyes Why Are You Blue", and "I'm Just Wild About Animal Crackers".

Early in January the law finally caught up with Richard Reese Whittemore, known and admired by a vast American public as "The Candy Kid". Whittemore, whom the press had already converted into a colorful gangster hero, faced definite charges on six murders and was credited with several other heroic deeds. Shortly after "The Candy Kid" was brought to the bar, the police captured Gerald Chapman and for days the front page of the *Daily News* was torn between two loves. Just as these stories were beginning to lose luster, Earl Carroll, noted producer of musical extravaganzas, came to the rescue with the party of the decade. The word "orgy" was well loved in the city room but previous to Mr. Carroll's famous party there had been nothing really worthy of the name.

During the course of a lavish spread for his Broadway friends, Mr. Carroll achieved his masterpiece by having Joyce

Hawley, one of his chorus ladies, appear in a bathtub filled with sparkling champagne. The guests then proceeded to consume the wine and Miss Hawley was left at her best. This outcome, she later explained, was more than she had bargained for and Mr. Carroll was brought up on what are politely known as "charges." Gleefully, the *News* plastered itself with inspired headlines, heavily adjectived accounts of the orgy and pictures of the prominent participants.

When this item had been wrung dry the *News* turned to the romance of the decade, l'Affaire Peaches. For several years, Edward Browning, a wealthy real estate operator, had been a realiable source of copy with his penchant for publicity and young girls. Now he had offered to share his gold with a plump, baby-faced, fifteen-year-old shopgirl known to a thrilled public as "Peaches." "Daddy's" marriage with "Peaches" was perfect tabloid stuff and while the *News* went into ecstasy the public throbbed happily with the realization of a dream.

Before spring had run into summer, another bedroom sensation mounted the front page. Kip Rhinelander, wealthy member of an old New York clan, had married an attractive girl of striking dark complexion. Several months later, Kip said, he was amazed to discover that his bride had a sound racial reason for her complexion and he sued her for divorce claiming that she had misrepresented herself as a Caucasian. The outraged lady contested on the grounds that Kip must have known it all along. The town was torn by the exciting question of how much a husband can reasonably be expected to know. Although the story was filled with potential dynamite on the racial question, the *News* neatly sidestepped the central issue carrying along with daily accounts of the thrilling happenings in court. When the trial reached its climax as Mrs. Rhinelander stripped before the judge to demonstrate the validity of her contention, the *News* was unable to rise to the heights with a picture such as the *Graphic* printed, but the event was described to a crisp.

In July the biggest crime story of the decade broke. Attempting to stimulate circulation, the staff of Hearst's tabloid *Daily Mirror* hit upon a murder case which had been forgotten for almost four years. On September 14, 1922 in New Brunswick, New Jersey, the bodies of Reverend Edward Hall and his choir-singing sweetheart, Eleanor Mills, had been found in what appeared to be a successful suicide pact. The matter was investigated by a coroner's inquest but nothing was found which cast enough suspicion to justify a trial and the case was closed. By producing some "new evidence", the *Mirror*'s agents succeeded in having Hall's widow, Mrs. Frances Stevens Hall, arrested on July 28, 1926 and the sordid mess was dragged into court. In retrospect one can hardly fail to be surprised that this run-of-the-mill murder story was able to arouse such tremendous interest but the story was picked up by every important paper in the country and for months the eyes of the press were focused on the little court in New Brunswick.

For the *Daily News* it was the story of the year as far as total amount of copy is concerned. On July 29, 1926 the *News* broke the story with a resume of the case accompanied by two pages of pictures showing the locale and the principals. The next day the story took up the entirety of the first four pages and page six carried a map of the murder region. Until August seventh the Hall-Mills case was featured daily upon the front page and it stopped then only because a butcher's daughter had catapulted herself to fame by swimming the English Channel. Gertrude Ederle was fine news but she couldn't compete with the lurid details of the New Brunswick trial and on August eighth the *News* reverted to Hall-Mills matters. There it remained until August twentieth when it gave way to rhapsodic comment on the Irving Berlin–Ellen Mackay nuptials, the union of "Tin-Pan Alley and Park Avenue."

Then came a story which topped all. It held the spotlight for only three days but during this time the *News* was almost a one-story paper. And well it might be, for America's heartbeat had paused. Early on the morning of August 23rd Rudolph Valentino died.

Not content with the inherent richness of the story, the *News* attempted to magnify the colossal with the suggestive front page headline:

VALENTINO POISONED

(Broadway Hears Doctors Deny.)

The second page was headed with:

VALENTINO DIES WITH SMILE
AS LIPS TOUCH PRIEST'S CRUCIFIX

and the next six pages were filled with accounts of the "Sheik's" romantic life and untimely death. His life story was entitled RUDY LEAPED FROM RAGS TO WORLD HERO. The day's sole editorial was a sentimental tribute ending with the words, "A typically American Romance ends with the career of Rudolph Valentino."

For the next day's issue the art department created a front-page masterpiece which lacked only a halo to make it a perfect Piet. Valentino was pictured at length upon his richly flowered bier while a young lady kneeled at his feet praying the lament that was in a million hearts. Page two presented a story by Norma Talmadge entitled VALENTINO AS I KNEW HIM and the screen star had known him well. There was still enough copy left in the story to fill the first three pages of the August 26th edition.

New York turned out 2,000,000 strong and roared itself hoarse "welcoming" Gertrude Ederle on August 28th. Broadway was covered with a record tonnage of confetti and the *News* that day was little more than a cheer for the Channel conqueress. Another big demonstration provided the meat for the issue of August 31st when Valentino's funeral was witnessed by 100,000. On September third a local record was set with SEVEN KILLINGS IN 15 HOURS and then the *News* reverted to the Hall-Mills case which was still good for a daily streamer. Then came the Dempsey-Tunney fight in Philadelphia to claim the first three pages for September 22nd, 23rd, and 24th.

On October fifth a great romance was shattered when PEACHES QUITS BROWNING but two days later the *News* was able to restore its confidence in the power of true love. "Bud" Stillman announced that he was about to share his father's millions with Lena Wilson, a woodcutter's daughter. These two stories took care of October.

From the first of November until the fifth of December the *News* front page stayed in New Brunswick to cover the closing testimony in the Hall-Mills trial. Mrs. Hall was pronounced not guilty on December fourth and was permitted to slide back into obscurity. Again Daddy Browning came to the rescue. This time he was being sued by Mary Spas, who claimed that he had inflicted brutalities upon her.

So it went through the winter until March 21, 1927 when the Snyder-Gray hammer murder broke. Although the trial was not scheduled to open until April 18th the *News* started its build-up in March with front page headlines such as

GRAY'S 4 LOVES and GRAY DID IT ALL, Says Ruth. This story received the most sensational treatment ever accorded a crime by the *News*. Signed articles were extracted from Judd Gray, the sad-faced corset salesman, and his sweetheard Ruth Snyder, who had combined talents in killing her husband after making practical financial arrangements. In June, Ruth was executed and the *News* accomplished its most noted camera coup with the printing of a picture taken in the death chamber just after the current had been turned on. The prison authorities had requested that no pictures be taken but the *News* photographer, answering a higher call, strapped a camera to his ankle and succeeded in taking one of the most gruesome pictures ever printed in a newspaper. A storm of protest was aroused but the *News* could afford disapproval of an action which sold an estimated 500,000 extra copies of paper.

These grotesque excitements which agitated the *Daily News* were only a reflection of the frenzy which was spreading through American life as the decade neared its climax. Business went mad with the intoxication of soaring profits, morals exploded into a "new freedom" and the daily press roared forth a harmonizing chant of accelerating sensationalism which reached its climax in May 1927 when a young aviator was lifted from obscurity to the summit of fame and mass worship. In its excitement over the "Lone Eagle" the press attained a peak of ballyhoo beyond which it could not climb. Nobody could be given greater fame than Lindbergh; no story could be inflated with greater mounds of copy; no public could be stimulated to more intense hysteria; no ecstasy could be further prolonged.

Two years later the business balloon collapsed and the frenzy was over. Overnight the spirit of the country changed more profoundly than it had in many years. The confidence and sense of ultimate security which had characterized American life even after the World War was shattered by the stuning severity and persistence of economic hardship. Thrust into a new and frightening period, the people turned their interest upon serious matters, for reality pressed at every turn.

Era of Wonderful Nonsense

by Allen Churchill

The 1920's have been given many nicknames: the Jazz Age, Roaring Twenties, Turbulent Twenties, Teeming Twenties, Whoopee Era, Fabulous Decade, Lawless Decade. But maybe the best designation of all is the Era of Wonderful Nonsense.

The peak of the nonsense—wonderful or not—came after 1925. The second half of the glorious decade produced such wacky characters as Alvin "Shipwreck" Kelly, the flagpole sitter. Calling himself the Luckiest Fool Alive, this ex-sailor first perched atop a pole on a St. Louis building for seven days. Over succeeding months, he more than doubled that time to become, despite considerable competition, the nation's No. 1 flagpole sitter. Most of the flagpoles Shipwreck adorned were at least fifty feet high. In the words of that bright new magazine *The New Yorker,* he sat up there "etched in magnificent loneliness."

How did the fellow do it? Shipwreck's chair was a rubber-covered wooden seat strapped tightly to the round flagpole ball. He took only fluids—milk, coffee, broth—hoisted up to him in a bucket. He slept with thumbs anchored into two holes bored into the wooden seat. During one sleet storm he used a hatchet to chip ice from his body.

The flagpoles were usually atop hotels, for Shipwreck's endurance feats brought much business. People peered up at him from the street, and any who paid fifty cents could ride to the roof for a closer view. One who did this was a redheaded flapper, aged eighteen. As she stood there, the man next to her said, "He's nothing but a damn fool." "He is not," she replied angrily. "He knows just what he's doing." She then slapped the man's face.

Informed of this episode by a note in his food bucket, thirty-two-year-old Shipwreck expressed a natural desire to meet the girl. She was hoisted up to him by a rope around her midriff, and the two pitched woo in mid-air. When Shipwreck climbed down they got married.

More madness came from the high-powered activities of promoter C. C. Pyle, whose many stunts included a transcontinental foot race, starting on the West Coast. Newspapers dubbed it the Bunion Derby. In New York, another promoter hired Madison Square Garden for a multi-event marathon. In one corner was a group of nonstop talkers; newspapers called this the Noun and Verb Rodeo. In another, a rocking-chair derby. And so on. These assorted marathons were open twenty-four hours a day and in the early hours of the morning revelers from New York's five thousand speakeasy night clubs dropped in to gape at the fun.

Not all was nonsense in the Nonsense Era. For unabashed sadism there were the dance marathons in which young couples danced around and around, with only a few minutes of each hour for sleep. Often dancers passed out from sheer exhaustion in partners' arms. By the rules, they had to be awakened and they usually came up screaming and clawing. "This," one reporter stated, "is known as 'going squirrelly,' and it gives everyone lots of laughs."

The top nonsense story of the Era of Wonderful Nonsense was the saga of Peaches and Daddy. Each of its widely publicized installments turned out to be goofier than the one before. Daddy was millionaire Edward West Browning, elderly New York real-estate dealer. He had a penchant (the word one newspaper used) for very young girls, on whom he liked to bestow pet names. The night he met pudgy fifteen-year-old Frances Belle Heenan, Daddy announced, "I'm going to call you Peaches, because you look like peaches and cream to me." Then he instructed her to "Call me Daddy." He married Peaches in the spring of 1926. A horde of reporters, photographers, and sob sisters followed them everywhere. CROWDS TRAMPLE PEACHES, a tabloid shrieked when the bride celebrated her sixteenth birthday by shopping along Fifth Avenue. Six months later Peaches packed her finery and departed dear old Dad. Naturally, reporters covered the event.

Daddy and Peaches had turned into what Damon Runyon called Homo Saps. That is, they'd do anything for publicity. Instead of racing home to mother, Peaches went to the office of a top-flight ghost writer. She gave him material for a scorching story called "My Honeymoon With Daddy." Daddy, too, dug up a ghost writer, to give his side of the drama to another tabloid. Next, the pair hired relays of ghost writers to whom they told new and differing stories. "Nothing

Era of Wonderful Nonsense

more sensational or fantastic has ever appeared in newspapers," says an authority.

Peaches sued for a legal separation, asking $300 a week in alimony. The Peaches-Daddy trial at White Plains, New York, in January, 1927, became the silliness sensation of the decade. The *New York Times* carried the testimony on page one, while the tabloids whipped up lurid coverage. A mob seethed outside the courthouse, with women abandoning baby carriages in order to push inside.

Courtroom testimony alternated between the funny and the salacious. Peaches turned out to be a typical flapper, while Daddy bounded to the witness chair like an actor taking a curtain call. His lawyer immediately asked, "You are a sane man, aren't you?" Daddy answered with an emphatic, "Yes." With Peaches crying bitterly, the judge decided against her, and the whole business sank into oblivion.

Mass hysteria swept to a morbid crest in 1926, with the death of movie actor Rudolph Valentino, the Sheik of Sheiks. Despite his slinky appearance, the screen lover in private life was a quiet fellow; he liked to call his wives "Boss." The latest of these had persuaded Rudy to break his lucrative contract with Paramount Pictures. Restless without work, in need of money, he began a personal-appearance tour of big-city theaters. He collapsed when he reached New York and was rushed to a hospital. In an operation for appendicitis, doctors also found two perforated gastric ulcers. With this, pneumonia, pleurisy, and peritonitis set in. Glossy-haired Rudy was doomed.

When he died, hysteria broke loose. Thirty thousand people, their emotions churned higher by skillful press-agentry, descended on Frank E. Campbell's Memorial Chapel, where the actor lay in state attired in immaculate evening dress. Plateglass windows were smashed and women trampled. With order restored, one hundred and fifty persons a minute began filing past the bier. The line of mourners never seemed to slacken.

Nonsense songs, fads, silly sayings reflected the atmosphere. On the vaudeville stage, comedians got laughs with the brand new She-Was-Only jokes: "She was only a farmer's daughter, but she sure did know her oats"; "She was only a doctor's daughter, but my how she operated"; "She was only a bootlegger's daughter, but I love her still"; "She was only a cab-driver's daughter, but oh, you auto meet her."

College boys in raccoon coats raced the roads in Model T

flivvers, the sides covered with slogans like Rattle of the Century, Girls Wanted, Plus-Four Brakes, Ain't She Sweet?, Handle With Hooks—No Care. Sheiks and shebas bought bright yellow slickers, spent hours stenciling them with contemporary catch phrases: Thanks for the Buggy Ride; Don't Step On It, It Might Be Lon Chaney; Show Me the Way to Go Home. Flappers and boy friends brought the ukelele into prominence, as fingers whipped the elementary instrument through a frenzied "Sheik of Araby" or "Who Stole My Heart Away?"

New slang popped up. A cute flapper was "a beaut," or the "cat's meow," "cat's whiskers," or "cat's pajamas." Her boy friend was a "cakeater," "jazzbo," jellybean," or "lounge lizard." Anything a flapper or jellybean liked was "nifty," or "the nuts." Rapture was expressed by "hot diggity dog," or "hot diggity." A tough guy was a "hard-boiled egg"; a stupid girl a "dumbbell," or "Dumb Dora." At a wild party, the flapper who hoisted skirts in a wicked Charleston was urged on by cries of "Get hot! Get hot!"

At the close of a happy date, a flip flapper would say to her sheik, "Thanks for the buggy ride." To tell him off, she'd snap, "Go fly a kite." If the cakeater made her laugh, she'd giggle, "Ooo, you slaughter me!" A pet expression of disbelief was, "It's the bunk." Or, "Banana oil." "Well, for crying out loud" meant incredulity.

Liquor, bathtub gin, or bootleg hooch was "booze," "giggle water," "giggle soup." Speakeasies were "whoopee parlors." Anything strange was "goofy," anyone strange a "goof." To add emphasis a sheba breathed fervently, "I should hope to tell you!" or "And *how!*" The girl never said yes or no. Sometimes she'd give a long-drawn-out "Ab-so-lute-ly," or "Pos-i-tive-ly." Other times it was a scramble of both "Abso*tive*-ly" or "Pos-a-*loot*-ly."

Revolution in Baseball: Ruth Reaches New York

by Robert W. Creamer

America was in social revolution as the 1920s began—Prohibition went into effect on January 16, eleven days after the announcement of Ruth's sale to the Yankees—and baseball turned around as radically as the country did. The game changed more between 1917 and 1921 than it did in the next forty years. Despite the high-profile presence of such outstanding batters as Cobb, Wagner, Lajoie, Speaker, Jackson and a few others, during the first two decades of the century hitting was a lesser art in a game that honored pitching and low scores. The term "inside" baseball was almost sacred, and John McGraw was its high priest. It meant playing for a run, a single run. You bunted safely, stole second, went to third on a sacrifice and scored on a fly ball to win 1–0. An exaggeration, of course, but that was the ideal. Even after the cork-center ball was introduced in 1910, tight baseball continued to dominate.

All this changed after the war, after Ruth's breakthrough in 1919. It was not a gradual evolution but sudden and cataclysmic. Baseball statistics give dramatic evidence of this. For fifteen seasons before 1919, major league batters as a group averaged around .250. By 1921 that figure had jumped above .285, and it remained steadily in the .280s throughout the 1920s. With this increase in hitting came an increase in scoring. Before 1920 it was a rare year when more than two or three men in both leagues batted in 100 runs; but in 1921 fifteen players did it, and the average for the 1920s was fourteen a year. Earned-run averages, the measure of a pitcher's run-suppressing ability, shot upward. Before 1919 the average annual ERA was about 2.85. In 1921 it was over 4.00, and it stayed in that generous neighborhood through the decade.

What caused the explosion? The end of the war, Ruth, money and the lively ball. Attendance in 1919 rose for every one of the sixteen major league teams, in some instances doubling and even tripling. The release from war was largely responsible for the first burst of interest, and then Ruth's home run hitting came into focus. Babe was the most exciting aspect of the 1919 season, even more than the pennant races. New fans bubbling into the ballparks could not begin to appreciate the austere beauty of a well-pitched game, but they thrilled vicariously to the surging erectile power of the Ruthian home run. They wanted more. They wanted hits and they wanted runs, lots of hits and lots of runs. They wanted homers. The owners, delighted by the windfall at the ticket windows, were happy to give them what they wanted. They instituted legislation against the myriad trick pitches, like the spitball, that tended to befuddle batters, and they pepped up the ball. No hard irrefutable facts exist to verify this—indeed, a laboratory test in August 1920 "proved" the ball had not been changed—but the data cited in the preceding paragraph seem overwhelming circumstantial evidence.

Too, Ruth's full free swing was being copied more and more, and so was his type of bat, thinner in the handle and whippier, in principle something like a golf club. (Early in his career Ruth used a massive 52-ounce bat, but this slimmed down as Ruth himself ballooned.) Strategy and tactics changed. A strikeout heretofore had been something of a disgrace—reread "Casey at the Bat." A batter was supposed to protect the plate, get a piece of the ball, as in the cognate game of cricket. In Ruth's case, however, a strikeout was only a momentary, if melodramatic, setback. Protecting the plate declined in importance, along with the sacrifice and the steal (the number of stolen bases in 1921 was half the prewar average). The big hit, the big inning blossomed.

With them, so did attendance. It had been a good year in 1919, but 1920 was marvelous. Attendance went up again in every city in the majors except Detroit (the Tigers fell to seventh place that year) and Boston, where bitterness had replaced the Royal Rooters. Seven clubs established new all-time attendance highs in 1920, and the Yankees set a new major league record. The old record was 910,000, by the 1908 New York Giants. No other club had ever drawn as high as 700,000, and for most of them yearly attendance was usually well under 500,000. In 1919 the Yankees had been like John the Baptist, preparing the way for the Lord. They were a powerful team, and their pre-Ruth batting order of Home Run Baker, Wally Pipp, Duffy Lewis, Ping Bodie, Roger Peckinpaugh, Del Pratt et al. was dubbed Murderers' Row by a newspaper cartoonist. The name seemed justified when the Yanks led the major leagues in home runs, with 45—only 16 more than Ruth hit by himself for Boston. They were in the race for the pennant a good part of the season, finished a respectable third and drew 619,000, more than 20 per cent above their previous high. But in 1920, with Ruth, they were in the pennant race all season long, finished a much closer third, hit 115 home runs (Babe had 54 of them) and drew phenomenally. The Polo Grounds had a seating capacity then of 38,000, and capacity was reached and surpassed time and again. The Yankees passed the Giants' old record in mid-summer, became the first major league team ever to draw a million people, and ended the season with 1,289,422, almost 380,000 better than the previous high. The Giants drew well too, surpassing their 1908 mark themselves, and the two clubs together drew 2,219,031 to the Polo Grounds, almost a million more than ever before.

Ruth was made for New York. It has been said that where youth sees discovery, age sees coincidence, and perhaps the retrospect of years makes Ruth's arrival in Manhattan in 1920 seem only a fortuitous juxtaposition of man and place in time. Nonetheless, Ruth in that place at that time was discovery. And adventure. And excitement. And all the concomitant titillations. One of his famous nicknames, the Bambino, came about because New York's polyglot immigrants, and their children, found themselves strangely excited by Ruth and baseball. Many of those riding the subways and elevated trains and streetcars up to the thin northern neck of Manhattan where the Polo Grounds was, or who talked about Ruth on street corners and in the neighborhood stores, were Italian. The rhythm and alliteration and connotative impact of the Italian word for babe, *bambino*, made the nickname a natural. In time, headlines would say simply, "BAM HITS ONE."

Ruth did not come to New York as a Yankee until the day the club left for Jacksonville and spring training. He had dawdled in California, occasionally sounding off about getting more money from the deal, and sidestepped New York on the way back. In Boston he tried to wangle a percentage of the sale price from Frazee. He smoked cigars in a show window to promote the cigar factory, even smoking three cigars at the same time. He basked in the sad adulation of Red Sox fans at a testimonial dinner given in his honor at the Hotel Brunswick by the David J. Walsh Collegiate Club.

Finally, on February 28, he took a train for New York to

join the rest of the Yankee contingent at Pennsylvania Station, where the team was to catch the 6:20 sleeper to Florida. He did not appear in the station until ten past six, but when he did a mob of fans crowded around him trying to touch him or shake hands. Autograph hounds happily were still a rarity in those days. Ruth, hulking over the people around him, beamed, shook hands, exchanged greetings and obviously enjoyed the stir he was creating. He was wearing a heavy leather coat and was clinging to a new set of golf clubs he had bought in California.

The affable Ping Bodie took him around and made a great show of introducing him formally to each of the Yankee players, even though Babe knew most of them already. When a club official parceled out five dollars in expense money to each player, Bodie said it would add up to just about enough for one fair-sized pot. Ruth grinned and said, "Let's get a game going." On the train he passed around Babe Ruth cigars and smoked some himself, as well as pulling at a handsome meerschaum pipe he said had cost him $12. He chewed gum incessantly ("He always had something in his mouth," Lee Allen wrote) and talked freely about his switch from the Red Sox to the Yankees. He cursed Frazee. When someone asked if he had managed to get part of the sale price from the Boston owner, he roared, "The son of a bitch wouldn't even see me."

In Jacksonville, whose chamber of commerce had advertised Ruth and the Yankees throughout Florida like a circus, he played golf with Bob Shawkey and Del Pratt and on one hole mis-hit the ball so badly he broke the head off his club. In early practice sessions at the ballpark he worked out at third base and surprised the other players with his lefthanded agility. His winter of golf and baseball in California had left him in pretty good shape. His weight was just about 200. He quickly became an accepted member of the team and enjoyed himself hugely clowning about in practice. One day when the chunky five-foot, eight-inch, 195-pound Bodie cut in front of him to take a grounder away, Ruth yelled in mock anger, grabbed Bodie, turned him upside down, dropped him on the grass and sat on him. He and Bodie got along well. They were roommates and often ate together. Bodie had been considered the biggest eater on the club before Ruth came along, but now he admitted defeat. "Anybody who eats three pounds of steak and a bottle of chili sauce for a starter has got me," he said. Not everything was jovial. Ruth got fed up with the biting jibes of a spectator one afternoon and went into the stands after him. The man stood his ground and pulled a knife. Ernie Shore, then with the Yankees, pulled Ruth away, and the fan left quietly.

Off the field, except for an occasional round of golf with other players, Babe was gone most of the time. Lee Allen described Ruth years later as "a large man in a camel's hair coat and camel's hair cap, standing in front of a hotel, his broad nostrils sniffing at the promise of the night." The essence of that vivid picture suited him in spring training in 1920. There was an outsize complement of reporters from New York's dozen or more newspapers in camp, most of them here because of Ruth, and they had trouble catching up to him off the field.

He was never around. When the team would come into a town on its way north, the players' luggage would be delivered to the hotel and left in the lobby. Each player would pick up his own bag and take it to his room. But Ruth would go from the train directly into town, looking for a girl he knew, or knew of, or hoped to know. In the hotel the good-natured Bodie would pick up his bag and the Babe's and carry both up to their room. Ruth might look into the room for a change of clothing during his visit, but he was gone most of the time, and more often than not Bodie would dutifully bring Babe's luggage back downstairs when it was time to leave. An enterprising reporter, scraping around for some sort of new angle on the Babe, approached Bodie one day and asked him to talk about Ruth.

"I don't know anything about him," Bodie said.

"You room with him. What's he like when you're alone with him?"

"I don't room with him," Bodie said, in a remark that entered baseball legend. "I room with his suitcase."

One trip from Jacksonville down to Miami proved so riotous—Ruth, still hazy one morning, ran into a palm tree chasing a fly ball—that Ruppert never again let the Yankees play a spring-training game in that city. In any case, Ruth started slowly and did not hit his first home run until April 1. Happily, Ruppert was there and was delighted by the homer, which was especially Ruthian. The fence was 429 feet from the plate and ten feet high, and the ball cleared it by 50 feet. Ruth hit more homers and lifted his batting average above .300 before the season began, but even so it was not a particularly good spring for the Yankees. Bodie, beset by personal problems, jumped the club in March and did not return until the season was well under way. Another outfielder, the colorful Chick Fewster, was hit in the head by a pitched ball and was so badly hurt he was unable to speak for nearly a month. He was eventually sent north to Baltimore for surgery to remove a blood clot and was out almost all season. Before he was hurt, Fewster had inspired a choice bit of sports-page doggerel:

> *Said slim Chick Fewster to big Babe Ruth,*
> *I haven't had a hit since Hector was a youth.*
> *Said big Babe Ruth to slim Chick Fewster,*
> *You don't hit the ball as hard as you uster.*

With Bodie and Fewster gone, Ruth asked Huggins if he could play center field. He said he did not want to play left or right because he might run into the short outfield walls in the Polo Grounds. "I'll get myself all smashed up going after a fly ball," he said. Huggins acceded to the request, and Ruth made his regular season debut with the Yankees as a center fielder, although it was not an auspicious debut. The Yankees opened in Philadelphia against the Athletics, and Ruth gave the last-place A's the game-winning runs when he dropped a fly ball in the eighth inning with two men on base and two out. At bat all he could produce were two meek singles.

Joe Dugan, the Philadelphia third baseman (known as Jumping Joe for his practice of jumping the ball club at irregular intervals), hit the fly ball Ruth dropped, which pleased Dugan, who liked a laugh. He felt Ruth's muff could not be ignored. After the game he scraped around and found a brown derby, in those days a symbol of ineptitude. (Al Smith had not yet made it nationally famous as a political trademark.) He had it wrapped up and the next afternoon a messenger brought it to the field when Ruth came to bat in the first inning. Such presentations were not uncommon, and the umpire dutifully called time. The other players gathered around and Ruth opened the package. When he lifted out the brown derby, the crowd and the players and even the umpires howled with laughter. Huggins tensed, waiting for Ruth's famous temper to explode. But after staring at the derby in stunned surprise for a moment, Ruth grinned, put it on and waved to the crowd.

His graceful acceptance of the joke did not help him at bat. He struck out three times and did not get a hit. The

Yankees went on to Boston for three games before returning to New York for their home opener, and before his old fans Ruth's slump continued. And the Yankees lost three straight to the Red Sox.

When the club began its home season in New York a big crowd was on hand to see the hero's debut. Again there was disappointment. Ruth pulled a muscle in his rib cage in batting practice, hurt it again striking out in the first inning, and to the chagrin of the crowd left the game.

"How do you like that?" complained a fan. "I come all the way from Red Hook and they take him out five minutes after the game starts."

Babe was out for several days, disappointing big crowds on the first weekend of the season, and when he did get back he struck out twice in one game and made another error. Then the Red Sox came to town and in the opener of a five-game series beat the Yankees for the fourth straight time in the young season. New York was becoming uneasy. The Ruthless Red Sox, as they were being called, were leading the league with a 10–2 record, while the Yankees were in the second division. The Babe had not hit a single homer. Maybe Frazee was right. After all, Boston had finished sixth with Ruth the year before.

On Saturday, May 1, a skeptical crowd came to see the second game of the series with the Red Sox. And that was the day Babe started. With Huggins, coaching at third, shrilling, "Come on, big boy!" Ruth hit his first home run of the year, a truly amazing drive far over the Polo Grounds roof, even farther than the one he had hit there the September before for his record-breaking 28th home run. The Yankees shut out Boston, 6–0, won two of the remaining three games, and were on their way. The Red Sox balloon went pffft. Frazee's depleted team slipped and slipped and eventually finished fifth with a 72–81 record, while Ruth and the Yankees began their climb to glory.

Babe's home runs came with exciting regularity—he had 12 before the end of May, far more than anyone had ever hit in one month before—and the crowds followed. On Sunday, May 16, a record 38,600 jammed the Polo Grounds, and 15,000 others had to be herded away by police when the ticket windows were shut down well before game time. Ruth hit another dozen homers in June, and his batting average climbed as sensationally as his home run total. On June 20 it was .345; on June 28, .359; on July 1, .372. It was up to .385

by July 11—he hit safely in 26 straight games—and peaked at .391 on August 4. After that the fires banked somewhat, and he finished the season at .376, fourth in the league behind Sisler (.407), Speaker (.388) and Jackson (.382).

All around the league, fans jammed the ballparks to see him, and they booed their own pitchers whenever Ruth was given a base on balls, which happened often (he had 148 walks in the 142 games he played that season). Because he was walked so often, Huggins moved him up from fourth to third in the batting order and put Bob Meusel, a good cleanup hitter, in the fourth spot. Most of the bases on balls Ruth received were intentional, or all but intentional, and with good reason, for it seemed almost impossible to get him out. Typical was a game in June when the Yankees were losing, 5–3, to Boston in the eighth inning. The Yanks had men on first and third with one out, Ruth up. The Red Sox wanted to walk him, but a walk would fill the bases, put the winning run on first and move the tying runs to scoring position at second and third. So they pitched to him, and Ruth tripled against the exit gate in deep right center to drive in both runners. Meusel doubled Ruth home, Pratt singled Meusel home, and the Yankees won, 7–5.

As the season wore on, the bases on balls became more frequent. On July 11 Ruth went to bat four times against Howard Ehmke of Detroit and took his bat from his shoulder only twice. In the first inning, with men on second and third and no one out, he walked on four straight pitches. In the third, with the bases empty, he swung and missed at the first pitch and hit a home run on the second. In the fifth and seventh innings, both times with the bases empty, he walked on four straight pitches. The crowd booed the walks.

He still had occasional bad days. He extended his hitting streak to 26 straight games in the first half of a doubleheader (before a capacity crowd on a Tuesday afternoon) but ended the streak when he walked twice and struck out twice in the second game. When he struck out on his last time at bat, which meant the streak was all over, he smashed his bat on the ground so hard that it broke. Such failures, which seemed rare, inspired one more bit of Ruthian verse:

There was a man in our town
Who was a baseball fan;
And who was always in his seat
Before the game began;

And every time the Yanks were here,
And Ruth came up to bat
And failed to bust the ball, he rose
And yelled and waved his hat.

He tied his own record of 29 homers on July 15. He hit his record-breaking 30th (the first time anyone ever hit that many in a season) on July 19 in the second game of a doubleheader, hit another in the same game and the next afternoon hit another. In those two games he made out only once; the rest of the time he either hit a home run or received a base on balls.

By the end of July he had 37. Maintaining that pace would have carried him past 60, but he slowed drastically and hit only seven during the next five weeks. In September he came alive again and hit ten in his last 24 games to finish with 54. Second to him was Sisler, with 19. The National League champion had 15.

His performance in 1920 is a baseball landmark. He batted .376, hit 54 home runs, nine triples, 36 doubles, scored 158 runs, batted in 137, stole 14 bases. His slugging average was .847, still the major league record. Sports researcher George Russell Weaver, quoted by David Willoughby in his book *The Super Athletes*, said it was the best single season any major league hitter has ever had. Weaver based his opinion on a comparison of Ruth's home run performance with that of the league as a whole. As an example, Weaver noted that Bill Terry's oft-cited batting average of .401 in 1930 was achieved in a season when the league as a whole batted .303; Terry's performance was therefore nowhere near as impressive as Honus Wagner's .354 in 1908, when the league as a whole batted only .239. Only five men batted over .300 in 1908, whereas more than fifty battled over .300 in 1930. When Ruth hit his 54 home runs in 1920, Weaver noted, only one other team in the league hit more than 44.

Popular Music of the Decade

by David Ewen

"It don't mean a thing if you ain't got that swing"

Possibly the most apt way of describing the 1920's is to call it the "jazz age." By "jazz" we are not here referring to the real product marketed first in New Orleans and then in Chicago and New York, by such giant jazzmen as Louis Armstrong, Bix Beiderbecke, or Duke Ellington. "Jazz," in connection with the twenties, as we are using it here, was the synthetic variety being produced in quantity in Tin Pan Alley. Ballads were still holding their own—love ballads particularly—and in the 1920's Irving Berlin was showing his mastery of the genre with such gems as "All Alone," "What'll I Do?," "All by Myself," and "Remember." But the ballad was getting plenty of competition from a more dynamic kind of song, a song more expressive of the twenties, which had captured public imagination and enthusiasm. It was exciting in its rhythmic pulse and changing meters, in its compulsive beat and dramatic accentuations, in its blues harmonies and jazz colorations. The appeal of this kind of number stemmed from its rhythmic momentum and kinesthetic force rather than from the beauty of the melody.

George Gershwin was one of the first to evolve this kind of jazz song and make it popular—with such numbers as "I'll Build a Stairway to Paradise," "Do It Again," "Fascinating Rhythm," "Fidgety Feet," and "Clap Yo' Hands." Other composers, following his direction, were also accentuating the beat and pulse of their writing and minimizing the sentiment of the lyric. There was Fred Fisher, whose "Dardanella" anticipated boogie-woogie with its recurring bass rhythm. Zez Confrey's rags are examples of this kind of jazz music—"Dizzy Fingers," "Kitten on the Keys," and "Stumbling." In the concert hall this kind of jazz found a receptive audience through the more ambitious symphonic works of George Gershwin, John Alden Carpenter, and Ferde Grofé.

The popularity of this restlessly rhythmic and nervously accented kind of song brought on a new abandon in social dance; and this new frenetic type of social dance, in turn, stimulated the writing of still other dynamically rhythmic tunes. The tango, the waltz and the fox trot—so popular before World War I—were followed in the 1920's by dances that were far more uninhibited in motions, far more in tune with the febrile spirit of the 1920's.

First there was the shimmy, the earliest dance expression of the jazz age. This was a demonstration of quivering shoulders and thighs, which was supposed to have originated on the Barbary Coast and then become popular in the dives of Chicago. The distinction of having been the first to make the shimmy famous on Broadway was hotly disputed by Gilda Gray and Bea Palmer, each of whom was celebrated for her shimmy performances. Gilda Gray had been a protégée of Sophie Tucker, who took the then-unknown dancer with her into a Sunday-night concert at the Winter Garden in 1918. There Gilda Gray did a shimmy to the music of "St. Louis Blues;" with which she became the talk of the town. She kept doing the shimmy in the Broadway Theater after that—a star of the *Ziegfeld Follies of 1922* where her shimmy was performed to the strains of " 'Neath the South Sea Moon" and "It's Getting Dark on Old Broadway." Bea Palmer had also won her spurs as a shimmy artist in 1918—in the *Ziegfeld Follies*, in which she did her dance to "I Want to Learn to Jazz Dance."

There is a third claimant for the honors of first making the shimmy popular on the stage—Mae West. She had seen the shimmy (or, as it was then known, the "shimmy shawobble") in a Negro café in Chicago. A couple "got out on the floor," Mae West recalled in her autobiographical *Goodness Had Nothing to Do with It*, "and stood in one spot, with hardly any movement of the feet, and just shook their shoulders, torsos, breasts, and pelvises. We thought it was funny and were terribly amused by it. But there was a naked, aching sensual agony about it too." The next day, in vaudeville, Mae West improvised a dance like that for her act, and a week after that she performed the dance during her vaudeville appearances in Milwaukee. Finally she came to New York with it—in the Rudolf Friml musical *Sometime*, which opened on Broadway on October 4, 1918. "Mae West," reported Sime

Silverman of *Variety,* "bowled them over with her songs and her dance known in the joints as the shimmy shawobble." There was also a fourth exponent of the shimmy, and to some she was the queen of the brood—Ann Pennington, whose shimmying was the main attraction of the *George White Scandals* of 1919 and 1920.

From the stage, the shimmy passed on into the ballroom and even the home. Everybody was shimmying now—or, as a Dave Stamper number from the *Ziegfeld Follies of 1919* put it, "The World Is Going Shimmy Mad." The shimmy was glorified by Tin Pan Alley in such song hits as "Indianola," and "I Wish I Could Shimmy like My Sister Kate."

Then in 1923 the shimmy was rudely brushed aside by a new dance craze—the Charleston, a fast fox trot introduced in the all-Negro revue *Runnin' Wild.* The nationwide fame of the song "Charleston" accompanying this dance—the work of Cecil Mack and Jimmy Johnson—was a powerful factor in spreading the vogue of the Charleston all around the country. The vibrations of a thousand people doing the Charleston was believed to have caused the collapse of the floor at the Pickwick Club in Boston, a disaster that cost fifty lives. Nevertheless, the Charleston continued to thrive. At the Roseland ballroom on Broadway, a Charleston marathon dragged on for almost twenty-four hours. And one of the big scenes in the motion picture *Our Dancing Daughters* in 1928 showed Joan Crawford doing the Charleston.

In or about 1926, the black bottom superseded the Charleston. The phrase "black bottom" probably referred to the muddy bottom of the Swanee River, and the movements of the dance suggested the dragging of feet through the mud. In any event, Alberta Hunter is the one credited as its creator, having copyrighted it in 1926, and was the first to feature it successfully on the stage. The dance quickly made the rounds of burlesque, vaudeville, musical comedy, dance halls, and night clubs. One of the big production numbers in the *Scandals of 1926* was a black-bottom number—the song was by De Sylva, Brown, and Henderson and the dance was performed by the former shimmy queen Ann Pennington.

The jazz age in Tin Pan Alley emphasized the beat and the accent rather than the melody. For this reason the main distributor of Tin Pan Alley's music in the 1920's was not the singer any longer but the jazz band or orchestra. In the 1910's sheet music used to feature prominently the photographs of Nora Bayes, Al Jolson, Eddie Cantor, or Sophie Tucker; in the 1920's it concentrated on popular bandleaders. These orchestras, while hardly jazz "combos" in the New Orleans or Chicago meaning of the term, nevertheless did make effective use of jazz colors, effects, and rhythms; and many of the performers in these bands and orchestras had once been steeped in the traditions of genuine jazz.

The music of the commercial jazz band or orchestra differed from the New Orleans variety in that the emphasis lay not on improvisation but on formal arrangements. During the 1920's, the commercial jazz orchestras featured the songs of Tin Pan Alley in brilliant instrumental arrangements that made these numbers as effective for listening pleasure as for dancing. These jazz orchestras were featured prominently in night clubs, dance halls, public auditoriums, hotels, over radio and on records, in revues and musical comedies. It was now the jazz band—even more than the singing star of the stage—who would carry the songs of Tin Pan Alley throughout the United States. And it was now the band or orchestra leaders who would become the idols of a musical public.

Paul Whiteman and His Orchestra became the first of these great-name bands. For many years Whiteman had played the viola in the Denver Symphony. While performing his job there he used to enjoy gathering some of his colleagues into rag sessions. One day he dropped into a nightspot featuring New Orleans jazz. He was so taken with this music that then and there he decided to turn from symphonic to popular music. In 1917 he organized his first band. After World War I he enlarged it and called it the Paul Whiteman Orchestra. An appearance at the Alexandria Hotel in Los Angeles was so successful that the engagement lasted more than a year. Then Whiteman hired Ferde Grofé as his orchestrator and pianist. Grofé, like Whiteman, had served a long apprenticeship in serious music before turning to jazz. The merger of Whiteman and Grofé marked the real beginnings of Whiteman's fame. With Grofé's ingenious and colorful orchestrations, and Whiteman's carefully prepared performances, the Whiteman Orchestra began gathering triumph after triumph by performing the popular songs of the day. Paul Whiteman's recording of "Whispering" in 1920 sold more than a million and a half records and was largely responsible for the immense success of that song. His rendition of "Three O'Clock in the Morning" in 1922 proved another substantial disk seller. At various times celebrated jazz artists were members of the Whiteman Orchestra, including Bix Beiderbecke, Red Nichols, Jimmy and Tommy Dorsey, and Joe Venuti; and among the vocalists affiliated with the ensemble from time to time were Mildred Bailey and the then-unknown Bing Crosby.

Besides selling millions of records, the Whiteman Orchestra appeared as a headline act in vaudeville and was starred in such revues as the *Follies* and the *Scandals*. In 1923 it made a triumphant tour of Europe. Over a period of years its performances at the Palais Royal made that night club one of the most successful on the Great White Way. Paul Whiteman was, indeed, the "king of jazz"—and that was the name used for the motion picture in which he and his orchestra appeared.

Whiteman's epoch-making achievement was a concert at Aeolian Hall in New York on February 12, 1924. For this "All-American Music Concert," jazz was featured from several different vantage points. Part of the program consisted of Tin Pan Alley songs in Ferde Grofé's arrangements; part was made up of semiclassical pieces dressed up in jazz costume. The most significant contribution, however, came from those compositions in a symphonic-jazz idiom in which composers used the jazz style and idiom within the framework of serious musical structures. In this last category was found Gershwin's *Rhapsody in Blue,* commissioned for this very concert by Whiteman, and introduced by the Paul Whiteman Orchestra with the composer at the piano. Here the audience heard not a jazz arrangement nor an adaptation of a serious piece of music nor a popular piece in symphonic raiment, but an original work by a serious musical creator using jazz with artistic intent and with all the resources of good music at his command. "Somewhere in the middle of the score, I began crying," Whiteman later confessed. "When I came to myself I was eleven pages along, and until this day I cannot tell you how I conducted that far."

The *Rhapsody in Blue* gave meaning to Whiteman's concert, and it was the only work on the program that aroused the audience to a high pitch of excitement. For the *Rhapsody in Blue*—more than any other musical composition—caught the "roaring twenties" in tones in the same way that the Offenbach cancan reflected the French Second Empire and the waltz of Johann Strauss the Austria of the Hapsburgs. And the 1920's recognized at once that here was its testament, here its song of songs. Paul Whiteman's first recording for Victor sold a million disks in a few months' time. Before long the *Rhapsody in Blue* was heard on the stage, over the radio, in the concert hall, in the ballet theater and motion-picture palace, and then on the talking screen. It made Gershwin the most famous and most financially affluent serious composer in America. It brought a new stature to Paul Whiteman, who from then on used the slow melody of the *Rhapsody* as his theme music. Tin Pan Alley, which had thus far produced so many distinguished songs, had now witnessed one of its native sons producing a concert masterwork.

The success of Paul Whiteman—who was earning about ten thousand dollars a week for his personal appearances—made the jazz orchestra a welcome headliner in vaudeville and a star in the stage shows of leading movie houses. In the middle 1920's there were more than twenty such orchestras touring the vaudeville circuit. Many a celebrated vaudeville act that formerly had been satisfied with a piano accompanist now used full-sized jazz bands. The interest in jazz bands or jazz orchestras became so keen that one vaudeville theater—Proctor's Fifth Avenue—conducted amateur jazz-band contests.

Paul Whiteman's Orchestra encouraged some of its rivals to penetrate the concert hall with jazz performances of their own. Vincent Lopez and his orchestra offered a concert at the Metropolitan Opera House in 1925, featuring a symphonic potpourri entitled *The Evolution of the Blues,* in which Lopez played the *Maple Leaf Rag* and the number that became his signature, "Nola." Though intended for the church, Lopez studied the piano from his boyhood days on. After three years of religious studies, he decided to exchange music for religion. He started playing the piano in Brooklyn saloons, beer halls and honky-tonks. In or about 1917 he was engaged as pianist and bandleader at the Pekin Restaurant in New York City, to become the youngest such maestro in the business; it was there and then that he played "Nola" for the first time. He held the job right through the era of World War I. When Prohibition threw the Pekin Restaurant out of business, Lopez and his band toured the vaudeville circuit. In 1921 they went to the Hotel Pennsylvania, there to initiate radio's first remote pickup. His salutation, "Hello, everybody, this is Lopez speaking," became as famous as the strains of his theme music. Besides his performances at the hotel, Lopez and his band were heard in vaudeville, stage shows, and at the Casa Lopez.

Neither Lopez' performance at the Metropolitan Opera, nor similar presentations by other bands in places like Carnegie Hall, achieved anything like the significance of Paul Whiteman's 1924 concert at Aeolian Hall. The main reason for this is that none of these concerts was able to produce a work in jazz idiom of the stature of the *Rhapsody in Blue*. The programs were generally filled with jazz treatments of classics and semiclassics. To provide jazz trimmings to pieces like the *Song of India*, or *Scheherazade*, or *Liebestraum*, or the *Dance of the Hours* merely demeaned and vulgarized good music without contributing an iota to the advancement of either popular music or jazz. This practice reached a low in taste with jazz versions of "The Star-Spangled Banner," the hymn "Rock of Ages," and the Spiritual "Deep River"; and it plunged to the depths of impropriety with a jazzed-up version of Chopin's "Funeral March" from the *Piano Sonata in B-flat Minor*. From across the ocean the eminent English music critic Ernest Newman bellowed, "Paws off!" while in Paris the French Society of Composers issued a formal protest.

But offering Tin Pan Alley tunes in fresh, attractive jazz orchestrations was something else again. In the 1920's the science of jazz orchestration advanced by leaps and bounds. In order to get its songs played by the leading bands, Tin Pan Alley was compelled to hire experts at instrumentation to prepare special arrangements for different orchestras, usually arrangements suiting the individual style of each ensemble. Many of these orchestrations were extraordinarily skillful. Tin Pan Alley's music was thus acquiring a new depth and dimension in orchestrations featured by ensembles led by Ben Bernie, Ted Lewis, Abe Lyman, Leo Reisman, Fred Waring, and many others, as well as Whiteman and Lopez. There were even some authorities who liked to regard these orchestrations as a new art form in music. Fritz Kreisler and Leopold Stokowski, for example, found a good deal to admire in this type of commercial jazz. Hiram K. Motherwell, a noted journalist, had this to say about jazz orchestration: "I like to think that it is a perfect expression of the American city, with its restless bustle and motion, its multitude of unrelated details, and its underlying rhythmic progress towards a vague Somewhere. Its technical resourcefulness continually surprises me, and its melodies at their best delight me."

There were, to be sure, severe critics—mainly among educators and the clergy. To John Roach Straton of the Calvary Baptist Church in New York City, this kind of jazz represented "music of the savage, intellectual and spiritual debauchery, utter degradation." The president of the Christian and Missionary Alliance Conference charged that because of jazz, "American girls of tender age are approaching jungle standards." One educator maintained that "if we permit our boys and girls to be exposed indefinitely to this pernicious influence, the harm that will result may tear to pieces our whole social fabric."

Jazz, in terms of big-name bands, remained unaffected by attack or criticism. The vogue swept right into the 1930's, when a new group of outstanding ensembles came to the fore—headed by the Dorsey brothers, Glenn Miller, Harry James, and Benny Goodman, the crowned "king of swing."

Many of the big-name bands—like the big-time singers of vaudeville and musical comedy—used identifying theme songs from Tin Pan Alley. Just as Lopez had "Nola" and Whiteman the slow section of the *Rhapsody in Blue,* Tommy Dorsey had "I'm Getting Sentimental Over You"; Glenn Miller, "Moonlight Serenade"; Ted Lewis, "When My Baby Smiles at Me"; Ben Bernie, "Au Revoir, Pleasant Dreams"; Wayne King, "The Waltz You Saved for Me"; Kay Kyser, "Thinking of You."

Before the 1920's were over, a soothing antidote to the hyperthyroid accents and rhythms of commercial jazz had been introduced with Rudy Vallee's crooning. Sober, soft-toned, relaxed, crooning was almost like the musical warning that the inebriation of the twenties was dissipating and that the hangover of the thirties was just around the corner. To Tin Pan Alley, the greatest importance of the vogue for crooning lay in the fact that—like Jolson, Cantor, Nora Bayes, and Sophie Tucker before him—Rudy Vallee was a maker of hit songs.

Vallee started out in music by forming a band called the Yale Collegians when he was at Yale University. After leaving college, he organized the Connecticut Yankees, and in 1928 he and his band were engaged for the Heigh-Ho Club. There Vallee introduced his familiar "heigh-ho" salutation and began to use a megaphone (from then on his trademark) to amplify his small voice. After that Vallee and the Connecticut Yankees played in vaudeville, in musical comedies and revues, in motion pictures, and over the radio. For his very first broadcast on the Fleischmann Hour in 1929, he began using his identifying theme song "My Time Is Your Time." Over the radio, as well as in his public appearances, his enormous personal appeal and his infectious crooning style brought national popularity to new songs and long-forgotten songs. Among them were "I'm Just a Vagabond Lover," "Betty Co-Ed," "Stein Song," "There's a Tavern in the Town," "Good Night, Sweetheart," and Irving Berlin's "Say It Isn't So."

Before long, Rudy Vallee became involved in a "battle of crooners." A competitor, Will Osborne, came up with a claim that it was he and not Vallee who had invented the style of singing. Partly stimulated by their keen scent for a provocative news item, partly by the maneuvers of a publicity agent, journalists gave wide coverage to the feud. Now Osborne challenged Vallee to a ten-round fight to decide the issue; now he tried to instigate litigation for a half-million-dollar libel suit that never really got off the ground; now he had his lawyers issue an injunction to prevent the publication of Vallee's autobiography *Vagabond Dreams Come True*. Legal methods failing, Osborne tried to reduce Vallee's huge success with the University of Maine's "Stein Song" to the ridiculous by featuring on one of his programs a number titled "I'd Like to Break the Neck of the Man Who Wrote the Stein Song."

Vallee countered Osborne's acts, maneuvers, and attacks by pointing out that Osborne had just been a drummer when he, Vallee, had hired him, that he had taught Osborne his own approaches, techniques, and musical arrangements, and that he had started Osborne off on his career as a crooner by letting him take over the leadership of the Vallee orchestra while Vallee was out in Hollywood making a movie. "How this feud is going to end, nobody can guess," remarked the New York *Daily Mirror*. Then treating the whole affair with the facetiousness it deserved, the *Mirror* added: "Maybe the boys will hurl plums at forty paces, handfuls of confetti at a city block." What the feud ultimately accomplished was to give Osborne a good deal of publicity without in any way weakening Vallee's own position as the public's favorite crooner.

"Looking at the world through rose-colored glasses"

During the 1920's the Broadway musical theater—the operetta, musical comedy, and the revue—began displacing vaudeville as Tin Pan Alley's prime showcase for new songs. The musical theater was now enjoying an era of unprecedented boom. The number of productions mounted were steadily increasing. Some seasons realized the opening of as many as fifty musicals, with four or five premières a night when the season was at its height. Staging and costuming had grown increasingly lavish; casts were studded with stars more plentifully than ever. Stage approaches and techniques had become slicker, dialogue and humor more sophisticated.

The opportunities offered to new creative talent by the expanding musical theater were increasing. Financial rewards were prodigious for those whose work was liked by the public. The percentage of box-office successes among produced musicals had never before—and has rarely since—been so high. With production costs low in relation to the admission prices, a musical that ran a hundred performances could expect to break even; a run of two hundred performances represented a profitable production; a three-hundred or four-hundred performance run was a smash hit. Even though the thousand-performance was as t unknown, producing musicals in the 1920's was for the most part a profitable business.

With so many shows being put on the boards all the time, Tin Pan Alley had a ready-made market in which to display its wares. A song that went well on Broadway was sure to get recorded and heard over the radio—all of which spelled big sheet-music and record sales and large subsidiary revenues.

Except for the stars themselves, perhaps no single element of the musical theater was better calculated to bring audiences to the box office than a hit song. There was more than a single instance in the 1920's when a song—becoming a sudden hit—changed for the better the fortunes of a musical production. This happened in 1920 to *Mary* because it had Louis Hirsch's "Love Nest"; to *Little Jesse James* in 1923 because its score included Harry Archer's "I Love You"; to *The Girl Friend* of Rodgers and Hart in 1926 because the public had grown to like the title number and "Blue Room." Cole

Porter's *The Gay Divorce* in 1932 became known as the "Night and Day show," and *Take a Chance,* also in 1932, as the "Eadie Was a Lady show." In each instance a song changed the tide of fortune for a production that at first looked as if it was doomed. Jerome Kern's *Roberta* in 1933 also might have had an early closing were it not for "Smoke Gets In Your Eyes."

There was much to attract and hold an audience's fascinated interest in those 1920 musicals: from the pulchritude of the chorus girls to the stupendous effects achieved by the large production numbers; from the comedy of stars like Ed Wynn, Victor Moore, or W. C. Fields to the tapping toes of Ann Pennington, Fred and Adele Astaire, and later on, Bill Robinson. But what usually made the house electric and created a spell over the audience—what carried to the stage that touch of magic that once witnessed was never forgotten—were the times that the right song found the right singer. This was a marriage heaven-made—a marriage that made Tin Pan Alley and Broadway one.

This miracle took place in 1920 in Jerome Kern's *Sally* when Marilyn Miller brought an unforgettable glow and radiance to "Look for the Silver Lining." *Sally* was an expensive Ziegfeld production planned to glorify the one and only Marilyn Miller, whom Ziegfeld regarded as the most beautiful woman in the world and as the most glamorous personality in the musical theater of that day. Petite to the point of being precious, with a small voice which nevertheless exerted a hypnotic spell—and with a grace of body movement that was music in itself and a quality that was nothing short of ethereal—Marilyn Miller gave to her role and to the song "Look for the Silver Lining" a "curious enchantment," as P. G. Wodehouse and Guy Bolton later recalled, "that no reproduction in other lands or other mediums ever captures."

Something of Marilyn Miller's incandescence and magic flooded the stage of *Oh, Kay!* when Gertrude Lawrence sang George and Ira Gershwin's "Someone to Watch over Me." Gertrude Lawrence was a London star who was seen in the United States for the first time in *Charlot's Revue,* an importation. Broadway producers then began a scramble to get her to appear in an American-written musical comedy. Out of all the offers that came her way, she accepted that of Alex A. Aarons to appear in *Oh, Kay!*. And the reason she accepted it was that Gershwin was its composer and she wanted to sing Gershwin's songs. For *Oh, Kay!* produced in 1926, Gershwin wrote one of his most poignant love ballads—"Someone to Watch over Me." When Gertrude Lawrence sang it, she forthwith became one of the great ladies of the American musical theater.

"Bill"—music by Jerome Kern, words by P. G. Wodehouse—had to wait a number of years to be heard and appreciated, and it waited all that time because it could not find the right performer. "Bill" had been written in 1919 for *Oh, Lady, Lady*, but it was dropped when the proper place for it in the show—and the proper singer—could not be found. Kern then tried to fit it into *Sally*, but it was just not the right material for Marilyn Miller's small voice, and once again Kern had to admit defeat.

Then, in 1927, a dark-haired, soulful-eyed litle girl with a throb in her voice was chosen for the role of the half-caste Julie in *Show Boat*. Her name was Helen Morgan. Kern knew when he auditioned her that here at last was the one to sing "Bill." The song was interpolated into the score—even though all the other musical numbers had lyrics by Oscar Hammerstein II—and "Bill" became Helen Morgan's song. Her plaintive, touching delivery has often been imitated but never really equaled.

There were many such wonderful stage moments between 1920 and 1930 when the right song and the right singer coalesced: Al Jolson singing "April Showers" in *Bombo* in 1921; Eddie Cantor with "Dinah" in *Kid Boots* in 1923 and with "Makin' Whoopee" in *Whoopee* in 1928; Grace Moore—her glamorous career in opera still ahead of her—presenting Irving Berlin's "What'll I Do?" in the *Music Box Revue of 1924;* Libby Holman's deep-throated wail of Ralph Rainger's "Moanin' Low" in the first *Little Show* in 1929 and of Johnny Green's "Body and Soul" in *Three's a Crowd* in 1930; Ruth Etting in her poignant presentation of "Love Me or Leave Me," a Donaldson song interpolated into *Whoopee*; the cataclysmic way in which Ethel Merman exploded in Gershwin's "I Got Rhythm" in *Girl Crazy* in 1930.

Tin Pan Alley's ace composers were now producing individual songs and full scores for the Broadway musical theater rather than concentrating their maximum productivity on numbers intended primarily for sheet-music distribution. Jerome Kern, for example. He came fully into his own as a Broadway composer in the 1910's. Then, in the 1920's, he went on to the heights of theatrical greatness.

One day, in 1914, Kern visited Dreyfus' office at Harms to play his songs from *The Girl from Utah* for Victor Herbert. When Kern finished playing a score that had included "They Didn't Believe Me," Herbert told Dreyfus: "This man will inherit my mantle."

Kern fulfilled this prophecy by dominating the musical theater in the 1910's and 1920's, and by revolutionizing it not once but twice. In the middle 1910's he joined with P. G. Wodehouse and Guy Bolton to evolve a new kind of musical comedy—intimate, informal, economical, sophisticated, thoroughly American. These productions came to be known as the "Princess Theater shows" because that was the theater where they were given. The most successful were *Very Good Eddie* in 1915, *Oh, Boy* in 1917, and *Oh, Lady, Lady* in 1918. Kern's surpassing melodic charm yielded in these productions several remarkable songs, among which were "Babes in the Wood," "Nodding Roses," "Till the Clouds Roll By" (a title later used to name the Kern screen biography), and "The Magic Melody." Carl Engel, one of America's most distinguished musicologists, described "The Magic Melody" as "the opening chorus of an epoch" and went on to say of Kern: "A young man gifted with musical talent and unusual courage has dared to introduce into his tune a modulation which has nothing extraordinary in itself, but which marked a change, a new regime in American popular music. . . . It was a relief, a liberation."

Kern continued growing and developing. He wrote the music for the lavishly mounted Ziegfeld production *Sally*, in 1920. Marilyn Miller, the star of *Sally*, returned in 1925 to be the heroine in still another Jerome Kern musical, *Sunny*, where she sang "Who?" and "D'ye Love Me?" Then, two years later, Kern wrote the music for a production that once again invoked a new era for the musical theater—*Show Boat*.

With a book by Oscar Hammerstein II based on Edna Ferber's novel, *Show Boat* became the first musical to side-step the accepted ritual of musical comedy and to use only those materials that could do justice to a play rich in atmosphere and local color, in characterizations, in dramatic interest. Here in *Show Boat* was one of the first and one of the most successful experiments to make every song basic to the development of character and story. But above and beyond that, "Ol' Man River," "Bill," "You Are Love," "Make Believe," "Why Do I Love You?" and "Can't Help Lovin' Dat Man" flooded the popular song with a glow and humanity and a deeper emotion than it had heretofore known. Songs like these—especially "Ol' Man River"—were lifted to the status of folk music. To this day, Kern's score remains a vibrant and unforgettable experience in the theater; to this day *Show Boat*, as a whole, remains a classic whose "grandeur and eloquence," as one critic said of it, "seem to increase with the passing of time."

The Princess Theater shows and *Show Boat* broke new ground for the American musical theater. This cannot be said of most of the musicals of the 1920's for which George Gershwin wrote the music and Ira Gershwin the lyrics. Except for *Strike Up the Band!*, which came when the 1920's were just about over, Gershwin's musical comedies up to 1930 followed the accepted rule that a plot was there just to provide a means of offering songs, dances, humor, and production numbers. Indeed, the plots of these 1920 Gershwin musicals had little distinction and less originality. These musicals were contrived to offer entertainment. Any device was acceptable if it gave the stars an opportunity to shine, and provided songs that could be sung and danced to.

But there was one significant way in which Gershwin's musical comedy differed from most of those of the 1920's— and that was in the quality of the score. There was little obeisance made to formula, cliché, conventional procedures. George Gershwin could not operate that way. With his continual search for ever subtler effects, Gershwin brought to the best popular songs of these musicals a new concept of harmonic and rhythmic writing, a new pattern to the melodic line, which only Kern at his best could equal.

The first of these Gershwin musicals of the 1920's was *Lady Be Good*, in 1924, starring Fred and Adele Astaire. For this production Gershwin created "Fascinating Rhythm," infectious for its changing meters, the title song, whose repeated triplets in cut time produced a novel melodic effect, and "So Am I," with its personalized lyricism. No wonder then that the critic of the New York *Sun* described this music as "brisk, inventive, gay, nervous, delightful." But good as the score was, it would have been richer still had another song written for that show been allowed to stay in the production after the out-of-town tryouts. "The Man I Love"—its descending chromaticism providing an enchanting background for a poignant blues melody—is probably the most famous song Gershwin wrote, and it is one of his best. When *Lady*

Be Good tried out, the song—intended for Adele Astaire in the opening scene—was found to slow up the action and was killed. A few years later, Gershwin thought of interpolating it into the first version of *Strike Up the Band!* Once again it was dropped. There were also plans afoot to have Marilyn Miller sing it in *Rosalie,* but these never jelled. Finally issued by Harms as an independent number, "The Man I Love" left Tin Pan Alley to become popular, first in London, then in Paris, and finally at its home base—especially in performances by Helen Morgan. By the time the second version of *Strike Up the Band!* had been crystallized and the show carried into New York City, "The Man I Love" had become too popular to be used. If any single number out of Tin Pan Alley can be said to have become a classic, its permanent survival assured, that number is "The Man I Love."

Not the least of the significance of *Lady Be Good* lay in the fact that this was the first show for which Ira Gershwin wrote all the lyrics for his brother's music. Previously he and George had collaborated only on random numbers. From *Lady Be Good* on, the songs of every important Gershwin musical comedy were a joint effort by the brothers. Just as George proved inimitable in his music, so Ira, in his masterful and subtle versification, became one of the top lyricists of his time.

There was hardly a Gershwin musical in the 1920's, even among the failures, which did not boast at least one song that stood out prominently from its context like pure gold in the company of brass. In 1925, *Tip Toes* boasted "Looking for a Boy," "That Certain Feeling," and "Sweet and Low Down." *Oh, Kay!,* in 1926, was a veritable treasure trove, with "Maybe," "Clap Yo' Hands," "Do, Do, Do," "Someone to Watch over Me," and "Fidgety Feet." *Funny Face,* in 1928, had "'S Wonderful," "He Loves and She Loves," and "The Babbitt and the Bromide," the last of which was particularly remarkable for its lyrics. In *Rosalie,* in 1928, "How Long Has This Been Going On?" was heard, while *Show Girl,* in 1929, offered "So Are You" and "Liza." "Liza" was sung not only on the stage (by Ruby Keeler) but also (for the first few nights at any rate) from the audience, where Al Jolson would jump from his seat to address a second chorus of the song to his wife.

The last of the successful traditional musical comedies by the Gershwin brothers was *Girl Crazy* in 1930. Here were born not only several extraordinary songs, but also a remarkable new musical-comedy star in the person of Ethel Merman. One-time typist in Astoria, Long Island, Ethel Merman (originally named Ethel Zimmerman) had made spasmodic appearances as a singer at small night clubs, weddings, parties, and at the Paramount Theater in Brooklyn. Without ever having appeared on Broadway, she auditioned for George Gershwin and was seized for the part of Kate Fothergill for *Girl Crazy*. Her first number there was "Sam and Delilah," which she delivered with shrill, metallic tones that electrified the audience. Later she brought down the house with "I Got Rhythm." She also sang "Boy, What Love Has Done to Me," in a resplendent score that included "Embraceable You" (sung by Ginger Rogers in her first Broadway starring role), "But Not for Me," and "Bidin' My Time."

Meanwhile, earlier in 1930, with *Strike Up the Band!* the Gershwins parted company for the first time with musical-comedy stereotypes and tried to explore new horizons for the theater. This musical was a gay takeoff on war and international politics—the book by Morrie Ryskind and George S. Kaufman tapping a vein of satire altogether fresh and novel in American musical comedy. The Gershwin music also found new resources in such songs as the title number, with its satirical overtones and with the ballad "Soon."

Finally, in 1931, came *Of Thee I Sing!*, the first musical comedy to win the Pulitzer Prize. The book by George S. Kaufman and Morrie Ryskind here made sport of politics in Washington, D. C., and a presidential election. There were hit songs such as the title number, "Love Is Sweeping the Country" and the satirical "Wintergreen for President." But with this came all kinds of choral numbers, orchestral interludes, and large musical episodes (made up of recitatives, songs, and choruses) with which musical comedy acquired new size and dimension. "George Gershwin," wrote Brooks Atkinson, "has compounded a score that sings in many voices, simmers with ideas, and tells the story more resourcefully than the book. . . . It has very nearly succeeded in liberating the musical-comedy stage from the mawkish and feeble-minded formula that has long been considered inevitable."

Irving Berlin's first significant Broadway assignment after World War I came in 1919 with songs for the *Ziegfeld Follies* of that year. One was "A Pretty Girl Is Like a Melody," sung by John Steel, and used as background music for a stunning parade of *Follies* beauties, each representing some such musical classic as "Traumerei," "Humoresque," or "Elégie." "A Pretty Girl Is Like a Melody" became the theme song of the *Follies*. It is also the song heard most often at fashion shows and beauty contests all over the world. This was also the edition of the *Follies* in which Eddie Cantor presented the suggestive "You'd Be Surprised," and in which Van and Schenck sang "Mandy," which Berlin had previously written for *Yip, Yip, Yaphank*.

In 1927, Berlin once again served as composer-lyricist for the *Follies*, this time providing all the numbers (except for one or two interpolations)—the first time in the history of the *Follies* that one man was required to perform this chore. To the production Berlin contributed "It's Up to the Band" sung by the Brox Sisters and "Shaking the Blues Away" with which Ruth Etting made her *Follies* bow. (But the big song of this edition was not a Berlin number but an interpolation by Eddie Cantor—Walter Donaldson's "My Blue Heaven.")

Between 1921 and 1925, Berlin wrote the book, music, and lyrics for four editions of a splendiferous new revue that offered serious competition to the *Follies*. This was called the *Music Box Revue*, named after the Music Box Theater, a handsome new auditorium on Forty-fifth Street that opened with the première of the first *Music Box Revue*. "Such ravishingly beautiful tableaux, such gorgeous costumes, such a wealth of comedy and spectacular freshness, such a piling of Pelion on Ossa of everything that is decorative, dazzling, harmonious, intoxicatingly beautiful in the theater—all that and more was handed out in a program that seemed to have no ending." This was the way the editor of *Theater Magazine* described the show, which opened for a year's run on September 22, 1921. Berlin's top-flight score included one of his all-time favorites, "Say It with Music," and one of his last and best exercises in ragtime, "Everybody Step."

The other three editions—in 1922, 1923, and 1924—were even more lavish in costuming, scenery, production numbers, and stars. Here, as in the first production, Berlin's songs were a prime attraction—such songs as "Pack Up Your Sins," "Lady of the Evening," "Crinoline Days," "What'll I Do?" and "All Alone." The last two were made particularly memorable as sung by Grace Moore, a fledgling at the time.

During the 1920's, Berlin wrote the music for only one musical comedy. This was *The Cocoanuts*, a zany musical about the Florida real-estate boom and the phonies that helped promote it. With their improvisations and ad-libs, the Four Marx Brothers, the stars of the show, made a shambles of plot, dialogue, and situations (as George S. Kaufman had originally put them down on paper).

Season after season, Broadway was enriched by the labors of Tin Pan Alley's troubadours. Jean Schwartz wrote the scores for the *Passing Show of 1921* and *Artists and Models of 1923*. Albert von Tilzer provided the music for one of the leading musical-comedy successes of the early 1920's—*The Gingham Girl* in 1922. J. Fred Coots produced the songs for *Sally, Irene and Mary* in 1922, as well as the scores for the 1924 and 1925 editions of *Artists and Models*, for *A Night in Paris*, and the musical comedy *Sons o' Guns*. Harry Ruby was the composer of *Helen of Troy, New York*, of *The Ramblers*, and of *Animal Crackers*, the last of which was another Marx Brothers escapade. Harry Tierney created the score for *Kid Boots*, which starred Eddie Cantor in 1923, and *Rio Rita*, a spectacle that helped open the new Ziegfeld Theater on Sixth Avenue in 1927; the music of still another Eddie Cantor triumph, *Whoopee*, was the work of Walter Donaldson.

The neophytes of Tin Pan Alley, as well as its experienced hands, were now directing their main interest and attention through Broadway channels. Of these newcomers none was more productive in the 1920's than the team of De Sylva, Brown, and Henderson. Before joining forces as a trio of songwriters and coming to Broadway, each of the men had individually achieved Tin Pan Alley renown. Buddy De Sylva began writing lyrics while he was still going to college, some of which interested Al Jolson, who interpolated them in his Winter Garden shows. When De Sylva received his first Tin Pan Alley royalty check—it read sixteen thousand dollars—he decided to drop college and pursue his songwriting future more actively. He found a job at Remick's, in whose employ he wrote lyrics for George Gershwin's first musical comedy *La, La, Lucille*, in 1919. In the next few years De Sylva provided words for the music of Kern, Victor Herbert, Gershwin, and many others. His biggest hits included Kern's "Look for the Silver Lining," Herbert's "A Kiss in the Dark," Gershwin's "Somebody Loves Me," Louis Silvers' "April Showers," and "If You Knew Susie" (the last was an Eddie Cantor specialty and was one of the rare instances in which De Sylva wrote his own music).

Lew Brown worked for the publishing house of Albert von Tilzer. There for a number of years he wrote lyrics to Albert von Tilzer's melodies. These included: "I'm the Lonesomest Gal in Town" in 1912; the World War I ballad "I May Be Gone for a Long, Long Time"; the nonsense song "Oh, By Jingo"; and "I Used to Love You." After World War I, Lew Brown's lyrics were set by composers other than Von Tilzer.

In 1922, his lyric "Georgette" (which Ted Lewis and his band introduced that year in the *Greenwich Village Follies*) had a melody by Ray Henderson.

Henderson had studied music at the Chicago Conservatory of Music, and while there he supported himself by playing popular piano with jazz bands and at parties. Occasionally he appeared in vaudeville in an act that included an Irish tenor and a Jewish comedian. Finally arriving at the decision that his forte was composing music, Henderson came to New York City and for a while worked as Leo Feist's song plugger. After that he worked as staff pianist and arranger for Fred Fisher and later on for Shapiro-Bernstein. It was Bernstein who encouraged Henderson to concentrate on songwriting and arranged for Lew Brown to work with him. Their first collaboration, "Georgette," was a minor success. After 1922, Henderson collaborated with other lyricists. With Mort Dixon and Billy Rose he wrote "That Old Gang of Mine," which was published by Irving Berlin in 1923 and introduced that year in the *Ziegfeld Follies* by Van and Schenck. For a number of months this song sold thirty thousand copies a day regularly. "Alabamy Bound," with words by Buddy De Sylva and Bud Green, sold more than a million copies following its publication in 1925. "Five Feet Two, Eyes of Blue" and "I'm Sitting on Top of the World"—both of which also appeared in 1925—also did extraordinarily well, the latter particularly after Al Jolson adopted it as one of his favorites.

When George Gershwin left the *Scandals* in 1924 to concentrate on musical comedies, George White engaged the team of De Sylva, Brown, and Henderson to replace him. Though Henderson had previously worked with both De Sylva and with Brown, the *Scandals of 1925* was the first time that the three men worked as a creative unit. It was truly an unusual combination. While De Sylva and Brown were lyricists and Henderson a composer, each member provided the other two with significant guidance, advice, and ideas; it could truly be said that each of their songs was a three-way collaboration, in the strictest meaning of that term.

De Sylva, Brown, and Henderson hit their full creative stride in several editions of the *Scandals*, with songs like "The Birth of the Blues," "Black Bottom," "Lucky Day," and "The Girl Is You." While employed by George White, De Sylva, Brown, and Henderson also planted their feet more solidly in Tin Pan Alley by forming their own publishing outfit that issued not only their stage music but also a series of hit songs not intended for any specific production, such as "It All Depends on You" in 1926 and "Just a Memory" in 1927.

During the year of 1927, George White produced no new edition of the *Scandals*. This was the year that De Sylva, Brown, and Henderson chose to invade musical comedy. This debut took place with *Good News*, one of the year's leading box-office attractions, a musical show reflecting the fascination of the 1920's for college life and its shenanigans. Among its principal songs were "The Varsity Drag," the title number "Good News," and "The Best Things in Life Are Free"—the last of which provided the title for the screen biography of De Sylva, Brown, and Henderson in 1956.

In *Hold Everything*, in 1928, De Sylva, Brown, and Henderson turned from college to boxing. In *Follow Through*, in 1929, they invaded the world of country clubs and golf. In *Flying High*, in 1930, they turned to air pilots and aviation. Each show had its quota of important song hits. The cream of the crop were: "You're the Cream in My Coffee"; "Button Up Your Overcoat"; "You Are My Lucky Star"; "Thank Your Father"; and "Wasn't It Beautiful While It Lasted?"

Another significant neophyte to emerge from Tin Pan Alley and achieve his full creative powers on Broadway was Vincent Youmans. Like Kern and Gershwin, he may well be regarded as a Max Dreyfus discovery. Twenty-two-year-old Youmans was the composer of a single published song when Max Dreyfus took him under his wing at Harms by employing him as staff pianist and song plugger. Youmans had been educated to be an engineer, and just before World War I he worked as a clerk in a Wall Street brokerage house. His ambition to become a popular composer was first nurtured when, as a navy man, he wrote and produced shows for naval personnel. One of the numbers he wrote during this period became popular with army and navy bands and was frequently played throughout the war. But after the war it became an even greater favorite outside the armed forces when Youmans adapted the melody for the song "Hallelujah."

How valuable Youmans regarded his apprenticeship under Max Dreyfus in Tin Pan Alley was proved by his own statement that "in less than a year I got something that money couldn't buy." He was talking about experiences as a song salesman that taught him first hand some of the secrets that made a song "tick" with the public. He then wrote his first musical-comedy score in collaboration with Paul Lannin, *Two Little Girls in Blue*. Ira Gershwin wrote all of the lyrics, and through Ira, Youmans was able to bring his music to George Gershwin's notice. George, impressed with what he heard, used his influence to get producer Alex A. Aarons to mount it on Broadway. The show opened on May 3, 1922, ran for more than a year, and yielded a modest hit song in "Oh Me, Oh My, Oh You." Youmans was on his way.

In 1923 came *Wildflower* for which Otto Harbach and Oscar Hammerstein II wrote book and lyrics; its score was a joint effort by Youmans and Herbert Stothart. *Wildflower* was an even greater box-office success than *Two Little Girls in Blue*. It ran for almost five hundred performances, and out of it came not one but two song hits, "Bambalina" and the title number.

Between 1925 and 1927, Youmans' two greatest stage triumphs, and two finest scores, made him one of the giant figures in the American musical theater. *No, No, Nanette*, in 1925, ran a year on Broadway, enjoyed over six hundred and fifty performances in London, and was seen throughout the rest of the civilized world in presentations by seventeen companies. Two of Youmans' standards were heard here: "Tea for Two" and "I Want to Be Happy." Two other Youmans standards—"Sometimes I'm Happy" and "Hallelujah"—were written for *Hit the Deck*, which opened on Broadway in 1927.

Hit the Deck was Youmans' last successful Broadway musical for which he wrote the entire score; but it was not the last of his Broadway productions for which he created song classics. In fact, one of his greatest fiascos—*Great Day*, which lasted only thirty-six performances—had no less than three Youmans gems: the title song, "More than You Know," and "Without a Song." *Smiles* in 1930 (sixty-three performances) introduced "Time on My Hands." *Through the Years* in 1932 (twenty performances) was the source of the title number—the composer's own favorite among his creations—and "Drums in My Heart." With *Take a Chance* the same year—for which Youmans wrote "Rise 'n

Shine"—Youmans finally was able to break his losing streak on Broadway. *Take a Chance* was a moderate success, but that success was not exclusively Youmans' since part of the score was the work of Richard A. Whiting.

Woman as Consumer: Advertising in the 1920s

by Stuart Ewen

Looking at the ads of the 1920s, one sees how the feminist demand for equality and freedom for women was appropriated into the jargon of consumerism. A classic example of commercialized feminism was a 1929 campaign in which the American Tobacco Company attempted "to induce women to smoke [cigarettes] in public places." George W. Hill, owner of American Tobacco, had contracted Edward Bernays to run the campaign, hoping to expunge the "hussy" label from women who smoked publicly. The smoking taboo among women, Bernays reasoned, was of deep psychological significance. Accordingly, he consulted the psychoanalyst, A. A. Brill, for advice. Brill's explanation was this:

> Some women regard cigarettes as symbols of freedom. . . . Smoking is a sublimation of oral eroticism; holding a cigarette in the mouth excites the oral zone. It is perfectly normal for women to want to smoke cigarettes. Further the first women who smoked probably had an excess of masculine components and adopted the habit as a masculine act. But today the emancipation of women has suppressed many of the feminine desires. More women now do the same work as men do. . . . Cigarettes, which are equated with men, become torches of freedom.

Brill's analysis, particularly his last statement, caught Bernays' imagination. "I found a way to help break the taboo against women smoking in public," he explained. "Why not a parade of women lighting torches of freedom—smoking cigarettes." Utilizing the feminist motif, and enlisting the support of "a leading feminist," Ruth Hale, Bernays had a contingent of cigarette-puffing women march in the 1929 Easter parade, down Fifth Avenue in New York. "Our parade of ten young women lighting 'torches of freedom' on Fifth Avenue on

Easter Sunday as a protest against woman's inequality caused a national stir," Bernays proclaimed. "Front-page stories in newspapers reported the freedom march in words and pictures."[1]

A "liberated" woman of the 1929 vintage appeared in ads such as this one for Hoover vacuum cleaners:

> I was the woman whose husband gave her each Christmas some pretty trinket. The woman whose youth was slipping away from her too fast. The woman whose cleaning burdens were too heavy.... In one short year I have discovered that youth need not go swiftly—that cleaning duties need not be burdensome. For last Christmas my husband did give me a *Hoover*.[2]

Other ads drew even more directly from libertarian language. Toastmaster proclaimed itself "The *Toaster* that FREED 465,000 HOMES. . . . From ever watching, turning or burning toast."[3]

Although according to the ideology of American business, the American woman was to remain identified with the home, it was a home whose definition had been severely altered by the explosion in production and distribution. No longer the repository of craft and self-sustaining values, the home of the 1920s saw the massive influx of industrial goods and values which made most of those crafts superfluous. Advertisers were quite conscious of the competition between new manufactured goods and older forms of home products and production. Their ads, they felt, must dramatize this competition and ceremonialize the victory of the new life style. *Printers' Ink*, the center of theory for the ad industry, turned often to such a task. The journal reinforced the need to substitute factory-made consumables for many of the products which had been produced traditionally as a part of women's activities. Speaking of the practice of bread baking in the home, *Printers' Ink* writer G. A. Nichols described it as the "greatest impediment to progress" that the biscuit industry confronted. The biscuit campaigns, he asserted, must utilize "antidote" methods, debunking bread baking, while at the same time "it will have to educate the people into using more biscuits."[4]

Other ads gave a slight twist to such a strategy. Rather than debunk the old ways outright, they offered the possibility of fusing old preferences and practices with new products. After telling how Fels-Naptha Soap made the boiling of clothes unnecessary, one ad gave ambivalent respect to the *old* way of doing things:

> Boil clothes with Fels-Naptha if you wish. Women have been used to boiling clothes for so long that to many it seems too good to be true that Fels-Naptha makes the dirt let go in water of any temperature.[5]

Here, while the soap certainly reduced the drudgery of housework, it also introduced an altered world view. Where wives in earlier families had held much "finger knowledge" about the right and wrong way of doing things, ads like this for Fels-Naptha reduced their knowledge to superstition. Old preferences appeared as "respected" but at the same time *useless* prejudices of a bygone era. Judgment and knowledge had been removed as all but a ceremonial or "fanciful" aspect of women's home activity.

While some, like Christine Frederick, heralded the entry of the machine-age into the home as a "household revolution" which freed women from toil,[6] the reduction in time for housework seems to have been elusive for many women. Despite the introduction of goods and machines which tended to routinize and take the "guess work" out of housework, sociologist Ruth Lindquist found, in her 1930 studies of the American family, that housework was still seen by most women as a general source of fatigue and worry. These women felt no more relieved than in the premechanized days of house-tending. "It is something of a paradox," she observed, "that a deluge of labor-saving devices, new sources of power, more commercial agencies in the community and an actual decrease in the size of families have not prevented homemaking from being more than a fulltime job."[7]

* * * * *

As women were encouraged to accept a self-definition of home manager, their corporately defined role also required that they continually manage and define themselves. Within the widespread association of women and the home, the modern housewife remained wageless in her capacity of "quartermaster." Operating in what she was told was her "proper" sorts to ensure her livelihood. While the skills of her mother place, she was encouraged to maintain a barter system of and grandmother had been productive, her own were increasingly depicted as tricks of the flesh.

The women in ads were constantly observing themselves, ever self-critical. Throughout the twenties, a noticeable proportion of magazine ads directed at women depicted them looking into mirrors.[8] Even in the midst of efficient home management women were reminded that it was their appearance more than their organizational capacities which would ensure fidelity in particular and home security in general. Just as men were encouraged to cultivate their appearance to impress the boss, for women the imperative of beauty was directly linked to the question of job security—their *survival*, in fact, depended upon their ability to keep a husband, ads continually reminded women—or more precisely, the wage that he brought home to underwrite their managerial role. In one ad for a highly mechanized and rationalized Boone kitchen cabinet (replete with coffee mill, swinging stool, card index, daily reminder, timer-clock, disappearing ironing board, knife sharpener and bread board) women were assured that central to this kitchen work-place was a "mirror—for that hasty glance." It was taken for granted that personal appearance was a central category of their job.[9]

Just as the modern woman was expected to spend the family income in making the home, sociologists Groves and Ogburn noted that she also had to "decide how to spend her personality . . . to bring the family and herself the greatest quantity of satisfaction."[10] Her personality and looks were integrated into her other multifarious commodified skills of survival and were posed as the way to vie in a world where her concrete productive capacities had nearly evaporated, and where "keen and critical" glances constantly threatened her. As her homemaking skills had been reconstituted into a process of accumulating mass-produced possessions, her sexuo-economic capacities were reinforced on a commercial plane. An ad for Woodbury Soap (1922) offered women "the possession of a beautiful skin" which might arm them to meet a hostile world "proudly—confidently—without fear."[11] Another Woodbury ad warned women that "a man expects to find daintiness, charm, refinement in the woman he knows," and that in order to maintain his pleasure, a woman must constantly spend on her appearance. The ad went so far as to warn, "And when some unpleasant little detail mars this conception of what a woman should be—nothing quite effaces his involuntary disappointment."[12] Another ad suggested that life-long marriage and security were "beauty's reward" and might be effected by using Pompeian Night Cream.[13]

The real insecurity women felt about "what a woman should be" is clearly manipulated in these ads of the twenties. As woman's social role became increasingly defined in terms of consumption—a job which required no more than an obedience to the dictates of the marketplace—the core of the modern housewife's success lay in her ability to charm and bewitch. Naturally here too industry played an indispensable role. As one ad for Madame Surilla Perfume noted, "very often the subtlety of an exquisity odeur, and not the lady herself, does the befuddling."[14] From the field of social psychology, advertising had borrowed the notion of the *social self* as a prime weapon in its arsenal. Here people defined themselves in terms set by the approval or disapproval of others. In its particular economic definition of womanhood, consumer ideology relied heavily on this notion.

In the middle of her mechanically engineered kitchen, the modern housewife was expected to be overcome with the issue of whether her "self," her body, her personality were viable in the socio-sexual market that defined her job. Ads of the 1920s were quite explicit about this narcissistic imperative. They unabashedly used pictures of veiled nudes and women in auto-erotic stances to encourage self-comparison and to remind women of the primacy of their sexuality. A booklet advertising feminine beauty aids had on its cover a picture of a highly scrubbed, powdered and decorated nude. The message of the title was explicit: "Your Masterpiece—Yourself." Women were being educated to look at themselves as things to be created competitively against other women: painted and sculpted with the aids of the modern market.[15]

Carl B. Naether, an ad man whose contributions included the most widely-read study of the twenties on how to advertise to women, encouraged the implementation of such tactics in advertising. Using an ad for pearls as an example, Naether discussed the message that the picture conveyed. The illustration showed a woman wearing a breast-length strand of pearls. With one hand she fondled her bosom. According to Naether, this represented an effective way of making women self-conscious about their bodies and of directing this self-consciousness toward consumption. "They [the pearls] center attention on those parts of the feminine body which they encircle and touch," he explained. "Thus," he continued, the ad "ingeniously compares women with these precious adornments, attributing to the former the qualities possessed by the latter." Locating female beauty in the realm of consumable objects, Naether argued, the ad would elicit "feelings of vanity and pride," which were central to the sexually competitive nature of the modern woman.[16] Sensuality had been reformulated into something resembling the cash nexus.

Even women well into motherhood were assured by advertisers that they might maintain the kind of youthful beauty that would guarantee their social security. H. W. Gossard Corsets could preserve "that line of beauty which girlhood claims as its own—that curve which Hogarth the artist pronounces the most beautiful in all creation . . . that line which, curving in gently at the waist, sweeps in graceful rhythm over the hip and down kneeward." Ads like this one used romantic and literary prose to simulate a seduction, suggesting to women that as they were being productively displaced by the marvels of the machine age, they might rely on their trump card, aesthetic supremacy. Thus a Gossard Corset might secure for women, who had undergone both childbirth and years of housekeeping, a body which would maintain Hogarth's raptures: a "line which makes woman's form the most perfect on earth."[17]

The pursuit of beauty through consumption was numbered among the modern skills of survival for women. While married women in fact entered the labor market with increasing frequency, the dominant ideology told them to look homeward for their proper role. Thus, there was a tension between women as wage earners and the ideal of *woman* which was essentially wageless. Separating men from women around the issue of who should bring in the wage, the advertising ideology brought them together through commodity-based sexuality. This was where the wage process was reconciled with a home which still sustained itself on a barter system.

Still bound to a patriarchal yoke, American women faced a level of insecurity which made ads for youth, beauty and sensuality an effective and meaningful part of their environment. Marketing research of the twenties seems to bear this out. One survey, done in small Midwestern towns where wives were likely to be actually home-bound while husbands brought in a wage, reflects the receptivity toward ads. Performed in nine towns in Kansas, Missouri, Nebraska, and Iowa, the survey showed that in 1926 a great majority of women said that they paid a "good" or "great deal" of attention to advertising. Their predilection was strongly in favor of the national ads seen in magazines over the local ads of newspapers.[18] Divested of survival capacities of her own, advertising's woman relied on commodities to secure a social bond with a family which was losing its productive intrarelationship.

For the modern woman the alleged managerial responsibility of consumption had little objective content, and the survival tactic of allurement became appended to it as the most conspicuous form of self-definition. Now even mothers must rely on Palmolive Soap's school-girl skin in order to ensure the support of the entire family, children included. One ad, with Oedipal implications, showed a beautiful young mother submitting to her boy-child's scrutiny and pleasure. Through the use of Palmolive, women were told, they could maintain themselves as "His first Love."[19] As ads documented the transition from the productive-knowledge of traditional home activity to the discipline of industrial capitalism, women's creative roles were increasingly displaced. The advertised duties of the *wife* became intertwined with the last home industry—marital sex.

> Woman's deep-seated instinct urging her to the use of perfumes is a manifestation of a fundamental law of biology. *The first duty of woman is to attract.* . . . It does not matter how clever or independent you may be, if you fail to influence the men you meet, consciously or unconsciously, you are not fulfilling your fundamental duty as a woman. . . .[20]

Despite the managerial lingo which had come to be applied to womanhood, the inadequacy and insecurity of such an "industrialized" role was reflected in the overbearing call for sexual skills. If consumption management was a *role* of work, sexuality was, for women, a *duty* of leisure. The two, work and leisure, could not be separated. Consumption provided an idiom for the unity of the two.

1. Edward Bernays, *Biography of an Idea: Memoirs of a Public Relations Counsel* (1965), pp. 386-387
2. *Saturday Evening Post*, December 14, 1929.
3. *Saturday Evening Post*, December 7, 1929.
4. G. A. Nichols, "When Your Customers Are Competitors," *Printers' Ink*, CXI (May 13, 1920), p. 52.
5. *Ladies' Home Journal*, May 1922.
6. Christine McGaffey Frederick, *Selling Mrs. Consumer* (1929),

p. 169.

7. Ruth Lindquist, *The Family in the Present Social Order* (1931), pp. 43, 49.

8. In an informal survey of *Ladies' Home Journal* and *Saturday Evening Post* ads through the 1920s, I have found that between eight and ten ads per issue depict a woman at or looking into a mirror. Many of these ads are *not* for cosmetic products.

9. *Ladies' Home Journal*, March 1926.

10. Ernest Groves and William Fielding Ogburn, *American Marriage and Family Relationships* (1928), p. 51.

11. *Ladies' Home Journal*, January 1922.

12. *Ladies' Home Journal*, May 1922.

13. *Ladies' Home Journal*, January 1922.

14. Carl A. Naether, *Advertising to Women* (1928), p. 252.

15. *Ibid.*, p. 248.

16. *Ibid.*, p. 129.

17. *Ibid.*, p. 100.

18. Mary E. Hoffman, *The Buying Habits of Small-Town Women* (1926), p. 11.

19. *Ladies' Home Journal*, July 1928.

20. Denys Thompson, *Voices of Civilisation: An Enquiry into Advertising* (1943), p. 132. This copy is from a perfume advertisement.

Smoking and Dancing as Symbols of Liberation

by Paula S. Fass

Smoking was perhaps the one most potent symbol of young woman's testing of the elbow room provided by her new sense of freedom and equality. Prostitutes and women in liberated bohemian and intellectual sets had been known to flaunt their cigarettes publicly and privately before the twenties. But in respectable middle-class circles, and especially among young women, smoking, like rouging, was simply not done. Throughout the twenties, smoking could still provoke heated commentary, and for many young women, to smoke in public was a welcome form of notoriety. Although young women in college did not initiate the smoking habit, they increasingly took advantage of the cigarette as a symbol of liberation and as a means of proclaiming their equal rights with men. More importantly, within the college community they had the support of peer-group opinion. Among the young, smoking for women became widely accepted during the twenties, and while smoking remained an issue, as the decade wore on it became an acceptable and familiar habit among college women.[1]

Smoking is not a sexual activity in itself. In the abstract, it is morally neutral. In the context of the specific values of American society, however, it was both morally value-laden and sexually related. Like cosmetics, smoking was sexually suggestive and associated with disreputable women or with bohemian types who self-consciously rejected traditional standards of propriety and morality. College administrators objected to smoking because it undermined an ideal of proper female behavior and decency. As the Dean of Women at Ohio State University noted, smoking was simply not "done in the best circles," and it was, in the words of the Dean of Rhode Island State College, "an unladylike act." In 1927, when four girls were dismissed from a female seminary in the Midwest, the administration admitted that smoking did not make them "bad girls" but claimed that such behavior would undermine commonly accepted standards of decency and might lead to other socially objectional practices.[2] The implication was clear. The objection to women's smoking was based on traditional criteria of proper conduct for women; once one of these was questioned, all of them would be questioned.

The right to smoke was denied to women as part of the double standard of morality. The implicit fear was that smoking would have an immoral effect on women because it removed one further barrier from the traditional differentiation of the roles and behaviors of the sexes. Smoking implied a promiscuous equality between men and women and was an indication that women could enjoy the same vulgar habits and ultimately also the same vices as men. It further eroded a tradition that held women to be morally superior to men. Moreover, the kind of woman who smoked in the period before the twenties was disreputable or defiant, and smoking was therefore associated with immorality. Thus, one correspondent of the UCLA paper objected to popular cigarette ads featuring women smoking because they lowered the moral "tone of the paper." Those who objected to smoking could give no specific moral definition to the habit. They were forced instead to argue that smoking was simply "unladylike."[3] The opponents of smoking were ultimately helpless when the young rejected the insincerity and dubious distinctions of such conventions.

These associations and conventions underlay the almost unanimous reaction to what became a *cause célèbre* in the twenties, the lifting of the no-smoking ban at Bryn Mawr College. That action brought the issue out into the open and reflected the growing acceptance of smoking in the college community. When in 1925 President Marion Edwards Park, in response to pressure from the student body, opened smoking rooms at various points on the campus, the day of the smoking young woman had dawned. The Bryn Mawr gesture was, of course, more symptomatic than revolutionary, but it was important nevertheless because it provided official sanction to what had been unofficially countenanced by the peer group and because it came in response to community demands. That it occurred at Bryn Mawr, one of the bastions of prestige and respectability, made the action all the more powerful in the public imagination. Bryn Mawr was, in fact, not the first school to permit women to smoke on campus, but President Park had done her deed with a flourish of publicity and well-poised liberality. Similar requests for smoking rights by Vassar and Wellesley students and by women at Brown had been rejected by school officials.[4]

Moreover, Park's action came at a time when most schools had strong anti-smoking ordinances. At Mt. Holyoke and Smith, for example, the penalty for smoking on or near the campus was suspension. At Nebraska Wesleyan Teachers College women who smoked were refused certificates of teaching. Indeed, some schools that did not have such regulations because the issue had not heretofore been raised began to impose them in the twenties. Rules have no rationale when the behavior they are meant to control does not exist, and smoking had not been a problem. Vassar College, which had no anti-smoking rule before, imposed one in 1925, and in 1926 so did the University of California at Berkeley.[5]

Park's liberal gesture provoked consternation among deans of women throughout the country. In effect, she had given official recognition to the prevalance of the habit among college women. The reactions were predictable, for they reflected the disparity between traditional perceptions and newly accepted habits. Administrators reacted by linking custom to morality. The young severed custom from morality and regarded the antipathy to smoking for women as a meaningless convention, long overdue for revision. At Kansas State Teachers College, President W. A. Brandenberg reacted with anger: "Nothing has occurred in higher education that has so shocked our sense of social decency as the action at Bryn Mawr." At Northwestern University, the Dean of Women announced that should a girl be found smoking anywhere on the campus, in town, or even at her home, she would be summarily dismissed for immoral behavior. In her view, "nice girls" did not smoke. "Any girl I catch smoking anywhere and at any time will not be permitted to remain in college," declared the Dean at Rhode Island State College after dismissing two girls who were caught. When the Dean of Women at Minnesota heard about the action at Bryn Mawr, she quickly formulated a policy; "Smoke and leave school." When asked whether she would ever follow Bryn Mawr's lead and permit women at the University of Minnesota to smoke, Dean E. E. Nichols answered unequivocally, "Never." So pressing did the urgency of the issue now appear that in 1925 the presidents of the Eastern women's colleges met to discuss smoking rules.[6]

But the young rejected the standards of propriety that governed the actions of the administrations. They overwhelmingly accepted the right of women to smoke in the 1920's, and smoking received the approval of most college papers. It was probably not true everywhere and among all youths: women at Coe College, Iowa, for example, were still shocked when a female guest lecturer smoked publicly and with abandon.[7] But it became increasingly true at the larger nondenominational schools for women, in coeducational universities, and even in high schools. Starting first in the East and then becoming general on the West Coast, the new freedom penetrated to the heart of the Midwest, and even into the South where women were probably viewed more traditionally than elsewhere. At the University of Texas, for example, between 1920 and 1925 there was a marked increase in smoking among coeds and an important liberalization of opinion among male and female students about whether smoking was wrong for women. By 1927, North Carolina's Duke *Chronicle* carried a large ad for Old Golds in which two young women were portrayed eagerly enjoying their smokes. By the end of the decade, smoking for women had become legitimate. When women were given permission to smoke at Stanford in 1927, the editor of the UCLA newspaper noted that only six years before the women's editor at Stanford had caused a scandal and was nearly dismissed for even suggesting that women should be allowed to smoke.[8]

It is impossible to know how many young women smoked habitually or occasionally during the twenties. Precise statistics are unavailable, but it is clear that smoking was becoming more popular among college women. At Ohio State one-third of the coeds admitted smoking at least occasionally, and an ad-hoc survey of weekending women at Bowdoin College revealed that there were as many women who smoked one brand, Luckies, as all those who did not smoke at all. One knowledgeable fraternity leader at Rhode Island State College declared, "Practically all the girls smoke."[9] But this seems unlikely. In many ways, knowing how many women smoked is unnecessary. Smoking is no more a necessary expression of female freedom than sexual intercourse alone is a gauge of sexual activity. More important than the extent of smoking was the increasing sense that women could smoke if they chose to and the breaking away by the young from traditional proscriptions governing female behavior and connecting smoking with immorality. In 1925, noting that the Dean of Women at the University of Texas was surprised and outraged to find that coeds were smoking, the editor of the *Daily Illini* chided, "The girls are beginning to smoke! Good Gracious, Annabelle! They have been smoking for months and years. One only has to be a boy and answer the continued demands for 'a drag' or a cigarette to know that smoking has with the fair young co-eds long ceased to be a practice. It is an art, and one of their most perfectly practiced ones. All co-eds at the University do not smoke but neither do all the boys." He explained that women who did not smoke failed to do so either because they did not like the taste, or because they did not yet consider it "quite lady-like," but certainly "morals never came in for consideration on this score. It is taste, social and olfactory." Furthermore, those girls who did not smoke themselves rarely "score anyone else for smoking."[10]

Women and men on the campuses of the twenties proclaimed that women had a right to smoke if they pleased: "If a man can enjoy his coke more by smoking as he drinks it, why isn't it logical to assume that a woman can enjoy hers more when it is accompanied by a cigarette?" asked one woman correspondent at Illinois. "Why shouldn't a woman have a taste for cigarettes just as a man has? It is not the smoking that breaks down the bonds of convention between men and women . . . a woman can command just as much respect with a cigarette in her mouth as without." At New York University women claimed their rights by announcing that they would hold a smoker rather than a traditional tea. The Dean was outraged and prohibited the event, but the women went ahead with their plans anyway. Blanchard and Manasses found that 80% of the young women they questioned approved of smoking for women. In marked contrast, only 26% of the parents approved.[11]

Except for occasional facetious comments about lost male prerogatives, women's smoking generally received the approval of college editors on two grounds. In the first place, the papers took a critical attitude toward all attempts to reform or regulate conduct in the name of moral uplift. Invariably hostile to the pseudo-reforms that abounded in the twenties with the prevailing fears about moral degeneration, editors thus defended the rights of men or women to smoke as an expression of their right to self-determination in morals and behavior. Editors were quick to point out that those who objected to drinking would soon find in smoking another fertile realm for regulation. Smoking for men and women was

Smoking and Dancing as Symbols of Liberation 177

for the young a personal issue of preference, not morality. The editor of the *Daily Illini* rebuked those who would regulate smoking among women and asserted that the silly "antismoking attempts of moral guardians, usually self appointed, to paint the nasty weed in crimson stain of immorality are a great joke." "Smoking by women," the editor at Louisiana State observed, "is entirely a question of attitude, of personal taste, and possibly of hygiene." The coed, he noted, "reasons quite logically that there is nothing in cigarette smoking which is degrading or immoral, and that, in the final analysis, there is very little difference between a man's smoking and a woman's smoking." Attempts to legislate this form of behavior, like all moral reforms, he continued, were "worse than useless," because they would only be an added inducement for women to flaunt their defiance.[12]

Second, the specific question of women's smoking was defended on the broad grounds of female equality and a woman's inherent right to indulge her tastes just as men had always done. "In this day," one Illinois correspondent asserted, "one has a perfectly good right to ask why men should be permitted to smoke while girls are expelled for doing it." In this, editors and correspondents went beyond the smoking issue to object to discriminatory regulations of all kinds that restricted women's freedom to a larger degree than men's. "Paternalism in colleges," the editor of the *Ohio State Lantern* announced, "is nowhere as pronounced as maternalism. It seems that in nearly every coeducational college in the country, the regulations affecting co-eds are far more drastic and far more circumscribing than the regulations for men. . . . Is this 'new freedom' and 'equality of the sexes' a chimera? Are men really better able to take care of themselves than women? Is the co-ed an inferior sort of person who must have a guardian as if she were feeble-minded or insane? Almost every coeducational school in the country answers 'No' in its classrooms but 'Yes' in its regulations." The double standard, not completely dead even among the young, was quickly losing its theoretical rationale and with that its efficacy as a guide to behavior. The *Barnard Bulletin,* always quick to defend women's rights and equality in intellectual matters, made clear the relationship between intellectual and social equality. Noting that "instructors in any state normal college in Nebraska will be refused leaves of absence to study or attend the Universities of Columbia, Chicago and Northwestern hereafter, because the testimony of those who have been students and the news items in the daily press show that cigarette smoking is common among women in these institutions," the editor announced that although women had not yet been spanked and sent to bed, "they were being cloistered from tobacco and research."[13] The editor had made a telling point. How could one hope to separate the classroom from the campus?

Women in the twenties had appropriated the right to indulge in a previously tabooed behavior. Noting the revolution in women's behavior that had taken place in the span of ten years between 1920 and 1930, Blanchard and Manasses observed: "The 1920 co-ed, if her spirit was bold, may have tried a cigarette or two, surreptitiously, but she certainly could not have risked her reputation by smoking in public, and such a gesture would have been considered serious enough to have secured her dismissal from the halls of learning. To expel women students for smoking in this year of grace would sadly deplete the college and university enrollments. . . . She does not even need to feel defiant about it; it is no longer a sign of adolescent rebellion against authority, but a piece of completely commonplace behavior." By 1933 Eunice Fuller Barnard found that cigarettes had already become "outdated" as symbols of woman's new freedom.[14]

Youth in the twenties denied that certain kinds of behavior were worse for women than for men and they rejected the notion that smoking involved a question of morality or propriety. Undoubtedly, many women began to smoke in the twenties because it was a glamorous affectation and somewhat naughty. They thus welcomed the sexual connotation that lingered around smoking and incorporated such sexual suggestiveness as part of their right.[15] By the end of the decade what had been risqué became merely another sphere of permissible behavior and, like the rights to sexual expression, it had been appropriated by women in their newer sense of freedom and the expanded concept of social equality.

In the twenties, young men and women danced whenever the opportunity presented itself. Unquestionably the most popular social pastime, dancing was, of all potentially questionable and morally related behavior, the least disreputable in the view of the young. For most youths dancing was not even questionable but a thoroughly respectable and almost compulsory form of socializing. Even at denominational schools, where dancing continued to be regarded as morally risky by officials, students clamored for a relaxation of the older bans as they asked officials to give up outdated "prejudiced feelings" and respond to "the bending of current public opinion."[16] A dance was an occasion. It was a meeting ground between young men and women. It was a pleasurable recreation. But above all it was a craze.

The dancers were close, the steps were fast, and the music was jazz. And because popular forms of dancing were intimate and contorting, and the music was rhythmic and throbbing, it called down upon itself all the venom of offended respectability. Administrative officials as well as women's clubs and city fathers found the dancing provocative and indecent and tried at least to stop the young from engaging in its most egregious forms, if not from the dances entirely.[17] But the young kept on dancing.

They started during the war years, and they danced through the decade. Dancing would leave its stamp on the twenties forever, and jazz would become the lingering symbol for an era. But whatever its symbolic value during the twenties and thereafter, dancing and jazz were forms of recreation, even a means of peer-group communication, that youth appropriated to itself.[18] Dancing was, in the words of one survey of student life, the "chief social diversion of college men and women," and school officials unanimously acknowledged that it was the most popular and universally indulged social activity. Almost all fraternity and university social affairs revolved around mixed dancing. Advertisements for dancing instruction appeared in most college papers. At the high schools, too, dancing was a prime occasion for socializing. One simply had to know how to dance to be sociable, and to be popular one had to know how to dance well. The ability to dance was both a sign of belonging to the world of youth and a necessary accomplishment if one wished to take part in the activities of that world. "I adore to dance" was a common remark among high-school girls. When asked what her favorite recreation was, the Vice-President of the Associated Women Students at UCLA answered quickly, "Of course, I adore dancing, who doesn't?" The fact that a man was a "divine dancer" made him an attractive date and added much to his social reputation, whatever his other possible assets or liabilities.[19]

The dances the young enjoyed most were the ones most criticized by adults. The shimmy and the toddle, which had become popular during the war, started the decade and the young on their dancing way. They were followed by the collegiate, the charleston, the black bottom, the tango. The dances brought the bodies and faces of the partners too dangerously close for the comfort of the older folks. Dimmed lights added to the mood. Because of the novelty of the rhythms and the "indecent" motions involved, most of the adverse comments came at the beginning of the decade. As the era progressed, less was said, but not because the dancing stopped. The dancing went on, probably becoming more and not less popular and certainly more hectic.[20] While the steps changed in fad fashion and increased in variety, they remained basically the same—exciting, sensuous, and always to the accompaniment of jazz. The older generation was no less opposed, but by working through the public opinion of the young they found a means of controlling what they considered its most indecent extremes. The young tempered the extremes to meet the adult criticism, but they were really calling the tune.

In the early twenties, college papers, noting administrative opposition to the dancing forms, advised students to reform themselves to forestall administrative interference. Student organizations, especially women's leagues, put the most offensive steps under interdict. But while the editor of the *Daily Illini*, for example, called the shimmy "that insult to our whole moral code," he was careful to distinguish it from the less extreme toddle, which he, like the Women's League and the Student Council, endorsed.[21] Above all, no editor was willing to condemn dancing in general or the jazz music that accompanied it. These they approved as wholesome pastimes.

Some letters to the editor in the early period took issue with the whole mode of dancing and observed that the toddle as well as the shimmy undermined respectability. Such dancing, critics noted, and jazz music generally, had once been known only in the "Black and Tan districts of Chicago or the East Tenderloin in New York." A college professor called jazz degenerate because it "expresses hysteria, incites idleness, revelry, dissipation, destruction, discord and chaos."[22] In the long run, those who believed all kinds of jazz dancing were offensive proved more perceptive, for once the rhythm of the music was accepted and approved as it was by the young, the dancing forms appropriate to the music logically followed. By accepting the sensuous and exciting rhythms of modern jazz and its well-known association with the least savory parts of the cities, the young accepted as respectable what their elders logically could not, the excitement and those very qualities of indecency that they formally disdained.

The young made jazz music and jazz dancing a part of their social world and identified with the jazz medium. It became not dancing itself that demonstrated conformity to the peer group but a certain kind of dancing. As a would-be versifier put it,

> Jazz and the bunch jazz with you
> Dance and you're by yourself,
> The mob thinks it's jake
> To shimmy and shake,
> For the old fashioned stuff's on the shelf.

"How many men," asked a *Daily Illini* correspondent, "would take a modest, sedate looking girl to a dance and brook the comment of his friends, 'Does Miss Innocence Toddle?'" In an editorial entitled "Heaven Protect Jazz," the *Illini* observed: "A college existence without jazz would be like a child's Christmas without Santa Claus." "Jazz conglomerates are second nature to us now. We have them after every meal in every fraternity and boarding house, on scores of phonographs during the off hours of the morning, at the movies in the afternoons and evenings, at the game, in the music shops, at the dance halls. . . . Without the assurance of jazz from September to June it would be folly to matriculate." College students, the *Ohio State Lantern* noted, were "jazz inebriates."[23]

As with the use of cosmetics, there were within the larger approval of jazz music and jazz dancing limits and standards of respectability consciously set by the young. "Students as a whole do not tolerate dances that savor of the indecent," an Ohio State editor declared. Reinforced by continuous administrative threats, the young carved out a realm of propriety within the jazz medium which only the ultra set on campus dared bypass. At the University of California at Los Angeles, the student editor noted that there were no rules or restrictions on dancing imposed by the administration: "Student sentiment is the only restriction we have, but it has never thus far failed to maintain a very desirable plane of conduct. Of our own accord, through several years of custom, we have built up a tradition for thoroughly snappy, thoroughly wholesome dance." The editor went on to warn students not to jeopardize this self-control. "Let's plan to make all measures unnecessary." After chaperones at Louisiana State caused a rumpus by condemning the favored dancing forms, the administration decided that they would no longer "bear the responsibility of censoring improper dancing." In response, students successfully formed a "committee of representative students . . . to formulate a set of 'self-chaperoning' rules, thus making each student the other's chaperone and responsible for his own actions." And when the editor at Duke University urged the Methodist board of governors to ease regulations and approve university-sponsored dances, he promised that students would responsibly patrol themselves: "Dancing is not degrading. . . . To be sure there are steps which could never inspire poetry, or music or grace, but they can be removed. A standard could be set and anything that fell below the standard could be removed."[24]

By agreeing to regulate themselves, the young defined the medium within which that regulation took place. They did not conform to the administrative view of what kind of dancing and music was aesthetically attractive or morally wholesome. They took upon themselves the task of defining the sphere, and within that sphere they imposed regulations of their own. At the University of Minnesota, for example, couples who were dancing in an objectionable fashion were given a card, distributed by the Women's Self-Government Association and the Association of Minnesota Upperclassmen, which read, "We do not dance cheek-to-cheek, shimmy or dance other extreme dances. You must not. A second note will cause your public removal from the hall. Help keep us the Minnesota Standard." Occasional disregard of the rules on the dance floor was noted and condemned in the papers with the wise warning that should such behavior continue and become general the whole enterprise would be endangered. At Ohio State, an editorial entitled "Watch Your Step" made this clear: "Recent rumpus over dancing should make clear to students that they are being watched, constantly, closely and critically."[25]

The administration had not left the young unguarded. Rather, they gave them the freedom to censure their own behavior. At Illinois, officials responded to allegations of indecent dancing by imposing a tight chaperone system, which the student newspaper, noting "Authority's Debut at Dances," condemned as "little more than a police system," but which it wisely recognized was a drastic measure to be followed by even worse unless the young took stock of their own conduct.

"If the first show of authority does not impress itself sufficiently to throw the right amount of scare into the few who have made its interference necessary," then there would be a move to abandon all dancing. Even those few who would effectively reject all standards had to conform if this most prized of social sports was to survive. At Louisiana State, the editor similarly warned students that the system of self-regulation was by no means "the last resort" and that "a desperate faculty" would find other means "to make its naughty students behave."[26]

By agreeing to impose rules against extreme varieties of dancing, the young had, however, approved what authorities could not logically approve and what, consistent with an older standard, most denominational schools continued to resist—the jazz medium that was offensive to traditional concepts of decency. The young had, in effect, redefined what was proper according to their own tastes. Dancing for the youth of the twenties was not merely a pleasurable recreation; it was a way of assimilating to their own uses one of the truly new artistic forms of twentieth-century America. It was a form that expressed the uninhibited quality of the new century, its accelerated pace and attention to sensuous movement. The young were surely not alone in their approval, but in identifying with jazz, they both expressed their right to make the choice and as significantly (and symbolically) gave respectability to the content. What was involved was style and sensibility, not philosophy or ideology, but it was a profound redirection all the same. In the name of decency the young mellowed the rhythms and smoothed out some of jazz's more raw passions, transforming the rude into the stylish. But the jazz embraced by the young in the twenties was also an expression and an outlet for the new tempo of American culture, its heterogenous sources, and its more open sexuality.

1. For the heated debate about smoking in the early twenties, see, for example, the on-going discussion in the letters-to-the-editor column of the *Daily Illini*, Spring, 1920, especially April 14, 15, 16, 1920, and the editorials of April 15 and 17. Also, *Ohio State Lantern*, November 22, 1926; *Cornell Sun*, November 30, 1926, "Innocents Abroad."

2. *Ohio State Lantern*, November 30, 1925, p. 1; Dean of Rhode Island College, quoted in Duke *Chronicle*, December 17, 1924, "College Collections"; seminary incident cited in *Daily Illini*, April 14, 1920, letter to the editor. Dismissals or suspensions for smoking violations were frequent; see *New Student*, June 21, 1924, p. 6, for dismissal of three women at Smith College.

3. *UCLA Daily*, November 30, 1927, letter to the editor. See also

Daily Illini, April 17, 1920, letter to the editor, which denounces the tendency of putting women on pedestals and links this idealization to smoking bans, and April 15, 1920, letter to the editor, which asserts that smoking undermines an ideal of "pure womanhood"; also remarks by the Dean of Women at Rhode Island State College, quoted in Duke *Chronicle,* December 17, 1924, "College Collections."

At UCLA the dean asserted, "The question is not is it right or is it wrong for women to smoke, but rather, does smoking on the campus cast reflections upon the good name of the University? While smoking among women is becoming more and more common, as yet it is not accepted by the mass of people as the correct thing to do. . . . It is the duty of the students to uphold the ideals of the mass of the people"; *UCLA Daily,* October 14, 1927.

4. Barnard College, for example, had more liberal rules than those at Bryn Mawr, but they had not been similarly publicized; see *Barnard Bulletin,* April 24, 1924. At M.I.T., women had been given permission to smoke just prior to the action at Bryn Mawr; see *New Student,* October 28, 1925. For rejection of petitions at Vassar and Wellesley, see *New Student,* January 19, 1924, December 9, 1925; *Daily Illini,* January 26, 1926.

5. *New Student,* January 31, 1925, p. 1, January 19, 1924, January 10, 1925, p. 3, January 21, 1925, p. 1; *Cornell Sun,* November 29, 1926, "Innocents Abroad." Vassar lifted the ban on smoking the next year on petition by students; see *Daily Princetonian,* March 2, 1926.

6. Quoted in *New Student,* December 9, 1925, p. 3; *New Student,* October 28, 1925; quoted in *New Student,* December 9, 1925, p. 3; quoted in Duke *Chronicle,* December 17, 1924, "College Collections"; quoted in *Ohio State Lantern,* November 30, 1925, p. 1; quoted in *New Student,* December 9, 1925, p. 3. For Eastern college meeting, see *New Student,* October 28, 1925. As early as 1921, smoking was one of the topics discussed at a conference of deans of Western colleges at Berkeley. The deans agreed that they should do something before the problem became "serious"; see, LSU *Reveille,* November 25, 1921, p. 7. By 1925, the problem had become serious; see *Ohio State Lantern,* November 30, 1925, p. 1.

7. *New Student,* November 18, 1925, p. 1.

8. *UCLA Daily,* February 18, 1927; Duke *Chronicle,* October 10, 1927, for Old Golds ad. For prevalence of smoking, see C. M. Whitlow, "Attitudes and Behavior of High School Students," *American Journal of Sociology,* 40 (1935), 492; R. H. Edwards, J. M. Artman and Galen Fisher, *Undergraduates* (Garden City, N.Y., 1928), p. 181; *Daily Illini,* November 10, 1925. Brogan found that the frequency of women's smoking and the permissive attitude toward smoking increased significantly at the University of Texas, but that permissiveness still lagged behind Northern institutions. At the University of Chicago, the habit was more common and approved earlier than at the Southern school. Smoking at Texas increased in frequency from fifteenth to tenth among bad practices among women between 1922 and 1924. See A. P. Brogan, "Group Estimates of the Frequency of Misconduct," *International Journal of Ethics,* 34 (1923–24), 259–260, 266–270. By 1927, *The Reveille* of Louisiana State University, a Deep-South school, was remarking that coeds were learning the habit of "bumming" cigarettes just like their brothers; see February 26, 1927.

9. For Ohio State, see *New Student,* December 19, 1925, p. 1. For

similar results at Mr. Holyoke and Wellesley, *New Student*, November 18, 1925. For Bowdoin survey, *Cornell Sun*, February 22, 1927, "Innocents Abroad." Rhode Island State leader quoted in Duke *Chronicle*, December 17, 1924, "College Collections."

10. *Daily Illini*, November 10, 1925.

11. *Daily Illini*, April 12, 1924, letter to the editor; New York University incident reported in *UCLA Daily*, October 12, 1925; Phyllis Blanchard and Carlyn Manasses, *New Girls for Old* (New York, 1930), pp. 66, 68. In a referendum on smoking at Wellesley College, 80% of the women were in favor of allowing women to smoke; see *Daily Illini*, January 24, 1926.

12. *Daily Illini*, September 22, 1925; LSU *Reveille*, March 9, 1928. For lost male prerogative, see, for example, *UCLA Daily*, November 17, 1922; *Cornell Sun*, January 17, 1925, January 9, 1926; LSU *Reveille*, November 13, 1925. See also the interview of LSU cadets on the question of women's smoking in *The Reveille*, December 1, 1925, p. 5. On the whole, the attitudes were of humorous condescension and objections were largely limited to the fear that coeds would soon be bumming cigarettes. No one was morally outraged.

For general approval by male editors, see *Daily Princetonian*, March 2, 1926; *Daily Illini*, September 22, 1925, March 11, 1921. Also LSU *Reveille*, March 9, 1928, which links banning smoking with banning drinking. In fact, all smoking, for men as well as women, was prohibited at Syracuse early in the decade; see *Cornell Sun*, March 14, 1921. Most editors believed that women had a right to smoke but some still asserted that "most of them smoke simply because it has come to be considered smart and the thing to do. With them it is incense burned in worship of the god of fashion"; *Ohio State Lantern*, November 22, 1926.

13. *Daily Illini*, April 14, 1920, letter to the editor; *Ohio State Lantern*, August 19, 1925; *Barnard Bulletin*, February 24, 1922. At Rhode Island State College, students circulated a petition of remonstrance against school authorities who had dismissed coeds for smoking. The action, students believed, was patently unjust because it punished women for what male students could do with impunity; see Duke *Chronicle*, December 17, 1924, "College Collections."

14. Blanchard and Manasses, *New Girls*, p. 2; Eunice Fuller Barnard, "The New Freedom of the College Girl," *New York Times Magazine* (March 19, 1933), p. 8. See also "Youth in College," *Fortune*, 13 (1936) 99–102. According to Walter Buck, the decrease in the disapproval of smoking for women between 1923 and 1933 was significant, a change of 20%. Moreover, this was true of under-classmen, freshmen and sophomores, as well as seniors and juniors, indicating that the new approbation was already incorporated into the mores of high-school students; see "A Measurement of Changes in Attitudes and Interests of University Students Over a Ten-Year Period," *Journal of Abnormal and Social Psychology*, 31 (1936), 16. Brogan found that although there was a decided decline in the tendency to differentiate between what was bad for women and men, the double standard still lingered. Smoking, for example, was at all times still considered worse for women than for men, but the differences were narrowing; see A. P. Brogan, "Moral Valuations About Men and Women," *International Journal of Ethics*, 35 (1925), 120–121.

15. See the *Daily Illini*, April 14, 1925, letter to the editor: "Every

girl likes to appear just a bit daring and just a bit worse than she really is. To pretend a thing is not immoral yet unconventional is to invite her to do one of the things she likes best; breaking the conventions."

A history could be written about the changes in cigarette advertisements. Where at the beginning of the decade photos showed women in the same room while men smoked, by the end of the decade women were not only smoking themselves, but many ads concentrated on the act of men offering or lighting women's cigarettes. There were constant overtones of sexual intimacy. The association between cigarettes and sexuality was not overlooked by the advertisers. One ad for Camels (in the *American Mercury*) featured two young couples, in the chic Fitzgerald-Zelda manner, in close proximity, with the provocative title, "Pleasure Ahead," and continued, "Those who love life for its own sake instinctively choose the cigarette which gives them the greatest pleasure." By the late twenties, women, often starlets, were used as spokesmen for the cigarette brands and their sexual and languorous manners usually implied much more than that they merely indulged a taste for tobacco.

16. See petition by denominational University of Richmond students, in the Duke *Chronicle*, April 14, 1926, "Wayside Wares"; also, F. W. Reeves, *The Liberal Art Colleges* (Chicago, 1932), p. 403. At Duke, students voted overwhelmingly, 704 to 6, for university-sponsored dances; *The Chronicle*, December 1, 1926. Despite this, however, the Methodist board of governors refused to lift the official ban against the school sponsoring such events; see March 30, 1927. For popularity of dancing, see Blanchard and Manasses, *New Girls*, p. 16; Robert Cooley Angell, *The Campus* (New York, 1928), p. 165; Edwards *et al.*, *Undergraduates*, pp. 185–189. The investigators called dancing "the chief social diversion of college men and women" (p. 185). Newspaper after newspaper documents the fact that dancing was an invariable part of college life. At the University of Wisconsin, there were approximately 30 all-college dances and 80 fraternity dances sponsored each month; see *New Student*, January 31, 1925. The *Daily Illini* editor scolded students at the University of Michigan for permitting their dance fervor to interfere with attendance at a football game, both the dance and the game being scheduled for the same day; see February 14, 1923. See also the statement by the Dean of the University of Kansas in the Duke *Chronicle*, November 13, 1924, "College Collections."

The popularity of dancing was by no means restricted to the colleges. High-school students were avid disciples of the dance craze. In general, more girls than boys danced. According to Whitlow, of 623 students at a high school in Cheyenne Wells, Colorado, 53% of the girls and 27% of the boys danced frequently, and 32% of the girls and 29% of the boys danced occasionally; "Attitudes and Behavior of High School Students," 493.

Even by the 1930's, although the frequency of dancing had subsided, the popularity remained strong. Dancing was still the most desirable kind of social recreation. See Robert C. Angell, "The Trend Toward Greater Maturity Among Undergraduates Due to the Depression," *School and Society*, 38 (1932), 394.

Of all morally "bad" practices, dancing was consistently ranked least bad by men and women in Brogan's studies; see A. P. Brogan, "A Study of Statistical Ethics," *International Journal of Ethics*, 33 (1922–1923), 122–126. It was also the most frequently indulged by women, second only to gossip; see Brogan, "Group Estimates," 259. Among men, its frequency was slightly lower (262). See also Joseph K. Johnson and Kingsley Davis, "An Attempt to Discover Change in Moral Attitudes of High School Students," *International Journal of Ethics*, 44 (1934), 244–251. According to the investigators, dancing was ranked least bad of all practices among high-school students throughout the period 1926–1932.

17. The city of Syracuse prohibited jazz bands and jazz dancing; see *Cornell Sun*, February 22, 1921, p. 1. So did East St. Louis; see *Daily Illini*, February 8, 1921, p. 1. At Columbus, Ohio, the city appointed a dance censor in the early twenties; see *Ohio State Lantern*, February 9, 1920. He was reported to be aghast at the fact that the "majority of boys and girls were dancing cheek-to-cheek." See also the rumpus caused by cheek-to-cheek dancing at Louisiana State, *The Reveille*, May 5, 1919.

18. See the cartoon, *Cornell Sun*, May 21, 1921; *Ohio State Lantern*, January 12, 1920. The jazz lingo was catchy and used in youth parlance for a variety of descriptions other than music. To call someone jazzy or snappy was a mark of approval. At UCLA, things highly favored were called "jazzy," at Ohio State, "snappy" or "peppy." On the enormous popularity of jazz, see *Ohio State Lantern*, January 12, 1920, November 30, 1920.

19. Edwards *et al.*, *Undergraduate*, p. 185; quoted in *UCLA Daily*, October 23, 1929. For dancing and the high-school girl, see Margaret V. Kiely, "The Significance of the Dean to the High School Girl," *Seventh Yearbook, NASSP*, 1923, p. 115. Among the requirements listed by coeds at Ohio State as basic to their ideal man was the ability to dance well; see *Ohio State Lantern*, April 25, 1923, p. 1. University of Washington women noted that in order to be popular one had to know how to dance; see *UCLA Daily*, March 15, 1929. See also *Daily Nebraskan*, reprinted in *Daily Illini*, October 19, 1921. The dean at Ohio State said that she often feared that girls would marry men simply because they were such wonderful dancers without considering their other qualifications; see *Ohio State Lantern*, April 26, 1921.

In instructing potential freshmen about the situation they could expect to find when they arrived at college, Kate W. Jameson and F. C. Lockwood, *The Freshman Girl* (New York, 1925), noted that "of fundamental importance to the girl in her relations with the men of the community are problems in dancing" (p. 93). At the University of Minnesota, "practically all evening parties are dancing parties," according to Jessie S. Ladd, "Recreation and the University Mixer," NEA *Proceedings*, 1922, p. 733.

20. The editor of the *Ohio State Lantern*, September 19, 1919, noted that city officials were issuing orders against certain kinds of dancing: "No more of this snuggling up and dreaming around the room; no more shimmying and shivering to nervous music; no more of this head-to-head business. Actually, it is demanded that there be some air space between the people who are doing the dancing. Isn't it cruel? What's to become of the evenings of those accustomed to cheek-to-cheek to a soothing sea of jazz?" At Smith College, girls were forbidden to practice the charleston in their dorm rooms because it was disturbing so many girls. At the State College for Women in Atlanta, Georgia, a floor caved in when 500 girls tried furiously to learn the latest dance steps, but at Oberlin College the dance was already taught in gym

classes; see *New Student,* January 27, 1926, pp. 1, 3; also *Daily Princetonian,* January 25, 1926. At the University of Kansas, a move was under way to have the latest steps taught in class; see Duke *Chronicle,* November 13, 1924, "College Collections." For the fast-paced changes in dancing, see LSU *Reveille,* June 18, 1927.

21. *Daily Illini,* December 19, 1920, January 22, 1921. The Women's League at Illinois, for example, reacted to the warnings of school officials by requesting the presidents of fraternities and sororities and the captains of other residence units (for unorganized students) to carry the message to their groups in order to insure that the extreme steps would be avoided; see *Daily Illini,* October 13, 1920. Later in the same year, the Women's Panhellenic at Illinois (an inter-sorority council) put a ban on "improper dancing" and called for the raising of standards and an end to the lights-out policy; see April 14, 1920, p. 1.

22. *Daily Illini,* December 21, 1920, letter to the editor; May 10, 1921, p. 1. See also the response to "Dad Elliott," who called dancing in college "one of the greatest menaces to the moral standards of our young people"; October 3, 1922.

23. Jingle in *Daily Illini,* April 20, 1920; *Daily Illini,* February 18, 1921, letter to the editor; January 22, 1921; *Ohio State Lantern,* November 30, 1920. See also *Ohio State Lantern,* January 24, 1922, January 12, 1920; Duke *Chronicle,* October 13, 1926.

24. *Ohio State Lantern,* February 10, 1920; *UCLA Daily,* December 14, 1923; LSU *Reveille,* February 13, 1920, p. 1, and editorial; Duke *Chronicle,* March 30, 1927.

25. Quoted in Ladd, "University Mixer," p. 735; *Ohio Lantern,* February 11, 1920. See also *UCLA Daily,* December 21, 1921. Many feared that other immoral behavior, including petting and drinking, went along with the dancing; see, for example, *Cornell Sun,* March 24, 1926; LSU *Reveille,* November 2, 1928.

26. *Daily Illini,* October 15, 1920; LSU *Reveille,* June 2, 1926.

Film as Big Business

by Lewis Jacobs

In 1918 the movie industry was shaken by a serious loss of patronage because of the influenza epidemic and the absence of millions of men at the front or in training camps. The public's distaste for war films after the Armistice was also a threat to the industry's well-being. But the setback was only temporary. Recouping their losses, producers quickly resumed expansion and consolidation. Inter-organizational rivalry attained proportions that made the old trust war seem petty. Having realized its fundamental large-scale characteristics, the industry began its ten years of growth as a big business —a growth to be intensified, in the closing years, by the sudden revolutionary addition of sound.

Unrivaled by foreign films during the four war years, American films were firmly established not only at home but in all parts of the globe—even in India, western Asia, and Africa. In 1919 American motion pictures exclusively were being shown in South America; in Europe ninety per cent of the movies shown originated in the United States. Hollywood had become the unquestioned motion picture center of the world.

The post-war period was one of unrestraint in business as in life generally. To be important a thing had to be big—and so the movie became one of the biggest things in American civilization. Everything connected with it was inflated, materially and psychologically. Companies, studios, productions, theatres, salaries, sales, advertising—all took on gigantic proportions. Excesses were characteristic of the hysteria and booming prosperity of "the jazz age."

Profits, huge though they were, were not big enough to finance the vast undertakings of these years. Wall Street banking houses, issuing stock lavishly, poured millions into the laps of the merging film companies to meet their ever-expanding needs. New men from Wall Street, educated in finance, became the overseers of the motion picture business.

Characteristic of the new managerial figures were two directors of a new and powerful company, Loew's: W. C. Durant, at that time also head of General Motors Corporation, and Harvey Gibson, president of the Liberty National Bank. Kuhn, Loeb and Company had already entered the field to back Famous-Players-Lasky; now the Du Ponts and the Chase National Bank undertook to finance Edgar Selwyn and Samuel Goldwyn, "the late Samuel Goldfish, not dead but legally annihilated" (January 1, 1919), in their new enterprise, Goldwyn Pictures. Loew, Pathé, and Fox listed stock on the New York Stock Exchange for public investment: this was the latest business method of getting much capital quickly. By 1925 stock issues had been floated also for Metro-Goldwyn and Universal.

Fiercely fighting for greater outlets for their productions, and to block the outlets of competitors, companies were ever at each other's throats. It was "company eat company." As the lords of finance grappled, minor companies were badly mangled. The steady expansion of the industry was marked by the continual attacks and counterattacks of First National versus Paramount versus Fox versus Universal versus Metro versus the independents. It was a new kind of warfare in the industry—large-scale economic warfare between powerful organizations for the control and monopoly of the motion picture business.

During the first years after the war the control of distribution was the major goal. Benjamin Schulberg effected the incorporation of the United Artists Company in order to distribute productions of directors and stars "too expensive for any single company to maintain on a permanent pay roll." The directors and stars were the "Big Four": Mary Pickford, Douglas Fairbanks, Charles Chaplin, and D. W. Griffith. Another distribution combination was Associated Producers, consisting of independent director-producers: Thomas Ince, Allan Dwan, George Loane Tucker, Mack Sennett, Marshall Neilan, Maurice Tourneur, J. Parker Read, Jr., and King Vidor. This group merged in 1921 with First National as their producers, and became known as Associated First National. Vitagraph, which had bought out the pioneers Kalem and Lubin during the war, was itself bought out in 1925 by Warner Brothers, a new company, which in 1929 absorbed First National as well. Goldwyn bought out the Triangle Corporation studio in Culver City, and in 1924 formed Metro-Goldwyn-Mayer. Meanwhile William Randolph Hearst launched Cosmopolitan Productions, which distributed through Metro-Goldwyn-Mayer.

The block-booking system, broken in 1918, was re-established. The exhibitors organized in angry groups to fight it, but their struggle was on the whole desultory. Distribution became increasingly centralized within the power of the major producing companies. These companies, having fought bitterly for the control of production through distribution, carried the fight into the field of exhibition. Control of exhibition assured not only a definite number of theatre outlets for productions, but a longer length of life and definite revenues on which to base future productions. Control of exhibition became a major means to keep rival productions off the screen and thus force competing companies out of business.

Just as Fox had been able to fight the Motion Picture Patents Company because of his ownership of theatres, so now First National was in an advantageous position to fight Paramount. First National, during the years 1919–1921, had some 3,400 theatres, some of them being among the largest and most important in the United States. Zukor, of Paramount, saw at once that he would have to enter the field of exhibition if Paramount was to be victorious, and he quickly began buying up theatres. Brilliant and ruthless as a business executive, he aroused increasing bitterness in his attempt to get, as nearly as the law allowed, a monopoly on movie theatres. He bought out thousands of theatres in small and large towns, and even acquired stock in the rival First National Company so that he could "bore from within." Endorsed by a national administration that believed in leaving business to its own tactics, he stopped at nothing to gain his ends.

Zukor's most formidable rival next to First National proved to be a new producer-exhibitor combination launched in 1920. This consisted of a theatre circuit that had been one of Paramounts chief customers, Loew's, and Metro, a new producing company. Paramount, Metro, and First National now fought savagely for big theatre control, squeezing many of the large independent theatre owners out of business, and forcing to the wall independent producers who had no theatre holdings. The situation was soon so acute that the independent exhibitors rose up frantically against the exhibition-distribution-production combinations. In 1921, at a national convention in Minneapolis, the independent Motion Picture Theatre Owners Association (M.P.T.O.) and the independent producers sought a way of checking monopoly operations, but their intentions bore little fruit.

The Federal Trade Commission filed complaints against Paramount and its affiliated corporation, studios, and individuals on the ground that in producing, distributing, and in addition owning from four to five hundred theatres, they were violating the trust laws. The proceedings temporarily halted Zukor's operations within First National but did not stop him from continuing his expansion policy, nor did it prevent his conquest of First National later.

Constant litigation and mutual accusation were giving the industry bad publicity and placing its leaders in a critical position. This was coming moreover at a bad time for other unforeseen factors were cutting in on the movies' soaring profits. Business conditions in general were depressed; this was not helped by the sudden strong competition of foreign films which were so far superior to Hollywood productions that many reasoned that they ought to be suppressed on this ground alone. At about the same time a wave of agitation for federal censorship of movies was gaining strength. Added to this was a series of scandals that aggravated the increasing animosity against the movie makers. For the first time in its history, the box office wavered. Many independent minor companies were forced to suspend operations under the pressure of the times. Others sought ways and means to maintain their power. The most essential item was to adjust the industrial and moral disputes amicably and thus forestall government interference or federal censorship.

In 1922 an organization was formed for self-regulation, both on the moral front and on the business front. The name of the organization, the Motion Picture Producers and Distributors Association, significantly omitted mention of exhibitors.

The industry selected Will H. Hays, a "distinguished and financially uninterested citizen," as president of their organization. Hays had first become known for his work in publicizing the Indiana State Council of Defense. An active worker and organizer in the triumphant Republican Party in 1920, he had come into national prominence as Postmaster-General in Harding's Cabinet. As head of the Motion Picture Producers and Distributors Association, Will Hays now became "the buffer between industry and the public."

The association immediately set up rules for arbitration and exhibitor units to eliminate monopoly practices and establish ethical standards. Just how far-reaching its reforms were can be judged from the fact that in 1925, three years after the association was formed, Vitagraph withdrew, on the grounds that theatres were still producer-owned.

The battle for control of exhibition continued unabated, the aim of the combinations being to acquire the best first-run houses and chain theatre circuits throughout the nation.

Mergers became the new economic order. Independent corporations and individuals were eliminated or submerged as the operations of production, distribution and exhibition became more and more interlocked and concentrated into the control of a few. Within a few years nearly all the major and first-run houses in the United States and Canada had been acquired by Paramount, Loew's, Inc. (Metro-Goldwyn-Mayer), and the large circuits affiliated with the First National group. Fox and Universal had outlets on a lesser scale. By 1927, with close to 6 exchanges in 46 key American cities, and 20,000 theatres, exhibition had become almost entirely monopolized by chain theatres, all in the hands of the major producer-distributor-exhibitor combinations. The following year Zukor was finally successful in weakening First National's control by acquiring one of its largest chains, the Katz-Balaban circuit. This was merged with his other theatre interests in the Publix Corporation, which ostensibly separated his production and exhibition activities.

The producer-distributor-exhibitor combination deeply influenced the industry's functioning. It minimized the roles of production and distribution and made exhibition the controlling factor in the industry. Producers who owned the most important chain of theatres controlled the source of receipts. This assured them in advance of an income upon which they could figure production budgets. Under the producer-distributor-exhibitor combination, the main channels of distribution and exhibition became virtually closed to newcomers or independents; for them, only the cheapest of markets remained. This control of outlets confined competition to the few major combinations. Under the new order financial dependence on Wall Street increased enormously and the vast resources now at the disposal of these million dollar movie combines led to a higher degree of extravagance and waste. Spending became the motto as never before; costs and prices reached new prohibitive highs.

In this era of extravagance producers competed intensively in building elaborate and luxurious showplaces. With a speed suggestive of the growth of the old nickelodeons, mammoth theatres accommodating thousands of people—at least three times as many as before—appeared throughout the country. In New York City the Capitol Theatre, completed in November 1919, had 5,300 seats. It had carpeted floors, costumed ushers, upholstered seats, eleven rock-crystal chandeliers, and the grandeur of Empire-period furnishings. Commented *Photoplay*, "The mezzanine floor looks as if it had been designed for eight-day bicycle races." Grauman's Egyptian and Chinese Theatres in Hollywood rivaled even this. Other New York palaces included Loew's State and, later, Roxy's, Paramount, and the Radio City Music Hall.

Expensive theatres in downtown districts of the metropolitan cities were regarded as safe investments, since the country was experiencing a building and real-estate boom in these years. Even neighborhood movie houses became luxurious. In 1928 alone, $161,930,000 was spent on new theatres; the total number of theatres at that time was about 20,500. In hundreds of towns the moving picture theatre had become the outstanding building.

Admission prices, despite sharp competition, were forced upward. Movies were no longer "the poor man's show" but the "universal American entertainment." Downtown theatres charged from 65 cents to $1.00. *Broken Blossoms* in 1919 got a record price of $3.00 a seat for its première. Second-run houses in the neighborhoods charged 25, 35, and 55 cents. Even fifth-run houses in poor side streets now charged 10 or 15 cents. The nickel no longer gave one entrance to the movie world.

To meet competition, exhibitors added elaborate stage presentations and novelties to the regular movie program. "Roxy" set an example when he introduced "prologues" consisting of operatic soloists, seventy-five-piece symphony orchestras, and a *corps de ballet* in 1925 in the Strand Theatre. Producer-exhibitors everywhere emulated his showmanship. The practice of offering elaborate stage shows spread so rapidly that after a few years these "prologues" became despised as "poisonous clichés." Extra attractions became so long and numerous that Richard Watts, movie critic of the New York *Herald Tribune*, protested,

> Heaven knows it is not my intention to cheer overlustily for the film little theatre when you consider some of the exhibits they have offered lately; but at least they

are about the only retreats left for the quaint ancients who want to see a motion picture.

Despite such animosity, "prologues" continued to flourish on a lavish scale.

Like exhibition and distribution, movie making also became a huge and extravagant undertaking practicable only for the wealthiest and strongest companies. The cost of picture making had grown from $1,00,000 for *The Birth of a Nation* in 1915 to millions for comparable spectacle productions. *Ben Hur,* said to have been the most expensive film ever made, cost $6,000,000.[1] The expense of the average picture likewise doubled and trebled. In 1920 the average five-reel feature cost from $40,000 to $80,000; "specials" of six to nine reels, from $100,000 to $200,000. By 1929 the average five-reeler was costing up to $200,000. To paraphrase Heywood Broun, it was not only that movies represented the views of big business; the movies now were big business.

The profits to be made from expensive pictures were obviously limited once the peak of theatre expansion had been reached. *The Ten Commandments,* costing close to $2,000,000, netted about $750,000 as road-show profits, and *The Covered Wagon,* costing under $350,000, netted over $1,500,000 on the road. It became apparent that the really steady income was to be got from the comparatively inexpensive productions—pictures graded as "program" or "B" pictures. The costlier "specials" were to function as "prestige films," productions that would keep the name of the producing company a favorite with public and exhibitor alike.

Now that profits were soaring, extravagance pervaded the film studios. Salaries reached fabulous amounts. Outstanding directors received from $20,000 to $50,000 for one film; screen writers, $1,000 to $2,500 a week and $10,000 to $25,000 for a novel or play adaptation. Among all the individuals involved, however, perhaps the star enjoyed the biggest income. The early post-war years saw his salary mounting at an alarming pace. William S. Hart netted $900,000 in two years, and got $2,225,000 for nine productions in the succeeding two years. Goldwyn paid Geraldine Farrar $10,000 a week; Metro topped the scale with a salary of $13,000 a week to Nazimova, then at the height of her screen fame. Nazimova's contract provided for a lump sum of $65,000 to be paid in

[1] According to *Variety,* April 18, 1925.

weekly installments; a limit of five weeks was placed on each picture, and for each day over that she was to be paid accordingly.

By 1923 the boom in salaries had created a new financial rating in the film world. Actor-producers—Harold Lloyd, Douglas Fairbanks, Charles Chaplin, Norma Talmadge, Mary Pickford, and one or two others—drew incomes ranging into the millions. If the salaries commanded by stars seemed preposterous, fan interest in the stars appeared to make them worth the money. It was estimated in 1919 that a quarter of a million dollars was spent annually on correspondence between stars and fans.

The standard pay for supporting players was now $600 a week and up—a big jump from the average of $100 to $200 a week in 1916. Leading men received $1,000 a week and more, less than female stars, who were considered more important. The high salary became so widely regarded as an index of a player's value that nearly everyone exaggerated the amounts received. So pronounced did this tendency become, owing to the activity of press agents, that Heywood Broun, writing in *The New York World* in 1922, was moved to remark,

> When an actor tells you how much he received, you discount his figure by 5 per cent and arrive at the approximate truth. This ratio does not hold with players from motion pictures. Time is required to take their figures and work out the answer. Nobody can very well be expected to divide a given sum by 11½ in his head.

Stars began forming their own production companies. If an actor or actress incorporated, it was the sign of success. William S. Hart, Anita Stewart, Norma Talmadge, Charles Chaplin, Douglas Fairbanks, Charles Ray, Clara Kimball Young, Sessue Hayakawa, Roscoe Arbuckle, Frank Keenan, and Agnes Ayres were a few of the many notables who flung themselves into production. Because of the lack of exhibition and distribution facilities and of poor management, few of them succeeded. Having amassed fortunes as stars, many lost their wealth promptly as producers.

As costs of production mounted and control settled into the hands of Wall Street bankers, the producer-supervisor was brought into the studio to oversee production. This new kind of executive, appointed by the Eastern financiers, was to assume more and more power, making the director, stars, and other movie workers mere pawns in production, of which he assumed full charge. The producer-supervisors set about making "entertainment the public wants." They had little creative imagination and were ruled by practical concerns. "Higher quality within one's means," the adage of the best of the old producers, was changed by these new Hollywood executives into "higher means within one quality."

The reign of the director by 1926 thus came to an end. Producer-supervisors, taking over the reins of production, began to supply the ideas, select the talent, choose the director, and steer the entire policy and conception of pictures according to their points of view. Business men and executives, but not craftsmen, they began to emphasize the more obvious aspects of their commodities, telling the exhibitor—and through him the public—what to look for in a picture. Movies were analyzed for the following selling points: (1) "Names"—that is, stars; (2) "Production Value"—elaborate sets, big crowds, and other proofs of great expense; (3) "Story Value"—the huge price paid for the original and its great reputation as a novel or play; (4) "Picture Sense"—a conglomeration of all these items; (5) "Box Office Appeal"—plenty of all the standardized values which had proved successful in years past.

All prospective films had to conform to these criteria of the producer-supervisor. He discovered that the quickest way to sell pictures in advance and to produce them rapidly was to duplicate the most recent successes. Thus what became known as the "cycle" in motion pictures, the unit of which was the "formula" picture, was born. The scheme was so "sure-fire" that producers found themselves not only aping the successful pictures of their competitors but even duplicating their own hits.

Production methods under this rigid system became mechanized; the "assembly line" appeared in Hollywood. The resulting standardization of pictures caused the downfall of the most important directors during the late twenties. The various branches of production were divided and specialized so specifically and minutely that directors had a lessening opportunity to contribute to the whole. Most directors became "glorified foremen" under the producer-supervisors.

As the director was shorn of his creative power, films became increasingly monotonous. Men with a passion for the movies and with promising talents were turned into orderlies, taking orders from superiors far less imaginative. The efforts of creative individuals to break through the limits set by the studios' new production chiefs were in most cases futile. The choice of the director himself now depended on considerations that had little connection with the movie art. As early as June 1921, *Photoplay* told the story of how executives of a company discussed a new director:

> "He'll make good," insisted the chief director of the company. "But he never directed pictures," said another director a bit jealously. "What makes you think he's going to be so wonderful?" "He's the man that invented the short-vamp shoe over in Paris a dozen years ago," said the boss director seriously.

Competition as well as expensive contracts and big capital investments demanded that production be kept going at all costs. The necessity to meet schedules often forced a producer to assign a second-rate director to a certain film, although the producer knew beforehand that the film would then be mediocre. There was only a limited supply of acknowledged and experienced first-rate directors available. When a second-rate director was assigned to a film, the safest procedure was to instruct him to imitate the style of a more talented director as closely as possible. It was not uncommon for a director to be told outright to copy the effect or trick or mannerism of some more distinguished craftsman. Indeed, if a lesser director who was getting a relatively low salary could do this effectively, he was a great commercial asset to his employer. At the same time, of course, the more esteemed directors were continually asked to repeat their own successful efforts.

The result of all such commercialization was the hindrance and misdirection of motion picture progress. Bad pictures, if they made money, were held up as models of perfection, while a good film that received less notice because of its lack of "star appeal," its poor publicity, or its unusual theme was overlooked and even abhorred as "arty." As Gilbert Seldes declared,[2]

> ... on the rare occasions when a director cuts loose from his own or established moving-picture tradition and does something new his work will be taken as a dreadful

[2] *The Nation*, July 27, 1927.

warning or an enviable example, depending on the box-office receipts.

This was the state of affairs in the movie industry when an apparently insignificant event began a movement that was soon to revolutionize the business. On August 26, 1926, Warner Brothers, in a desperate effort to ward off bankruptcy, premièred a novelty, the first motion picture with sound accompaniment, *Don Juan*. Its opening at the Manhattan Opera House in New York City was made the more auspicious by Will Hays' address, recorded on the film's sound track, welcoming sound to the world of cinema. The innovation did not at first greatly alarm the industry. But the sound film was welcomed by the movie audiences, and soon Warner Brothers, surviving its financial troubles, was making real profits in its pioneering. *Don Juan* was quickly followed by *The Better 'Ole* and *When a Man Loves*, both of which had synchronized musical scores, and by a number of short sound films that featured the voices of famous singers: Schumann-Heink, Gigli, Mary Lewis, Alda.

The enthusiasm of the public for the sound film was so pronounced that the other companies got together to decide what action to take regarding this invention which they had so far ignored and, confidentially, expected to fail. The five major companies resolved to fight the "Warner Vitaphone peril" on the grounds that:

1. Present equipment would have to be discarded, and expensive talking equipment would have to be bought.
2. Such equipment could be obtained only by paying royalties to a competitor.
3. Obeisance to Warner Brothers meant loss of prestige.
4. The technique of production would have to change radically.
5. Long-term contracts with "silent" stars and directors might prove to be frozen liabilities.

If their opposition proved unavailing, these companies were prepared to rush the installation of sound apparatus for their own use. This alternative was encouraged by Western Electric, the backers of Warner Brothers, since Western Electric was eager to come to terms with the larger companies in view of the greater profits that such an alliance would make possible.

While the major companies were making up their minds about sound, Warner Brothers advanced and consolidated its position by presenting to the public, on October 6, 1927, the first feature film with synchronized speech as well as music and other sound: *The Jazz Singer*. The audience responded riotously to Al Jolson's "Come on, Ma! Listen to this . . ." in a natural, intimate voice. People were even more fascinated by his speech than by his singing. Warner Brothers immediately added "dialogue sequences" to three more sound movies then in the making: *The Lion and the Mouse, Glorious Betsy,* and *Tenderloin*.

The other companies meanwhile still hesitated to accept sound pictures as more than a temporary fad. Their situation was the more complicated and precarious because of the flood of other new inventions, each of which was hailed as revolutionary: Color, Grandeur-Screen, Three-Dimension. Each new discovery sent a new shock through the already nervous industry, and few companies wanted to jump one way or the other. For a time the only producer besides Warner that definitely accepted sound was Fox, who launched his own more flexible system, Movietone, in 1927.

Until May 15, 1928, Warner and Fox were the only two studios in the field of sound pictures. After that time the public's enthusiasm for the sound film could no longer be denied or ignored. The entire industry, now in a panic, rushed into the production of sound pictures, hoping to make up for lost time; overnight Hollywood became frantic with the mad race to catch up with Warner. The remainder of the year was full of chaos, conjecture, and confusion. As in motion pictures' earliest days, quantity alone counted. The novelty of talking and sound had enchanted the nation, and producers could not keep up with the demand for sound pictures.

Major companies at first tried to play the game from all sides. Their production schedules included part-talkies, all-talkies, sound films, and silent films, the common supposition being that eventually the talkie would merely share the screen with the silent movie. But as time went on and more theatres were wired for sound, it became apparent that the talkies were entirely supplanting the "silents." With theatre patronage mounting from 60,000,000 in 1927 to 110,000,000 in 1929, largely because of sound, the hundred-per-cent talkie became recognized as the established form for all future productions.

The motion picture industry now proceeded to dig the

grave of the silent picture. Millions of dollars having been invested in sound, all the resources of advertising, publicity, and direct appeals to audiences were used to kill the silent film and establish the talkie. The campaign was reminiscent of Paramount's earlier launching of features to replace the one- and two-reelers of pre-war times. Before long, like features in their early days, talkies became the norm. People took them for granted, and could hardly remember when talkies did not exist.

Hollywood set itself to solve as rapidly as possible the new financial and technical problems that sound posed. Technological unemployment and rapid labor turnover were prime worries. Thousands of extras were thrown out of work because of the new vogue of drawing-room talkie dramas. Musicians by the hundreds were unable to find jobs either in theatre orchestras, now eliminated, or in the studios which had formerly employed them during the shooting of scenes to induce the desired mood in players (a use of music now completely impracticable). "Gag" men and title writers were dropped from the pay rolls as playwrights and dialogue writers were added. Broadway and "Tin Pan Alley" were ransacked for talkie talent, while directors, actors, and writers who had made reputations in the "silents" were put to tests that few of them could pass. Changes in lighting equipment also eliminated a great many studio electricians; for where it had formerly taken fifty men to handle the lights on a big set, with the new incandescents only four or five men were now needed to do this work. Salaries throughout the studios decreased markedly as new and less expensive Broadway personnel were hired. Within an amazingly short time, once the new sound studios were equipped and a clearer understanding was reached as to the type of talent needed, there was a rapid readjustment in the industry.

While in the midst of these stabilization activities, the motion picture industry like the rest of the nation was shocked by the stock-market crash of 1929. Panic gripped Hollywood as fortunes were lost overnight, the building boom collapsed, and motion picture companies' big theatre holdings and real-estate investments swiftly depreciated. But despite the national turmoil and widespread fears, the box-office receipts of theatres continued the climb they had started with the innovation of sound. Wall Street gazed in astonishment at what appeared to be a "depression-proof" industry. The "resistance" of the movie to the stock-market debacle so impressed Wall

Street interests that during the following years they were to struggle with more resolution than ever to gain control of the movie industry.

Thus the motion picture survived and even profited despite two acute crises within two years: the advent of sound and the onset of the depression. Its commerce now exceeded a billion and a half dollars a year. The end of the silent movie had closed an era of tremendous and fantastic expansion. Economic progress in the industry was henceforth to take the form of a greater concentration of its resources.

Trials of the Twenties

by Paul Sann

Sand, Sex and Scandal

On April 12, 1922, Roscoe Conklin Arbuckle emerged from a courtroom in San Francisco and told the press:

"This is the most solemn moment of my life. My innocence of the hideous charge preferred against me has been proved . . . I am truly grateful to my fellow men and women. My life has been devoted to the production of clean pictures for the happiness of children. I shall try to enlarge my field of usefulness so that my art shall have a wider service."

That's not the way it worked out. Hollywood never let Fatty Arbuckle enlarge his "field of usefulness" until it was too late. The round comedian's $5,000-a-week career had actually ended September 5, 1921, during a boozy midday party in a suite in the St. Francis Hotel in the City of Hills. It ended when Arbuckle, conveniently attired in pajamas and bathrobe, adjourned to a bedroom with pretty Virginia Rappe, a delicately beautiful actress and model. The girl, twenty-three, died four days later and the State of California blamed it on "external pressure" applied by Arbuckle during a sexual adventure. The cause of death was peritontis following a rupture of the bladder.

The incident rocked Hollywood on its foundations. The silent screen counted 35,000,000 cash customers per week at the time and the studios weren't relying solely on the kiss-proof, drink-proof, sin-proof Western hero to lure them in. Not at all. The fan who wanted something more current than the 200 per cent purity of William S. Hart or Jack Holt had a nice selection of bedroom epics to draw from. Hollywood somehow knew about the revolution in manners and morals right from the start; the cameras had been grinding away on the New Freedom since the war's end. The once-delicate subject of divorce and the general loosening of the marital ties had produced some spicy items on celluloid and with them some caustic comments from women in clubs and men in cloth. Fighting the twin threats of boycott and censorship, the studios dreaded a live scandal even more than their own juicy canned product. The irony was that the big blow finally came not from one of the screen's more frolicsome lover boys but from a hefty comic whose work on film was the soul of good clean Mack Sennett slapstick.

Fatty Arbuckle's ordeal—and Hollywood's—lasted through not one but three trials. The star contended all along that Miss Rappe's torn bladder grew out of a chronic condition aggravated by bootleg hootch, but the State's witnesses furnished more lurid headlines. Miss Bambina Maud Delmont testified that there were screams from the hotel room and then Arbuckle emerged, giggling with the girl's hat tilted on the side of his head, and said, "Go in and get her dressed and take her back to the Palace. She makes too much noise." The witness said she found Miss Rappe all but naked, moaning "I'm dying, I'm dying," and writhing in pain. Alice Blake, a showgirl, supported Miss Delmont's story. "We tried to dress her," she said, "but found her clothing torn to shreds. Her shirtwaist, underclothes and even her stockings were ripped and torn so that one could hardly recognize what garments they were."

The women thought Miss Rappe might have had too much to drink, among other things, so they put her into a cold bath. Doctors called by the defense testified that the bath could have ruptured the bladder. The actress, while she lingered, had furnished no clues to the bedroom scene beyond telling a nurse that she been intimate with the fun-loving 350-pound comedian. The first jury stood 10–2 for acquittal after 43 hours, so a mistrial was declared. The second stood 10–2 for conviction and was dismissed after 44 hours. The third panel took just 6 minutes to clear the pink-faced defendant of manslaughter and observed:

"Acquittal is not enough for Roscoe Arbuckle. We feel a great injustice has been done him and there was not the slightest proof to connect him in any way with the commission of any crime."

Miss Rappe's fiancé, director Henry Lehrman, saw it another way from the start.

"Virginia had the most remarkable determination," Lehrman said, "She would rise from the dead to defend her person from indignity. As for Arbuckle, this is what comes of taking vulgarians from the gutter and giving them enormous salaries and making idols of them. Some people don't know how to get a kick out of life, except in a beastly way. They are the ones who participate in orgies that surpass the orgies of degenerate Rome."

The studios, watching the box office, endorsed the Lehrman view not just by blacklisting Arbuckle but by junking his unreleased movies. It was questionable in any case whether those pictures could have been sold: exhibitors everywhere had marked the oversized star guilty long before the third jury had acquitted him.

Arbuckle changed his name to William Goodrich—somebody said he should have made it Will B. Good—and got some casual work as a director but eleven years passed before anyone let him act. Warner Brothers put him in some two-reel comedies in 1933, shooting in New York. He finished one on June 30 and said, "This is the happiest day of my life." In the morning he was dead—felled in his sleep by a heart attack. He was forty-six. Today you can see his old pie-in-the-face comedies on afternoon television programs aimed at the kiddie audience. The TV people figured, correctly, that the younger set couldn't possibly be contaminated by the pre-Rappe Arbuckle.

Murder for Fun

"Everybody is a potential murderer . . ."
—CLARENCE DARROW

One afternoon in the spring of 1924, two youths drew up in front of the Harvard School for Boys in the Chicago suburb of South Side Kenwood. They had been plotting the "perfect murder" for seven months. They had no particular victim in mind until little Bobby Franks, a neighbor of theirs, came by. He seemed an excellent candidate. Would Bobby like a ride home? The boy eagerly said yes. He held Dickie Loeb and Nathan Leopold in awe. Loeb, eighteen, the University of Michigan's youngest graduate, was doing postgraduate work at the University of Chicago, Leopold, nineteen, Phi Beta Kappa, had a B.S. from Chicago and was taking a law course there now. They were *cum laude* all the way.

Bobby Franks was always flattered when they talked to him. He hopped into the car.

It was the beginning of the big horror saga of the Lawless Decade. It would turn the nation's insides.

Loeb and Leopold took their fourteen-year-old admirer within a few blocks of his home in Hyde Park and then stuffed a gag into his mouth and crashed a heavy cold chisel against his skull four times. Then they drove idly over to the marshy wasteland near Hegewisch and carried the still-warm body into a culvert alongside the Pennsylvania Railroad tracks. They held the head under swamp water for a while to make sure all life had fled. Then they poured hydrochloric acid on the face to make identification hard. Then they wedged the body, all but the feet, into a drain pipe obscured by shrubbery and weeds. After that, they drove to a restaurant and got some sandwiches. Their labors, however casual and unhurried, had made them hungry.

That night the two intellectual prodigies sipped liquor and played cards at Leopold's home until midnight, but took time to call Jacob Franks and inform him that his son had been kidnaped. They told Franks, a wealthy retired pawnbroker, that he would receive mailed instructions as to how to get the boy back—and for how much.

Franks notified the police.

Detectives called him back at noon the next day—May 22. Two workmen taking a shortcut through a culvert had found the body of a boy; the police wanted Franks to come and look at it. Franks said no, he had heard from the kidnapers. Bobby was fine and was about to be returned for $10,000—$2,000 in "old twenties" and $8,000 in "old fifties." But later, tortured by anxiety, Franks sent his brother-in-law to the Hegewisch Morgue and heard the horrible truth.

There was no shortage of clues in the "perfect murder."

Leopold, son of a millionaire lake transport executive, had dropped his glasses during the burial scene without bothering to recover them. It took the police eight days, but they found the oculist who made them. Leopold denied the glasses were his but the empty case betrayed him. Then he said he must have lost them in the culvert weeks ago, while studying bird life there. But it had rained hard for days before the murder and the glasses were spotless.

That didn't shake Leopold. "He was a nice little boy," he said airily. "What motive did I have for killing him? I didn't need the money; my father is rich. Whenever I want money all I have to do is ask him for it. And I earn money myself teaching ornithology." Besides, he had an alibi for May 21. He said he and Dickie Loeb were out in his car all afternoon. He said they got a bottle of gin and picked up two girls—"May" and "Edna"—and went joy-riding. Loeb, son of a vice-president of Sears, Roebuck & Co., told the same story. But the Leopold chauffeur said Nathan's Willys-Knight never left the garage on May 21. And while all this was going on two cub reporters on the *Chicago Daily News,* Jim Mulroy and Al Goldstein, were checking samples of Leopold's typing against a ransom note Bobby Franks' father had received. The type seemed to match; Leopold's Underwood portable, found in a lagoon later, would bear this out.

The handsome, well-manered Loeb, a self-styled amateur criminologist, cracked first. He had offered detectives some theories on the murder early in the investigation, before his arrest; now he told them all about it. It was only a lark, really; he and Babe wanted to see what turmoil a "perfect murder" would create in a city like Chicago. Lord knows they didn't dislike Bobby Franks; he seemed like a nice kid. But Loeb was critical of Leopold, whom he called "Babe." He said he never approved of Babe's perverted sex habits.

Leopold, a small, round-shouldered boy with bulging eyes, said Loeb was a Superman type and had made him his slave. He said Dickie planned the murder.

The families sent for Clarence Darrow. He was sixty-eight and very tired, but he didn't like capital punishment. He had saved 104 men from the death penalty. He would save two boys now and then quit.

Darrow for the Defense

> "A man who lives, not by what he loves but what he hates, is a sick man."
> —ARCHIBALD MACLEISH

There was no need to prove anything against the twisted killers of Bobby Franks, but the State of Illinois put each and every gruesome fact into the record in endless array as the newspapers screamed the eye-for-an-eye theme. Clarence Darrow countered with a small battalion of alienists, psychiatrists and neurologists, and for thirty-three days the nation heard all about the wondrous, inexplicable ways of the billion-cell labyrinth we call the brain. Darrow's best witness wasn't even in the courtroom during those hot summer days; his real star was Freud. Darrow did not argue that the honor students before the bar didn't know right from wrong; he argued that they didn't know what they were doing because they were sick in their brilliant heads. But Darrow didn't plead insanity. He pleaded mental illness.

It was something new in courtroom spectacles, another trail-blazer for the New Era. The human brain was on trial in Chicago and some fancy words got in the papers. Darrow offered evidence that Leopold was a paranoiac with a severe manic drive, and Loeb a dangerous schizophrenic. The lawyer made much of the fact that a governess forcibly introduced Leopold to sex when he was fourteen and a chauffeur performed the same disservice for Loeb. He noted that they had super-normal intelligences, but emotionally weren't past the age of seven. He noted that Loeb existed in a world of fantasy, alternately imagining himself a frontiersman in pioneer days or the master criminal of our times. He said the boys didn't make sense: just for kicks, they cheated at bridge, broke automobile windows, fired an abandoned building, and looted fraternity houses when they had all the money they could use.

Darrow talked for two days. He talked about fathers and sons. He quoted from Housman's "A Shropshire Lad":

> *The night my father got me*
> *his mind was not on me;*
> *He did not play his fancy*
> *to muse if it should be*
> *the son you see.*

"No one knows what will be the fate of the child he begets," Darrow told the court. "This weary world goes on begetting . . . and all of it is blind from beginning to end. I don't know what it was that made these boys do this mad act, but I know there is no reason for it. I know they did not beget themselves . . . We are all helpless . . . But when you are pitying the father and the mother of poor Bobby Franks, what about the fathers and mothers of all the boys and all the girls who tread a dangerous maze in darkness from birth to death? . . . I am sorry for all fathers and all mothers. The mother who looks into the blue eyes of her little baby cannot help musing of the end of the child, whether it will be crowned with the greatest promises that mind can imagine—or whether he will meet death upon the scaffold. All she can do is to rear him with love and with care, to watch over him tenderly, and to meet life with hope and trust and confidence, and to leave the rest with fate."

Darrow argued that the scaffold was not the answer to the ills that beset Loeb and Leopold or the others like them in all the cities and towns everywhere.

"Do you think you can cure the hatreds and the maladjustments of the world by hanging them?" he asked. "You simply show your ignorance and your hate when you say it. You may heal and cure hatred with love and understanding, but you can only add fuel to the flames with cruelty and hating."

Here Darrow wept.

The defendants had sat impassively through the horror of the State's presentation and through the moving rhetoric of the masterful advocate pleading for their lives. At times they had seemed bored, but now Darrow got to them. He said he could think of a scene even more macabre than the one in the culvert—"I can think of taking two boys . . . irresponsible, weak, diseased . . . penning them in a cell, checking off the days, the hours and the minutes, until they be taken out and hanged."

Dickie Loeb shuddered. Babe Leopold got hysterical and had to be taken out of the courtroom. When the boy came back Darrow returned to his theme:

"Wouldn't it be a glorious day for Chicago, wouldn't it be a glorious triumph for the State's Attorney, wouldn't it be a glorious triumph for justice in this land, wouldn't it be a glorious illustration of Christianity, and kindness and charity? I can picture them awakened in the gray light of morning, furnished a suit of clothes by the State, led to the scaffold, and fitting tight, black caps down over their heads, stood on a trap door, the hangman pressing a spring, so that it gives way under them; I can see them fall through space—and— stopped by a rope around their necks."

John R. Caverly, Chief Justice of the Criminal Court of Cook County, had a hard decision to make. He had heard the case himself, without a jury. He had heard the murder of Bobby Franks described as the most heinous in Illinois' history. He had heard the Battle of the Head Shrinkers—a most puzzling thing because the State's witnesses, equally qualified, countered every point made by the defense's learned experts. He knew the agony of the parents on both sides. He knew what passions had boiled up; his bailiffs had to break up near-riots outside the courtroom as the people battled for seats. He could sense what they were there for. Should he call for the hangman?

The sentence came in two parts:

For the murder of Bobby Franks, life.

For kidnapping the boy, ninety-nine years.

Darrow had won.

The Word, the Book and Mr. Bryan

> *"With flying banners and beating drums we are marching backward to the glorious age of the sixteenth century, when bigots lighted fagots to burn the men who dared to bring any intelligence and enlightenment and culture to the human mind."*
>
> —CLARENCE DARROW,
> on the Monkey Trial

Freckled-faced John T. Scopes, 24, taught science (and a little football on the side) in the drowsy Tennessee town of Dayton. One day in 1925 he read his class this sentence from Hunter's *Civic Biology:* "We have now learned that animal forms may be arranged so as to begin with the simple one-celled forms and culminate with a group which includes man himself." Scopes knew he would get arrested. He had talked to three lawyers about it over some soda pop in Robinson's Drugstore on Main Street. Tennessee had a brand new law—first in the nation—making it a crime to "teach any theory that denies the story of the Divine creation of man as taught in the Bible." So a Special Grand Jury quickly indicted the upstart teacher for his assault on the beliefs and dignity of the state.

William Jennings Bryan, three-time candidate for the presidency, one-time Secretary of State and long-time Defender of the Word, laid aside his ventures in Florida real estate and hastened to the Volunteer State as the volunteer prosecutor in the case.

When old Clarence Darrow heard this, he made tracks for the Cumberland Country too, bringing along two other eminent Counsels-for-the-Defense, Dudley Field Malone and

Arthur Garfield Hays. Protestant Dayton, population 1,500, rallied to stand foursquare against the arriving infidel horde. The town blossomed out with signs that summer:

> READ YOUR BIBLE DAILY
> SWEETHEART, COME TO JESUS
> BE SURE YOUR SINS
> WILL FIND YOU OUT
> YOU NEED GOD IN YOUR
> BUSINESS
> PREPARE TO MEET THY MAKER
> GOD IS LOVE
> WHERE WILL YOU SPEND
> ETERNITY?

Beneath these banners, strung across the narrow streets near Judge J. Raulston's musty old courthouse, evangelists and hot-dog vendors competed with Bible salesmen and purveyors of "ice-cold" lemonade (you could get corn likker too, if you knew the right vendor). By wagon, mule, horse or foot, the oldest settlers and the Holy Rollers came down from the hills. An atmosphere of carnival, weighted with serious things, overtook the town. So many reporters flocked in that twenty-two telegraph operators had to be imported to send out their frontline dispatches in the Battle of Fundamentalism vs. Evolution.

Judge Raulston, six feet of solid Bible-taught stock, and self-introduced as "jist a reg'lar mountaineer jedge," set himself up with a strong supply of chewing gum and two flunkies to wield fans over his ample dome. He had a spittoon by his feet and a ten-foot banner hung behind his head, facing the jury. It said, READ YOUR BIBLE!

The aging Bryan, bald and paunchy and visibly suffering in the fetid Dayton heat after his pleasant and profitable sojourn in the Florida lagoons, appeared coatless in a tufted white shirt with a starched front. He carried his own palm leaf fan and a three-gallon graniteware jug for water. Darrow shed his coat, too, exposing wide lavender suspenders over a blue summer shirt. When the heat got him he would make his way into the line of the electric fans; the Tennessee-financed breezes were being wafted in directions away from the defense table.

The Judge opened court with a prayer and announced that counsel would be addressed by honorary titles—"general" for prosecution lawyers and "colonel" for the defenders of John Thomas Scopes. Darrow let that pass, but not the form of the opening. "I object to the turning of this court into a meeting-house," he said. Overruled, he observed later that in forty years he had never before "heard God called in to referee a court trial."

The state put on Howard Morgan, fourteen, a pupil of the defendant, to lay bare the nature of the crime. It was plain that the boy liked his teacher but he had to tell the whole truth and nothing but.

"He said that the earth was once a hot, molten mass, too hot for plant or animal life to exist upon it; in the sea the earth cooled off; there was a little germ of one-celled organism formed, and this organism kept on revolving and from this was man."

When Darrow asked Howard whether he thought this intelligence had damaged him in any way, the boy said, "Oh, no sir."

The judge sent the jurors out, listened to defense references to such items as the Paleozoic era, the Heidelberg Man and the Cro-Magnons and said no, he couldn't see the purpose of any evidence by a bunch of imported scientists. Darrow argued that testimony tracing the human specimen back to his beginnings, maybe 600,000 years ago, was indeed pertinent. The Judge said no, everybody knew, or should know, that God created man 6,000 years ago; it was in the Bible. The exchange grew rather heated—

> RAULSTON: I hope that counsel intends no reflection upon this court.
> DARROW: Your Honor, of course, is entitled to hope.

That cost Darrow a citation for contempt but he got off with an apology, the "Jedge" observing that the Book taught him that "it was godly to forgive." With his learned witnesses declared null, void and irrelevant, "Colonel" Darrow surprised everyone and called William Jennings Bryan for the defense, as an expert on the Bible. Now the stage was set for high drama. The courtroom could not safely hold the throng that wanted to see the Plumed Knight of Fundamentalism take up the sword against the Infidel Darrow, so the judge moved the trial to the lawn. There, on a platform built under the maple trees, the fetid July heat wouldn't go over 100 degrees—except under the Bryan collar—on July 20, 1925.

The Drama on the Lawn

> *"The Bible states it. It must be so."*
> —WILLIAM JENNINGS BRYAN

On the lawn at Dayton, with the whole world watching, Clarence Darrow and William Jennings Bryan acted out the classic Science vs. Religion conflict of the century. The timing was right; everything else was going under the microscope for open examination in the twenties, why not the Bible? The casting was perfect; the principals were men of formidable convictions, each in his own way. The record would tell:

DARROW: Do you claim that everything in the Bible should be literally interpreted?
BRYAN: I believe everything in the Bible should be accepted as it is given there.
DARROW: Now, you say, the big fish swallowed Jonah, and he remained there how long—three days—and then he spewed him upon the land . . . Do you believe that He made them—that He made such a fish and that it was big enough to swallow Jonah?
BRYAN: Yes, sir. Let me add: One miracle is just as easy to believe as another.
DARROW: Do you believe Joshua made the sun stand still?
BRYAN: I believe what the Bible says.
DARROW: Now, Mr. Bryan, have you ever pondered what would have happened to the earth if it had stood still?
BRYAN: No, the God I believe in could have taken care of that, Mr. Darrow.
DARROW: You believe the story of the flood to be a literal interpretation.
BRYAN: Yes, sir.

Attorney General E. T. Stewart protested when Darrow tried to get the witness to fix the date of the flood. Bryan broke in: "These gentlemen . . . did not come here to try this case. They came here to try revealed religion. I am here to defend it, and they can ask me any question they please." There was loud applause and when Darrow remarked on it Bryan accused him of insulting the people of Tennessee. Darrow in turn accused Bryan of insulting "every man of science and learning in the world because he does not believe in your fool religion."

The examination went on. Did Bryan know there were ancient civilizations and ancient religions going back long before Biblical times? "I have never felt it necessary to look up competing religions," the witness said. Did Bryan believe God confused the tongues of the men building the Tower of Babel because he was afraid they were reaching unto heaven? "Something like that . . ." the witness said. The Attorney General wanted to know the purpose of this line of questioning but Bryan, not Darrow, answered him.

> BRYAN: The purpose is to cast ridicule on everybody who believes in the Bible, and I am perfectly willing that the world shall know that these gentlemen have no other purpose than ridiculing every Christian who believes in the Bible.
>
> DARROW: We have the purpose of preventing bigots and ignoramuses from controlling the education of the United States and you know it, and that is all.

Bryan said he was "simply trying to protect the word of God against the greatest atheist or agnostic in the States." The gallery, more like a camp-meeting, cheered again.

The questioning turned to the Garden of Eden.

> DARROW: Mr. Bryan, do you believe that the first woman was Eve?
> BRYAN: Yes.
> DARROW: Do you believe she was literally made out of Adam's rib?
> BRYAN: I do.
> DARROW: Do you believe that after Eve ate the apple, or gave it to Adam, whichever way it was, that God cursed Eve, and at that time decreed that all womankind thenceforth and forever should suffer the pains of childbirth in the reproduction of the earth?

This led to the most vehement clash of the day, Darrow and Bryan shaking their fists at each other before the examination could proceed. It didn't matter. In essence one answer of Bryan's stood for all: "The Bible states it; it must be so." When Darrow talked about geology, he got this answer: "I am more interested in the Rock of Ages than in the age of rocks." When he talked about the manifold discoveries of science over the years, shedding light on our beginnings, Bryan stood on "the Word as it is written."

> DARROW: You don't care how old the earth is, how old man is, and how long the animals have been here?
> BRYAN: I am not much interested in that.
> DARROW: You have never made an investigation to find out.
> BRYAN: No, sir, I have never.

Judge Raulston mercifully called a halt to the unequal encounter the next morning. He said no purpose was being served by it because all the jury had to decide was whether man was made by God or descended from "a lower order of animals." And "General" Bryan, wearied by his last-ditch defense of the True Faith against "the greatest infidel of his age," did not pursue a threat he had made to put Darrow on the stand. It hardly mattered. There could only be one verdict and the shirt-sleeved hillbilly jury didn't tarry over it. The boy over there in the bow tie, the pagan Scopes, was guilty as charged. Genesis had triumphed over Darwin in Dayton, Tennessee. The monkey was on the run.

The Aftermath

> *"He came into life a hero, a Galahad, in bright and shining armor. He was passing out a poor mountebank."*
> —H. L. MENCKEN, *on Bryan*

Judge John T. Raulston robbed the Monkey Trial of one element of suspense present in all trials. He told the jury in advance that if it found for the State he would fine John T. Scopes one hundred dollars—"our practice in whiskey cases." This assessment, of course, failed to bring home the desired lesson to the defendant. "Your Honor," Scopes said, "I feel that I have been convicted for violation of an unjust statute. I will continue to oppose this law in any way I can. Any other action would be a violation of my ideal of academic freedom."

Darrow went up into the Big Smoky Mountains in search of some fresh air.

The victor, Bryan, sixty-five and tired, retired to a friend's home in Dayton to read his clippings. What he read could not have cheered him. He found even his pearly tones under attack. "The corrosion of nearly three decades became apparent at once," W. O. McGeehan had wired the *New York Herald* from the courtroom. "Once the voice had in it the qualities of brazen trumpets, but the resonance had gone from the brass." And that was Sunday School–mild alongside what H. L. Mencken had filed to the *Baltimore Sun*:

> The old boy grows more and more pathetic. He has aged greatly during the past few years and begins to look elderly and enfeebled . . . Once he had one leg in the White House and the nation trembled under his roars. Now he is a tinpot pope in the Coca-Cola belt and a brother to the forlorn pastors who belabor half-wits in the galvanized iron tabernacles behind the railroad yards.

Bryan could expect that from such a notorious non-believer as Mencken. He knew Mencken. What he could not expect was the nationwide scorn heaped on the Monkey Trial outside of the Bible Belt. The drama at Dayton had come out as a farce instead of a holy thing. In the Year of Our Lord 1925, it had to; the clock couldn't be turned back, not even for William Jennings Bryan. Tennessee, of course, did stand firm for the Word. While it threw out the Scopes conviction because the "Jedge" erred in setting the sentence instead of letting the jury do it, the State Supreme Court did uphold the evolution law itself.

But by then it was too late for Bryan to savor his victory. He was dead. He died of apoplexy on July 26, five days after the trial, six days after his ordeal on the stand against the wily Darrow. He was buried in Arlington National Cemetery with the nation's best.

The Murders in Lovers Lane

> *"Everybody is a potential murderer. I've never killed anyone, but I frequently get satisfaction reading the obituary notices."*
>
> —CLARENCE DARROW

The *New York Daily Mirror* broke out on July 17, 1926, with a front page that was lively and also exclusive:

HALL-MILLS MURDER
MYSTERY BARED

To get the full flavor of it you had to reassemble the cast of characters in the four-year-old crime.

First the dead:

The Rev. Mr. Edward Wheeler Hall, forty-one, stubby and balding, rector of the Protestant Episcopal Church of St. John the Evangelist in New Brunswick, New Jersey.

Mrs. Eleanor Mills, thirty-four, petite, pretty and vivacious, mother of two children, soloist in the Rev. Mr. Hall's choir.

They had been slain under a crabapple tree in De Russey's Lane on the old Phillips Farm, near their homes, on Friday night, September 16, 1922. A .32 calibre slug had passed through the rector's brain. The killer or killers had shot the blond choir singer three times and then slashed her throat. The deed done, somebody arranged the bodies in a position of decorous intimacy and scattered over them selections from the burning love missiles of Eleanor Mills to her "true heart," Edward Hall.

And now the living:

Mrs. Frances Stevens Hall, dumpy, plain, severe-looking wife of the pastor, seven years his senior.

Willie and *Henry Stevens*, her devoted brothers.

Henry de la Bruyere Carpender, her cousin, member of the New York Stock Exchange.

James Mills, husband of the slain woman, eleven years older, janitor in the school and sexton of St. John's, raising a family on thirty-five dollars a week.

Jane Gibson, "The Pig Woman," chief witness in the rather casual 1922 investigation and due to serve as the State's prime weapon in the new case.

Mrs. Hall and her brothers and cousin were indicted in the double murder because of the *Mirror* story. The newspaper charged that they had bribed police and witnesses and sweet-talked the local prosecutor to escape prosecution in 1922.

The trial in November and December turned the eyes of the nation to the white-marble courthouse at Sommerville, New Jersey. The newspaper sent three hundred reporters, augmented by a small army of "experts"—Mary Roberts Rinehart, Billy Sunday, Peggy Hopkins Joyce, and Eleanor

Mills' husband James, himself, and his flapper daughter, Charlotte, to mention a few. The sixty leased wires set up in the basement spewed out words in a torrent—5,000,000 in the first eleven days, 9,000,000 in the full eighteen trial days, 12,000,000 in the twenty-four days in which the spectacle stayed on the front pages. Even *The New York Times* had four stenographers on the scene, so that not a single word-fit-to-print would get away.

The Hall-Mills story, an orgy of murder, intrigue, and purple passion without equal in the Lawless Decade, owed much of its celebrity to the fact that the departed had committed their emotions to paper so freely. "Sweetheart, my true heart," Eleanor Mills had written, "I could crush you— oh, I am so happy tonight! I'm not pretty. I know there are girls with more shapely bodies, but I'm not caring what they have. I have the greatest part of all blessings, a noble man's deep, true, eternal love, and my heart is his, my life is his; poor as my body is, scrawny as my skin may be; but I am his forever. How impatient I am and will be! I want to look up into your dear face for hours as you touch my body close."

Hall's letters, a smoking cache sold to the newspapers by the widower Mills for five hundred dollars, made it plain that the little soprano's ardor was well matched. "Darling wonder heart," the pastor had written, "I just want to crush you for two hours. I want to see you Friday night alone by our road; where we can let out, unrestrained, that universe of joy and happiness that will be ours." He called Mrs. Mills his "Gypsy Queen" and signed himself "D.T.L.," the German *Deiner Treuer Lieber,* translated Thy True Lover. The sexton's wife called the rector by the shorter, more explicit "Babykins."

The special prosecutor, State Senator Alexander Simpson, offered the jury this thesis: when the struggling pastor married Frances Hall, "he got position, wealth, and refinement" but "he found he was in a chill, cold household" and took up with the gay and zestful Eleanor. Mrs. Hall came upon some of the pastor's passionate incoming mail, overheard the rendezvous made by phone that ghastly night, assembled her kin and stage-managed the execution of the sinners. Simpson had eighty-four witnesses to expand on this story but his case hinged on one person alone—Mrs. Jane Gibson.

The Pig Woman, fifty-six and dying of cancer, had to testify from an iron hospital bed. She was attended by a nurse and doctor and as she croaked out her story the smell of iodoform and formaldehyde suffused a trial chamber made for

280 people and packed with 500. The witness, who raised Poland China pigs, said that on the fatal night she was riding her mule Jenny down De Russey's Lane on a kind of patrol because thieves had rustled two rows of corn from her farm. She said the moon was "shinin' bright and pretty" and she saw Mrs. Hall and Willie Stevens get out of an auto and go into the orchard, so she tied up Jenny and went "peeking and peeking and peeking." She said she heard many voices—"the men were talking and the woman said very quick, 'explain those letters.'"

Q—(by Simpson) What did you hear the men say? *A*—They were saying "God damn it" and everything else. All that kind of stuff.

Q—Did you hear more than one man say anything? *A*—Someone was hitting, hitting, hitting. I could hear somebody's wind going out, and somebody said, "Ugh." Then somebody said, "God damn it, let go." A man hollered . . . then somebody threw a flash toward where they were hollering . . . I see something glitter and I see a man and I see another man like they were wrestling together. [The witness paused while the nurse applied cold cream to her parched lips.] I heard a shot . . . then I heard something fall heavy. Then I run for the mule . . .

Q—Did you hear a woman's voice after you heard the shot? *A*—One said, "Oh, Henry," easy, very easy; and the other began to scream, scream, scream so loud, "Oh my, oh my, oh my," so terrible loud.

The Pig Woman said she heard three more shots and then mounted Jenny and hurried away from the ghastly tableau under the apple tree.

Neither Mrs. Hall nor her brothers showed any emotion during this recital, but the Pig Woman's own mother showed plenty. The aged crone sat in a front row muttering, "She's a liar, she's a liar, she's a liar," as the grisly story unfolded. The seven-man "million-dollar" defense battery addressed itself to that point at once by bringing out discrepancies in the Gibson story of 1922, as told to a Grand Jury, and the 1926 testimony. Then came damaging items bearing on the witness's vaunted memory for detail. She couldn't remember where she had married, whether she had been divorced, whether she had known certain gentlemen named by the defense. The point could not have escaped the jury: if Jane Gibson couldn't remember the men in her life, husbands or otherwise, how could she retain after four years every detail of that horror-filled night in De Russey's Lane?

Then Senator Clarence E. Case, handling the cross-examination, returned to the murder scene. He wanted to know why Mrs. Gibson hadn't thought of getting help when she heard a woman screeching in the Lane. He got a curious answer from the ashen-gray witness on the bed. She said she thought she detected a Negro among the men in the clearing and she figured that the screaming woman there had got into trouble by going out with the Negro. "When I see a white woman with a colored man," she said, "it serves them right."

There were only a few more questions. As the Pig Woman was lifted from the bed to a stretcher to go back to the hospital, she shook her finger at Frances Hall and gasped: "I've told the truth, so help me God, and you know it, you know it!" Then she fell back in a sweat.

The Iron Widow

> "Mrs. Hall is not an emotionless woman, she is a pent-up woman."
> —DUDLEY NICHOLS, *New York World*

Some of the newspapers had a name for Frances Hall, the rich and dignified matron of New Brunswick. They called her The Iron Widow. She made the headline label stand up. She took the Trial of the Century in stride. What went on inside was her affair; her emotions were her own. On the outside, she betrayed nothing. She heard her husband's torrid letters to Eleanor Mills read in court; she sat impassive. She heard a dozen witnesses say that *everybody* knew about the affair between the pastor and the choir singer for oh, a year or two; she never winced. She heard that someone saw Eleanor Mills sitting on the rector's lap in the vestry at St. John's; she heard that the rector used to slip into the dingy Mills apartment when James Mills was working in the church and the children were in school; she betrayed nothing. She heard a grim recital of the events of September 16, 1922. How she couldn't sleep because the Reverend Hall didn't come home; how she went to the church to look for him; how she called the police at 6:00 A.M. and asked if any "casualties" had been reported; how she met James Mills in the morning and asked him if his wife was home . . . She heard Jane Gibson and looked her straight in the eye. She heard them all; her steel reserve never cracked.

And now she heard Henry Stevens' testimony only as another spectator in the packed courtroom; her big brother could take care of himself. He said he was at his home in Lavallette at the time of the murders. The bluefish were running in Barnegat Bay that weekend and he wouldn't miss that for the world. He was there, fifty miles away, and he had witnesses to prove it, just as the State had witnesses to prove he was in New Brunswick.

There was some concern on Mrs. Hall's features as the eccentric Willie Stevens took the stand. People always made fun of Willie. He rode around town with Engine Co. No. 3, wearing his own oversized red helmet, and he ran errands for the firemen and bought them things out of his forty-dollar allowance. Sometimes he rode the laundry wagon to pass the time, looking so comical in his wing collar. People said he wasn't altogether right in the head and he was a burden to Mrs. Hall.

But Willie, a pudgy fellow with a walrus mustache and a chowder head, took good care of himself on the stand. If he was the village idiot, you'd never know it from his testimony. He was calm, courteous, direct, and the soul of patience. He had the air of a man who wanted to help the prosecutor if he possibly could. He had no hard feelings. Where was he on the night of the murders? He was in his room, sir. He just went out for a little while, sir, when his sister asked him to go to the church with her and look for the Reverend. In the morning, when he heard that Mr. Hall was dead, he dropped his *New York Times* and cried. Willie got good notices in the papers. Dudley Nichols, the *World* man, later a top Hollywood writer and producer, noted Willie's "childish delight" in courtroom theatricals and the "irresponsible rotundity" about him. He seemed like "a small boy" to Nichols. Willie, in a word, set the stage perfectly for his sister.

Poised, well-bred, a touch of white in the collar over her black widow's weeds, Mrs. Hall answered the questions evenly as they were put by Robert H. McCarter, former Attorney General of the State and one of its top trial lawyers and now part of the "million-dollar" defense. (It cost $400,000 actually.)

Q—Now, Mrs. Hall, did you kill your husband? *A*—I did not.

Q—Did you play any part in that dreadful tragedy? *A*—I did not.

Was Eleanor Mills once in her own Sunday school class? Yes. Did she pay the bills when Eleanor Mills had a kidney operation early in 1922? Yes. Did she send flowers for her room? Yes. Did she drive Mrs. Mills home from the hospital? Yes. Did she sometimes invite Mrs. Mills along on family picnics? Yes. Did she have any but the kindliest feelings towards Eleanor Mills in all that time? No, sir. Did she ever have the least occasion to suspect her husband and the choir singer? Certainly not.

Prosecutor Simpson, five feet tall but a giant in the courtroom, took over. He moved close to Mrs. Hall. He had lots of questions. He tore into every angle of her story. Could she swear she was not in De Russey's Lane with her brothers that night? Absolutely. Did she tell James Mills the next morning that she thought the Reverend and Mrs. Mills had met with foul play? No, she didn't think she had. Was there a scratch on her face that morning, as a witness testified? No, sir. Why had she sent her brown cloth coat to a dyer in Philadelphia after the murder? She needed a coat for the mourning period and always sent things to that firm. Was the coat stained with anything? Certainly not. Why did she ask the police about "casualties" when her husband failed to return home that night? "It means accidents," she said. "It means death also, doesn't it?" Simpson stormed back. "I do not know that it does," the witness said. Was Reverend Hall always "a loving, affectionate husband"? The lady replied, almost audibly, with one word: "Always."

Now there were tears in her eyes. It was plain that the Iron Widow through the long nightmare, had some good memories to go with the bad.

Despite the mass of testimony, the jury was out only five hours. The verdict was not guilty. There remained only some details: The standing indictment against Henry Carpender would be thrown out. Mrs. Hall and her brothers would sue the *Daily Mirror* for three million dollars and accept an out-of-court settlement. Phil Payne, the managing editor who broke the story, would die the next year in the disappearance of the monoplane Old Glory flying to Rome. The Pig Woman would die four years later. The widow and her family would retreat into the close-knit privacy they had always known.

Somebody figured out that the words filed out of Somerville on the Hall-Mills story could have filled twenty-two novels.

This was undoubtedly so, but there was no last chapter in the mountain of prose. The question would go down through the years: Who killed the little pastor and his favorite choir singer?

Murder for Money

> *"Ruth Snyder was so like the woman across the street that many an American husband was soon haunted by the realization that she also bore an embarrassing resemblance to the woman across the breakfast table."*
> —ALEXANDER WOOLLCOTT

It was the year of the Long Count, starring Dempsey and Tunney. It was the year of the Atlantic flights, starring Lucky Lindy. It was the year of the Home Run, starring Babe Ruth. It was the year of the Executions at Charlestown, starring Sacco and Vanzetti. It was the year of the Unwed Mother, starring Nan Britton and Warren Harding. But 1927 began with the sordid story of a straying suburban housewife and a fun-loving corset salesman. Ruth Snyder and Judd Gray became quite famous by taking a sash weight to Albert Snyder and then fighting bitterly over who had the idea in the first place. They made murder—and possibly even illicit love—unpopular that year.

The deed was unfurled on a Sunday morning in March in the Snyder row house in Queens Village, New York. Mrs. Snyder, bound and gagged, pounded on her daughter's door shortly after 2:00 A.M. and screamed, "Get help!" Lorraine, nine, called a neighbor. Snyder, $115-a-week art editor of *Motor Boating* magazine, lay smashed to death on his bed. His wife blamed a burglar; she said the man also hit her over the head and tied her up. But all the things she listed as stolen turned up in secret caches around the house and the unemotional Mrs. Snyder cracked that night. She named Judd Gray as her collaborator in the badly fumbled murder plot—"Poor Judd," she said. "I promised not to tell"—and the police found him upstate in a Syracuse hotel.

The traveling salesman professed total innocence. "My word, gentlemen," he said, "when you know me better you'll see how utterly ridiculous it is for a man like me to be in the clutches of the law. Why, I've never even been given a ticket for speeding." But he wasn't nearly as hard to break as his paramour. He confessed on the train going back. He said that when the time came to smite Snyder, he weakened and had to have help from Mrs. Snyder. She had said that her courage departed at the appointed hour and Gray—she used to call him "Lover Boy"—had to wield the bludgeon all by himself.

Ruth Brown Snyder, thirty-two, was a slim and nicely curved peroxide blond with good features marred only by a hard jaw and an icy look. Henry Judd Gray, thirty-four, who had a wife and eleven-year-old daughter in Orange, New Jersey, wore shell-rimmed glasses and had a mild, gentle look. He could have passed for a Sunday School teacher.

The tragic journey began in the summer of 1925 when a mutual friend introduced the Queens matron to the corset impresario in a restaurant in midtown Manhattan. Mrs. Snyder, oddly, happened to be in the market for a corselette and Gray took her back to his office. "She removed her dress and I tried on a garment to see if it was the right size," he said, "and she was very badly sunburned and I offered to get some lotion to fix her shoulders, and . . ."

Thereafter the pair met in hotels with much regularity and compared notes on married life and items like that. The plot on Albert Snyder's life—and some companion discussions about taking out a fat insurance policy on the easy-going artist—thickened amid a strong romantic aura and ample helpings from bootleg whiskey. But there would never be any agreement on the details: the lovebirds squabbled bitterly in court that April.

End of the Affair

> *"Does not he to whom you betray another know that you will at another time do as much for him?"*
>
> —MICHEL DE MONTAIGNE

The trial of Ruth Snyder and Judd Gray in the Queens County Courthouse at Long Island City started out like a replay at the Hall-Mills story. The chamber overflowed with outside observers, some of them holdovers from the elaborate newspaper coverage of the earlier epic. The list included Mary Roberts Rinehart, Billy Sunday, David Belasco, D. W. Griffith, Peggy Hopkins Joyce (presumably as an expert on marriage), Will Durant (then on the best-seller lists with *The Story of Philosophy*), Dr. John Roach Straton, and Aimee Semple McPherson.

The latter pair drew the strongest moral and religious lessons from the murder melodrama. Dr. Straton's examination of the record satisfied him that "literally every one of the Ten Commandments" had been trampled along the tawdry path of crime. Sister Aimee used the columns of the *New York Evening Graphic* to enjoin God to teach young men to say, "I want a wife like mother—not a Red-Hot Cutie." It took brass for "The Beautiful Sister Aimee of the Silver Tongue" to utter such a lofty sentiment within a year after starring in a red-hot scandal of her own, but nobody was surprised.

The proceedings opened with violently conflicting presentations. Edgar F. Hazleton, Mrs. Synder's counsel told the jury he would show that not only Gray but also the late Albert Snyder had contributed to his fair client's descent into the morass. He said that Snyder "drove love from out that house" by pining over a departed sweetheart of his youth and that Gray worked out the murder and the $50,000 double-indemnity insurance policy that sweetened the package.

"We will prove to you," Hazleton said, "that Ruth Snyder is not the demi-mondaine that Gray would like to paint her, but that she is a real loving wife, a good wife; that it was not her fault that brought about the condition that existed in that home..."

Samuel L. Miller, one of Gray's attorneys, had it the other way. He offered the jury "the most tragic story that has ever gripped the human heart." He said Gray was such a peace-abiding citizen that Ruth Synder had to give him fifteen or twenty shots of whiskey to steel him for the murder.

"He was dominated by a cold, heartless, calculating master mind and master will," Miller said. "He was a helpless mendicant of a designing, deadly, conscienceless, abnormal woman, a human serpent, a human fiend in the guise of a woman. He became inveigled and drawn into this hopeless chasm, when reason was gone, when mind was gone, when manhood was gone, and when his mind was weakened by lust and passion."

Ruth Snyder took the stand in a simple black frock characterized by the ladies among the 120 working reporters as "chic but decorous." She said Synder spent most of his time on such manly sports as boating and fishing and barely took her out, except to an occasional movie, but she maintained the best possible home for him nonetheless. She said she was the one who read the Bible to their daughter Lorraine and took her to Sunday school.

Then Hazleton came to the chance meeting with Gray and the hurry-up romance that ensued. "He was in about the same boat I was," Mrs. Snyder testified, a microphone carrying her words to the overflow throng in the corridors. "He said he was not happy (at home)." She said Gray drank heavily when they went to hotels or such Prohibition-time resorts as the Frivolity Club or the Monte Carlo but she hardly ever finished a drink and didn't even smoke. She swore that Gray got her to take out the heavy insurance policies on Snyder. "Once," she said, "he sent me poison and told me to give it to my husband." When the witness came to the murder itself she lost her composure and wept, while the stone-faced Gray suddenly came to life and chattered eagerly to his legal battery.

On cross-examination, Assistant District Attorney Charles W. Froessel hit hard on the men in Ruth Snyder's life, including other roving salesmen of her acquaintance, but the witness swore Gray was her only lover. The women in the courtroom, hostile to Mrs. Snyder from the beginning, snickered often during this line of questioning but the prosecutor didn't spare the woman in the chair.

Q—You thought that while you were carrying on with the defendant Gray you were putting it all over on your husband, didn't you? *A*—No, I did not.

Q—You thought you were doing him a favor? *A*—No, I did not.

Q—You knew you were doing wrong, did you not? *A*—Yes.

Q—He had full confidence in you, did he not, Madam? *A*—Yes.

Q—And you betrayed that confidence, did you not? *A*—I did not.

Q—Well, you betrayed it with Gray, did you not? *A*—Yes.

Q—You hated your husband, did you not? *A*—No, I did not.

Q—You loved him? *A*—I didn't love him but I didn't hate him.

Q—Of course, you did nothing in your married life to make your husband unhappy, did you? *A*—No.

Q—In other words, you want the jury to believe that you

were a perfect lady. Your answer is that you did nothing to make your husband unhappy. *A*—Not that he knew about it.

The big, hulking prosecutor took the witness over every step of the way, up to the murder, detail by detail, tearing her story to shreds. When he let her go she staggered from the stand badly shaken.

Judd Gray took the uneasy seat five minutes later, wearing a double-breasted business suit touched off by a white handkerchief in the lapel pocket. Occasionally he would glance from the stand to his aged mother, Mrs. Margaret Gray, sitting alongside no less a personage than Nora Bayes, the actress, there to see some real-life drama. Gray said he was perfectly happy at home until Ruth Snyder entered his life in search of a corselette. He said he hardly knew her well when she started talking about disposing of her husband. "We had a terrific argument over the thing."

Gray's recital transformed his ex-lover into a modern Borgia and made Albert Snyder, up to a point, the most durable of husbands. The salesman said Mrs. Synder—he called her "Momsie" in better times—once tried to kill Snyder with gas because nothing happened when she put knockout pills in his prune whip. "I told her I thought she was crazy," he testified. He said she gave Snyder poison for a case of hiccups but it only made him violently ill. "I said to her," Gray swore, "that was a hell of a way to cure hiccups." He said that when she told him about another abortive gas attempt he "criticized her sorely." He said she tried to kill Snyder with overdoses of sleeping powders at least twice. He said that once she showed him some arsenic with which she was going to spice "the Governor's" diet and another time she asked him if he would shoot Snyder for her. Gray said the woman simply wore him down to the point where he couldn't refuse when she asked him to bludgeon the artist to death. He said she worked out the insurance policies herself. He said she struck the first blow with the sash weight. Here Ruth Snyder sobbed so heavily that Gray glanced her way.

As the salesman finished, the dead man's brother, Warren Schneider, collapsed in the corridor outside and his wife's screams pierced the little courtroom, so Supreme Court Justice Townsend Scudder called an adjournment.

When the summations came, Gray wept over his attorney's eloquent appeal to the jury and Mrs. Snyder broke down when District Attorney Richard S. Newcombe likened her to a "wild beast of the jungle."

The jury deliberated ninety-eight minutes before condemning the once-loving pair. It was not a hard verdict to reach; no double prosecution had ever received quite as much help from the defendants themselves.

Gray went to the electric chair professing contentment. His wife, who had shunned him since the day of his arrest, sent him a letter of forgiveness—co-signed by her mother—as the end neared. When he got it, he said, "I am ready to go. I have nothing to fear."

Ruth Snyder died, on that bleak night of January 12, 1928, with a prayer on her lips. She had said in the Death House earlier that God had forgiven her and she hoped the world would.

"Those Anarchist Bastards"

> ". . . Never in our full life could we hope to do such a work for tolerance, for justice, for man's understanding of men as we do by accident . . . That last moment belongs to us— that agony is our triumph."
> —VANZETTI, *from the Death Cell*

There was a crowd of reporters waiting on the State House steps in Boston when Governor Alvan Tufts Fuller arrived to conduct the day's business on August 23, 1926.

"It's a beautiful morning, boys, isn't it?" he said, smiling broadly.

"The Governor seems in excellent health and spirits," *The New York Times* man wired his paper.

But there was a strong question that day about the health and spirits of two other men in Massachusetts—Nicola Sacco and Bartolomeo Vanzetti, anarchists. They were in the Death House at Charleston Prison waiting to keep an on-and-off date with the electric chair. They might have been pardoned a little uneasiness on that beautiful morning. It was meant to be their last.

The long, tortured night of Sacco and Vanzetti began with their arrest on May 5, 1920. The Red Raids were then in progress and the police questioned them about a memorial meeting for Andrea Salsedo, an anarchist who had plunged fourteen stories to his death from the Department of Justice offices in New York after an eight-week grilling. Sacco and

Vanzetti both had loaded pistols on them and on May 7 the police began to ask if they knew anything about a hold-up murder in South Braintree on April 15. A five-man bandit band had seized a $15,776.51 payroll belonging to the Slater & Morrill shoe factory after shooting down paymaster Frederick A. Parmenter and guard Alessandro Berardelli. Sacco and Vanzetti denied knowledge of the crime.

Questioned about an earlier payroll holdup, in Bridgewater, Sacco produced a time-clock alibi: he was at his bench in the Stoughton shoe factory where he was an edge trimmer. But Vanzetti, a fish peddler, was tried in the Bridgewater holdup. The judge in the case was the Hon. Webster Thayer, an aging pillar of the Back Bay aristocracy and a violent foe of all things radical. His charge to the jury included an injunction which, while horrid in a judicial sense, was quite popular at the time. "This man, although he may not actually have commited the crime attributed to him," Judge Thayer said, "is nevertheless morally culpable, because he is the enemy of our existing institutions . . . the defendant's ideals are cognate with crime." Even though thirty witnesses testified that he was in Plymouth when the crime took place, Vanzetti was convicted and sentenced to twelve to fifteen years in prison.

Judge Thayer, now sixty-four, also presided in Dedham the following spring when Vanzetti and his friend Sacco were tried in the South Braintree case. The Commonwealth produced an array of eyewitnesses who placed the two aliens at the scene. For the defense, nine witnesses from Boston put Sacco there on the day of the crime; the clerk of the Italian Consulate testified that he came in that day to inquire about getting a passport to Italy. In Vanzetti's case, six witnesses placed him in Plymouth that afternoon on his door-to-door rounds. The prosecution had 61 witnesses and the defense 107. The jury had to determine where the weight of truth lay.

The two men in the steel cage—both radicals, both slackers who had fled to Mexico during the war; Vanzetti with a brand-new criminal record in the Bridgewater holdup—were found guilty. The jury deliberated six and a half hours but the case reverberated around the world for the next six years. During that time, evidence piled upon evidence to throw massive doubts on the conviction, but Judge Thayer denied successive motions for a new trial, including one based on a convicted murderer's story that he could name the gang that committed the crime.

There were strong suggestions that the little Yankee Judge

had something more than a mild distaste for the convicted men. While turning down the appeals, he had freely referred to Sacco and Vanzetti as "Dagos" and "Sons of Bitches" in the confines of his golf club. During a Dartmouth football game he was overheard saying to a friend, "Did you see what I did to those anarchistic bastards?" Robert Benchley, the writer, quoted a mutual New England friend—"Webster has been saying those anarchist bastards down in Boston were trying to intimidate him." Frank P. Sibley of the *Boston Globe*, dean of the Massachusetts reporters, said that in thirty-five years around the courts he had never seen anything like Judge Thayer's handling of the Sacco-Vanzetti trial. "His whole manner, his whole attitude, seemed to be that the jurors were there to convict the men," Sibley wrote. Louis Stark of *The New York Times* said that in February, 1922, Thayer had said to him, "I hope *The New York Times* is not going on the side of these anarchists." Stark said the judge revealed to him an overwhelming abhorrence of radicals and foreigners. Other reporters also documented that point but it couldn't help win a new trial. The judge passing on that detail was Webster Thayer.

The Last Days of Sacco and Vanzetti

> *"I have known Judge Thayer all my life. . . . He is a narrow-minded man; he is a half-educated man; he is an unintelligent man; he is carried away with his fear of Reds. . . ."*
> —WILLIAM G. THOMPSON, *for the Defense*

On April 9, 1927, the eyes of the world were focused on a little courtroom in New England. The day of sentence finally had arrived. When Nicola Sacco was asked what he had to say, he replied in halting English that his friend Vanzetti would speak for both of them. But then the immigrant factory hand looked up at the shriveled old man on the bench and words poured forth:

"I never knew, never heard, even read in history anything so cruel as this Court. After seven years' prosecuting they still consider us guilty. And these gentle people here are arrayed with us in this court today.

"I know the sentence will be between two classes, the oppressed class and the rich class, and there will be always collision between one and the other. We fraternize the people with the books, with the literature. You persecute the people, tyrannize them and kill them. We try the education of people always. You try to put a path between us and some other nationality that hates each other. That is why I am here today on this bench, for having been of the oppressed class. Well, you are the oppressor . . .

"You know it, Judge Thayer—you know all my life, you know why I have been here, and after seven years that you have been persecuting me and my poor wife, and you still today sentence us to death. I would like to tell all my life, but what is the use?"

Vanzetti, forty-one, a prize student in Italy before he came to the United States—laborer, peddler, bricklayer, quarry worker, rope mill hand, and strike leader in this country, was even more eloquent than Sacco.

". . . I am not only innocent of these two crimes," he said, "but I never commit a crime in my life. I have never steal and I have never kill and I have never spilt blood and I have fought against the crime and I have fought and I have sacrificed myself even to eliminate the crimes that the law and the church legitimate and sanctify.

"This is what I say: I would not wish to a dog or to a snake, to the most low and misfortunate creature of the earth—I would not wish to any of them what I have had to suffer for things that I am not guilty of. But my conviction is that I have suffered for things that I am guilty of. I am suffering because I am a radical and indeed I am a radical; I have suffered because I was an Italian and indeed I am an Italian; I have suffered more for my family and for my beloved than for myself; but I am so convinced to be right that if you could execute me two times and if I could be reborn two other times I would live again to do what I have done already. I have finished—thank you."

Judge Thayer noted in a wispy voice that Massachusetts' Supreme Judicial Court had upheld the verdicts and that death was mandatory. He set the week of July 10 for the executions but protests mounted with such force that Governor Fuller granted a reprieve until August 10 so that a special advisory commission could look into the case for him. He named Abbott Lawrence Lowell, president of Harvard University, Dr. Samuel W. Stratton, president of the Massachusetts Institute of Technology and ex–Probate Judge Robert Grant.

The Lowell Commission went over the record and heard a mass of testimony—some from prosecution witnesses recanting their 1921 stories, some throwing doubts on the veracity and character of other state witnesses, some backing the trial witnesses who had placed Sacco in Boston on the day of the South Braintree holdup, eighteen saying Vanzetti sold them fish in Plymouth that day, some to the effect that the court interpreter erred in translating key testimony. One witness swore that before the trial the man later made foreman of the jury had said, "Damn them, they ought to hang anyway."

Except for noting "a grave breach of official decorum" in Judge Thayer's oft-quoted off-the-bench remarks, the Lowell Commission found nothing to suggest a miscarriage of justice. The Governor accepted the findings but on August 10 he granted a twelve-day reprieve for final legal moves. The stay reached the Death House in Charlestown Prison just fifty-one minutes ahead of the executioner and served to touch off violent Sacco-Vanzetti demonstrations all over the world. There were forty persons hurt in a London riot. There were street fights in Paris and disorders outside the American Consulate in Geneva. The American flag was burned before our Consulate in Casablanca. There were riots in Berlin, Warsaw, Buenos Aires, Mexico, Cuba, Japan, Brest, Marseilles and Argentina. Throngs wearing black mourning bands marched in Boston and New York. The voices of George Bernard Shaw, Albert Einstein, H. G. Wells, Romain Rolland, Anatole France and John Galsworthy joined with those of the American writers and intellectuals pleading for clemency. Heywood Broun, till then a leisurely observer of the American scene, tore into the Lowell Commission in his *New York World* column:

"What more can the immigrants from Italy expect? It is not every person who has a president of Harvard University throw the switch for him. If this is lynching, at least the fish-peddler and his friend, the factory hand, may take unction to their souls that they will die at the hands of men in dinner jackets or academic gowns, according to the conventionalities required by the hour of execution." The *World*, supposedly an oasis of liberalism in those days, held out succeeding Broun columns when he refused to write about more tranquil subjects than the two Italians in Death Row. Eventually it led to his leaving the paper.

Sacco and Vanzetti died on August 23, 1927. Governor Fuller spent the "beautiful morning" and the rest of the day entertaining eleventh-hour appeals for the doomed men, but did not act. The Commonwealth put an armed garrison around Charlestown Prison—thousands demonstrated to the last second—and the switch fell on schedule. Later Louis Stark summed it up this way: "The tragedy for the Sacco-Vanzetti case is the tragedy of three men—Judge Thayer, Governor Fuller, and President Lowell—and their inability to rise above the obscene battle that raged for seven long years around the heads of the shoemaker and the fish peddler."

It was greater than that. It was the tragedy of the whole United States in the Lawless Decade, because it happened in the very Cradle of Liberty and it suggested that in those days, in some places, the government itself held the law lightly.

New Social Types

by Elizabeth Stevenson

The opportunities and the pressures of a new age created new kinds of people. Whether or not there was freedom and a new chance for all—and there was not—there existed an erroneous but cheering belief that there was change ahead. The openness of the future and the accessibility, as it seemed, of success produced a froth upon the times, and many short-lived, heedless, sometimes graceful, careers danced upon this foam of confidence. A later, more solid time that would have more real opportunity would lack this effervescence, which was a unique attribute to the twenties. An English observer characterized a conspicuous part of the population: "Dancing as aimlessly as gnats in winter sunshine it brings to bear on the jolly business of being *ephemeridae* the same hard and cheerful efficiency that it uses in its money making."[1] Observers from overseas were keen, but never got in quite right. They assumed in Americans a hard, deliberate choice in the universal career of money-making with other choices discarded, whereas, for Americans, there was nothing else they knew, and they put into money-making the traits reserved in Europe for other careers: sports, gambling, politics, status-creation, even remotely, a kind of esthetics.

The most effervescent symbol of the twenties was the flapper. She was a new American girl, a new woman, a new arrangement of the elements of sex and love. She no longer exists; she existed for only a few years in the mid- and late twenties, but during that short epoch she was a completely defined and recognizable type. In the twenties she was suddenly there, it seemed, and welcome.

Yet the flapper evolved.[2] She was born perhaps in the experiences some few women had in the war of 1917–18, when all sorts of freedoms and equalities with men occurred during the exigencies of Red Cross and other welfare work among the soldiers or particularly in the excitements of entertaining them. Travel, informality, closeness of contact between the two sexes in situations of danger changed the relations between men and women, at least for short periods in certain places; and some of this carried over into the period after the war, buried at first, but asserting itself at last with impudence and self-assurance.

Mary Pickford was not a flapper, and the Mary Pickford type of sweet, confiding, shy, and yet gay innocent female dominated the early after-the-war covers and illustrations in the *Saturday Evening Post*, which may be taken as a place to watch for the flapper's arrival. A change appears first in the familiarity of the boy and girl on the innocuous covers. In a Norman Rockwell painting for the issue of March 12, 1921, the girl is more kittenish than hoydenish; her hair, her dress, her attitude are soft and tentative, but she is unafraid and a little bold, whereas the boy whose hand she is holding—to tell his fortune—is awkward. She looks into his eyes with confidence and no assumption of consequences to her boldness. A year later, in a cover by Thomas H. Webb for the issue of May 13, 1922, the closeness of the boy and the girl, while still playful, is more self-conscious; he is standing close in an attitude of embrace, ostensibly showing her how to hold a bow and arrow; her dress is beginning to be tomboyish: a skirt and sweater, the sweater belted in leather, an Indian beaded band across her forehead. Her glance backward at the young man—awkward boy no longer—is more conscious of possible consequences of this exciting intimacy.

During 1922 and 1923 the girls in the stories still wear soft, full dresses, rather awkwardly long. Sometimes the heroine in sweater and skirt wears her hair in a long, thick braid down her back. Older women wear ample clothes, which denote maturity. In 1924 there is a change in an occasional cover or illustration. Out of the cover of January 5, 1924, a gambling girl looks straight at you. Her dress is the slightest, flimsiest silk, cut low and square-necked, thin straps over her shoulders. Her bobbed hair is almost hidden by a soft, wide, shirred bandeau of the same silken material as the slight, slim gown. She handles gambling counters as she sits at a table; the look she gives says that she handles her life as a gamble, too.

Dresses in many of the stories remain rather indefinitely long, but the nice young girl's position in society is infinitely free and easy; one story shows the heroine sitting at her ease at a drug counter, exchanging pleasantries good-naturedly and unselfconsciously with the sleek young man behind the counter. A boy and a girl in an Alice Duer Miller story sit at ease upon a beach. They wear the new bathing suits; his is one-piece, armless, but high-necked; hers is one-piece, reaching a few inches down the thigh, the skirt of the suit gaily and boldly striped. She has on some kind of stocking below the knees and slippers. As late as January, 1925, a cover shows a fond and fatuous portrait of a Mary Pickford girl who has long corkscrew curls trailing down to a soft and modest neckline. But inside the same issue, on the first page after the cover, there is a bold girl in a hosiery ad who seems to herald a new age. She is perched carelessly but gracefully upon a glossy mahogany table, dangling one silken leg off the edge. Her hair is softly waved and bobbed and her dress is sleeveless and short, held up by straps that look like flowers. Her slippers are slight things with pointed toes. At this moment the flapper is here, and all girls, the good ones and the bad ones, try to be flappers; the time is the end of the year 1925 and the early part of 1926. So long did it take her to come. Girls with skirts short to the knees or just below the knees became frequent if not universal.

In a story in the issue of April 3, 1926, there is a girl who is the very type: a girl seen in a careless pose, her back to us, on tiptoes, her dress hem hitting the back of her knees, her waist low and bloused. On her head is a cloche hat with a soft brim. Another story shows the same kind of girl dancing the Charleston, the caption comments, "with imagination and abandon." Girls, by this time, are shown putting on lipstick in public, confident of their own importance, and displaying a breezy independence of opinion. Many girls try to be flappers. The generic flapper is the nice girl who is a little fast, who takes the breath of staid observers with her flip spontaneity, her short-lived likes and dislikes, her way of skating gaily over thin ice. Would-be flappers are often heartless little ignoramuses, gum-chewing, vulgar, wearing ridiculous clothes, imitating a mode in second-rate style; others are overdecorated, costly, gangsters' girl friends. Many girls of the mid-twenties, however, grew up, finished school, fell in love, married, all without any whiff of the style of the type—yet bobbing their hair, doing up their hems, learning to Charleston.

By 1925 the phenomenon of the flapper was so conspicuous that many words were put on paper analyzing her. In 1920, before the full-blown type existed, Scott Fitzgerald gave a book of short stories the title *Flappers and Philosophers*. A magazine like *The New Republic*, given to the seri-

New Social Types

ous study of politics and economics, had space on September 9, 1925, for a piece by Bruce Bliven, an attempt to describe the new girl. Bliven thought he knew how she made up her face and what she wore and told it in a piece called "Flapper Jane":

> She is frankly, heavily made up, not to imitate nature, but for an altogether artificial effect—pallor mortis, poisonously scarlet lips, richly ringed eyes—the latter looking not so much debauched (which is the intention) as diabetic....
>
> [Her clothes] ... were estimated the other day by some statistician to weight two pounds. Probably a libel; I doubt if they come within half a pound of such bulk. Jane isn't wearing much this summer. If you'd like to know exactly, it is: one dress, one step-in, two stockings, two shoes. [No petticoat, no brassiere, of course, no corset.][3]

The flapper seemed the most notable new character upon the scene. She attracted the most attention. When she smoked a cigarette conspicuously on a public street, reporters made a front-page story of the incident. She rallied a whole new circle of male types around her. Her beaus, boys in Joe College clothes, or sharp young gentlemen in belted jackets and new Van Heusen soft collars, and trousers with wide flapping legs, shared her good times, learning to drink in a dry age, dancing the fox-trot in roadhouses, riding about in rattletrap flivvers or expensive Marmons, going to the movies and the speakeasies, traveling across the Atlantic to a gay, superficial Europe that seemed to belong to Americans. Oddly, the particular, identifiable flapper faded away very quickly, to be replaced, so that the fact was hardly noticed, by another. She and her boy friend, after a short season of gaiety, a year or two or more, vanished and became part of a solid, respectable, and inconspicuous mass of settled, older, married folks, upholding the standards of the good life as sketched so preposterously and winningly in Sinclair Lewis' *Babbitt*. Flappers and Babbitts had to be rather well off. Unprosperous folks did not have the time or cash to belong to either types so the double layer of gay young people and stuffily proper middle-aged ones was after all very thin, the two-tiered icing upon the cake of the age.

N. W. Ayer & Sons took a full-page advertisement in the

Saturday Evening Post on January 10, 1925, to state the facts of life that fed business. A drawing showed three young people striding forward clothed in confidence and pride as well as of the costumes of youthful success: two girls wearing dresses belted low and carelessly across the hips, the boy in a pinched-in jacket and loose fitting trousers and wide-brimmed fashionable hat. The copy read:

> You may regard the new generation as amusing or pathetic; as a bit tragic, or rather splendid. You may consider their manners crude, their ideals vague, their clothes absurd. Their cynical, humorous discussions of social conditions may stir you to admiration or fill you with helpless rage.
>
> But it is useless to deny that these youngsters have a definite bearing on the thought, literature and customs of our day. And particularly do they exert a powerful influence on buying habits and the movement of merchandise.
>
> The tremendous increase in the sales of cosmetics and silk stockings in the last ten years is a revelation of power. . . . Practically all men's clothes are young men's clothes. Most frocks are designed for young women.
>
> Today they are careless of tradition, heedless of responsibility. But tomorrow these young women will be home executives. These young men will conduct our businesses. They will buy enormous quantities of every conceivable kind of staple merchandise.

The flapper fascinated because she flaunted respectability. But respectability usually caught up with her. There was another type of the time who fascinated because he really broke through the crust of respectability and showed the hellishness down below. This was the garish gangster. He exerted a strong pull of half-denied interest upon the solid middle group, for he showed in his awful, destructive, yet sometimes stylish and purposeful activity traits in human nature that everyone felt the tug of, but usually denied.

The age was held spellbound by the gangster, but in most of the territory of the twenties, the gangster was an exotic, seldom seen, only talked about. He was rampant in restricted areas. In Chicago he was most blatant. Solid citizens in comfortable beds had no reason, or so it seemed, to fear him.

(Poor folks feared him, those out of the swing of the general prosperity.) He attracted as well as terrified. The point has been made that the gangster, in his perfected and organized form, was the businessman as the businessman wished to be but dared not be, without restrictions or aims but those of power alone. He was therefore a caricature in burning-bright and ruthless shape of what all the good, small men praised and desired in success. But this is to make Babbitt into a bigger, freer creature than he was. Babbitt was the middling mover and servicer of society, not the maker and organizer and producer. The real makers and producers were larger, more unhampered men whom the Babbitts did not really know at all, although they flattered themselves that they modeled themselves upon such men. What the gangster meant to the good, tight, well-behaved middling Babbitt was an extension of personality. Superficially, Babbitt deplored the fact that such people existed, but he never exerted himself to control the gangster till the end of the period; then his own world and the gangster's both ended.

A dying gangster, shot by rivals in Chicago, kicked at the hospital attendant who was helping to carry him on a stretcher, aiming at the face of the man who represented society to him, saying, "Take that, you dirty son of a bitch." This was his "valediction"; and, once pronounced, "he fell back and died."[4]

Gangster dominance in certain areas showed in an uncontrolled violence. Gang-killings in Chicago accelerated:

1924—16 men shot to death
1925—46 men shot to death
1926—76 men shot to death

In these particular killings only six men were brought to trial. All were acquitted except one, who certainly went out of his way to be offensive: "Sam Vinci, who pushed public settlement of quarrels a little too far. He drew a .45 automatic during an inquest on his brother Mike and shot John Minatti dead, his explanation being that it had begun to look as if the jury were going to set Minatti free, and he did not wish this to happen. Vinci went to Joliet Penitentiary for twenty-five years."[5]

The epitome of gangsterism was Al Capone, in his flashy clothes and freehanded spending of a fat bankroll for friends and for the poor, his killings, his organization of liquor into a gigantic business at the top of a great terror-ridden pyramid. His operations by the end of the twenties had given him a fortune of probably forty million dollars and his organization an income of a hundred million a year.[6] Capone showed a chilling public display of power in taking over and remaking one innocuous suburban town, Cicero, Illinois. Capone's men supported the Republican ticket of Cicero and then took over the city completely. Capone moved into Cicero to line its streets with gambling places, which gave him one certain supply of money. He made the Hawthorne Inn his personal headquarters, covered its doors and windows with steel shutters, and turned its second floor into a sort of castle from which he looked down upon the activities of his personal domain.

> Mayor Klenha and his circle dispiritedly endured what they had brought upon themselves. Now it was Capone's voice that was listened to; his orders transcended law. Police, city officials and local businessmen took instructions direct from the Hawthorne Inn.
>
> Once when Klenha had failed to carry out a command, Capone paid him a personal call, knocked him down the steps of the City Hall and kicked him repeatedly as he scrambled up. A policeman stood watching the assault, twirled his night stick and strolled off.[7]

The twenties created the flapper and the gangster, who were exceptional and notable. It created also the middle businessman, who enjoyed being part of a great, undifferentiated average. The normal view was from the middle. However, the colorful off-shoots of the age, the types with bright or angular distinctions, enlivened Babbitt's satisfactions.

The work of the professional entertainers pierced through the blandness of the time. So excellent were the entertainers of the twenties that a later time remembered them and forgot the middle people. Yet in entertainment, perhaps most in entertainment, there were contradictions. There were two popular kinds of entertainment in the twenties: one that soothed and edified and put to sleep; another that inflamed, sharpened, and intensified emotions and wills.

An advertisement of Universal Pictures in the *Saturday Evening Post* of January 19, 1924, signed by the president of the company, Carl Laemmle, states exactly what producers of entertainment thought the broad audience wanted, and what for the most part that audience thought it wanted:

> I don't want to go to the theatre to weep. No, and I don't like death scenes. I don't like to see the hero shot or hanged, or the heroine die in the arms of her lover when they can just as well live and send you home with pleasant impressions and memories.

While the techniques of movie-making improved during the late years of the silent pictures and a few producers made movies of enduring intellectual brilliance to go with the better technical means, a blandness in agreement with Carl Laemmle's prescription crept over much that was offered, a placidity of entertainment suited apparently for the happy people of Middletown.

But strangely enough, it was entertainers of a kind of demoniac possession who were the ones best loved. Lon Chaney in his career was an example. In a series of horror movies, his special and intense gift burned out the dross of preposterous surroundings and left an impression of purity and genius. Edmund Wilson found Chaney's American motion picture *The Unholy Three* not far below the acknowledged German masterpiece of the type, *Dr. Caligari*, and "admirably acted. . . . [In] its parrots that cannot talk, its misanthropic midget, its infernal scene around the Christmas tree where the tranquil benevolence of a family circle serves as a mask for the murderers, it is quite comparable in imagination to the German nightmare."[8]

Wilson, beginning to exercise an individual gift for criticism, assessed motion pictures or nightclub entertainers as seriously as a new poem by T. S. Eliot or a novel by F. Scott Fitzgerald. In the enthusiastic proliferation of living, doing, being, without forethought or afterthought, there did not lack some minds such as Wilson's who saw that this life was all of a piece and all interesting. The American environment itself was as rewarding a study as American books or paintings or buildings. Wilson found the contemplation of the nightclub hostess Texas Guinan well worthwhile: "This prodigious woman, with her pearls, her glittering bosom, her abundant beautifully bleached yellow coiffure, her formidable trap of shining white teeth, her broad bare back behind its grating of green velvet, the full-blown peony as big as a cabbage exploding on her broad green thigh."[8] Wilson saw in her raucous salute "Hello sucker" an honesty and a spirit that many in the busy age lacked and that was refreshing and good in itself.

Gilbert Seldes, another new critic of the anonymous or popular or vulgar arts, praised Al Jolson. "Mr. Jolson sublimely lives. His daemon attends. He is ageless and radiant and terrible."[10] Seldes was writing for a highbrow audience in a highbrow magazine, *The Dial*. An anonymous critic in the same magazine attested devotion to "Krazy Kat." "Here is a veritable creation."[11] A comic-strip artist, a popular singer, a motion-picture actor, a gifted director—such individuals drew vitality from the general life of the time and gave that life form and style. Such people were an irritation as well as a stimulation to the general viewer. Main Street life flattened out angularities. Its environment encouraged sameness rather than difference. Yet Main Street kept always a sneaking admiration for those others, the outrageous, the different, the entertaining. Entertainers and entertainments flourished just beyond the borders of the well-regulated areas where the numerous, sincerely imitative Main Streeters or Middle-towners lived.

So a director like von Stroheim or an actor like Chaney lighted up the mediocre scene of the movies, or a Texas Guinan the tawdriness of the places where bad liquor was sold. In other fields, other gifted individuals were not lacking. The unknown and almost interchangeable jazz musicians of Chicago and New York played in reeking, sweating, ugly surroundings, but achieved a kind of lighthearted innocence of aspiration and single-minded ambition. The scene of the speakeasy itself, the nightclub hostess' and jazz player's world, a stronghold owned by gangsters, serving rotgut liquor, charging outrageous prices, provided a stage for creativity. With the exception of O'Neill, it was the lighter, more popular side of Broadway that attained first-rate quality. Edmund Wilson wrote about "The Follies" in August, 1923, in *The Dial*:

> ... Ann Pennington has been added, so that, with Cantor and Gilda Gray, you have perhaps the three highest pressure performers in the city all under the same canvas. The tempo of the show is now uniform and it is the same as that of life outside. It is New York in terms of

entertainment—the expression of extreme nervous intensity to the tune of complicated harmonies. When you take the subway after the theatre, it speeds you straight with a crash to your goal, like a song by Eddie Cantor; and in the roar of the nocturnal city, driven rhythmically for all its confusion, you catch hoarse echoes of Gilda Gray singing her incomparable Come Along!

In September, 1923, Seldes wrote in *The Dial:* "One man on the American stage, and one woman, are possessed—Al Jolson and Fanny Brice. Their demons are not of the same order, but together they represent all we have of the Great God Pan, and we ought to be grateful for it."

Appreciation for the gifted and "possessed" entertainers came most literally from the highbrow press, not at all from the *Saturday Evening Post,* which existed to smooth away the sharp perceptions of its middle people, who yet, almost ashamedly, enjoyed Jolson and Brice and Chaney and Krazy Kat. The best entertainment of the twenties was brilliant and extreme because it played itself out against its audience, not for it.

One must put off any solid analysis of the world of Middletown and the possible reactions against it that were valid and not merely hectic. But here, in glancing at the types twisted into shape by a divided world, at the flappers, the businessmen of middling range but extreme monotony of type, at lurid gangsters, and at brilliant entertainers often wasting talents upon poor material, one can study the binding world of knowing and feeling in which they all lived.

It was a new civilization trying with young energy to be one. After having been thin, poor, scattered, it found itself rich and influential, its spiritual means not quite grown up to the occasion. Some of the ways people bound themselves together were commendable and even noble, others were pathetic or improper or harmful. The popular culture that wrapped around this people was made up only in part of older elements of tradition from smaller regional cultures or of the successive traditions of immigrant waves. These elements spread thin and lacked depth and force for the children of the old settlers and the children of the new settlers living in new conditions. The new popular culture built itself up out of the pristine elements of life that this young generation found itself immersed in. The going quickly from place to place, the hearing of news almost as soon as an event occurred, the sense that all the parts of a large continental country were tied together—these new facts changed people. Making the change radical was the way goods were bought and sold.

The world of persuasion, in a society whose business, as President Coolidge said, was business, *was* the new tradition—lacking any other—in which people lived and felt close to one another and knew themselves one people. The very means by which this unity and closeness were accomplished—transportation, communication, persuasion—were part of the culture.

It has become a commonplace notion that an uncritical, ambitious, rising culture becomes itself through imitating the life of advertisements. In the twenties in such a typical magazine as the *Saturday Evening Post* one can see it begin to happen. What people ate, what soap they used, what clothes they wore, what they did for amusement, what thrilled them with a sense of adventure—in advertisements all these things were invented, named, joined together, in a continuous pageant of life to be emulated. The young industry made life exciting for a people eager to improve themselves and their families. That the being better and the doing better was worked for the benefit of corporations selling goods was slurred over willingly both by the sellers and the buyers. It was a conspiracy happily self-imposed. A sampling illustrates the way the new world of goods and ideas hit the eye and the mind of the casual reader.

A Cream of Wheat ad in the *Saturday Evening Post* of March 12, 1921, made gentle fun of the hick farmer who held up a box of cereal and exclaimed, "Empty, by Heck," as he stood by his pot-bellied stove, his kindling in an empty Cream of Wheat case. This was a way of including all the people in the knowingness of the brand name—even those isolated like the farmer. This approach was quickly abandoned. Increasingly, the advertisements painted the consumer as sharp, sophisticated, more sophisticated than the advertiser believed him to be, but therefore sophisticated as the consumer wished himself to be. Taught like a lesson, plainly and pointedly emphasized again and again, as if for a bright but lagging child, was the new importance of the brand name. In the issue of May 13, 1922, the Victrola ad asks the reader to look for the label: "Important: look for these trademarks. Under the lid. On the label." The Campbell's Soup ad says firmly, "Look for the Red and White label." In the same issue of January 5, 1924, the Del Monte foods ad reads:

> You can be just as sure of quality in canned fruits as you want to be.
>
> It's the easiest thing in the world. There's only one condition—you must *know* what you want. Then make sure you get it. Quality is bought only through knowledge—and *not* by chance.
>
> That's why it is so important to insist on a brand like *Del Monte.*

Simple insistence gave way to enticement, the association of all sorts of allied advantages to the basic good ensured by the product. An Ivory Soap ad of January 5, 1924, showed a young woman playing the piano surrounded by five attentive men. She had bare arms, her dress had a square low neckline, its fabric fell straight and soft, in simple lines. She wore a bandeau across her forehead to catch and hold her short hair. Another smaller picture showed her among her beauty aids in her bathroom: cleanliness was of course understood, but attractiveness was stressed. The ad states: "In Sally Jollyco's own gleaming white bathroom lies one of the chief secrets of her charm."

Magazine advertisements sold ideas as well as products. A full-page display on January 5, 1924, sold "California—Where Success Means More." It pictured an idyllic valley farmhouse surrounded by orchards; in the foreground of the picture were a youthful father and mother and a little girl with an armload of flowers.

> Many people plan to succeed, and then come to California. California invites you to succeed here. People who can make good somewhere else can make good in California and in many cases do it more quickly. California is developing faster than any other section of the country. ... There is, on the average, an automobile for every family and every farm. Modern kitchen conveniences are common in the country. Rural homes are on smooth highways. Even the humblest abodes are flower-clad, and can nestle against great foothills beneath mild skies. ...
>
> California spends money to be better. Better roads, better schools, better parks. A $12,000,000 bond issue

was recently voted by San Francisco for a greater public school program. California spends money to be happy and comfortable. . . .

Success means more in California because children are given advantages here. Success means more because the average Californian sees his youngsters grow heavier and taller than the nation's average. . . .

There is comfortable room in California for 26,000,000 more people.

The very means of communication and transportation that bound together the parts of the country, a comparatively old East and a comparatively new West, were romanticized in advertising.

A General Electric advertisement of Mazda Lamps in the issue of January 10, 1925, conveyed a relationship between the homely electric lamp of household use and the lamps used to light airplanes to dangerous landings at night. A dramatic picture showed a biplane, as if seen from above, square-winged, single-engined, its two searchlights on: "When the mail plane swoops down from the sky at night, it sails into a flood of light that makes landings safe as at noon. For the air mail landings, the Laboratories have developed Mazda Lamps of ten thousand watts."

Radio in thousands of homes linked people in simultaneous enjoyment and excitement. Advertising was from the first the skeleton upon which the enjoyment and excitement were fleshed. An ad for radio batteries, in the *Saturday Evening Post* of January 5, 1924, showed two boys with earphones on, grinning with excitement at each other, one saying, "There's another station we never had!" The advertiser's comment, patronizing, encouraging, was: "Fishing for the new ones—that's half the fun, isn't it?"

Another radio-batteries ad, for Willard Batteries, on January 10, 1925, conveyed the communion of people listening to new programs carried regularly by large and powerful stations, a standardization in listening and enjoying that was a pleasure.

> When "The King of the Ivories" is tickling the keys at WOS—
> When WOR comes rolling in from the East and KFI, in its turn brings greetings from the Pacific coast—
> When your Saturday evening dance from WTAM is

making just the biggest kind of hit—remember that Willard Radio Batteries are contributing to your enjoyment—

Advertising was false in promising more than the seller delivered to the buyer, but it was false also in seeming to be a world to which real life must bring itself into relation. It was false to particular American life and it was false to particular human nature in its blandness, narrowness, its smoothing away of individual corners and all inconvenient or tragic exultations or despairs. It was so pervasive a surface, so willingly adjusted to by many people that it was like a lowered, limited horizon. Strong emotions and fierce beliefs were stoppered down so that when they burst forth they rushed out with violence and exaggeration.

The true twenties, the real twenties, was a society of contrast, of an amazing sameness and acceptance, and also of violent emphasis, revolt, and jagged and exceptional development. The violence and waywardness of achievement were ways of reacting against an impervious blanket of satisfaction. Yet the rejecters and the accepters shared a similarity of confidence encouraged by the widespread sense of national and personal security, It was a security that seemed to roll around and lap all the contingencies of life; it included patronage (pity or scorn) for other peoples and was so basic as not to know itself: Hopes and ambitions were thought not to have limitations,

1. Cyril H. Bretherton, *Midas, or the United States and the Future* (London, K. Paul, Trench, Trubner & Co., 1926), p. 66.
2. For instance, in the pages of the *Saturday Evening Post*, a product of the popular culture, in illustrations, advertisements, cover drawings, from 1921 to 1926, the flapper evolved until she finally existed.
3. *The New Republic*, Sept. 9, 1925.
4. Kenneth Allsop, *The Bootleggers and Their Era* (New York, Doubleday & Co., 1961), p. 98.
5. *Ibid.*, p. 57.
6. *Ibid.*, p. 199.
7. *Ibid.*, p. 64.
8. *The New Republic*, Vol. 44, p. 124.
9. *The New Republic*, Sept. 9, 1925.
10. *The Dial*, Nov., 1921.
11. *The Dial*, "Comment," unsigned, July, 1920.

Lyrics

A Typographical Note

Since the metrical character of a song lyric is established by the music, it is not always possible to reprint a lyric apart from its musical setting in such a way as to demonstrate its rhythmic vitality. Nevertheless, I have tried to indicate some sense of the meter by printing the lyrics to emphasize the rhyme. Compared with meter in poetry, meter in song lyrics is more intimately connected with rhyme.

The punctuation used in sheet music—where the lyrics are presumably "heard" rather than read—is typically inadequate for the printed page; therefore, I have frequently modified or supplemented the punctuation for the sake of clarity.

Ain't We Got Fun? (1921)

*Lyrics by Gus Kahn and Raymond B. Egan
Music by Richard A. Whiting*

Verse One

Bill collectors gather
Round and rather
Haunt the cottage next door,
Men the grocer and butcher sent,
Men who call for the rent.

But within a happy chappy
And his wife of only a year
Seem to be so cheerful,
Here's an earful
Of the chatter you hear.

Refrain One

Ev'ry morning.
Ev'ry eve-ning,
Ain't we got fun?
Not much money,
Oh, but honey,
Ain't we got fun?

The rent's unpaid, dear;
We haven't a bus;
But smiles were made, dear,
For people like us.

In the winter,
In the summer,
Don't we have fun?
Times are bum and
Getting bummer,
Still we have fun.

There's nothing surer,
The rich get rich and the poor get children.
In the meantime,
In between time,
Ain't we got fun?

Verse Two

Just to make their trouble
Nearly double,
Something happened last night.
To their chimney a gray bird came;
Mr. Stork is his name.

And I'll bet two pins
A pair of twins
Just happened in with the bird.
Still they're very
Gay and merry—
Just at dawn I heard.

Refrain Two

Ev'ry morning,
Ev'ry eve-ning,
Don't we have fun?
Twins and cares, dear,
Come in pairs, dear,
Don't we have fun?

We've only started
As mommer and pop.
Are we downhearted?
I'll say that we're not.

Landlord's mad and
Getting madder,
Ain't we got fun?
Times are bad and
Getting badder,
Still we have fun.

There's nothing surer,
The rich get rich and the poor get laid off.
In the meantime,
In between time,
Ain't we got fun?

Verse Three

When the man who sold 'em
Carpets told 'em
He would take them away,
They said, "Wonderful, here's our chance—
Take them up and we'll dance."

And when burglars came and robb'd them,
Taking all their silver, they say
Hubby yell'd, "We're famous,
For they'll name us
In the papers today."

Refrain Three

Night or daytime,
It's all playtime,
Ain't we got fun?
Hot or cold days,
Any old days,
Ain't we got fun?

If wifey wishes
To go to a play,
Don't wash the dishes,
Just throw them away.

Street car seats are
Awful narrow,
Ain't we got fun?
They won't smash up
Our Pierce Arrow,
We ain't got none.

They've cut my wages,
But my income tax will be so much smaller.
When I'm paid off,
I'll be laid off,
Ain't we got fun?

Second Hand Rose (1921)

Lyrics by Grant Clarke
Music by James F. Hanley

Verse

Father has a bus'ness,
Strictly second hand,
Everything from toothpicks
To a baby grand.
Stuff in our apartment
Came from Father's store,
Even things I'm wearing,
Someone wore before.
It's no wonder that I feel abused,
I never have a thing that ain't been used:

Refrain One

I'm wearing second hand hats,
Second hand clothes,
That's why they call me
Second Hand Rose.
Even our piano in the parlour,
Father bought for ten cents on the dollar.
Second hand pearls,
I'm wearing second hand pearls,
I never get a single thing that's new.
Even Jake the plumber, he's the man I adore,
He had the nerve to tell me he's been married before.
Everyone knows
That I'm just Second Hand Rose
From Second Avenue.

Two

I'm wearing second hand shoes,
Second hand hose,
All the girls hand me

Their second hand beaux.
Even my pajamas when I don 'em
Have somebody else's 'nitials on 'em.
Second hand rings,
I'm sick of second hand things,
I never get what other girlies do.
Once while strolling thru the Ritz, a girl got my goat:
She nudged her friend and said, "Oh look! There's my old fur coat."
Everyone knows
That I'm just Second Hand Rose
From Second Avenue.

The Best Things in Life Are Free (1927)

*Lyrics and Music by Buddy DeSylva,
Lew Brown, and Ray Henderson*

Verse

There are so many kinds of riches,
And only one of them is gold.
The wealth you miss,
Remember this:
Worthwhile things cannot be bought or sold.

Refrain

The moon belongs to ev'ryone,
The best things in life are free.

The stars belong to ev'ryone,
They gleam there for you and me.

The flowers in Spring,
The robins that sing,
The sunbeams that shine,
They're yours, they're mine!

And love can come to ev'ryone,
The best things in life are free.

Can't Help Lovin' Dat Man
(1927)

Lyrics by Oscar Hammerstein II
Music by Jerome Kern

Verse

Oh listen, sister,
I love my mister man,
And I can't tell yo' why.
Dere ain't no reason
Why I should love dat man.
It must be sumpin'
Dat de angels done plan.
De chimbley's smokin',
De roof is leakin' in,
But he don't seem to care.
He can be happy
With jes' a sip of gin.
I even love him
When his kisses got gin.

Refrain

Fish got to swim and
Birds got to fly,
I got to love one
Man till I die,
Can't help lovin' dat man of mine.

Tell me he's lazy,
Tell me he's slow,
Tell me I'm crazy,
Maybe, I know.
Can't help lovin' dat man of mine.

When he goes away,
Dat's a rainy day,
And when he comes back
Dat day is fine,
The sun will shine.

He can come home as
Late as can be,
Home without him ain't
No home to me,
Can't help lovin' dat man of mine.

Let's Do It (Let's Fall in Love) (1928)

Lyrics and Music by Cole Porter

Verse

When the little bluebird
Who has never said a word
Starts to sing: "Spring, spring";
When the little blue-bell
In the bottom of the dell
Starts to ring: "Ding, ding";
When the little blue clerk,
In the middle of his work
Starts a tune
To the moon
Up above,
It is nature, that's all,
Simply telling us to fall
In love.

Refrain One

And that's why birds do it, bees do it,
Even educated fleas do it,*
Let's do it,
Let's fall in love.

In Spain, the best upper sets do it,
Lithuanians and Letts do it,
Let's do it,
Let's fall in love.

*Although now normally sung at the beginning of Refrain One, lines 1 and 2, slightly altered, actually belong toward the end of Refrain Four, which is rarely performed. Porter's original first two lines of Refrain One contain ethnic references now considered offensive:

And that's why Chinks do it, Japs do it,
  Up in Lapland, little Laps do it . . .

and they are no longer used.

The Dutch in old Amsterdam do it,
Not to mention the Finns.
Folks in Siam do it,
Think of Siamese twins.

Some Argentines,
Without means, do it.
People say, in Boston even beans do it,
Let's do it,
Let's fall in love.

Refrain Two

The nightingales in the dark do it,
Larks, k-razy for a lark, do it,
Let's do it,
Let's fall in love.

Canaries caged in the house do it,
When they're out of season, grouse do it,
Let's do it,
Let's fall in love.

The most sedate barnyard fowls do it,
When a chantacleer cries.
High-browed old owls do it,
They're supposed to be wise.

Penguins in flocks,
On the rocks, do it,
Even little cuckoos in their clocks do it,
Let's do it,
Let's fall in love.

Refrain Three

Romantic sponges, they say, do it,
Oysters down in Oyster Bay do it,
Let's do it,
Let's fall in love.

Cold Cape Cod clams, 'gainst their wish, do it,
Even lazy jelly-fish do it,
Let's do it,
Let's fall in love.

Electric eels, I might add, do it,
Though it shocks 'em, I know.
Why ask if shad do it?
Waiter, bring me shad roe.

In shallow shoals,
English soles do it,
Gold fish, in the privacy of bowls, do it,
Let's do it,
Let's fall in love.

Refrain Four

The dragon flies, in the reeds, do it,
Sentimental centipedes do it,
Let's do it,
Let's fall in love.

Mosquitos, heaven forbid, do it,
So does ev'ry katydid do it,
Let's do it,
Let's fall in love.

The most refined lady-bugs do it,
When a gentleman calls.
Moths in your rugs, do it,
What's the use of mothballs?

Locusts in trees do it,
Bees do it,
Even highly educated fleas do it,
Let's do it,
Let's fall in love.

Refrain Five

The chimpanzees in the zoos do it,
Some courageous kangaroos do it,
Let's do it,
Let's fall in love.

I'm sure giraffes, on the sly, do it,
Heavy hippopotami do it,
Let's do it,
Let's fall in love.

Let's Do It (Let's Fall in Love)

Old sloths who hang down from twigs do it,
Though the effort is great.
Sweet guinea-pigs do it,
Buy a couple and wait.

The world admits
Bears in pits do it,
Even pekineses in the Ritz do it,
Let's do it,
Let's fall in love.

Look for the Silver Lining
(1920)

Lyrics by Buddy DeSylva
Music by Jerome Kern

Verse One

Please don't be offended
If I preach to you awhile.
Tears are out of place in
Eyes that were meant to smile.
There's a way to make
Your very biggest troubles small.
Here's the happy secret of it all:

Refrain

Look for the silver lining
Whene'er a cloud appears in the blue.
Remember somewhere the sun is shining,
And so the right thing to do
Is make it shine for you.
A heart full of joy and gladness
Will always banish sadness and strife,
So always look for the silver lining,
And try to find the sunny side of life.

Verse Two

As I wash my dishes,
I'll be following your plan,
Till I see the brightness
In ev'ry pot and pan.
I am sure your point
Of view will ease the daily grind,
So I'll keep repeating in my mind:

Repeat Refrain

Makin' Whoopee (1928)

Lyrics by Gus Kahn
Music by Walter Donaldson

Verse

Ev'ry time I hear that march from Lohengrin*
I am always on the outside lookin' in.
Maybe that is why I see the funny side
When I see a fall'n brother take a bride.
Weddings make a lot of people sad,
But if you're not the groom they're not so bad.

Refrain

Another bride,
Another June,
Another sunny
Honeymoon,
Another season,
Another reason
For makin' whoopee!

A lot of shoes,
A lot of rice,
The groom is nervous,
He answers twice.
It's really killing
That he's so willing
To make whoopee.

Picture a little love nest,
Down where the roses cling.

*Alternate verse

Ev'rytime I hear that dear old wedding march
I feel rather glad I have a broken arch.
I have heard a lot of married people talk,
And I know that marriage is a long, long walk.
To most people weddings mean romance,
But I prefer a picnic or a dance.

Picture the same sweet love nest,
Think what a year can bring.

He's washing dishes
And baby clothes,
He's so ambitious
He even sews.
But don't forget, folks,
That's what you get, folks,
For makin' whoopee!

Refrain Two

Another year
Or maybe less,
What's this I hear?
Well, can't you guess?
She feels neglected,
And he's suspected
Of makin' whoopee.

She sits alone
Most ev'ry night,
He doesn't phone her,
He doesn't write.
He says he's "busy,"
But she says, "Is he?"
He's making whoopee.

He doesn't make much money,
Only five thousand per.
Some judge who thinks he's funny
Says, "You'll pay six to her."

He says, "Now, judge,
Suppose I fail."
The judge says, "Budge
Right into jail.
You'd better keep her,
I think it's cheaper
Than makin' whoopee!"

The Man I Love (1924)

Lyrics by Ira Gershwin
Music by George Gershwin

Verse

When the mellow moon begins to beam,
Ev'ry night I dream a little dream,
And of course Prince Charming is the theme,
The he for me.
Although I realize as well as you,
It is seldom that a dream comes true,
To me it's clear
That he'll appear.

Refrain

Someday he'll come along,
The man I love;
And he'll be big and strong,
The man I love;
And when he comes my way,
I'll do my best to make him stay.

He'll look at me and smile,
I'll understand;
And in a little while
He'll take my hand;
And though it seems absurd,
I know we both won't say a word.

Maybe I shall meet him one day,
Maybe Monday,
Maybe not.
Still I'm sure to meet him Sunday,
Maybe Tuesday
Will be my good-news day.

He'll build a little home,
Just meant for two,

From which I'll never roam,
Who would, would you?
And so all else above,
I'm waiting for the man I love.

Mountain Greenery (1926)

Lyrics by Lorenz Hart
Music by Richard Rodgers

Verse One

On the first of May
It is moving day.
Spring is here,
So blow your job—
Throw your job
Away.
Now's the time to trust
To your wanderlust.
In the city's dust you wait,
Must you wait?
Just you wait.

Refrain One

In a mountain greenery,
Where God paints the scenery,
Just two crazy people together.

While you love your lover, let
Blue skies be your coverlet;
When it rains we'll laugh at the weather.

And if you're good
I'll search for wood,
So you can cook
While I stand look-ing.

Beans could get no keener re-
Ception in a beanery.
Bless our mountain greenery home!

Verse Two

Simple cooking means

More than French cuisines.
I've a banquet
Planned which is
Sandwiches
And beans,
Coffee's just as grand
With a little sand.
Eat and you'll grow fatter, boy,
S'matter, boy?
'Atta boy!

Refrain Two

In a mountain greenery,
Where God paints the scenery,
Just two crazy people together.

How we love sequestering
Where no pests are pestering,
No dear mama holds us in tether!

Mosquitos here
Won't bite you, dear;
I'll let them sting
Me on the fing-er.

We could find no cleaner re-
Treat from life's machinery,
Than our mountain greenery home!

Interlude (Patter)

He: When the world was young,
 Old Father Adam with sin would grapple,
 So we're entitled to just one apple—
 I mean to make apple sauce.

She: Underneath the bough
 We'll learn a lesson from Mister Omar;
 Beneath the eyes of no Pa and no Ma,
 Old Lady Nature is boss.

He: Washing dishes,
 Catching fishes
 In the running stream—
 We'll curse the smell o'
 Citronella

Mountain Greenery

    Even when we dream.

She: Head upon the ground,
     Your downy pillow is just a boulder.

He: I'll have new dimples before I'm older;
     But life is peaches and cream.

Encore (to the music of the 3rd and 4th stanzas of the Refrain)

It's quite all right
To sing all night.
I'll sit and play
My ukule-le.

You can bet its tone
Beats a Jascha Haifetz tone.
Bless our mountain greenery home!

Refrain Three

In a mountain greenery
Where God paints the scenery,
With the world we haven't a quarrel.

Here a girl can map her own
Life without a chaperone.
It's so good it must be immoral.

It's not amiss
To sit and kiss.
For me and you
There are no blue . . . laws.

Life is more delectable
When it's disrespectable.
Bless our mountain greenery home!

Star Dust (1929)

Lyrics by Mitchell Parish
Music by Hoagy Carmichael

Verse

And now the purple dusk of twilight time
Steals across the meadows of my heart.
High up in the sky the little stars climb,
Always reminding me that we're apart.

You wandered down the lane and far away,
Leaving me a song that will not die;
Love is now the star dust of yesterday,
The music of the years gone by.

Refrain

Sometimes I wonder why I spend the lonely night
Dreaming of a song.
The melody
Haunts my reverie,
And I am once again with you,
When our love was new
And each kiss an inspiration,
But that was long ago.
Now my consolation
Is in the star dust of a song.

Beside a garden wall, when stars are bright,
You are in my arms.
The nightingale
Tells his fairy tale
Of paradise, where roses grew.
Tho' I dream in vain,
In my heart it will remain:
My star dust melody,
The memory of love's refrain.

Tea for Two (1924)

Lyrics by Irving Caesar
Music by Vincent Youmans

Verse

I'm discontented
With homes that are rented,
So I have invented
   My own;
Darling, this place is
A lover's oasis,
Where life's weary chase is
   Unknown,

Far from the cry of the city,
Where flowers pretty
   Caress the streams,
Cosy to hide in,
To live side by side in;
Don't let it abide in
   My dreams.

Refrain

Picture you
Upon my knee,
Just tea for two
And two for tea,
Just me for you
And you for me
   Alone.

Nobody near us
To see us or hear us,
No friends or relations
On weekend vacations,
We won't have it known, dear,
That we own a
   Telephone, dear.

Day will break,
And you'll awake
And start to bake
A sugar cake
For me to take
For all the boys to see.

We will raise a family,
A boy for you,
A girl for me.
Oh can't you see
How happy we
Would be?

That New-Fangled Mother of Mine (1924)

Lyrics by Desmond Carter
Music by George Gershwin

Verse One

Lots of people's mothers
Are silver-haired and sweet,
But finally there are others,
And mine you want to meet.
You never find her knitting,
She has no silver hair,
You never find her sitting
Beside my vacant chair.
I stay at home, but mother's never there.

Refrain One

That new-fangled mother of mine,
That glass-spangled mother of mine.
While others sit at home
In Ireland or Tennessee,
She's more inclined to roam—
She's more at home with Hennessey.
And thanks to that mother of mine,
The nightclubs I have to resign
'Cause I hate to have to answer
That the exhibition dancer
Is that new-fangled mother of mine.

Verse Two

First she took to henna.
Of that I wasn't fond,
But she contracted then a
Severe attack of blonde.
And how I blushed and tingled
The day her hair was bobbed,
But when she came home shingled

Of joy my day was robbed.
I crumpled up and absolutely sobbed.

Refrain Two

That new-fangled mother of mine,
That star-spangled mother of mine.
You don't know what she's like,
She's one among a million.
Upon my motor bike,
She occupies the pillion.
And thanks to that mother of mine,
All fancy dress balls I decline
Since I found that the bacchante
In the costume rather scanty
Was that new-fangled mother of mine.

The Varsity Drag (1927)

*Lyrics and Music by Buddy DeSylva,
Lew Brown, and Ray Henderson*

Verse

We've always thought,
Knowledge is naught;
We should be taught
To dance.

Right here at Tait,
We're up to date;
We teach a great
New dance.

Don't think that I brag,
I speak of the Drag.

Why should a sheik
Learn how to speak
Latin and Greek
Badly?

Give him a neat
Motto complete,
"Say it with feet
Gladly!"

First lesson right now;
You'll love it, and how—
You'll love it!

Refrain

Here is the Drag,
See how it goes;
Down on the heels,
Up on the toes.
That's the way to do the Varsity Drag.

Hotter than hot,
Newer than new!
Meaner than mean,
Bluer than blue,
Get's as much applause as waving the Flag!

You can pass
Many a class,
Whether you're dumb or wise,
If you all
Answer the call,
When your professor cries:
"Everybody

"Down on the heels,
Up on the toes,
Stay after school,
Learn how it goes;
Everybody do the Varsity Drag."

I Can't Give You Anything But Love (1928)

Lyrics by Dorothy Fields
Music by Jimmy McHugh

Verse One

Gee, but it's tough to be broke, kid;
It's not a joke, kid,
It's a curse.
My luck is changing, it's gotten
From simply rotten
To something worse.

Who knows, someday I will win, too,
I'll begin to
Reach my prime?
Now though I see what our end is,
All I can spend is
Just my time.

Refrain

I can't give you anything but love, baby,
That's the only thing I've plenty of, baby.

Dream a-while,
Scheme a-while,
We're sure to find
Happiness
And I guess
All of those things you've always pined for.

Gee, I'd like to see you looking swell, baby,
Diamond bracelets Woolworth doesn't sell, baby.
Till that lucky day, you know darned well, baby,
I can't give you anything but love.

Verse Two

Rome wasn't built in a day, kid;

You have to pay, kid,
For what you get.
But I am willing to wait, dear,
Your little mate, dear,
Will not forget.

You have a lifetime before you,
I'll adore you,
Come what may.
Please don't be blue for the present,
When it's so pleasant
To hear you say:

Repeat Refrain

I Guess I'll Have To Change My Plan (1929)

Lyrics by Howard Dietz
Music by Arthur Schwartz

Verse One

I beheld her and was conquered at the start,
And placed her on a pedestal apart:
I planned the little hideaway
That we would share some day.
When I met her I unfolded all my dream
And told her how she'd fit into my scheme
Oh what bliss is.
Then the blow came,
When she gave her name
As "Mrs."

Refrain One

I guess I'll have to change my plan.
I should have realized there'd be another man!
I overlooked that point completely
Until the big affair began.
Before I knew where I was at,
I found myself
Upon the shelf,
And that was that.
I tried to reach the moon, but when I got there,
All that I could get was the air.
My feet are back upon the ground,
I've lost the one girl I found.

Refrain Two

I guess I'll have to change my plan.
I should have realized there'd be another man!
Why did I buy those blue pajamas
Before the big affair began?
My boiling point is much too low

For me to try
To be a fly
Lothario!
I think I'll crawl right back into my shell,
Dwelling in my personal Hell.
I'll have to change my plan around,
I've lost the one girl I found.

Verse Two

But on second thought this resignation's wrong.
Most women want the one who comes along
With love that's secret and more true
Than they're accustomed to.
And besides it gives a most romantic edge
When one is sort of hanging on the ledge
Of abysses.
So methinks I
Do not mind if she's
A Mrs.

Refrain Three

I guess I'll have to change my plan.
Supposing after all there is another man:
I'm glad I bought those blue pajamas
Before the enterprise began.
For all is fair in love and war,
And love's a war—
That makes it fair-
Er all the more.
Forbidden fruit I've heard is better to taste.
Why should I let this go to waste?
My conscience to the wind is tossed—
I've found the one girl I've lost.

Button Up Your Overcoat
(1928)

*Lyrics and Music by Buddy DeSylva,
Lew Brown, and Ray Henderson*

Verse One

Listen, big boy!
Now that I've got you made,
Goodness, but I'm afraid
Something's gonna happen to you.

Listen, big boy!
You've got me hooked and how!
I would die if I should lose you now.

Refrain One

Button up your overcoat
When the wind is free.
Take good care of yourself,
You belong to me!

Eat an apple ev'ry day;
Get to bed by three.
Take good care of yourself,
You belong to me!

Be careful crossing streets,
Oo-oo!
Don't eat meats,
Oo-oo!
Cut out sweets,
Oo-oo!
You'll get a pain and ruin your tum-tum!

Keep away from bootleg hooch
When you're on a spree.
Take good care of yourself,
You belong to me.

Verse Two

Listen, girl friend!
You've knocked me off my feet.
I think you're very sweet
Making such a fuss about me.

Listen, girl friend!
Now that I'm fond of you,
I'm afraid I'm gonna worry too.

Refrain Two

Button up your overcoat
When the wind is free.
Take good care of yourself,
You belong to me!

Wear your flannel underwear
When you climb a tree.
Take good care of yourself,
You belong to me!

Don't sit on hornets' tails,
Oo-oo!
Or on nails,
Oo-oo!
Or third rails,
Oo-oo!
You'll get a pain and ruin your tum-tum!

Don't go out with college boys
When you're on a spree.
Take good care of yourself,
You belong to me.

Stories

The Egg

by Sherwood Anderson

My father was, I am sure, intended by nature to be a cheerful, kindly man. Until he was thirty-four years old he worked as a farm hand for a man named Thomas Butterworth whose place lay near the town of Bidwell, Ohio. He had then a horse of his own and on Saturday evenings drove into town to spend a few hours in social intercourse with other farm hands. In town he drank several glasses of beer and stood about in Ben Head's saloon—crowded on Saturday evenings with visiting farm hands. Songs were sung and glasses thumped on the bar. At ten o'clock father drove home along a lonely country road, made his horse comfortable for the night and himself went to bed, quite happy in his position in life. He had at that time no notion of trying to rise in the world.

It was in the spring of his thirty-fifth year that father married my mother, then a country school teacher, and in the following spring I came wriggling and crying into the world. Something happened to the two people. They became ambitious. The American passion for getting up in the world took possession of them.

It may have been that mother was responsible. Being a school teacher she had no doubt read books and magazines. She had, I presume, read of how Garfield, Lincoln, and other Americans rose from poverty to fame and greatness and as I lay beside her—in the days of her lying-in—she may have dreamed that I would someday rule men and cities. At any rate she induced father to give up his place as a farm hand, sell his horse and embark on an independent enterprise of his own. She was a tall silent woman with a long nose and troubled gray eyes. For herself she wanted nothing. For father and myself she was incurably ambitious.

The first venture into which the two people went turned out badly. They rented ten acres of poor stony land on Grigg's Road, eight miles from Bidwell, and launched into chicken raising. I grew into boyhood on the place and got my first impressions of life there. From the beginning they were impressions of disaster and if, in my turn, I am a gloomy man inclined to see the darker side of life, I attribute it to the fact that what should have been for me the happy joyous days of childhood were spent on a chicken farm.

One unversed in such matters can have no notion of the many and tragic things that can happen to a chicken. It is born out of an egg, lives for a few weeks as a tiny fluffy thing such as you will see pictured on Easter cards, then becomes hideously naked, eats quantities of corn and meal bought by the sweat of your father's brow, gets diseases called pip, cholera, and other names, stands looking with stupid eyes at the sun, becomes sick and dies. A few hens and now and then a rooster, intended to serve God's mysterious ends, struggle through to maturity. The hens lay eggs out of which come other chickens and the dreadful cycle is thus made complete. It is all unbelievably complex. Most philosophers must have been raised on chicken farms. One hopes for so much from a chicken and is so dreadfully disillusioned. Small chickens, just setting out on the journey of life, look so bright and alert and they are in fact so dreadfully stupid. They are so much like people they mix one up in one's judgments of life. If disease does not kill them they wait until your expectations are thoroughly aroused and then walk under the wheels of a wagon—to go squashed and dead back to their maker. Vermin infest their youth, and fortunes must be spent for curative powders. In later life I have seen how a literature has been built up on the subject of fortunes to be made out of the raising of chickens. It is intended to be read by the gods who have just eaten of the tree of the knowledge of good and evil. It is a hopeful literature and declares that much may be done by simple ambitious people who own a few hens. Do not be led astray by it. It was not written for you. Go hunt for gold on the frozen hills of Alaska, put your faith in the honesty of a politician, believe if you will that the world is daily growing better and that good will triumph over evil, but do not read and believe the literature that is written concerning the hen. It was not written for you.

I, however, digress. My tale does not primarily concern itself with the hen. If correctly told it will center on the egg. For ten years my father and mother struggled to make our chicken farm pay and then they gave up that struggle and began another. They moved into the town of Bidwell, Ohio, and embarked in the restaurant business. After ten years of worry with incubators that did not hatch, and with tiny—and in their own way lovely—balls of fluff that passed on into seminaked pullethood and from that into dead henhood, we threw all aside and packing our belongings on a wagon drove down Griggs's Road toward Bidwell, a tiny caravan of hope looking for a new place from which to start on our upward journey through life.

We must have been a sad looking lot, not, I fancy, unlike refugees fleeing from a battlefield. Mother and I walked in the road. The wagon that contained our goods had been borrowed for the day from Mr. Albert Griggs, a neighbor. Out of its sides stuck the legs of cheap chairs and at the back of the pile of beds, tables, and boxes filled with kitchen utensils was a crate of live chickens, and on top of that the baby carriage in which I had been wheeled about in my infancy. Why we stuck to the baby carriage I don't know. It was unlikely other children would be born and the wheels were broken. People who have few possessions cling tightly to those they have. That is one of the facts that make life so discouraging.

Father rode on top of the wagon. He was then a bald-headed man of forty-five, a little fat and from long association with mother and the chickens he had become habitually silent and discouraged. All during our ten years on the chicken farm he had worked as a laborer on neighboring farms and most of the money he had earned had been spent for remedies to cure chicken diseases, on Wilmer's White Wonder Cholera Cure or Professor Bidlow's Egg Producer or some other preparations that mother found advertised in the poultry papers. There were two little patches of hair on father's head just above his ears. I remember that as a child I used to sit looking at him when he had gone to sleep in a chair before the stove on Sunday afternoons in the winter. I had at that time already begun to read books and have notions of my own and the bald path that led over the top of his head was, I fancied, something like a broad road, such a road as Caesar might have made on which to lead his legions out of Rome and into the wonders of an unknown world. The tufts of hair that grew above father's ears were, I thought, like forests. I fell into a half-sleeping, half-waking state and dreamed I was a tiny thing going along the road into a far beautiful place where there were no chicken farms and where life was a happy eggless affair.

One might write a book concerning our flight from the

chicken farm into town. Mother and I walked the entire eight miles—she to be sure that nothing fell from the wagon and I to see the wonders of the world. On the seat of the wagon beside father was his greatest treasure. I will tell you of that.

On a chicken farm where hundreds and even thousands of chickens come out of eggs surprising things sometimes happen. Grotesques are born out of eggs as out of people. The accident does not often occur—perhaps once in a thousand births. A chicken is, you see, born that has four legs, two pairs of wings, two heads or what not. The things do not live. They go quickly back to the hand of their maker that has for a moment trembled. The fact that the poor little things could not live was one of the tragedies of life to father. He had some sort of notion that if he could but bring into henhood or roosterhood a five-legged hen or a two-headed rooster his fortune would be made. He dreamed of taking the wonder about to county fairs and of growing rich by exhibiting it to other farm hands.

At any rate he saved all the little monstrous things that had been born on our chicken farm. They were preserved in alcohol and put each in its own glass bottle. These he had carefully put into a box and on our journey into town it was carried on the wagon seat beside him. He drove the horses with one hand and with the other clung to the box. When we got to our destination the box was taken down at once and the bottles removed. All during our days as keepers of a restaurant in the town of Bidwell, Ohio, the grotesques in their little glass bottles sat on a shelf back of the counter. Mother sometimes protested but father was a rock on the subject of his treasure. The grotesques were, he declared, valuable. People, he said, liked to look at strange and wonderful things.

Did I say that we embarked on the restaurant business in the town of Bidwell, Ohio? I exaggerated a little. The town itself lay at the foot of a low hill and on the shore of a small river. The railroad did not run through the town and the station was a mile away to the north at a place called Pickleville. There had been a cider mill and pickle factory at the station, but before the time of our coming they had both gone out of business. In the morning and in the evening busses came down to the station along a road called Turner's Pike from the hotel on the main street of Bidwell. Our going to the out-of-the-way place to embark in the restaurant business was mother's idea. She talked of it for a year and

The Egg

then one day went off and rented an empty store building opposite the railroad station. It was her idea that the restaurant would be profitable. Traveling men, she said, would be always waiting around to take trains out of town and town people would come to the station to await incoming trains. They would come to the restaurant to buy pieces of pie and drink coffee. Now that I am older I know that she had another motive in going. She was ambitious for me. She wanted me to rise in the world, to get into a town school and become a man of the towns.

At Pickleville father and mother worked hard as they always had done. At first there was the necessity of putting our place into shape to be a restaurant. That took a month. Father built a shelf on which he put tins of vegetables. He painted a sign on which he put his name in large red letters. Below his name was the sharp command—"EAT HERE"—that was so seldom obeyed. A showcase was bought and filled with cigars and tobacco. Mother scrubbed the floor and the walls of the room. I went to school in the town and was glad to be away from the farm and from the presence of the discouraged, sad-looking chickens. Still I was not very joyous. In the evening I walked home from school along Turner's Pike and remembered the children I had seen playing in the town school yard. A troop of little girls had gone hopping about and singing. I tried that. Down along the frozen road I went hopping solemnly on one leg. "Hippity Hop To The Barber Shop," I sang shrilly. Then I stopped and looked doubtfully about. I was afraid of being seen in my gay mood. It must have seemed to me that I was doing a thing that should not be done by one who, like myself, had been raised on a chicken farm where death was a daily visitor.

Mother decided that our restaurant should remain open at night. At ten in the evening a passenger train went north past our door followed by a local freight. The freight crew had switching to do in Pickleville and when the work was done they came to our restaurant for hot coffee and food. Sometimes one of them ordered a fried egg. In the morning at four they returned northbound and again visited us. A little trade began to grow up. Mother slept at night and during the day tended the restaurant and fed our boarders while father slept. He slept in the same bed mother had occupied during the night and I went off to the town of Bidwell and to school. During the long nights, while mother and I slept, father cooked meats that were to go into sandwiches for the lunch baskets of our boarders. Then an idea in regard to getting up in the world came into his head. The American spirit took hold of him. He also became ambitious.

In the long nights when there was little to do father had time to think. That was his undoing. He decided that he had in the past been an unsuccessful man because he had not been cheerful enough and that in the future he would adopt a cheerful outlook on life. In the early morning he came upstairs and got into bed with mother. She woke and the two talked. From my bed in the corner I listened.

It was father's idea that both he and mother should try to entertain the people who came to eat at our restaurant. I cannot now remember his words, but he gave the impression of one about to become in some obscure way a kind of public entertainer. When people, particularly young people from the town of Bidwell, came into our place, as on very rare occasions they did, bright entertaining conversation was to be made. From father's words I gathered that something of the jolly innkeeper effect was to be sought. Mother must have been doubtful from the first, but she said nothing discouraging. It was father's notion that a passion for the company of himself and mother would spring up in the breasts of the younger people of the town of Bidwell. In the evening bright happy groups would come singing down Turner's Pike. They would troop shouting with joy and laughter into our place. There would be song and festivity. I do not mean to give the impression that father spoke so elaborately of the matter. He was as I have said an uncommunicative man. "They want some place to go. I tell you they want some place to go," he said over and over. That was as far as he got. My own imagination has filled in the blanks.

For two or three weeks this notion of father's invaded our house. We did not talk much, but in our daily lives tried earnestly to make smiles take the place of glum looks. Mother smiled at the boarders and I, catching the infection, smiled at our cat. Father became a little feverish in his anxiety to please. There was no doubt, lurking somewhere in him, a touch of the spirit of the showman. He did not waste much of his ammunition on the railroad men he served at night but seemed to be waiting for a young man or woman from Bidwell to come in to show what he could do. On the counter in the restaurant there was a wire basket kept always filled with eggs, and it must have been before his eyes when the idea of being entertaining was born in his brain. There was something pre-natal about the way eggs kept themselves connected with the development of his idea. At any rate an egg ruined his new impulse in life. Late one night I was awakened by a roar of anger coming from father's throat. Both mother and I sat upright in our beds. With trembling hands she lighted a lamp that stood on a table by her head. Downstairs the front door of our restaurant went shut with a bang and in a few minutes father tramped up the stairs. He held an egg in his hand and his hand trembled as though he were having a chill. There was a half insane light in his eyes. As he stood glaring at us I was sure he intended throwing the egg at either mother or me. Then he laid it gently on the table beside the lamp and dropped on his knees besides mother's bed. He began to cry like a boy and I, carried away by his grief, cried with him. The two of us filled the little upstairs room with our wailing voices. It is ridiculous, but of the picture we made I can remember only the fact that mother's hand continually stroked the bald path that ran across the top of his head. I have forgotten what mother said to him and how she induced him to tell her of what had happened downstairs. His explanation also has gone out of my mind. I remember only my own grief and fright and the shiny path over father's head glowing in the lamp light as he knelt by the bed.

As to what happened downstairs. For some unexplainable reason I know the story as well as though I had been a witness to my father's discomfiture. One in time gets to know many unexplainable things. On that evening young Joe Kane, son of a merchant of Bidwell, came to Pickleville to meet his father, who was expected on the ten o'clock evening train from the South. The train was three hours late and Joe came into our place to loaf about and to wait for its arrival. The local freight train came in and the freight crew were fed. Joe was left alone in the restaurant with father.

From the moment he came into our place the Bidwell young man must have been puzzled by my father's actions. It was his notion that father was angry at him for hanging around. He noticed that the restaurant keeper was apparently disturbed by his presence and he thought of going out. However, it began to rain and he did not fancy the long walk to town and back. He bought a five-cent cigar and ordered a cup of coffee. He had a newspaper in his pocket and took it out and began to read. "I'm waiting for the evening train. It's late," he said apologetically.

For a long time father, whom Joe Kane had never seen before, remained silently gazing at his visitor. He was no doubt suffering from an attack of stage fright. As so often happens in life he had thought so much and so often of the situation that now confronted him that he was somewhat nervous in its presence.

For one thing, he did not know what to do with his hands. He thrust one of them nervously over the counter and shook hands with Joe Kane. "How-de-do," he said. Joe Kane put his newspaper down and stared at him. Father's eye lighted on the basket of eggs that sat on the counter and he began to talk. "Well," he began hesitatingly, "well, you have heard of Christopher Columbus, eh?" He seemed to be angry. "That Christopher Columbus was a cheat," he declared emphatically. "He talked of making an egg stand on its end. He talked, he did, and then he went and broke the end of the egg."

My father seemed to his visitor to be beside himself at the duplicity of Christopher Columbus. He muttered and swore. He declared it was wrong to teach children that Christopher Columbus was a great man when, after all, he cheated at the critical moment. He had declared he would make an egg stand on end and then when his bluff had been called he had done a trick. Still grumbling at Columbus, father took an egg from the basket on the counter and began to walk up and down. He rolled the egg between the palms of his hands. He smiled genially. He began to mumble words regarding the effect to be produced on an egg by the electricity that comes out of the human body. He declared that without breaking its shell and by virtue of rolling it back and forth in his hands he could stand the egg on its end. He explained that the warmth of his hands and the gentle rolling movement he gave the egg created a new center of gravity, and Joe Kane was mildly interested. "I have handled thousands of eggs," father said. "No one knows more about eggs than I do."

He stood the egg on the counter and it fell on its side. He tried the trick again and again, each time rolling the egg between the palms of his hands and saying the words regarding the wonders of electricity and the laws of gravity. When after a half hour's effort he did succeed in making the egg stand for a moment he looked up to find that his visitor was no longer watching. By the time he had succeeded in calling Joe Kane's attention to the success of his effort the egg had again rolled over and lay on its side.

Afire with the showman's passion and at the same time a

The Egg

good deal disconcerted by the failure of his first effort, father now took the bottles containing the poultry monstrosities down from their place on the shelf and began to show them to his visitor. "How would you like to have seven legs and two heads like this fellow?" he asked, exhibiting the most remarkable of his treasures. A cheerful smile played over his face. He reached over the counter and tried to slap Joe Kane on the shoulder as he had seen men do in Ben Head's saloon when he was a young farm hand and drove to town on Saturday evenings. His visitor was made a little ill by the sight of the body of the terribly deformed bird floating in the alcohol in the bottle and got up to go. Coming from behind the counter father took hold of the young man's arm and led him back to his seat. He grew a little angry and for a moment had to turn his face away and force himself to smile. Then he put the bottles back on the shelf. In an outburst of generosity he fairly compelled Joe Kane to have a fresh cup of coffee and another cigar at his expense. Then he took a pan and filling it with vinegar, taken from a jug that sat beneath the counter, he declared himself about to do a new trick. "I will heat this egg in this pan of vinegar," he said. "Then I will put it through the neck of a bottle without breaking the shell. When the egg is inside the bottle it will resume its normal shape and the shell will become hard again. Then I will give the bottle with the egg in it to you. You can take it about with you wherever you go. People will want to know how you got the egg in the bottle. Don't tell them. Keep them guessing. That is the way to have fun with this trick."

Father grinned and winked at his visitor. Joe Kane decided that the man who confronted him was mildly insane but harmless. He drank the cup of coffee that had been given him and began to read his paper again. When the egg had been heated in vinegar father carried it on a spoon to the counter and going into a back room got an empty bottle. He was angry because his visitor did not watch him as he began to do his trick, but nevertheless went cheerfully to work. For a long time he struggled, trying to get the egg to go through the neck of the bottle. He put the pan of vinegar back on the stove, intending to reheat the egg, then picked it up and burned his fingers. After a second bath in the hot vinegar the shell of the egg had been softened a little but not enough for his purpose. He worked and worked and a spirit of desperate determination took possession of him. When he thought that at last the trick was about to be consummated the delayed train came in at the station and Joe Kane started to go nonchalantly out the door. Father made a last desperate effort to conquer the egg and make it do the thing that would establish his reputation as one who knew how to entertain guests who came into his restaurant. He worried the egg. He attempted to be somewhat rough with it. He swore and the sweat stood out on his forehead. The egg broke under his hand. When the contents spurted over his clothes, Joe Kane, who had stopped at the door, turned and laughed.

A roar of anger rose from my father's throat. He danced and shouted a string of inarticulate words. Grabbing another egg from the basket on the counter, he threw it, just missing the head of the young man as he dodged through the door and escaped.

Father came upstairs to mother and me with an egg in his hand. I do not know what he intended to do. I imagine he had some idea of destroying it, of destroying all eggs, and that he intended to let mother and me see him begin. When, however, he got into the presence of mother something happened to him. He laid the egg gently on the table and dropped on his knees by the bed as I have already explained. He later decided to close the restaurant for the night and to come upstairs and get into bed. When he did so he blew out the light and after much muttered conversation both he and mother went to sleep. I suppose I went to sleep also, but my sleep was troubled. I awoke at dawn and for a long time looked at the egg that lay on the table. I wondered why eggs had to be and why from the egg came the hen who again laid the egg. The question got into my blood. It has stayed there, I imagine, because I am the son of my father. At any rate, the problem remains unsolved in my mind. And that, I conclude, is but another evidence of the complete and final triumph of the egg—at least as far as my family is concerned.

"There's Money in Poetry"

by Konrad Bercovici

On the transatlantic steamer a stoutish man of about fifty, bald-headed and blue-eyed, extended a hand as big as a ham and introduced himself:

"Levine is my name. What is yours? I am in the silk business; what is your business?"

I mumbled that my business was of no importance. After dinner, when the coffee was brought in, the purser and the captain of the boat greeted me and sat down at our table for a few moments. I introduced my companion, who, being overawed that such important personages should be on friendly terms with me, asked again:

"What did you say your business was?"

My answer was very vague. Puzzled, Mr. Levine looked at me with suspicion.

An hour later Levine tapped me familiarly on the shoulder.

"Say, I found out what you are. They tell me you're a writer. Why the hell didn't you tell me so? That's nothing to be ashamed of! That's happened even in my family, Good night."

The following day Mr. Levine had made up his mind to tell me the story of his life. Instead of discouraging him I egged him on. It was better to get through with it. When a man has made up his mind to tell you the story of his life there is no escape. The longer you make him wait for the occasion the more ornate his story will be . . . and the more untrue. Nothing is so boring as the invented romance of unimaginative people.

After dinner I went up on deck, sat down on a chair beside him, and said:

"You wanted to tell me something? Go ahead, Levine, let's hear."

Levine hemmed and hawed.

"To make a long story short, it was this way. I'm going to tell it to you briefly, but from soup to nuts, as they say.

"To begin with, Kantrowitz, who is also in the silk business, is an old friend of mine who came to America about the same time I came, twenty years ago. We were both in the same business. Sometimes there was a little competition between us. Sometimes we had a little fight, a little squabble, a little quarrel; but when I thought we had parted forever, Kantrowitz buys a little property up in the Bronx and lets me know that there is another lot beside it which can be had for the same price he had paid, and we build the same kind of house, so it should cost cheaper, the architect and everything else, and we remain friends forever again for a long time. He has what he has, I have what I have, and the families are friends and everything is all right.

"When the time comes and silk is good one of his sons, the oldest one, as soon as he has finished high school goes into his father's business. A-one all around, and falls in love with a girl of the neighborhood, and gets married to her, moves over to Washington Heights, and is doing very fine. That oldest boy of Kantrowitz is the spit image of his father. What his father had done at twenty he does at twenty. What his father has done at forty he will do at forty. A regular fellow. The kind of a son a man wishes to have not a stranger.

"But the other son, Izzy—with him it's not so good. What's happened was that when Izzy was twelve or thirteen years old and was still in school they printed in the school paper a poem written by Izzy himself, which was called 'Indian Wind.' And so Kantrowitz goes around and shows it to everybody that his son is a poet, and frames it and hangs it up in the office. You could not talk to Kantrowitz for five minutes without he should show you the poem of his son framed and hung up on the wall. I came to talk business. He showed me Izzy's picture. And it made the older son good and angry. What if he hadn't written poetry, wasn't he a good son?

"That's all very nice and fine for a boy thirteen years old, and not born in this country, who writes poems that get printed in the papers; the whole neighborhood is proud of him. He is a celebrity already. But the boy finishes high school, and the father wants he should come into his business, and Izzy wouldn't even hear about it. Then it is not so good. He wants to be a poet.

"Well, for a year or so we didn't know nothing about it and didn't know how much Kantrowitz was worried and all the quarrels in the family. Kantrowitz is a proud man, a self-made man, and keeps a secret what is not so nice in his

"There's Money in Poetry"   299

family. But when the boy got to be eighteen, nineteen years old and was still doing nothing except writing poetry, I had a look at him because he was coming every night to my house to read to my Margaret his poems. So I says to him one day:

" 'Izzy, what's going to be the end of it? When are you going into business? Poetry is no business for a Kantrowitz. You got to consider the family!'

"So Izzy looks at me as if I had called his father names, and he shrugged his shoulders as if what I said was talking maybe Chinese; and when he goes away, my daughter asks me what business have I got to talk to Izzy like that, and she tells me Izzy is a great poet. So I says to her that I knew that already, that I saw the poem that got printed in the school magazine years ago, but what had that got to do with business? And a boy that comes round to my house, I want I should know what he is doing. Loafers should come into my house yet!

"So a week passes, and another week, and Kantrowitz comes up to my office one day, and I can see he is very worried. So I says to him:

" 'How's business, Kantrowitz?'

"Kantrowitz says business is all right. So I ask him how was the health? And he says that was all right, too. I wondered what could be worrying him. Finally, he tells me it's about Izzy. That a boy like this could happen in his family— with the best of examples always before him! His father and brother in business, all his family in business, and everybody in business, and he should just loaf, and does nothing. I talk to him and I talk to him, he says, and it's like talking to the wall. And what would the end be, he asks me, with tears in his eyes.

"So I consoled him and said don't worry; it would all come out all right, with a father like you and a brother. . . . I know Izzy is not a bad boy.

"All the time I wanted to tell him that the fault is really with Kantrowitz, for he had turned the boy's mind by showing the poem and hanging it up in his office, so that he got a swelled head and thinks that he is better than everybody. But even if I didn't tell him, Kantrowitz understood that that was what I meant, so he said:

" 'I know it was my own fault. But I was so proud. How should I know what is going to happen? How should I know that he will not want to do what I will tell him and write poetry forever!'

" 'Don't worry,' I told him, 'things will come out all right. Izzy is of good family and blood is thicker than water. There ain't been any poet in your family yet?' I ask.

" 'No,' says Kantrowitz. 'Have you ever heard of such a thing in my family? No bankrupts and no poets.'

"That evening when I came home and found Izzy sitting near my daughter on a couch and reading to her poetry from a paper, I got very angry, and I said to him that he had no business to worry his father and mother and shame his family and loaf and write poetry and that I was the best friend of the family and wouldn't have said a word but he had no business to sit near my Margaret on a couch and read poetry to her. And I gave it to him good and hard. First he should go and make a man of himself, and then you should talk to my daughter. So Izzy gets angry, and my Margaret talks to me as she has never talked before—says she is in America, and not in Russia. So I said to my Margaret that for women it was all right; if she wanted to read poetry or do anything honest she wanted, it was all right, but for a boy whose family was in business it was a ruination. So he shouldn't come any more to our house.

"I thought I knew my Margaret, that she wouldn't see him because she wouldn't do what her father didn't want her to do. And everything was all right. But we are in America. Women got independent even from their families that supports them. Of course for women that work independence is O.K. But it turned out O.K. as you will hear later; even if I almost died, and it is even the reason I took a trip to the old country.

"But you should have seen Kantrowitz then. He worried more in a week than his father had worried in a lifetime. And his father was the kind that spoke politics and carried the world on his shoulders. He worried more about that boy's future than he did about business. He would sit in my office and cry like a baby. His boy was no good! His son was getting worse from year to year. And already he was twenty-one, with no thought of anything at all, and happy only when a poem of his got printed somewheres in the magazines.

"Margaret used to read it to me when it appeared, and when she read it, it sounded all right, but it was always about flowers and rivers and such things, so I said to her one day:

" 'Look. In five years that he writes poetry, show me what he has done. There is maybe two pages in a magazine. Was that enough work for a man in five years? Nobody has nothing against a man writing poetry . . . but after business, when you got a little time. Nobody could write poetry eight hours a day, and even the Socialists say a man got to work eight hours a day.'

"So she sighs and looks at me as if to say 'you know nothing,' and from then on she stops showing me his poetry, and I stop talking about him. And Kantrowitz just loses his head that such a misfortune should happen in his house; that one of his sons shouldn't want to do anything serious. And it breaks my heart. To all the worries a man got in business there should yet come such a thing in America. Poetry!

"And then one day Kantrowitz comes into my office, and I could see right away from how he acted that he was very happy. The biggest order couldn't have made him so happy. No. And so I think what could have happened to him! I am in conference with my salesmen, but I stop the conference and I call him aside and say:

"'What is it, Kantrowitz? Tell me quick. I'm dying.'

"But he was so excited he could hardly talk, and finally he says:

"'You were right, Levine. You were right. My Izzy has come to his senses. Blood is thicker than water. This morning he took a position with the A.G.B. Silk Company, and he is going on the road in a week! That boy has saved my life.' And Kantrowitz cries like a baby.

"It made me very happy. I couldn't tell you how happy it made me. The biggest order of silk couldn't have done it. A man got feelings even if he is in business, you know. And so I tell Kantrowitz I have a big conference on, but the conference could wait for to-morrow. And the two of us went down town and we had a good bottle of wine over it, and we hadn't been so happy together in a long time, talking about the old country and about people we knew and about everything. We hadn't done so bad in this country. We have made money. Everything was all right. And our children were all right. There was nothing to worry about and blood was thicker than water.

"I went home and told the good news to my wife. But when Margaret, my daughter, hears that Izzy has come to his senses and is going on the road she begins to cry and cry as if she had heard the worst news. So you never can understand women, I think to myself. Nobody ever did. So how should I know what she cried about? But I knew she did not cry for happiness. I knew that. There is a great difference. So

I let her alone and think maybe she cries because he goes on the road and she wouldn't see him no more as often. For I knew that she did meet him even if I had ordered the contrary. Girls are independent in this country, and a father that knows gives an order and then closes the eyes when he isn't obeyed.

"A month later, Izzy comes back from the road. He is a new man. He has cut his hair short. His clothes are pressed. The A.G.B. silk people are very satisfied with him. I called them up on the telephone and asked them how it goes with him. So I think to myself now if he should come to talk to my Margaret I won't say anything; for I understood that Margaret didn't dislike him. But what do you think happens. When he comes to talk to her, she wouldn't speak to him. She is angry that he should be no more a poet! Women got political rights but they are as foolish as ever. They don't want bread, they want jewelry . . . poetry.

"So he goes back on the road, and his father is very happy, and tells me that the boy learned in two months the business better than anybody could have learned it in ten years. Why not? Silk was in the Kantrowitz family for two hundred years. The boy knew silk just as somebody coming from a family of musicians knows music. He was just born with it. He didn't have to go to school to learn it and know the difference between silk and cotton. But I say nothing, and the father is happy, and everything is all right. Kantrowitz was crazy about the boy. About poetry that was not in the family I understand he should have made such a noise and hang up the picture on the wall. But about silk! How could a Kantrowitz not know silk?

"Meanwhile every morning as I go out of my house I see letters coming from the road to my Margaret, so I say nothing. The boy goes back and forth on the road. Each time he comes back, he sees Margaret. Sometimes she talks to him one way and sometimes she talks to him another way, hot, cold, but I say nothing. Watch and see. I always believe blood is thicker than water. And there ain't been no poet yet in my family neither.

"Meanwhile his brother, who has been partners with the father, has gone into business for himself. Izzy comes home and goes into partnership with his father. And his father you couldn't talk to him, he was so proud of Izzy. He spoiled that boy twenty-four hours a day. He was afraid Izzy would go back to poetry.

"Now there comes out a new kind of silk, and every wholesaler in town gets the sample. Izzy looks at that piece of silk and touches it and smells it and caresses it. You ain't never seen such things the boy did with that piece of silk! The wholesaler had given it a name—I don't know what—but Izzy looks at the silk and smells it, and presses it to his cheeks and to his lips like he was crazy, and then he says again:

" 'Indian Wind!' And his eyes were sparkling, and his face was red just like he was drunk from touching that piece of silk. Just like that. 'Indian Wind!'

"And when he sends an order he asks that they should print 'Indian Wind' all around the selvages of the silk, and pack it in a special kind of tinted silk paper.

"And 'Indian Wind' becomes such a craze that the women would have nothing but 'Indian Wind' and wouldn't buy silk that didn't have marked around it 'Indian Wind,' even if it was exactly the same. And the orders fly to Kantrowitz, until it almost put everybody else in the business out of the business. 'This is the same silk as the other,' I explain to customers. But they don't want nothing only 'Indian Wind.' And then Kantrowitz becomes very proud and shows to everybody that comes in the office that first poem which was still hanging on the wall with the name 'Indian Wind.' And when I come to see him, he tells me:

" 'Levine, you were right. Such a boy I got!'

"And I give the man right. You got to be straight. When the man is right he is right even when it hurts your business.

"And so Izzy begins to come a little more often to the house. Business grows. Kantrowitz and Son were making lots of money. He and Margaret go out, and he spends money like water. I say nothing. Sometimes they were happy, sometimes they were not. One day they come home and say they got married. Just like that. They wanted no wedding, no ceremony. That boy was always a little peculiar, even if he was a success in business. It made me very happy and it saved me a lot of money, because the father of the girl pays the expenses of the wedding. And for business reasons I would have had to give a wedding supper of five hundred plates at ten dollars apiece. Count it up, please. And in this country you never know when a child of yours marries what the family is. And here I have known Izzy since he was a little boy and he was such a great success and had turned out to be A-one with such a mind like his, calling a silk 'Indian Wind.' With such ideas he had! And we were all very happy.

"The season over, people from the silk mills began to come around with new samples. I am very busy picking the new samples; and when Kantrowitz comes in I can see from his face that he is not so very happy.

"'What is it?' I ask him.

"'It's my Izzy,' he answers. 'He ain't come to the office in three days.'

"'For why?' I asks him.

"'I telephone and telephone, and he answers that he is very busy at home and that I should leave him alone; that he is too busy to come to the office. Levine,' Kantrowitz tells me, 'he is your son also a little, now. What can you do?'

"I came home and I didn't tell my wife nothing; for what's the use of worrying her!

"But when a man has got an only daughter and nothing else in the world except his business and he is no more young, I can assure you whatever I ate that night was poison. What does Izzy mean by not coming to the office for three days and answering his own father that he has no time? No time for business! How is that possible?

"So I ask my wife whether she has seen Margaret, and she said that she had telephoned her up and asked her to come, and Margaret said she was too busy; not to disturb her. So I remembered my Margaret was never satisfied that Izzy should not be a poet any more, and my blood got cold. You never can tell with women.

"So after dinner I couldn't hold out no more, so I said to my wife that I had to go somewhere very important to a lodge meeting and I get into the first taxi and go down town to Washington Square where they live. In the taxi I think and think what could it be; and wonder why they should have chosen to live in such a place. There are nicer houses in Washington Heights and still nicer ones in the Bronx. Why should they live in Washington Square? Even if he was in business, still he was a little peculiar, and Margaret, even if she was my daughter, she, too, had crazy ideas in the head. So I get out of the taxi and ring the bell with my heart so heavy as if I was going to visit a sick relative or going to a creditors' meeting of a bankrupt firm. When the maid opens the door and I come in, my heart becomes twenty times heavier than it already was; for there sits Izzy at a table and across from him sits my Margaret, and Izzy has again got long hair and smokes a pipe, and the table is just full of books. And the whole house was not like the home of a business man. The furniture was different. Full of couches and candlesticks. Why candlesticks when there is electricity and not like in the old country?

"'Just a minute, Pop,' Izzy tells me, and he reads poetry from a book and gets terribly excited because Margaret does not agree. When Izzy gets through, Margaret says:

"'Just a minute, Papa. Sit down a minute.' And she reads another poem to me from a book.

"So I can see that the sickness has again come upon them, and I wonder that this can be a daughter of mine and a son of Kantrowitz that I have known so well for so many years. I saw ruin before me! If a hole should have opened before me I should have jumped in. They paid no attention to me at all, as if I didn't exist. Izzy takes out another book and reads. Margaret takes out another book and reads back. And they fight and quarrel about things I don't understand at all. And he smokes a pipe and she smokes a cigarette. And I feel I am going to die. My heart sinks. Then I can hold out no longer, so I get up and cry:

"What is the matter with you children? Izzy! Again? You forget you are a married man. Izzy, again poetry! What's to become of you?'

"And so Izzy looks at me as if I was the greatest dumb-bell ever lived on God's earth. Then he smiles at me, and picks up a book, and I can tell you that in one moment all my happiness comes back with a rush. Between the leaves of the book were pieces of sample silk, and they were looking through poetry books to find another name as good as 'Indian Wind' for the new silks! So you see poetry pays in business. But you got to be an American boy and know how to make use of it . . . and not like them old country poets that starved in garrets.

"But I got very sick, and the doctor orders a rest. So I think I will visit my people in the old country.

"So why didn't you tell me that you are a writer? That's nothing to be ashamed of."

Night Club

by Katharine Brush

Promptly at quarter of ten P.M. Mrs. Brady descended the steps of the Elevated. She purchased from the newsdealer in the cubbyhole beneath them a next month's magazine and a to-morrow morning's paper and, with these tucked under one plump arm, she walked. She walked two blocks north on Sixth Avenue; turned and went west. But not far west. Westward half a block only, to the place where the gay green awning marked Club Français paints a stripe of shade across the glimmering sidewalk. Under this awning Mrs. Brady halted briefly, to remark to the six-foot doorman that it looked like rain and to await his performance of his professional duty. When the small green door yawned open, she sighed deeply and plodded in.

The foyer was a blackness, an airless velvet blackness like the inside of a jeweller's box. Four drum-shaped lamps of golden silk suspended from the ceiling gave it light (a very little) and formed the jewels: gold signets, those, or cuff-links for a giant. At the far end of the foyer there were black stairs, faintly dusty, rippling upward toward an amber radiance. Mrs. Brady approached and ponderously mounted the stairs, clinging with one fist to the mangy velvet rope that railed their edge.

From the top, Miss Lena Levin observed the ascent. Miss Levin was the checkroom girl. She had dark-at-the-roots blonde hair and slender hips upon which, in moments of leisure, she wore her hands, like buckles of ivory loosely attached. This was a moment of leisure. Miss Levin waited behind her counter. Row upon row of hooks, empty as yet, and seeming to beckon—wee curved fingers of iron—waited behind her.

"Late," said Miss Levin, "again."

"Go wan!" said Mrs. Brady. "It's only ten to ten. *Whew!* Them *stairs!*"

She leaned heavily, sideways, against Miss Levin's counter,

and, applying one palm to the region of her heart, appeared at once to listen and to count. "Feel!" she directed then in a pleased voice.

Miss Levin obediently felt.

"Them stairs," continued Mrs. Brady darkly, "with my bad heart, will be the death of me. Whew! Well, dearie? What's the news?"

"You got a paper," Miss Levin languidly reminded her.

"Yeah!" agreed Mrs. Brady with sudden vehemence. "I got a paper!" She slapped it upon the counter. "An' a lot of time I'll get to *read* my paper, won't I now? On a Saturday night!" She moaned. "Other nights is bad enough, dear knows—but *Saturday* nights! How I dread 'em! Every Saturday night I say to my daughter, I say, 'Geraldine, I can't,' I say, 'I can't go through it again, an' that's all there is to it,' I say. 'I'll quit!' I say. An' I *will*, too!" added Mrs. Brady firmly, if indefinitely.

Miss Levin, in defense of Saturday nights, mumbled some vague something about tips.

"Tips!" Mrs. Brady hissed it. She almost spat it. Plainly money was nothing, nothing at all, to this lady. "I just wish," said Mrs. Brady, and glared at Miss Levin, "I just wish *you* had to spend one Saturday night, just one, in that dressing room! Bein' pushed an' stepped on and near knocked down by that gang of hussies, an' them orderin' an' bossin' you 'round like you was *black*, an' usin' your things an' then sayin' they're sorry, they got no change, they'll be back. Yah! They *never* come back!"

"There's Mr. Costello," whispered Miss Levin through lips that, like a ventriloquist's, scarcely stirred.

"An' as I was sayin'," Mrs. Brady said at once brightly, "I got to leave you. Ten to ten, time I was on the job."

She smirked at Miss Levin, nodded, and right-about-faced. There, indeed, Mr. Costello was. Mr. Billy Costello, manager, proprietor, monarch of all he surveyed. From the doorway of the big room, where the little tables herded in a ring around the waxen floor, he surveyed Mrs. Brady, and in such a way that Mrs. Brady, momentarily forgetting her bad heart, walked fast, scurried faster, almost ran.

The door of her domain was set politely in an alcove, beyond silken curtains looped up at the sides. Mrs. Brady reached it breathless, shouldered it open, and groped for the electric switch. Lights sprang up, a bright white blaze, intolerable for an instant to the eyes, like sun on snow. Blinking, Mrs. Brady shut the door.

The room was a spotless, white-tiled place, half beauty shop, half dressing room. Along one wall stood washstands, sturdy triplets in a row, with pale-green liquid soap in glass balloons afloat above them. Against the opposite wall there was a couch. A third wall backed an elongated glass-topped dressing table; and over the dressing table and over the washstands long rectangular sheets of mirror reflected lights, doors, glossy tiles, lights multiplied....

Mrs. Brady moved across this glitter like a thick dark cloud in a hurry. At the dressing table she came to a halt, and upon it she laid her newspaper, her magazine, and her purse—a black purse worn gray with much clutching. She divested herself of a rusty black coat and a hat of the mushroom persuasion, and hung both up in a corner cupboard which she opened by means of one of a quite preposterous bunch of keys. From a nook in the cupboard she took down a lace-edged handkerchief with long streamers. She untied the streamers and tied them again around her chunky black alpaca waist. The handkerchief became an apron's baby cousin.

Mrs. Brady relocked the cupboard door, fumbled her keyring over, and unlocked a capacious drawer of the dressing table. She spread a fresh towel on the plate-glass top, in the geometrical centre, and upon the towel she arranged with care a procession of things fished from the drawer. Things for the hair. Things for the complexion. Things for the eyes, the lashes, the brows, the lips, and the finger nails. Things in boxes and things in jars and things in tubes and tins. Also, an ash tray, matches, pins, a tiny sewing kit, a pair of scissors. Last of all, a hand-printed sign, a nudging sort of sign:

NOTICE!
These articles, placed here for your convenience, are the property of the *maid*.

And directly beneath the sign, propping it up against the looking-glass, a china saucer, in which Mrs. Brady now slyly laid decoy money: two quarters and two dimes, in four-leaf-clover formation.

Another drawer of the dressing table yielded a bottle of bromo seltzer, a bottle of aromatic spirits of ammonia, a tin of sodium bicarbonate, and a teaspoon. These were lined up on a shelf above the couch.

Mrs. Brady was now ready for anything. And (from the grim, thin pucker of her mouth) expecting it.

Music came to her ears. Rather, the beat of music, muffled, rhythmic, remote. *Umpa-um*, umpa-um, umpa-um—Mr. "Fiddle" Baer and his band, hard at work on the first foxtrot of the night. It was teasing, foot-tapping music; but the large solemn feet of Mrs. Brady were still. She sat on the couch and opened her newspaper; and for some moments she read uninterruptedly, with special attention to the murders, the divorces, the breaches of promise, the funnies.

Then the door swung inward, admitting a blast of Mr. "Fiddle" Baer's best, a whiff of perfume, and a girl.

Mrs. Brady put her paper away.

The girl was *petite* and darkly beautiful; wrapped in fur and mounted on tall jewelled heels. She entered humming the ragtime song the orchestra was playing, and while she stood near the dressing table, stripping off her gloves, she continued to hum it softly to herself:

"Oh, I know my baby loves me,
I can tell my baby loves me."

Here the dark little girl got the left glove off, and Mrs. Brady glimpsed a platinum wedding ring.

" 'Cause there ain't no maybe—"
In my baby's
Eyes."

The right glove came off. The dark little girl sat down in one of the chairs that faced the dressing table. She doffed her wrap, casting it carelessly over the chair back. It had a cloth-of-gold lining, and "Paris" was embroidered in curlicues on the label. Mrs. Brady hovered solicitously near.

The dark little girl, still humming, looked over the articles "placed here for your convenience," and picked up the scissors. Having cut off a very small hangnail with the air of one performing a perilous major operation, she seized and used the manicure buffer, and after that the eyebrow pencil. Mrs. Brady's mind, hopefully calculating the tip, jumped and jumped again like a taximeter.

"Oh I know my baby loves me—"

The dark little girl applied powder and lipstick belonging to herself. She examined the result searchingly in the mirror and sat back, satisfied. She cast some silver *Klink! Klink!* into Mrs. Brady's saucer, and half rose. Then, remembering something, she settled down again.

The ensuing thirty seconds were spent by her in pulling off her platinum wedding ring, tying it in a corner of a lace handkerchief, and tucking the handkerchief down the bodice of her tight white velvet gown.

"There!" she said.

She swooped up her wrap and trotted toward the door, jewelled heels merrily twinkling.

" 'Cause there ain't no maybe

The door fell shut.

Almost instantly it opened again, and another girl came in. A blonde, this. She was pretty in a round-eyed, babyish way; but Mrs. Brady, regarding her, mentally grabbed the spirits of ammonia bottle. For she looked terribly ill. The round eyes were dull, the pretty, silly little face was drawn. The thin hands, picking at the fastenings of a specious beaded bag, trembled and twitched.

Mrs. Brady cleared her throat. "Can I do something for you, miss?"

Evidently the blonde girl had believed herself alone in the dressing room. She started violently and glanced up, panic in her eyes. Panic, and something else. Something very like murderous hate—but for an instant only, so that Mrs. Brady, whose perceptions were never quick, missed it altogether.

"A glass of water?" suggested Mrs. Brady.

"No," said the girl, "no." She had one hand in the beaded bag now. Mrs. Brady could see it moving, causing the bag to squirm like a live thing, and the fringe to shiver. "Yes!" she cried abruptly. "A glass of water—please—you get it for me."

She dropped on to the couch. Mrs. Brady scurried to the water cooler in the corner, pressed the spigot with a determined thumb. Water trickled out thinly. Mrs. Brady pressed harder, and scowled, and thought, "Something's wrong with this thing. I mustn't forget, next time I see Mr. Costello—"

When again she faced her patient, the patient was sitting erect. She was thrusting her clenched hand back into the beaded bag again.

She took only a sip of the water, but it seemed to help her

quite miraculously. Almost at once colour came to her cheeks, life to her eyes. She grew young again—as young as she was. She smiled up at Mrs. Brady.

"Well!" she exclaimed. "What do you know about that!" She shook her honey-coloured head. "I can't imagine what came over me."

"Are you better now?" inquired Mrs. Brady.

"Yes. Oh, yes. I'm better now. You see," said the blonde girl confidentially, "we were at the theatre, my boy friend and I, and it was hot and stuffy—I guess that must have been the trouble." She paused, and the ghost of her recent distress crossed her face. "God! I thought that last act *never* would end!" she said.

While she attended to her hair and complexion, she chattered gaily to Mrs. Brady, chattered on with scarcely a stop for breath, and laughed much. She said, among other things, that she and her "boy friend" had not known one another very long, but that she was "ga-ga" about him. "He is about me, too," she confessed. "He thinks I'm grand."

She fell silent then, and in the looking-glass her eyes were shadowed, haunted. But Mrs. Brady, from where she stood, could not see the looking-glass; and half a minute later the blonde girl laughed out and began again. When she went out she seemed to dance out on little winged feet; and Mrs. Brady, sighing, thought it must be nice to be young . . . and happy like that.

The next arrivals were two. A tall, extremely smart young woman in black chiffon entered first, and held the door open for her companion; and the instant the door was shut, she said, as though it had been on the tip of her tongue for hours, "Amy, what under the sun *happened?*"

Amy, who was brown-eyed, brown-bobbed-haired, and patently annoyed about something, crossed to the dressing table and flopped into a chair before she made reply.

"Nothing," she said wearily then.

"That's nonsense!" snorted the other. "Tell me. Was it something she said? She's a tactless ass, of course. Always was."

"No, not anything she said. It was—" Amy bit her lip. "All right! I'll tell you. Before we left your apartment I just happened to notice that Tom had disappeared. So I went to look for him—I wanted to ask him if he'd remembered to tell the maid where we were going—Skippy's subject to croup, you know, and we always leave word. Well, so I went into the kitchen, thinking Tom might be there mixing cocktails—and there he was—and there *she* was!"

The full red mouth of the other young woman pursed itself slightly. Her arched brows lifted. "Well?"

Her matter-of-factness appeared to infuriate Amy. "He was *kissing* her!" she flung out.

"Well?" said the other again. She chuckled softly and patted Amy's shoulder, as if it were the shoulder of a child. "You're surely not going to let *that* spoil your whole evening? Amy *dear!* Kissing may once have been serious and significant—but it isn't nowadays. Nowadays, it's like shaking hands. It means nothing."

But Amy was not consoled. "I hate her!" she cried desperately. "Red-headed *thing!* Calling me 'darling' and 'honey,' and s-sending me handkerchiefs for C-Christmas—and then sneaking off behind closed doors and k-kissing my h-h-husband . . ."

At this point Amy quite broke down, but she recovered herself sufficiently to add with venom, "I'd like to slap her!"

"Oh, oh, oh," smiled the tall young woman, "I wouldn't do that!"

Amy wiped her eyes with what might well have been one of the Christmas handkerchiefs, and confronted her friend. "Well, what *would* you do, Claire? If you were I?"

"I'd forget it," said Claire, "and have a good time. I'd kiss somebody myself. You've no idea how much better you'd feel!"

"I don't do—" Amy began indignantly; but as the door behind her opened and a third young woman—red-headed, ear-ringed, exquisite—lilted in, she changed her tone. "Oh, hello!" she called sweetly, beaming at the newcomer via the mirror. "We were wondering what had become of you!"

The red-headed girl, smiling easily back, dropped her cigarette on the floor and crushed it out with a silver-shod toe. "Tom and I were talking to 'Fiddle' Baer," she explained. "He's going to play 'Clap Yo' Hands' next, because it's my favourite. Lend me a comb, will you, somebody?"

"There's a comb there," said Claire, indicating Mrs. Brady's business comb.

"But imagine using it!" murmured the red-headed girl. "Amy, darling, haven't you one?"

Amy produced a tiny comb from her rhinestone purse. "Don't forget to bring it when you come," she said, and stood up. "I'm going out, I want to tell Tom something."

She went.

The red-headed young woman and the tall black-chiffon one were alone, except for Mrs. Brady. The red-headed one beaded her incredible lashes. The tall one, the one called Claire, sat watching her. Presently she said, "Sylvia, look here." And Sylvia looked. Anybody, addressed in that tone, would have.

"There is one thing," Claire went on quietly, holding the other's eyes, "that I want understood. And that is, *'Hands off!'* Do you hear me?"

"I don't know what you mean."

"You do know what I mean!"

The red-headed girl shrugged her shoulders. "Amy told you she saw us, I suppose."

"Precisely. And," went on Claire, gathering up her possessions and rising, "as I said before, you're to keep away." Her eyes blazed sudden white-hot rage. "Because, as you very well know, he belongs to *me*," she said, and departed, slamming the door.

Between eleven o'clock and one Mrs. Brady was very busy indeed. Never for more than a moment during those two hours was the dressing room empty. Often it was jammed, full to overflowing with curled cropped heads, with ivory arms and shoulders, with silk and lace and chiffon, with legs. The door flapped in and back, in and back. The mirrors caught and held—and lost—a hundred different faces. Powder veiled the dressing table with a thin white dust; cigarette stubs, scarlet at the tips, choked the ash-receiver. Dimes and quarters clattered into Mrs. Brady's saucer—and were transferred to Mrs. Brady's purse. The original seventy cents remained. That much, and no more, would Mrs. Brady gamble on the integrity of womankind.

She earned her money. She threaded needles and took stitches. She powdered the backs of necks. She supplied towels for soapy, dripping hands. She removed a speck from a teary blue eye and pounded the heel on a slipper. She curled the straggling ends of a black bob and a gray bob, pinned a velvet flower on a lithe round waist, mixed three doses of bicarbonate of soda, took charge of a shed pink-satin girdle, collected, on hands and knees, several dozen fake pearls that had wept from a broken string.

She served chorus girls and schoolgirls, gay young matrons and gayer young mistresses, a lady who had divorced four husbands, and a lady who had poisoned one, the secret (more or less) sweetheart of a Most Distinguished Name, and the Brains of a bootleg gang. . . . She saw things. She saw a yellow check, with the ink hardly dry. She saw four tiny bruises, such as fingers might make, on an arm. She saw a girl strike another girl, not playfully. She saw a bundle of letters some man wished he had not written, safe and deep in a brocaded handbag.

About midnight the door flew open and at once was pushed shut, and a gray-eyed, lovely child stood backed against it, her palms flattened on the panels at her sides, the draperies of her white chiffon gown settling lightly to rest around her.

There were already five damsels of varying ages in the dressing room. The latest arrival marked their presence with a flick of her eyes and, standing just where she was, she called peremptorily, "Maid!"

Mrs. Brady, standing just where *she* was, said, "Yes, miss?"

"Please come here," said the girl.

Mrs. Brady, as slowly as she dared, did so.

The girl lowered her voice to a tense half-whisper. "Listen! Is there any way I can get out of here except through this door I came in?"

Mrs. Brady stared at her stupidly.

"Any window?" persisted the girl. "Or anything?"

Here they were interrupted by the exodus of two of the damsels-of-varying-ages. Mrs. Brady opened the door for them—and in so doing caught a glimpse of a man who waited in the hall outside, a debonair, old-young man with a girl's furry wrap hung over his arm, and his hat in his hand.

The door clicked. The gray-eyed girl moved out from the wall, against which she had flattened herself—for all the world like one eluding pursuit in a cinema.

"What about that window?" she demanded, pointing.

"That's all the farther it opens," said Mrs. Brady.

"Oh! And it's the only one—isn't it?"

"It is."

"Damn," said the girl. "Then there's *no* way out?"

"No way but the door," said Mrs. Brady testily.

The girl looked at the door. She seemed to look *through* the door, and to despise and to fear what she saw. Then she looked at Mrs. Brady. "Well," she said, "then I s'pose the only thing to do is to stay in here."

She stayed. Minutes ticked by. Jazz crooned distantly, stopped, struck up again. Other girls came and went. Still the gray-eyed girl sat on the couch, with her back to the wall and her shapely legs crossed, smoking cigarettes, one from the stub of another.

After a long while she said, "Maid!"

"Yes, miss?"

"Peek out that door, will you, and see if there's anyone standing there."

Mrs. Brady peeked, and reported that there was. There was a gentleman with a little bit of a black moustache standing there. The same gentleman, in fact, who was standing there "just after you came in."

"Oh, Lord," sighed the gray-eyed girl. "Well . . . I can't stay here all *night*, that's one sure thing."

She slid off the couch, and went listlessly to the dressing table. There she occupied herself for a minute or two. Suddenly, without a word, she darted out.

Thirty seconds later Mrs. Brady was elated to find two crumpled one-dollar bills lying in her saucer. Her joy, however, died a premature death. For she made an almost simultaneous second discovery. A saddening one. Above all, a puzzling one.

"Now what for," marvelled Mrs. Brady, "did she want to walk off with them *scissors*?"

This at twelve-twenty-five.

At twelve-thirty a quartette of excited young things burst in, babbling madly. Al of them had their evening wraps with them; all talked at once. One of them, a Dresden china girl with a heart-shaped face, was the centre of attention. Around her the rest fluttered like monstrous butterflies; to her they addressed their shrill exclamatory cries. "Babe," they called her.

Mrs. Brady heard snatches: "Not in this state unless . . ." "Well, you can in Maryland, Jimmy says." "Oh, there must be some place nearer than . . ." "Isn't this *marvellous*?" "When did it happen, Babe? When did you decide?"

"Just now," the girl with the heart-shaped face sang softly, "when we were dancing."

The babble resumed, "But listen, Babe, what'll your mother and father . . . ?" "Oh, never mind, let's hurry. "Shall we be warm enough with just these thin wraps, do you think? Babe, will you be warm enough? Sure?"

Powder flew and little pocket combs marched through bright marcels. Flushed cheeks were painted pinker still.

"My pearls," said Babe, "are *old*. And my dress and my slippers are *new*. Now, let's see—what can I *borrow*?"

A lace handkerchief, a diamond bar pin, a pair of earrings were proffered. She chose the bar pin, and its owner unpinned it proudly, gladly.

"I've got blue garters!'" exclaimed another girl.

"Give me one, then," directed Babe. "I'll trade with you. . . . There! That fixes that."

More babbling, "Hurry! Hurry up!" . . . "Listen, are you *sure* we'll be warm enough? Because we can stop at my house, there's nobody home." "Give me that puff, Babe, I'll powder your back." "And just to think a week ago you'd never even met each other!" "Oh, hurry *up*, let's get *started!*" "I'm ready." "So'm I." "Ready, Babe? You look adorable." "Come on, everybody."

They were gone again, and the dressing room seemed twice as still and vacant as before.

A minute of grace, during which Mrs. Brady wiped the spilled powder away with a damp gray rag. Then the door jumped open again. Two evening gowns appeared and made for the dressing table in a bee line. Slim tubular gowns they were, one silver, one palest yellow. Yellow hair went with the silver gown, brown hair with the yellow. The silver-gowned, yellow-haired girl wore orchids on her shoulder, three of them, and a flashing bracelet on each fragile wrist. The other girl looked less prosperous; still, you would rather have looked at her.

Both ignored Mrs. Brady's cosmetic display as utterly as they ignored Mrs. Brady, producing full field equipment of their own.

"Well," said the girl with the orchids, rouging energetically, "how do you like him?"

"Oh-h—all right."

"Meaning, 'Not any,' hmm? I suspected as much!" The girl with the orchids turned in her chair and scanned her companion's profile with disapproval. "See here, Marilee," she drawled, "are you going to be a damn fool *all* your life?"

"He's fat," said Marilee dreamily. "Fat, and—greasy, sort of. I mean, greasy in his mind. Don't you know what I mean?"

"I know *one* thing," declared the girl with orchids. "I know

Who He Is! And if I were you, that's all I'd need to know. *Under the circumstances.*"

The last three words, stressed meaningly, affected the girl called Marilee curiously. She grew grave. Her lips and lashes drooped. For some seconds she sat frowning a little, breaking a black-sheathed lipstick in two and fitting it together again.

"She's worse," she said finally, low.

"Worse?"

Marilee nodded.

"Well," said the girl with orchids, "there you are. It's the climate. She'll never be anything *but* worse, if she doesn't get away. Out West, or somewhere."

"I know," murmured Marilee.

The other girl opened a tin of eye shadow. "Of course," she said drily, "suit yourself. She's not *my* sister."

Marilee said nothing. Quiet she sat, breaking the lipstick, mending it, breaking it.

"Oh, well," she breathed finally, wearily, and straightened up. She propped her elbows on the plate-glass dressing-table top and leaned toward the mirror, and with the lipstick she began to make her coral-pink mouth very red and gay and reckless and alluring.

Nightly at one o'clock Vane and Moreno dance for the Club Français. They dance a tango, they dance a waltz; then, by way of encore, they do a Black Bottom, and a trick of their own called the Wheel. They dance for twenty, thirty minutes. And while they dance you do not leave your tables—for this is what you came to see. Vane and Moreno. The New York thrill. The sole justification for the five-dollar couvert extorted by Billy Costello.

From one until half-past, then, was Mrs. Brady's recess. She had been looking forward to it all the evening long. When it began—when the opening chords of the tango music sounded stirringly from the room outside—Mrs. Brady brightened. With a right good will she sped the parting guests.

Alone, she unlocked her cupboard and took out her magazine—the magazine she had bought three hours before. Heaving a great breath of relief and satisfaction, she plumped herself on the couch and fingered the pages. Immediately she was absorbed, her eyes drinking up printed lines, her lips moving soundlessly.

The magazine was Mrs. Brady's favourite. Its stories were true stories, taken from life (so the editor said); and to Mrs. Brady they were live, vivid threads in the dull, drab pattern of her night.

Each in His Generation

by Maxwell Struthers Burt

Every afternoon at four o'clock, except when the weather was very bad—autumn, winter, and spring—old Mr. Henry McCain drove up to the small, discreet, polished front door, in the small, discreet, fashionable street in which lived fairly old Mrs. Thomas Denby; got out, went up the white marble steps, rang the bell, and was admitted into the narrow but charming hall—dim turquoise-blue velvet panelled into the walls, an etching or two: Whistler, Brangwyn—by a trim parlour-maid. Ten generations, at least, of trim parlour-maids had opened the door for Mr. McCain. They had seen the sparkling victoria change, not too quickly, to a plum-coloured limousine; they had seen Mr. McCain become perhaps a trifle thinner, the colour in his cheeks become a trifle more confined and fixed, his white hair grow somewhat sparser, but beyond that they had seen very little indeed, although, when they had left Mr. McCain in the drawing-room with the announcement that Mrs. Denby would be down immediately, and were once again seeking the back of the house, no doubt their eyebrows, blonde, brunette, or red, apexed to a questioning angle.

In the manner of youth the parlour-maids had come, worked, fallen in love and departed, but Mr. McCain, in the manner of increasing age, had if anything grown more faithful and exact to the moment. If he were late the fraction of five minutes, one suspected that he regretted it, that it came near to spoiling his entire afternoon. He was not articulate, but occasionally he expressed an idea and the most common was that he "liked his things as he liked them"; his eggs, in other words, boiled just so long, no more—after sixty years of inner debate on the subject he had apparently arrived at the conclusion that boiled eggs were the only kind of eggs permissible—his life punctual and serene. The smallest manifestation of unexpectedness disturbed him. Obviously that was one reason why, after a youth not altogether constant, he had become so utterly constant where Mrs. Denby was concerned. She had a quality of perenniality, charming and assuring, even to each strand of her delicate brown hair. Grayness should have been creeping upon her, but it was not. It was doubtful if Mr. McCain permitted himself, even secretly, to wonder why. Effects, fastidious and constant, were all he demanded from life.

This had been going on for twenty years—this afternoon call; this slow drive afterward in the park; this return by dusk to the shining small house in the shining small street; the good-by, reticently ardent, as if it were not fully Mr. McCain's intention to return again in the evening. Mr. McCain would kiss Mrs. Denby's hand—slim, lovely, with a single gorgeous sapphire upon the third finger. "Good-by, my dear," he would say, "you have given me the most delightful afternoon of my life." For a moment Mrs. Denby's hand would linger on the bowed head; then Mr. McCain would straighten up, smile, square his shoulders in their smart, young-looking coat, and depart to his club, or the large, softly lit house where he dwelt alone. At dinner he would drink two glasses of champagne. Before he drained the last sip of the second pouring he would hold the glass up to the fire, so that the bronze coruscations at the heart of the wine glowed like fireflies in a gold dusk. One imagined him saying to himself: "A perfect woman! A perfect woman—God bless her!" Saying "God bless" any one, mind you, with a distinct warming of the heart, but a thoroughly late-Victorian disbelief in any god to bless. . . . At least, you thought as much.

And, of course, one had not the slightest notion whether he—old Mr. Henry McCain—was aware that this twenty years of devotion on his part to Mrs. Denby was the point upon which had come to focus the not inconsiderable contempt and hatred for him of his nephew Adrian.

It was an obvious convergence, this devotion of all the traits which composed, so Adrian imagined, the despicable soul that lay beneath his uncle's unangled exterior; undeviating self-indulgence; secrecy; utter selfishness—he was selfish even to the woman he was supposed to love; that is, if he was capable of loving any one but himself—a bland hypocrisy; an unthinking conformation to the dictates of an unthinking world. The list could be multiplied. But to sum it up, here was epitomized, beautifully, concretely, the main and minor vices of a generation for which Adrian found little pity in his heart; a generation brittle as ice; a generation of secret diplomacy; a generation that in its youth had covered a lack of bathing by a vast amount of perfume. That was it—! That expressed it perfectly! The just summation! Camellias, and double intentions in speech, and unnecessary reticences, and refusals to meet the truth, and a deliberate hiding of uglinesses!

Most of the time Adrian was too busy to think about his uncle at all—he was a very busy man with his writing: journalistic writing; essays, political reviews, propaganda—and because he was busy he was usually well-content, and not uncharitable, except professionally; but once a month it was his duty to dine with his uncle, and then, for the rest of the night, he was disturbed, and awoke the next morning with the dusty feeling in his head of a man who has been slightly drunk. Old wounds were recalled, old scars inflamed; a childhood in which his uncle's figure had represented to him the terrors of sarcasm and repression; a youth in which, as his guardian, his uncle had deprecated all first fine hot-bloodednesses and enthusiasms; a young manhood in which he had been told cynically that the ways of society were good ways, and that the object of life was material advancement; advice which had been followed by the stimulus of an utter refusal to assist financially except where absolutely necessary. There had been willingness, you understand, to provide a gentleman's education, but no willingness to provide beyond that any of a gentleman's perquisites. That much of his early success had been due to this heroic upbringing, Adrian was too honest not to admit, but then—by God, it had been hard! All the colour of youth! No time to dream—except sorely! Some warping, some perversion! A gasping, heart-breaking knowledge that you could not possibly keep up with the people with whom, paradoxically enough, you were supposed to spend your leisure hours. Here was the making of a radical. And yet, despite all this, Adrian dined with his uncle once a month.

The mere fact that this was so, that it could be so, enraged him. It seemed a renunciation of all he affirmed; an implicit falsehood. He would have liked very much to have got to his feet, standing firmly on his two long, well-made legs, and have once and for all delivered himself of a final philippic. The philippic would have ended something like this:

"And this, sir, is the last time I sacrifice any of my good hours to you. Not because you are old, and therefore think you are wise, when you are not; not because you are blind and besotted and damned—a trunk of a tree filled with dry rot that presently a clean wind will blow away; not because your opinions, and the opinions of all like you, have long ago been proven the lies and idiocies that they are; not even because you haven't one single real right left to live—I haven't come to tell you these things, although they are true; for you are past hope and there is no use wasting words upon you; I have come to tell you that you bore me inexpressibly. (That would be the most dreadful revenge of all. He could see his uncle's face!) That you have a genius for taking the wrong side of every question, and I can no longer endure it. I dissipate my time. Good-night!"

He wouldn't have said it in quite so stately a way, possibly; the sentences would not have been quite so rounded, but the context would have been the same.

Glorious; but it wasn't said. Instead, once a month, he got into his dinner-jacket, brushed his hair very sleekly, walked six blocks, said good-evening to his uncle's butler, and went on back to the library, where, in a room rich with costly bindings, and smelling pleasantly of leather, and warmly yellow with the light of two shaded lamps, he would find his uncle reading before a crackling wood fire. What followed was almost a formula, an exquisite presentation of stately manners, an exquisite avoidance of any topic which might cause a real discussion. The dinner was invariably gentle, persuasive, a thoughtful gastronomic achievement. Heaven might become confused about its weather, and about wars, and things like that, but Mr. McCain never became confused about his menus. He had a habit of commending wine. "Try this claret, my dear fellow, I want your opinion. . . . A drop of this Napoleonic brandy won't hurt you a bit." He even sniffed the bouquet before each sip; passed, that is, the glass under his nose and then drank. But Adrian, with a preconceived image of the personality back of this, and the memory of too many offences busy in his mind, saw nothing quaint or amusing. His gorge rose. Damn his uncle's wines, and his mushrooms, and his soft-footed servants, and his house of nuances and evasions, and his white grapes, large and outwardly perfect, and inwardly sentimental as the generation whose especial fruit they were. As for himself, he had a recollection of ten years of poverty after leaving college; a recollection of sweat and indignities; he had also a recollection of some poor people whom he had known.

Afterward, when the dinner was over, Adrian would go

home and awake his wife, Cecil, who, with the brutal honesty of an honest woman, also some of the ungenerosity, had early in her married life flatly refused any share in the ceremonies described. Cecil would lie in her small white bed, the white of her boudoir-cap losing itself in the white of the pillow, a little sleepy and a little angrily perplexed at the perpetual jesuitical philosophy of the male. "If you feel that way," she would ask, "why do you go there, then? Why don't you banish your uncle utterly?" She asked this not without malice, her long, violet, Slavic eyes widely open, and her red mouth, a trifle too large, perhaps, a trifle cruel, fascinatingly interrogative over her white teeth. She loved Adrian and had at times, therefore, the right and desire to torture him. She knew perfectly well why he went. He was his uncle's heir, and until such time as money and other anachronisms of the present social system were done away with, there was no use throwing a fortune into the gutter, even if by your own efforts you were making an income just sufficiently large to keep up with the increased cost of living.

Sooner or later Adrian's mind reverted to Mrs. Denby. This was usually after he had been in bed and had been thinking for a while in the darkness. He could not understand Mrs. Denby. She affronted his modern habit of thought.

"The whole thing is so silly and adventitious!"

"What thing?"

Adrian was aware that his wife knew exactly of what he was talking, but he had come to expect the question. "Mrs. Denby and my uncle." He would grow rather gently cross. "It has always reminded me of those present-day sword-and-cloak romances fat businessmen used to write about ten years ago and sell so enormously—there's an atmosphere of unnecessary intrigue. What's it all about? Here's the point! Why, if she felt this way about things, didn't she divorce that gentle drunkard of a husband of hers years ago and marry my uncle outright and honestly? Or why, if she couldn't get a divorce—which she could—didn't she leave her husband and go with my uncle? Anything in the open! Make a break—have some courage of her opinions! Smash things; build them up again! Thank God nowadays, at least, we have come to believe in the cleanness of surgery rather than the concealing palliatives of medicine. We're no. longer—we modern people—afraid of the world; and the world can never hurt for any length of time any one who will stand up to it and tell it courageously to go to hell. No! It comes back and licks hands.

"I'll tell you why. My uncle and Mrs. Denby are the typical moral cowards of their generation. There's selfishness, too. What a travesty of love! Of course there's scandal, a perpetual scandal; but it's a hidden, sniggering scandal they don't have to meet face to face; and that's all they ask of life, they, and people like them—never to have to meet anything face to face. So long as they can bury their heads like ostriches! . . . Faugh!" There would be a moment's silence; then Adrian would complete his thought. "In my uncle's case," he would grumble in the darkness, "one phase of the selfishness is obvious. He couldn't even get himself originally, I suppose, to face the inevitable matter-of-fact moments of marriage. It began when he was middle-aged, a bachelor—I suppose he wants the sort of Don Juan, eighteen-eighty, perpetual sort of romance that doesn't exist outside the brains of himself and his like. . . . Camellias!"

Usually he tried to stir up argument with his wife, who in these matters agreed with him utterly; even more than agreed with him, since she was the escaped daughter of rich and stodgy people, and had insisted upon earning her own living by portrait-painting. Theoretically, therefore, she was, of course, an anarchist. But at moments like the present her silent assent and the aura of slight weariness over an ancient subject which emanated from her in the dusk, affronted Adrian as much as positive opposition.

Why don't you try to understand me?"

"I do, dearest!"—a pathetic attempt at eager agreement.

"Well, then, if you do, why is the tone of your voice like that? You know by now what I think. I'm not talking convention; I believe there are no laws higher than the love of a man for a woman. It should seek expression as a seed seeks sunlight. I'm talking about honesty; bravery; a willingness to accept the consequences of one's acts and come through; about the intention to sacrifice for love just what has to be sacrificed. What's the use of it otherwise! That's one real advance the modern mind has made, anyhow, despite all the rest of the welter and uncertainty."

"Of course, dearest."

He would go on. After a while Cecil would awake guiltily and inject a fresh, almost gay interest into her sleepy voice. She was not so unfettered as not to dread the wounded esteem of the unlistened-to male. She would lean over and kiss Adrian.

"Do go to sleep, darling! What's the sense? Pretty soon your uncle will be dead—wretched old man! Then you'll never have to think of him again." Being a childless woman, her red, a trifle cruel mouth would twist itself in the darkness into a small, secretive, maternal smile.

But old Mr. Henry McCain didn't die; instead he seemed to be caught up in the condition of static good health which frequently companions entire selfishness and a careful interest in oneself. His butler died, which was very annoying. Mr. McCain seemed to consider it the breaking of a promise made fifteen or so years before. It was endlessly a trouble instructing a new man, and then, of course, there was Adlington's family to be looked after, and taxes had gone up, and Mrs. Adlington was a stout woman who, despite the fact that Adlington, while alive, had frequently interrupted Mr. McCain's breakfast newspaper reading by asserting that she was a person of no character, now insisted upon weeping noisily every time Mr. McCain granted her an interview. Also, and this was equally unexpected, since one rather thought he would go on living forever, like one of the damper sort of fungi, Mr. Denby came home from the club one rainy spring night with a slight cold and died, three days later, with extraordinary gentleness.

"My uncle," said Adrian, "is one by one losing his accessories. After a while it will be his teeth."

Cecil was perplexed. "I don't know exactly what to do," she complained. "I don't know whether to treat Mrs. Denby as a bereaved aunt, a non-existent family skeleton, or a released menace. I dare say now, pretty soon, she and your uncle will be married. Meanwhile, I suppose it is rather silly of me not to call and see if I can help her in any way. After all, we do know her intimately, whether we want to or not, don't we? We meet her about all the time, even if she wasn't motoring over to your uncle's place in the summer when we stop there."

So she went, being fundamentally kindly and fundamentally curious. She spoke of the expedition as "a descent upon Fair Rosamund's tower."

The small, yellow-panelled drawing-room, where she awaited Mrs. Denby's coming, was lit by a single silver vase-lamp under an orange shade and by a fire of thin logs, for the April evening was damp with a hesitant rain. On the table, near the lamp, was a silver vase with three yellow tulips in it, and Cecil, wandering about, came upon a double photograph frame, back of the vase, that made her gasp. She picked it up and stared at it. Between the alligator edgings, facing each other obliquely, but with the greatest amity, were Mr. Thomas Denby in the fashion of ten years before, very handsome, very well-groomed, with the startled expression which any definite withdrawal from his potational pursuits was likely to produce upon his countenance, and her uncle-in-law, Mr. Henry McCain, also in the fashion of ten years back. She was holding the photographs up to the light, her lips still apart, when she heard a sound behind her, and, putting the frame back guiltily, turned about. Mrs. Denby was advancing toward her. She seemed entirely unaware of Cecil's malfeasance; she was smiling faintly; her hand was cordial, grateful.

"You are very good," she murmured. "Sit here by the fire. We will have some tea directly."

Cecil could not but admit that she was very lovely; particularly lovely in the black of her mourning, with her slim neck, rising up from its string of pearls, to a head small and like a delicate white-and-gold flower. An extraordinarily well-bred woman, a sort of misty Du Maurier woman, of a type that had become almost non-existent, if ever it had existed in its perfection at all. And, curiously enough, a woman whose beauty seemed to have been sharpened by many fine-drawn renunciations. Now she looked at her hands as if expecting Cecil to say something.

"I think such calls as this are always very useless, but then—"

"Exactly—but then! They mean more than anything else in the world, don't they? When one reaches fifty-five one is not always used to kindness. . . . You are very kind. . . ." She raised her eyes.

Cecil experienced a sudden impulsive warmth. After all, what did she or any one else know about other peoples' lives? Poor souls! What a base thing life often was!

"I want you to understand that we are always so glad, both Adrian and myself. . . . Anytime we can help in any way, you know—"

"Yes, I think you would. You—I have watched you both. You don't mind, do you? I think you're both rather great people—at least, my idea of greatness."

Cecil's eyes shone just a little; then she sat back and drew together her eager, rather childish mouth. This wouldn't do! She had not come here to encourage sentimentalization. With a determined effort she lifted her mind outside the circle of commiseration which threatened to surround it. She deliberately reset the conversation to impersonal limits. She was sure that Mrs. Denby was aware of her intention, adroitly concealed as it was. This made her uncomfortable, ashamed. And yet she was irritated with herself. Why should she particularly care what this woman thought in ways as subtle as this? Obvious kindness was her intention, not mental charity pursued into tortuous by-paths. And, besides, her frank, boyish cynicism, its wariness, revolted, even while she felt herself flattered at the prospect of the confidences that seemed to tremble on Mrs. Denby's lips. It wouldn't do to "let herself in for anything"; to "give herself away." No! She adopted a manner of cool, entirely reflective kindliness. But all along she was not sure that she was thoroughly successful. There was a lingering impression that Mrs. Denby was penetrating the surface to the unwilling interest beneath. Cecil suspected that this woman was trained in discriminations and half-lights to which she and her generation had joyfully made themselves blind. She felt uncomfortably young; a little bit smiled at in the most kindly of hidden ways. Just as she was leaving, the subversive softness came close to her again, like a wave of too much perfume as you open a church-door; as if some one were trying to embrace her against her will.

"You will understand," said Mrs. Denby, "that you have done the very nicest thing in the world. I am horribly lonely. I have few women friends. Perhaps it is too much to ask— if you could call again sometimes. Yes . . . I would appreciate it so greatly."

She let go of Cecil's hand and walked to the door, and stood with one long arm raised against the curtain, her face turned toward the hall.

"There is no use," she said, "in attempting to hide my husband's life, for every one knows what it was, but then—yes, I think you will understand. I am a childless woman, you see; he was infinitely pathetic."

Cecil felt that she must run away, instantly. "I do—" she said brusquely. "I understand more than other women. Perfectly! Good-by!"

She found herself brushing past the latest trim parlour-maid, and out once more in the keen, sweet, young dampness. She strode briskly down the deserted street. Her fine bronze eyebrows were drawn down to where they met. "Good Lord! Damn!"—Cecil swore very prettily and modernly—"What rotten taste! Not frankness, whatever it might seem outwardly; not frankness, but devious excuses! Some more of Adrian's hated past-generation stuff! And yet—no! The woman was sincere—perfectly! She had meant it—that about her husband. And she *was* lovely—and she was fine, too! It was impossible to deny it. But—a childless woman! About that drunken tailor's model of a husband! And then— Uncle Henry! . . ." Cecil threw back her head; her eyes gleamed in the wet radiance of a corner lamp; she laughed without making a sound, and entirely without amusement.

But it is not true that good health is static, no matter how carefully looked after. And, despite the present revolt against the Greek spirit, Time persists in being bigotedly Greek. The tragedy—provided one lives long enough—is always played out to its logical conclusion. For every hour you have spent, no matter how quietly or beautifully or wisely, Nemesis takes toll in the end. You peter out; the engine dulls; the shining coin wears thin. If it's only that it is all right; you are fortunate if you don't become greasy, too, or blurred, or scarred. And Mr. McCain had not spent all his hours wisely or beautifully, or even quietly, underneath the surface. He suddenly developed what he called "acute indigestion." "Odd!" he complained, "and exceedingly tiresome! I've been able to eat like an ostrich all my life." Adrian smiled covertly at the simile, but his uncle was unaware that it was because in Adrian's mind the simile applied to his uncle's conscience, not his stomach.

It *was* an odd disease, that "acute indigestion." It manifested itself by an abrupt tragic stare in Mr. McCain's eyes, a whiteness of cheek, a clutching at the left side of the breast; it resulted also in his beginning to walk very slowly indeed. One day Adrian met Carron, his uncle's physician, as he was leaving a club after luncheon. Carron stopped him. "Look here, Adrian," he said, "is that new man of your uncle's—that valet, or whatever he is—a good man?"

Adrian smiled. "I didn't hire him," he answered, "and I couldn't discharge him if I wanted—in fact, any suggestion of that kind on my part, would lead to his employment for life. Why?"

"Because," said Carron, "he impresses me as being rather young and flighty, and some day your uncle is going to die suddenly. He may last five years; he may snuff out to-morrow. It's his heart." His lips twisted pityingly. "He prefers to call it by some other name," he added, "and he would never send for me again if he knew I had told you, but you ought to know. He's a game old cock, isn't he?"

"Oh, very!" agreed Adrian. "Yes, game! Very, indeed!"

He walked slowly down the sunlit courtway on which the back door of the club opened, swinging his stick and meditating. Spring was approaching its zenith. In the warm May afternoon pigeons tumbled about near-by church spires which cut brown inlays into the soft blue sky. There was a feeling of open windows; a sense of unseen tulips and hyacinths; of people playing pianos. . . . Too bad, an old man dying that way, his hand furtively seeking his heart, when all this spring was about! Terror in possession of him, too! People like that hated to die; they couldn't see anything ahead. Well, Adrian reflected, the real tragedy of it hadn't been his fault. He had always been ready at the slightest signal to forget almost everything—yes, almost everything. Even that time when, as a sweating newspaper reporter, he had, one dusk, watched in the park his uncle and Mrs. Denby drive past in the cool seclusion of a shining victoria. Curious! In itself the incident was small, but it had stuck in his memory more than others far more serious, as concrete instances are likely to do. . . . No, he wasn't sorry; not a bit! He was glad, despite the hesitation he experienced in saying to himself the final word. He had done his best, and this would mean his own release and Cecil's. It would mean at last the blessed feeling that he could actually afford a holiday, and a little unthinking laughter, and, at thirty-nine, the dreams for which, at twenty-five, he had never had full time. He walked on down the courtway more briskly.

That Saturday night was the night he dined with his uncle. It had turned very warm; unusually warm for the time of year. When he had dressed and had sought out Cecil to say good-by to her he found her by the big studio window on the top floor of the apartment where they lived. She was sitting in the window-seat, her chin cupped in her hand, looking out over the city, in the dark pool of which lights were beginning to open like yellow water-lilies. Her white arm gleamed in the gathering dusk, and she was dressed in some diaphanous blue stuff that enhanced the bronze of her hair. Adrian took his place silently beside her and leaned out. The air was very soft and hot and embracing, and up here it was very quiet, as if one floated above the lower clouds of perpetual sound.

Cecil spoke at last. "It's lovely, isn't it?" she said. "I should have come to find you, but I couldn't. These first warm nights! You really understand why people live, after all, don't you? It's like a pulse coming back to a hand you love." She was silent a moment. "Kiss me," she said, finally. "I—I'm so glad I love you, and we're young."

He stooped down and put his arms about her. He could feel her tremble. How fragrant she was, and queer, and mysterious, even if he had lived with her now for almost fifteen years! He was infinitely glad at the moment for his entire life. He kissed her again, kissed her eyes, and she went down the stairs with him to the hall-door. She was to stop for him at his uncle's after a dinner to which she was going.

Adrian lit a cigarette and walked instead of taking the elevator. It was appropriate to his mood that on the second floor some one with a golden Italian voice should be singing "Louise." He paused for a moment. He was reminded of a night long ago in Verona, when there had been an open window and moonlight in the street. Then he looked at his watch. He was late; he would have to hurry. It amused him that at his age he should still fear the silent rebuke with which his uncle punished unpunctuality.

He arrived at his destination as a near-by church clock struck the half-hour. The new butler admitted him and led him back to where his uncle was sitting by an open window; the curtains stirred in the languid breeze, the suave room was a little penetrated by the night, as if some sly, disorderly spirit was investigating uninvited. It was far too hot for the wood fire—that part of the formula had been omitted, but otherwise each detail was the same. "The two hundredth time!" Adrian thought to himself. "The two hundredth time, at least! It will go on forever!" And then the formula was altered again, for his uncle got to his feet, laying aside the evening paper with his usual precise care. "My dear fellow," he began, "so good of you! On the minute, too! I—" and then he stumbled and put out his hand. "My glasses!" he said.

Adrian caught him and held him upright. He swayed a little. "I— Lately I have had to use them sometimes, even when not reading," he murmured. "Thank you! Thank you!"

Adrian went back to the chair where his uncle had been sitting. He found the glasses—gold pince-nez—but they were broken neatly in the middle, lying on the floor, as if they had dropped from someone's hand. He looked at them for a moment, puzzled, before he gave them back to his uncle.

Each in His Generation

"Here they are, sir," he said. "But—it's very curious. They're broken in such an odd way."

His uncle peered down at them. He hesitated and cleared his throat. "Yes," he began; then he stood up straight, with an unexpected twist of his shoulders. "I was turning them between my fingers," he said, "just before you came in. I had no idea—no, no idea! Shall we go in? I think dinner has been announced."

There was the sherry in the little, deeply cut glasses, and the clear soup, with a dash of lemon in it, and the fish, and afterward the roast chicken, with vegetables discreetly limited and designed not to detract from the main dish; and there was a pint of champagne for Adrian and a mild white wine for his uncle. The latter twisted his mouth in a dry smile. "One finds it difficult to get old," he said. "I have always been very fond of champagne. More aesthetically I think than the actual taste. It seems to sum up so well the evening mood—dinner and laughter and forgetting the day. But now—" he flicked contemptuously the stem of his glass—"I am only allowed this uninspired stuff." He stopped suddenly and his face twisted into the slight grimace which Adrian in the last few weeks had been permitted occasionally to see. His hand began to wander vaguely over the white expanse of his shirt.

Adrian pushed back his chair. "Let me—!" he began, but his uncle waved a deprecating hand. "Sit down!" he managed to say. "Please!" Adrian sank back again. The colour returned to his uncle's cheeks and the staring question left his eyes. He took a sip of wine.

"I cannot tell you," he observed with elaborate indifference, "how humiliating this thing is becoming to me. I have always had a theory that invalids and people when they begin to get old and infirm, should be put away some place where they can undergo the unpleasant struggle alone. It's purely selfish—there's something about the sanctity of the individual. Dogs have it right—you know the way they creep off? But I suppose I won't. Pride fails when the body weakens, doesn't it, no matter what the will may be?" He lifted his wine-glass. "I am afraid I am giving you a very dull evening, my dear fellow," he apologized. "Forgive me! We will talk of more pleasant things. I drink wine with you! How is Cecil? Doing well with her painting?"

Adrian attempted to relax his own inner grimness. He responded to his uncle's toast. But he wished this old man, so very near the mysterious crisis of his affairs, would begin to forego to some extent the habit of a lifetime, become a little more human. This ridiculous "façade"! The dinner progressed.

Through an open window the night, full of soft, distant sound, made itself felt once more. The candles, under their red shades, flickered at intervals. The noiseless butler came and went. How old his uncle was getting to look, Adrian reflected. There was a grayness about his cheeks; fine, wire-like lines about his mouth. And he was falling into that sure sign of age, a vacant absent-mindedness. Half the time he was not listening to what he, Adrian, was saying; instead, his eyes sought constantly the shadows over the carved sideboard across the table from him. What did he see there? What question was he asking? Adrian wondered. Only once was his uncle very much interested, and that was when Adrian had spoken of the war and the psychology left in its train. Adrian himself had not long before been released from a weary round of training-camps, where, in Texas dust, or the unpleasant resinous summer of the South, he had gone through a repetition that in the end had threatened to render him an imbecile. He was not illusioned. As separate personalities, men had lost much of their glamour for him; there had been too much sweat, too much crowding, too much invasion of dignity, of everything for which the world claimed it had been struggling and praying. But alongside of this revolt on his part had grown up an immense pity and belief in humanity as a mass—struggling, worm-like, aspiring, idiotic, heroic. The thought of it made him uncomfortable and at the same time elate.

His uncle shook a dissenting head. On this subject he permitted himself mild discussion, but his voice was still that of an old, wearied man, annoyed and bewildered. "Oh, no!" he said. "That's the very feature of it that seems to me most dreadful; the vermicular aspect; the massed uprising; the massed death. About professional armies there was something decent—about professional killing. It was cold-blooded and keen, anyway. But this modern war, and this modern craze for self-revelation! Naked! Why, these books—the young men kept their fingers on the pulses of their reactions. It isn't clean; it makes the individual cheap. War is a dreadful thing; it should be as hidden as murder." He sat back, smiled. "We seem to have a persistent tendency to become serious to-night," he remarked.

Serious! Adrian saw a vision of the drill-grounds, and

smiled sardonically; then he raised his head in surprise, for the new butler had broken all the rules of the household and was summoning his uncle to the telephone in the midst of dessert. He awaited the expected rebuke, but it did not come. Instead, his uncle paused in the middle of a sentence, stared, and looked up. "Ah, yes!" he said, and arose from his chair. "Forgive me, Adrian, I will be back shortly." He walked with a new, just noticeable, infirmness toward the door. Once there he seemed to think an apology necessary, for he turned and spoke with absent-minded courtesy.

"You may not have heard," he said, "but Mrs. Denby is seriously ill. Her nurse gives me constant bulletins over the telephone."

Adrian started to his feet, then sat down again. "But—" he stuttered—"but—is it as bad as all that?"

"I am afraid," said his uncle gently, "it could not be worse." The curtain fell behind him.

Adrian picked up his fork and began to stir gently the melting ice on the plate before him, but his eyes were fixed on the wall opposite, where, across the shining table, from a mellow gold frame, a portrait of his grandfather smiled with a benignity, utterly belying his traditional character, into the shadows above the candles. But Adrian was not thinking of his grandfather just then, he was thinking of his uncle—and Mrs. Denby. What in the world—! Dangerously ill, and yet here had been his uncle able to go through with—not entirely calmly, to be sure; Adrian remembered the lack of attention, the broken eye-glasses; and yet, still able to go through with, not obviously shaken, this monthly farce; this dinner that in reality mocked all the real meaning of blood-relationship. Good Lord! To Adrian's modern mind, impatient and courageous, the situation was preposterous, grotesque. He himself would have broken through to the woman he loved, were she seriously ill, if all the city was cordoned to keep him back. What could it mean? Entire selfishness on his uncle's part? Surely not that! That was too inhuman! Adrian was willing to grant his uncle exceptional expertness in the art of self-protection, but there was a limit even to self-protection. There must be some other reason. Discretion? More likely, and yet how absurd! Had Mr. Denby been alive, a meticulous, a fantastic delicacy might have intervened, but Mr. Denby was dead. Who were there to wound, or who left for the telling of tales? A doctor and the servants. This was not altogether reasonable, despite what he knew of his uncle. Here was some oddity of psychology he could not follow. He heard the curtains stir as his uncle reentered. He looked up, attentive and curious, but his uncle's face was the mask to which he was accustomed.

"How is Mrs. Denby?" he asked.

Mr. McCain hesitated for the fraction of a second. "I am afraid, very ill," he said. "Very ill, indeed! It is pneumonia. I—the doctor thinks it is only a question of a little time, but—well, I shall continue to hope for the best." There was a metallic harshness to his concluding words. "Shall we go into the library?" he continued. "I think the coffee will be pleasanter there."

They talked again of the war; of revolution; of the dark forces at large in the world.

Though that hour or two Adrian had a nakedness of perception unusual even to his sensitive mind. It seemed to him three spirits were abroad in the quiet, softly-lit, book-lined room; three intentions that crept up to him like the waves of the sea, receded, crept back again; or were they currents of air? or hesitant, unheard feet that advanced and withdrew? In at the open windows poured at times the warm, enveloping scent of the spring; pervading, easily overlooked, lawless, persistent, inevitable. Adrian found himself thinking it was like the presence of a woman. And then, overlapping this, would come the careful, dry, sardonic tones of his uncle's voice, as if insisting that the world was an ordinary world, and that nothing, not even love or death, could lay disrespectful fingers upon or hurry for a moment the trained haughtiness of the will. Yet even this compelling arrogance was at times overtaken, submerged, by a third presence, stronger even than the other two; a presence that entered upon the heels of the night; the ceaseless murmur of the streets; the purring of rubber tires upon asphalt; a girl's laugh, high, careless, reckless. Life went on. Never for a moment did it stop.

"I am not sorry that I am getting old," said Mr. McCain. "I think nowadays is an excellent time to die. Perhaps for the very young, the strong—but for me, things are too busy, too hurried. I have always liked my life like potpourri. I liked to keep it in a china jar and occasionally take off the lid. Otherwise one's sense of perfume becomes satiated. Take your young girls; they remain faithful to a love that is not worth being faithful to—all noise, and flushed laughter, and open doors." Quite unexpectedly he began to talk in a way he had

Each in His Generation

never talked before. He held his cigar in his hand until the ash turned cold; his fingers trembled just a little.

"You have been very good to me," he said. Adrian raised startled eyes. "Very good. I am quite aware that you dislike me"—he hesitated and the ghost of a smile hovered about his lips—"and I have always disliked you. Please!" He raised a silencing hand. "You don't mind my saying so? No. Very well, then, there is something I want to tell you. Afterward I will never mention it again. I dare say our mutual dislike is due to the inevitable misunderstanding that exists between the generations. But it is not important. The point is that we have always been well-bred toward each other. Yes, that is the point. You have always been a gentleman, very considerate, very courteous, I cannot but admire you. And I think you will find I have done the best I could. I am not a rich man, as such things go nowadays, but I will hand you on the money that will be yours quite unimpaired, possibly added to. I feel very strongly on that subject. I am old-fashioned enough to consider the family the most important thing in life. After all, we are the only two McCains left." He hesitated again, and twisted for a moment his bloodless hands in his lap, then he raised his eyes and spoke with a curious hurried embarrassment. "I have sacrificed a great deal for that," he said. "Yes, a great deal."

The soft-footed butler stood at his elbow, like an actor in comedy suddenly cast for the role of a portentous messenger.

"Miss Niles is calling you again, sir," he said.

"Oh, yes!—ah—Adrian, I am very sorry, my dear fellow. I will finish the conversation when I come back."

This time the telephone was within earshot; in the hall outside. Adrian heard his uncle's slow steps end in the creaking of a chair as he sat down; then picking up the receiver. The message was a long one, for his uncle did not speak for fully a minute; finally his voice drifted in through the curtained doorway.

"You think . . . only a few minutes?

". . . Ah, yes! Conscious? Yes. Well, will you tell her, Miss Niles?—yes, please listen very carefully—tell her this. That I am not there because I dared not come. Yes; on her account. She will understand. My heart—it's my heart. She will understand. I did not dare. For her sake, not mine. Tell her that. She will understand. Please be very careful in repeating the message, Miss Niles. Tell her I dared not come because of my heart. . . . Yes; thank you. That's it. . . . What? Yes, I will wait, Miss Niles."

Adrian, sitting in the library, suddenly got to his feet and crossed to the empty fireplace and stood with his back to it, enlightenment and a puzzled frown struggling for possession of his face. His uncle's heart! Ah, he understood, then! It was discretion, after all, but not the kind he thought—a much more forgiveable discretion. And, yet, what possible difference could it make should his uncle die suddenly in Mrs. Denby's house? Fall dead across her bed, or die kneeling beside it? Poor, twisted old fool, afraid even at the end that death might catch him out; afraid of a final undignified gesture.

A motor blew its horn for the street crossing. Another girl laughed; a young, thin, excited girl, to judge by her laughter. The curtains stirred and again there was that underlying scent of tulips and hyacinths; and then, from the hall outside, came the muffled thud of a receiver falling to the floor. Adrian waited. The receiver was not picked up. He strode to the door. Crumpled up over the telephone was old Mr. McCain.

Cecil came later. She was very quick and helpful, and jealously solicitous on Adrian's account, but in the taxicab going home she said the one thing Adrian had hoped she wouldn't say, and yet was sure she would. She belonged to a sex which, if it is honest at all, is never reticently so. She believed that between the man she loved and herself there were no possible mental withdrawals. "It is very tragic," she said, "but much better—you know it is better. He belonged to the cumberers of the earth. Yes, so much better; and this way, too!"

In the darkness her hand sought his. Adrian took it, but in his heart was the same choked feeling, the same knowledge that something was gone that could not be found again, that, as a little boy, he had had when they sold, at his father's death, the country place where he had spent his summers. Often he had lain awake at night, restless with the memory of heliotrope, and phlox, and mignonette, and afternoons quiet except for the sound of bees.

The Cracked Teapot

by Charles Caldwell Dobie

For the twentieth time, Finderson, with an inconceivably swift glide past the kitchen window, convinced himself that the woman's husband had not yet left the kitchen. What ailed the man? A farmer dawdling about his hearthstone during the plowing season was a new experience. . . . Should he go on to the next farmhouse or wait a little longer? For his purpose one place was as good as another, and it was absurd to shiver outside in the biting northwest gale when all he needed was a warm kitchen cleared of men folk. Yet, a curious stubbornness of purpose held him to his original intention—he fell back again behind the futile shelter of the beehives.

There was something malicious in the unexpectedness of the wind which exasperated Finderson: it seemed absurd for an inland valley, blossom-starred to a point of softness, to be raked by such a sharp-toothed gale. He had thought to find the tempest that had followed him from San Francisco routed by the hills, but, instead, the pools of tranquillity beyond seemed determined to draw in deep gusts from the sea. In his home country, March had always been a thing of brittle humor, harsh, but, on the whole, forthright; here in California, he told himself, nature could smile and stab in one breath.

After all, any countryside was for midsummer achievement. The most squalid city byway held infinitely more cheer and comfort at the other seasons. A slow dribble of well chosen curses escaped him: What had possessed him to flee the vicious delights of the town in such sudden panic? He had faced police clean-ups before, in fact so often that his reform technic was perfect. Any crook with human intelligence could rise above the most gigantic reform wave in existence; it was usually the rank beginners who fell victims to these noisy gestures toward civic purity. Could it be that he was growing old and jumpy? . . . Old! And he not out of his thirties! Yet the suggestion gave him a fleeting sense of weariness and he fell back in the tall grass, his half-closed lids upturned to the intense and biting sunlight.

A sickening nostalgia swept him. He wanted to feel the paved streets of the town beneath his discreet tread. What a place of supreme delight the city was, after all! Crowds, crowds, everywhere! Crowds intent on forthright wickedness or covert indiscretions; crowds ripe for dishonor or betrayal; crowds furtive and fawning, crowds bold to a point of insecurity! Crowds of suckers, crowds of fools, crowds of innocents! Crowds wary and wise and self-sufficient!

Back in the city, at this moment, he would have been standing apart, screened by a thicket of pretenses, watching humanity skim heedlessly by, waiting patiently to take aim and bring low a plump victim; sitting, to be precise, as was his early morning custom in one of the devil's playgrounds—a public square. If his pockets, under such a circumstance, were quite empty, it added zest to the game. There was a sporting quality in the speculation as to who among the throng would provide him with his next meal and whether he would break his fast at noon or evening. And the uncertainty of the means accomplishing his end added *its* note: Would he win by persuasion, blackmail, or force? . . . Ah, yes, the town had its flavor! . . . At a farmhouse, one kicked one's heels together until the men were afield—beyond that, there were no intriguing uncertainties. If food were your object, you asked boldly; if you found plunder within reach, you threatened or grasped it without ado. In short, it was a tepid performance made tolerable by balmy weather; without this compensation, it became dull to a point of exasperation.

He peered up between a lattice, shaped by his fingers, at the interlocking boughs of a prune orchard in the final stages of its clean-white blossoming. Immediately above him thin lines of harried bees battled with the gale to achieve security for their hoard. Silly fools, piling up treasure for others! . . . Well, that was life—industry and plunder in a continuous ironic succession. He laughed slyly, with the satisfaction of a man who unexpectedly finds his philosophy reinforced and justified.

The wind, in spite of its bite, began to lull his senses, and, in a shivering drowse, he felt a sudden atmospheric vehemence fill the air with flecks of white. A blizzard! Could it be possible? . . . In answer, a shower of prune petals brushed his cheek and he opened his eyes wide to see the ground become frosted with conquered blossoms instead of snow crystals. For a moment he felt disappointed. Just how long had it been since he had seen snow fall? . . . Oh, yes, he remembered—that day in Minnesota when he had stumbled through a white hurricane to the first farmhouse. He could see the woman now, opening the door, blond and cool to look at . . . pale eyes and skin and hair. He had been younger, then. *Cool to look at!* But her looks hadn't fooled him! . . . He'd almost forgotten her. Well, after all, the countryside occasionally did have promise in an off season. Especially when a man was young!

The clipped barking of a dog roused him. He sat up. The bark of the dog receded. Finderson came to his feet. The figure of a man was melting into a swift distance.

At last the woman was alone!

She was younger than he had fancied—ripely young, not blond and cool like the woman in Minnesota, but dark and flashing. Her glance winged toward him boldly and fell suddenly in a flutter of instinctive fear. He liked this contradiction of manner: it fed his vanity, for one thing, and it carried a hint of pliability. She made a closing movement with the door, but he had taken care to thrust his foot against the jamb. He knew the tricks of the trade: with a woman one had only to achieve a hearing and the rest was easy. Besides, his appearance was disarming. Tatters and battered foot-gear and an unkempt beard might have served the passing generation of panhandlers, but Finderson was a modern, he believed in the psychology of clothes and safety razors.

She let him in, of course, but her eyes continued their alternate flashes of audacity and fear. In the end, boldness triumphed and she fastened a questioning gaze upon him. Aware of her scrutiny, he contrived an air of amazing ingenuousness. She brought coffee first and a plate of biscuit, lingering for a moment, as if to say:

"Well, why don't you tell me about yourself?"

But he was too clever; he knew the value of piqued curiosity. Instead, he began to talk about the weather. She agreed that it was cold for March.

"Cold!" he echoed. "Why, a minute ago I thought it was snowing—with the wind and the air full of prune-petals. I tell you it was a pretty sight! I thought I was a kid again . . . I made believe I was lost in a blizzard!"

The interrogative manner left her. At the first shot he had struck the bull's-eye with this kid stuff! . . . And then the blossom talk—that always fetched a woman! Suddenly he was quickened out of his depression. This was the life!—angling for victims, watching them nibble discreetly at the bait thrown out, taking care to hide in the shadows so as not to frighten them. He'd tell the world that the preliminaries were interesting!

She turned her back on him for the first time since he had entered, and he heard the click of eggs broken into a pan. She was talking, too. She'd never seen snow fall. She often wondered what it was like. He must have come from the East—or the mountains.

He laughed. If she called Kansas east! . . . *Kansas!* She seemed disappointed. . . . That was years ago he reassured her—since then he had been all over. . . . *Everywhere?* . . . Yes—everywhere worth mentioning.

She brought him the eggs swimming in pungent bacon fat and she sat down opposite him with her hands clasped upon the table, her lips parted. He knew these countryside women, hungry for news. He narrowed his eyes upon her. She drew away with a little flutter of the eyelids and he turned his attention discreetly to his plate.

"Yes," he repeated. "I've been everywhere—seen everything!"

She released a sharp breath. "Some folks get it all!" she said.

Pretty and unhappy! flashed through Finderson's mind. The prospect grew better and better. It might be worth his while to stick around for a few days. Of course, a lot depended on the husband. . . . He began to wonder whether man and wife had a joint bank account: that always made things easier. But it really didn't matter. The affair in Minnesota had gone through without that. But there the husband had been a dumbbell—a poor creature.

"I don't suppose your husband needs any help," he broke out suddenly.

"You mean you want a job? . . . *You!*"

He mistook her incredulity for scorn. "Well, and why not?" he flashed back, tightening up his biceps. "Here, feel that arm! Pretty fit, eh?"

She put a hand, half timid, half bold, upon the prideful swell of flesh, and her touch sent a tremor through him. He snapped his teeth together. He didn't like anything to unsteady him before he laid his wires. In his profession skirts should always remain incidental—a means to an end.

"You're fit enough," she agreed. "It wasn't that. But I don't believe you ever worked—not really."

"How do you think I get by?"

"Oh, I dunno. I guess you just kinda talk things out of folks. . . . You're the first strange man I ever fed in the kitchen. Usually I hand it out to them. My husband doesn't like me to go even that far."

His mind closed nimbly over this fact. Was the husband discreet or merely jealous? . . . At any rate, the woman had broken her rule. He'd scored in the preliminaries, anyway. He concealed his satisfaction under a cloak of emphatic approval.

"He's right!" he agreed heartily. "You can't tell who you're taking in. Look at me, now. I might be a thief, for all you know. Or—or worse!"

"Well, you wouldn't get much here!" she flung back with a laugh.

He glanced about. "No? . . . Why, I'd say you looked pretty prosperous, if you asked me."

"Maybe that's the reason. You see, Jim ain't one of the careless kind."

She baffled him, somewhat. He couldn't tell whether she was simple or extraordinarily shrewd. A little of both, perhaps, he decided. . . . Well, the woman in Minnesota was a good deal that way. She had wit enough to fool her husband, at any rate. . . .

"You mean he doesn't leave money lying around loose?" he shot out directly. "Well, some thieves ain't particular—they'd lift anything that ain't tied down. . . . I knew a bad man in Minnesota once who stole a farmer's wife!" He chuckled at the memory, regarding her through narrowed lids.

She stood opposite him with a gesture of curious defiance. "Stole her! I'd like to see any man steal me, against my will!"

He roared mirthfully. "You don't mean you think he just picked her up and carried her away, do you? That wasn't his game. He kidded her and she fell for him. The husband bought him off—to get rid of him."

"Oh!" she said, midway between relief and scorn, "I thought you were talking about a case like this—a strange man coming to a farmhouse for food."

He looked at her with clear triumph. "I am—it began that way."

She flushed deeply. He felt a sense of power, as if he could make her dance to any tune he cared to pipe. . . . She turned from him, and, in a voice that seemed to betray a realization of unplumbed degradations, she answered coldly: "That wouldn't be Jim's way. He'd plug the man who did him up full of holes."

Her words were puzzling. You didn't know whether she were warning or daring you. Some women were like that, Finderson thought again, mentally repeating the phrase. He felt vaguely that she was already defending herself against him. He liked the idea—it made him feel powerful. But the picture she was drawing of Jim, with her lightning strokes, was disturbing. Finderson was sure that, if he wished to stay on, it could be arranged. Help was always scarce at this time of year in the country. But that meant work. It wasn't often that he found a prospect worth even a pretense at industry. Yet something challenged him. It was as if she had said:

"My husband is a man, anyway. You couldn't get the best of him! . . . Besides, deep down, you're a coward!"

Yes, that was it: pride and scorn and a challenge all mixed in one. She was like a slack tide, full of uncertainties. She might turn in any direction. He began rapidly to sketch the possibilities. Would the game be worth the candle? Instinctively, under the urge of this inward question, his eyes swept the kitchen in furtive appraisal. His glance trailed past the enormous range to the pots and kettles hanging in a straight line just under the north window, and, presently, it halted, briefly, significantly, as it fell upon the cupboard. He tore a thick slice of bread from the loaf at his elbow as he said levelly:

"My mother had a teapot like that once."

The woman turned. "Which teapot?" she asked.

"The cracked one—on the top shelf."

The start she gave was almost imperceptible, yet it sufficed. All that there remained to discover, now, was the extent of the hoard which the cracked teapot concealed. He found his vague speculations of the previous moment shattered by their sudden contact with a concrete fact. The prospect of immediate loot always sharpened Finderson's desire for tangibilities: he was not a man to let a bird in the hand go flying.

The woman turned away without another word. If he had wanted a confirmation of the teapot's office, she could not have given him a better answer. But her assumption that he

The Cracked Teapot

would be dull enough to be deceived by silence piqued him and he observed in a louder tone:

"Well, perhaps my mother's wasn't just like that one. But it was cracked, anyway. . . . Every woman seems to have a cracked teapot somewhere about. . . . I always wonder what they use them for."

She faced him again. "What did your mother use hers for?"

He stared for a moment in silent surprise. He hadn't expected her to counter in this fashion. What was he waiting for, anyway? He narrowed his eyes, swiftly measuring the distance from cupboard to sink, at the same time calculating how many feet lay between table, cupboard and doorway. . . . Would it be possible to accomplish the business without violence? Ordinarily, he would have hoped so, especially as the woman had fed him. But, somewhere, quite suddenly she irritated him—she, with her questions! . . . He'd like to show her a thing or two! She wouldn't be so calm and insolent when he got through with her!

"You haven't answered me yet," the woman was saying.

Her insistence rather won him: besides, it would be diverting to give her a little more line before he pulled up. "What did my mother use *her* cracked teapot for?" he echoed. His reply hung unsteadily in the balance, but, finally, he broke into a chuckling little laugh as he said: "Why, she hid money in it, of course—hid it from my father."

"I thought so!" escaped her.

He felt an impulse to fly to the defense of his sex. "Oh, my father didn't abuse her—he didn't drink or anything like that. And he was a good provider. It was a kind of game with her, I guess. She just liked to slip it over. You see, she made a sly dollar here and there, selling eggs to the grocer or a chicken now and then to the neighbors. I used to think she got more kick out of spending *that* money than all the rest put together."

"Naturally," the woman assented dryly.

Her composure roused him afresh. Should he seize the cracked teapot without further ado, or stay awhile and worry her? . . . In the end he chose to stay and, at once he broke out brutally:

"I stole my first money from that teapot. When I found my mother didn't miss it, I tried again. In the end, I cleaned her out of every penny and bolted." He gave a hard laugh. "There's no training school for crooks like the home!"

She made an instinctive movement toward the cupboard. With calm insolence he began to take off his coat. The wind outside was still shrieking and there was no necessity for immediate departure—the cracked teapot would be in its place an hour from now—next week, for that matter. Besides, he hadn't yet decided on a course of action. There were such infinite possibilities in sharing a woman's secret—the secret she kept from her husband. He sat down again, drawing his chair toward the stove.

"Suppose you bring me that cracked teapot," he drawled. "Come, now, don't be stubborn. I'd like to have a look inside."

She was shaking with mingled fear and rage, but she did as she was bidden. Finderson went back to the table again.

He lifted the lid, sprawling forward with his elbows on the table. She stood apart, her breast rising and falling in a sort of rhythmic protest. He overturned the teapot with a brutal movement. There was more in it than he had fancied.

"Well, well!" he chuckled. "You'd have a harder job explaining this to Jim than I thought. . . . Do you know, I believe I'll stay. . . . I think a few weeks of the simple life would just set me up right."

He could see that she was frightened—that she'd rather die, almost, than explain that cracked teapot to Jim, yet she kept up a deceitful bravado. He had seen his mother like that once, trembling upon the verge of betrayal. He remembered it as if it were yesterday. He had come in from some prolonged truancy to find her ready and waiting for him, switch in hand. The cracked teapot lay on the table and at one side a piece of silver glistened. "I'll learn yer to keep out of sight like this for half a day!" his mother had shouted at him. "Didn't I tell yer when yer went out this morning that Hattie Beals wanted eggs? I had to put on my things and run every step of the way there and back myself!"

She was quite beside herself with rage and she brought the whip across his legs with a vehemence he had never imputed to her. He backed into a corner and she followed close upon him, making the air hum with wasted lashes. In a last desperate remonstrance he had shouted at her, without the slightest hope of victory:

"If you touch me again I'll tell Father! I'll tell Father about that cracked teapot!"

From that moment he had her in his power. She hid the teapot, of course, hoping to blot from his mind the memory of her weakness, but the fact lay between them like an unsheathed sword. In an eye's twinkling he had become a successful blackmailer. He never had to mention the teapot again. But he grew to realize that every concession he wrung from her was traceable to a single source. By the end of the week he had discovered the cracked teapot's new hiding place, and before a month had gone by he had added thievery to his accomplishments. *A good training school for crooks?* ... He'd tell the world it was. He didn't blame his mother—he didn't blame the woman before him. Their husbands? ... No, he didn't blame them, either. But he'd like to see them slip over moral talk where he was concerned.

He heard the woman moving about in a nonchalant attempt to appear engrossed in her household duties. He had to admire her pluck—most women would have whimpered. She'd be harder to manage than the woman in Minnesota. But that only gave the game zest. As to her husband's readiness with a gun—well, he'd heard the wind blow before. Besides, there was a technic even in disillusioning husbands: it was lightning flashes of truth that induced violence—the reality standing out suddenly against a dark background of deceits. It was different if one raised the light slowly as one turned up the wick of a lamp, letting the eye become gradually accustomed to the situation. Even the futile husband of that woman in Minnesota might have been nasty if he had been abruptly surprised. Finderson knew how to get on with men—how first to disarm and then despoil them. In many ways they were easier than the women.

He noticed that the woman was listening: the faint, faraway bark of a dog floated across the fields. She came and stood opposite him.

"That," she said, pointing in the direction of the sound, "is my husband coming back again."

The smile he threw at her had a wolfish quality. "He'll be surprised to see me, won't he?"

"You mean—you mean you ain't afraid?"

"Are you?"

"I told you at the start he didn't like me to feed strangers."

"You can't be blamed if a man pushes his way into your kitchen, can you?"

"You're really not going to stay?"

"I was thinking of it.... Is Jim a hard boss?"

"Why, you don't suppose I'll let him hire you, do you?"

"How will you stop it?"

"I'll tell him you're a thief!"

He stood up. "Like you are!"

"It's my money!" she cried passionately.

"Why do you hide it—sneak it, then?"

A dark flush mounted to her forehead. "Do you expect a woman to *ask* for every nickel?"

"No—there ain't much difference between a beggar and a thief. . . . But you could fight for it!"

"Fight!" she sneered. "That's just it!"

He laughed. "You're too lazy, of course. . . . Well, that's the way I figure it."

She took a step toward him. "If men make thieves of women, why that's their lookout!"

He fell back before her advance like an archer taking perfect aim. "What about making thieves of children? . . . Where do you suppose I got my first ideas about easy money? . . . Wait until *your* kid watches you drop swag into a cracked teapot!"

She brought her apron up over her head with a quick movement that was half shame, half reticence. He went toward her, tearing the covering from her face. The look she gave him betrayed her secret. He felt a curious impotence—as if the shaft he had sent winging toward her had been turned back on him. He turned awkwardly away, slipping into his coat again. The sound of the barking dog came nearer. He wondered what he had better do.

A child! A boy . . . perhaps a girl. . . . Somehow, the wings of his imagination sped upward for a fluttering moment, lighting on a vague, intangible hope, an impersonal hope that he could not define. It had nothing to do with him and yet it was in every part of his being—a sort of vicarious impulse toward perfection. It was like smiling back at a babe. As wistful and irrational and full of faith as that—and almost as fleeting.

Instantly he felt ashamed of his weakness. Like a boy caught in an act of gentleness, he began to swagger again. He looked at the woman sharply. She had recovered from her confusion and her face had a new dignity as if she felt herself standing on firmer ground. But, he knew, even now, that her integrity still hung in the balance. This knowledge completely recaptured his old insolence. What did he care?

The money, lying on the table, meant nothing. There were other farmhouses with cracked teapots. But he would tramp many a mile without a chance to match the general prospect before him. The thrill of the woman's touch still shook him, but his pride discounted this circumstance. He admitted difficulties, but tough propositions always had challenged him—won him. In town, among his associates he had been noted for his ability to put over the impossible. He liked to get his teeth into the hide of intrenched respectability. He liked to pull people down to his level. . . . Already he hated this woman's husband—hated his complacency. He was a man who ordered his wife to keep the door closed against vagabondage, was he? . . . Well, one could see how she obeyed.

The barking of the dog came nearer and nearer. The woman was regarding him with a sort of anxious terror.

"Why don't you go?" she cried out suddenly. "Why don't you take the money and leave?"

"Money—I don't want your money!" he said with a sneer. "I want your husband to give me a job. . . . You act as if you were afraid to have me around."

She faced him desperately. "If you don't leave I'll lie about you!" she shrilled. "I'll tell my husband you insulted me."

"Try it," he returned coolly. "You know what he'll say. 'What did you let him in for?'"

"But he'll settle with you first."

"Perhaps, but I won't have to live with him after, and you will. . . . 'Now if you'd done what I told you,' that's what you will hear! morning, noon, and night!"

"How do you know so much about it?"

"Oh, I've lived with some married couples," he said, ironically.

"With—with that family in Minnesota, you were telling me about? . . . I knew you were that man!"

He answered with a venomous laugh. She turned suddenly white and sat down. A heavy step clattered along the low, rickety porch.

"That's Jim!" she said in a frightened whisper.

He threw back his head. "Call him in! I'm ready for him!"

She began to scream with diabolic vehemence—like a woman in the grip of nightmare. The door flew open: Finderson made a quick movement toward his hip pocket.

They stood glaring at each other, Jim's head thrust slightly forward, a pistol already in his hand. Every muscle of the two men was taut with instinctive hostility of males unsettled by a woman. Finderson had to admit that the man opposite him would prove an equal match, but he had worsted better men in his day. He was dealing with a man quick to settle an account but, once past the point of violence, one who would have the sense to think in terms of expediency. Finderson knew that he must direct his first move toward the drawn pistol. He was clever enough to keep his hand suggestively where it had flown at the first hint of danger—on his hip pocket, but he decided against anything beyond a hint of readiness. How could he get the woman's husband to put up his gun? . . . Quite suddenly it flashed upon Finderson that the unborn child was his strongest ally; upon the child hung the whole adventure; the child that would one day be watching its mother drop marital plunder into a cracked teapot. He spoke calmly, yet with the cautious lightness of a skater aware of the thinness of the ice. "This kind of a scene ain't the best thing in the world for the little lady, is it?' " he drawled significantly.

Jim stared, looked at his wife, put up his pistol. Finderson had won the first victory.

The interrogative silence fell again; Finderson was determined that this time the woman should break it. Already, with his usual facility, he was framing replies to any charges she might make. The more desperate her claims the more convinced he would be that he had her in his power. Her weakness would be in proportion to the extent of her lies. He knew enough about innocence to know that it came pretty near being invincible. You couldn't confuse a man who hadn't trespassed. And she knew, as well as he did, that she couldn't bring a single charge against him. Beyond suggesting that she fetch him the cracked teapot, he hadn't even given her an arrogant order. The cracked teapot! It lay upturned upon the table with its loot circling it. He wondered just what she *would* say about that. If she would only lie! . . . If she would only lie, both she and her husband were as good as delivered into his hands. He wouldn't even have to prove himself—the candor and fearlessness of his replies would save him, would win the husband over. The man couldn't help but see he was telling the truth. Yes, it would be as simple as that. He had been accused too many times of misdeeds—falsely or otherwise, not to know the confidence with which one faced empty charges.

The woman would lie and Finderson would reply calmly, truthfully, to every accusation. The husband would question her then, his voice tinged with baffled suspicion. At this she would protest too much, become hysterical. Then Finderson would step in:

"It doesn't matter. . . . I understand. . . . It's her condition. . . . I'm the oldest of ten—I know all about such things."

She'd never stand up under that. Jim would be embarrassed, ashamed, grateful. She'd fling herself out of the room, weeping. Then over a pipe the men would talk self-consciously of far-removed topics. He'd stay on, of course—that was inevitable, for a week, a month—until he'd accomplished his twofold purpose. . . . Before he had finished with them both, Jim would be glad to come through handsomely. Jim wouldn't flash a gun again. That moment had passed.

The woman had risen, in a moment she would be speaking. Finderson's lip curled with satisfaction. The lies were to begin.

"I dunno what's the matter with me," she began. "I just had a sort of sinking feeling. . . . I was that scared!" Finderson blinked in confusion. "This man—he wants a job! . . . I told him to wait."

That was the woman for you! You never could tell about a woman. A moment before she had been screaming out at him, asking him to go! Now, she was calmly giving in to him. Did she want him to stay or was she trying to confuse him?

Finderson could have predicted the husband's course down to a hair's breadth. But this woman! Damn her, you'd never be sure of her!

Jim was talking to him—asking him where he'd come from. Did he really want a job?

Well, he could play her game: he could confuse her with the unexpected. Besides, in the long run, a little urging from Jim would strengthen his position. . . . No, he didn't want a job. He just had been longing for a warm hour by the fire. He'd be moving on right away.

A nasty frown was curdling Jim's forehead and his questioning glance traveled between his wife and Finderson with unpleasant directness. Finally his eyes fell upon the silver coins encircling the cracked teapot. The woman saw it. What would she say, now? How would she explain the presence of the money to her husband?

"You don't want to forget your money!" She was talking to *him*, Finderson.

Finderson gasped. Imagine her having the wit to get around it like that. God, she was clever! . . . She'd have made a magnificent pal! For the second time she had disarmed him with an unlooked-for move.

"Forget my money?" he drawled. "Any old time! . . . That's all I've got between me and the sheriff." He turned to Jim. "I was just counting it up."

He scooped the coins loosely into his coat pocket. Jim's face cleared and Finderson knew that the implication of resources had raised him immeasurably in the other's eyes.

"That's a fool way to carry money," Jim commented. "Don't you realize how many crooks there are in the world?"

Finderson looked directly at the woman. "You're right!" he laughed. "There's a new one born every minute!"

She flushed.

Finderson made a pretense of moving toward the door. The woman's husband took the pipe out of his mouth. "I'd like it fine, if you'd stay!" he exclaimed with some warmth. "It ain't often I run into a likely man. . . . I want to apologize for that pistol stuff. Of course, soon as I really seen yer I realized you was all right. . . . But, then, when a woman hollers, yer know. . . . And then the wife— Well, I guess yer know how things is with her."

He broke off in confusion and Finderson found the words that he had planned only a few moments ago rising to his lips:

"Yes, I understand. . . . I'm the oldest of ten. . . . I know about such things!"

"That's another reason I'd like yer to stay," Jim mumbled awkwardly. "I could pick up a lotta rotten trash—but well, at a time like this I wanta feel comfortable about the man who's here with me and the wife—you know!"

Finderson smiled inwardly. This woman's husband was too easy! Yes, easier than that man in Minnesota. He glanced at the woman; she had the look of a fluttering bird charmed by a reptile, at once terrified and expectant. A sense of his power over the two people standing before him almost brought a chuckle to his lips. He liked the sensation of Jim's importunities.

"Oh, I guess I'd better be on my way," he murmured, continuing his pretense of departure. "I ain't much of a hand to settle down."

His eyes fell again on the woman. She had caught up the cracked teapot and she was holding it almost fiercely at her breast.

"Couldn't yer stay on for a couple of weeks?" Jim was saying. "A week even?—it would help out lots."

The Cracked Teapot

Finderson cleared his throat to answer, and at that moment the cracked teapot fell in a shattered heap to the floor.

He stood motionless, the assent to Jim's final plea frozen. He didn't look at the woman—he didn't have to, she had spoken to him through the crashing sound of the smashed teapot. It was as if she had said:

"I've smashed it, do you understand, smashed it for good and all. Will you stay, now, and ruin everything? *I* don't matter and *you* don't matter and *Jim* don't matter, but *can't* you see—won't you see?"

Yes, he did. The woman was throwing her child to him—throwing the only thing that mattered out of danger. Would he catch it or let it fall? And, as before, the wings of his imagination sped upward in a fluttering moment of vague, intangible hope, that impersonal hope that was a sort of vicarious impulse toward perfection.

"Not for a couple of weeks—a week even?" the woman's husband was repeating.

This time he *did* look at her, searchingly. Her answer burned through her glance like a candle's flicker—a sputtering flame of courage that grew steadily in power.

Finderson shook his head. "No. . . . I've got to get back to town. . . . This here country stuff ain't in my line."

A Jazz-Age Clerk

by James T. Farrell

I

Jack Stratton worked from ten to eight answering telephone calls in the Wagon Department of the Continental Express Company. What he liked best about his job was his lunch hour from one to two. Ordinarily, clerks went to lunch at twelve o'clock, and he believed that people seeing him on the streets between one and two might figure that he was a lad with a pretty good job, because one o'clock was the time when many businessmen took their lunch in order to avoid the noonday jams in the Loop.

One sunny day in early spring Jack went out to lunch. He felt good. He would have felt even better if only his faded powder-blue suit were not so old, and if only it were already the next pay day, because then he hoped to be able to make a down payment and get a new suit on the installment plan. When he had got this powder-blue suit, he'd thought that it was the real thing. All the cake-eaters were wearing them. But it was a cheap suit that had faded quickly. And his brown hat, fixed square-shaped the way the cakes were wearing them, was old and greasy from the stacomb that he smeared on his hair every day. Yes, he would have been feeling much better if he were dogged out in a new outfit. Well, he would some day, he decided. He walked toward Van Buren Street.

It was a narrow, dusty street, with garages, a continental filling station and terminal, and the rear ends of old office buildings and restaurants. On the other side he spotted a girl, and told himself that she was so hot she could start a new Chicago fire all by herself. He snapped his fingers and watched her pass. Daddy! He burst into song:

Teasing eyes, teasing eyes,
You're the little girl that sets my heart afire...

Teasing! He expressed his feelings with a low whistle. He guessed that working in the Loop had its advantages. At least there were plenty of shebas to look at. He shifted his gait into a hopping two-step. Self-conscious, he checked himself. People might laugh at him in the street, just as Gas-House McGinty, Heinie Mueller, and some of the others in the office laughed at him. Some day he would like to show them, clean up on a few of the wise-aleck clerks. And he would, too! They were dumb, that was all, and they didn't know what was the real thing in the world today. They didn't have enough sense to be cake-eaters. And nicknaming him Jenny, like they had. Someday he would Jenny them! He began walking in a kind of waltzing dance step, his body quivering as he moved. Another song burst into his thoughts, Tiger Rose.

Sadness and self-pity drove the half-sung chorus out of his mind. He wanted girls, a girl, and he wanted money to spend on clothes so that he could impress the broads, and to spend on dances, dates, going places. But he was only making eighty-five dollars a month. That was more than he had expected when he started looking for a job, and he couldn't kick. He knew fellows who only made their fifteen a week. But his pay wasn't any too much. And since his old man was out of work, most of his jack had to go to his mother toward keeping up the home. Gee, he wished that the old man would find another job, and then he could have a little more to spend.

He saw an athletically built blonde, who was just bow-wows, the kind to look at and weep. He jerked his shoulders in rhythm and sang:

I'm runnin' wild, I'm runnin' wild,
I lost control . . .

Now, if there would only be some mama like that in the restaurant, and if he could only get next to her.

The restaurant where he usually ate was owned by a Greek, and was a small establishment with a tile floor and an imitation marble counter. He took a counter seat in the front, several stools removed from the nearest customer. Kitty, the slatternly peroxide-blonde waitress, greeted him with a yellow-toothed yawn, and at the same time she rubbed a fat hand over her low forehead. He looked up at her face; it was crusted with powder.

"Hello," he said.

A customer got up and went to the glass case to pay his

check. Kitty left Jack, collected, rang the cash register, deposited the silver in the drawer, and returned. The expression on her face was stupid, bored. Jack snapped his fingers, rolled his eyes, and sang a jazz song.

"What yuh want today, Dapper Dan?" she asked.

"Ham and coffee."

Swinging her head sidewise, she shouted the sandwich order to the chef. Other customers left and she collected. He was the only one remaining in the restaurant. Suddenly he was conscious of his shabbiness. He reached down to touch the raggedy cuffs of his bell-bottom trousers. He felt the thinness at the right elbow of his coat. Kitty slid a ham sandwich at him, and then she slopped a cup of coffee across the counter.

"Big times tonight!" he said while applying mustard to his sandwich.

"Huh?" she mumbled lifelessly.

"Dance at the South Hall out in Englewood where I live," he said, biting into his sandwich.

"Takin' yours along?" she asked lackadaisically.

"I told her to keep the home fires burning tonight. I like a little variety and change, sister."

His shoulders swung to the singing of a few lines from The Darktown Strutters' Ball.

"Cancha sing something that's new," Kitty said petulantly.

"I just learned this one this week at the Song Shop on Quincy Street. Listen!"

>   No, no, Nora, nobody but you, dear,
>   You know, Nora, yours truly is true, dear . . .

"Aha!" he interrupted with a leer.

>   And when you accuse me of flirting

"Like that?" he interpolated with a lascivious wink.

>   I wouldn't, I couldn't, I love you so,
>   I've had chances, too many to mention . . .

"Always get chances," he interposed.

>   Never give them a bit of attention.
>   No, no, Nora. No? No?

"Nice tune," Kitty said dopily as Jack bent down to drink coffee.

"Fast! And tonight I'm grabbing myself a keen number and stepping myself right up over those blue clouds into heaven."

"You're conceited."

He finished his sandwich. His coffee cup was half full. He looked at the cuts of pie in the dessert case before him. He dug his hand into his right trouser pocket. He swallowed his coffee in one gulp and slid off the stool. He paid Kitty fifteen cents, which she rang up.

"Toodle-oo!"

" 'Bye, sheik," she said patronizingly.

II

Overhead, the elevated trains thundered, drowning out the racket of street traffic. He stood on the sidewalk, hands in pockets, hat tilted, watching the crowd. He decided that today he'd sit in the lobby of a good hotel instead of going to the Song Shop and listening to the new tunes being sung. It would be restful.

If he only had on decent clothes, he could sit in a lobby and seem like a young fellow, maybe, with a rich old man or a good job that paid a big salary. A man in a hurry bumped into him and, hastening on, snottily suggested that he quit taking up the whole sidewalk. Jack looked after him, shrugged his shoulders, laughed. He bent his eyes on the moving legs of a girl ahead of him. He realized that if he got his shoes shined, he would improve his appearance. He hated to spend the dime, though, because when he got home tonight he could shine his own shoes. But his appearance would be improved, and he wouldn't look quite so poor. It was all in accordance with the principles of clever dressing. Always have on something new, outstanding or shiny, a loud tie, a clean shirt, a new hat, shined shoes, and then something else you were wearing that was shabby wouldn't be so noticed. He applied his principle by dropping into a shoe-shine parlor.

A young Negro energetically shined his shoes, and Jack day-dreamed about how he would stroll nonchalantly into the lobby of the Potter Hotel and find himself a chair that he could slump into, just so natural. He could spread his legs out so that the first thing anyone noticed about him would be his shined shoes. His thoughts leaped. Wouldn't it be luck if some ritzy queen fell for him! It would just be ... delicious. Daddy! His mood lifted.

Adventure-bound, hopeful and gay, he hustled toward the new Potter Hotel. His courage deserted him as he passed the uniformed doorman who stood with a set and frowning face, seeming to tell Jack that he wasn't wanted. He paused at the entrance to the enormous lobby, with its gold decorations, its hanging diamond-like chandeliers, its lavish display of comfortable furniture. He told himself in awe that it was like a palace. He noticed men and women, sitting, standing, moving around, talking, reading newspapers, and for a moment he felt as if he were in a moving picture world, the hero in a picture walking into this hotel lobby like a palace fit for the richest of kings or businessmen. He skirted several bellboys and found a chair in a corner, but it was not obscure, because there was a passageway all round the lobby and many people would pass him while he sat. A feeling of awe, as if he were in a church where talking was not permitted, filled his consciousness. He wished that he hadn't come here where he didn't belong, and at the same time he was glad that he'd come.

Several yards away from him he noticed a gray-haired man in a gray suit, whose pleasingly wrinkled face seemed calm, contented, mellowed. He tried to make himself seem as calm and as at ease as this man. For want of something to do, he ran the palm of his hand through his greasy hair; it was meticulously parted in the center. He sedulously drew out his dirty handkerchief to wipe the grease off his hand. To his right, he heard a well-dressed fellow discussing the stock market with a friend. A bellboy wended in and out, intoning:

"Call for Mr. Wagner ... Call for Mr. Wagner ... Call for Mr. Wagner ... Call for Mr. Wagner ... Mr. Wagner please..."

He was unable to chase out his confusion of feelings in this alien atmosphere of the well-dressed, the well-fed, the prosperous. He wished he could live a life that had as much glitter as there must be in the lives of these people. He thought how some day he wanted to be able to sit in a swanky hotel lobby like this one, well-dressed, and have a bell hop pass along calling out his name. He tried to visualize himself, a little older, a successful rich businessman in the lobby with the bellboy droning for him.

"Call for Mr. Stratton ... Call for Mr. John Stratton ... Call for Mr. John Stratton ... Mr. John Stratton..."

And it would be some millionaire on the wire waiting to close an important deal that would net him a handsome piece of change. He'd close the deal and come back to wait for a mama. Maybe she'd be some hot movie actress like Gloria Swanson who would be like the sweetheart of the world in her pictures. And he would be waiting for this movie actress more beautiful than even Gloria Swanson, thinking how when he had been nothing but a punk clerk at the express company he'd come to sit in the same lobby, wearing shabby clothes, dreaming of the day when things would happen to him.

He watched a tall and handsome young fellow stroll by. Must be collegiate! Must have had his gray suit made to order and have paid fifty, seventy-five bucks for it, maybe even more. The threads of his daydream suddenly snapped. All the confidence went out of him, so that he felt shaky, trembly. He wished again that he hadn't come here. He felt as if everyone in the lobby were looking at him, knowing he didn't belong and wanting to see him tossed out on his can. He looked unobtrusively at two snappily dressed young fellows on his left. They were out of earshot, but he wondered what they were saying. They probably had everything they wanted and did anything they cared to do, had automobiles, money on which to date up queens ... everything. The one wearing a Scotch tweed suit drew out a fat cigar, removed the band, smelled the cigar, bit off the end, lit it like a businessman in a movie. If only his life were that of a hero in the movies! Ah! That was class, the way that fellow in the tweeds had pulled out his cigar and lit it. Yes, when his own dream ship came in and he could afford to smoke four-bit cigars, he would have to remember to light them the way that fellow did.

"Call for Mr. O'Flaherty ... Call for Mr. Al O'Flaherty ... Call for Mr. Al O'Flaherty ... Call for Mr. Al O'Flaherty ..."

Wouldn't it be the dogs to be paged like that on important business calls! But he had no right even to think of such things. It wouldn't ever be for him. His lot in life deepened his wretchedness. He hadn't had anything to start on. Father and mother with no dough. One year in high school, and that without clothes, no athletic ability, no money, nothing that could get him into fraternities and make the girls go for him. But, gee, in high school there'd been all kinds of hot and classy girls! Only why should they have looked at an unimportant freshman like himself? And anyway, that was all over. Now he was working at a job with no future. Maybe he ought to be glad for what he had, but, gee, he couldn't help feeling that some guys got all the breaks, while he got almost none. All these people, they belonged to a world he would never enter.

A bellboy coming toward him. Gee! He sat stricken in a paralyzing fright. He pushed back the dirty cuffs of his shirt so that they were invisible. He tried to think up a reason he could give for being in the lobby when the bell hop came and questioned him. He'd say he was waiting for somebody who was staying at the hotel. But they could check up on the name. He'd say he was waiting for a friend coming in from New York who was going to stay here. The bellboy coming! He wanted to get up and leave. He had no will. He was so afraid that he began to sweat under the armpits, and his forehead perspired. Coming!

The bellboy passed by his chair as if no one were sitting in it, and bent down to speak with the calm-faced man. The man rose and followed the bellboy across the lobby. Jack again pulled out his soiled handkerchief, crushed it into a ball so that it couldn't be noticed, and wiped his forehead.

He watched a slim, voluptuous blonde woman cross the lobby. She was the dogs, the snake's hips, and the stars all rolled into something in a black dress. Those lips of hers. She had lip-appeal, sister, lip-appeal, sex-appeal, and she had it, and she was like a shower of stars. Looked like a woman some rich bird had put in the velvet. He followed her tantalizing, sensuous movements with thirsting eyes. She was a trifle taller than he, he guessed . . . but . . . hot . . . She sat down beside a middleaged man in a conservative blue suit, crossed her legs. . . . Legs! Wouldn't he like to have the bucks to buy the most expensive stockings money could buy for those legs! She lit a cigarette and he bet himself that it was an expensive Turkish cigarette. Oh, sister!

Tantalizing, he told himself, not removing his eyes from her legs.

Yes, all he wanted was the money to have a mama like that. There wasn't a movie queen in Hollywood that had a nickel on that one. He imagined that she was his woman, seated beside him, talking to him, saying that she would rather have lunch at the Fraternity Row today. She was saying she was crazy, just crazy, about him and didn't care two cents for anyone else in the world. She was wild for him. . . .

"Call for Mr. Jones . . . Mr. Jones please! . . . Mr. Jones!"

The voice of the bellboy was like a jolt, awakening him. He looked at his Ingersoll watch. Two minutes to two. He'd be late, and Collins, his boss, might bawl the hell out of him, and then the fellows in the office would razz him, call him Jenny, the drugstore cowboy. He placed his hat on carefully and moved swiftly out of the lobby. Hurrying along the street, he fell into a dance step. Then he ran until he pulled up, winded. Four minutes after two. What excuse could he give Collins? He paused to look at a girl in pink. Nice! He unwittingly broke into song.

I'm Al-a-ba-ma bound . . .

He again worried about himself, thought of the things he wanted and couldn't have. He started running, hoping that Collins wouldn't bawl him out. Two seven!

Hey! Taxi!

by Edna Ferber

Nervous old ladies from Dubuque, peering fearfully at the placard confronting them as they rode in Ernie's taxi, waxed more timorous still as they read it. It conveyed a grisly warning. Attached thereto was a full-face photograph of Ernie. Upon viewing this, their appraising glance invariably leaped, startled, to where Ernie himself loomed before them in the driver's seat on the other side of the glass partition. Immediately there swept over them an impulse to act upon the printed instructions.

POLICE DEPARTMENT
CITY OF NEW YORK

ERNEST STEWIG

This is a photograph of the authorized driver. If another person is driving this cab notify a policeman.

Staring limpidly back at one from the official photograph was a sleek, personable, and bland young man. This Ernest Stewig who basked in police approval was modishly attired in a starched white collar, store clothes and a not-too-rakish fedora. Trust me, he said.

From a survey of this alleged likeness the baffled eye swung, fascinated, to the corporeal and workaday Ernie seated just ahead, so clearly outlined against the intervening glass.

A pair of pugnacious red ears outstanding beneath a checked gray and black cap well pulled down over the head; a soft blue shirt, somewhat faded; or, in winter, a maroon sweater above whose roll rose a powerful and seemingly immovable neck. Somewhere between the defiant ears and the monolithic neck you sensed a jaw to which a photograph could have done justice only in profile. You further felt that situate between the cap's visor and the jaw was a pair of eyes before which the seraphic gaze of the pictured Ernie would have quailed. The head never moved, never turned to right or left; yet its vision seemed to encompass everything. It was like a lighthouse tower, regnant, impregnable, raking the maelstrom below with a coldly luminous scrutiny.

About the whole figure there was something pantherlike—a quietly alert, formidable, and almost sinister quality—to convey which was in itself no mean achievement for a young man slouched at the wheel of a palpably repainted New York taxicab.

Stewig. Stewig! The name, too, held a degree of puzzlement. The passenger's brain, rejecting the eye's message, sent back a query: Stewig? Isn't there a consonant missing?

Just here the n.o.l. from Dubuque had been known to tap on the glass with an apprehensive but determined forefinger.

"Young man! Young man! Is this your taxicab you're driving?"

"What's that?"

"I said, are you driving this taxi?"

"Well, who'd you think was driving it, lady?"

"I mean are you the same young man as in the picture here?"

Then Ernie, to the horror of his fare, might thrust his head in at the half-open window, unmindful of the traffic that swirled and eddied all about him.

"Me? No. I'm a couple of other guys," he might say, and smile.

In spite of sweater, cap, jaw, ears, and general bearing, when Ernie smiled you recognized in him the engaging and highly sartorial Ernest Stewig photographically approved by the local constabulary. Apologetic and reassured, the passenger would relax against the worn leather cushion.

About Ernie there was much that neither police nor passenger knew. About police and passenger there was little that Ernie did not know. And New York was the palm of his hand. Not only was Ernie the authorized driver of this car; he was its owner. He had bought it secondhand for four hundred dollars. Its four cylinders made rhythmic music in his ears. He fed it oil, gas, and water as a mother feeds her babe. He was a member in good standing of the United Taxi Men's Association. He belonged to Mickey Dolan's Democratic Club for reasons more politic than political.

In his left coat pocket he carried the gray-bound booklet

which was his hack driver's license—a tiny telltale pamphlet of perhaps a dozen pages. At the top of each left-hand page was printed the word VIOLATION. At the top of each right-hand page was the word DISPOSITION. If, during the year, Ernie had been up for speeding, for parking where he shouldn't, for wearing his hackman's badge on his left lapel instead of his right, for any one of those myriad petty misdemeanors which swarm like insects above a hackman's head, that small crime now would appear inevitably on the left-hand page, as would his punishment therefor on the right-hand.

Here it was, November. The pages of Ernie's little gray book were virgin.

It must not be assumed that this was entirely due to the high moral plane on which Ernie and his four-cylinder, secondhand cab (repainted) moved. He was careful, wise, crafty, and almost diabolically gifted at the wheel. When you rode with Ernie you got there—two new gray hairs, perhaps, and the eye pupils slightly dilated—but you got there. His was a gorgeous and uncanny sense of timing. You turned the green-light corner just one second before the sanguine glare of the stop light got you. Men passengers of his own age, thirtyish, seemed to recognize a certain quality in his manipulation of the wheel. They said, "What outfit were you with?"

There were many like him penduluming up and down the narrow tongue of land between the Hudson and the East River. He was of his day: hard, tough, disillusioned, vital, and engaging. He and his kind had a pitying contempt for those grizzled, red-faced old fellows whose hands at the wheel were not those of the mechanic, quick, deft, flexible, but those of the horseman, bred to the reins instead of the steering gear. These drove cautiously, their high-colored faces set in anxiety, their arms stiffly held. Theirs were rattling old cars for which they had no affection and some distrust. They sat in the driver's seat as though an invisible rug were tucked about their inflexible knees. In their eyes was an expectant look—imploring, almost—as though they hoped the greasy engine would turn somehow, magically, into a quadruped. Past these, Ernie's car flashed derisively.

Up and down, up and down the little island he raced. New York swore at him, growled at him, confided in him, overtipped him, undertipped him, borrowed money from him, cheated him, rewarded him, bribed him, invited him to crime. His knowledge of New York was fearful. He forever was talking of leaving it. He complained of the dullness of business, of the dullness of life. He never talked to you unless you first talked to him, after which you had some difficulty in shutting him up. He had a sweet, true, slightly nasal tenor which he sometimes obligingly loaned to college boys with an urge to harmonize while on a New York week end. His vocabulary in daily use consisted of perhaps not more than two hundred words. He was married. He was fond of his wife, Josie. His ambition, confided under the slightest encouragement, was to open a little country hotel somewhere up the river, with a quiet but brisk bar and liquor business on the side. To this end he worked fifteen hours a day; toward it he and Josie saved his money. It was to be their idyl.

"Yeh, hackin', there's nothing in it. Too many cabs, see? And overhead! Sweet jeez, lookit. Insurance thirty bucks a month and you got to pay it. If you ain't got your sticker every month—yeh, that's it, that blue paper on the windshield, see?—you're drove off the street by the cops and you get a ticket. Sure. You gotta insure. Garage, twenty-five. Paint your car once a year anyway is fifty. Oil and gas, two-fifty a day. Five tires a year and a good shoe sets you back plenty. That says nothing about parts and repairs. Where are you, with anyway fifteen hunnerd a year and nearer two grand? No, I only got just this one hack. No, I wouldn't want no jockey. I drive it alone. They don't play square with you, see? It ain't worth the worry of an extra bus. Yeh, I see aplenty and hear aplenty. Keep your eyes and ears open in the hackin' game, and your mouth shut, and you won't never get into a jam is the way I figger."

Strange fragments of talk floated out to Ernie as he sat so stolidly there at the wheel, looking straight ahead:

"Don't! There! I've lost an earring."

". . . five dollars a quart . . ."

". . . sick and tired of your damn nagging . . ."

". . . You do trust me, don't you, babe?"

Up and down, up and down, putting a feverish city to bed. Like a racked and restless patient who tosses and turns and moans and whimpers, the town made all sorts of notional demands before finally it composed its hot limbs to fitful sleep.

Light! cried the patient. Light!

All right, said Ernie. And made for Broadway at Times Square.

I want a drink! I want a drink!

Sure, said Ernie. And stopped at a basement door with a little slit in it and an eye on the other side of the slit.

I want something to eat!

Right, said Ernie. And drove to a place whose doors never close and whose windows are plethoric with roast turkeys, jumbo olives, cheeses, and sugared hams.

It's hot! It's hot! I want to cool off before I go to sleep!

Ernie trundled his patient through the dim aisles of Central Park and up past the midnight velvet of Riverside Drive.

One thing more. Under his seat, just behind his heels and covered by the innocent roll of his raincoat, Ernie carried a venomous fourteen-inch section of cold, black, solid iron pipe. Its thickness was such that the hand could grasp it comfortably and quickly. A jack handle, it was called affectionately.

Though he affected to be bored by his trade he deceived no one by his complaints; not even himself. Its infinite variety held him; its chanciness; the unlimited possibilities of his day's vagaries. Josie felt this. Josie said, "You'll be hackin' when you're sixty and so stiff-knuckled your fingers can't wrap around the wheel."

"Sixty, I'll be pushing you in a wheel chair if you don't take off some that suet."

They loved each other.

Saturday. Any day in Ernie's life as a hackman might bring forth almost anything, and frequently did. But Saturday was sure to. Saturday, in winter, was a long hard day and night, yet Ernie always awoke to it much as a schoolboy contemplates his Saturday, bright and new-minted. It held all sorts of delightful possibilities.

Saturday, in late November. Having got in at 4 A.M., he awoke at noon, refreshed.

Josie had been up since eight. She did not keep hackman's hours. Josie's was a rather lonely life. She complained sometimes, but not often; just enough to keep Ernie interested and a little anxious. A plump, neat woman with slim, quick ankles; deep-bosomed; a careful water wave; an excellent natural cook; she dressed well and quietly, eschewing beige with a wisdom that few plump women have. Ernie took pride in seeing her smartly turned out on their rare holidays together. A lonely and perforce an idle wife, she frequented the movies both afternoon and evening, finding in their shadowy love-making and lavishness a vicarious thrill and some solace during Ernie's absence.

His breakfast was always the same. Fruit, toast, coffee— the light breakfast of a man who has had his morning appetite ruined by a late lunch bolted before going to bed. Josie had eaten four hours earlier. She lunched companionably with him as he breakfasted. It was, usually, their only meal together. As she prepared it, moving deftly about the little kitchen in her print dress and wave pins, Ernie went up on the roof, as was his wont, to survey the world and to fool for five minutes with Big Bum, the family police dog, named after Ernie's pet aversion, the night traffic cop at the corner of Forty-fifth and Broadway. He it was who made life hard for hackmen between the hours of nine-thirty and eleven, when they were jockeying for the theater break.

The Stewigs' flat was one of the many brownstone walk-ups in West Sixty-fifth Street, a sordid and reasonably respectable row of five-story ugliness whose roofs bristled with a sapling forest of radio aerials. A little rickety flight of stairs and a tiny tar-papered shed led to an exhilarating and unexpected view of sky and other low-lying roofs, a glimpse of the pocket-edition Statue of Liberty on top of the Liberty Storage Warehouse, and even a bit of the Hudson if you leaned over the parapet and screwed your neck around.

Ernie liked it up there. It gave him a large sense of freedom, of dominance. He and Big Bum tussled and bounded and rolled about a bit within the narrow confines of their roof world. They surveyed the Western Hemisphere. Big Bum slavered and pawed and bowed and scraped his paws and wagged his tail and shimmied his flanks and went through all the flattering and sycophantic attitudes of the adoring canine who craves male company, being surfeited with female.

"Ernie!" a voice came up the airshaft. "Coffee's getting cold!"

Big Bum threw his whole heart into his effort to hold his master on the roof. He bared his fangs, growled, set his forefeet menacingly. Ernie slapped him on the rump, tousled his muzzle, tickled his stomach with a fond toe.

"Come on, Bum."

"Aw, no!" said Bum, with his eyes. "Let's not pay any attention to her. Couple of men like us."

"Ernie! Don't beef to me if your toast is leather."

"Come on, Bum." Down they went to domesticity.

"What time'll you be home, do you think?"

"How should I know?"

"You couldn't stop by for dinner, could you, late? Nice little steak for you, maybe, or a pork tenderloin and lemon pie?"

"On a Saturday? You're cuckoo!"

"Well, I just thought."

"Yeh! Don't go bragging."

They had discussed a child in rare conjugal moments. "Wait," Ernie had said, "till we got the place up the river with a back yard for the kid like I had time I was little and lived in Jersey, and he can fool with Bum and like that. Here, where'd he be but out on the street being run over?"

"Yes," said Josie, not too delicately. "Let's wait till I'm fifty."

She bade him good-by now, somewhat listlessly. "Well, anyway, you're not working tomorrow, are you, Ernie? Sunday?"

"No. Give the other guy a chance tomorrow. We'll go somewheres."

They did not kiss one another good-by. After seven years of marriage they would have considered such daytime demonstration queer, not to say offensive.

One o'clock. Over to the garage on Sixty-ninth for the hack. Gas, oil, and water. These services he himself performed, one of the few taxi men to whom the engine of a car was not as mysterious and unexplored as the heavenly constellations. It was a saying among hackmen that most of them did not know what to do when the engine was boiling over. Ernie's car had been cleaned during the morning. Still, he now extracted from beneath the seat cushion a flannel rag with which he briskly rubbed such metal parts as were, in his opinion, not sufficiently resplendent.

He had fitted the car with certain devices of his own of which he was extremely proud. Attached to the dashboard, at the right, was a little metal clip which held his pencil. Just below the meter box hung a change slot such as streetcar conductors wear. It held dimes, quarters, and nickels and saved Ernie much grubbing about in coat pockets while passengers waited, grumbling.

Out through the broad, open door of the garage and into the lemon-yellow sunshine of a sharp November Saturday. A vague nostalgia possessed him momentarily. Perhaps they were burning leaves on some cross street that still boasted an anemic tree or two. Saturday afternoons in Jersey—Jeez, it's a great day for football, he thought, idly, and swung into Sixty-eighth Street toward the Park.

Two elderly, gray-haired women twittered wrenlike at the curb in front of a mountainous apartment house near Central

Park West. They looked this way and that. At sight of Ernie's cab they fluttered their wings. He swooped down on them. They retreated timidly, then gave him the address and were swallowed in the maw of his taxi.

Two o'clock. Ernie's Saturday had begun.

The number they had given was on Lexington Avenue in the Fifties. It turned out to be a small motion-picture theater.

"This where you meant, lady?"

They fumbled with the door. Ernie reached in, opened it. They stepped out, stiffly. The fare was fifty-five cents. One wren handed him a minutely folded green bill. He tapped the change slot three times and gave her two dimes and a quarter. The wren put the three coins into a small black purse. From the same purse she extracted a five-cent piece and offered it to him. He regarded it impersonally, took it.

A little superstitious shiver shook him. A swell start for a Saturday, all right. What those two old birds want to come 'way over here to a bum movie for, anyway! Curious, he glanced at the picture title. *Souls for Sale.* That didn't sound so hot. Oh, well, you couldn't never tell what people done things for. He tucked the folded bill into his upper left coat pocket. He always did that with his first fare, for luck.

Off down the street. Might pick up a matinee fare one the hotels on Madison. He came down to Forty-seventh, jockeyed along the Ritz. Little groups of two and three stood on the steps and came languidly down to the sidewalk at the Madison Avenue entrance. Orchids, fur, sheer silk stockings; British topcoats, yellow sticks: au 'voir, darling . . . awfly nice. . . . The doorman hailed him.

Two of the orchids skipped into his car. They waved good-by to a coat. Whyn't the big stiff come along with'm, pay their fare and maybe a decent tip instead of the dime these kind of mice give a guy?

"Listen, driver, can't you go faster?"

"Doing the best I can. You can't go through the lights."

Turn around the middle of the street front of the theater if the cop wasn't looking. Yeh, he wasn't. "Forty-five cents."

"I've got it, dear. Please let me. Don't fuss. We're so late."

Oh, my Gawd!

The winning orchid handed him a dollar. He flipped a nickel and two quarters into his palm, turned to look hard. "That's all right," said the orchid. They skipped into the theater. Well, that was more like it. Cute couple kids, at that.

He headed down Eighth Avenue toward the loft district in

the Thirties between Eighth and Fifth. The fur and cloak-and-suit manufacturers were rushed with late Saturday orders to be delivered, to be shipped. Little dark men ran up and down with swatches, with bundles, with packages of fur and cloth and felt. Take me down to Tenth and Fifth. Take me up to Thirty-second and Third. I want to go to Eighty-eight University Place.

It was tough driving through the packed, greasy streets. You couldn't make time, but they were generous with their tips. Ernie preferred to stay all afternoon in and out of the cloak-and-suit district. Being too far downtown, he headed uptown again toward the Thirties. In Thirteenth Street, going west, vacant, he had a call from a gimlet-eyed young man at the curb in front of an old brick building. The young man leaned very close to Ernie. He made no move to enter the taxi. He glanced quickly up and down the street. He said to Ernie, quietly:

"Take a sack of potatoes?"

"Sure," said Ernie. "Where to?"

"Broadway and Nine'y-foist."

"Sure," said Ernie.

The gimlet-eyed young man nodded ever so slightly toward an unseen figure behind him. There emerged quickly from the doorway a short, mild-looking blond man. He carried a suitcase and a brown-paper corded bundle. His strong short arms were tense-muscled under the weight of them. It was as though they held stone. He deposited these gently in the bottom of the cab. Glup-glup, came a soft gurgle. The younger man vanished as the little fellow climbed ponderously into the taxi. He reappeared carrying still another brown bundle. He sagged under it.

"Fi' bucks for you," he said to Ernie. "Take Ninth Avenue."

"Sure," said Ernie.

The young man closed the taxi door and disappeared into the brick building. Ernie and the mild blond fellow and the suitcase and the two stout, brown-paper parcels sped up Ninth Avenue, keeping always on the far side of an occasional traffic cop and observing all road rules meticulously.

The uptown Broadway address reached, the man paid him his fare and the five dollars. Ernie sat stolidly in his seat while the little man wrestled with suitcase and bundles. Not him! They wouldn't catch Ernie carrying the stuff with his own hands. As the bundles touched the curb he stepped on the gas and was off, quickly. He headed down Broadway again.

A plump, agitated little woman in an expensive-looking black fur coat hailed him at Eighty-fifth. "Take me to Eight-fifty-five West End. And I'm late for a bridge game."

"That's terrible," said Ernie, grimly. She did not hear him. She perched on the edge of the seat, her stout silken legs crossed at the ankles, both feet beating a nervous tattoo.

Ernie whirled west on Eighty-fifth, then north up West End. The dressy woman climbed laboriously out. She handed Ernie his exact fare and scurried into the marble-and-plush foyer of Number Eight-fifty-five.

"And I hope you lose your shirt," Ernie remarked feelingly.

He took out the five-dollar bill that the man had given him for carrying the sack of potatoes, smoothed it, and placed it in his billfold. Then he remembered the bill in his upper left coat pocket—his first fare given him by the fluttery old ladies bent on seeing *Souls for Sale*. He fished down with two fingers, extracted the bill, smoothed it, and said piously, "For the jeez!"

It was a ten-dollar bill. His mind jolted back. He pieced the events of the past two hours into neat little blocks. Hm. Gosh! Fifteen bones clean, he could call it a day and knock off and go home and have dinner with Josie. There was no possibility of returning the ten-dollar bill to its owner, even if he had thought remotely of so doing—which he emphatically had not.

The blue-and-gold doorman, guardian of Number Eight-fifty-five, now approached Ernie. "What you sticking around here blocking up this entrance?"

Ernie looked up absently. He tucked his bills tidily into the folder, rammed the folder into his hip pocket. "Do you want me to move on?" he inquired humbly.

"You heard me." But the doorman was suspicious of such meekness.

Ernie shifted to first. He eyed the doorman tenderly. "And just when I was beginning to love you," he crooned.

Four-fifteen. He bumbled slowly around the corner on Eighty-sixth and across to Columbus. Might go home, at that. No, Jo wouldn't be there, anyway. A white-tiled coffeeshop. A great wire basket of golden-brown doughnuts in the window, flaky-looking and flecked with powdered sugar. Pretty cold by now. Ernie stamped his feet. Guess he'd go in; have a cup of hot coffee and a couple sinkers.

There were other hackmen in the steaming little shop with its fragrance of coffee and its smell of sizzling fat. They did not speak to Ernie, nor he to them. The beverage was hot and stimulating. He ate three crullers. Feeling warm and gay, he climbed into the driver's seat again. He'd stick around a couple hours more. Then he'd go home and give the other guy a chance.

Down to Columbus Circle, across Fifty-ninth, down Seventh, across Fifty-seventh to Madison. Down Madison slowly. Not a call. Nearly five o'clock.

A girl gave him a call. Tall, slim, pale. Not New York. She had been standing at the curb. Ernie had seen her let vacant cabs go by. As she gave him the number she smiled a little. She looked him in the eye. Her accent was not New Yorkese. She got in. The number she had given turned out to be an office building near-Fortieth.

"Wait here," she said and smiled again and looked into Ernie's eyes.

"Long?"

"No, just a minute. Please."

It didn't look so good. Still, he'd wait a couple minutes, anyway. Wonder was there another exit to this building.

She came out almost immediately. "The office was closed," she explained.

Ernie nodded. "Yeh, five o'clock, and Saturday afternoon. Close one o'clock."

She got into the taxi, gave another number. Ernie recognized it as that of still another office building. That, too, probably would be closed, he told her. He turned his head a little to look at her through the window.

She smiled and put her head on one side.

"I want to try, anyway." Then, as Ernie turned to face forward again, his hand on the gear shift, "Could I trouble you for a match?"

Hm. Thought so. When they asked you for a match, anything might happen. He gave her a light. She took it, lingeringly, and kept the matches. You want me to take you to that number, girlie? Yes. She did not resent the girlie. He took her to the number. Wait, please. In a minute she was back. Her voice was plaintive, her brow puckered.

"Seems like everybody's away," she said. She got in. "I

love riding in taxis. I'm crazy about it." Her *I* was *Ah*. Her *ou* was double *o*, or nearly.

"You from out of town?"

"I'm from Birmingham. I'm all alone in town. I guess you better take me to my hotel. The Magnolia Hotel, West Twenty-ninth."

He started for it, waiting for the next move from his fare. She pushed down the little seat that folded up, one of a neat pair, against the front of the taxi. She changed over to it and opened the sliding window, leaning out a little.

"My train doesn't go till ten o'clock tonight, and I haven't a thing to do till then."

"That's too bad," said Ernie.

"If I keep my room after six they charge for it. It's almost half-past five now. And my train doesn't go till ten and I haven't a thing to do."

"Yeh?"

"If I got my suitcase and checked out, would you be back down here at six?" They had reached the hotel entrance.

"Sure," said Ernie. She stepped out, her slim ankles teetering in high heels. She turned to go.

"Ninety cents, girlie," said Ernie. She gave him a dollar. Her hand touched his.

"Six o'clock," she repeated. "Right here."

"Sure," said Ernie.

He drove briskly over to the manufacturing section again. They were great taxi riders, those little paunchy men, and a fare there around six o'clock meant a good call up to the Bronx, or over to Brooklyn. The manufacturers worked late now in the height of the season. Six o'clock and often seven. On the way he got a call to Twelfth Street, came back to the Thirties, and there picked up a Bronx call just as he had hoped. This was his lucky day, all right. Breaking good. Wonder was that Birmingham baby standing on the curb, waiting.

He drove briskly and expertly in and out of the welter of traffic. His fare wanted some newspapers, and Ernie obligingly stopped at a newsstand and got them for him—*Sun, Journal, Telegram*. The man read them under the dim light inside the cab, smoking fat black cigars the while. The rich scent of them floated out to Ernie even through the tightly closed windows. A long cold ride, but Ernie didn't mind. He deposited his fare in front of a gaudy new apartment house far uptown.

"Cold night, my boy," said the man.

"I'll say!" A fifty-cent tip. The fare had left the newspapers in the taxi. Ernie selected the *Journal*. He drove to a near-by lunchroom whose sign said Jack's Coffee Pot. Another cup of coffee and a ham-on-rye. He read his paper and studied its pictures, believing little of what he read. Sometimes, though rarely, he discussed notorious tabloid topics with a fellow worker, or with a talkative fare, or a lunchroom attendant. His tone was one of sly but judicious wisdom. In a murder trial he was not deceived by the antics of principals, witnesses, lawyers, or judges. "Yeh, well, that baby better watch herself, because she can't get away with that with no jury. Blonde or no blonde, I bet she fries."

Seven-thirty. Guessed he'd start downtown and get around the Eighties by eight o'clock, pick up a nice theater fare. Wonder if that Birmingham baby was waiting yet. No. Too late. Looked as mild as skim-milk, too. Never can tell, and that's a fact. He'd have to tell Jo about that one. Uh—no, guess he wouldn't, at that. Mightn't believe him. Women.

Central Park West. He turned in at Sixty-seventh, picked up a theater fare for Forty-fifth Street. Hoped that big bum on the corner Forty-fifth would leave him turn right, off Broadway. From Fifty-first to Forty-fifth his progress became a crawl, and the crawl became a series of dead stops punctuated by feeble and abortive attempts to move. The streets were packed solid. The sidewalks were a moving mass. Thousands of motors, tens of thousands of lights, hundreds of thousands of people.

Ernie sat unruffled, serene, watchful at his wheel. He rarely lost his temper, never became nervous, almost never cursed. It was too wearing. Hacking was no job for a nervous man. It was eight-thirty when he deposited his fare in front of the theater. Sometimes, on a good night, you could cover two theater calls. But this was not one of those nights. He went west to Ninth Avenue on his way to dinner uptown. Ninth would be fairly clear going. But at Forty-seventh and Ninth he reluctantly picked up a call headed for a nine-o'clock picture show. Oh, well, all right.

By nine he was again on his way uptown. He liked to eat dinner at Charley's place, the Amsterdam Lunch, on Amsterdam near Seventy-seventh. He could have stopped very well for a late dinner at home. But you never could tell. Besides, Jo getting a hot meal at nine—for what! The truth was that his palate had become accustomed to the tang of the pungent stews, the sharp sauces, and the hearty roughage of the lunchroom and the sandwich wagons. When possible he liked to drive uptown to Charley's, out of the welter of traffic, where he could eat in nine-o'clock peace.

Charley was noted for his Blue Plate, 65¢. He gave you stew or roast and always two fresh vegetables. Spinach and asparagus; corn and string beans. His peas were fresh. No canned stuff at Charley's. His potatoes were light and floury. Josie was an excellent cook. Yet, on the rare occasions when he ate at home, he consumed the meal listlessly, though dutifully. She went to endless trouble. She prepared delicate pastry dishes decorated with snarls of meringue or whipped cream. She cut potatoes into tortured shapes. She beat up sauces, stuffed fowl. Yet Ernie perversely preferred Smitty McGlaughlin's lunch wagon at Seventh and Perry.

Charley's long, narrow slit of a shop was well filled. There were only two empty stools along the glass-topped counter. Ernie had parked his car, one of a line of ten taxis, outside the Amsterdam Lunch.

"What's good eating tonight, Charley?" Ernie swung a leg over the stool at the counter.

Charley wore an artless toupee, a clean white apron, a serious look. "Baked breast of lamb with peas and cauliflower and potatoes."

Ernie ordered it, and it was good. Rich brown gravy, and plenty of it. But even if, in Charley's momentary absence, you had made your own choice, you would not have gone wrong. Boiled ham knuckle, baked beans, Ger. fr., 50¢. Broiled lamb chops, sliced tomatoes, Fr. fr., 55¢. As you ate your Blue Plate there smirked up at you, through the transparent glass shelf below, sly dishes of apple pie, custards, puddings, cakes. Here you heard some of the gossip of the trade—tales of small adventure told in the patois of New York.

"I'm going east on Thirty-eighth, see, and the big harp standing there sees me, starts bawling me out, see? 'What the hell,' I says, 'what's eating into you?' Well, he comes up slow, see, stops traffic and walks over to me slow, looking at me, the big mick! 'Want a ticket, do you?' he says. 'Looking for it, are you?' he says. 'Asking for it? Well, take that,' he says, 'and like it.' Can you match that, the big . . .'" There followed a stream of effortless obscenity almost beautiful in its quivering fluidity.

Usually, though, the teller emerged triumphant from these verbal or fistic encounters. "They give me a number up in

Harlem. You ought to seen the pans on them. Scared you. When we get there it's in front of a light. So one of them pokes their head out of the window and says it ain't the place. It's in the next block, halfway. Well, then I know I'm right. I reach for the old jack handle under the seat and I climb down and open the door. 'Oh, yes it is,' I says. 'This is the right place, all right, and you're getting out.' At that the one guy starts to run. But the other swings back so I clip him one in the jaw. I bet he ain't come to yet—lookit the skin of my knuckles. . . ."

His fellow diners listened skeptically and said he was an artist, thus conveying that he was a romancer of high imagination but low credibility. "Come on!" they said. "I heard you was hackin' at Mott Street Ferry all evening."

Ernie paid for his meal, took a toothpick, and was on his way downtown for the theater break. Might as well make a day of it. Get a good rest tomorrow. It was a grim business, this getting in line for the eleven-o'clock show crowd. The cops wouldn't let you stand, they wouldn't let you move. You circled round and round and round, east on Thirty-eighth, back to Broadway, chased off Broadway by the cops, east again, back up Broadway, over to Eighth. "Come on! Come on! Come *on!*" bawled the cop, when you tried to get into Forty-fourth. "Come on! Come *on! Come on!*" chasing you up to Forty-sixth, on Eighth.

Ernie picked up a call in Forty-fourth. They wanted to go downtown to one of those Greenwich Village dumps. Pretty good call. Uptown again, and down again. He stopped at Smitty's and had a hamburger sandwich and a cup of coffee. Cold night, all right. How's hackin'? Good!

One o'clock. Might as well go over to the Sucker Clubs around the West Fifties. Saturday night you could pick up a 33⅓. One of the boys had cleaned up a hundred dollars one night last week. You picked up a call that wanted to go to a night club, a club where there was enough to drink. You took him in, if he looked all right to you, and you handed him over to the proprietor and you parked your hack outside and you came in, comfortably, and waited—you waited with one eye on him and the other on the cash register. And no matter what he spent, you got your 33⅓ per cent. One, two, three hundred.

Ernie cruised about a bit, but with no luck. Half-past one. Guessed he'd call it a day and go home to old Jo and the hay. Early, though, for a Saturday night. Pretty fair day.

He cruised across Fifty-first Street, slowly, looking carefully up at the grim old shuttered houses, so quiet, so quiet. A door opened. A bar of yellow light made a gash in the blackness. Ernie drew up at the curb. A man appeared at the top of the stairs. He was supporting a limp bundle that resembled another man. The bundle had legs that twisted like a scarecrow's.

"Hello, Al," said Ernie.

"Hey," called the man, softly, "give me a hand, will you?"

Ernie ran up the stairs, took the scarecrow under the left arm as the man had it under the right arm. The bundle said, with dignity, "Cut the rough stuff, will you, you big ape!"

Ernie, surprised, looked inquiringly at Al. "His head is all right," Al explained. "He ain't got no legs, that's all."

Together they deposited the bundle in Ernie's hack. Ernie looked at the face. It was scarred again and again. There were scars all over it. Old scars. It was Benny Opfer.

"There!" said Al, affably, arranging the legs and stepping back to survey his handiwork. "Now, then. The address . . ."

"I'll give my own address," interrupted Mr. Opfer, with great distinctness, "you great big so-and-so."

Al withdrew. The yellow gash of light showed again briefly; vanished. The house was dark, quiet.

Benny Opfer gave his address. It was in Brooklyn.

"Oh, say," protested Ernie, with excusable reluctance, "I can't take no call to Brooklyn this time of night."

"Do you know who I am?" Ernie was no weakling; but that voice was a chill and horrid thing, coming even as it did from the limp and helpless body.

"Yeh, but listen, Mr. Opfer—"

"Brooklyn." He leaned forward ever so little by an almost superhuman effort of will. "I'm a rich man. When I was fourteen I was earning a hundred dollars a week."

"That right!" responded Ernie wretchedly.

"Do you know how?"

"Can't say I do."

"Gunning," said Mr. Benny Opfer modestly. And sank back. They went to Brooklyn.

Arrived at the far Brooklyn destination, "I ain't got any money," announced Mr. Benny Opfer with engaging candor, as Ernie lifted him out.

"Aw, say, listen," objected Ernie plaintively. He hoisted Mr. Benny Opfer up the steps and supported him as he fitted the key.

"Get you some," Opfer promised him. "She's always got fi' dollars stuck away someplace. You wait."

"I'll wait inside," Ernie declared stoutly.

Ernie stood outside in the cold November morning. He looked up at a lighted upper window of the Brooklyn house. Sounds floated down, high shrill sounds. He waited. He mounted the steps again and rang the bell, three long hard rings. He came down to the street again and looked up at the window. 'Way over to Brooklyn, and then gypped out of his fare! He rang the bell again and again.

The window sash was lifted. A woman's head appeared silhouetted against the light behind it. "Here!" she called softly. Something dropped at Ernie's feet. It was the exact fare. Benny Opfer, limp as to legs, had been levelheaded enough when it came to reading the meter.

Half-past three.

Ernie was on his way home, coming up Third Avenue at a brisk clip. A man and a girl halted him. The girl was pretty and crying. The man gave an address that was Riverside at One Hundred and Eighteenth Street. The streets were quiet now. Quiet. Sometimes New York was like that for one hour, between three-thirty and four-thirty. The front window was open an inch or two.

"You don't need him," said the man. "He's all washed up. You stick to me and everything'll be all right. He never was on the level with you, anyway."

"I'm crazy about him," whimpered the girl.

"You'll be crazy about me in a week. I'm telling you."

An early morning el train roared down her reply.

Cold. Getting colder all the time. Sitting here since one o'clock today. Today! Yesterday. Ernie sank his neck into his sweater and settled down for the grind up to One Hundred and Eighteenth. Last fare he'd take, not if it was the governor of New York State, he wouldn't.

The man and the girl got out. The girl's head drooped on the man's shoulder. The man paid Ernie. She wouldn't sit so pretty with that bimbo if the size of his tip was any sign and, if it wasn't, what was?

No more hackin' this night. He turned swiftly into Broadway.

Tired. Dead-tired. Kind of dreamy, too. This hackin'. Enough to make you sick to your stomach. Taking everybody home and putting them to bed. Just a goddam wet nurse, that's what. One Hundred and Fifteenth. Tenth. His eye

Hey! Taxi!

caught a little line of ice that formed a trail down the middle of Broadway. The milk wagon that came down from the station at One Hundred and Twenty-fifth Street. The melting ice inside these trickled through the pipe to the pavement, making a thin line of ice in the cold November morning. One Hundredth. Ninety-fifth.

Half-past four.

The sound of a tremendous explosion. The crash of broken glass. Ernie, relaxed at the wheel, stiffened into wakeful attention. It was still dark. He drove swiftly down to Nineteenth Street. The remains of a white-painted milk wagon lay scattered near the curb. Broken glass was everywhere. A horse lay tangled in the reins. The sound of groans, low and unceasing, came from within the shattered wagon. Fifty feet away was a powerful car standing upright and trim on the sidewalk.

Ernie drew up, got out. All about, in the towering apartment houses lining the street, windows were flung open. Heads stuck out. Police whistles sounded. No policeman appeared. Ernie went over to the cart; peered in. A man lay there, covered with milk and blood and glass. Chunks of glass stuck in his cheeks, in his legs. They were embedded in his arms. He was bleeding terribly and groaning faintly as he bled. More faintly. Men appeared—funny fat men and lean men in pajamas with overcoats thrown on.

"Here, give me a hand with this guy," commanded Ernie. "He's bleeding to death."

No one came forward. Blood. They did not want to touch it. Ernie looked up and around. He saw a figure emerge from the queerly parked automobile and walk away, weaving crazily.

"Hey, get that bird," cried Ernie, "before he gets away. He's the one hit the wagon. Must of been going eighty miles an hour, the way this outfit looks."

A slim, pale young fellow, fully dressed, detached himself from the crowd that had now gathered—still no police—walked quickly across the street—seemed almost to flow across it, like a lean cat. He came up behind the man who had emerged from the reckless automobile. Swiftly he reached into his back hip pocket, took from it a blackjack, raised his arm lightly, brought it down on the man's head. The man crumpled slowly to the pavement. The pale young fellow vanished.

The groans within the shattered wagon were much fainter.

"Give me a hand here," commanded Ernie again. "One you guys. What's eating you! Scared you'll get your hands dirty! Must of all been in the war, you guys."

Someone helped him bundle the ludicrous yet terrible figure into the taxi. Ernie knew the nearest hospital, not five minutes away. He drove there, carefully yet swiftly. The groans had ceased. Men in white uniforms received the ghastly burden.

Ernie looked ruefully at the inside of his hack. Pools of red lay on the floor, on the cushions; ran, a viscid stream, down the steps.

At the garage, "I won't clean no car like that," declared the washer.

"All right, sweetness, all right," snarled Ernie. "I'll clean it tomorrow myself."

The washer peered in, his eyes wide. "Jeez, where'd you bury him!" he said.

Josie was asleep, but she awoke at his entrance, as she almost always did.

"How'd you make out, Ernie?"

"Pretty good," replied Ernie, yawning. "Made a lot of jack."

"You rest till late," Josie murmured drowsily. "Then in the afternoon we'll maybe go to a movie or somewhere. There's *Ride 'em Cowboy* at the Rivoli."

"The West," said Ernie, dreamily, as he took off his socks. "That's the place where I'd like to go. 'Ride 'em, cowboy!' That's the life. Nothing ever happens in this town."

Bernice Bobs Her Hair

by F. Scott Fitzgerald

After dark on Saturday night one could stand on the first tee of the golf-course and see the country-club windows as a yellow expanse over a very black and wavy ocean. The waves of this ocean, so to speak, were the heads of many curious caddies, a few of the more ingenious chauffeurs, the golf professional's deaf sister—and there were usually several stray, diffident waves who might have rolled inside had they so desired. This was the gallery.

The balcony was inside. It consisted of the circle of wicker chairs that lined the wall of the combination clubroom and ballroom. At these Saturday-night dances it was largely feminine; a great babble of middle-aged ladies with sharp eyes and icy hearts behind lorgnettes and large bosoms. The main function of the balcony was critical. It occasionally showed grudging admiration, but never approval, for it is well known among ladies over thirty-five that when the younger set dance in the summer-time it is with the very worst intentions in the world, and if they are not bombarded with stony eyes, stray couples will dance weird barbaric interludes in the corners, and the more popular, more dangerous girls will sometimes be kissed in the parked limousines of unsuspecting dowagers.

But, after all, this critical circle is not close enough to the stage to see the actors' faces and catch the subtler byplay. It can only frown and lean, ask questions and make satisfactory deductions from its set of postulates, such as the one which states that every young man with a large income leads the life of a hunted partridge. It never really appreciates the drama of the shifting, semicruel world of adolescence. No; boxes, orchestra-circle, principals, and chorus are represented by the medley of faces and voices that sway to the plaintive African rhythm of Dyer's dance orchestra.

From sixteen-year-old Otis Ormonde, who has two more years at Hill School, to G. Reese Stoddard, over whose bureau at home hangs a Harvard law diploma; from little

Madeleine Hogue, whose hair still feels strange and uncomfortable on top of her head, to Bessie MacRae, who has been the life of the party a little too long—more than ten years—the medley is not only the center of the stage but contains the only people capable of getting an unobstructed view of it.

With a flourish and a bang the music stops. The couples exchange artificial, effortless smiles, facetiously repeat *"la-de-dad-da* dum-*dum,"* and then the clatter of young feminine voices soars over the burst of clapping.

A few disappointed stags caught in midfloor as they had been about to cut in subsided listlessly back to the walls, because this was not like the riotous Christmas dances—these summer hops were considered just pleasantly warm and exciting, where even the younger marrieds rose and performed ancient waltzes and terrifying fox trots to the tolerant amusement of their younger brothers and sisters.

Warren McIntyre, who casually attended Yale, being one of the unfortunate stags, felt in his dinner-coat pocket for a cigarette and strolled out onto the wide, semidark veranda, where couples were scattered at tables, filling the lantern-hung night with vague words and hazy laughter. He nodded here and there at the less absorbed and as he passed each couple some half-forgotten fragment of a story played in his mind, for it was not a large city and every one was Who's Who to every one else's past. There, for example, were Jim Strain and Ethel Demorest, who had been privately engaged for three years. Every one knew that as soon as Jim managed to hold a job for more than two months she would marry him. Yet how bored they both looked, and how wearily Ethel regarded Jim sometimes, as if she wondered why she had trained the vines of her affection on such a wind-shaken poplar.

Warren was nineteen and rather pitying with those of his friends who had gone East to college. But, like most boys, he bragged tremendously about the girls of his city when he was away from it. There was Genevieve Ormonde, who regularly made the rounds of dances, house-parties, and football games at Princeton, Yale, Williams, and Cornell; there was black-eyed Roberta Dillon, who was quite as famous to her own generation as Hiram Johnson or Ty Cobb; and, of course, there was Marjorie Harvey, who besides having a fairylike face and a dazzling, bewildering tongue was already justly celebrated for having turned five cart-wheels in succession during the last pump-and-slipper dance at New Haven.

Bernice Bobs Her Hair

Warren, who had grown up across the street from Marjorie, had long been "crazy about her." Sometimes she seemed to reciprocate his feeling with a faint gratitude, but she had tried him by her infallible test and informed him gravely that she did not love him. Her test was that when she was away from him she forgot him and had affairs with other boys. Warren found this discouraging, especially as Marjorie had been making little trips all summer, and for the first two or three days after each arrival home he saw great heaps of mail on the Harveys' hall table addressed to her in various masculine handwritings. To make matters worse, all during the month of August she had been visited by her cousin Bernice from Eau Claire, and it seemed impossible to see her alone. It was always necessary to hunt round and find some one to take care of Bernice. As August waned this was becoming more and more difficult.

Much as Warren worshipped Marjorie, he had to admit that Cousin Bernice was sorta dopeless. She was pretty, with dark hair and high color, but she was no fun on a party. Every Saturday night he danced a long arduous duty dance with her to please Marjorie, but he had never been anything but bored in her company.

"Warren"—a soft voice at his elbow broke in upon his thoughts, and he turned to see Marjorie, flushed and radiant as usual. She laid a hand on his shoulder and a glow settled almost imperceptibly over him.

"Warren," she whispered, "do something for me—dance with Bernice. She's been stuck with little Otis Ormonde for almost an hour."

Warren's glow faded.

"Why—sure," he answered half-heartedly.

"You don't mind, do you? I'll see that you don't get stuck."

" 'Sall right."

Marjorie smiled—that smile that was thanks enough.

"You're an angel, and I'm obliged loads."

With a sigh the angel glanced round the veranda, but Bernice and Otis were not in sight. He wandered back inside, and there in front of the women's dressing-room he found Otis in the center of a group of young men who were convulsed with laughter. Otis was brandishing a piece of timber he had picked up, and discoursing volubly.

"She's gone in to fix her hair," he announced wildly. "I'm waiting to dance another hour with her."

Their laughter was renewed.

"Why don't some of you cut in?" cried Otis resentfully. "She likes more variety."

"Why, Otis," suggested a friend, "you've just barely got used to her."

"Why the two-by-four, Otis?" inquired Warren, smiling.

"The two-by-four? Oh, this? This is a club. When she comes out I'll hit her on the head and knock her in again."

Warren collapsed on a settee and howled with glee.

"Never mind, Otis," he articulated finally. "I'm relieving you this time."

Otis simulated a sudden fainting attack and handed the stick to Warren.

"If you need it, old man," he said hoarsely.

No matter how beautiful or brilliant a girl may be, the reputation of not being frequently cut in on makes her position at a dance unfortunate. Perhaps boys prefer her company to that of the butterflies with whom they dance a dozen times an evening, but youth in this jazz-nourished generation is temperamentally restless, and the idea of fox-trotting more than one full fox trot with the same girl is distasteful, not to say odious. When it comes to several dances and the intermissions between she can be quite sure that a young man, once relieved, will never tread on her wayward toes again.

Warren danced the next full dance with Bernice, and finally, thankful for the intermission, he led her to a table on the veranda. There was a moment's silence while she did unimpressive things with her fan.

"It's hotter here than in Eau Claire," she said.

Warren stifled a sigh and nodded. It might be for all he knew or cared. He wondered idly whether she was a poor conversationalist because she got no attention or got no attention because she was a poor conversationalist.

"You going to be here much longer?" he asked, and then turned rather red. She might suspect his reasons for asking.

"Another week," she answered, and stared at him as if to lunge at his next remark when it left his lips.

Warren fidgeted. Then with a sudden charitable impulse he decided to try part of his line on her. He turned and looked at her eyes.

"You've got an awfully kissable mouth," he began quietly.

This was a remark that he sometimes made to girls at college proms when they were talking in just such half-dark as this. Bernice distinctly jumped. She turned an ungraceful red and became clumsy with her fan. No one had ever made such a remark to her before.

"Fresh!"—the word had slipped out before she realized it, and she bit her lip. Too late she decided to be amused, and offered him a flustered smile.

Warren was annoyed. Though not accustomed to have that remark taken seriously, still it usually provoked a laugh or a paragraph of sentimental banter. And he hated to be called fresh, except in a joking way. His charitable impulse died and he switched the topic.

"Jim Strain and Ethel Demorest sitting out as usual," he commented.

This was more in Bernice's line, but a faint regret mingled with her relief as the subject changed. Men did not talk to her about kissable mouths, but she knew that they talked in some such way to other girls.

"Oh, yes," she said, and laughed. "I hear they've been mooning round for years without a red penny. Isn't it silly?"

Warren's disgust increased. Jim Strain was a close friend of his brother's, and anyway he considered it bad form to sneer at people for not having money. But Bernice had had no intention of sneering. She was merely nervous.

II

When Marjorie and Bernice reached home at half after midnight they said good night at the top of the stairs. Though cousins, they were not intimates. As a matter of fact Marjorie had no female intimates—she considered girls stupid. Bernice on the contrary all through this parent-arranged visit had rather longed to exchange those confidences flavored with giggles and tears that she considered an indispensable factor in all feminine intercourse. But in this respect she found Marjorie rather cold; felt somehow the same difficulty in talking to her that she had in talking to men. Marjorie never giggled, was never frightened, seldom embarrassed, and in fact had very few of the qualities which Bernice considered appropriately and blessedly feminine.

As Bernice busied herself with toothbrush and paste this night she wondered for the hundredth time why she never had any attention when she was away from home. That her family were the wealthiest in Eau Claire, that her mother entertained tremendously, gave little dinners for her daughter before all dances and bought her a car of her own to drive round in, never occurred to her as factors in her home-town social success. Like most girls she had been brought up on the warm milk prepared by Annie Fellows Johnston and on novels in which the female was beloved because of certain mysterious womanly qualities, always mentioned but never displayed.

Bernice felt a vague pain that she was not at present engaged in being popular. She did not know that had it not been for Marjorie's campaigning she would have danced the entire evening with one man; but she knew that even in Eau Claire other girls with less position and less pulchritude were given a much bigger rush. She attributed this to something subtly unscrupulous in those girls. It had never worried her, and if it had her mother would have assured her that the other girls cheapened themselves and that men really respected girls like Bernice.

She turned out the light in her bathroom, and on an impulse decided to go in and chat for a moment with her aunt Josephine, whose light was still on. Her soft slippers bore her noiselessly down the carpeted hall, but hearing voices inside she stopped near the partly opened door. Then she caught her own name, and without any definite intention of eavesdropping lingered—and the thread of the conversation going on inside pierced her consciousness sharply as if it had been drawn through with a needle.

"She's absolutely hopeless!" It was Marjorie's voice. "Oh, I know what you're going to say! So many people have told you how pretty and sweet she is, and how she can cook! What of it? She has a bum time. Men don't like her."

"What's a little cheap popularity?"

Mrs. Harvey sounded annoyed.

"It's everything when you're eighteen," said Marjorie emphatically. "I've done my best. I've been polite and I've made men dance with her, but they just won't stand being bored. When I think of that gorgeous coloring wasted on such a ninny, and think what Martha Carey could do with it—oh!"

"There's no courtesy these days."

Mrs. Harvey's voice implied that modern situations were too much for her. When she was a girl all young ladies who belonged to nice families had glorious times.

"Well," said Marjorie, "no girl can permanently bolster up a lame-duck visitor, because these days it's every girl for herself. I've even tried to drop her hints about clothes and things, and she's been furious—given me the funniest looks.

She's sensitive enough to know she's not getting away with much, but I'll bet she consoles herself by thinking that she's very virtuous and that I'm too gay and fickle and will come to a bad end. All unpopular girls think that way. Sour grapes! Sarah Hopkins refers to Genevieve and Roberta and me as gardenia girls! I'll bet she'd give ten years of her life and her European education to be a gardenia girl and have three or four men in love with her and be cut in on every few feet at dances."

"It seems to me," interrupted Mrs. Harvey rather wearily, "that you ought to be able to do something for Bernice. I know she's not very vivacious."

Marjorie groaned.

"Vivacious! Good grief! I've never heard her say anything to a boy except that it's hot or the floor's crowded or that she's going to school in New York next year. Sometimes she asks them what kind of car they have and tells them the kind she has. Thrilling!"

There was a short silence, and then Mrs. Harvey took up her refrain: "All I know is that other girls not half so sweet and attractive get partners. Martha Carey, for instance, is stout and loud, and her mother is distinctly common. Roberta Dillon is so thin this year that she looks as though Arizona were the place for her. She's dancing herself to death."

"But, mother," objected Marjorie impatiently, "Martha is cheerful and awfully witty and an awfully slick girl, and Roberta's a marvellous dancer. She's been popular for ages!"

Mrs. Harvey yawned.

"I think it's that crazy Indian blood in Bernice," continued Marjorie. "Maybe she's a reversion to type. Indian women all just sat round and never said anything."

"Go to bed, you silly child," laughed Mrs. Harvey. "I wouldn't have told you that if I'd thought you were going to remember it. And I think most of your ideas are perfectly idiotic," she finished sleepily.

There was another silence, while Marjorie considered whether or not convincing her mother was worth the trouble. People over forty can seldom be permanently convinced of anything. At eighteen our convictions are hills from which we look; at forty-five they are caves in which we hide.

Having decided this, Marjorie said good night. When she came out into the hall it was quite empty.

III

While Marjorie was breakfasting late next day Bernice came into the room with a rather formal good morning, sat down opposite, stared intently over and slightly moistened her lips.

"What's on your mind?" inquired Marjorie, rather puzzled.

Bernice paused before she threw her hand-grenade.

"I heard what you said about me to your mother last night."

Marjorie was startled, but she showed only a faintly heightened color and her voice was quite even when she spoke.

"Where were you?"

"In the hall. I didn't mean to listen—at first."

After an involuntary look of contempt Marjorie dropped her eyes and became very interested in balancing a stray corn-flake on her finger.

"I guess I'd better go back to Eau Claire—if I'm such a nuisance." Bernice's lower lip was trembling violently and she continued on a wavering note: "I've tried to be nice, and—and I've been first neglected and then insulted. No one ever visited me and got such treatment."

Marjorie was silent.

"But I'm in the way, I see. I'm a drag on you. Your friends don't like me." She paused, and then remembered another one of her grievances. "Of course I was furious last week when you tried to hint to me that that dress was unbecoming. Don't you think I know how to dress myself?"

"No," murmured Marjorie less than half-aloud.

"What?"

"I didn't hint anything," said Marjorie succinctly. "I said, as I remember, that it was better to wear a becoming dress three times straight than to alternate it with two frights."

"Do you think that was a very nice thing to say?"

"I wasn't trying to be nice." Then after a pause: "When do you want to go?"

Bernice drew in her breath sharply.

"Oh!" It was a little half-cry.

Marjorie looked up in surprise.

"Didn't you say you were going?"

"Yes, but—"

"Oh, you were only bluffing!"

They stared at each other across the breakfast-table for a moment. Misty waves were passing before Bernice's eyes, while Marjorie's face wore that rather hard expression that she used when slightly intoxicated undergraduates were making love to her.

"So you were bluffing," she repeated as if it were what she might have expected.

Bernice admitted it by bursting into tears. Marjorie's eyes showed boredom.

"You're my cousin," sobbed Bernice. "I'm v-v-visiting you. I was to stay a month, and if I go home my mother will know and she'll wah-wonder—"

Marjorie waited until the shower of broken words collapsed into little sniffles.

"I'll give you my month's allowance," she said coldly, "and you can spend this last week anywhere you want. There's a very nice hotel—"

Bernice's sobs rose to a flute note, and rising of a sudden she fled from the room.

An hour later, while Marjorie was in the library absorbed in composing one of those non-committal, marvellously elusive letters that only a young girl can write, Bernice reappeared, very red-eyed and consciously calm. She cast no glance at Marjorie but took a book at random from the shelf and sat down as if to read. Marjorie seemed absorbed in her letter and continued writing. When the clock showed noon Bernice closed her book with a snap.

"I suppose I'd better get my railroad ticket."

This was not the beginning of the speech she had rehearsed up-stairs, but as Marjorie was not getting her cues—wasn't urging her to be reasonable; it's all a mistake—it was the best opening she could muster.

"Just wait till I finish this letter," said Marjorie without looking round. "I want to get it off in the next mail."

After another minute, during which her pen scratched busily, she turned round and relaxed with an air of "at your service." Again Bernice had to speak.

"Do you want me to go home?"

"Well," said Marjorie, considering, "I suppose if you're not having a good time you'd better go. No use being miserable."

"Don't you think common kindness—"

"Oh, please don't quote 'Little Women'!" cried Marjorie impatiently. "That's out of style."

"You think so?"

"Heavens, yes! What modern girl could live like those inane females?"

"They were the models for our mothers."

Marjorie laughed.

"Yes, they were—not! Besides, our mothers were all very well in their way, but they know very little about their daughters' problems."

Bernice drew herself up.

"Please don't talk about my mother."

Marjorie laughed.

"I don't think I mentioned her."

Bernice felt that she was being led away from her subject.

"Do you think you've treated me very well?"

"I've done my best. You're rather hard material to work with."

The lids of Bernice's eyes reddened.

"I think you're hard and selfish, and you haven't a feminine quality in you."

"Oh, my Lord!" cried Marjorie in desperation. "You little nut! Girls like you are responsible for all the tiresome colorless marriages; all those ghastly inefficiencies that pass as feminine qualities. What a blow it must be when a man with imagination marries the beautiful bundle of clothes that he's been building ideals around, and finds that she's just a weak, whining, cowardly mass of affectations!"

Bernice's mouth had slipped half open.

"The womanly woman!" continued Marjorie. "Her whole early life is occupied in whining criticisms of girls like me who really do have a good time."

Bernice's jaw descended farther as Marjorie's voice rose.

"There's some excuse for an ugly girl whining. If I'd been irretrievably ugly I'd never have forgiven by parents for bringing me into the world. But you're starting life without any handicap—" Marjorie's little fist clenched. "If you expect me to weep with you you'll be disappointed. Go or stay, just as you like." And picking up her letters she left the room.

Bernice claimed a headache and failed to appear at luncheon. They had a matinée date for the afternoon, but the headache persisting, Marjorie made explanation to a not very downcast boy. But when she returned late in the afternoon she found Bernice with a strangely set face waiting for her in her bedroom.

"I've decided," began Bernice without preliminaries, "that maybe you're right about things—possibly not. But if you'll tell me why your friends aren't—aren't interested in me I'll see if I can do what you want me to."

Marjorie was at the mirror shaking down her hair.

"Do you mean it?"

"Yes."

"Without reservations? Will you do exactly what I say?"

"Well, I—"

"Well nothing! Will you do exactly as I say?"

"If they're sensible things."

"They're not! You're no case for sensible things."

"Are you going to make—to recommend—"

"Yes, everything. If I tell you to take boxing-lessons you'll have to do it. Write home and tell your mother you're going to stay another two weeks."

"If you'll tell me—"

"All right—I'll just give you a few examples now. First, you have no ease of manner. Why? Because you're never sure about your personal appearance. When a girl feels that she's perfectly groomed and dressed she can forget that part of her. That's charm. The more parts of yourself you can afford to forget the more charm you have."

"Don't I look all right?"

"No; for instance, you never take care of your eyebrows. They're black and lustrous, but by leaving them straggly they're a blemish. They'd be beautiful if you'd take care of them in one-tenth the time you take doing nothing. You're going to brush them so that they'll grow straight."

Bernice raised the brows in question.

"Do you mean to say that men notice eyebrows?"

"Yes—subconsciously. And when you go home you ought to have your teeth straightened a little. It's almost imperceptible, still—"

"But I thought," interrupted Bernice in bewilderment, "that you despised little dainty feminine things like that."

"I hate dainty minds," answered Marjorie. "But a girl has to be dainty in person. If she looks like a million dollars she can talk about Russia, ping-pong, or the League of Nations and get away with it."

"What else?"

"Oh, I'm just beginning! There's your dancing."

"Don't I dance all right?"

"No, you don't—you lean on a man; yes, you do—ever so slightly. I noticed it when we were dancing together yesterday. And you dance standing up straight instead of bending over a little. Probably some old lady on the side-line once told you that you looked so dignified that way. But except with a very small girl it's much harder on the man, and he's the one that counts."

"Go on." Bernice's brain was reeling.

"Well, you've got to learn to be nice to men who are sad birds. You look as if you'd been insulted whenever you're thrown with any except the most popular boys. Why, Bernice, I'm cut in on every few feet—and who does most of it? Why, those very sad birds. No girl can afford to neglect them. They're the big part of any crowd. Young boys too shy to talk are the very best conversational practice. Clumsy boys are the best dancing practice. If you can follow them and yet look graceful you can follow a baby tank across a barb-wire sky-scraper."

Bernice sighed profoundly, but Marjorie was not through.

"If you go to a dance and really amuse, say, three sad birds that dance with you; if you talk so well to them that they forget they're stuck with you, you've done something. They'll come back next time, and gradually so many sad birds will dance with you that the attractive boys will see there's no danger of being stuck—then they'll dance with you."

"Yes," agreed Bernice faintly. "I think I begin to see."

"And finally," concluded Marjorie, "poise and charm will just come. You'll wake up some morning knowing you've attained it, and men will know it too."

Bernice rose.

"It's been awfully kind of you—but nobody's ever talked to me like this before, and I feel sort of startled."

Marjorie made no answer but gazed pensively at her own image in the mirror.

"You're a peach to help me," continued Bernice.

Still Marjorie did not answer, and Bernice thought she had seemed too grateful.

"I know you don't like sentiment," she said timidly.

Marjorie turned to her quickly.

"Oh, I wasn't thinking about that. I was considering whether we hadn't better bob your hair."

Bernice collapsed backward upon the bed.

IV

On the following Wesnesday evening there was a dinner-dance at the country club. When the guests strolled in Bernice found her place-card with a slight feeling of irritation. Though at her right sat G. Reece Stoddard, a most desirable and distinguished young bachelor, the all-important left held only Charley Paulson. Charley lacked height, beauty, and social shrewdness, and in her new enlightenment Bernice decided that his only qualification to be her partner was that he had never been stuck with her. But this feeling of irritation left with the last of the soup-plates, and Marjorie's specific instruction came to her. Swallowing her pride she turned to Charley Paulson and plunged.

"Do you think I ought to bob my hair, Mr. Charley Paulson?"

Charley looked up in surprise.

"Why?"

"Because I'm considering it. It's such a sure and easy way of attracting attention."

Charley smiled pleasantly. He could not know this had been rehearsed. He replied that he didn't know much about bobbed hair. But Bernice was there to tell him.

"I want to be a society vampire, you see," she announced coolly, and went on to inform him that bobbed hair was the necessary prelude. She added that she wanted to ask his advice, because she had heard he was so critical about girls.

Charley, who knew as much about the psychology of women as he did of the mental states of Buddhist contemplatives, felt vaguely flattered.

"So I've decided," she continued, her voice rising slightly, "that early next week I'm going down to the Sevier Hotel barber-shop, sit in the first chair, and get my hair bobbed." She faltered, noticing that the people near her had paused in their conversation and were listening; but after a confused second Marjorie's coaching told, and she finished her paragraph to the vicinity at large. "Of course I'm charging admission, but if you'll all come down and encourage me I'll issue passes for the inside seats."

There was a ripple of appreciative laughter, and under cover of it G. Reece Stoddard leaned over quickly and said close to her ear: "I'll take a box right now."

She met his eyes and smiled as if he had said something surpassingly brilliant.

"Do you believe in bobbed hair?" asked G. Reece in the same undertone.

"I think it's unmoral," affirmed Bernice gravely. "But, of

course, you've either got to amuse people or feed 'em or shock 'em." Marjorie had culled this from Oscar Wilde. It was greeted with a ripple of laughter from the men and a series of quick, intent looks from the girls. And then as though she had said nothing of wit or moment Bernice turned again to Charley and spoke confidentially in his ear.

"I want to ask you your opinion of several people. I imagine you're a wonderful judge of character."

Charley thrilled faintly—paid her a subtle compliment by overturning her water.

Two hours later, while Warren McIntyre was standing passively in the stag line abstractedly watching the dancers and wondering whither and with whom Marjorie had disappeared, an unrelated perception began to creep slowly upon him—a perception that Bernice, cousin to Marjorie, had been cut in on several times in the past five minutes. He closed his eyes, opened them and looked again. Several minutes back she had been dancing with a visiting boy, a matter easily accounted for; a visiting boy would know no better. But now she was dancing with some one else, and there was Charley Paulson headed for her with enthusiastic determination in his eye. Funny—Charley seldom danced with more than three girls an evening.

Warren was distinctly surprised when—the exchange having been effected—the man relieved proved to be none other than G. Reece Stoddard himself. And G. Reece seemed not at all jubilant at being relieved. Next time Bernice danced near, Warren regarded her intently. Yes, she was pretty, distinctly pretty; and to-night her face seemed really vivacious. She had that look that no woman, however histrionically proficient, can successfully counterfeit—she looked as if she were having a good time. He liked the way she had her hair arranged, wondered if it was brilliantine that made it glisten so. And that dress was becoming—a dark red that set off her shadowy eyes and high coloring. He remembered that he had thought her pretty when she first came to town, before he had realized that she was dull. Too bad she was dull—dull girls unbearable—certainly pretty though.

His thoughts zigzagged back to Marjorie. This disappearance would be like other disappearances. When she reappeared he would demand where she had been—would be told emphatically that it was none of his business. What a pity she was so sure of him! She basked in the knowledge that no other girl in town interested him; she defied him to fall in love with Genevieve or Roberta.

Warren sighed. The way to Marjorie's affections was a labyrinth indeed. He looked up. Bernice was again dancing with the visiting boy. Half unconsciously he took a step out from the stag line in her direction, and hesitated. Then he said to himself that it was charity. He walked toward her—collided suddenly with G. Reece Stoddard.

"Pardon me," said Warren.

But G. Reece had not stopped to apologize. He had again cut in on Bernice.

That night at one o'clock Marjorie, with one hand on the electric-light switch in the hall, turned to take a last look at Bernice's sparkling eyes.

"So it worked?"

"Oh, Marjorie, yes!" cried Bernice.

"I saw you were having a gay time."

"I did! The only trouble was that about midnight I ran short of talk. I had to repeat myself—with different men of course. I hope they won't compare notes."

"Men don't," said Marjorie, yawning, "and it wouldn't matter if they did—they'd think you were even trickier."

She snapped out the light, and as they started up the stairs Bernice grasped the banister thankfully. For the first time in her life she had been danced tired.

"You see," said Marjorie at the top of the stairs, "one man sees another man cut in and he thinks there must be something there. Well, we'll fix up some new stuff to-morrow. Good night."

"Good night."

As Bernice took down her hair she passed the evening before her in review. She had followed instructions exactly. Even when Charley Paulson cut in for the eighth time she had simulated delight and had apparently been both interested and flattered. She had not talked about the weather or Eau Claire or automobiles or her school, but had confined her conversation to me, you, and us.

But a few minutes before she fell asleep a rebellious thought was churning drowsily in her brain—after all, it was she who had done it. Marjorie, to be sure, had given her her conversation, but then Marjorie got much of her conversation out of things she read. Bernice had bought the red dress, though she had never valued it highly before Marjorie dug it out of her trunk—and her own voice had said the words, her own lips had smiled, her own feet had danced. Marjorie nice girl—vain, though—nice evening—nice boys—like Warren—Warren—Warren—what's-his-name—Warren—

She fell asleep.

V

To Bernice the next week was a revelation. With the feeling that people really enjoyed looking at her and listening to her came the foundation of self-confidence. Of course there were numerous mistakes at first. She did not know, for instance, that Draycott Deyo was studying for the ministry; she was unaware that he had cut in on her because he thought she was a quiet, reserved girl. Had she known these things she would not have treated him to the line which began "Hello, Shell Shock!" and continued with the bathtub story—"It takes a frightful lot of energy to fix my hair in the summer—there's so much of it—so I always fix it first and powder my face and put on my hat; then I get into the bathtub, and dress afterward. Don't you think that's the best plan?"

Though Draycott Deyo was in the throes of difficulties concerning baptism by immersion and might possibly have seen a connection, it must be admitted that he did not. He considered feminine bathing an immoral subject, and gave her some of his ideas on the depravity of modern society.

But to offset that unfortunate occurrence Bernice had several signal successes to her credit. Little Otis Ormonde pleaded off from a trip East and elected instead to follow her with a puppylike devotion, to the amusement of his crowd and to the irritation of G. Reece Stoddard, several of whose afternoon calls Otis completely ruined by the disgusting tenderness of the glances he bent on Bernice. He even told her the story of the two-by-four and the dressing-room to show her how frightfully mistaken he and every one else had been in their first judgment of her. Bernice laughed off that incident with a slight sinking sensation.

Of all Bernice's conversation perhaps the best known and most universally approved was the line about the bobbing of her hair.

"Oh, Bernice, when you goin' to get the hair bobbed?"

"Day after to-morrow maybe," she would reply, laughing.

"Will you come and see me? Because I'm counting on you, you know."

"Will we? You know! But you better hurry up."

Bernice, whose tonsorial intentions were strictly dishonorable, would laugh again.

"Pretty soon now. You'd be surprised."

But perhaps the most significant symbol of her success was the gray car of the hypercritical Warren McIntyre, parked daily in front of the Harvey house. At first the parlor-maid was distinctly startled when he asked for Bernice instead of Marjorie; after a week of it she told the cook that Miss Bernice had gotta holda Miss Marjorie's best fella.

And Miss Bernice had. Perhaps it began with Warren's desire to rouse jealousy in Marjorie; perhaps it was the familiar though unrecognized strain of Marjorie in Bernice's conversation; perhaps it was both of these and something of sincere attraction besides. But somehow the collective mind of the younger set knew within a week that Marjorie's most reliable beau had made an amazing face-about and was giving an indisputable rush to Marjorie's guest. The question of the moment was how Marjorie would take it. Warren called Bernice on the 'phone twice a day, sent her notes, and they were frequently seen together in his roadster, obviously engrossed in one of those tense, significant conversations as to whether or not he was sincere.

Marjorie on being twitted only laughed. She said she was mighty glad that Warren had at last found some one who appreciated him. So the younger set laughed, too, and guessed that Marjorie didn't care and let it go at that.

One afternoon, when there were only three days left of her visit, Bernice was waiting in the hall for Warren, with whom she was going to a bridge party. She was in rather a blissful mood, and when Marjorie—also bound for the party—appeared beside her and began casually to adjust her hat in the mirror, Bernice was utterly unprepared for anything in the nature of a clash. Marjorie did her work very coldly and succinctly in three sentences.

"You may as well get Warren out of your head," she said coldly.

"What?" Bernice was utterly astounded.

"You may as well stop making a fool of yourself over Warren McIntyre. He doesn't care a snap of his fingers about you."

For a tense moment they regarded each other—Marjorie

scornful, aloof; Bernice astounded, half-angry, half-afraid. Then two cars drove up in front of the house and there was a riotous honking. Both of them gasped faintly, turned, and side by side hurried out.

All through the bridge party Bernice strove in vain to master a rising uneasiness. She had offended Marjorie, the sphinx of sphinxes. With the most wholesome and innocent intentions in the world she had stolen Marjorie's property. She felt suddenly and horribly guilty. After the bridge game, when they sat in an informal circle and the conversation became general, the storm gradually broke. Little Otis Ormonde inadvertently precipitated it.

"When you going back to kindergarten, Otis?" some one had asked.

"Me? Day Bernice gets her hair bobbed."

"Then your education's over," said Marjorie quickly. "That's only a bluff of hers. I should think you'd have realized."

"That a fact?" demanded Otis, giving Bernice a reproachful glance.

Bernice's ears burned as she tried to think up an effectual comeback. In the face of this direct attack her imagination was paralyzed.

"There's a lot of bluffs in the world," continued Marjorie quite pleasantly. "I should think you'd be young enough to know that, Otis."

"Well," said Otis, "maybe so. But gee! With a line like Bernice's—"

"Really?" yawned Marjorie. "What's her latest bon mot?"

No one seemed to know. In fact, Bernice, having trifled with her muse's beau, had said nothing memorable of late.

"Was that really all a line?" asked Roberta curiously.

Bernice hesitated. She felt that wit in some form was demanded of her, but under her cousin's suddenly frigid eyes she was completely incapacitated.

"I don't know," she stalled.

"Splush!" said Marjorie. "Admit it!"

Bernice saw that Warren's eyes had left a ukulele he had been tinkering with and were fixed on her questioningly.

"Oh, I don't know!" she repeated steadily. Her cheeks were glowing.

"Splush!" remarked Marjorie again.

"Come through, Bernice," urged Otis. "Tell her where to get off."

Bernice Bobs Her Hair

Bernice looked round again—she seemed unable to get away from Warren's eyes.

"I like bobbed hair," she said hurriedly, as if he had asked her a question, "and I intend to bob mine."

"When?" demanded Marjorie.

"Any time."

"No time like the present," suggested Roberta.

Otis jumped to his feet.

"Good stuff!" he cried. "We'll have a summer bobbing party. Sevier Hotel barber-shop, I think you said."

In an instant all were on their feet. Bernice's heart throbbed violently.

"What?" she gasped.

Out of the group came Marjorie's voice, very clear and contemptuous.

"Don't worry—she'll back out!"

"Come on, Bernice!" cried Otis, starting toward the door.

Four eyes—Warren's and Marjorie's—stared at her, challenged her, defied her. For another second she wavered wildly.

"All right," she said swiftly, "I don't care if I do."

An eternity of minutes later, riding down-town through the late afternoon beside Warren, the others following in Roberta's car close behind, Bernice had all the sensations of Marie Antoinette bound for the guillotine in a tumbrel. Vaguely she wondered why she did not cry out that it was all a mistake. It was all she could do to keep from clutching her hair with both hands to protect it from the suddenly hostile world. Yet she did neither. Even the thought of her mother was no deterrent now. This was the test supreme of her sportsmanship, her right to walk unchallenged in the starry heaven of popular girls.

Warren was moodily silent, and when they came to the hotel he drew up at the curb and nodded to Bernice to precede him out. Roberta's car emptied a laughing crowd into the shop, which presented two bold plate-glass windows to the street.

Bernice stood on the curb and looked at the sign, Sevier Barber-Shop. It was a guillotine indeed, and the hangman was the first barber, who, attired in a white coat and smoking a cigarette, leaned nonchalantly against the first chair. He must have heard of her; he must have been waiting all week, smoking eternal cigarettes beside that portentous, too-often-mentioned first chair. Would they blindfold her? No, but they would tie a white cloth round her neck lest any of her blood—nonsense—hair—should get on her clothes.

"All right, Bernice," said Warren quickly.

With her chin in the air she crossed the sidewalk, pushed open the swinging screen-door, and giving not a glance to the uproarious, riotous row that occupied the waiting bench, went up to the first barber.

"I want you to bob my hair."

The first barber's mouth slid somewhat open. His cigarette dropped to the floor.

"Huh?"

"My hair—bob it!"

Refusing further preliminaries, Bernice took her seat on high. A man in the chair next to her turned on his side and gave her a glance, half lather, half amazement. One barber started and spoiled little Willy Schuneman's monthly haircut. Mr. O'Reilly in the last chair grunted and swore musically in ancient Gaelic as a razor bit into his cheek. Two bootblacks became wide-eyed and rushed for her feet. No, Bernice didn't care for a shine.

Outside a passer-by stopped and stared; a couple joined him; half a dozen small boys' noses sprang into life, flattened against the glass; and snatches of conversation borne on the summer breeze drifted in through the screen-door.

"Lookada long hair on a kid!"

"Where'd yuh get 'at stuff? 'At's a bearded lady he just finished shavin'."

But Bernice saw nothing, heard nothing. Her only living sense told her that this man in the white coat had removed one tortoise-shell comb and then another; that his fingers were fumbling clumsily with unfamiliar hairpins; that this hair, this wonderful hair of hers, was going—she would never again feel its long voluptuous pull as it hung in a dark-brown glory down her back. For a second she was near breaking down, and then the picture before her swam mechanically into her vision—Marjorie's mouth curling in a faint ironic smile as if to say: "Give up and get down! You tried to buck me and I called your bluff. You see you haven't got a prayer."

And some last energy rose up in Bernice, for she clenched her hands under the white cloth, and there was a curious narrowing of her eyes that Marjorie remarked on to some one long afterward.

Twenty minutes later the barber swung her round to face

the mirror, and she flinched at the full extent of the damage that had been wrought. Her hair was not curly, and now it lay in lank lifeless blocks on both sides of her suddenly pale face. It was ugly as sin—she had known it would be ugly as sin. Her face's chief charm had been a Madonna-like simplicity. Now that was gone and she was—well, frightfully mediocre—not stagy; only ridiculous, like a Greenwich Villager who had left her spectacles at home.

As she climbed down from the chair she tried to smile—failed miserably. She saw two of the girls exchange glances; noticed Marjorie's mouth curved in attenuated mockery—and that Warren's eyes were suddenly very cold.

"You see"—her words fell into an awkward pause—"I've done it."

"Yes, you've—done it," admitted Warren.

"Do you like it?"

There was a half-hearted "Sure" from two or three voices, another awkward pause, and then Marjorie turned swiftly and with serpentlike intensity to Warren.

"Would you mind running me down to the cleaners?" she asked. "I've simply got to get a dress there before supper. Roberta's driving right home and she can take the others."

Warren stared abstractedly at some infinite speck out the window. Then for an instant his eyes restly coldly on Bernice before they turned to Marjorie.

"Be glad to," he said slowly.

VI

Bernice did not fully realize the outrageous trap that had been set for her until she met her aunt's amazed glance just before dinner.

"Why, Bernice!"

"I've bobbed it, Aunt Josephine."

"Why, child!"

"Do you like it?"

"Why, Ber-nice!"

"I suppose I've shocked you."

"No, but what'll Mrs. Deyo think to-morrow night? Bernice, you should have waited until after the Deyo's dance—you should have waited if you wanted to do that."

"It was sudden, Aunt Josephine. Anyway, why does it matter to Mrs. Deyo particularly?"

"Why, child," cried Mrs. Harvey, "in her paper on 'The

Foibles of the Younger Generation' that she read at the last meeting of the Thursday Club she devoted fifteen minutes to bobbed hair. It's her pet abomination. And the dance is for you and Marjorie!"

"I'm sorry."

"Oh, Bernice, what'll your mother say? She'll think I let you do it."

"I'm sorry."

Dinner was an agony. She had made a hasty attempt with a curling-iron, and burned her finger and much hair. She could see that her aunt was both worried and grieved, and her uncle kept saying, "Well, I'll be darned!" over and over in a hurt and faintly hostile tone. And Marjorie sat very quietly, intrenched behind a faint smile, a faintly mocking smile.

Somehow she got through the evening. Three boys called; Marjorie disappeared with one of them, and Bernice made a listless unsuccessful attempt to entertain the two others—sighed thankfully as she climbed the stairs to her room at half past ten. What a day!

When she had undressed for the night the door opened and Marjorie came in.

"Bernice," she said, "I'm awfully sorry about the Deyo dance. I'll give you my word of honor I'd forgotten all about it."

" 'Sall right," said Bernice shortly. Standing before the mirror she passed her comb slowly through her short hair.

"I'll take you down-town to-morrow," continued Marjorie, "and the hairdresser'll fix it so you'll look slick. I didn't imagine you'd go through with it. I'm really mighty sorry."

"Oh, 'sall right!"

"Still it's your last night, so I suppose it won't matter much."

Then Bernice winced as Marjorie tossed her own hair over her shoulders and began to twist it slowly into two long blond braids until in her cream-colored negligée she looked like a delicate painting of some Saxon princess. Fascinated, Bernice watched the braids grow. Heavy and luxurious they were, moving under the supple fingers like restive snakes—and to Bernice remained this relic and the curling-iron and a to-morrow full of eyes. She could see G. Reece Stoddard, who liked her, assuming his Harvard manner and telling his dinner partner that Bernice shouldn't have been allowed to go to the movies so much; she could see Draycott Deyo exchanging glances with his mother and then being conscientiously charitable to her. But then perhaps by to-morrow Mrs. Deyo would have heard the news; would send round an icy little note requesting that she fail to appear—and behind her back they would all laugh and know that Marjorie had made a fool of her; that her chance at beauty had been sacrificed to the jealous whim of a selfish girl. She sat down suddenly before the mirror, biting the inside of her cheek.

"I like it," she said with an effort. "I think it'll be becoming."

Marjorie smiled.

"It looks all right. For heaven's sake, don't let it worry you!"

"I won't."

"Good night, Bernice."

But as the door closed something snapped within Bernice. She sprang dynamically to her feet, clenching her hands, then swiftly and noiselessly crossed over to her bed and from underneath it dragged out her suitcase. Into it she tossed toilet articles and a change of clothing. Then she turned to her trunk and quickly dumped in two drawerfuls of lingerie and summer dresses. She moved quietly, but with deadly efficiency, and in three-quarters of an hour her trunk was locked and strapped and she was fully dressed in a becoming new travelling suit that Marjorie had helped her pick out.

Sitting down at her desk she wrote a short note to Mrs. Harvey, in which she briefly outlined her reasons for going. She sealed it, addressed it, and laid it on her pillow. She glanced at her watch. The train left at one, and she knew that if she walked down to the Marborough Hotel two blocks away she could easily get a taxicab.

Suddenly she drew in her breath sharply and an expression flashed into her eyes that a practised character reader might have connected vaguely with the set look she had worn in the barber's chair—somehow a development of it. It was quite a new look for Bernice—and it carried consequences.

She went stealthily to the bureau, picked up an article that lay there, and turning out all the lights stood quietly until her eyes became accustomed to the darkness. Softly she pushed open the door to Marjorie's room. She heard the quiet, even breathing of an untroubled conscience asleep.

She was by the bedside now, very deliberate and calm. She acted swiftly. Bending over she found one of the braids of Marjorie's hair, followed it up with her hand to the point nearest the head, and then holding it a little slack so that the sleeper would feel no pull, she reached down with the shears and severed it. With the pigtail in her hand she held her breath. Marjorie had muttered something in her sleep. Bernice deftly amputated the other braid, paused for an instant, and then flitted swiftly and silently back to her own room.

Down-stairs she opened the big front door, closed it carefully behind her, and feeling oddly happy and exuberant stepped off the porch into the moonlight, swinging her heavy grip like a shopping-bag. After a minute's brisk walk she discovered that her left hand still held the two blond braids. She laughed unexpectedly—had to shut her mouth hard to keep from emitting an absolute peal. She was passing Warren's house now, and on the impulse she set down her baggage, and swinging the braids like pieces of rope flung them at the wooden porch, where they landed with a slight thud. She laughed again, no longer restraining herself.

"Huh!" she giggled wildly. "Scalp the selfish thing!"

Then picking up her suitcase she set off at a half-run down the moonlit street.

Mendel Marantz–
Housewife

by David Freedman

"What is a landlord? A bore! He asks you one question all the time—Rent! What is rent? A fine you pay for being poor. What is poverty? Dirt—on the surface. What is riches? More dirt—under the surface. Everybody wants money. Money! What is money? A disease we like to catch but not to spread. Just wait, Zelde! The time will come! I'll be a landlord on Riverside Drive! We'll have our own home—"

"In the cemetery!" Zelde said bitterly.

"Not so fast," Mendel replied, sipping his tea. "Cheer up, Zelde! What is pessimism? A match. It burns the fingers. What is hope? A candle. It lights the way. You never can tell yet! What is life? A see-saw. Today you're poor and tomorrow—"

"You starve!" Zelde muttered, as she rubbed a shirt vigorously against the wash-board.

With a sudden impulse she slapped the shirt into the tub, dried her hands on the apron, and, resting her fists on her hips, turned to Mendel.

"Why shouldn't I be mad?" she began, replying to a previous question. "Here I stand like a fool scrubbing my life away, from morning till night-time, working like a horse, cooking, washing, sewing, cleaning and everything. And for what? For this I eloped with you from a rich father? Did you marry me—or hire me?"

"I stole you. Now I got to pay the penalty. What is love? A conquest. What is marriage? An inquest. Don't worry; your father was no fool. He made believe he didn't see us run away. We felt romantic—and he got off cheap! What is romance? Soap-bubbles. They look nice, but taste rotten."

"Never mind! Mister Mendel Marantz, I know you too good. You talk a lot to make me forget what I was saying. But this whole business must come to a finish right here and there!

"You talked into yourself you're a great man, so you don't

want to work and you don't want to listen. Sarah sweats in the factory, Hymie peddles papers, Nathan works by the telegrams. And what do you do? You sit like a king and drink tea and make jokes—and nothing! I betcha you're waiting Jakie, Lena and Sammy should grow up so you'll send them to work for you too!"

Mendel shrugged his shoulders.

"What's a woman's tongue? A little dog's tail. It wags too much!"

"I know what I talk. You hate work like poison. You like better to smoke a cigaret and close your eyes and invent schemes how to get rich quick. But you'll get crazy quicker!"

"Zelde, you're a old woman. You don't understand. All I need is one drop of luck and that drop will sweeten our whole ocean of troubles. If only one of my inventions succeeds, none of us will have to work. Then Sarah will have dowry. What is dowry? Every man's price. And we'll move out of the fish-market. What is success? Fifth Avenue. What is failure? Fifth floor.

"Someday, you'll see. I'll be president of the Refillable Can Company and save the world millions in tin. Just wait!"

"And who'll buy bread in the meantime? Mendel, remember what I tell you. Knock out this craziness from your head. Forget about this can business!"

Mendel's dignity was roused.

"Crazy! That's what you all are! You and all your relatives think I got water on the brain!" He pointed with conviction to his brow. "But up here is the refillable can. Zelde, you see it? It's in the brain, the whole scheme. Up here is full with ideas, plans and machinery. Thinking, scheming, planning all the time. It don't let me sleep. It don't let me eat. It don't let me work. And I should forget it—ah?

"You're all jealous because God was good to me. He gave your brother Morris a shoe factory, your cousin Joe He gave a real estate, your sister Dora a rich husband. But God gave me *brains*—and that none of you got!"

Mendel paced the floor excitedly.

Zelde stood silent and bit her lip. For years she had heard the same flow of rhetoric, the same boast of intellect, and the same trust in luck. The net result was always an evasion of work, and the responsibility shifted back to her and the children.

Mendel Marantz had brains, all right. Otherwise, how could he have existed so long without working?

He always confused her with clever phrases and blurred the issue by creating fictitious ones. And he always succeeded in infecting her with his dreams, until she let him dream on while she did the work. It was that way when they had the candy-stand which her brother Gershon bought for them; it was that way when they kept a vegetable-store which sister Dora financed and later reduced to a push-cart; and it was that way now when they had nothing.

By trade a mechanic, by inclination an inventor, and by nature a dreamer, Mendel abhorred the sordid commonplaces of labor and dreaded the yoke of routine. He had been everything from an insurance agent to a night watchman in rapid succession, and had invented at least a hundred different devices for the betterment of civilization while changing jobs. None of these inventions had as yet received proper recognition, least of all from Zelde. But that could not discourage him to such a point as to drive him to work.

He really believed in his powers. That was the tragedy of it. All geniuses have an unalterable faith in their greatness. But so have most cranks. And Zelde was not sure as to which of the two species Mendel belonged.

She was sure of one thing—that the family was hovering perilously near the brink. A single feather added to its burdens and it would topple over. Mendel might take it lightly, but she knew better. She had seen families in that neighborhood crumble to ruin over night. She had known many who—like Mendel—started as harmless dreamers, hopeful idlers, and ended—God forbid—as gamblers, drunkards, and worse.

"How was it with Reznick? Every day he had a scheme to make millions while his wife got sick working in the shop. She died working, and the children went to an orphan asylum and he still wanted to make millions. So he made a corner on the coffee-market and he lost everything what everybody else had, and the only way they could stop him from signing checks with Rockefeller's name was to send him to Bellevue.

"Or Dittenfass? Wasn't he the picture of Mendel? Didn't he hate work like poison, and didn't he pay for it? He thought he was smarter from the rest. Didn't his wife used to told him, 'Dittenfass, look out!'? But he laughed only. He looked out for himself only. And one day she threw in his eyes vitriol! That's what she threw in his eyes, and then he couldn't look any more!

"You can't be too smart. Didn't Karneol try? And it's two

years she's waitin' already with swollen eyes he should come back. But he's got to serve three more.

"The best smartness is to do a day's work. If you wait it shall happen miracles—it happens! But the wrong way!"

Zelde knew. She wished she didn't know.

"Maybe you can invent something to make you work," she offered as a possible solution. "Somebody else with your brains could make a fortune. Why don't you make at least a living?"

"Brains make ideas; fools can make money. That's why your relatives are rich. What is business? Blind man's bluff. They shut your eyes and open your pockets!"

"Again you mix me up," she said warily, sensing this new attempt to befuddle the issue. "What's the result from all this? You joke and we starve. It's lucky Sarah works. If not, we would all be thrown out in the street, already."

At this moment Sarah entered. She was pale and tired from the climb of stairs. She dropped her hat languidly on the couch and sank into a chair.

Zelde was too surprised to speak. It was only one-thirty. She never expected Sarah before six. An ominous thought flitted through her mind. She looked anxiously at her daughter. Sarah's gaze shifted to the floor.

An oppressive silence gathered over them. Then Sarah tried to mumble something. But Zelde understood without hearing. Her heart had told her.

"It's slack! Everybody laid off. Sarah, too!"

What she had dreaded most had happened. The family of Marantz was now over the brink. Zelde stood crushed by the thought of the morrow. Sarah sat staring vacantly, her chin against her clenched hand. Mendel stopped smoking to appear less conspicuous.

Four female eyes detected him, however, and scorched him with their gaze.

The handwriting on the wall was unnecessarily large.

Mendel Marantz knew that his crisis was at hand.

Zelde spoke.

"That settles it. Either tomorrow you go to work or go altogether! Yessir! You, I mean, mister!"

Mendel had faced crises before. Some he had overcome with a jest, others with a promise, still others with a pretence at work until the novelty wore off. But there was a grimness in Zelde's manner this time that looked fatal. Nothing but a permanent job and lifelong drudgery could save him now. But that would also destroy him.

Tying him down to a position was like hitching a lion to a cart. His mind could not travel on tracks. It was too restive and spirited. He could never repeat an act without discovering how much easier it might be done by machinery, and immediately he set himself to invent the necessary machine. That was why he could not be a tailor. After he once threaded a needle, he started to devise a simple instrument for doing it, and in the meantime lost his job. And that happened in every case.

His head was so full of ideas that he often had to stand still to keep his balance. His mind sapped all of his powers and left him powerless for work. In order to work he would have to stop thinking. He might just as well stop living. Idleness was as essential a part of his make-up as industry was of Zelde's.

"I wasn't made for work," he said with finality. "I mean— for just plain work. Some people work with their feet, others with their hands. I work with my head. You don't expect I shall sit like Simon, the shoemaker, every day, and hit nails till I get consumption. One—two—three, I invent a machinery which hits nails, cuts leather, fits heels, makes patches, and I sit down and laugh on the world. I can't work like others, just as others can't work like me!"

"You can make me believe night is day and black is white, but it won't help you. It's a new rule in this house from today on—those who work, eat; those who don't, don't. If you think you can invent food, go ahead. So long I live my children is not going to starve. From today on I'm the father from this family. If you don't want to go to work—I will!"

Mendel was skeptical.

"What is a woman?" he thought. "A lot of thunder, but a little rain."

Still, the shower was more drenching than he supposed.

"Tomorrow morning I go back to be a dressmaker by fancy dresses. Sarah, you come with me. I learn you a real trade."

Then she turned to Mendel with a sneer.

"You thought I play around in the house, didn't you? All right! Now you stay home and play like I did. You want to eat? Cook, yourself. You think in the house it's easy? You'll find out different. Send the children to school, go up on the roof to hang clothes, run down with the garbage five floors, buy groceries, wash underwear, mend stockings, press shirts, scrub floors—go on! Have a good time, and I'll pay the bills!"

Mendel admitted that Zelde had worn for some time the family trousers, but he believed that he still wore the belt. However, her inexorable decision disillusioned him. He admitted having been caught slightly off his guard. He had never suspected that a type of work existed so near him, into which he might be forced out of sheer necessity. Not that he intended to do it! But still—

"What is a woman?" he reconsidered. "Lightning. It's nice and bright till it hits you."

The next morning Mendel discovered perpetual motion. The children had taken possession of the house. He dodged flying pillows, tripped over upset furniture, slipped on greasy garbage from an overturned can, found salt in his coffee and something sharper on his seat. He kept constantly moving to avoid falling objects and fell into others. He had planned to have nothing to do with the house, but the house was having a great deal to do with him.

The youngsters seemed to be under the impression that with Zelde all law and order had passed away. Mendel found it hard work to change their minds. It was monotonous to spank Lena, then Jakie, then Sammy. Then over again. It would be better to send them off to school. But they had to be dressed and fed and washed for that!

He was tempted to snatch his hat and coat and leave the house. But what would he do in the streets?

He hesitated, gritted his teeth, and set to work by scrubbing Jakie's face till it resembled a carrot.

"What's a wife?" he muttered, and Lena started at the question. "A telescope! She makes you see stars!" And some soap got into his eye.

"Sammy, don't you never marry?" he exclaimed with a profound look of warning at the frightened little boy. "What is marriage? First a ring on the finger and later—on the neck. Lena, stop pulling Jakie's hair. She's like her mother. Don't do that, Sammy. A table-cloth ain't a handkerchief! Ai! Little children, little troubles; big children, big troubles. What is children? Life insurance. Some day they pay you back—when you're dead. But you like them anyhow. Such is life! You know it's tough, but you try it once, anyway.

"After all, what is life? A journey. What is death? The goal. What is man? A passenger. What is woman? Freight.

"Jakie, you bad boy! Don't cry, Lena. He didn't mean it. Here's an apple. Go to school. Sammy, get off the banister! Look out, children! It's a step missing down there! Who's crying? Jakie, give her back the apple! Did you ever hear such excitements? My goodness!"

Mendel, perspired, exhausted, sank into a chair.

"I'm working, after all," he noted with surprise. "If this lasts, I don't."

But the trials of Mendel Marantz had only begun. The sensation of womanhood did not thrill his bosom, and the charms of housekeeping failed to allure him. A home like a warehouse on moving-day tumbled about him. The beds were upset, the table and floor were littered with breakfast leavings, the cupboard was bare, the dishes were piled in the sink, the dust had gathered already as if cleaning were a lost art, and the general atmosphere was one of dejection, confusion, chaos. The magic touch of the housewife revealed itself by its absence.

Zelde had now proved to him conclusively that her presence and service were essential to his comfort. As if he had ever questioned the fact. Why did she go to all this trouble to drive home a point?

"Zelde, a glass tea," he used to say, and the tea stood steaming hot before him. "Zelde, it's a draft. Shut up the window," and presently the draft was gone.

"Zelde—" he would call, leaning back in his chair, but why torture himself with things that were no more?

That night when Zelde arrived, masculine and businesslike, through with work and ready for supper, she beheld a pitiful spectacle.

The house was in hopeless disorder. The children had managed that. The cat was on the table and Jakie was under it, while Lena kept him there with her foot. Sammy's eye had been darkened by a flying saucer which Hymie let go in a moment of abandon. Everything was where it should not be. The kitchen furniture had been moved into the dining room and the feather beds were in the wash-tub.

Mendel was nowhere within the range of Zelde's call.

"Where is papa?" she asked sharply, after calming the youngsters with her two convincing hands. "Everything is upside down. I betcha he didn't do a thing all day. My goodness, that man will make me crazy!"

A crashing sound as of dishes in hasty descent issued from the next room.

Zelde and her retinue rushed to the scene of disaster. With one foot in the sink and the other on the wash-tub Mendel Marantz was poised on high, searching through the closet. Dishes, pans, bottles and rags lay scattered in ruined fragments beneath him.

Zelde blazed.

"Gozlen!" she almost shrieked. "What do you want up there!"

Mendel steadied himself. His heart having missed a beat, he waited a moment, then answered quietly, "Iodin."

"What for iodin, what for?" She was still furious, but also a little anxious.

"A small scratch," he explained without moving. "My finger got caught—under the meat-chopper."

"Oi! You clumsy! And what's all the rags and the water on the floor?"

"To put by my side and my leg. I—slipped and—the gas-range fell on me. My ankle turned around. The soup was good and hot. Maybe you got something for burns?"

Zelde was a little less furious and a little more anxious.

"Then what are you climbing on the walls for? Go in bed. Go—you look broken in pieces!"

She sighed heavily and shook her head.

"After all, he's only a man," she soliloquized. "What can you expect? He don't know if he's alive!"

She continued to scold, but nursed him tenderly.

"How is it? You're a inventor, and you don't know how to light the gas without blowing up the house? A man who can't help nobody else can't help himself!"

After a pause she said, "Maybe I should stay home? Ah?"

"Maybe," he murmured weakly.

Zelde vacillated.

"So what'll be if I stay home?" she prodded.

"It'll be better."

"That I know, but what'll be with you?"

"I'll get well."

"And—?" She expected him not only to recover, but to reform.

"And if I get well I'll feel good. What is health? A garden. What is sickness? A grave. What is a good wife? A gardener. What is a bad wife? A grave-digger."

"He's as bad as ever," she thought.

She finally resolved, "It's not such a terrible! He won't die from it and we can't live from it. He'll learn a lesson and I'll earn a living."

And the experiment continued.

It was very hard on Mendel. It was harder on Sarah and hardest on Zelde. But time subdued Mendel's protests and improved his work.

Zelde was surprised at his altered attitude of gradual submission. It almost alarmed her. She had never really intended this radical change to last. She had expected Mendel to rebel more and more violently as time went on and finally to make a break for his freedom and exclaim, "I'm sick and tired of this slavery. I'm going to work!"

Instead he was getting actually to like it. By degrees Zelde found less to do in the house after her return from the shop. True, his work was crude and slovenly to her practiced eye. She never would have cleaned dishes as he did, with a whisk-broom, or swept dirt under the table, or boiled soup in a coffee-pot, or wiped the floor with a perfectly good skirt.

But withal, Mendel was doing things, and as his domestic craftsmanship improved, Zelde grew more disappointed and depressed. She felt that he was planning to displace her permanently. She pictured him bending over the wash-tub as she used to do; or arranging the dishes in the closet, which was once her favorite diversion; or scouring the pots and pans as only she knew how, and a genuine feeling of envy and longing seized her.

"Thief!" she was tempted to cry. "Go out from my kitchen! Give me back my apron and let alone my housework!"

For she had become nothing more than a boarder in that home, to be tolerated merely because she earned the rent. She saw the children only at supper-time, and they looked curiously at her as if they hardly recognized her.

At table all eyes were turned to pa.

"Papa, Sammy took my spoon!"

"Take his," Mendel decreed.

"Pa, I want some more meat!"

"Take mine."

"Pop, Lena stealed my bread!"

"Take hers."

"Pa-ah! The thoup ith too hot. I tan't eat it!" Jakie complained, and turned a bruised tongue to his father.

"Take some water from the sink," was Mendel's motherly advice.

Zelde felt like a stranger. They did not seem to know that she was present. She tried to interfere.

"Don't put water in soup, Jakie! Better blow on it."

But the little boy slipped down from the chair without noticing her, wriggled out from under the table, and soon returned, gaily carrying a cup of sink-water.

Her maternal instinct rebelled.

"No!" she said warningly, as Jakie tilted the cup over the plate of bean-soup.

But the child, with his eyes fixed on Mendel, poured the contents bravely.

Zelde slapped his hand, and the cup fell with a clatter. It was not a hard blow, but an impulsive one. It created a strained and awkward silence. Jakie burst into tears. He ran to Mendel and buried his little face in daddy's lap. Lena began to whimper in sympathy.

Something snapped in Zelde. Her appetite was gone. She rose and went into the bedroom and shut the door behind her.

She did not want them to hear her sobs.

It had all turned out so different!

Instead of driving Mendel to work she had driven herself into exile. Mendel the housewife was now further from ever getting a man's job than Mendel the idler had ever been. Zelde felt she had made a grave mistake. Rather should she have permitted him to idle and mope—he would have tired of it eventually—than that he should be wrongly occupied and contented.

If only she could undo what she had done, she'd be satisfied.

"After all, a house to manage is for a woman," she began, bent upon re-establishing the old order. "A man should do housework? It can make him crazy yet!"

"I believe you," Mendel conceded.

"It don't look like housework should agree with you," she observed.

"Looks is deceiving."

There was a pause. A good deal of understanding passed between them.

"Mendel, hard work will kill you yet," she insisted.

"So will idleness—in the long run. What is death? An appointment. You got to keep it some time."

"But you don't look good."

"I don't feel bad."

Zelde became a little dizzy. Did he mean to say that he intended to stick to housework? She tried to tempt him.

"Wouldn't you like, like you used to, to have nothing to do, and sit and cross your legs, and, without you should move, somebody should bring you hot tea?"

Mendel blew rings of smoke at the ceiling.

Zelde continued, scarcely breathing.

"And wouldn't you like to lie on the couch with your hands together behind your head and look on the sky from the window and dream what a great inventor you are?"

An impressive silence followed. On Mendel's face were fleeting traces of an inner struggle.

"And—I'll clean the house," she added softly to clear any doubts that he might still have.

Mendel shook his head.

"It'll be too hard for you," he said gallantly.

"It's not such a terrible!"

"I haven't the heart to let you," he complained feebly.

"You'll get over it."

His tone became firmer.

"No! Housework is not for a woman. Like the Masora says, 'Be good to your wife and give your children to eat.' That means a man should clean the house and cook for his children. What is a wife? A soldier. Her place is on the field. What is a husband? A general. His place is at home!"

Zelde was chagrined.

"So this is the future what you aimed for?" she chided. "To be a washerwoman and a porter! Pooh! You ought to be ashamed to look on my face! Think what people say! They don't know which is what! If I am the husband or if you are the wife or how!"

Mendel carefully rolled a new cigarette. There was a plaintive note in her anger. He could afford to be defiant.

"Didn't you make me to stay home and work? So! I'm working! What is work? Pleasure!— If you know how!"

And he struck a match.

Zelde sat down to avoid falling down.

"Work is pleasure," echoed through her mind like an explosion. Maybe solitary confinement at home every day had gone to his head. Or maybe—maybe—! She slowly repeated to herself his sally. "What is work? Pleasure!" and "What is pleasure?" she wondered. The shock of the answer almost made her scream.

So that was it! She had suspected something, but *that*

would never have occurred to her in a million years. Those floor-brushes that she found the other day under the bed, and the mop and the tin pail. They did not belong to the house. To whom *did* they belong? She had certainly seen them somewhere before. Now she knew! At the janitor's!

"No wonder he likes to stay home," she muttered to herself. "I should have knew; it's a bad sign if Mendel likes work all of a sudden!"

Her suspicions were still hypothetical, but fragments of evidence were fast falling in to shape an ominous and accusing picture.

One day, upon her return from work, Zelde found Mendel sitting near the window, restfully smoking a cigarette. His legs were crossed under his apron and his arms were folded over his lap. He gazed wistfully out upon the city.

Zelde looked about her in astonishment. The house was tidy, the kitchen spick and span, the wash dried and ironed, the floor freshly scrubbed. A model housewife would have envied the immaculate perfection of the work.

Zelde gasped. So early in the day and already through with all his work! And what work!

"Sarah, I wonder who did it," she finally said to her daughter when she had somewhat regained her composure.

Her groping suspicions now became a startling conviction. Evidence fairly shrieked at her from every corner.

"Only a woman could do this," she thought, overcome by the shock of the revelation.

"Who do you think?" Sarah asked innocently.

"Did you see the way she looks at me?" Zelde exclaimed with mounting fury. "No wonder she laughs in my face. No wonder she tells all the neighbors, 'Such a fool! She works and he plays!' No wonder!"

"What are you talking about?" Sarah inquired, bewildered.

"Never mind! Your father knows what I mean! *She* did it! Rifke! The janitor's wife! I know her, all right. She made eyes to Mister Mendel Marantz lots of times! She's older from me by four years, but she paints up like a sign and makes her hair Buster Brown and thinks the men die for her. Ask your father. He knows!"

Mendel sat dumbfounded. His eyes opened like mouths.

"Don't make believe you're innocent. I know you men too good," Zelde broke out violently. "I slave like a dog and that dirty old—" Tears of rage stifled her. But with a swift change of tone she added, her finger shaking under Mendel's nose,

"Mister Marantz, remember, you'll be sorry for this." And she walked out of the room.

Mendel was sorry for her. He turned a puzzled face to Sarah. "When the house was upside down she said I made her crazy. Now when it's fixed up she tried to make me crazy! What's a wife? An epidemic. If it don't break out here, it breaks out there!"

The next day Zelde fidgeted at her work. She was prompted to fling it aside, rush home, and catch them together—Mendel and Rifke—and pull out the old vixen's hair and scratch out her eyes. But she bided her time. Mendel was, no doubt, expecting a surprise attack and perhaps had warned his paramour to stay away.

Zelde decided to be wily. She would make believe that she had forgotten and forgiven. But how could she?

That night, on the landing of the fourth floor, she met Rifke coming down from the fifth. There were only two tenants on the fifth floor—Mrs. Peril Tzvack, a widow who hated Rifke and would never let her into her house, and Mendel Marantz. From which of the two was Rifke coming?

As Zelde entered her home the same neatness, the same cleanliness and smartness stung her sight. In fact, she herself could not have done better. To be honest—not even as good. The house was a mirror of spotlessness. It was so obviously the accomplishment of the wicked woman she had met on the stairs that Zelde spent a tortured and sleepless night.

She went to work the next morning with a splitting headache, and mists swam before her eyes as she tried to sew. Weird thoughts revolved in her mind. If it were only a question of Mendel, she would not hesitate a moment to leave him forever. But the children! A daughter of marriageable age and the tiny ones! What would people say? And even Mendel. True, there was no excuse—absolutely none—for his abominable treachery. She would never forgive him! Still, Rifke, that superannuated flirt, was the kind of woman that could turn any man's head! With that double chin of hers and the shaved neck and a dimple like a funnel in her cheek! That's what the men liked!

After all, Mendel was a helpless male, all alone in a house. He probably did not know the first thing about housekeeping and would have starved or been buried in dirt if he had not appealed to somebody to help him. And Rifke was just the type to take advantage of a defenceless man in such a predicament. She doubtless opened her eyes at him like two coal-scuttles, and pursed her lips—she had a way of doing it which gave the women of the neighborhood heart failure. And Mendel must have been grateful and kind to her for her assistance, and she must have mistaken his attitude for something else. She always misunderstood kindness from men.

So that's how Mendel managed to clean the house so well! And that's why work was pleasure to him! Judging by the amount and quality of the work Rifke was doing for him, their affection for each other must have developed to an alarming degree.

Zelde visualized the hateful scenes of faithlessness in which Mendel probably danced fawningly about Rifke, the fifty-three-year-old "vamp," who cleaned dishes and washed clothes for him as a reward. She must have nudged him with her elbow while she boiled the wash and said invitingly, "Mendel, dear, why are you blind to beauty?"

And Mendel, edging closer, must have answered, "What is beauty? Wine! The older it gets, the rarer it is!" Then pressing his cheek against hers, he undoubtedly added, with tenderness, "You're so fat! It's a pleasure to hold you around! What is a man? Dynamite. What is a woman? A burning match. What is passion? The explosion!"

"Stop it! Your whiskers tickle me," she probably replied with a coquettish laugh, and slapped him playfully over the hands with a rinsed shirt.

But she was only jesting, and was perhaps ecstatic with joy when Mendel courageously kissed her on the cheek despite her protests, and exclaimed, "What is a kiss? A smack for which you turn the other cheek!" And she probably turned it.

Then Rifke amorously rested her head on his chest and looked up with those devilish eyes of hers, and, linking her plump arms about his neck, she whispered, "Love me, Mendel, love me! I am yours!"

And Mendel, planting his feet more solidly to bear her weight, and carried away by the flames of desire, must have gripped her in his passionate embrace and murmured in a throaty voice, "What is love? A broom. It sweeps you away!"

"What's the matter with you, Zelde?" cried Marcus, the tailor, biting the thread from a seam. "You stitched the skirt to a sleeve and you're sewing up the neck of the waist!

"You look white like a ghost!"

Zelde drew herself up, as out of a lethargy.

"Eh! W—where am I? Oh!"

And her face sank into her palms.

Instantly there was a tumult in the shop.

A startled group of frightened men and women gathered about her.

But Zelde regained her self-control without aid, and pale and faint though she was, she smiled weakly to reassure them all.

"It's nothing. A dizziness. I'm better," she said. But Sarah insisted upon taking her home at once.

"That's right," Marcus advised. "Go home and take a hot tea with lemon. It'll sweat you out."

He added in an undertone to his neighbor, "It's a shame! Such a fine woman! She's got a husband who's a nix!"

Zelde refused to have Sarah accompany her home.

"We can't afford you shall lose a half day," she argued. But the real reason was that she did not wish her daughter to behold her father's infamy.

At eleven o'clock Zelde left. As she neared the house her breath became short and rapid. She stumbled several times going up the stairs. She stopped at the door.

Was it voices or was it her imagination?

No. Yes. It was. A man's voice, then a woman's laughter, then some—oh! She could stand it no longer. She broke wildly into the room and dislodged a bulky person who had been leaning against the door. Zelde stood electrified.

It was Rifke. And she was laughing in her face! And there was Mendel. And the janitor, too—Rifke's husband. And two men! With stovepipe hats and cutaways and spats! Detectives, no doubt! Brought by the janitor to catch his wife and arrest Mendel! Oh, heavens! And there was Morton, Mendel's nephew, a lawyer!

"Oi! A lawyer in the case!" she moaned to herself. "Then everything is lost!"

Zelde was ready to drop, but Mendel took her by the hand, and she heard him say, "This is my wife. It's all her fault. She drove me to it."

"We want you to come with us now," one of the strangers said to Mendel.

"What's the matter here, anyhow?" Zelde exclaimed at last.

"I got to go with these people," Mendel replied. "But you can ask—Rifke," he added significantly. "She knows all about it."

Mendel, his nephew and the two gentlemen departed before Zelde had time to protest. She turned with burning eyes to Rifke—the hussy!

"I wish they could take my husband where they take yours," Rifke began by way of explanation. "You don't know what kind of a husband you got. It's gonna be in all the papers. He did something. Those men what was here watched him, and when they seen it they jumped up like crazy."

"What did he do?" Zelde asked in great alarm. "I betcha you made him to do it."

"I? He says you made him. I only brought up the people. They knock by me in the door. They say, 'Do Mendel Marantz live here? Where is it?' So I bring them up."

"What for did you bring them up—what for? A blind one could see it's detectives!" Zelde muttered angrily.

"How shall I know it who they are? When they came in your husband turned white like milk. 'Are you the man which done it?' they ask him, and he says, shivering, 'Yes.'"

Zelde wrung her hands.

"What for did he say 'Yes'—what for?"

"Because it's true," Rifke explained.

"What's true?"

"That he done it."

"What did he done—what? You'll make me crazy yet. Why don't you tell me."

"But I told you already!"

"When did you told me—when? You're talkin' and talkin' and it don't come out nothing! What happened here? What did they want here? Why is your husband here? Why are you here? Why were they here? What's the matter here, altogether, anyway?"

"It's a whole lot the matter—with you!" Rifke exclaimed impatiently. "Come over here and look and maybe it'll open your eyes!"

She led the dazed Zelde into the kitchen.

"You see it?" Rifke asked triumphantly, pointing out a mass of wrinkled canvas in the middle of the room.

"What shall I see?" Zelde answered skeptically. "Rags, I see!"

"But under the rags!" Rifke insisted. She lifted the canvas. Zelde stood completely bewildered. Her eyes opened wide, then her face reddened. A feeling of indignation welled up in her.

"You can't make a fool from me!" she began at last with rising momentum. "What do you show me—what? An ashcan on wheels! What's that got to do with you and my husband? Don't think I don't know! You show me this, I should forget *that!*"

Rifke began to perspire. She mopped her face with her apron as she struggled to keep calm.

"You don't know what I'm talkin' about and I don't know what you're talkin' about. It's mixed up, everything! Where do you see a ash-can? This ain't a ash-can! It looks, maybe, like it. But it ain't. All my friends should have such ash-cans! It's a wonder in the world!"

Zelde's head was reeling.

"So what is it, I'm asking you?" she gasped helplessly.

"It's a whole business!" Rifke replied. "We seen it, my husband Shmeril and me and the people which was here. Your husband showed us. He winds up the can like a phonograph and it begins to play. The dishes go in dirty and they come out clean like after a bath. You see it? On these straps the dishes take a ride. They go in from the back and come out on the front. When it's finished the dishes, your husband opens the box—I thought a man will jump out from it—but it's only wheels and straps and wires and pipes inside! Did you ever?

"Then he pulls off the feet and the box sits down on the floor, and he takes out the straps from the back door and puts in such a board with bumps and brushes, and he turns the handle and the box rides around like a automobile and washes up the floor till it shines! I tell you the people was standing and looking—I thought their eyes would fall out!

"Then your husband stands up the box and puts back the feet and takes out the bumpy board and sticks in a whole machinery with pipes and wheels and winds up the machine and pumps in fresh water and throws in all the old clothes, and you hear inside such a noises, and then the clothes come out like frankfurters, clean and washed and ready to hang! Such a business! You don't have to work no more! It works itself! I wouldn't mind to have such a box by me!"

Zelde, dumb with amazement, gazed at the mute, ugly monster before her. She recognized the wheels from the old baby-carriage; the legs were from her kitchen chair; the handle from the stove. And now she remembered the can, the brushes, and the mops that Rifke had probably discarded, and that Mendel had used in the creation of this freak.

So this was the rival she had been jealous of, the usurper of her rights!

"It makes in five minutes what I do a whole day," Rifke

rambled along. "They call it such a fancy name—Combination House-Cleaner. It cleans everything. The strangers is from a company which goes to make millions cans like this.

"You're gonna be rich, Mrs. Marantz!

"Who would think from house-cleaning you could get rich! Here I'm cleaning houses for twenty-nine years and I never thought from such a scheme! You gotta have luck, I tell you!"

"And I thought all the time it was Rifke! Oi, Mendel, you must think I'm such a fool!"

"Forget it. If not for you I never would have did what I done. You made me to do it."

"I didn't, Mendel."

She added in a caressing tone:

"Your laziness did it, Mendel. You invented that machine because you were too lazy to work."

"What's a wife? An X-Ray. She knows you through and through!"

Fame for Mr. Beatty

by James Norman Hall

I

William C. Dow and company, wholesale drygoods merchants, occupied a fourteen story building covering half the block between Commercial and East River streets. The business offices of the firm were on the fourth floor. Here were to be found the sales manager with his staff, the manager of imports with his, the advertising manager with his. The remainder of the fourth floor, considerably more than half of it, was taken up by the accounting department, a miniature city laid out in orderly, rectangular fashion, with narrow passageways for streets and wire cages for houses, each of them six feet by six, each of them with its occupant. In one of the cages farthest from the main corridor was a man who had been in the employ of the Dow company for more than twenty years. His name was Herbert Beatty.

It would be difficult to describe Mr. Beatty in any vivid manner. To say that he was quietly dressed, that his linen was immaculate and his boots carefully polished, is not to distinguish him from thousands of other self-respecting bookkeepers. Observing him in a crowd—but this is unthinkable: the most curious observer of human nature, touching elbows with him in a crowd, would not have noticed him, unless—which is equally unthinkable—Mr. Beatty had been guilty of some act of gross and unusual conduct, and even then the eccentricity would have been remembered rather than the man himself.

He was a lonely man, without close friends or any living relatives, so far as he knew, and his life flowed on from year to year in unbroken monotony. Although he spent forty-five hours weekly in his little wire enclosure, he neither spoke nor thought of it as a cage. He entered it, six mornings out of seven, as willingly as a bee enters its hive, and much more punctually. Having dusted off his boots with a flannel cloth which he kept in a drawer, he slipped into his black alpaca office-coat. Then he marked out with a neat cross, in red ink, the date of the previous day on the calendar—two crosses on a Monday. Then he opened the ledgers in which he took such pride, and was immediately engrossed in his work. This was purely of a routine nature, as familiar to him as breathing, quite as necessary, and almost as instinctively performed. He was rarely disturbed, had no decisions to make and was never asked for his opinion about anything.

At twelve-thirty he went out to lunch. He patronized always the same white-tiled restaurant on East River Street, a large, clean, impersonal sort of place catering to the employees of the wholesale houses in the vicinity. An immense sign on the wall of this restaurant read: "We serve more than three-thousand lunches daily, between the hours of twelve and two." During the past ten years Mr. Beatty himself had alone been served with that number of lunches: three-thousand lettuce sandwiches, three-thousand pieces of custard pie, three-thousand glasses of milk. But although his order was the same, summer and winter, none of the waitresses ever remembered what it was or appeared to recognize him as an old patron.

In winter he spent the whole of his luncheon hour in this place reading the *Morning Post*. On fine days in summer, he would go, after his meal, to a small park near the City Hall, two blocks distant. There he would buy a bag of salted peanuts, and after eating a few of them would give the rest to the pigeons that frequented the square. They would eat out of his hand, perch on his outstretched arm, even on his head. He liked to think that they were his pigeons, and he enjoyed the moment of attention they brought him from other midday loungers in the park. When he had doled out the last of the peanuts, he dusted the salt from his fingers and sat down to enjoy his newspaper.

Mr. Beatty was one of the numberless army of men and women who have made possible the success of the modern American newspaper, whose reading is confined almost entirely to its columns. It amused him, instructed him, thought for him. He found there satisfaction for all his modest needs, spiritual and cultural. He turned first to the comic section, smiling over the adventures of Mutt and Jeff and the vicissitudes of the Gump family. These people were real to him, and he followed their fortunes closely from day to day. Next he read the editorial of Dr. Francis Crake whom he admired and respected as a philosopher of genius. Another feature of the *Morning Post* was the Enquirer's column. The enquirer sauntered daily through the streets, asking of four people, chosen more or less at random, some question of current interest. Their replies, together with a small photograph of each individual, were then printed in the column. Mr. Beatty's interest never waned in this feature of his favorite newspaper. Indeed, there was so much on every page to engage his attention that his luncheon hour passed in a flash of time. At twenty minutes past one he would leave the park and before the half-hour had struck was again at his desk and at work.

II

One sultry midsummer day while he was enjoying his usual noontime recreation in the park, a young man wearing horn-rimmed spectacles and with a camera slung over his shoulder sat down on the bench beside him. Mr. Beatty was not aware of this at the moment, for he was in the midst of Dr. Crake's editorial for the day: "Clothes as an Index of Personality." In three short paragraphs Dr. Crake had evolved his philosophy on this subject. "Show me a man who is slovenly in his dress and I will show you one that is slovenly in his morals. A clean collar is the index of a clean mind. It matters not how modest your income, or how humble your station in life, you cannot afford to be indifferent to the appearance you present to your fellow men. Neatness pays. It is investment at compound interest in the Bank of Success, and it will bring in dividends when you least expect them." So Dr. Crake in his first paragraph. Mr. Beatty heartily approved of these opinions and he thought, not without a touch of pride, that Dr. Crake would have approved of him.

Upon turning the page of his paper he noticed his companion on the bench. The young man nodded cordially.

"A scorcher, isn't it?" he said.

Mr. Beatty was slightly startled. It was not often that a stranger spoke to him.

"Yes, it *is* warm," he replied, a little apologetically, as though he were somehow to blame for the heat.

"Hottest day this summer," said the young man. "What do you suppose the thermometer at the *Morning Post* building registered at noon?"

"Oh, I couldn't say. I fancy it was pretty high?"

"One hundred and two in the shade; and it's hotter than

that, inside. Press-room like a furnace, city-room worse. Glad I didn't have to stay there."

"Are you—do you mean that you are employed on the *Morning Post?*"

"Yes. I run what we call the Enquirer's column. You may have read it sometimes?"

"Oh, yes! Well! Isn't that remarkable! Why, I always—"

"Well, that's my job on the *Post*, or one of them. I'm supposed to be working at it now. You know, that is really why I sat down on this bench. The question for to-morrow is, 'Do you favor Restricted Immigration?' When I saw you sitting here I thought, there's a man, if I'm not mistaken, who has views on this subject. Would you mind letting me have them, Mr.—but you haven't told me your name, I think?"

"Beatty. Herbert Beatty."

"Are you in business in the city?"

"Yes. I'm a bookkeeper with William C. Dow and company."

"That's fine! We'll be glad to have a man of your profession represented in the Enquirer's column. You don't object, do you, Mr. Beatty? You know, you can tell me precisely what you think our immigration policy should be. The *Post* wishes to offer its readers the opinions of intelligent men on both sides of the question."

Never, not even in his most sanguine moments, had it occurred to Mr. Beatty that he might one day be called upon to express, publicly, his opinion of any question. Now that the opportunity had come, he was dazed, stupefied. The sound of the young man's voice came to him with a strange, far-off effect. He understood in a dreamlike way that this reporter was preparing to direct the attention of a city of two million inhabitants to his, Herbert Beatty's, views upon a matter of great public concern. He watched, fascinated, while the young man drew a notebook from his pocket, slipped off the rubber band, opened it on his knee. What could he say? What *were* his views? Dr. Crake had dealt with this subject in one of his editorials only a few weeks before. If only he could remember what he had said, perhaps it would help him to—

Of a sudden he was conscious that the young man was speaking.

"I suppose you think there is something to be said on both sides, Mr. Beatty?"

"Oh, yes! I—you see—you have taken me a little by surprise. One doesn't like to be too sure—I hardly know—perhaps—"

"But wouldn't it, in your opinion, be a good thing if the government were to adopt a fairly cautious restriction policy, say for the next twenty-five years?"

"Well, yes, I believe it would."

"We would know by that time where we stand, don't you think, with respect to the great foreign-born population already in America? With this information to guide us, we could then decide what our future policy should be."

Mr. Beatty heartily agreed with this. It seemed to him a sound way of looking at the matter. The reporter made some rapid entries in his notebook, snapped on the rubber band, and clipped his pencil to his waistcoat pocket.

"Thanks very much, Mr. Beatty. You're the fourth man I've interviewed to-day. The views of the other three were rather extreme, both for and against restricted immigration. I'm glad to have found one man who favors moderation—a wise middle course. Now then, you'll let me take your photograph? We like to print these with the replies in the column. I'll not be ten seconds. If you'll stand there—a little more this way—Good! That will do. Snap! That's done it! Thanks once more, Mr. Beatty. To-morrow the whole city will know your views on the immigration problem, and I'll venture to say that nine out of ten men will agree with them. Well, good-bye, I must be getting along."

III

Mr. Beatty was conscious of a feeling of profound relief as he entered his enclosure at the bookkeeping department. He rearranged the articles on his desk, flicked an imaginary fleck of dust from his adding-machine, and resharpened a pencil whose point had been a little blunted with use during the morning. So great was the virtue in these familiar practices, and so strong the habits of a lifetime, that he was then able to resume his work with a certain measure of calm.

But his pleasantly disquieting thoughts returned at five o'clock. They seemed to be awaiting him in the street below, and occupied his mind to the exclusion of everything else. He entered the stream of homeward-bound pedestrian traffic, letting it carry him where it would, and presently found himself in front of the *Morning Post* building. One of the plate-glass windows bore an inscription in gold lettering: "The *Morning*

Post. Your Paper—Everybody's Paper. Guaranteed Circulation Over 450,000." He gazed at this for some time as he thought over the events of the day. He could recall vividly the appearance of the young reporter, and the kind of notebook he had used—opening at the end, with wide spaces between the ruled lines—and the round blue pencil with the nickle pocket-clip. But he could not remember at all clearly the details of the interview. How long had it lasted? Five minutes? Ten minutes? Probably not more than five. The reporter had worked rapidly. . . . He had seemed pleased with his replies. . . . But just what was it he had said? . . . A circulation of four-hundred-fifty thousand! And likely twice that many people actually read the *Post*.

After his customary solitary supper, Mr. Beatty went to a moving-picture theater for the seven-o'clock show. He returned to his lodgings at nine and went to bed. The following morning he awoke at a quarter to five, an hour before his usual time. It was impossible to sleep again, so he shaved, dressed, and went downstairs. The sky was cloudless; it would be another sweltering day. A horse-drawn milk wagon was just then making its rounds; otherwise the street was deserted.

The stationery shop where he usually bought his morning paper was not yet opened. He went on to another several blocks distant, but that too was closed. The papers had already been delivered there; they were lying on the doorstep, loosely wrapped in a brown paper cover. Mr. Beatty looked up and down the street; there was no one in view. Quickly opening his penknife he cut the cord of the parcel and drew forth a copy of the *Post*. Then he discovered that he had only a penny, a quarter, and a half-dollar in his pocket, and the price of the *Post* was three cents. He left the quarter on top of the parcel and hurried back to his lodgings where Mrs. Halleck, his landlady, was standing in the entryway.

"Good morning, Mr. Beatty! Well! You *are* an early bird this morning! Wherever have you been at this time of day? My! Ain't this heat awful? I don't know what's goin' to happen if we don't have some rain soon to cool things off. You got the morning paper already?"

He murmured a hasty reply, went up to his room on the third floor, and shut and locked the door. Then he opened his paper at the editorial page.

ENQUIRER'S COLUMN

Question for the day: "Do you favor Restricted Immigration?" Herbert Beatty, bookkeeper, with William C. Dow & Company, 400 Commercial Street.

"One hesitates in pronouncing an opinion upon a question of such far-reaching importance, but it would seem advisable that we should now adopt a cautious, well balanced policy of restriction until such time as we shall have been able to assimilate the immense foreign-born population already on our shores. Twenty-five years hence we shall have gathered sufficient data with regard to our immigration policy to enable us to decide with some measure of confidence what our future policy should be."

Mr. Beatty's photograph gazing at him from the page, and the print of his own name looked so strange that he could hardly believe them his. He read the interview again, and a third and a fourth time. He had not been able to recall, before, just how he had worded his reply; he had been a little confused, of course, at the moment of the interview, and surprised at the suddenness of the question put to him by the reporter. What a faculty that young man had shown for getting immediately at the gist of his thought! That was a reporter's business, to be sure, but this one must be a particularly gifted interviewer. His own interview had been given the place of honor at the top of the column. He now turned to the views of the others:

Morris Goldberg, haberdasher, 783 Fourth Avenue.

"I don't think we've got room for any more foreigners in the United States. We ought to put the lid on tight, now. Business has been poor since the war, and there's too much competition already."

H. Dwight Crabtree, pastor, the Division Street Baptist Church.

"I often think of America as a great melting-pot where all the various splendid elements which go to make up our Democracy are being fused, and the composite type, American, made perfect in the sight of the Father of us all. No, let us not forbid them, these brothers of ours from over the seas. Let us rather say: 'Welcome, ye poor and oppressed! We have room for you and more than room! Bask here in God's sunlight! Enjoy our opportunities! Partake of our fellowship! And may you bequeath to your children a rich heritage of health and love and beauty in this glorious land, America!"

John J. Canning, architect, 45 First National Bank building.

"This question would have been timely fifty years ago. My answer then would have been: 'I favor exclusion, not restriction.' That is my answer to-day."

Over his breakfast at the dairy lunch-room at the corner, Mr. Beatty again read the interviews, gaining the conviction as he compared them, that his was by far the most sensible of the four. It was pleasant to think of the thousands of men who would that day read his opinions, learn of his name— college professors, lawyers, doctors, government officials, perhaps Dr. Crake himself. He remembered now that Dr. Crake, too, had counseled moderation in dealing with the question of restricted immigration. He would be pleased to see his views upheld in the Enquirer's column. He could fancy him saying, "Now *there's* a man that knows what he is talking about."

The walk to the office on this memorable August morning was like a dream to him. Every newsboy at every corner seemed particularly anxious to sell him papers, and every passerby seemed to look at him with interest, with respect. He fancied several times that he had been recognized. He was almost afraid to enter the Dow building, and gave a sigh of relief when he was safe within his enclosure at the end of the corridor. He found it difficult to keep his mind on his work. The roar of traffic from the street was like a universal voice of acclaim loud with the name, Beatty—so loud, in fact, that he did not at first hear the voice of a small boy standing at the little window in front of his desk.

"Mr. Beatty! Mr. Dow wants to see you, Mr. Beatty."

He looked up quickly.

"Who did you say?"

"Mr. William Dow wants to see you. He says you are to come up at once if you are not too busy."

Arriving at the fourth floor the boy who had escorted him pointed to a glazed door at the end of a passageway.

"Mr. Dow is in there," he said, and left him.

Mr. Beatty hesitated for a moment, then timidly ap-

Fame for Mr. Beatty

proached the door and knocked, very gently. Receiving no reply he knocked again, a trifle more firmly.

"Come in!"

Mr. Dow was busy with his morning correspondence. He finished the dictation of a letter before looking up.

"Good morning," he said. "Yes?"

"I beg your pardon, sir. I was told that you wished to see me."

"Oh, yes. Are you Mr. Beatty? I've just been reading your little interview in the *Post*. It was yours, I believe?"

"Yes, sir. That is—"

"I rather liked your reply to that question, Mr. Beatty. I merely wanted to tell you this. But just what do you mean by 'a cautious, well-balanced policy of restriction'? How would you put it into effect, supposing you had the power?"

"Oh, I should hardly like to say, sir. I haven't thought so very much— Perhaps—"

"How would you begin? What nationalities do you think should be first restricted? Poles? Italians? Russian Jews?"

"Well, yes, perhaps the Russians—but I can't say that I am quite sure—"

Mr. Dow gave him a thoughtful appraising glance.

"How long have you been with us, Mr. Beatty?"

"Twenty years, sir, the fourteenth of last April."

His employer pursed his lips in a soundless whistle.

"Have you! As long as that? What do you think of our Accounting department? Is it efficiently managed?"

"Why, yes, I believe so, sir. At least—that is, I am sure that you know much better than I do."

"Have you any suggestions to make as to how it might be bettered?"

"Oh, no, sir!"

Mr. Dow gazed silently out of the window for a moment.

"Well, I'm glad to have had this opportunity for a little chat with you, Mr. Beatty. That's all for the present. Thanks for coming up."

IV

On a November afternoon, several years later, Mr. Beatty, having fed his pigeons in City Hall park, dusted the salt from his fingers with his handkerchief, and sat down to his customary after-luncheon perusal of the *Morning Post*. It was a raw, blustery day, too chilly for comfort out of doors. He decided that hereafter he would spend his luncheon hour at the restaurant. But this was not to be. The following day he came down with an attack of bronchial pneumonia. Within a week he was dead.

Mrs. Halleck, his landlady, was genuinely sorry to lose so old and dependable a lodger, but she could not afford to let sentimental regrets interfere with re-letting at once her third-floor-front, one of the best rooms in the house. Her new lodger, a law-school student, moved in immediately. She had the room all ready for him but had forgotten to remove from the wall a bit of cardboard which hung by a string by the side of the bed. A newspaper clipping, yellow with age, was pasted on it. The young man glanced idly at it as he took it down. "One hesitates," he read, "in pronouncing an opinion on a question of such far-reaching importance, but it would seem advisable that we should now adopt—"

Whistling softly to himself, the new lodger arranged his belongings. He crumbled the piece of cardboard and threw it in the waste-paper basket. He hung a Maxfield Parrish picture in its place. The light was just right for it there.

The Golden Honeymoon

by Ring W. Lardner

Mother says that when I start talking I never know when to stop. But I tell her the only time I get a chance is when she ain't around, so I have to make the most of it. I guess the fact is neither one of us would be welcome in a Quaker meeting, but as I tell Mother, what did God give us tongues for if He didn't want we should use them? Only she says He didn't give them to us to say the same thing over and over again, like I do, and repeat myself. But I say:

"Well, Mother," I say, "when people is like you and I and been married fifty years, do you expect anything I say will be something you ain't heard me say before? But it may be new to others, as they ain't nobody else lived with me as long as you have."

So she says:

"You can bet they ain't, as they couldn't nobody else stand you that long."

"Well," I tell her, "you look pretty healthy."

"Maybe I do," she will say, "but I looked even healthier before I married you."

You can't get ahead of Mother.

Yes, sir, we was married just fifty years ago the seventeenth day of last December and my daughter and son-in-law was over from Trenton to help us celebrate the Golden Wedding. My son-in-law is John H. Kramer, the real estate man. He made $12,000 one year and is pretty well thought of around Trenton; a good, steady, hard worker. The Rotarians was after him a long time to join, but he kept telling them his home was his club. But Edie finally made him join. That's my daughter.

Well, anyway, they come over to help us celebrate the Golden Wedding and it was pretty crimpy weather and the furnace don't seem to heat up no more like it used to and Mother made the remark that she hoped this winter wouldn't be as cold as the last, referring to the winter previous. So

Edie said if she was us, and nothing to keep us home, she certainly wouldn't spend no more winters up here and why didn't we just shut off the water and close up the house and go down to Tampa, Florida? You know we was there four winters ago and staid five weeks, but it cost us over three hundred and fifty dollars for hotel bill alone. So Mother said we wasn't going no place to be robbed. So my son-in-law spoke up and said that Tampa wasn't the only place in the South, and besides we didn't have to stop at no high price hotel but could rent us a couple rooms and board out somewheres, and he had heard that St. Petersburg, Florida, was *the* spot and if we said the word he would write down there and make inquiries.

Well, to make a long story short, we decided to do it and Edie said it would be our Golden Honeymoon and for a present my son-in-law paid the difference between a section and a compartment so as we could have a compartment and have more privatecy. In a compartment you have an upper and lower berth just like the regular sleeper, but it is a shut in room by itself and got a wash bowl. The car we went in was all compartments and no regular berths at all. It was all compartments.

We went to Trenton the night before and staid at my daughter and son-in-law and we left Trenton the next afternoon at 3.23 P.M.

This was the twelfth day of January. Mother set facing the front of the train, as it makes her giddy to ride backwards. I set facing her, which does not affect me. We reached North Philadelphia at 4.03 P.M. and we reached West Philadelphia at 4.14, but did not go into Broad Street. We reached Baltimore at 6.30 and Washington, D.C., at 7.25. Our train laid over in Washington two hours till another train come along to pick us up and I got out and strolled up the platform and into the Union Station. When I come back, our car had been switched on to another track, but I remembered the name of it, the La Belle, as I had once visited my aunt out in Oconomowoc, Wisconsin, where there was a lake of that name, so I had no difficulty in getting located. But Mother had nearly fretted herself sick for fear I would be left.

"Well," I said, "I would of followed you on the next train."

"You could of," said Mother, and she pointed out that she had the money.

"Well," I said, "we are in Washington and I could of borrowed from the United States Treasury. I would of pretended I was an Englishman."

Mother caught the point and laughed heartily.

Our train pulled out of Washington at 9.40 P.M. and Mother and I turned in early, I taking the upper. During the night we passed through the green fields of old Virginia, though it was too dark to tell if they was green or what color. When we got up in the morning, we was at Fayetteville, North Carolina. We had breakfast in the dining car and after breakfast I got in conversation with the man in the next compartment to ours. He was from Lebanon, New Hampshire, and a man about eighty years of age. His wife was with him, and two unmarried daughters and I made the remark that I should think the four of them would be crowded in one compartment, but he said they had made the trip every winter for fifteen years and knowed how to keep out of each other's way. He said they was bound for Tarpon Springs.

We reached Charleston, South Carolina, at 12.50 P.M. and arrived at Savannah, Georgia, at 4.20. We reached Jacksonville, Florida, at 8.45 P.M. and had an hour and a quarter lay over there, but Mother made a fuss about me getting off the train, so we had the darky make up our berths and retired before we left Jacksonville. I didn't sleep good as the train done a lot of hemming and hawing, and Mother never sleeps good on a train as she says she is always worrying that I will fall out. She says she would rather have the upper herself, as then she would not have to worry about me, but I tell her I can't take the risk of having it get out that I allowed my wife to sleep in an upper berth. It would make talk.

We was up in the morning in time to see our friends from New Hampshire get off at Tarpon Springs, which we reached at 6.53 A.M.

Several of our fellow passengers got off at Clearwater and some at Belleair, where the train backs right up to the door of the mammoth hotel. Belleair is the winter headquarters for the golf dudes and everybody that got off there had their bags of sticks, as many as ten and twelve in a bag. Women and all. When I was a young man we called it shinny and only needed one club to play with and about one game of it would of been a-plenty for some of these dudes, the way we played it.

The train pulled into St. Petersburg at 8.20 and when we got off the train you would think they was a riot, what with all the darkies barking for the different hotels.

I said to Mother, I said:

"It is a good thing we have a place picked out to go to and don't have to choose a hotel, as it would be hard to choose amongst them if every one of them is the best."

She laughed.

We found a jitney and I give him the address of the room my son-in-law had got for us and soon we was there and introduced ourselves to the lady that owns the house, a young widow about forty-eight years of age. She showed us our room, which was light and airy with a comfortable bed and bureau and washstand. It was twelve dollars a week, but the location was good, only three blocks from Williams Park.

St. Pete is what folks calls the town, though they also call it the Sunshine City, as they claim they's no other place in the country where they's fewer days when Old Sol don't smile down on Mother Earth, and one of the newspapers gives away all their copies free every day when the sun don't shine. They claim to of only give them away some sixty-odd times in the last eleven years. Another nickname they have got for the town is "the Poor Man's Palm Beach," but I guess they's men that comes there that could borrow as much from the bank as some of the Willie boys over to the other Palm Beach.

During our stay we paid a visit to the Lewis Tent City, which is the headquarters for the Tin Can Tourists. But maybe you ain't heard about them. Well, they are an organization that takes their vacation trips by auto and carries everything with them. That is, they bring along their tents to sleep in and cook in and they don't patronize no hotels or cafeterias, but they have got to be bona fide auto campers or they can't belong to the organization.

They tell me they's over 200,000 members to it and they call themselves the Tin Canners on account of most of their food being put up in tin cans. One couple we seen in the Tent City was a couple from Brady, Texas, named Mr. and Mrs. Pence, which the old man is over eighty years of age and they had came in their auto all the way from home, a distance of 1,641 miles. They took five weeks for the trip, Mr. Pence driving the entire distance.

The Tin Canners hails from every State in the Union and in the summer time they visit places like New England and the Great Lakes region, but in the winter the most of them comes to Florida and scatters all over the State. While we was down there, they was a national convention of them at

Gainesville, Florida, and they elected a Fredonia, New York, man as their president. His title is Royal Tin Can Opener of the World. They have got a song wrote up which everybody has got to learn it before they are a member:

> "The tin can forever! Hurrah, boys! Hurrah!
> Up with the tin can! Down with the foe!
> We will rally round the campfire, we'll rally once again,
> Shouting, 'We auto camp forever!'"

That is something like it. And the members has also got to have a tin can fastened on to the front of their machine.

I asked Mother how she would like to travel around that way and she said:

"Fine, but not with an old rattle brain like you driving."

"Well," I said, "I am eight years younger than this Mr. Pence who drove here from Texas."

"Yes," she said, "but he is old enough to not be skittish."

You can't get ahead of Mother.

Well, one of the first things we done in St. Petersburg was to go to the Chamber of Commerce and register our names and where we was from as they's great rivalry amongst the different States in regards to the number of their citizens visiting in town and of course our little State don't stand much of a show, but still every little bit helps, as the fella says. All and all, the man told us, they was eleven thousand names registered, Ohio leading with some fifteen hundred-odd and New York State next with twelve hundred. Then come Michigan, Pennsylvania and so on down, with one man each from Cuba and Nevada.

The first night we was there, they was a meeting of the New York–New Jersey Society at the Congregational Church and a man from Ogdensburg, New York State, made the talk. His subject was Rainbow Chasing. He is a Rotarian and a very convicting speaker, though I forget his name.

Our first business, of course, was to find a place to eat and after trying several places we run on to a cafeteria on Central Avenue that suited us up and down. We eat pretty near all our meals there and it averaged about two dollars per day for the two of us, but the food was well cooked and everything nice and clean. A man don't mind paying the price if things is clean and well cooked.

On the third day of February, which is Mother's birthday,

we spread ourselves and eat supper at the Poinsettia Hotel and they charged us seventy-five cents for a sirloin steak that wasn't hardly big enough for one.

I said to Mother: "Well," I said, "I guess it's a good thing every day ain't your birthday or we would be in the poorhouse."

"No," says Mother, "because if everyday was my birthday, I would be old enough by this time to of been in my grave long ago."

You can't get ahead of Mother.

In the hotel they had a card-room where they was several men and ladies playing five hundred and this new fangled whist bridge. We also seen a place where they was dancing, so I asked Mother would she like to trip the light fantastic toe and she said no, she was too old to squirm like you have got to do now days. We watched some of the young folks at it awhile till Mother got disgusted and said we would have to see a good movie to take the taste out of our mouth. Mother is a great movie heroyne and we go twice a week here at home.

But I want to tell you about the Park. The second day we was there we visited the Park, which is a good deal like the one in Tampa, only bigger, and they's more fun goes on here every day than you could shake a stick at. In the middle they's a big bandstand and chairs for the folks to set and listen to the concerts, which they give you music for all tastes, from Dixie up to classical pieces like Hearts and Flowers.

Then all around they's places marked off for different sports and games—chess and checkers and dominoes for folks that enjoys those kind of games, and roque and horseshoes for the nimbler ones. I used to pitch a pretty fair shoe myself, but ain't done much of it in the last twenty years.

Well, anyway, we bought a membership ticket in the club which costs one dollar for the season, and they tell me that up to a couple years ago it was fifty cents, but they had to raise it to keep out the riffraff.

Well, Mother and I put in a great day watching the pitchers and she wanted I should get in the game, but I told her I was all out of practice and would make a fool of myself, though I seen several men pitching who I guess I could take their measure without no practice. However, they was some good pitchers, too, and one boy from Akron, Ohio, who could certainly throw a pretty shoe. They told me it looked like he would win the championship of the United States in

The Golden Honeymoon

the February tournament. We come away a few days before they held that and I never did hear if he win. I forget his name, but he was a clean cut young fella and he has got a brother in Cleveland that's a Rotarian.

Well, we just stood around and watched the different games for two or three days and finally I set down in a checker game with a man named Weaver from Danville, Illinois. He was a pretty fair checker player, but he wasn't no match for me, and I hope that don't sound like bragging. But I always could hold my own on a checker-board and the folks around here will tell you the same thing. I played with this Weaver pretty near all morning for two or three mornings and he beat me one game and the only other time it looked like he had a chance, the noon whistle blowed and we had to quit and go to dinner.

While I was playing checkers, Mother would set and listen to the band, as she loves music, classical or no matter what kind, but anyway she was setting there one day and between selections the woman next to her opened up a conversation. She was a woman about Mother's own age, seventy or seventy-one, and finally she asked Mother's name and Mother told her her name and where she was from and Mother asked her the same question, and who do you think the woman was?

Well, sir, it was the wife of Frank M. Hartsell, the man who was engaged to Mother till I stepped in and cut him out, fifty-two years ago!

Yes, sir!

You can imagine Mother's surprise! And Mrs. Hartsell was surprised, too, when Mother told her she had once been friends with her husband, though Mother didn't say how close friends they had been, or that Mother and I was the cause of Hartsell going out West. But that's what we was. Hartsell left his town a month after the engagement was broke off and ain't never been back since. He had went out to Michigan and become a veterinary, and that is where he had settled down in Hillsdale, Michigan, and finally married his wife.

Well, Mother screwed up her courage to ask if Frank was still living and Mrs. Hartsell took her over to where they was pitching horse-shoes and there was old Frank, waiting his turn. And he knowed Mother as soon as he seen her, though it was over fifty years. He said he knowed her by her eyes.

"Why, it's Lucy Frost!" he says, and he throwed down his shoes and quit the game.

Then they come over and hunted me up and I will confess I wouldn't have knowed him. Him and I is the same age to the month, but he seems to show it more, some way. He is balder for one thing. And his beard is all white, where mine has still got a streak of brown in it. The very first thing I said to him, I said:

"Well, Frank, that beard of yours makes me feel like I was back north. It looks like a regular blizzard."

"Well," he said, "I guess yourn would be just as white if you had it dry cleaned."

But Mother wouldn't stand that.

"Is that so!" she said to Frank. "Well, Charley ain't had no tobacco in his mouth for over ten years!"

And I ain't!

Well, I excused myself from the checker game and it was pretty close to noon, so we decided to all have dinner together and they was nothing for it only we must try their cafeteria on Third Avenue. It was a little more expensive than ours and not near as good, I thought. I and Mother had about the same dinner we had been having every day and our bill was $1.10. Frank's check was $1.20 for he and his wife. The same meal wouldn't of cost more than a dollar at our place.

After dinner we made them come up to our house and we all set in the parlor, which the young woman had give us the use of to entertain company. We begun talking over old times and Mother said she was a-scared Mrs. Hartsell would find it tiresome listening to we three talk over old times, but as it turned out they wasn't much chance for nobody else to talk with Mrs. Hartsell in the company. I have heard lots of women that could go it, but Hartsell's wife takes the cake of all the women I ever seen. She told us the family history of everybody in the State of Michigan and bragged for a half hour about her son, who she said is in the drug business in Grand Rapids, and a Rotarian.

When I and Hartsell could get a word in edgeways we joked one another back and forth and I chafed him about being a horse doctor.

"Well, Frank," I said, "you look pretty prosperous, so I suppose they's been plenty of glanders around Hillsdale."

"Well," he said, "I've managed to make more than a fair living. But I've worked pretty hard."

"Yes," I said, " and I suppose you get called out all hours of the night to attend births and so on."

Mother made me shut up.

Well, I thought they wouldn't never go home and I and Mother was in misery trying to keep awake, as the both of us generally always takes a nap after dinner. Finally they went, after we had made an engagement to meet them in the Park the next morning, and Mrs. Hartsell also invited us to come to their place the next night and play five hundred. But she had forgot that they was a meeting of the Michigan Society that evening, so it was not till two evenings later that we had our first card game.

Hartsell and his wife lived in a house on Third Avenue North and had a private setting room besides their bedroom. Mrs. Hartsell couldn't quit talking about their private setting room like it was something wonderful. We played cards with them, with Mother and Hartsell partners against his wife and I. Mrs. Hartsell is a miserable card player and we certainly got the worst of it.

After the game she brought out a dish of oranges and we had to pretend it was just what we wanted, though oranges down there is like a young man's whiskers; you enjoy them at first, but they get to be a pesky nuisance.

We played cards again the next night at our place with the same partners and I and Mrs. Hartsell was beat again. Mother and Hartsell was full of compliments for each other on what a good team they made, but the both of them knowed well enough where the secret of their success laid. I guess all and all we must of played ten different evenings and they was only one night when Mrs. Hartsell and I come out ahead. And that one night wasn't no fault of hern.

When we had been down there about two weeks, we spent one evening as their guest in the Congregational Church, at a social give by the Michigan Society. A talk was made by a man named Bitting of Detroit, Michigan, on How I Was Cured of Story Telling. He is a big man in the Rotarians and give a witty talk.

A woman named Mrs. Oxford rendered some selections which Mrs. Hartsell said was grand opera music, but whatever they was my daughter Edie could of give her cards and spades and not made such a hullaballoo about it neither.

Then they was a ventriloquist from Grand Rapids and a young woman about forty-five years of age that mimicked different kinds of birds. I whispered to Mother that they all sounded like a chicken, but she nudged me to shut up.

After the show we stopped in a drug store and I set up the refreshments and it was pretty close to ten o'clock before we finally turned in. Mother and I would of preferred tending the movies, but Mother said we mustn't offend Mrs. Hartsell, though I asked her had we came to Florida to enjoy ourselves or to just not offend an old chatterbox from Michigan.

I felt sorry for Hartsell one morning. The women folks both had an engagement down to the chiropodist's and I run across Hartsell in the Park and he foolishly offered to play me checkers.

It was him that suggested it, not me, and I guess he repented himself before we had played one game. But he was too stubborn to give up and there while I beat him game after game and the worst part of it was that a crowd of folks had got in the habit of watching me play and there they all was, looking on, and finally they seen what a fool Frank was making of himself, and they began to chafe him and pass remarks. Like one of them said:

"Who ever told you you was a checker player!"

And:

"You might maybe be good for tiddle-de-winks, but not checkers!"

I almost felt like letting him beat me a couple games. But the crowd would of knowed it was a put up job.

Well, the women folks joined us in the Park and I wasn't going to mention our little game, but Hartsell told about it himself and admitted he wasn't no match for me.

"Well," said Mrs. Hartsell, "checkers ain't much of a game anyway, is it?" She said: "It's more of a children's game, ain't it? At least, I know my boy's children used to play it a good deal."

"Yes, ma'am," I said. "It's a children's game the way your husband plays it, too."

Mother wanted to smooth things over, so she said:

"Maybe they's other games where Frank can beat you."

"Yes," said Mrs. Hartsell, "and I bet he could beat you pitching horse-shoes."

'Well," I said, "I would give him a chance to try, only I ain't pitched a shoe in over sixteen years."

"Well," said Hartsell, "I ain't played checkers in twenty years."

"You ain't never played it," I said.

"Anyway," says Frank, "Lucy and I is your master at five hundred."

Well, I could of told him why that was, but had decency enough to hold my tongue.

It had got so now that he wanted to play cards every night and when I or Mother wanted to go to a movie, any one of us would have to pretend we had a headache and then trust to goodness that they wouldn't see us sneak into the theater. I don't mind playing cards when my partner keeps their mind on the game, but you take a woman like Hartsell's wife and how can they play cards when they have got to stop every couple seconds and brag about their son in Grand Rapids?

Well, the New York–New Jersey Society announced that they was goin to give a social evening too and I said to Mother, I said:

"Well, that is one evening when we will have an excuse not to play five hundred."

"Yes," she said, "but we will have to ask Frank and his wife to go to the social with us as they asked us to go to the Michigan social."

"Well," I said, "I had rather stay home than drag that chatterbox everywheres we go."

So Mother said:

"You are getting too cranky. Maybe she does talk a little too much but she is good hearted. And Frank is always good company."

So I said:

"I suppose if he is such good company you wished you had of married him."

Mother laughed and said I sounded like I was jealous. Jealous of a cow doctor!

Anyway we had to drag them along to the social and I will say that we give them a much better entertainment than they had given us.

Judge Lane of Paterson made a fine talk on business conditions and a Mrs. Newell of Westfield imitated birds, only you could really tell what they was the way she done it. Two young women from Red Bank sung a choral selection and we clapped them back and they gave us Home to Our Mountains and Mother and Mrs. Hartsell both had tears in their eyes. And Hartsell, too.

Well, some way or another the chairman got wind that I was there and asked me to make a talk and I wasn't even going to get up, but Mother made me, so I got up and said:

"Ladies and gentlemen," I said. "I didn't expect to be called on for a speech on an occasion like this or no other occasion as I do not set myself up as a speech maker, so will have to do the best I can, which I often say is the best anybody can do."

Then I told them the story about Pat and the motorcycle, using the brogue, and it seemed to tickle them and I told them one or two other stories, but altogether I wasn't on my feet more than twenty or twenty-five minutes and you ought to of heard the clapping and hollering when I set down. Even Mrs. Hartsell admitted that I am quite a speechifier and said if I ever went to Grand Rapids, Michigan, her son would make me talk to the Rotarians.

When it was over, Hartsell wanted we should go to their house and play cards, but his wife reminded him that it was after 9:30 P.M., rather a late hour to start a card game, but he had went crazy on the subject of cards, probably because he didn't have to play partners with his wife. Anyway, we got rid of them and went home to bed.

It was the next morning, when we met over to the Park, that Mrs. Hartsell made the remark that she wasn't getting no exercise so I suggested that why didn't she take part in the roque game.

She said she had not played a game of roque in twenty years, but if Mother would play she would play. Well, at first Mother wouldn't hear of it, but finally consented, more to please Mrs. Hartsell than anything else.

Well, they had a game with a Mrs. Ryan from Eagle, Nebraska, and a young Mrs. Morse from Rutland, Vermont, who Mother had met down to the chiropodist's. Well, Mother couldn't hit a flea and they all laughed at her and I couldn't help from laughing at her myself and finally she quit and said her back was too lame to stoop over. So they got another lady and kept on playing and soon Mrs. Hartsell was the one everybody was laughing at, as she had a long shot to hit the black ball, and as she made the effort her teeth fell out on to the court. I never seen a woman so flustered in my life. And I never heard so much laughing, only Mrs. Hartsell didn't join in and she was madder than a hornet and wouldn't play no more, so the game broke up.

Mrs. Hartsell went home without speaking to nobody, but Hartsell stayed around and finally he said to me, he said:

"Well, I played you checkers the other day and you beat

me bad and now what do you say if you and me play a game of horse-shoes?"

I told him I hadn't pitched a shoe in sixteen years, but Mother said:

"Go ahead and play. You used to be good at it and maybe it will come back to you."

Well, to make a long story short, I give in. I oughtn't to of never tried it, as I hadn't pitched a shoe in sixteen years, and I only done it to humor Hartsell.

Before we started, Mother patted me on the back and told me to do my best, so we started in and I seen right off that I was in for it, as I hadn't pitched a shoe in sixteen years and didn't have my distance. And besides, the plating had wore off the shoes so that they was points right where they stuck into my thumb and I hadn't throwed more than two or three times when my thumb was raw and it pretty near killed me to hang on to the shoe, let alone pitch it.

Well, Hartsell throws the awkwardest shoe I ever seen pitched and to see him pitch you wouldn't think he would ever come nowheres near, but he is also the luckiest pitcher I ever seen and he made some pitches where the shoe lit five and six feet short and then schoonered up and was a ringer. They's no use trying to beat that kind of luck.

They was a pretty fair size crowd watching us and four or five other ladies besides Mother, and it seems like, when Hartsell pitches, he has got to chew and it kept the ladies on the anxious seat as he don't seem to care which way he is facing when he leaves go.

You would think a man as old as him would of learnt more manners.

Well, to make a long story short, I was just beginning to get my distance when I had to give up on account of my thumb, which I showed it to Hartsell and he seen I couldn't go on, as it was raw and bleeding. Even if I could of stood it to go on myself, Mother wouldn't of allowed it after she seen my thumb. So anyway I quit and Hartsell said the score was nineteen to six, but I don't know what it was. Or don't care, neither.

Well, Mother and I went home and I said I hoped we was through with the Hartsells as I was sick and tired of them, but it seemed like she had promised we would go over to their house that evening for another game of their everlasting cards.

Well, my thumb was giving me considerable pain and I felt

kind out of sorts and I guess maybe I forgot myself, but anyway, when we was about through playing Hartsell made the remark that he wouldn't never lose a game of cards if he could always have Mother for a partner.

So I said:

"Well, you had a chance fifty years ago to always have her for a partner, but you wasn't man enough to keep her."

I was sorry the minute I had said it and Hartsell didn't know what to say and for once his wife couldn't say nothing. Mother tried to smooth things over by making the remark that I must of had something stronger than tea or I wouldn't talk so silly. But Mrs. Hartsell had froze up like an iceberg and hardly said good night to us and I bet her and Frank put in a pleasant hour after we was gone.

As we was leaving, Mother said to him: "Never mind Charley's nonsense, Frank. He is just mad because you beat him all hollow pitching horse-shoes and playing cards."

She said that to make up for my slip, but at the same time she certainly riled me. I tried to keep ahold of myself, but as soon as we was out of the house she had to open up the subject and begun to scold me for the break I had made.

Well, I wasn't in no mood to be scolded. So I said:

"I guess he is such a wonderful pitcher and card player that you wished you had married him."

"Well," she said, "at least he ain't a baby to give up pitching because his thumb has got a few scratches."

"And how about you," I said, "making a fool of yourself on the roque court and then pretending your back is lame and you can't play no more!"

"Yes," she said, "but when you hurt your thumb I didn't laugh at you, and why did you laugh at me when I sprained my back?"

"Who could help from laughing!" I said.

"Well," she said, "Frank Hartsell didn't laugh."

"Well," I said, "why didn't you marry him?"

"Well," said Mother, "I almost wished I had!"

"And I wished so, too!" I said.

"I'll remember that!" said Mother, and that's the last word she said to me for two days.

We seen the Hartsells the next day in the Park and I was willing to apologize, but they just nodded to us. And a couple days later we heard they had left for Orlando, where they have got relatives.

I wished they had went there in the first place.

Mother and I made it up setting on a bench.

"Listen, Charley," she said. "This is our Golden Honeymoon and we don't want the whole thing spoilt with a silly old quarrel."

"Well," I said, "did you mean that about wishing you had married Hartsell?"

"Of course not," she said, "that is, if you didn't mean that you wished I had, too."

So I said:

"I was just tired and all wrought up. I thank God you chose me instead of him as they's no other woman in the world who I could of lived with all these years."

"How about Mrs. Hartsell?" says Mother.

"Good gracious!" I said. "Imagine being married to a woman that plays five hundred like she does and drops her teeth on the roque court!"

"Well," said Mother, "it wouldn't be no worse than being married to a man that expectorates towards ladies and is such a fool in a checker game."

So I put my arm around her shoulder and she stroked my hand and I guess we got kind of spoony.

They was two days left of our stay in St. Petersburg and the next to the last day Mother introduced me to a Mrs. Kendall from Kingston, Rhode Island, who she had met at the chiropodist's.

Mrs. Kendall made us acquainted with her husband, who is in the grocery business. They have got two sons and five grandchildren and one great-grandchild. One of their sons lives in Providence and is way up in the Elks as well as a Rotarian.

We found them very congenial people and we played cards with them the last two nights we was there. They was both experts and I only wished we had met them sooner instead of running into the Hartsells. But the Kendalls will be there again next winter and we will see more of them, that is, if we decide to make the trip again.

We left the Sunshine City on the eleventh day of February, at 11 A.M. This give us a day trip through Florida and we seen all the country we had passed through at night on the way down.

We reached Jacksonville at 7 P.M. and pulled out of there at 8:10 P.M. We reached Fayetteville, North Carolina, at nine o'clock the following morning, and reached Washington, D.C., at 6:30 P.M., laying over there half an hour.

We reached Trenton at 11:01 P.M. and had wired ahead to my daughter and son-in-law and they met us at the train and we went to their house and they put us up for the night. John would of made us stay up all night, telling about our trip, but Edie said we must be tired and made us go to bed. That's my daughter.

The next day we took our train for home and arrived safe and sound, having been gone just one month and a day.

Here comes Mother, so I guess I better shut up.

Manicure

by Margaret Kernochan Leech

Saturday afternoons wrought subtle changes in the salons of Leon and Jules (Specialists in the Artistry of Coiffure). To a superficial observer all was as usual. In every orchid and green compartment a feminine form, lavishly bibbed in fresh white linen, sat before the mirror of the toilet table. Sharp little clicks came from the snapping irons of the artists in marcel. Heads were deftly molded in the plasticene dampness of finger waves. Cold cream was competently smeared on heated faces, to a murmur of "Just relax, please, madame. Lie perfectly quiet and relax." In the booths devoted to permanent waves sat ladies with heads grotesquely bristling into huge painful coronets, like Russian headdresses. Miss Nina and Miss Hazel ran back and forth. "What's the matter with that cold air?" "Just a minute, madame. No, I'm not going to leave you alone. It's only the steam, it won't burn you." In rows outside the compartments the little manicure tables were crowded. Indeed, on Saturday afternoons there were so many manicures that clients often had to be "started" on stray chairs placed in the narrow aisles, with bowls of hot soapy water perilously poised on their knees.

Whatever the subtle changes of Saturday afternoons, they did not diminish the number of patrons who thronged the salons of Leon and Jules. On the contrary, these last hours of the week supported their tradition of amazing success—contributed to explain the country house toward which Mr. Leon sped at one o'clock each Saturday in a comfortable motor car with a uniformed chauffeur. For Mr. Leon—there was no Mr. Jules, and if there ever had been he was lost in the dimness of legend—did not remain in the salons on Saturday afternoons. That was a part of the subtle changes. None of "his ladies" was expected to be there.

Downstairs in the foyer of the great hotel in which the establishment of Leon and Jules was housed swirled a flux of expensive gayety. By the entrance to the Florentine Room, a fixed point in the restless tide, stood Mr. Peter Koch, the handsome assistant manager of the hotel, smiling affably under his slight mustache. Eddies of smartly gowned women broke and rippled around him. For though his connection with the hotel was of only a year's standing, Mr. Koch had already made his impression. It was inevitable, with that face and that figure, that he should have done so. Many women paused to speak to him as he bent forward deferentially from the waist, smiled, nodded, noted things on a pad. "But, certainly, Madame, I will arrange everything. No, no, no, you must not trouble at all. I will speak to Louis myself, *parole d'honneur*. I will arrange it personally. It will be a pleasure to do it—for you, madame."

He would glance at Madame with his full, excitable eyes, which the large lids could veil so quickly. And she, if her companion happened to be another woman, would murmur a moment later, "Isn't he marvelous? I'm afraid it's running into a flirtation. I ought to be ashamed to let him look at me the way he does."

Under the small felt hats which bobbed in the foyer or bowed across small tables in the Florentine Room were many heads shingled and waved in the salons of Leon and Jules. But none of these women ascended on Saturday afternoons. A new invasion, unfamiliar on week days, crowded the orchid compartments. These were the women who worked five afternoons of the week. On the sixth they repaired the ravages of time and exertion.

The Saturday afternoon patrons were persons well up in the world. Here were buyers, smartly dressed and deftly rouged. Here were well-informed private secretaries, in dark woolen dresses. Here were women executives with lines of worry between their brows. They looked prosperous, even affluent. But some grade was lacking—some glaze of exquisiteness which leisure and years of infinite luxury impart. On Saturday afternoons there was none of the casual elegance of an enameled cigarette case, of a glimpse of *binche* at the bosom, of a square emerald sliding negligently around a thin finger. And it might have been observed that on Saturday afternoons the deference of the girls at Leon and Jules fell a shade short. For these woman were not silken creatures from some incredible Aladdin's palace. After all, they worked for a living. They might be wise and friendly, but they were not opening doors of vivid life, they were not clear windows through which to peep into a fairyland of riches. The young persons with the soft names—Miss Rose, Miss Nina, Miss Adele, Miss Hazel, Miss Blanche—were a little bored when Saturday afternoon came.

Miss Nina was terribly bored. She was not the prettiest of the girls at Leon and Jules, by any means. She brushed her short brown hair forward to soften her face; for, though she was only twenty-four, it was rather a pinched little face, dark skinned. Her green-blue eyes looked surprisingly light between black lashes. Her lips were thin and avid, and she carried her head high.

But, if she was not remarkably pretty, Miss Nina undeniably had a way with her. Her figure was supple, and she had tiny feet with steep little insteps. She swished her skirts slightly when she walked. Dressed for the street in a carmine frock and hat and a plain black coat, she looked quite striking. She rouged her drooping little mouth very red, and this made her eyes look brighter and her skin less drab. The men's eyes turned as she passed through the lobby of the great hotel with her mincing, rather affected walk. It was the sort of walk which takes cognizance of the fact that men's eyes often turn.

Miss Nina was proud of working at Leon and Jules. She had striven for this job through years of initiation in lesser shops. Here she made breathless contact with something she desired, something on which her spirit fed. She looked hungrily at the women who came to the salons, appraised their jewels, their dresses, listened rapturously while they prattled of their travels, beaux, parties, appointments, shopping.

When occasion arose Miss Nina could do more than listen. She could join in the conversation—about the cabarets, the theaters. Her evenings were not always dull. To her less conservative customers—gay débutantes, lively married women—she hinted as much: cocktails, champagne, a midnight roof. Sometimes, bending confidentially over a white hand, Nina forgot that her name was really Nellie, forgot her tiny tawdry flat, forgot long evenings spent in making clothes, or in washing, ironing, and repairing them. Almost she was able to identify herself with the other woman, to please the men that the other woman pleased, to shine in the glitter of her good fortune. They sat, half whispering, like two friends. There was only a narrow green table between them.

When the long fantasy of her day was over Miss Nina slipped into her street clothes. Nor was disillusionment immediate. The carmine dress and hat were more becoming than the white linen uniform. She rouged her lips very carefully and buttoned her gloves and took her square, shiny black purse. In the elevator she was no longer Miss Nina of Leon and Jules—she was, with some faint impertinence of lifted chin, a guest of the great hotel. The moment of traversing the foyer was pure magic every evening. Through the luxurious corridor she moved, gazing about her with her astonishingly light eyes, as though she were looking for someone. Outside the Florentine Room, where music sounded and people still lingered over teacups among potted palms, stood Mr. Peter Koch, handsome, erect, deferential. Their eyes just met before she smiled at the doorman and was whirled into the street.

Miss Nina wandered around the airless little cloakroom, munching a very late lunch of an olive-and-cream-cheese sandwich. She was hoping that Miss Rose would forget that she had been gone quite half an hour; for her distaste for the ugly cloakroom was less than her distaste for the boredom of Saturday afternoon. Her mouth drooped as she washed her hands and dried them slowly with a towel secreted from the salons, with *Leon and Jules* straggling across it in green chain-stitching. She licked her thumb and forefinger and twisted an upturned sickle of hair on each cheek. Then from the breast of her white uniform she drew a square envelope, addressed in an angular handwriting, foreign and precise. There was more of the handwriting inside. Miss Nina ran her eyes along the lines, drawing in her chin with a mysterious little smile.

"Miss Nina! Miss Nina!" The voice of Miss Rose, officiating at the appointment desk, came sharply up the stairs. Miss Nina frowned, thrust the letter into its hiding place, and minced down the stairs on her steep little feet. "Your lady's waiting," Miss Rose informed her crossly. "Manicure. Second table."

Miss Nina stifled a yawn. She took from a shelf her small crowded tray of manicure necessaries; she filled a bowl with hot soapy water. "Second table, madame. Right this way," Miss Rose prompted the woman who had asked for Miss Nina. Her tone was a trifle brisk and businesslike, for even on a Saturday afternoon this was not an impressive customer. It was less an indication of appearance than of manner. She seemed oddly confused, ill at ease in the orchid and green salons. She stood by the appointment desk, looking about her with an exaggerated assumption of indifference. But, at Miss Rose's direction, she now moved to the second table, her head raised, as one who has outfaced many situations. Miss Nina came tripping toward her; deposited her tray and the bowl of soapy water on the glass-topped table; laid a fresh towel over the small cushion; snapped on the green-shaded light.

"Good-afternoon, madame!" she said in her eager voice. Miss Nina's eyes ran curiously over the customer. She was a new one, a stranger. Miss Nina, who had an excellent memory for faces, couldn't remember ever having seen her in the shop. She was a blonde woman, with large pale-brown eyes. The light on the table struck the flat planes of her face, cleft by fine lines about her eyes and mouth. She had neatly rubbed her thin cheeks with a brickish, dusty-looking rouge. Between the fur bands of her coat collar there was a glint of metal cloth. She laid on the table a pair of fresh kid gloves and a bag worked in blue glass beads with a German silver mounting. Miss Nina quickly appraised the blouse, the new gloves, the beaded bag, the hat—blue velvet with a rhinestone ornament. There was that about them which spoke of Sunday, of occasion. Tissue paper seemed to rustle faintly around them. They were her "best" things. Miss Nina's upper lip curled slightly, briefly, as she took the woman's left hand, a capable hand with large shapely nails. She ran her file experimentally around the littlest one.

"Not much shorter, madame?" she suggested. The woman shook her head.

"You have very lovely nails. Very lovely nails, madame," said Miss Nina absently. With mechanical skill the long file moved around the nails, shaping them. The left hand, the finger tips dabbed with salve, was consigned to the bowl of water. Miss Nina shifted her shoulders, glanced cursorily at the customers seated at the other manicure tables. She took up the right hand, smothering another yawn.

The woman spoke so suddenly that Miss Nina was startled. Her voice had a queer husky quality, very pleasant. "Do you know a girl named Adele that used to work here?"

"Why, yes," said Miss Nina, and bit her lip. "Why, yes, of course. Yes, Adele was here for a good while, I guess, about a year or two."

"She's not here any more, is she? Do you ever see her?"

pursued the woman. Her large hazel eyes were fixed on Miss Nina's face.

The girl looked up briefly. "No," she said, twisting a fragment of cotton around an orange-wood stick. "Not any more. Not for—oh, two or three months. I haven't seen her since she left."

"You didn't know her very well?" asked the woman, and again Miss Nina looked at her.

"Why, yes—" she began hesitatingly. Then she gave a little laugh and leaned confidentially over the woman's hand. "Why, I'll tell you how it was, madame. Adele was my girl friend. Then we had a little fuss. She said something I didn't like. Will you have the white under your nails? We don't talk now." Miss Nina poked among the articles on her tray for an emery board. "You knew Adele, madame? I mean, you were one of her customers? I didn't think—"

"No," said the blonde woman. "I've never been here before. Quite some place you have, isn't it? I've never seen this Adele. But I've heard about her." She lowered her eyes, raised them again, moistening her lips. "I heard she got in some trouble here," she said, and waited.

"Well!" Miss Nina threw back her head with an explosive little laugh. "What do think of that? Well, some people say more than their prayers."

"I heard," said the blonde woman softly, "that Adele did."

"Oh, no, no." Miss Nina deprecated the entire report. "There isn't anything to that. Why, I can't believe there's anything to that. She just wanted a new place, madame. Some place handier to where she lives."

The woman shook her head slowly. "No. That wasn't it. She got in trouble on account of some man here in the hotel. She *had* to leave."

Miss Nina drew a quick breath. Her eyes darted around the shop. A drying machine whirred behind the curtains of the nearest compartment. There was a chatter of conversation. At near-by tables Miss Blanche and Miss Myrtle bent over their customers' hands. Their backs were concentrated, oblivious. Calmly above them lay a soft haze of cigarette smoke. Miss Nina picked up her orange-wood stick.

"Well, madame," she murmured, "you know all about it, don't you? Would you put your other hand in the water, please? I did hear some gossip myself, but I don't think there was anything to it. Nothing wrong, I mean, madame. Nothing really wrong."

"Foolish girl, wasn't she?" said the blonde woman. "Going up to his room here in the hotel and all. She might have known they'd find out."

Nina conceded the wisdom of this with a hunching of her shoulders and a sympathetic smile. "Well, of course, you know, madame"—her voice had dropped to an eager whisper—"some girls never think how things look. You know how they are, madame. That's what I always told Adele, she'd get in trouble if she didn't look out. I like a good time myself. But the idea, can you imagine, going to a man's room, in a hotel like this, too, where they're so careful. They have to be." Miss Nina paused, while she ran a soapy brush over the nicely groomed nails of the woman's left hand. "Will you have the medium polish, madame? Or do you prefer the very red?" Her fingers quivered among the bottles, chose on instruction the very red. She drew out the cork, with its tiny pendant brush, and began to paint the neat finger nails.

"I got disgusted with her," Miss Nina resumed. "That's how we came to have this falling out I spoke of. Going up to his room!" Miss Nina sniffed.

The blonde woman raised her hand, gazed intently at the shining red nails. "I suppose," she said, "you've seen this man she went with?"

"Seen him?" said Miss Nina. "Oh, yes. Yes, indeed, I've seen him." She cleared her throat. "Well, you see, madame, Adele and I had a little apartment together last year. East Thirty-first Street. A nice little place. This man—this friend of Adele's—used to come there, see? Then sometimes, you know, my boy friend would be there, and the four of us would go out somewheres, to dinner or a show or to dance somewheres. That's the way I got to know him. Of course, I wasn't paying any attention to him. I had a friend of my own." Miss Nina moved her shoulders expressing hauteur. "I could see all along he was getting sick of Adele. She was just crazy about him. Silly over him. And here he was with his wife and all—"

"So he has a wife?" said the woman. And her eyes opened very wide as she stared at the five red, shining nails of her left hand.

"Oh, sure." said Miss Nina. "I should say so. Believe me, he has a wife. Very delicate. Just relax your hand a little, madame. She's a very delicate woman. Lives in the country, New Jersey some place. If you could just let your hand lie quiet—that's better, thank you, madame. She's crazy about him. At least, that's what Adele used to say. He's just got to be home certain nights in the week. He has three children, too. He thinks the world of them. Quite a family man." Miss Nina laughed.

"Yes," said the woman. "It would seem that way. Well, that's hard on a man, a nagging wife."

Miss Nina was voluble, eager. "Yes, madame, that's just what I used to tell Adele. 'Adele,' I used to say to her, 'there's no use *your* nagging at him; he's got one like that already.' And I told her, 'He's a married man, that'll never bring you luck.' But she said, 'If you like them, what can you do?'"

The woman uttered a little exclamation that was not quite a laugh. But Miss Nina did not heed. "Well, finally, she heard about Adele—the wife did. So he came to Adele and told her she'd have to leave and go some place else, because his wife, see, would make trouble if she stayed here. So that was how it happened. That's the whole story."

"Yes," said the blonde woman. "Yes, that's what I heard happened. I live in Brooklyn, and I heard about it from friends of her married sister's. I heard she got going out with this man, and then she lost her place. They all thought it was too bad, she was such a nice girl." She leaned forward across the narrow table, her lips parted. "There couldn't—you're sure that was what happened, that his wife found out about it? You couldn't be wrong about that?"

"No, I'm sure," said Miss Nina. She snipped her little scissors delicately, decisively. "Sure that was what happened. He was always scared to death his wife would find out. Why, sometimes he used to break dates the last minute. She's sick, see, and she gets suspicious. I guess she gave it to him all right."

The woman sighed. "I wonder," she said, "if Adele ever sees him now?"

"No," said Miss Nina quickly. "No, she doesn't see him any more. Hasn't seen him since she left."

"But I thought," said the blonde woman in a puzzled tone, "that you and Adele weren't friends any more? How would you know if she saw him or not? You wouldn't—" she hesitated—"I don't suppose *you* ever see him, do you? To talk to, I mean?"

"Me?" cried Miss Nina. "Why, no. No, I'd never dream— Why, what made you think—?" She laid down her small sharp scissors and ran her fingers quickly across her upper lip. The blonde woman's eyes were lowered. They stared intently at the middle finger of her right hand. And, following her gaze, Miss Nina's eyes rested on a scarlet speck beside the finger nail, which grew to a tiny bubble of blood, spreading across the whiteness of the finger. "Oh, madame, I'm so sorry! How stupid of me! I don't know when I've done such a thing." With tremulous fingers she took the cork from a bottle of colorless fluid and moistened a scrap of cotton which she pressed against the tiny wound. "Terribly sorry, madame. I—I must be nervous to-day."

"That's all right," said the woman. Her voice was low and quiet. "We all make mistakes. I'm afraid I've upset you, talking about your girl friend. We'll drop the subject if you'd rather."

Miss Nina pressed her palms to her cheeks. "It upsets me awfully to cut a customer. No, no, madame, why should I mind talking about Adele? She's nothing to me any more. I don't care what she does. You needn't worry over her. She's got somebody else by now. She never cares long for anybody. That's why I was so sure, see, that she doesn't meet this man any more. Ah, you don't know what a fool she is!" Miss Nina's mouth was bitter. "Going up to his room here! If she had to see him, why couldn't she meet him some place else? I knew she'd get in trouble. I *told* her, 'Adele,' I said, 'a manager of a hotel has his position to consider. A big hotel like this, you want to be careful about going up there to see him; he can't always be telling you, don't come up to my room— how does that look for a man, to be the one to be careful?'" Miss Nina was breathing fast. "I'll tell you what's the trouble with Adele, madame. She's too easy. That's why, see, I know they don't see each other any more. A man gets sick of that, believe me."

The blonde woman bent her head. "Well, I should blame her," she said. "I should blame her. I guess every woman's been easy one time anyway—or wished she'd had the chance to be. I was easy once myself," she whispered, and her hand twitched in Miss Nina's clasp. "One time I was cashier in a hotel. There was a handsome fellow was one of the day clerks." She smiled wryly. "Well—"

She caught her lip between her teeth, with a long intake of breath, as though she were nerving herself to go on. "I fell for him," she said slowly. "A ton of bricks. I was nutty about him. His manners, you know. Always so polite and like that. He used to write me notes, lovely handwriting, like a copy book. He was educated in Europe. I'd carry those notes around with me for days—read them over and over again. He was crazy for women." She gave a nervous laugh of apology. "I thought he was crazy for me. Funny, isn't it? That's a mistake a lot of women make. Well—" After a minute she went on—"He had a wife. She was awfully delicate. That made her nagging and suspicious of him—the way they get. He couldn't bear to hurt her. And then there were the kids. He was so fond of his kids."

Miss Nina had stiffened. A confused hostility was hot in her narrowed eyes. Meeting that gaze, the woman flinched, looked away. Her lips trembled, and she bit at them to make them steady. "I stuck to him for six years," she said. "Six years out of my life. You wouldn't believe it. Every thought I had for that man, every breath I drew."

Miss Nina ran the scrub brush over the fingers of the woman's hand. Chill soapy water dripped through the fingers. Miss Nina squeezed them briefly in a towel.

"It's a bad thing to happen to a girl," said the woman. Her eyes were fastened on Miss Nina with a quivering intensity. They seemed to implore her to understand, to respond. But Miss Nina's eyes were as blank as two bits of pale-blue glass. "It's a bad thing," the woman went on, "getting mixed up with a married man. It gets a girl a bad name around. I could have married—oh, easy—before I got to going with this fellow. But after—well, after, it was different. No man's going to wait for a woman six years. Not these days. You can't blame them. And with the talk and all. There's always talk."

Miss Nina painted the last finger of the right hand with the very red polish. She thrust the cork into the bottle, busied herself with tidying her tray of small articles. The woman opened her beaded bag awkwardly with her left hand and took from it a mirror and a powder puff in a figured-silk handkerchief. She powdered her nose and straightened her hat. "Of course, I'm not out of the running yet," she said. She snapped her bag shut and took up her new gloves. She laughed lightly. "No, sir, I haven't given up hope yet."

But as she hesitated to rise it became clear that she had not yet finished. She was mustering the courage to go on. There was a minute of painful silence. "There's just one thing," she at least admitted. "I—I'm sorry you aren't friends with Adele any more. Because I was hoping you could take her a message from me. I—I got a feeling I wanted to tell her something."

Miss Nina had raised her tray. Now she set it down with a clatter. She took the edge of the table in both hands. "Tell me," she whispered. The light from the lamp flickered sharply in her eyes. "Tell me," she repeated.

"Well, you see, I guess I know him better than you do. This man Koch—" The name fell like a stone between them. And, seeing that the woman's face was white, Nina started sharply. In her thin young throat muscles twitched.

"Oh, my God!" said Nina. "You—you're not—"

For a moment they faced each other. Then the blonde woman understood. "No," she said, "I'm not. My God, do I look like a delicate wife? No, dearie, I never made it. But what I wanted to tell you was about her—Koch's wife. This sick wife of his that he can't bear to hurt." The woman swallowed, as though it hurt her. "She died four years ago," she said. "I happen to know that. You see? Well, that's all."

She did not look at Miss Nina now, stared instead at her new gloves and the blue-beaded bag. "He really did have the sick wife when I knew him. Yes, and the kids, too. Her family took them when she died. I guess he couldn't bear the idea of losing her," she said with a dreary smile. "She came in so handy."

The woman rose, moved toward the cashier's desk, her head raised, as one who has outfaced many situations. With uncertain fingers she fumbled in her bag for a crumpled bill. Outside the orchid and green salons she paused in the gloomy carpeted silence of the hotel corridor. Almost she turned back. Her lips twisted. She clenched her hands, turning her head in a panic of regret. Suddenly she pressed her stiffened palms over her eyes. She did not hear Miss Nina coming until she stood beside her.

"Oh," cried the blonde woman. There were tears in her big hazel eyes. "Oh, I shouldn't have told you. I did wrong to tell you. It's none of my business, I know, what you do. But I got so's I couldn't sleep, thinking of him giving out he was a married man—getting away with it time after time—other girls suffering the way he made me suffer." Tears spilled down her thin cheeks, across the dusty pink areas of rouge. She brushed them away angrily.

"I'm glad you told me," said Miss Nina in a queer little voice. Her aquamarine eyes were very light in her drab face.

"I only wish," she said slowly, "I only wish I had of known before."

The woman laid one hand on Miss Nina's arm. "Listen," she implored her. "Would you take a piece of advice? I'm older than you. Don't let this break your heart, dear. Go back to that boy friend you talked about. You get married, hear me? That's the only thing for a woman to do, get married—"

"Boy friend?" cried Miss Nina. She spat out the word in disgust. "Married? Say, what's getting married? Kids. No clothes. No fun. Washing and ironing, and mending his clothes instead of just your own. Cooking and cleaning and losing your looks. And him not as nice to you as before you were married." She thrust her face close to the blonde woman's. "I'm going to have things," she said. Her little voice was shrill and vibrant. "No thirty-dollar clerk for me when I marry. I've been studying, educating myself to speak nice, and everything. I gave the boy friend the air six months ago. Do you think I'm going to throw myself away?"

Before such indignation the woman gasped speechless. Her large hazel eyes, around which moisture still clung, looked at Nina with a hypnotized fascination which was almost fear. "What you just told me," said Nina grimly, "explains a lot of things. It's just what I needed." Her eyes narrowed as she looked at the woman. "I've got enough on Pete Koch to put him in State's prison." And absently, thoughtfully, her fingers tapped the corner of a white envelope which protruded at the bosom of her dress.

The blonde woman drew on her new kid gloves before she stumbled from the elevator. The big foyer seemed almost quiet. The woman glanced about her. In the cashier's cage, at the end of the long hotel desk, sat a very pretty girl. And, as the blonde woman looked, she saw that a tall man stooped attentively beside the cage. His back was toward the blonde woman. But she could see that he leaned forward eagerly, absorbed in his conversation with the pretty girl. The woman took an impulsive step toward him. "Oh, my God!" she whispered. The expression on her face might have been pity—as though these bland shoulders in the well-cut coat seemed suddenly pathetically vulnerable, unaware of dangers.

Then abruptly she turned and walked down the long corridor which led to the side entrance of the hotel. She kept clasping and unclasping her gloved hands as she walked. She was still laughing when she reached the street.

A Matter of Business

by Sinclair Lewis

Candee's sleeping porch faced the east. At sunrise every morning he startled awake and became a poet.

He yawned, pulled up the gray camping blanket which proved that he had once gone hunting in Canada, poked both hands behind his neck, settled down with a wriggling motion, and was exceedingly melancholy and happy.

He resolved, seriously and all at once, to study music, to wear a rose down to business, to tell the truth in his advertisements, and to start a campaign for a municipal auditorium. He longed to leap out of bed and go change the entire world immediately. But always, as sunrise blurred into russet, he plunged his arms under the blanket, sighed, "Funny what stuff a fellow will think of at six A.M.," yawned horridly, and was asleep. Two hours afterward, when he sat on the edge of the bed, rubbing his jaw in the hope that he could sneak out of shaving this morning, letting his feet ramble around independently in search of his slippers, he was not a poet. He was Mr. Candee of the Novelty Stationery Shop, Vernon.

He sold writing paper, Easter cards, bronze book-ends, framed color prints. He was a salesman born. To him it was exhilaration to herd a hesitating customer; it was pride to see his clerks, Miss Cogerty and the new girl, imitate his courtesy, his quickness. He was conscious of beauty. Ten times a week he stopped to gloat over a print in which a hilltop and a flare of daisies expressed all the indolence of August. But—and this was equally a part of him—he was delighted by "putting things over." He was as likely to speculate in a broken lot of china dogs as to select a stock of chaste brass knockers. It was he who had popularized Whistler in Vernon, and he who had brought out the "Oh My! Bathing Girl" pictures.

He was a soldier of fortune, was Candee; he fought under any flag which gave him the excuse. He was as much an adventurer as though he sat on a rampart wearing a steel corselet instead of sitting at a golden-oak desk wearing a blue-serge suit.

Every Sunday afternoon the Candees drove out to the golf club. They came home by a new route this Sunday.

"I feel powerful. Let's do some exploring," said Candee.

He turned the car off the Boulevard down one of the nameless hilly roads which twist along the edge of every city. He came into a straggly country of market gardens, jungles of dead weeds, unpruned crab-apple trees, and tall, thin houses which started as artificial-stone mansions and ended as unpainted frame shacks. In front of a tar-paper shanty there was a wild-grape arbor of thick vines draped upon second-hand scantlings and cracked pieces of molding. The yard had probably never been raked, but it displayed petunias in a tub salvaged from a patent washing machine. On a shelf beside the gate was a glass case with a sign:

ToYs FOR THEE CHILRUN.

Candee stopped the car.

In the case were half a dozen wooden dolls with pegged joints—an old-man doll with pointed hat, jutting black beard, and lumpy, out-thrust hands; a Pierrot with a prim wooden cockade; a princess fantastically tall and lean.

"Huh! Hand made! Arts-and-crafts stuff!" said Candee, righteously.

"That's so," said Mrs. Candee.

He drove on.

"Freak stuff. Abs'lutely grotesque. Not like anything I ever saw!"

"That's so," said Mrs. Candee.

He was silent. He irritably worked the air-choke, and when he found that it was loose he said, "Damn!" As for Mrs. Candee, she said nothing at all. She merely looked like a wife.

He turned toward her argumentatively. "Strikes me those dolls were darn ugly. Some old nut of a hermit must have made 'em. They were—they were ugly! Eh?"

"That's so," said Mrs. Candee.

"Don't you think they were ugly?"

"Yes, I think that's so," said Mrs. Candee, as she settled

down to meditate upon the new laundress who was coming to-morrow.

Next morning Candee rushed into his shop, omitted the report on his Sunday golf and the progress of his game which he usually gave to Miss Cogerty, and dashed at the shelf of toys. He had never thought about toys as he had about personal Christmas cards or diaries. His only specialty for children was expensive juveniles.

He glowered at the shelf. It was disordered. It was characterless. There were one rabbit of gray Canton flannel, two rabbits of papier-mâché, and nine tubercular rabbits of white fur. There were sixteen dolls which simpered and looked unintelligent. There were one train, one fire engine, and a device for hoisting thimblefuls of sand upon a trestle. Not that you did anything with it when you had hoisted it.

"Huh!" said Candee.

"Yes, Mr. Candee?" said Miss Cogerty.

"Looks like a side-street notions store. Looks like a racket shop. Looks like a—looks like— Aah!" said Candee.

He stormed his desk like a battalion of marines. He was stern. "Got to take up that bum shipment with the Fressen Paper Company. I'll write 'em a letter that'll take their hides off. I won't type it. Make it stronger if I turn the ole pen loose."

He vigorously cleared away a pile of fancy penwipers—stopping only to read the advertisement on an insurance blotter, to draw one or two pictures on an envelope, and to rub the enticing pale-blue back of a box of safety matches with a soft pencil till it looked silvery in a cross-light. He snatched his fountain pen out of his vest pocket. He looked at it unrelentingly. He sharpened the end of a match and scraped a clot of ink off the pen cap. He tried the ink supply by making a line of O's on his thumbnail. He straightened up, looked reprovingly at Miss Cogerty's back, slapped a sheet of paper on the desk—then stopped again and read his mail.

It did not take him more than an hour to begin to write the letter he was writing. In grim jet letters he scrawled:

FRESSEN COMPANY:
    GENTLEMEN,—I want you to thoroughly understand—

Twenty minutes later he had added nothing to the letter but a curlicue on the tail of the "d" in "understand." He was drawing the picture of a wooden doll with a pointed hat and a flaring black beard. His eyes were abstracted and his lips moved furiously:

"Makes me sick. Not such a whale of a big shop, but it's distinctive. Not all this commonplace junk—souvenirs and bum valentines. And yet our toys— Ordinary! Common! Hate to think what people must have been saying about 'em! But those wooden dolls out there in the country—they were ugly, just like Nelly said, but somehow they kind of stirred up the imagination."

He shook his head, rubbed his temples, looked up wearily. He saw that the morning rush had begun. He went out into the shop slowly, but as he crooned at Mrs. Harry MacPherson, "I have some new light-weight English envelopes—crossbar lavender with a stunning purple lining," he was imperturbable. He went out to lunch with Harry Jason and told a really new flivver story. He did not cease his bustling again till four, when the shop was for a moment still. Then he leaned against the counter and brooded:

"Those wooden dolls remind me of— Darn it! I don't know what they do remind me of! Like something— Castles. Gypsies. Oh, rats! Brother Candee, I thought you'd grown up! Hey, Miss Cogerty, what trying do? Don't put those Honey Bunny books there!"

At home he hurried through dinner.

"Shall we play a little auction with the Darbins?" Mrs. Candee yawned.

"No. I— Got to mull over some business plans. Think I'll take a drive by myself, unless you or the girls have to use the machine," ventured Candee.

"No. I think I might catch up on my sleep. Oh, Jimmy, the new laundress drinks just as much coffee as the last one did!"

"Yes?" said Candee, looking fixedly at a candle shade and meditating. "I don't know. Funny, all the wild crazy plans I used to have when I was a kid. Suppose those dolls remind me of that."

He dashed out from dinner, hastily started the car. He drove rapidly past the lakes, through dwindling lines of speculative houses, into a world of hazel-nut brush and small boys with furtive dogs. His destination was the tar-paper shack in front of which he had seen the wooden dolls.

He stopped with a squawk of brakes, bustled up the path to the wild-grape arbor. In the dimness beneath it, squatting on his heels beside a bicycle, was a man all ivory and ebony,

A Matter of Business

ghost white and outlandish black. His cheeks and veined forehead were pale, his beard was black and thin and square. Only his hands were ruddy. They were brick-red and thick, yet cunning was in them, and the fingers tapered to square ends. He was a mediæval monk in overalls, a Hindu indecently without his turban. As Candee charged upon him he looked up and mourned:

"The chain, she rusty."

Now Candee was the friendliest soul in all the Boosters' Club. Squatting, he sympathized:

"Rusty, eh? Ole chain kind of rusty! Hard luck, I'll say. Ought to use graphite on it. That's it—graphite. 'Member when I was a kid—"

"I use graphite. All rusty before I get him," the ghost lamented. His was a deep voice, and humorless and grave.

Candee was impressed. "Hard luck! How about boric acid? No, that isn't it—chloric acid. No, oxalic acid. That's it—oxalic! That'll take off the rust."

"Os-all-ic," murmured the ghost.

"Well, cheer up, old man. Some day you'll be driving your own boat."

"Oh! Say!"—the ghost was childishly proud—"I got a phonograph!"

"Have you? Slick!" Candee became cautious and inquisitive. He rose and, though actually he had not touched the bicycle, he dusted off his hands. Craftily: "Well, I guess you make pretty good money, at that. I was noticing—"

"Reason I turned in, I noticed you had some toys out front. Thought I might get one for the kids. What do you charge?" He was resolving belligerently, "I won't pay more than a dollar per."

"I sharge fifty cent."

Candee felt cheated. He had been ready to battle for his rights and it was disconcerting to waste all this energy. The ghost rose, in sections, and ambled toward the glass case of dolls. He was tall, fantastically tall as his own toy emperors, and his blue-denim jacket was thick with garden soil. Beside him Candee was rosy and stubby and distressingly neat. He was also uneasy. Here was a person to whom he couldn't talk naturally.

"So you make dolls eh? Didn't know there was a toy maker in Vernon."

"No, I am nod a toy maker. I am a sculptor." The ghost was profoundly sad. "But nod de kine you t'ink. I do not make chudges in plog hats to put on courthouses. I would lige to. I would make fine plog hats. But I am not recognize. I make epitaphs in de monooment works. Huh!" The ghost sounded human now, and full of guile. "I am de only man in dose monooment works dat know what 'R.I.P.' mean in de orizhinal Greek!"

He leaned against the gate and chuckled. Candee recovered from his feeling of being trapped in a particularly chilly tomb. He crowed:

"I'll bet you are, at that. But you must have a good time making these dolls."

"You lak dem?"

"You bet! I certainly do. I—" His enthusiasm stumbled. In a slightly astonished tone, in a low voice, he marveled, "And I do, too, by golly!" Then: "You— I guess you enjoy making—"

"No, no! It iss not enjoyment. Dey are my art, de dolls. Dey are how I get even wit' de monooment works. I should wish I could make him for a living, but nobody want him. One year now—always dey stand by de gate, waiting, and nobody buy one. Oh, well, I can't help dat! I know what I do, even if nobody else don't. I try to make him primitive, like what a child would make if he was a fine craftsman like me. Dey are all dream dolls. And me, I make him right. See! Nobody can break him!"

He snatched the Gothic princess from the case and banged her on the fence.

Candee came out of a trance of embarrassed unreality and shouted: "Sure are the real stuff. Now, uh, the—uh— May I ask your name?"

"Emile Jumas my name."

Candee snapped his fingers. "Got it, by golly!"

"*Pardon?*"

"The Papa Jumas dolls! That's their name. Look here! Have you got any more of these in the house?"

"Maybe fifty." Jumas had been roused out of his ghostliness.

"Great! Could you make five or six a day, if you didn't do anything else and maybe had a boy to help you?"

"Oh yez. No. Well, maybe four."

"See here. I could— I have a little place where I think maybe I could sell a few. Course you understand I don't know for sure. Taking a chance. But I think maybe I could. I'm J.T. Candee. Probably you know my stationery shop. I don't want to boast, but I will say there's no place in town that touches it for class. But I don't mean I could afford to pay you any fortune. But"—all his caution collapsed—"Jumas, I'm going to put you across!"

The two men shook hands a number of times and made sounds of enthusiasm, sounds like the rubbing of clothes on a washboard. But Jumas was stately in his invitation:

"Will you be so good and step in to have a lettle homemade wine?"

It was a one room, his house, with a loft above, but it contained a harp, a double bed, a stove, a hen that was doubtful of strangers, a substantial Mamma Jumas, six children, and forty-two wooden dolls.

"Would you like to give up the monument works and stick to making these?" glowed Candee, as he handled the dolls.

Jumas mooned at him. "Oh yez."

Ten minutes later, at the gate, Candee sputtered: "By golly! by golly! Certainly am pitching wild to-night. Not safe to be out alone. For first time in my life forgot to mention prices. Crazy as a kid—and I like it!" But he tried to sound managerial as he returned. "What do you think I ought to pay you apiece?"

Craftily Papa Jumas piped: "I t'ink you sell him for more than fifty cent. I t'ink maybe I ought to get fifty."

Then, while the proprietor of the Novelty Stationery Shop wrung spiritual hands and begged him to be careful, Candee the adventurer cried: "Do you know what I'm going to do? I'm going to sell 'em at three dollars, and I'm going to make every swell on the Boulevard buy one, and I'm going to make 'em pay their three bones, and I'm going to make 'em like it! Yes, sir! And you get two dollars apiece!"

It was not till he was on the sleeping porch, with the virile gray blanket patted down about his neck, that Candee groaned: "What have I let myself in for? And are they ugly or not?" He desired to go in, wake his wife, and ask her opinion. He lay and worried, and when he awoke at dawn and discovered that he hadn't really been tragically awake all night, he was rather indignant.

But he was exhilarated at breakfast and let Junior talk all through his oatmeal.

He came into the shop with a roar. "Miss Cogerty! Get the porter and have him take all those toys down to that racket shop on Jerusalem Alley that bought our candlestick remainders. Go down and get what you can for 'em. We're going to have— Miss Cogerty, we're going to display in this shop a line of arts-and-crafts dolls that for artistic execution and delightful quaintness— Say, that's good stuff for an ad. I'll put a ten-inch announcement in the *Courier*. I'll give this town one jolt. You wait!"

Candee did not forever retain his enthusiasm for Papa Jumas dolls. Nor did they revolutionize the nurseries of Vernon. To be exact, some people liked them and some people did not like them. Enough were sold to keep Jumas occupied, and not enough so that at the great annual crisis of the summer motor trip to Michigan, Candee could afford a nickel-plated spotlight as well as slip covers. There was a reasonable holiday sale through the autumn following, and always Candee liked to see them on the shelf at the back of the shop —the mediæval dolls like cathedral grotesques, the Greek warrior Demetrios; and the modern dolls—the agitated traffic policeman and the aviator whose arms were wings. Candee and Junior played explorer with them on the sleeping porch, and with them populated a castle made of chairs.

But in the spring he discovered Miss Arnold's batik lamp shades.

Miss Arnold was young, Miss Arnold was pretty, and her lamp shades had many "talking points" for a salesman with enthusiasm. They were terra-cotta and crocus and leaf green; they had flowers, fruit, panels, fish, and whirligigs upon them, and a few original decorations which may have been nothing but spots. Candee knew that they were either artistic or insane; he was excited, and in the first week he sold forty of them and forgot the Papa Jumas dolls.

In late April a new road salesman came in from the Mammoth Doll Corporation. He took Candee out to lunch and was secretive and oozed hints about making a great deal of money. He admitted at last that the Mammoth people were going to put on the market a doll that "had everything else beat four ways from the ace." He produced a Skillyoolly doll. She was simpering, star-eyed, fluffy, chiffon-clothed lady doll, and, though she was cheaply made, she was not cheaply priced.

"The Skillyoolly drive is going to be the peppiest campaign you ever saw. There's a double market—not only the kids, but all these Janes that like to stick a doll up on the piano, to make the room look dressy when Bill comes calling. And it's got the snap, eh?"

"Why don't you—? The department stores can sell more of these than I can," Candee fenced.

"That's just what we don't want to do. There's several of these fluff dolls on the market—not that any of them have the zip of our goods, of course. What we want is exclusive shops, that don't handle any other dolls whatever, so we won't have any inside competition, and so we can charge a class price."

"But I'm already handling some dolls—"

"If I can show you where you can triple your doll turnover, I guess we can take care of that, eh? For one thing, we're willing to make the most generous on-sale proposition you ever hit."

The salesman left with Candee samples of the Skillyoolly dolls, and a blank contract. He would be back in this territory next month, he indicated, and he hoped to close the deal. He gave Candee two cigars and crooned:

"Absolutely all we want is to have you handle the Skillyoolly exclusively and give us a chance to show what we can do. 'You tell 'em, pencil, you got the point!'"

Candee took the dolls home to his wife, and now she was not merely wifely and plump and compliant. She squealed.

"I think they're perfectly darling! So huggable—just sweet. I know you could sell thousands of them a year. You must take them. I always thought the Jumas dolls were hideous."

"They aren't so darn hideous. Just kind of different," Candee said, uncomfortably.

Next morning he had decided to take the Skillyoolly agency—and he was as lonely and unhappy about it as a boy who has determined to run away from home.

Papa Jumas came in that day and Candee tried to be jolly and superior.

"Ah, there, old monsieur! Say, I may fix up an arrangement to switch your dolls from my place to the Toy and China Bazaar."

Jumas lamented: "De Bazaar iss a cheap place. I do not t'ink they lige my t'ings."

"Well, we'll see, we'll see. Excuse me now. Got to speak to Miss Cogerty about—about morocco cardcases—cardcases."

He consulted Miss Cogerty and the lovely Miss Arnold of the batik lamp shades about the Skillyoolly dolls. Both of them squeaked ecstatically. Yet Candee scowled at a Skillyoolly standing on his desk and addressed her:

"Doll, you're a bunch of fluff. You may put it over these

sentimental females for a while, but you're no good. You're a rotten fake, and to charge two plunks for you is the darndest nerve I ever heard of. And yet I might make a thousand a year clear out of you. A thousand a year. Buy quite a few cord tires, curse it!"

At five Miss Sorrell bought some correspondence cards.

Candee was afraid of Miss Sorrell. She was the principal of a private school. He never remembered what she wore, but he had an impression that she was clad entirely in well-starched four-ply linen collars. She was not a person to whom you could sell things. She looked at you sarcastically and told you what she wanted. But the girls in her school were fervid customers, and, though he grumbled, "Here's that old grouch," he concentrated upon her across the showcase.

When she had ordered the correspondence cards and fished the copper address plate out of a relentless seal purse, Miss Sorrell blurted: "I want to tell you how very, very much I appreciate the Papa Jumas dolls. They are the only toys sold in Vernon that have imagination and solidity."

"Folks don't care much for them, mostly. They think I ought to carry some of these fluffy dolls."

"Parents may not appreciate them, and I suppose they're so original that children take a little time getting used to them. But my nephew loves his Jumas dolls dearly; he takes them to bed with him. We are your debtors for having introduced them."

As she dotted out, Candee was vowing: "I'm not going to have any of those Skillyoolly hussies in my place! I'm—I'll fight for the Jumas dolls! I'll make people like 'em, if it takes a leg. I don't care if I lose a thousand a year on them, or ten thousand, or ten thousand million tillion!"

It was too lofty to last. He reflected that he didn't like Miss Sorrell. She had a nerve to try to patronize him! He hastened to his desk. He made computations for half an hour. Candee was an irregular and temperamental cost accountant. If his general profit was sufficient he rarely tracked down the share produced by items. Now he found that, allowing for rent, overhead, and interest, his profit on Papa Jumas dolls in the last four months had been four dollars. He gasped:

"Probably could make 'em popular if I took time enough. But—four dollars! And losing a thousand a year by not handling Skillyoollys. I can't afford luxuries like that. I'm not in business for my health. I've got a wife and kids to look out for. Still, I'm making enough to keep fat and cheery on, entirely aside from the dolls. Family don't seem to be starving. I guess I can afford one luxury. I— Oh, rats!"

He reached, in fact, a sure, clear, ringing resolution that he would stock Skillyoolly dolls; that he'd be hanged if he'd stock Skillyoolly dolls; and that he would give nine dollars and forty cents if he knew whether he was going to stock them or not.

After the girls had gone out that evening he hinted to his wife: "I don't really believe I want to give up the Jumas dolls. May cost me a little profit for a while yet, but I kind of feel obligated to the poor old Frenchie, and the really wise birds—you take this Miss Sorrell, for instance—they appreciate—"

"Then you can't handle the Skillyoolly dolls?"

"Don't use that word! Skillyoolly! Ugh! Sounds like an old maid tickling a baby!"

"Now that's all very well, to be so superior and all—and if you mean that I was an old maid when we were married—"

"Why, Nelly, such a thought nev' entered my head!"

"Well, how could I tell? You're so bound and determined to be arbitrary tonight. It's all very well to be charitable and to think about that Jumas—and I never did like him, horrid, skinny old man!—and about your dolls that you're so proud of, and I still insist they're ugly, but I do think there's some folks a little nearer home that you got to show consideration for, and us going without things we need—"

"Now I guess you've got about as many clothes as anybody—"

"See here, Jimmy Candee! I'm not complaining about myself. I like pretty clothes, but I never was one to demand things for myself, and you know it!"

"Yes, that's true. You're sensible—"

"Well, I try to be, anyway, and I detest these wives that simply drive their husbands like they were pack-horses, but— It's the girls. Not that they're bad off. But you're like all these other men. You think because a girl has a new dancing frock once a year that she's got everything in the world. And here's Mamie crying her eyes out because she hasn't got anything to wear to the Black Bass dance, and that horrible Jason girl will show up in silver brocade or something, and Mamie thinks Win Morgan won't even look at her. Not but what she can get along. I'm not going to let you work and slave for things to put on Mamie's back. But if you're going to waste a lot of money I certainly don't see why it should go to a perfect stranger—a horrid old Frenchman that digs graves, or whatever it is—when we could use it right here at home!"

"Well, of course, looking at it that way—" sighed Candee.

"Do you see?"

"Yes, but—there's a principle involved. Don't know that I can make it clear to you, but I wouldn't feel as if I was doing my job honestly if I sold a lot of rubbish."

"Rubbish? Rubbish? If there's any rubbish it isn't those darling Skillyoolly dolls, but those wretched, angular Jumas things! But if you've made up your mind to be stubborn—and of course I'm not supposed to know anything about business! I merely scrimp and save and economize and do the marketing!"

She flapped the pages of her magazine and ignored him. All evening she was patient. It is hard to endure patience, and Candee was shaken. He was fond of his wife. Her refusal to support his shaky desire to "do his job honestly" left him forlorn, outside the door of her comfortable affection.

"Oh, I suppose I better be sensible," he said to himself, seventy or eighty times.

He was taking the Skillyoolly contract out of his desk as a cyclone entered the shop, a cyclone in brown velvet, white hair, and the best hat in Vernon—Mrs. Gerard Randall. Candee went rejoicing to the battle. He was a salesman. He was an artist, a scientist, and the harder the problem the better. Mechanically handing out quires of notepaper to customers who took whatever he suggested bored Candee as it would bore an exhibition aviator to drive a tractor. But selling to Mrs. Randall was not a bore. She was the eternal dowager, the dictator of Vernon society, rich and penurious and overwhelming.

He beamed upon her. He treacherously looked mild. He seemed edified by her snort:

"I want a penholder for my desk that won't look like a beastly schoolroom pen."

"Then you want a quill pen in mauve or a sea-foam green." Mrs. Randall was going to buy a quill pen, or she was going to die—or he was.

"I certainly do not want a quill pen, either mauve or pea-green or sky-blue beige! Quill pens are an abomination, and they wiggle when you're writing, and they're disgustingly common."

"My pens don't wiggle. They have patent grips—"

"Nonsense!"

"Well, shall we look at some other kinds?"

He placidly laid out an atrocious penholder of mother-of-pearl and streaky brass which had infested the shop for years.

"Horrible! Victorian! Certainly not!"

He displayed a nickel penholder stamped, "Souvenir of Vernon," a brittle, red wooden holder with a cork grip, and a holder of chased silver, very bulgy and writhing.

"They're terrible!" wailed Mrs. Randall.

She sounded defenseless. He flashed before her eyes the best quill in the shop, crisp, firm, tinted a faint rose.

"Well," she said, feebly. She held it, wabbled it, wrote a sentence in the agitated air. "But it wouldn't go with my desk set," she attempted.

He brought out a desk set of seal-brown enamel and in the bowl of shot he thrust the rose quill.

"How did you remember what my desk set was like?"

"Ah! Could one forget?" He did not look meek now; he looked insulting and cheerful.

"Oh, drat the man! I'll take it. But I don't want you to think for one moment that I'd stand being bullied this way if I weren't in a hurry."

He grinned. He resolved, I'm going to make the ole dragon buy three Jumas dolls—no, six! "Mrs. Randall, I know you're in a rush, but I want you to look at something that will interest you."

"I suppose you're going to tell me that 'we're finding this line very popular,' whatever it is. I don't want it."

"Quite the contrary. I want you to see these because they haven't gone well at all."

"Then why should I be interested?"

"Ah, Mrs. Randall, if Mrs. Randall were interested, everybody else would have to be."

"Stop being sarcastic, if you don't mind. That's my own province." She was glaring at him, but she was following him to the back of the shop.

He chirped: "I believe you buy your toys for your grandchildren at the Bazaar. But I want to show you something they'll really like." He was holding up a Gothic princess, turning her lanky magnificence round and round. As Mrs. Randall made an "aah" sound in her throat, he protested. "Wait! You're wrong. They're not ugly; they're a new kind of beauty."

"Beauty! Arty! Tea-roomy!"

"Not at all. Children love 'em. I'm so dead sure of it that I want— Let's see. You have three grandchildren. I want to send each of them two Papa Jumas dolls. I'll guarantee— No. Wait! I'll guarantee the children won't care for them at first. Don't say anything about the dolls, but just leave 'em around the nursery and watch. Inside of two weeks you'll find the children so crazy about 'em they won't go to bed without 'em. I'll send 'em up to your daughter's house and when you get around to it you can decide whether you want to pay me or not."

"Humph! You are very eloquent. But I can't stand here all day. Ask one of your young women to wrap up four or five of these things and put them in my car. And put them on my bill. I can't be bothered with trying to remember to pay you. Good day!"

While he sat basking at his desk he remembered the words of the severe schoolmistress, Miss Sorrell, "Only toys in Vernon that have imagination and solidity."

"People like that, with brains, they're the kind. I'm not going to be a popcorn-and-lemonade seller. Skillyoolly dolls! Any ten-year-old boy could introduce those to a lot of sentimental females. Takes a real salesman to talk Jumas dolls. And— If I could only get Nelly to understand!"

Alternately triumphant and melancholy, he put on his hat, trying the effect in the little crooked mirror over the water cooler, and went out to the Boosters' Club weekly lunch.

Sometimes the Boosters' lunches were given over to speeches; sometimes they were merry and noisy; and when they were noisy Candee was the noisiest. But he was silent to-day. He sat at the long table beside Darbin, the ice-cream manufacturer, and when Darbin chuckled invitingly, "Well, you old Bolshevik, what's the latest junk you're robbing folks for?" Candee's answer was feeble.

"That's all right, now! 'S good stuff."

He looked down the line of the Boosters—men engaged in electrotyping and roofing, real estate and cigar making; certified accountants and teachers and city officials. He noted Oscar Sunderquist, the young surgeon.

He considered: "I suppose they're all going through the same thing—quick turnover on junk *versus* building up something permanent, and maybe taking a loss; anyway, taking a chance. Huh! Sounds so darn ridiculously easy when you put it that way. Of course a regular fellow would build up the long-time trade and kick out cheap stuff. Only—not so easy to chase away a thousand or ten thousand dollars when it comes right up and tags you. Oh, gee! I dunno! I wish you'd quit fussing like a schoolgirl, Brother Candee. I'm going to cut it out." By way of illustrating which he turned to his friend Darbin. "Frank, I'm worried. I want some advice. Will it bother you if I weep on your shoulder?"

"Go to it! Shoot! Anything I can do—"

He tried to make clear to Darbin how involved was a choice between Papa Jumas and the scent pots of the Skillyoolly. Darbin interrupted:

"Is that all that ails you? Cat's sake! What the deuce difference does it make which kind of dolls you handle? Of course you'll pick the kind that brings in the most money. I certainly wouldn't worry about the old Frenchman. I always did think those Jumas biznai were kind of freakish."

"Then you don't think it matters?"

"Why, certainly not! Jimmy, you're a good business man, some ways. You're a hustler. But you always were erratic. Business isn't any jazz-band dance. You got to look at these things in a practical way. Say, come on; the president's going to make a spiel. Kid him along and get him going."

"Don't feel much like kidding."

"I'll tell you what I think's the matter with you, Jimmy; your liver's on the bum."

"Maybe you're right," croaked Candee. He did not hear the president's announcement of the coming clam-bake. He was muttering, in an injured way:

"Damn it! Damn it! Damn it!"

He was walking back to the shop.

He didn't want to go back; he didn't care whether Miss Cogerty was selling any of the *écrasé* sewing baskets or not. He was repeating Darbin's disgusted: "What difference does it make? Why all the fuss?"

"At most I'd lose a thousand a year. I wouldn't starve. This little decision—nobody cares a hang. I was a fool to speak to Nelly and Darbin. Now they'll be watching me. Well, I'm not going to let 'em think I'm an erratic fool. Ten words of approval from a crank like that Sorrell woman is a pretty thin return for years of work. Yes, I'll—I'll be sensible."

He spent the late afternoon in furiously re-arranging the table of vases and candlesticks. "Exercise, that's what I need, not all this grousing around," he said. But when he went home he had, without ever officially admitting it to himself that he was doing it, thrust a Jumas doll and a Skillyoolly into his pocket, and these, in the absence of his wife, he hid beneath his bed on the sleeping porch. With his wife he had a strenuous and entirely imaginary conversation:

"Why did I bring them home? Because I wanted to. I don't see any need of explaining my motives. I don't intend to argue about this in any way, shape, manner, or form!" He looked at himself in the mirror, with admiration for the firmness, strength of character, iron will, and numerous other virtues revealed in his broad nose and square—also plump—chin. It is true that his wife came in and caught him at it, and that he pretended to be examining his bald spot. It is true that he listened mildly to her reminder that for two weeks now he hadn't rubbed any of the sulphur stuff on his head. But he marched downstairs—behind her—with an imperial tread. He had solved his worry! Somehow, he was going to work it all out.

Just how he was going to work it out he did not state. That detail might be left till after dinner.

He did not again think of the dolls hidden beneath his bed till he had dived under the blanket. Cursing a little, he crawled out and set them on the rail of the sleeping porch.

He awoke, suddenly and sharply, at sunup. He heard a voice—surely not his own—snarling: "Nobody is going to help you. If you want to go on looking for a magic way out—go right on looking. You won't find it!"

He stared at the two dolls. The first sunlight was on the Skillyoolly object, and in that intolerant glare he saw that her fluffy dress was sewed on with cheap thread which would break at the first rough handling. Suddenly he was out of bed, pounding the unfortunate Skillyoolly on the rail, smashing her simpering face, wrenching apart her ill-jointed limbs, tearing her gay chiffon. He was dashing into the bedroom, waking his bewildered wife with:

"Nelly! Nelly! Get up! No, it's all right. But it's time for breakfast."

She foggily looked at her wrist watch on the bedside table, and complained, "Why, it isn't but six o'clock!"

"I know it, but we're going to do a stunt. D'you realize we haven't had breakfast just by ourselves and had a chance to really talk since last summer? Come on! You fry an egg and I'll start the percolator. Come on!"

"Well," patiently, reaching for her dressing gown.

While Candee, his shrunken bathrobe flapping about his shins, excitedly put the percolator together and attached it to the baseboard plug, leaving out nothing but the coffee, he chattered of the Boosters' Club.

As they sat down he crowed: "Nelly, we're going to throw some gas in the ole car and run down to Chicago and back, next week. How's that?"

"That would be very nice," agreed Mrs. Candee.

"And we're going to start reading aloud again, evenings, instead of all this doggone double solitaire."

"That would be fine."

"Oh, and by the way, I've finally made up my mind. I'm not going to mess up my store with that Skillyoolly stuff. Going to keep on with the Jumas dolls, but push 'em harder."

"Well, if you really think—"

"And, uh— Gee! I certainly feel great this morning. Feel like a million dollars. What say we have another fried egg?"

"I think that might be nice," said Mrs. Candee, who had been married for nineteen years.

"Sure you don't mind about the Skillyoolly dolls?"

"Why, no, not if you know what you want. And that reminds me! How terrible of me to forget! When you ran over to the Jasons' last evening, the Skillyoolly salesman telephoned the house—he'd just come to town. He asked me if you were going to take the agency, and I told him no. Of course I've known all along that you weren't. But hasn't it been interesting, thinking it all out? I'm so glad you've been firm."

"Well, when I've gone into a thing thoroughly I like to smash it right through. . . . Now you take Frank Darbin; makes me tired the way he's fussing and stewing, trying to find out whether he wants to buy a house in Rosebank or not. So you—you told the Skillyoolly salesman no? I just wonder— Gee! I kind of hate to give up the chance of the Skillyoolly market! What do you think?"

"But it's all settled now."

"Then I suppose there's no use fussing— I tell you; I mean a fellow wants to look at a business deal from all sides. See how I mean?"

"That's so," said Mrs. Candee, admiringly. As with a commanding step he went to the kitchen to procure another fried egg she sighed to herself, "Such a dear boy—and yet such a forceful man."

Candee ran in from the kitchen. In one hand was an egg,

in the other the small frying pan. "Besides," he shouted, "how do we know the Skillyoollys would necessarily sell so darn well? You got to take everything like that into consideration, and then decide and stick to it. See how I mean?"

"That's so," said Mrs. Candee.

The Dummy-Chucker

by Arthur Somers Roche

There were many women on East Fourteenth Street. With the seeing eye of the artist, the dummy-chucker looked them over and rejected them. Kindly-seeming, generously fat, the cheap movie houses disgorged them. A dozen alien tongues smote the air, and every one of them hinted of far lands of poverty, of journeys made and hardships undergone. No better field for beggary in all Manhattan's bounteous acreage.

But the dummy-chucker shook his head and shuffled ever westward. These were good souls, but—they thought in cents. Worse than that, they translated their financial thoughts into the pitiful coinage of their birthplaces. And in the pocket of the dummy-chucker rested a silver dollar.

A gaunt man, who towered high, and whose tongue held the cadences of the wide spaces, had slipped this dollar into the receptive hand of the dummy-chucker. True, it was almost a fortnight ago, and the man might have gone back to his Western home—but Broadway had yielded him up to the dummy-chucker. Broadway might yield up such another.

At Union Square, the dummy-chucker turned north. Past the Flatiron Building he shuffled, until, at length, the Tenderloin unfolded itself before him. These were the happy hunting-grounds!

Of course—and he glanced behind him quickly—there were more fly cops on Broadway than on the lower East Side. One of them had dug his bony fingers between the shabby collar of the dummy-chucker's coat and the lank hair that hung down his neck. He had yanked the dummy-chucker to his feet. He had dragged his victim to a patrol-box; he had taken him to a police station, whence he had been conveyed to Jefferson Market Court, where a judge had sentenced him to a sojourn on Blackwell's Island.

That had been ten days ago. This very day, the municipal ferry had landed the dummy-chucker, with others of his slinking kind, upon Manhattan's shores again. Not for a long time would the memory of the Island menu be effaced from the dummy-chucker's palate, the locked doors be banished from his mental vision.

A man might be arrested on Broadway, but he might also get the money. Timorously, the dummy-chucker weighed the two possibilities. He felt the dollar in his pocket. At a street in the Forties, he turned westward. Beyond Eighth Avenue there was a place where the shadow of prohibition was only a shadow.

Prices had gone up, but, as Finisterre Joe's bartender informed him, there was more kick in a glass of the stuff that cost sixty cents to-day than there had been in a barrel of the old juice. And, for a good customer, Finisterre Joe's bartender would shade the price a trifle. The dummy-chucker received two portions of the crudely blended poison that passed for whisky in exchange for his round silver dollar. It was with less of a shuffle and more of a stride that he retraced his steps toward Broadway.

Slightly north of Times Square, he surveyed his field of action. Across the street, a vaudeville house was discharging its mirth-surfeited audience. Half a block north, laughing groups testified that the comedy they had just left had been as funny as its press-agent claimed. The dummy-chucker shook his head. He moved south, his feet taking on that shuffle which they had lost temporarily.

"She Loved and Lost"—that was the name of the picture being run this week at the Concorde. Outside was billed a huge picture of the star, a lady who received more money for making people weep than most actors obtain for making them laugh. The dummy-chucker eyed the picture approvingly. He took his stand before the main entrance. This was the place! If he tried to do business with a flock of people that had just seen Charlie Chaplin, he'd fail. He knew! Fat women who'd left the twins at home with the neighbor's cook in order that they might have a good cry at the Concorde—these were his mutton-heads.

He reeled slightly as several flappers passed—just for practise. Ten days on Blackwell's hadn't spoiled his form. They drew away from him; yet, from their manners, he knew that they did not suspect him of being drunk. Well, hurrah for prohibition, after all! Drunkenness was the last thing people suspected of a hardworking man nowadays. He slipped his hand in his pocket. They were coming now—the fat women with the babies at home, their handkerchiefs still at their eyes. His hand slipped to his mouth. His jaws moved savagely. One thing was certain: out of to-day's stake he'd buy some decent-tasting soap. This awful stuff that he'd borrowed from the Island—

The stoutest woman paused; she screamed faintly as the dummy-chucker staggered, pitched forward, and fell at her short-vamped feet. Excitedly she grasped her neighbor's arm.

"He's gotta fit!"

The neighbor bent over the prostrate dummy-chucker.

"Ep'lepsy," she announced. "Look at the foam on his lips."

"Aw, the poor man!"

"Him so strong-looking, too!"

"Ain't it the truth? These husky-looking men sometimes are the sickliest."

The dummy-chucker stirred. He sat up feebly. With his sleeve, he wiped away the foam. Dazedly he spoke.

"If I had a bite to eat—"

He looked upward at the first stout woman. Well and wisely had he chosen his scene. Movie tickets cost fractions of a dollar. There is always some stray silver in the bead bag of a movie patron. Into the dummy-chucker's outstretched palm fell pennies, nickels, dimes, quarters. There was present to-day no big-hearted Westerner with silver dollars, but here was comparative wealth. Already the dummy-chucker saw himself again at Finisterre Joe's, this time to purchase no bottled courage but to buy decantered ease.

"T'ank, ladies," he murmured. "If I can get a bit to eat and rest up—"

"'Rest up!'" The shrill jeer of a newsboy broke in upon his pathetic speech. "Rest up again on the Island! That's the kind of a rest up you'll get, y' big tramp."

"Can't you see the man's sick?" The stoutest one turned indignantly upon the newsboy. But the scoffer held his ground.

"'Sick?' Sure he's sick! Eatin' soap makes anyone sick. Youse dames is easy. He's chuckin' a dummy."

"'A dummy?'"

The dummy-chucker sat a bit straighter.

"Sure, ma'am. That's his game. He t'rows phony fits. He eats a bit of soap and makes his mouth foam. Last week, he got pinched right near here—"

But the dummy-chucker heard no more. He rolled sidewise just as the cry: "Police!" burst from the woman's lips. He reached the curb, rose, burst through the gathering crowd, and rounded a corner at full speed.

He was half-way to Eighth Avenue, and burning lungs had slowed him to a jog-trot, when a motor-car pulled up alongside the curb. It kept gentle pace with the fugitive. A shrewd-featured young man leaned from its fashionably sloped wheel.

"Better hop aboard," he suggested. "That policeman is fat, but he has speed."

The dummy-chucker glanced over his shoulder. Looming high as the Woolworth Building, fear overcoming the dwarfing tendency of distance, came a policeman. The dummy-chucker leaped to the motor's running-board. He climbed into the vacant front seat.

"Thanks, feller," he grunted. "A li'l speed, please."

The young man chuckled. He rounded the corner into Eighth Avenue and darted north among the trucks.

At Columbus Circle, the dummy-chucker spoke.

"Thanks again, friend," he said. "I'll be steppin' off here."

His rescuer glanced at him.

"Want to earn a hundred dollars?"

"Quitcher kiddin'," said the dummy-chucker.

"No, no; this is serious," said the young man.

The dummy-chucker leaned luxuriously back in his seat.

"Take me *anywhere*, friend," he said.

Half-way round the huge circle at Fifty-ninth Street, the young man guided the car. Then he shot into the park. They curved eastward. They came out on Fifth Avenue, somewhere in the Seventies. They shot eastward another half-block, and then the car stopped in front of an apartment-house. The young man pressed the button on the steering-wheel. In respone to the short blast of the electric horn, a uniformed man appeared. The young man alighted. The dummy-chucker followed suit.

"Take the car around to the garage, Andrews," said the young man. He nodded to the dummy-chucker. In a daze, the mendicant followed his rescuer. He entered a gorgeously mirrored and gilded hall. He stepped into an elevator chauffeured by a West Indian of the haughtiest blood. The dummy-chucker was suddenly conscious of his tattered garb, his ill-fitting, run-down shoes. He stepped, when they alighted from the lift, as gingerly as though he trod on tacks.

A servant in livery, as had been the waiting chauffeur downstairs, opened a door. If he was surprised at his master's choice of guest, he was too well trained to show it. He did not rebel even when ordered to serve sandwiches and liquor to the dummy-chucker.

"You seem hungry," commented the young man.

The dummy-chucker reached for another sandwich with his left hand while he poured himself a drink of genuine Scotch with his right.

"*And* thirsty," he grunted.

"Go to it," observed his host genially.

The dummy-chucker went to it for a good ten minutes. Then he leaned back in the heavily upholstered chair which the man servant had drawn up for him. He stared round him.

"Smoke?" asked his host.

The dummy-chucker nodded. He selected a slim panetela and pinched it daintily between the nails of his thumb and forefinger. His host watched the operation with interest.

"Why?" he asked.

"Better than cuttin' the end off," explained the dummy-chucker. "It's a good smoke," he added, puffing.

"You know tobacco," said his host. "Where did you learn?"

"Oh, we all have our ups and downs," replied the dummy-chucker. "But don't get nervous. I ain't goin' to tell you that I was a millionaire's son, educated at Harvard. I'm a bum."

"Doesn't seem to bother you," said his host.

"It don't," asserted the dummy-chucker. "Except when the police butt into my game. I just got off Blackwell's Island this morning."

"And almost went back this afternoon."

The dummy-chucker nodded.

"Almost," he said. His eyes wandered around the room. "*Some* dump!" he stated. Then his manner became business-like. "You mentioned a hundred dollars—what for?"

The young man shrugged.

"Not hard work. You merely have to look like a gentleman, and act like—"

"Like a bum?" asked the dummy-chucker.

"Well, something like that."

The dummy-chucker passed his hand across his stubby chin.

"Shoot!" he said. "Anything short of murder—*anything*, friend."

His host leaned eagerly forward.

"There's a girl—" he began.

The dummy-chucker nodded.

"There always is," he interrupted. "I forgot to mention that I bar kidnaping, too."

"It's barred," said the young man. He hitched his chair a trifle nearer his guest. "She's beautiful. She's young."

"And the money? The coin? The good red gold?"

"I have enough for two. I don't care about her money."

"Neither do I," said the dummy-chucker; "so long as I get my hundred. Shoot!"

"About a year ago," resumed the host, "she accepted, after a long courtship, a young man by the name of—oh, let's call him Jones."

The dummy-chucker inhaled happily.

"Call him any darned thing you like," he said cheerily.

"Jones was a drunkard," said the host.

"And she married him?" The dummy-chucker's eyebrows lifted slightly.

"No. She told him that if he'd quit drinking she'd marry him. She stipulated that he go without drink for one year."

The dummy-chucker reached for a fresh cigar. He lighted it and leaned back farther in the comfortable chair.

"Jones," continued the young man, "had tried to quit before. He knew himself pretty well. He knew that, even with war-time prohibition just round the corner, he couldn't keep away from liquor. Not while he stayed in New York. But a classmate of his had been appointed head of an expedition that was to conduct exploration work in Brazil. He asked his classmate for a place in the party. You see, he figured that in the wilds of Brazil there wouldn't be any chance for drunkenness."

"A game guy," commented the dummy-chucker. "Well, what happened?"

"He died of jungle-fever two months ago," was the answer. "The news just reached Rio Janeiro yesterday."

The dummy-chucker lifted his glass of Scotch.

"To a regular feller," he said, and drank. He set his glass down gently. "And the girl? I suppose she's all shot to pieces?"

"She doesn't know," said the host quietly.

The dummy-chucker's eyebrows lifted again.

"I begin to get you," he said. "I'm the messenger from Brazil who breaks the sad news to her, eh?"

The young man shook his head.

"The news isn't to be broken to her—not yet. You see— well, I was Jones' closest friend. He left his will with me, his personal effects, and all that. So I'm the one that received the wire of his death. In a month or so, of course, it will be published in the newspapers—when letters have come from the explorers. But, just now, I'm the only one that knows it."

"Except me," said the dummy-chucker.

The young man smiled dryly.

"Except you. And you won't tell. Ever wear evening clothes?"

The dummy-chucker stiffened. Then he laughed sardonically.

"Oh, yes; when I was at Princeton. What's the idea?"

His host studied him carefully.

"Well, with a shave, and a hair-cut, and a manicure, and the proper clothing, and the right setting—well, if a person had only a quick glance—that person might think you were Jones."

The dummy-chucker carefully brushed the ashes from his cigar upon a tray.

"I guess I'm pretty stupid to-night. I still don't see it."

"You will," asserted his host. "You see, she's a girl who's seen a great deal of the evil of drink. She has a horror of it. If she thought that Jones had broken his pledge to her, she'd throw him over."

"'Throw him over?' But he's *dead*!" said the dummy-chucker.

"She doesn't know that," retorted his host.

"Why don't you tell her?"

"Because I want to marry her."

"Well, I should think the quickest way to get her would be to tell her about Jones—"

"You don't happen to know the girl," interrupted the other. "She's a girl of remarkable conscience. If I should tell her that Jones died in Brazil, she'd enshrine him in her memory. He'd be a hero who had died upon the battle-field. More than that—he'd be a hero who had died upon the battle-field in a war to which she had sent him. His death would be upon her soul. Her only expiation would be to be faithful to him forever."

"I won't argue about it," said the dummy-chucker. "I don't know her. Only—I guess your whisky has got me. I don't see it at all."

His host leaned eagerly forward now.

"She's going to the opera to-night with her parents. But, before she goes, she's going to dine with me at the Park

Square. Suppose, while she's there, Jones should come in. Suppose that he should come in reeling, noisy, *drunk*! She'd marry me to-morrow."

"I'll take your word for it," said the dummy-chucker. "Only, when she's learned that Jones had died two months ago in Brazil—"

"She'll be married to me then," responded the other fiercely. "What I get, I can hold. If she were Jones' wife, I'd tell her of his death. I'd know that, sooner or later, I'd win her. But if she learns now that he died while struggling to make himself worthy of her, she'll never give to another man what she withheld from him."

"I see," said the dummy-chucker slowly. "And you want me to—"

"There'll be a table by the door in the main dining-room engaged in Jones' name. You'll walk in there at a quarter to eight. You'll wear Jones' dinner clothes. I have them here. You'll wear the studs that he wore, his cuff-links. More than that, you'll set down upon the table, with a flourish, his monogrammed flask. You'll be drunk, noisy, disgraceful—"

"How long will I be all that—in the hotel?" asked the dummy-chucker dryly.

"That's exactly the point," said the other. "You'll last about thirty seconds. The girl and I will be on the far side of the room. I'll take care that she sees you enter. Then, when you've been quietly ejected, I'll go over to the *maître d'hôtel* to make inquiries. I'll bring back to the girl the flask which you will have left upon the table. If she has any doubt that you are Jones, the flask will dispel it."

"And then?" asked the dummy-chucker.

"Why, then," responded his host, "I propose to her. You see, I think it was pity that made her accept Jones in the beginning. I think that she cares for me."

"And you really think that I look enough like Jones to put this over?"

"In the shaded light of the dining-room, in Jones' clothes—well, I'm risking a hundred dollars on it. Will you do it?"

The dummy-chucker grinned.

"Didn't I say I'd do *anything*, barring murder? Where are the clothes?"

One hour and a half later, the dummy-chucker stared at himself in the long mirror of his host's dressing-room. He had bathed, not as Blackwell's Island prisoners bathe, but in a luxurious tub that had a head-rest, in scented water, soft as the touch of a baby's fingers. Then his host's man servant had cut his hair, had shaved him, had massaged him until color crept into the pale cheeks. The sheerest of knee-length linen underwear touched a body that knew only rough cotton. Silk socks, heavy, gleaming, snugly encased his ankles. Upon his feet were correctly dull pumps. That the trousers were a wee bit short mattered little. In these dancing-days, trousers should not be too long. And the fit of the coat over his shoulders—he carried them in a fashion unwontedly straight as he gazed at his reflection—balanced the trousers' lack of length. The short shirt-bosom gave freely, comfortably as he breathed. Its plaited whiteness enthralled him. He turned anxiously to his host.

"Will I do?" he asked.

"Better than I'd hoped," said the other. "You look like a gentleman."

The dummy-chucker laughed gaily.

"I feel like one," he declared.

"You understand what you are to do?" demanded the host.

"It ain't a hard part to act," replied the dummy-chucker.

"And you *can* act," said the other. "The way you fooled those women in front of the Concorde proved that you—"

"Sh-sh!" exclaimed the dummy-chucker reproachfully. "Please don't remind me of what I was before I became a gentleman."

His host laughed.

"You're all right." He looked at his watch. "I'll have to leave now. I'll send the car back after you. Don't be afraid of trouble with the hotel people. I'll explain that I know you, and fix matters up all right. Just take the table at the right hand side as you enter—"

"Oh, I've got it all right," said the dummy-chucker. "Better slip me something on account. I may have to pay something—"

His host laughed.

"You get nothing now," was the stern answer. "One hundred dollars when I get back here. And," he added, "if it should occur to you at the hotel that you might pawn these studs, or the flask, or the clothing for more than a hundred, let me remind you that my chauffeur will be watching one entrance, my valet another, and my chef another."

The dummy-chucker returned his gaze scornfully.

"Do I look," he asked, "like the sort of man who'd *steal*?"

His host shook his head.

"You certainly don't," he admitted.

The dummy-chucker turned back to the mirror. He was still entranced with his own reflection, twenty minutes later, when the valet told him that the car was waiting. He looked like a millionaire. He stole another glance at himself after he had slipped easily into the fur-lined overcoat that the valet held for him, after he had set somewhat rakishly upon his head the soft black-felt hat that was the latest accompaniment to the dinner coat.

Downstairs, he spoke to Andrews, the chauffeur.

"Drive across the Fifty-ninth Street bridge first."

The chauffeur stared at him.

"Who you givin' orders to?" he demanded.

The dummy-chucker stepped closer to the man.

"You heard my order?"

His hands, busily engaged in buttoning his gloves, did not clench. His voice was not raised. And Andrews must have outweighed him by thirty pounds. Yet the chauffeur stepped back and touched his hat.

"Yes, sir," he muttered.

The dummy-chucker smiled.

"The lower classes," he said to himself, "know rank and position when they see it."

His smile became a grin as he sank back in the limousine that was his host's evening conveyance. It became almost complacent as the car slid down Park Avenue. And when, at length, it had reached the center of the great bridge that spans the East River, he knocked upon the glass. The chauffeur obediently stopped the car. The dummy-chucker's grin was absolutely complacent now.

Down below, there gleamed lights, the lights of ferries, of sound steamers, and—of Blackwell's Island. This morning, he had left there, a lying mendicant. To-night, he was a gentleman. He knocked again upon the glass. Then, observing the speaking-tube, he said through it languidly.

"The Park Square, Andrews."

An obsequious doorman threw open the limousine door as the car stopped before the great hotel. He handed the dummy-chucker a ticket.

"Number of your car, sir," he said obsequiously.

"Ah, yes, of course," said the dummy-chucker. He felt in his pocket. Part of the silver that the soft-hearted women of the movies had bestowed upon him this afternoon found repository in the doorman's hand.

A uniformed boy whirled the revolving door that the dummy-chucker might pass into the hotel.

"The coat-room? Dining here, sir? Past the news-stand, sir, to your left. Thank you, sir." The boy's bow was as profound as though the quarter in his palm had been placed there by a duke.

The girl who received his coat and hat smiled as pleasantly and impersonally upon the dummy-chucker as she did upon the whiskered, fine-looking old gentleman who handed her his coat at the same time. She called the dummy-chucker's attention to the fact that his tie was a trifle loose.

The dummy-chucker walked to the big mirror that stands in the corner made by the corridor that parallels Fifty-ninth Street and the corridor that separates the tea-room from the dining-room. His clumsy fingers found difficulty with the tie. The fine-looking old gentleman, adjusting his own tie, stepped closer.

"Beg pardon, sir. May I assist you?"

The dummy-chucker smiled a grateful assent. The old gentleman fumbled a moment with the tie.

"I think that's better," he said. He bowed as one man of the world might to another, and turned away.

Under his breath, the dummy-chucker swore gently.

"You'd think, the way he helped me, that I belonged to the Four Hundred."

He glanced down the corridor. In the tea-room were sitting groups who awaited late arrivals. Beautiful women, correctly garbed, distinguished-looking men. Their laughter sounded pleasantly above the subdued strains of the orchestra. Many of them looked at the dummy-chucker. Their eyes rested upon him for that well-bred moment that denotes acceptance.

"One of themselves," said the dummy-chucker to himself.

Well, why not? Once again he looked at himself in the mirror. There might be handsomer men present in this hotel, but—was there any one who wore his clothes better? He turned and walked down the corridor.

The *maître d'hôtel* stepped forward inquiringly as the dummy-chucker hesitated in the doorway.

"A table, sir?"

"You have one reserved for me. This right-hand one by the door."

"Ah, yes, of course, sir. This way, sir."

He turned toward the table. Over the heads of intervening diners, the dummy-chucker saw his host. The shaded lights upon the table at which the young man sat revealed, not too clearly yet well enough, the features of a girl.

"A lady!" said the dummy-chucker, under his breath. "The real thing!"

As he stood there, the girl raised her head. She did not look toward the dummy-chucker, could not see him. But he could see the proud line of her throat, the glory of her golden hair. And opposite her he could see the features of his host, could note how illy that shrewd nose and slit of a mouth consorted with the gentle face of the girl. And then, as the *maître d'hôtel* beckoned, he remembered that he had left the flask, the monogrammed flask, in his overcoat pocket.

"Just a moment," he said.

He turned and walked back toward the corner where was his coat. In the distance, he saw some one, approaching him, noted the free stride, the carriage of the head, the set of the shoulders. And then, suddenly, he saw that the "some one" was himself. The mirror was guilty of the illusion.

Once again he stood before it, admiring himself. He summoned the face of the girl who was sitting in the dining-room before his mental vision. And then he turned abruptly to the check-girl.

"I've changed my mind," he said. "My coat, please."

He was lounging before the open fire when three-quarters of an hour later his host was admitted to the luxurious apartment. Savagely the young man pulled off his coat and approached the dummy-chucker.

"I hardly expected to find you here," he said.

The dummy-chucker shrugged.

"You said the doors were watched. I couldn't make an easy getaway. So I rode back here in your car. And when I got here, your man made me wait, so—here we are," he finished easily.

" 'Here we are!' Yes! But when you were there—I saw you at the entrance to the dining-room—for God's sake, why didn't you do what you'd agreed to do?"

The dummy-chucker turned languidly in his chair. He eyed his host curiously.

"Listen, feller," he said. "I told you that I drew the line at murder, didn't I?"

"'Murder'? What do you mean? What murder was involved?"

The dummy-chucker idly blew a smoke ring.

"Murder of faith in a woman's heart," he said slowly. "Look at me! Do I look the sort who'd play your dirty game?"

The young man stood over him.

"Bannon," he called. The valet entered the room. "Take the clothes off this—this bum!" snapped the host. "Give him his rags."

He clenched his fists, but the dummy-chucker merely shrugged. The young man drew back while his guest followed the valet into another room.

Ten minutes later, the host seized the dummy-chucker by the tattered sleeve of his grimy jacket. He drew him before the mirror.

"Take a look at yourself, you—bum!" he snapped. "Do you look, now, like the sort of man who'd refuse to earn an easy hundred?"

The dummy-chucker stared at himself. Gone was the debonair gentleman of a quarter of an hour ago. Instead, there leered back at him a pasty-faced, underfed vagrant, dressed in the tatters of unambitious, satisfied poverty.

"Bannon," called the host, "throw him out!"

For a moment, the dummy-chucker's shoulders squared, as they had been squared when the dinner jacket draped them. Then they sagged. He offered no resistance when Bannon seized his collar. And Bannon, the valet, was a smaller man than himself.

He cringed when the colored elevator-man sneered at him. He dodged when little Bannon, in the mirrored vestibule, raised a threatening hand. And he shuffled as he turned toward Central Park.

But as he neared Columbus Circle, his gait quickened. At Finisterre Joe's he'd get a drink. He tumbled in his pockets. Curse the luck! He'd given every cent of his afternoon earnings to doormen and pages and coat-room girls!

His pace slackened again as he turned down Broadway. His feet were dragging as he reached the Concorde moving-picture theater. His hand, sunk deep in his torn pocket, touched something. It was a tiny piece of soap.

As the audience filed sadly out from the teary, gripping drama of "She Loved and Lost," the dummy-chucker's hand went from his pocket to his lips. He reeled, staggered, fell. His jaws moved savagely. Foam appeared upon his lips. A fat woman shrank away from him, then leaned forward in quick sympathy.

"He's gotta fit!" she cried.

"Ep'lepsy," said her companion pityingly.

Romance in the Roaring Forties

by Damon Runyon

Only a rank sucker will think of taking two peeks at Dave the Dude's doll, because while Dave may stand for the first peek, figuring it is a mistake, it is a sure thing he will get sored up at the second peek, and Dave the Dude is certainly not a man to have sored up at you.

But this Waldo Winchester is one hundred per cent sucker, which is why he takes quite a number of peeks at Dave's doll. And what is more, she takes quite a number of peeks right back at him. And there you are. When a guy and a doll get to taking peeks back and forth at each other, why, there you are indeed.

This Waldo Winchester is a nice-looking young guy who writes pieces about Broadway for the *Morning Item*. He writes about the goings-on in night clubs, such as fights, and one thing and another, and also about who is running around with who, including guys and dolls.

Sometimes this is very embarrassing to people who may be married and are running around with people who are not married, but of course Waldo Winchester cannot be expected to ask one and all for their marriage certificates before he writes his pieces for the paper.

The chances are if Waldo Winchester knows Miss Billy Perry is Dave the Dude's doll, he will never take more than his first peek at her, but nobody tips him off until his second or third peek, and by this time Miss Billy Perry is taking her peeks back at him and Waldo Winchester is hooked.

In fact, he is plumb gone, and being a sucker, like I tell you, he does not care whose doll she is. Personally, I do not blame him much, for Miss Billy Perry is worth a few peeks, especially when she is out on the floor of Miss Missouri Martin's Sixteen Hundred Club doing her tap dance. Still, I do not think the best tap dancer that ever lives can make me take two peeks at her if I know she is Dave the Dude's doll, for Dave somehow thinks more than somewhat of his dolls.

He especially thinks plenty of Miss Billy Perry, and sends her fur coats, and diamond rings, and one thing and another, which she sends back to him at once, because it seems she does not take presents from guys. This is considered most surprising all along Broadway, but people figure the chances are she has some other angle.

Anyway, this does not keep Dave the Dude from liking her just the same, and so she is considered his doll by one and all, and is respected accordingly until this Waldo Winchester comes along.

It happens that he comes along while Dave the Dude is off in the Modoc on a little run-down to the Bahamas to get some goods for his business, such as Scotch and champagne, and by the time Dave gets back, Miss Billy Perry and Waldo Winchester are at the stage where they sit in corners between her numbers and hold hands.

Of course nobody tells Dave the Dude about this, because they do not wish to get him excited. Not even Miss Missouri Martin tells him, which is most unusual because Miss Missouri Martin, who is sometimes called "Mizzoo" for short, tells everything she knows as soon as she knows it, which is very often before it happens.

You see, the idea is when Dave the Dude is excited he may blow somebody's brains out, and the chances are it will be nobody's brains but Waldo Winchester's, although some claim that Waldo Winchester has no brains or he will not be hanging around Dave the Dude's doll.

I know Dave is very, very fond of Miss Billy Perry, because I hear him talk to her several times, and he is most polite to her and never gets out of line in her company by using cuss words, or anything like this. Furthermore, one night when One-eyed Solly Abrahams is a little stewed up he refers to Miss Billy Perry as a broad, meaning no harm whatever, for this is the way many of the boys speak of the dolls.

But right away Dave the Dude reaches across the table and bops One-eyed Solly right in the mouth, so everybody knows from then on that Dave thinks well of Miss Billy Perry. Of course Dave is always thinking fairly well of some doll as far as this goes, but it is seldom he gets to bopping guys in the mouth over them.

Well, one night what happens but Dave the Dude walks into the Sixteen Hundred Club, and there in the entrance, what does he see but this Waldo Winchester and Miss Billy Perry kissing each other back and forth friendly. Right away

Dave reaches for the old equalizer to shoot Waldo Winchester, but it seems Dave does not happen to have the old equalizer with him, not expecting to have to shoot anybody this particular evening.

So Dave the Dude walks over and, as Waldo Winchester hears him coming and lets go his strangle hold on Miss Billy Perry, Dave nails him with a big right hand on the chin. I will say for Dave the Dude that he is a fair puncher with his right hand, though his left is not so good, and he knocks Waldo Winchester bowlegged. In fact, Waldo folds right up on the floor.

Well, Miss Billy Perry lets out a screech you can hear clear to the Battery and runs over to where Waldo Winchester lights, and falls on top of him squalling very loud. All anybody can make out of what she says is that Dave the Dude is a big bum, although Dave is not so big, at that, and that she loves Waldo Winchester.

Dave walks over and starts to give Waldo Winchester the leather, which is considered customary in such cases, but he seems to change his mind, and instead of booting Waldo around, Dave turns and walks out of the joint looking very black and mad, and the next anybody hears of him he is over in the Chicken Club doing plenty of drinking.

This is regarded as a very bad sign indeed, because while everybody goes to the Chicken Club now and then to give Tony Bertazzola, the owner, a friendly play, very few people care to do any drinking there, because Tony's liquor is not meant for anybody to drink except the customers.

Well, Miss Billy Perry gets Waldo Winchester on his pegs again, and wipes his chin off with her handkerchief, and by and by he is all okay except for a big lump on his chin. And all the time she is telling Waldo Winchester what a big bum Dave the Dude is, although afterwards Miss Missouri Martin gets hold of Miss Billy Perry and puts the blast on her plenty for chasing a two-handed spender such as Dave the Dude out of the joint.

"You are nothing but a little sap," Miss Missouri Martin tells Miss Billy Perry. "You cannot get the right time off this newspaper guy, while everybody knows Dave the Dude is a very fast man with a dollar."

"But I love Mr. Winchester," says Miss Billy Perry. "He's so romantic. He is not a bootlegger and a gunman like Dave the Dude. He puts lovely pieces in the paper about me, and he is a gentleman at all times."

Now of course Miss Missouri Martin is not in a position to argue about gentlemen, because she meets very few in the Sixteen Hundred Club and anyway, she does not wish to make Waldo Winchester mad as he is apt to turn around and put pieces in his paper that will be a knock to the joint, so she lets the matter drop.

Miss Billy Perry and Waldo Winchester go on holding hands between her numbers, and maybe kissing each other now and then, as young people are liable to do, and Dave the Dude plays the chill for the Sixteen Hundred Club and everything seems to be all right. Naturally we are all very glad there is no more trouble over the proposition, because the best Dave can get is the worst of it in a jam with a newspaper guy.

Personally, I figure Dave will soon find himself another doll and forget all about Miss Billy Perry, because now that I take another peek at her, I can see where she is just about the same as any other tap dancer, except that she is red-headed. Tap dancers are generally blackheads, but I do not know why.

Moosh, the doorman at the Sixteen Hundred Club, tells me Miss Missouri Martin keeps plugging for Dave the Dude with Miss Billy Perry in a quiet way, because he says he hears Miss Missouri Martin make the following crack one night to her: "Well, I do not see any Simple Simon on your lean and linger."

This is Miss Missouri Martin's way of saying she sees no diamond on Miss Billy Perry's finger, for Miss Missouri Martin is an old experienced doll, who figures if a guy loves a doll he will prove it with diamonds. Miss Missouri Martin has many diamonds herself, though how any guy can ever get himself heated up enough about Miss Missouri Martin to give her diamonds is more than I can see.

I am not a guy who goes around much, so I do not see Dave the Dude for a couple of weeks, but late one Sunday afternoon little Johnny McGowan, who is one of Dave's men, comes and says to me like this: "What do you think? Dave grabs the scribe a little while ago and is taking him out for an airing!"

Well, Johnny is so excited it is some time before I can get him cooled out enough to explain. It seems that Dave the Dude gets his biggest car out of the garage and sends his driver, Wop Joe, over to the *Item* office where Waldo Winchester works, with a message that Miss Billy Perry wishes to see Waldo right away at Miss Missouri Martin's apartment on Fifty-ninth Street.

Of course this message is nothing but the phonus bolonus, but Waldo drops in for it and gets in the car. Then Wop Joe drives him up to Miss Missouri Martin's apartment, and who gets in the car there but Dave the Dude. And away they go.

Now this is very bad news indeed, because when Dave the Dude takes a guy out for an airing the guy very often does not come back. What happens to him I never ask, because the best a guy can get by asking questions in this man's town is a bust in the nose.

But I am much worried over this proposition, because I like Dave the Dude, and I know that taking a newspaper guy like Waldo Winchester out for an airing is apt to cause talk, especially if he does not come back. The other guys that Dave the Dude takes out for airings, do not mean much in particular, but here is a guy who may produce trouble, even if he is a sucker, on account of being connected with a newspaper.

I know enough about newspapers to know that by and by the editor or somebody will be around wishing to know where Waldo Winchester's pieces about Broadway are, and if there are no pieces from Waldo Winchester, the editor will wish to know why. Finally it will get around to where other people will wish to know, and after a while many people will be running around saying: "Where is Waldo Winchester?"

And if enough people in this town get to running around saying where is So-and-so, it becomes a great mystery and the newspapers hop on the cops and the cops hop on everybody, and by and by there is so much heat in town that it is no place for a guy to be.

But what is to be done about this situation I do not know. Personally, it strikes me as very bad indeed, and while Johnny goes away to do a little telephoning, I am trying to think up some place to go where people will see me, and remember afterwards that I am there in case it is necessary for them to remember.

Finally Johnny comes back, very excited, and says: "Hey, the Dude is up at the Woodcock Inn on the Pelham Parkway, and he is sending out the word for one and all to come at once. Good Time Charley Bernstein just gets the wire and tells me. Something is doing. The rest of the mob are on their way, so let us be moving."

But here is an invitation which does not strike me as a

good thing at all. The way I look at it, Dave the Dude is no company for a guy like me at this time. The chances are he either does something to Waldo Winchester already, or is getting ready to do something to him which I wish no part of.

Personally, I have nothing against newspaper guys, not even the ones who write pieces about Broadway. If Dave the Dude wishes to do something to Waldo Winchester, all right, but what is the sense of bringing outsiders into it? But the next thing I know, I am in Johnny McGowan's roadster, and he is zipping along very fast indeed, paying practically no attention to traffic lights or anything else.

As we go busting out the Concourse, I get to thinking the situation over, and I figure that Dave the Dude probably keeps thinking about Miss Billy Perry, and drinking liquor such as they sell in the Chicken Club, until finally he blows his topper. The way I look at it, only a guy who is off his nut will think of taking a newspaper guy out for an airing over a doll, when dolls are a dime a dozen in this man's town.

Still, I remember reading in the papers about a lot of different guys who are considered very sensible until they get tangled up with a doll, and maybe loving her, and the first thing anybody knows they hop out of windows, or shoot themselves, or somebody else, and I can see where even a guy like Dave the Dude may go daffy over a doll.

I can see that little Johnny McGowan is worried, too, but he does not say much, and we pull up in front of the Woodcock Inn in no time whatever, to find a lot of other cars there ahead of us, some of which I recognize as belonging to different parties.

The Woodcock Inn is what is called a roadhouse, and is run by Big Nig Skolsky, a very nice man indeed, and a friend of everybody's. It stands back a piece off the Pelham Parkway and is a very pleasant place to go to, what with Nig having a good band and a floor show with a lot of fair-looking dolls, and everything else a man can wish for a good time. It gets a nice play from nice people, although Nig's liquor is nothing extra.

Personally, I never go there much, because I do not care for roadhouses, but it is a great spot for Dave the Dude when he is pitching parties, or even when he is only drinking single-handed. There is a lot of racket in the joint as we drive up, and who comes out to meet us but Dave the Dude himself with a big hello. His face is very red, and he seems heated up no little, but he does not look like a guy who is meaning any harm to anybody, especially a newspaper guy.

"Come in, guys!" Dave the Dude yells. "Come right in!"

So we go in, and the place is full of people sitting at tables, or out on the floor dancing, and I see Miss Missouri Martin with all her diamonds hanging from her in different places, and Good Time Charley Bernstein, and Feet Samuels, and Tony Bertazzola, and Skeets Boliver, and Nick the Greek, and Rochester Red, and a lot of other guys and dolls from around and about.

In fact, it looks as if everybody from all the joints on Broadway are present, including Miss Billy Perry, who is all dressed up in white and is lugging a big bundle of orchids and so forth, and who is giggling and smiling and shaking hands and going on generally. And finally I see Waldo Winchester, the scribe, sitting at a ringside table all by himself, but there is nothing wrong with him as far as I can see. I mean, he seems to be all in one piece so far.

"Dave," I say to Dave the Dude, very quiet, "what is coming off here? You know a guy cannot be too careful what he does around this town, and I will hate to see you tangled up in anything right now."

"Why," Dave says, "what are you talking about? Nothing is coming off here but a wedding, and it is going to be the best wedding anybody on Broadway ever sees. We are waiting for the preacher now."

"You mean somebody is going to be married?" I ask, being somewhat confused.

"Certainly," Dave the Dude says. "What do you think? What is the idea of a wedding, anyway?"

"Who is going to be married?" I ask.

"Nobody but Billy and the scribe," Dave says. "This is the greatest thing I ever do in my life. I run into Billy the other night and she is crying her eyes out because she loves this scribe and wishes to marry him, but it seems the scribe has nothing he can use for money. So I tell Billy to leave it to me, because you know I love her myself so much I wish to see her happy at all times, even if she has to marry to be that way.

"So I frame this wedding party, and after they are married I am going to stake them to a few G's so they can get a good running start," Dave says. "But I do not tell the scribe and I do not let Billy tell him as I wish it to be a big surprise to him. I kidnap him this afternoon and bring him out here and he is scared half to death thinking I am going to scrag him.

"In fact," Dave says, "I never see a guy so scared. He is still so scared nothing seems to cheer him up. Go over and tell him to shake himself together, because nothing but happiness for him is coming off here."

Well, I wish to say I am greatly relieved to think that Dave intends doing nothing worse to Waldo Winchester than getting him married up, so I go over to where Waldo is sitting. He certainly looks somewhat alarmed. He is all in a huddle with himself, and he has what you call a vacant stare in his eyes. I can see that he is indeed frightened, so I give him a jolly slap on the back and I say: "Congratulations, pal! Cheer up, the worst is yet to come!"

"You bet it is," Waldo Winchester says, his voice so solemn I am greatly surprised.

"You are a fine-looking bridegroom," I say. "You look as if you are at a funeral instead of a wedding. Why do you not laugh ha-ha, and maybe take a dram or two and go to cutting up some?"

"Mister," says Waldo Winchester, "my wife is not going to care for me getting married to Miss Billy Perry."

"Your wife?" I say, much astonished. "What is this you are speaking of? How can you have any wife except Miss Billy Perry? This is great foolishness."

"I know," Waldo says, very sad. "I know. But I got a wife just the same, and she is going to be very nervous when she hears about this. My wife is very strict with me. My wife does not allow me to go around marrying people. My wife is Lola Sapola, of the Rolling Sapolas, the acrobats, and I am married to her for five years. She is the strong lady who juggles the other four people in the act. My wife just gets back from a year's tour of the Interstate time, and she is at the Marx Hotel right this minute. I am upset by this proposition."

"Does Miss Billy Perry know about this wife?" I ask.

"No." he says. "No. She thinks I am single-o."

"But why do you not tell Dave the Dude you are already married when he brings you out here to marry you off to Miss Billy Perry?" I ask. "It seems to me a newspaper guy must know it is against the law for a guy to marry several different dolls unless he is a Turk, or some such."

"Well," Waldo says, "if I tell Dave the Dude I am married after taking his doll away from him, I am quite sure Dave will be very much excited, and maybe do something harmful to my health."

Now there is much in what the guy says, to be sure. I am inclined to think, myself, that Dave will be somewhat disturbed when he learns of this situation, especially when Miss Billy Perry starts in being unhappy about it. But what is to be done I do not know, except maybe to let the wedding go on, and then when Waldo is out of reach of Dave, to put in a claim that he is insane, and that the marriage does not count. It is a sure thing I do not wish to be around when Dave the Dude hears Waldo is already married.

I am thinking that maybe I better take it on the lam out of there, when there is a great row at the door and I hear Dave the Dude yelling that the preacher arrives. He is a very nice looking pracher, at that, though he seems somewhat surprised by the goings-on, especially when Miss Missouri Martin steps up and takes charge of him. Miss Missouri Martin tells him she is fond of preachers, and is quite used to them, because she is twice married by preachers, and twice by justices of the peace, and once by a ship's captain at sea.

By this time one and all present, except maybe myself and Waldo Winchester, and the preacher and maybe Miss Billy Perry, are somewhat corned. Waldo is still sitting at his table looking very sad and saying "Yes" and "No" to Miss Billy Perry whenever she skips past him, for Miss Billy Perry is too much pleasured up with happiness to stay long in one spot.

Dave the Dude is more corned than anybody else, because he has two or three days' running start on everybody. And when Dave the Dude is corned I wish to say that he is a very unreliable guy as to temper, and he is apt to explode right in your face any minute. But he seems to be getting a great bang out of the doings.

Well, by and by Nig Skolsky has the dance floor cleared, and then he moves out on the floor a sort of arch of very beautiful flowers. The idea seems to be that Miss Billy Perry and Waldo Winchester are to be married under this arch. I can see that Dave the Dude must put in several days planning this whole proposition, and it must cost him plenty of the old do-re-mi, especially as I see him showing Miss Missouri Martin a diamond ring as big as a cough drop.

"It is for the bride," Dave the Dude says. "The poor loogan she is marrying will never have enough dough to buy her such a rock, and she always wishes a big one. I get it off a guy who brings it in from Los Angeles. I am going to give the bride away myself in person, so how do I act, Mizzo? I want Billy to have everything according to the book."

Well, while Miss Missouri Martin is trying to remember back to one of her weddings to tell him, I take another peek at Waldo Winchester to see how he is making out. I once see two guys go to the old warm squativoo up in Sing Sing, and I wish to say both are laughing heartily compared to Waldo Winchester at this moment.

Miss Billy Perry is sitting with him and the orchestra leader is calling his men dirty names because none of them can think of how "Oh, Promise Me" goes, when Dave the Dude yells: "Well, we are all set! Let the happy couple step forward!"

Miss Billy Perry bounces up and grabs Waldo Winchester by the arm and pulls him up out of his chair. After a peek at his face I am willing to lay six to five he does not make the arch. But he finally gets there with everybody laughing and clapping their hands, and the preacher comes forward, and Dave the Dude looks happier than I ever see him look before in his life as they all get together under the arch of flowers.

Well, all of a sudden there is a terrible racket at the front door of the Woodcock Inn, with some doll doing a lot of hollering in a deep voice that sounds like a man's, and naturally everybody turns and looks that way. The doorman, a guy by the name of Slugsy Sachs, who is a very hard man indeed, seems to be trying to keep somebody out, but pretty soon there is a heavy bump and Slugsy Sachs falls down, and in comes a doll about four feet high and five feet wide.

In fact, I never see such a wide doll. She looks all hammered down. Her face is almost as wide as her shoulders, and makes me think of a great big full moon. She comes in bounding-like, and I can see that she is all churned up about something. As she bounces in, I hear a gurgle, and I look around to see Waldo Winchester slumping down to the floor, almost dragging Miss Billy Perry with him.

Well, the wide doll walks right up to the bunch under the arch and says in a large bass voice: "Which one is Dave the Dude?"

"I am Dave the Dude," says Dave the Dude, stepping up. "What do you mean by busting in here like a walrus and gumming up our wedding?"

"So you are the guy who kidnaps my ever-loving husband to marry him off to this little red-headed pancake here, are you?" the wide doll says, looking at Dave the Dude, but pointing at Miss Billy Perry.

Well now, calling Miss Billy Perry a pancake to Dave the Dude is a very serious proposition, and Dave the Dude gets very angry. He is usually rather polite to dolls, but you can see he does not care for the wide doll's manner whatever.

"Say, listen here," Dave the Dude says, "you better take a walk before somebody clips you. You must be drunk," he says. "Or daffy," he says. "What are you talking about, anyway?"

"You will see what I am talking about," the wide doll yells. "The guy on the floor there is my lawful husband. You probably frighten him to death, the poor dear. You kidnap him to marry this red-headed thing, and I am going to get you arrested as sure as my name is Lola Sapola, you simple-looking tramp!"

Naturally, everybody is greatly horrified at a doll using such language to Dave the Dude, because Dave is known to shoot guys for much less, but instead of doing something to the wide doll at once, Dave says: "What is this talk I hear? Who is married to who? Get out of here!" Dave says, grabbing the wide doll's arm.

Well, she makes out as if she is going to slap Dave in the face with her left hand, and Dave naturally pulls his kisser out of the way. But instead of doing anything with her left, Lola Sapola suddenly drives her right fist smack-dab into Dave the Dude's stomach, which naturally comes forward as his face goes back.

I wish to say I see many a body punch delivered in my life, but I never see a prettier one than this. What is more, Lola Sapola steps in with the punch, so there is plenty on it.

Now a guy who eats and drinks like Dave the Dude does cannot take them so good in the stomach, so Dave goes "oof," and sits down very hard on the dance floor, and as he is sitting there he is fumbling in his pants pockets for the old equalizer, so everybody around tears for cover except Lola Sapola, and Miss Billy Perry, and Waldo Winchester.

But before he can get his pistol out, Lola Sapola reaches down and grabs Dave by the collar and hoists him to his feet. She lets go her hold on him, leaving Dave standing on his pins, but teetering around somewhat, and then she drives her right hand to Dave's stomach a second time.

The punch drops Dave again, and Lola steps up to him as

if she is going to give him the foot. But she only gathers up Waldo Winchester from the floor and slings him across her shoulder like he is a sack of oats, and starts for the door. Dave the Dude sits up on the floor again and by this time he has the old equalizer in his duke.

"Only for me being a gentleman I will fill you full of slugs," he yells.

Lola Sapola never even looks back, because by this time she is petting Waldo Winchester's head and calling him loving names and saying what a shame it is for bad characters like Dave the Dude to be abusing her precious one. It all sounds to me as if Lola Sapola thinks well of Waldo Winchester.

Well, after she gets out of sight, Dave the Dude gets up off the floor and stands there looking at Miss Billy Perry, who is out to break all crying records. The rest of us come out from under cover, including the preacher, and we are wondering how mad Dave the Dude is going to be about the wedding being ruined. But Dave the Dude seems only disappointed and sad.

"Billy," he says to Miss Billy Perry, "I am mighty sorry you do not get your wedding. All I wish for is your happiness, but I do not believe you can ever be happy with this scribe if he also has to have his lion tamer around. As Cupid I am a total bust. This is the only nice thing I ever try to do in my whole life, and it is too bad it does not come off. Maybe if you wait until he can drown her, or something—"

"Dave," says Miss Billy Perry, dropping so many tears that she seems to finally wash herself right into Dave the Dude's arms, "I will never, never be happy with such a guy as Waldo Winchester. I can see now you are the only man for me."

"Well, well, well," Dave the Dude says, cheering right up. "Where is the preacher? Bring on the preacher and let us have our wedding anyway."

I see Mr. and Mrs. Dave the Dude the other day, and they seem very happy. But you can never tell about married people, so of course I am never going to let on to Dave the Dude that I am the one who telephones Lola Sapola at the Marx Hotel, because maybe I do not do Dave any too much of a favor, at that.

Midwestern Primitive

by Ruth Suckow

Bert went flying over to get May Douglas to come to look at her table. It was all ready now, and she had to show it to some one. There was nobody at home who knew or cared about such things.

"May! Busy? Want to come and see the table now I've got it fixed?"

"Oh, yes!"

May was delighted. She left her ironing where it was and followed Bert with eager excitement. She thought that Bert Statzer was a wonder.

"We'll go right through the kitchen. Smells kind of good, don't it? There! Do you like it?"

"Bert!"

May was fairly speechless. She gazed at the table with fervent, faded eyes. It seemed to her the most beautiful thing she had ever seen. She didn't see how Bert had managed it—how she ever thought of such things and how she learned to do them. Bert was just a genius, that was all.

"You really think it looks nice?"

Bert drank in May's appreciation thirstily. She knew it didn't amount to much that May would admire anything she did; but she had to get appreciation from somewhere.

"I think it's just too beautiful for words. You little marvel! I just don't see how you do it." May sighed.

"Well, I'm glad you think it looks nice." Bert relaxed, with a long, gratified sigh, but stiffened again to say to Maynard, who had tagged them into the dining room, "Be careful, Maynard! If you move one of those things—!"

May was looking at everything: the little fringed napkins of pink crêpe, the tinted glass goblets which Bert had sent away for, the spray of sweet peas at every place, one pink and then the next one lavender, made of tissue paper—such a pretty idea! She had never seen any napkins like those. Bert went on talking excitedly.

"Well, if it's good enough for those folks, it'll be good enough for any one. I'll think I've accomplished something, May!"

"I don't see how it can help—"

"Oh, but I've never had any one like them here—any one really from away! It scares me. This looks nice to us, but these people have all seen things. Then, you know, they're going to have that famous writer with them. That's what I'm so excited about. If he likes it, then I thought maybe I could use his name. You know that'll help to get me known—if I can get his recommendation. Like those cold cream ads and everything—they're all doing that. Oh, I'm so excited, May! Feel my hands. Aren't they cold?"

"Why, you poor child!" May took Bert's tense, thin little hands and fondled them. "You don't need to feel that way. I don't see how anybody could ask for anything nicer. If *this* isn't good enough for them—"

"Oh, I know, but people like that who have been places and seen things—! Just the kind I've wanted to have come. I don't expect anybody *here* to appreciate this—anybody but you and Mrs. Elliott. Well, I don't care, I've done the best I could. Maynard, look *out!*"

Bert's face was still gratified but screwed with worry. She knew how she really wanted things to look. She wanted flowered curtains instead of these old ones, and little painted tables instead of this big old thing. . . . Here was this little stuck-in-the-mud burg always holding her back, and her mother, and Arlie. Well, *she* didn't intend to be stuck in the mud, anyway. She had put up her sign where tourists could see it: "Hillside Inn." It made people in town laugh. They wanted to know where the "hillside" was. She didn't care. People like these could appreciate. Her tea room, if the dinner to-day was a success, would attract others; "interesting people" would come—the kind of people she craved to know and among whom she really belonged—and finally she would make so much money that she could get them all out of Shell Spring, herself and Maynard and Arlie, and really go somewhere.

She burst out, "The only trouble is mother!" And that was true. Arlie would stay out—he didn't want folks like that to see him in his old working clothes—but mother thought she had to go in and entertain them, just the way she did with any one who came to the house. "I was so ashamed when those last people were here. The way mother came in—!

Now, of course, May, *I* know mother's good as gold, and means it the best in the world, but what do folks like that think of her? I can't get her to fix herself up or anything. She doesn't understand. 'Ach, well, if they don't like the way I look, then they can look at something they do like.' That's the way she is. She doesn't know one person from another, doesn't see why these people are any different from any others. (May kept making distressed little murmurs. She did know how Mrs. Hohenschuh was!) Now, May, I went and bought a nice up-to-date dress for her, like people are wearing, when I was in Dubuque last. She'd look nice in it if she'd wear it. But do you think she will? No, sir. 'Ach, I never wore anything like that, I'll stick to what I been wearing.' You don't know, May—" Bert's voice tightened into bitterness—"nobody does, they all talk about how good-natured mother is. They don't know how stubborn she can be. Honestly, if mother didn't want to move, I don't believe a *motorcycle* running into her could budge her one inch. She's just hopeless."

"Oh, well, Bert, it'll come out," May said soothingly.

"I suppose. But she gives these people who come here the wrong idea. I don't want them to think we're all like she is."

"They won't think that about you!"

Bert felt encouraged after May's visit. She was excited, flying around the kitchen, doing the last few things, watching out for Maynard so that he would keep his little suit clean. Where was mother? she thought in exasperation. Oh, there! out in the garden, *digging*. Bert had no time to run out after her now. She snatched a look at the clock. Almost time for them to get here! Oh, dear, but she did want everything just right. What was mother thinking of? Did she want to get caught looking like that? "Maynard, if you don't keep away from that table—!" Bert thought she would go crazy.

Then mother came waddling serenely into the house.

"Want I should help?"

"Not at this late date!"

That was all Bert was going to say. But she couldn't hold in; even if it was more of a triumph to be simply cold and cutting, she had to let it all out.

"Here I am working, trying to get everything nice, with everything all fixed, and you don't care. You just go on with your old digging out there in the garden and don't see or care!"

Mrs. Hohenschuh looked abashed. "Ach, well," she began;

then she retorted, "Well, I ain't wanted around here. You wouldn't be satisfied anyway with things the way I'd do them. Ach, all this fuss! What are you making all this fuss about? All this business!"

She finished with an angry mutter and waddled off to the door. Bert didn't know whether she was going to change her dress or not. Well, if she wanted them to catch her looking that way, if she didn't care, didn't know any better . . . Bert was left trembling with anger. She flew about the kitchen, put a few more nuts on each plate of salad, with shaking fingers changed her old apron for the bright green smock she was going to wear to do the serving—it was what they were wearing; it was like the one she'd seen in the photograph of "Betty Lee's Tea Room" in the cooking magazine.

She went into the dining room. The shining glasses twinkled up at her, the sweet peas were rosy and stiff, the dishes looked so nice, the little napkins were so pretty . . . was everything right? She had got ideas wherever she could, but was she sure? She wanted to show these people that even if she did live out here in Shell Spring, she knew how things ought to be. She was going to have a *real* tea room some day. She had never felt that she belonged in Shell Spring, among the people who lived there. If she could only have the kind of things that other people had, do things the way that other people did them! She was going to do it even if she was stuck here. It had to be right. Everything was so lovely. Her anger and fear changed into a shining glory. The whole table dazzled before her eyes. She caught hold of Maynard, who was tagging her. "Look, Maynard!" she cried. "Isn't our table pretty?" She snatched a kiss from him in her trembling happiness.

Then she heard a car outside on the road. Her heart gave a wild leap. The people were coming!

A large green car rolled up to the cement block that still stood in the thick green grass beside the road as a relic of horse and buggy days. Bert in her green smock was waiting. Her black eyes were shining under short black hair threaded with early white. It seemed to her that it took the people a long while to get out of the car. She had time to wonder and to agonize over the place; the old frame house—she wished they could have had it stuccoed—what would these people think? Then the people were out and coming up the walk, and she had a confused, eager sight of two men and three

Midwestern Primitive

women—one of them was the writer! One man was in advance, a large man with a rosy face and shell-rimmed glasses. He came toward her smiling. That must be the one who had ordered the dinner, Mrs. Elliott's friend, Mr. Drayton.

"Mrs. Statzer?" Yes, that was who he was. "We heard you gave such good meals here that we thought we'd have to stop and try one of them."

Bert was so pleased and flattered that she scarcely heard his introductions, forgot the names just as soon as he mentioned them. She had been trying from the first to pick out the writer. It was the tall man, then, with the thick gray hair. She hadn't expected him to look . . . like that, somehow—grand, or at least in artistic-looking clothes, a hat with a wide brim, or glasses on a cord, or something. She wanted to show him that she knew who he was, even if most of the people here in town didn't. They hadn't known whom she meant when she said Harry Whetstone was coming here. Well, she hadn't known, either, until Mrs. Elliott told her—but she did now. She held out her hand, alert and eager.

"Oh, this is the writer, is it? I certainly was honored when I heard we were going to entertain you. I haven't read any of your works yet, but I intend to—I don't get much time for reading."

"No hurry, no hurry," the writer said with affable nonchalance.

She was looking, too, at the women. She hadn't got the relationships between the women and men figured out yet. One looked older, one wore that smart little green dress and hat, and then there was that one who might be any age—where did *she* come in? They were looking around. "Isn't this lovely!" one of them was saying. What did they mean? Bert's brilliant eyes were watching them. They were pointing to that terrible old brown tile in which mother had some geraniums planted. "Look, Harry! Isn't that lovely?" They couldn't really think it was *lovely*. "Lovely" had a different, suspicious meaning as these women used it. Bert's eyes were devouring the details of their clothes. She led them into the house, burning with anxiety, sensitiveness, eagerness; she knew how many things were wrong.

"I suppose you folks would like to wash a little after your drive. We haven't any bathroom, I'm sorry to say. We want to have one, but this town is so slow, they've never piped the water out this far. But if you don't mind just washing in the old-fashioned wash-bowls—"

She hated that so. But they were nice about it.

"You know, you're out in the country," she said with a nervous laugh, "and you have to take us the way you find us."

She ushered the women into her best bedroom, the guest room off the parlor. This was the one room in the house in which she could take some pride. She had fixed it up with furniture she had painted herself, and she had put the stencil on the walls—all after the plan of the Model Bedroom in the household magazine for which she had taken subscriptions last winter.

"Now, if you'll just take off your hats and put them wherever you find a place." She was eager and flustered. "I'm afraid I'll have to ask you gentlemen to go upstairs." She was ashamed to take them up to her old room, full of horrid old dark furniture—was afraid, too, as she sped up the steep stairs ahead of them, although she knew it was all right, she had been up at four o'clock cleaning and getting the house ready. She banged the door of her mother's room shut as she went past. "Now I think you'll find everything—" She ran down.

The women were talking in the bedroom. She heard a soft laugh. She lingered in the front room, sensitive and alert, but she couldn't hear. The smartness of their clothes actually hurt her, showed her all kinds of unsuspected deficiencies in herself, although it pleased and gratified her too. They were the kind of people she wanted to know.

But when she went into the dining room and saw the table she was exultant again. "If you'll excuse me," she called, "I'm afraid I'll have to be in the kitchen." They were nice! Oh, dear. She had forgotten to ask the author to write in her visitor's book. She was going to have her book just as they did in the real Eastern tea rooms Mrs. Elliott had told her about. Well, there was time. The table looked so sweet! And yet she was obscurely hurt and smarting. She wasn't sure those women weren't laughing.

Arlie had come into the kitchen and was washing his hands. "Well, are they here?" he asked. He didn't exactly like their coming, or to have Bert always fussing around with things like this, but then, he was all right, he kept out of the way. Bert was taking the roast chicken from the oven. Roasted, not fried. "People in the East never think of *frying* chicken." Mrs. Elliott had never tasted fried chicken all the time that she was in the East. Bert wanted these people to be able to say they had eaten as good a meal here in the Hillside Inn as ever they had got in any city restaurant. She had followed the menus in the cooking magazine. She was so excited now that the ordeal was on that she felt herself working in a kind of tense calm. She gave Arlie his dinner in the back kitchen. These people would see that she knew how things should be done.

"You can come in to dinner now."

There was a moment of quiet and formality as she seated them. They didn't exclaim like those last people. "Well, well, I didn't know we were going to find a first-class hotel here in Shell Spring!" that other man had cried. She served them, wondering if she oughtn't to have got in Donna Peterson to help her—but then, Donna wouldn't "know," and she wanted things right. She tried to remember what things should go to the right and what to the left. When she went out to the kitchen she ordered Maynard to keep back. She was going to bring him in after the meal, all dressed up in his little new suit, and just introduce him. "This is my little boy Maynard." She had read, in a story, about a mother doing that.

Through her preoccupation with the food and the serving—wondering if everything tasted just right—she heard snatches of the conversation. The people seemed a little tired, maybe from that long drive. "Well, this is familiar." What did they mean by that? Did they like the little napkins, or were they laughing at them? But those napkins were exactly the kind that were used in all the tea rooms now! "Standardization, I tell you. It gets into all the corners." That meant nothing to Bert. They certainly must like those salads that May Douglas had said were simply too pretty to be eaten. Nice salads were things people here in town didn't fuss with—all those "do-dads" mother called them. The people were affable and talking among themselves, and yet Bert could sense that the dinner didn't seem to be going exactly as she had hoped that it would. She had somehow thought that they would be more astonished and delighted, and that they would take her right in with them. Her thin cheeks were flushed. In the kitchen it was as if she were working in a vacuum, not in that shining flush of triumph she knew and craved. How fast it was all going, how soon this great dinner would be over!

Mrs. Hohenschuh had come into the kitchen from the back

way. "Mother, you went and put on that old percale dress of yours, and I had that new one all laid out for you ready!" That seemed the crowning catastrophe. Bert suddenly began to tremble with anger. When she came in to the kitchen the next time she whispered furiously, "You aren't going to let those people see you in that! Since you had to go put it on, just to be stubborn, you can stay out of sight." How could she ever get anywhere with all this family to pull up after her? Mother looked like an old farm woman. Bert felt ready to cry and could scarcely bear to hear the quiet sound of the voices in the dining room.

The coffee cups were all set out on the little old sewing table that she was using for a serving table. She was going to serve her coffee with dessert, the right way. "Ach, let 'em have their coffee!" Mrs. Hohenschuh pleaded. She thought it was terrible to deprive people of coffee all through a meal. She didn't much mind Bert's reproaches. "Ach, Bert, she always gets so cross when she's got anything to do, I don't know." The old lady made off into the garden. But Bert knew how her mother was. It would be a miracle if she let any people get away without talking to them, and probably telling them the whole family history!

Bert took in the fragrant coffee and home-made ice cream. Well, they did like that! The woman in the cute green dress (she didn't seem to be the author's wife, after all; that was the one who didn't look nearly so much like "somebody"—it surprised Bert) said very flatteringly, "What delicious ice cream! Did you make it yourself?" The older woman—that was Mrs. Drayton—smiled up at Bert. The talk was freer now. The author seemed to be saying the least of any of them, though. That seemed funny to Bert. Mr. Drayton was lots more talkative and full of fun—peppier. She bet he could write awfully good stories, better than the other one, if he just wanted to.

She was almost happy, when she happened to look out of the window and saw mother climbing up from the cellar-way outside, lugging something—a bottle! Oh, for . . . Before she got a chance to go out to the kitchen the old lady came, shy but beaming, into the room, with a big bottle of dandelion wine. Bert was in torment. As if these people cared for anything like that!

But there mother stood and there was nothing to do but introduce her. Bert suffered agony. It was all the worse, somehow, that they were being so polite and nice. "This is my mother, Mrs. Hohenschuh." Mother began to beam at that. She loved to entertain people—that was all right, of course, but she had never learned that people didn't do things the way she used to, any more.

And mother was starting right in.

"Well, I thought it was mean you folks had to go all that time without your coffee, so I just brought you something else to drink. If you ain't afraid somebody's going to get after you—ach, it's all so funny these days—maybe you'll take a little drink of this wine. It's dandelion. I made it."

Bert couldn't stand it. She made for the kitchen. She sat down there, clenched her fists, and felt that she would actually fly to pieces.

The voices were louder in the dining room. She heard delighted laughter. Yes, now mother had an audience, and she was just laying herself out for them—Bert knew how! She burned with humiliation. The whole thing was spoiled. How could anybody in this town try to do things the way they ought to be done?

Her mother came smiling out to the kitchen.

"Where are them little glasses gone?"

"Mother, *why* did you have to go in there with that stuff?"

"Ach, what are you fussing about? They like it."

Bert got up and began feverishly to clean the messy plates and stack them together. She couldn't eat a thing herself, not even good little crisp bits of chicken that were left. Mother had got hold of the people now. She heard them leaving the dining room, and then the whole party trailed past the kitchen windows. Mother waddled in the lead. She was going to take them all out and show them her flower beds.

Maynard was whining. "Are you going to take me in and introduce me, mother?"

Bert looked at him, cold and remote.

"No."

They were all out in the garden. Mrs. Hohenschuh always thought it her duty as a hostess to take her guests out and show them everything she had. Here where she felt that she "had things nice," too—this place in town which she and Mr. Hohenschuh had bought when they moved in from the country—she could take real enjoyment with visitors, even if Bert did go on about the place and say how behind the times it was. But it was a long time since she had got hold of any people so appreciative as these.

"Well, I don't know as there's anything you folks'll care much about looking at (she didn't mean that; she said it in a rich, comfortable tone). I only got the same old kind of flowers I've always had, they ain't any of these new-fangled kinds with fancy names here."

"Oh, we adore seeing them!" the woman in the green dress cried enthusiastically.

Mrs. Hohenschuh beamed. "Well, I think they're pretty nice, they suit me, but there's lots of folks nowadays wants different things, I guess. Ja! Anyway, that don't worry me. I let 'em talk. I go on doing things the way I want to."

The people all laughed, and she was gratified.

"Well, here's what I got. I put in all these things myself. Bert, she don't want to bother, she's got too many irons in the fire all the time."

"This is lovely!"

Mrs. Hohenschuh stood fat and beaming while they looked and wandered about. She thought her garden was pretty nice—ja, you bet she did! And these folks all seemed to think so too. Why, they was awful nice folks! Why had Bert got so fussed over having them here to dinner? Why, they was real nice and common! That one in the green dress (she was older than she wanted to let on, too, Mrs. Hohenschuh shrewdly judged) did the most running around and palavering; but those other two, that husband and wife, enjoyed things just as much. The man in the glasses was *real* nice. So was his wife, although she didn't have so much to say. But those other two, she kind of liked the best of the bunch. The woman was real sensible, the things she said and the questions she asked; and the man kind of trailed around after the others and looked at things on his own account, the way Mrs. Hohenschuh liked to have folks do. That showed he wasn't putting it on, he was really enjoying himself.

Along with her answers and her explanations, Mrs. Hohenschuh managed to get in a good part of the family history. Bert had a fit when she told things like that; but Mrs. Hohenschuh never felt right until she'd—well, kind of given folks the facts and the right idea about the family. They'd hear it all anyway, so she might as well tell it herself.

"Have you had your garden long, Mrs. Hohenschuh?"

"Ja, ever since we moved into town. That's—how long is it, a'ready?—ach, it's twenty years, I guess! Bert, she was only just in high school. That was partly why we come. The boys, they didn't get to finish, but Pa he said Bert was to get her diploma, she was always the smartest, anyway. Ja, how old was Bert then? She's thirty-seven now. Ja, she's such a thin little sliver, I don't know, women seems to want to be that way now, but she's thirty-seven! Her and Arlie been married twelve years a'ready; and then this here little fellow's all they've got! Ach, I don't know!"

As she talked, in her deep comfortable voice rich with chuckles and drolleries of German inflection, she waddled about among the flower beds, pointing out this kind and that. "These? Moss roses, I call 'em. I guess that ain't the right name, some folks says not, but they grow just the same—ain't that so? Ja, the old lady Douglas over there, when she was living, she had to have the right names for all her plants, but I told her mine grew better'n hers did if I did call 'em wrong!" The moss roses in their flat matted bed on the hot earth were gay spots of scarlet and crimson, yellow, cerise, and white. They made one of the women think of the colors in patchwork quilts, she said.

"She's got the real old honest-to-God peppermint! I haven't smelled any of that for years."

"Peppermint? Ja, that I always have. That I like too."

The woman in the green dress came running and clutched the other younger woman. "Come here, Jean! I want to show you. The pump! Isn't that just right? And see here—all these little flower pots set out and slips started in them. Just see, this foliage stuff, this old red and green funny leaf stuff, my grandmother used to have that. And look back there! One of those big green wire flower stands that I suppose used to stand in the bay window. Didn't you just yearn to take your dolls promenading on that, and they wouldn't let you, because you might spoil the plants? Isn't this perfect?" Mrs. Hohenschuh had told them, "Ja, sure, you look around anywhere you want to; what's the use of hiding what you got?" Harry Whetstone had been enjoying the old lady's naïve revelations, but now he lounged about, poking into the woodshed where the light fell dim and dusty through a little square window high up in the wall, and into a toll shed where pans of seeds were set about in the midst of a clutter of ancient furniture. It was like going back thirty years.

There was a little apple orchard at the side, grown up to tall grass now; and there, on one of his silent excursions, he discovered a two-foot troll planted down in a tiny hollow with grass grown about the base as it binds in ancient tombstones, and a casual offering of fallen apples about his chipped feet. The woman in the green dress came running over.

"What have you found, Harry? *Oh!* Isn't that marvelous? Oh, Mrs. Hohenschuh, we've found something simply wonderful, won't you tell us what that is?"

"That? Ach, is that old thing still out there? Ja, it's funny, but then I don't know . . . Pa, he was the one that got that thing."

"It's German, isn't it?"

"Ja, it's German, all right. Pa, he come from the old country, he come over here when he was only eighteen years old. He had just twenty dollars when he landed in this country. Ja, it's German, that's what it is. Pa, he always wanted to fix up the back yard and make him a garden—that was why he got this funny fellow, that was one reason we moved into town when we did, because Pa wanted to fix up a place . . . ja, and then we hadn't lived here but a year or two when Pa got killed, he got run over, he was thinking of things the way he always done, and didn't hear the train coming . . . ja, that's the way of it!" But after a moment, she roused herself and went on, "Bert, she always had a fit over that fellow. She was the one took him out of the front yard and lugged him out here. But I don't know—" Mrs. Hohenschuh chuckled— "I always kind of liked the little fellow. He means good. You can see that. Well, I guess he's where she ain't likely to find him. She's too busy inside there to fool around out here. I'm the one does that."

Slowly, Mrs. Hohenschuh in the lead, they trailed away from the orchard. The troll, with his colors faded to dim faint tints and with curls chipped off his beard, stood smiling a one-sided but jovial smile at the rotting apples about his broken feet that had almost grown into the orchard ground.

Mrs. Hohenschuh picked one of each kind of flowers for every person. "Hold on, now! You ain't got any of the pansies yet." A circle of sticks set upright—little thin sticks with flaking bark—inclosed the colored pansies. The tiger lilies grew in a straggling bunch tied with twine. "Pick yourself some if you like 'em. Go ahead!" What else are flowers here for? "Here's a color you ain't got, if you like them zinnies, Mrs.—well, you'll have to excuse me, I can't remember all you folks's names." The sun shone down brightly on the garden, blaring out the hot colors of the moss roses, throwing clear antique shadows from the grape arbor, glinting and losing itself in coolness in the thick wet grass around the pump through which silent little streams of water soaked slowly. They all had a drink before they went into the house. The sides of the cold glass were frosted with wet. The family story was entwined with their wanderings among the paths of the garden, tangled with the colors of the flowers, and brightened over with sunshine.

The house seemed cool when they went inside.

"Oh, you don't want to go yet! Come in and set awhile and let's finish our visit."

Mrs. Hohenschuh led them into the parlor.

"There's lots of things you ain't seen yet."

Mrs. Drayton was tired, even Mr. Drayton—although still genial—was ready to stop; but the others seemed insatiable, and the writer most of all. Bert had heard her mother's invitation and burned with helpless shame. What else was mother going to show? There was no chance for her talk with the author. It was hopeless trying to lead mother off now. Bert followed the others into the front room.

"I'll show you Pa's picture, Mr.—ach, that name's gone again! Well, I guess you know I mean you, don't you? Sure! That's right."

She got down that old faded purple plush album that held all the family pictures: Bert and the boys when they were youngsters, Mr. Hohenschuh when he first came to this country, chance pictures of shamefaced hired men. The writer looked at all the pictures with a gravity that Bert couldn't fathom, Mr. Drayton laughed and made funny remarks about the clothes that pleased mother, and Mrs. Drayton looked at everything last with a pleased but tired smile; she wasn't quite in on all the things the others were, Bert thought. "Ja, look at that one! Ain't he funny-looking, though? He was a cousin of mine. Ja, now they all look funny." Bert sat and suffered. Maynard sidled into the room. He couldn't give up the promise of being introduced. They were all nice to him. The women smiled. But they went on making that fuss over mother.

When she had shown them the photographs she had to let them see her other things: the shells and the "curios" that she prized so, and that she kept on a shelf in the bookcase. "Look here! Did you ever see anything like this before?" How could they act so pleased, unless they were just false and putting it on to get mother to make a fool of herself? Bert could have cried. That shell! Of course they'd seen shells. They'd been everywhere. Those old feathers from the tail of the peacock they used to have out on the farm; the cocoanut husk with the stamps and address label on it; that big long German pipe; the glass paper-weight with the snowfall inside. What else could she find to show them? They were asking about fancy work. Did she ever make the real old knitted lace? Ja, not so much knit as crochet, though—wait, she'd show them! It would be just like her to ask them all up to her room to look through those terrible drawers—and if she did that Bert was ready to kill herself. That room of mother's (and it wasn't any use talking to her about it, Bert couldn't make her do a *thing*) with dresses hanging on nails, and quilts piled up in the corner, drawers filled with old shawls, pieces of cloth, silk gowns, baby dresses—a perfect museum!

Well, they weren't paying any attention to her and Maynard anyway, so Bert went back to the dining room. She might as well clear off the table. At least they were staying a long time and seemed to be enjoying themselves. In that way she supposed the dinner was a success. But she had thought that she could talk to them. It was she to whom they ought to be paying attention—she who appreciated them, and knew how different they were, and wanted to be like them; they couldn't really mean it when they made such a fuss over mother. They must be laughing at her. What could they see in all this old junk? That was the kind of stuff that Bert was trying so hard to get rid of. That was what the tea room was *for*—so that she could make some money, and get to know the right kind of folks, and maybe live like other people in other places. All the very awfullest things in the house— things *no*-body had any more! What kind of an idea of the family would they have? She looked into the parlor, and there was mother getting out all her old fancy work: that terrible piece, that huge table spread, with squarish horses and dogs and roosters crocheted into it, and they were saying "lovely"! She heard them.

"That dress! Isn't it perfect? The real thing."

"Oh, she's a jewel!"

"Lovely!"

They were going at last. They were very nice to Bert then, as if they realized that she had been neglected. The women sought her out in the dining room. "Such a good dinner you gave us!"

"Well, I'm glad you liked it. I didn't know..."

She followed them into the parlor, feeling appeased and excited again, even though she seemed to scent a tactful patronage. But they were all complimenting her now, and she drank in the praise, eagerly, but afraid to believe they meant it.

Mr. Drayton had taken her aside. "And what do we owe you for this fine meal you gave us?" he asked in a low, genial tone.

"Well . . . a dollar apiece," Bert said firmly. She had heard that all the city tea rooms charged a dollar and a quarter now. Of course, she couldn't ask quite as much as a city tea room, that had everything just up to snuff; but her dinner was good, and she knew it, and she was going to stick to business. He didn't seem to think that she was charging them too much, however. He counted out some bills and handed them right over to her. But when she came to look at them, there were too many—a five and an extra one!

"Oh, I can't—why, you've given me—"

He tapped her shoulder. "That's all right. Don't notice it. Doesn't begin to pay for the entertainment we've had here."

She still protested, flushed and happy, but he wouldn't listen to her; so she guessed there was nothing else for her to do.

She hadn't forgotten about the visitors' book. She got it out now. All the tea rooms in the East had those, Mrs. Elliott had said. She had seen several famous names in one place where she had eaten. It advertised the place; and then it was an honor, too, to think that such people had eaten there. Bert was a little bashful but determined.

"I hope you don't mind before you go." She laid down the new visitors' book, a notebook with black covers from the drug store, before the author. "I'd like to have you put your name in my book so other folks can see you've been here."

He didn't seem very much flattered about it, she thought, but anyway he wasn't going to refuse. How funny! She would have supposed it would please folks to be asked to do things like that. The others teased him a little. "You can't escape, Harry!" They seemed to think it was some sort of joke. Bert stood flushed, waiting and determined. She said generously that she wanted all the other names, too.

"Yes, I do. You're all along with Mr. Whetstone. Anyway, I know you're all . . ." She meant to say "important," or something of that kind, too; but she couldn't just seem to finish it.

"Well, go on, girls. Sign yourselves," Mr. Drayton commanded.

They all signed. Mrs. Drayton blushed when she did it.

Bert wasn't through with the author yet. Before she let him go she was going to get all she'd meant to get out of him.

"I wondered if you'd let me use your name, Mr. Whetstone."

He still had that funny, kind of bored way. His wife was really nicer.

"Say he ate with a large appetite, even mightier than usual," Mrs. Whetstone said.

But it seemed to Bert they were all amused.

She wanted to talk to the author about his books. She thought she ought to do that. "You know I never met an author before," she said. "I've always been wanting to, because—" she flushed—"well, I've always wanted to write myself. I always thought I could if I just had the time to do it."

"Don't," he assured her solemnly. But he wasn't as impressed as she had thought he would be. "It's much better to cook biscuits like those we devoured this noon. Infinitely better to make dandelion wine like your mother."

He was joking, of course. But Bert didn't like it. She had meant what she said, seriously, and she had thought he would encourage her.

Mrs. Hohenschuh came into the house, waddling and breathless.

"Dandelion wine!" she cried. "Ja, if you liked that, then you come back here and you'll get some of my wild grape this fall. You come and let *me* get you up a dinner. I'll give you some real genuine fried chicken and you won't have to wait all meal for your coffee."

They all laughed. They seemed to think that that was *funny*. The author said that he would certainly come! He'd wanted a meal like that for the last fifteen years. Mother had been out in the garden again. She had dug up some plants and wrapped them in newspapers, and brought some slips for the women to take along and set out.

"You take these with you. Sure, you go ahead!"

She parceled them out right and left and gave directions. The people went out to the car swamped with packages. They were thanking Mrs. Hohenschuh profusely, and promising to do just as she told them, laughing delightedly at everything she said. She went right up to the car with them, as she always did with people who were leaving. Bert stood back with the bills wadded up in her hot hand, and with Maynard beside her. They had complimented her on the dinner, done all she had asked of them; but she had thought that from *these* people—the kind she admired, not just the folks in town who had never known what she was after—she would get her own appreciation at last.

"Good-by, Mrs. Hohenschuh. We certainly enjoyed this."

"You come again, all of you. You just drop in any time you feel like it."

"I'm coming back some day to hear more of those stories," the writer warned her.

"Ach, them old-time stories? Ja, I know plenty of them!"

"And we're coming after that dinner, Mrs. Hohenschuh. Real old fried chicken. Remember! You've promised us."

Mr. Drayton took the wheel, the big engine started humming, the car rolled ahead. They waved—they were going.

"Good-by, Mrs. Statzer! . . . And Maynard!"

But they had to remember to call back that.

"Well!" Mrs. Hohenschuh said gratified, climbing back onto the walk. "They was real nice folks! I don't see why you made such a fuss over having them. You needn't. The other way would have been just as good."

"Look at your hands, mother!" Bert said bitterly.

"Ja, I know. I dug up them plants. Well, it don't matter now, they're gone anyway."

She waddled serenely to the house.

Bert stood looking after the car, still clutching her bills. She would be able to report to May that the dinner had been a success. The people had enjoyed themselves, they had paid her well, let her have their recommendations. Her tea room was started. But the thing she had wanted most of all, and waited for all her life—their appreciation—they had given to mother, who couldn't even understand or care for it. Bert didn't yet see what their idea was.

Selected Bibliography

Abels, Jules. *In the Time of Silent Cal.* New York: G.P. Putnam's Sons, 1969.
Allen, Frederick Lewis. *Only Yesterday.* New York: Harper & Brothers, 1931.
Allsop, Kenneth. *The Bootleggers and Their Era.* New York: Doubleday & Co., 1961.
Asbury, Herbert. *The Great Illusion: An Informal History of Prohibition.* Garden City, N.Y.: Doubleday & Co., 1950.
Barnouw, Erik. *A Tower in Babel: A History of Broadcasting in the United States.* New York: Oxford University Press, 1966.
Beard, Charles A., ed. *Whither Mankind?* New York: Longmans, Green and Co., 1928.
Brooks, Van Wyck. *Days of the Phoenix: The Nineteen-Twenties I Remember.* New York: E. P. Dutton & Co., 1957.
Bent, Silas. *Ballyhoo: The Voice of the Press.* New York: Boni and Liveright, 1927.
Chase, Stuart. *Men and Machines.* New York: The Macmillan Co., 1929.
Bessie, Simon Michael. *Jazz Journalism.* New York: Russell & Russell, 1969.
Cleaton, Irene, and Allen Cleaton. *Books and Battles: American Literature, 1920–1930.* Boston: Houghton, Mifflin, 1937.
Churchill, Allen. *Remember When.* New York: Golden Press, Inc., 1967.
Cowley, Malcolm. *Exile's Return: A Narrative of Ideas.* New York: W. W. Norton, 1934; revised edition, Viking, 1951.
Creamer, Robert W. *Babe: The Legend Comes to Life.* New York: Simon and Schuster, 1974.

SELECTED BIBLIOGRAPHY

Eastman, Edward Rae. *These Changing Times*. New York: The Macmillan Co., 1927.

Epstein, Ralph Cecil. *The Automobile Industry*. Chicago: A. W. Shaw Co., 1928.

Ewen, David. *The Life and Death of Tin Pan Alley*. New York: Funk and Wagnalls Co., 1964.

Ewen, Stuart. *Captains of Consciousness: Advertising and the Social Roots of the Consumer Culture*. New York: McGraw-Hill Book Co., 1976.

Fass, Paula S. *The Damned and the Beautiful: American Youth in the 1920's*. New York: Oxford University Press, 1977.

Galbraith, J.K. *The Great Crash: 1929*. Boston: Houghton, Mifflin, 1955.

Harriman, Margaret Case. *The Vicious Circle: The Story of The Algonquin Round Table*. New York: Rinehart & Co., 1951.

Hoffman, Frederick J. *The Twenties: American Writing in the Postwar Decade*. New York: The Free Press, 1949; revised edition, 1962.

Jacobs, Lewis. *The Rise of the American Film: A Critical History*. New York: Teachers College Press, 1968.

Knoles, George Harmon. *The Jazz Age Revisited: British Criticism of American Civilization during the 1920's*. Stanford: Stanford University Press, 1955.

Leighton, Isabel, ed. *The Aspirin Age 1919–1941*. New York: Simon and Schuster, 1949.

Leuchtenberg, William E. *The Perils of Prosperity, 1914–1932*. Chicago: University of Chicago Press, 1958.

Lynd, Robert S., and Helen Merrill Lynd. *Middletown: A Study in Contemporary American Culture*. New York: Harcourt, Brace & Co., 1929.

MacManus, Theodore Francis, and Norman Beasley. *Men, Money and Motors*. New York: Harper and Brothers, 1929.

Merz, Charles. *The Dry Decade*. Garden City, New York: Doubleday, Doran, 1931.

O'Brien, Edward J., ed. *The Best Short Stories of 1920*. Boston: Small Maynard & Co., 1920. Stories of each year of the decade are collected in individual volumes.

Osgood, Henry O. *So This Is Jazz*. Boston: Little, Brown & Co., 1926.

Prothro, James Warren. *The Dollar Decade: Business Ideas*

in the 1920's. Baton Rouge: Louisiana State University Press, 1954.

Robinson, David. *Hollywood in the Twenties*. New York: Paperback Library, 1968.

Sann, Paul. *The Lawless Decade*. New York: Crown Publishers, 1957.

Schubert, Paul. *The Electric Word: The Rise of Radio*. New York: The Macmillan Press, 1928.

Seldes, Gilbert. *The Seven Lively Arts*. New York: Harper and Brothers, 1924.

Sloat, Warren. *1929, America before the Crash*. New York: Macmillan Publishing Co., Inc., 1979.

Slosson, Preston William. *A History of American Life: The Great Crusade and After, 1914–1928*. New York: The Macmillan Co., 1930.

Soule, George Henry. *Prosperity Decade, 1917–1929*. New York: Rinehart and Co., 1947.

Stevenson, Elizabeth. *Babbitts and Bohemians: The American 1920's*. New York: The Macmillan Co., 1967.

Sullivan, Mark. *Our Times*. New York: The Macmillan Co., 1935.

Walker, Stanley. *The Night Club Era*. New York: Frederick A. Stokes Co., 1933.

Ware, Caroline F. *Greenwich Village, 1920–1930*. Boston: Houghton, Mifflin, 1935.

Whiteman, Paul, and Mary M. McBride. *Jazz*. New York: J.H. Sears & Co., 1926.

Williams, Blanche Colton, ed. *O. Henry Memorial Award Prize Stories of 1920*. Garden City, N.Y.: Doubleday, Doran and Co., Inc. Stories of each year of the decade are collected in individual volumes.

Wilson, Edmund. *The Twenties*. New York: Farrar, Straus & Giroux, 1975.

Wood, James Playsted. *The Story of Advertising*. New York: The Ronald Press Co., 1958.

Recommended Reading from MENTOR

- [ ] **THE READER'S COMPANION TO WORLD LITERATURE edited by Hornstein, Percy, and Brown.** An invaluable guide to the immortal masterpieces of writing, from the dawn of civilization to the present, compiled by a board of experts. Lists authors, titles, literary movements, technical terms, and phrases. (#ME1841—$2.95)

- [ ] **EIGHT GREAT COMEDIES edited by Sylvan Barnet, Morton Berman and William Burto.** Complete texts of the great comic plays from Aristophanes to Shaw, and essays on the comic view. (#ME1840—$2.50)

- [ ] **EIGHT GREAT TRAGEDIES edited by Sylvan Barnet, Morton Berman and William Burto.** The great dramatic literature of the ages, eight memorable tragedies by Aeschylus, Euripides, Sophocles, Shakespeare, Ibsen, Strindberg, Yeats and O'Neill. With essays on tragedy by Aristotle, Emerson and others. (#ME1768—$2.25)

- [ ] **MYTHOLOGY by Edith Hamilton.** A widely-read retelling of the Greek, Roman and Norse legends of love and adventure. "Classical mythology has long needed such a popular exposition and Miss Edith Hamilton has given us one in this volume, which is at once a reference book and a book which may be read for stimulation and pleasure."—*The New York Times* Illustrated. Charts. Index. (#ME1839—$2.25)

- [ ] **THE MENTOR BOOK OF SHORT PLAYS edited by Richard H. Goldstone and Abraham H. Lass.** A treasury of drama by some of the finest playwrights of the century that includes Anton Chekhov, Thornton Wilder, Tennessee Williams, Gore Vidal, Terence Ratigan and Paddy Chayefsky. (#ME1730—$2.25)

Buy them at your local bookstore or use coupon on next page for ordering.

World Literature Anthologies from MENTOR

☐ **CLASSIC SCENES edited and translated by Jonathan Price.** In this single volume are 48 outstanding examples of playwriting genius—all of them enticing invitations to both amateur and professional performers. Each scene is accompanied by commentary that sets the scene in historical perspective, places it within the body of the play, and explores the key aspects involved in bringing the characters and actors vividly alive. (#ME1779—$2.75)

☐ **STORIES OF THE AMERICAN EXPERIENCE edited by Leonard Kriegel and Abraham H. Lass.** Vivid insights into American life by some of our greatest writers, including Hawthorne, Melville, Twain, Harte, Crane, Shaw, Steinbeck, Faulkner, and other outstanding American writers. (#ME1605—$2.25)

☐ **MASTERS OF THE SHORT STORY edited by Abraham Lass and Leonard Kriegel.** Complete with individual biographical and critical forewords, here is a superlative gathering of twenty-seven great stories offering unforgettable insight into the greatest of literature. The great masters included are: Balzac, Pushkin, Poe, Gogol, Flaubert, Borges, Kafka and Camus. (#ME1744—$2.50)

☐ **POINTS OF VIEW: An Anthology of Short Stories, edited with Preface and Afterword by Kenneth R. McElheny and James Moffett.** A unique anthology including more than forty stories by such outstanding authors as James Joyce, Anton Chekhov, Katherine Anne Porter, Nathaniel Hawthorne, Fyodor Dostoyevsky, and others of similar caliber, grouped according to point of view of narration. (#ME1880—$2.95)

Buy them at your local bookstore or use this convenient coupon for ordering.

THE NEW AMERICAN LIBRARY, INC.,
P.O. Box 999, Bergenfield, New Jersey 07621

Please send me the MENTOR BOOKS I have checked above. I am enclosing $_____(please add 50¢ to this order to cover postage and handling). Send check or money order—no cash or C.O.D.'s. Prices and numbers are subject to change without notice.

Name _____

Address _____

City_____ State_____ Zip Code_____

Allow 4-6 weeks for delivery.
This offer is subject to withdrawal without notice.

MENTOR Books of Interest

☐ **THE ESSENTIAL MARX: The Non-Economic Writings edited, with new translations by Saul K. Padover.** This important selection of Marx's writings illumines his extraordinary analytical powers, amazing erudition, sensitivity, compassion, and humanity—how far beyond the world of economics Marx's intellect and insight extended. (#ME1709—$2.50)

☐ **THE ESSENTIAL ROUSSEAU newly translated by Lowell Bair; with an Introduction by Matthew Josephson.** The major contributions of the great 18th-century social philosopher whose ideas helped spark a revolution that still has not ended. Included are: The Social Contract, Discourse on Inequality, Discourse on the Arts and Sciences, and The Creed of a Savoyard Priest (from *Emile*). (#ME1719—$2.25)

☐ **THE ESSENTIAL ERASMUS, selected and translated with an Introduction and Commentary by John P. Dolan.** The first single volume in English to show the full range of thought of one of the great Catholic minds of the Renaissance.
(#MJ1673—$1.95)

☐ **THE PHILOSOPHY OF NIETZSCHE, edited with an Introduction by Geoffrey Clive.** A unique topical anthology of writings from the Oscar Levy English translation of 18 volumes and based on Karl Schlechta's new German edition of Nietzsche's works. (#ME1680—$2.25)

☐ **THE PHILOSOPHY OF ARISTOTLE translated by A. E. Wardman and J. L. Creed, with Introduction and Commentary by Renford Bambrough.** A new translation of the basic writings, including selections from the *Metaphysics, Logic, Physics, Psychology, Ethics, Politics,* and *Poetics*—relevant issues that still perplex and preoccupy philosophers of the present day.
(#ME1790—$2.50)

Buy them at your local

bookstore or use coupon

on next page for ordering.

NAL / ABRAMS' BOOKS
ON ART, CRAFTS AND SPORTS

in beautiful, large format, special concise editions—lavishly illustrated with many full-color plates.

- [ ] **NORMAN ROCKWELL: A Sixty Year Retrospective** by Thomas S. Buechner. (#G9969—$7.95)
- [ ] **THE PRO FOOTBALL EXPERIENCE** edited by David Boss, with an Introduction by Roger Kahn. (#G9984—$6.95)
- [ ] **DALI . . . DALI . . . DALI . . .** edited and arranged by Max Gérard, with an Introduction by Dr. Pierre Roumeguère. (#G9983—$6.95)
- [ ] **THE TIN CAN BOOK** by Hyla M. Clark. (#G9965—$6.95)
- [ ] **FANTASY: The Golden Age of Fantastic Illustration** by Brigid Peppin. (#G9971—$6.95)
- [ ] **THE FAMILY OF MAN: The Greatest Photographic Exhibition of All Time—503 Pictures from 68 Countries** created by Edward Steichen for The Museum of Modern Art with a Prologue by Carl Sandburg. (#G9999—$4.95)
- [ ] **THE GREAT AMERICAN T-SHIRT** by Ken Kneitel, Bill Maloney and Andrea Quinn. (#G9972—$5.95)
- [ ] **THE WORLD OF M. C. ESCHER** by J. L. Locher, G. W. Locher, H. S. M. Coxter, C. H. A. Broos, and M. C. Escher. (#G9970—$7.95)
- [ ] **MAGRITTE: Ideas and Images** by Harry Torczyner. (#G9963—$7.95)

Buy them at your local bookstore or use this convenient coupon for ordering.

THE NEW AMERICAN LIBRARY, INC.,
P.O. Box 999, Bergenfield, New Jersey 07621

Please send me the MENTOR and ABRAMS BOOKS I have checked above. I am enclosing $_____ (please add 50¢ to this order to cover postage and handling). Send check or money order—no cash or C.O.D.'s. Prices and numbers are subject to change without notice.

Name _____

Address _____

City_____ State_____ Zip Code_____

Allow 4-6 weeks for delivery.
This offer is subject to withdrawal without notice.